T0207084

Lecture Notes in Computer Science

Lecture Notes in Artificial Intelligence   14269

Founding Editor

Jörg Siekmann

Series Editors

Randy Goebel, *University of Alberta, Edmonton, Canada*
Wolfgang Wahlster, *DFKI, Berlin, Germany*
Zhi-Hua Zhou, *Nanjing University, Nanjing, China*

The series Lecture Notes in Artificial Intelligence (LNAI) was established in 1988 as a topical subseries of LNCS devoted to artificial intelligence.

The series publishes state-of-the-art research results at a high level. As with the LNCS mother series, the mission of the series is to serve the international R & D community by providing an invaluable service, mainly focused on the publication of conference and workshop proceedings and postproceedings.

Huayong Yang · Honghai Liu · Jun Zou ·
Zhouping Yin · Lianqing Liu · Geng Yang ·
Xiaoping Ouyang · Zhiyong Wang
Editors

Intelligent Robotics and Applications

16th International Conference, ICIRA 2023
Hangzhou, China, July 5–7, 2023
Proceedings, Part III

Springer

Editors
Huayong Yang
Zhejiang University
Hangzhou, China

Jun Zou 🆔
Zhejiang University
Hangzhou, China

Lianqing Liu 🆔
Shenyang Institute of Automation
Shenyang, Liaoning, China

Xiaoping Ouyang 🆔
Zhejiang University
Hangzhou, China

Honghai Liu 🆔
Harbin Institute of Technology
Shenzhen, China

Zhouping Yin
Huazhong University of Science
and Technology
Wuhan, China

Geng Yang 🆔
Zhejiang University
Hangzhou, China

Zhiyong Wang
Harbin Institute of Technology
Shenzhen, China

ISSN 0302-9743   ISSN 1611-3349 (electronic)
Lecture Notes in Artificial Intelligence
ISBN 978-981-99-6488-8   ISBN 978-981-99-6489-5 (eBook)
https://doi.org/10.1007/978-981-99-6489-5

LNCS Sublibrary: SL7 – Artificial Intelligence

© The Editor(s) (if applicable) and The Author(s), under exclusive license
to Springer Nature Singapore Pte Ltd. 2023

This work is subject to copyright. All rights are reserved by the Publisher, whether the whole or part of the material is concerned, specifically the rights of translation, reprinting, reuse of illustrations, recitation, broadcasting, reproduction on microfilms or in any other physical way, and transmission or information storage and retrieval, electronic adaptation, computer software, or by similar or dissimilar methodology now known or hereafter developed.
The use of general descriptive names, registered names, trademarks, service marks, etc. in this publication does not imply, even in the absence of a specific statement, that such names are exempt from the relevant protective laws and regulations and therefore free for general use.
The publisher, the authors, and the editors are safe to assume that the advice and information in this book are believed to be true and accurate at the date of publication. Neither the publisher nor the authors or the editors give a warranty, expressed or implied, with respect to the material contained herein or for any errors or omissions that may have been made. The publisher remains neutral with regard to jurisdictional claims in published maps and institutional affiliations.

This Springer imprint is published by the registered company Springer Nature Singapore Pte Ltd.
The registered company address is: 152 Beach Road, #21-01/04 Gateway East, Singapore 189721, Singapore

Paper in this product is recyclable.

Preface

With the theme "Smart Robotics for Sustainable Society", the 16th International Conference on Intelligent Robotics and Applications (ICIRA 2023) was held in Hangzhou, China, July 5–7, 2023, and designed to encourage advancement in the field of robotics, automation, mechatronics, and applications. It aimed to promote top-level research and globalize quality research in general, making discussions and presentations more internationally competitive and focusing on the latest outstanding achievements, future trends, and demands.

ICIRA 2023 was organized and hosted by Zhejiang University, co-hosted by Harbin Institute of Technology, Huazhong University of Science and Technology, Chinese Academy of Sciences, and Shanghai Jiao Tong University, co-organized by State Key Laboratory of Fluid Power and Mechatronic Systems, State Key Laboratory of Robotics and System, State Key Laboratory of Digital Manufacturing Equipment and Technology, State Key Laboratory of Mechanical System and Vibration, State Key Laboratory of Robotics, and School of Mechanical Engineering of Zhejiang University. Also, ICIRA 2023 was technically co-sponsored by Springer. On this occasion, ICIRA 2023 was a successful event after the COVID-19 pandemic. It attracted more than 630 submissions, and the Program Committee undertook a rigorous review process for selecting the most deserving research for publication. The Advisory Committee gave advice for the conference program. Also, they help to organize special sections for ICIRA 2023. Finally, a total of 431 papers were selected for publication in 9 volumes of Springer's Lecture Note in Artificial Intelligence. For the review process, single-blind peer review was used. Each review took around 2–3 weeks, and each submission received at least 2 reviews and 1 meta-review.

In ICIRA 2023, 12 distinguished plenary speakers delivered their outstanding research works in various fields of robotics. Participants gave a total of 214 oral presentations and 197 poster presentations, enjoying this excellent opportunity to share their latest research findings. Here, we would like to express our sincere appreciation to all the authors, participants, and distinguished plenary and keynote speakers. Special thanks are also extended to all members of the Organizing Committee, all reviewers for peer-review, all staffs of the conference affairs group, and all volunteers for their diligent work.

July 2023

Huayong Yang
Honghai Liu
Jun Zou
Zhouping Yin
Lianqing Liu
Geng Yang
Xiaoping Ouyang
Zhiyong Wang

Organization

Conference Chair

Huayong Yang   Zhejiang University, China

Honorary Chairs

Youlun Xiong   Huazhong University of Science and Technology, China

Han Ding   Huazhong University of Science and Technology, China

General Chairs

Honghai Liu   Harbin Institute of Technology, China

Jun Zou   Zhejiang University, China

Zhouping Yin   Huazhong University of Science and Technology, China

Lianqing Liu   Chinese Academy of Sciences, China

Program Chairs

Geng Yang   Zhejiang University, China

Li Jiang   Harbin Institute of Technology, China

Guoying Gu   Shanghai Jiao Tong University, China

Xinyu Wu   Chinese Academy of Sciences, China

Award Committee Chair

Yong Lei   Zhejiang University, China

Publication Chairs

Xiaoping Ouyang	Zhejiang University, China
Zhiyong Wang	Harbin Institute of Technology, China

Regional Chairs

Zhiyong Chen	University of Newcastle, Australia
Naoyuki Kubota	Tokyo Metropolitan University, Japan
Zhaojie Ju	University of Portsmouth, UK
Eric Perreault	Northeastern University, USA
Peter Xu	University of Auckland, New Zealand
Simon Yang	University of Guelph, Canada
Houxiang Zhang	Norwegian University of Science and Technology, Norway
Duanling Li	Beijing University of Posts and Telecommunications, China

Advisory Committee

Jorge Angeles	McGill University, Canada
Tamio Arai	University of Tokyo, Japan
Hegao Cai	Harbin Institute of Technology, China
Tianyou Chai	Northeastern University, China
Jiansheng Dai	King's College London, UK
Zongquan Deng	Harbin Institute of Technology, China
Han Ding	Huazhong University of Science and Technology, China
Xilun Ding	Beihang University, China
Baoyan Duan	Xidian University, China
Xisheng Feng	Shenyang Institute of Automation, Chinese Academy of Sciences, China
Toshio Fukuda	Nagoya University, Japan
Jianda Han	Nankai University, China
Qiang Huang	Beijing Institute of Technology, China
Oussama Khatib	Stanford University, USA
Yinan Lai	National Natural Science Foundation of China, China
Jangmyung Lee	Pusan National University, Korea
Zhongqin Lin	Shanghai Jiao Tong University, China

Hong Liu	Harbin Institute of Technology, China
Honghai Liu	University of Portsmouth, UK
Shugen Ma	Ritsumeikan University, Japan
Daokui Qu	Siasun Robot and Automation Co., Ltd., China
Min Tan	Institute of Automation, Chinese Academy of Sciences, China
Kevin Warwick	Coventry University, UK
Guobiao Wang	National Natural Science Foundation of China, China
Tianmiao Wang	Beihang University, China
Tianran Wang	Shenyang Institute of Automation, Chinese Academy of Sciences, China
Yuechao Wang	Shenyang Institute of Automation, Chinese Academy of Sciences, China
Bogdan M. Wilamowski	Auburn University, USA
Ming Xie	Nanyang Technological University, Singapore
Yangsheng Xu	Chinese University of Hong Kong, China
Huayong Yang	Zhejiang University, China
Jie Zhao	Harbin Institute of Technology, China
Nanning Zheng	Xi'an Jiaotong University, China
Xiangyang Zhu	Shanghai Jiao Tong University, China

Contents – Part III

Advanced Underwater Robot Technologies

Innovative Design and Performance Evaluation of Robot Mechanisms

Evaluation of Wearable Robots for Assistance and Rehabilitation

3D Printing Soft Robots

Perception and Manipulation
of Dexterous Hand for Humanoid Robot

Dexterous Hand-Object Interaction Control Based on Adaptive Impedance Algorithm

Changqu Wu[1], Zhuang Wang[1], Yuqiu Zhang[2], Xiaolong Ma[1], Hailiang Meng[1], and Guanjun Bao[1(✉)]

[1] Zhejiang University of Technology, Hangzhou 310023, China
gjbao@zjut.edu.cn
[2] College of Biomedical Science and Engineering, South China University of Technology, Guangzhou 510000, China

Abstract. Aiming at the problem of contact force control of objects with different dynamic characteristics in the process of hand-object interaction of dexterous hands, this paper proposes a contact force control algorithm of dexterous hands based on admittance control, which combines the adaptive rate of admittance parameters and takes the calculation amount of environmental (grasping object) dynamic model as feedforward input. In the process of interaction between hands and objects, the adaptability of objects is maintained to achieve the flexible grasp of objects with different dynamic characteristics. In addition, in order to deploy the control algorithm in the actual physical system, this paper designs and develops the layered control system of multi-fingered dexterous hand. Finally, in order to verify the effectiveness of the control algorithm and control system studied in this paper, Experiments were designed for multi-sensor data acquisition, joint Angle closed-loop control, fingertip Cartesian space pose control and contact force control of objects with different dynamic characteristics. The experimental results show that the control system studied in this paper can collect data from the multi-sensor system of the multi-fingered dexterous hand, and can conduct closed-loop control of joint Angle and fingertip pose according to the data acquisition results. In addition, the control effect of contact force between the dexterous finger end and objects with different dynamic characteristics is verified by experiments. Thus, the effectiveness of position control and force control algorithms for dexterous hands is verified.

Keywords: dexterous hand · admittance control

1 Introduction

In the automation of industrial production and the intelligence in unstructured environment, robots have played an important role. As the end-effector of robots, multi-fingered dexterous hand has gradually become a research hotspot in the field of robotics due to its high adaptability and dexterity. At present, many experts and scholars have carried out research and development on the human-like multi-fingered dexterous hand. At the same time, the combination of human-like multi-finger-like dexterous hand with

© The Author(s), under exclusive license to Springer Nature Singapore Pte Ltd. 2023
H. Yang et al. (Eds.): ICIRA 2023, LNAI 14269, pp. 3–14, 2023.
https://doi.org/10.1007/978-981-99-6489-5_1

machine vision, arm-hand combination system and intelligent operating system has also become a new research trend in the field. The control system and control algorithm of the dexterous hand determine the degree of completion of these grasping and operating tasks. Therefore, the design and research of the control algorithm and control system of the multi-finger dexterous hand plays a very important role in the grasping and operating tasks of the dexterous hand. Due to the complex working environment of humanoid multi-finger-like dexterous hand, it is impossible for researchers to take all kinds of working conditions into account when building control systems. In some unknown environments, dexterous hands cannot complete predetermined grasping and operating tasks, which greatly limits the practical application of humanoid multi-finger-like dexterous hands. Therefore, the research on the control algorithm and control system of human-like multi-finger dexterous hand needs to be further strengthened. A stable and efficient control strategy is the key to ensure the humanoid multi-fingering dexterous hand to complete the grasping task [1, 2].

According to whether the humanoid multi-finger-dexterous hand is in contact with the environment, the working space of multi-finger-dexterous hand can be divided into two parts: free space and constrained space [3].In free space, there is no force on the dexterous hand and there is no constraint problem. Only the position control of the dexterous hand is needed [4]; In constrained space, fingers are in contact with the outside world. Besides position control, the contact force between the fingers of dexterous hands and the environment should also be controlled. For dexterous hand compliance control in the process of hand/object interaction, it is mainly divided into direct force control (force/position mixed control) and interrelay control (impedance control) [5].

Hybrid force control is mainly oriented towards specific control tasks. It was proposed by Mason, Craig et al., and its core idea is the decoupling control of the robot's end position and contact force [6, 7]. In this algorithm, the robot workspace is divided into force subspace and position subspace, and corresponding stiffness selection matrix is introduced [8], position and force are controlled in different subspaces. The impedance control, which is more suitable for flexible grasping with dexterous hands, was originally proposed by Hogan in 1985 [9]. Impedance control is actually an indirect impedance relationship established between the contact force and position, thus incorporating force control and position control into the same framework. For different task requirements, different impedance parameters are selected to achieve compliance control. For example, Lasky et al. proposed a secondary performance index based on the force tracking error, and took the index as the correction of position control, which improved the accuracy of force tracking [10].Seraji et al. used an adaptive impedance control strategy to change the value of impedance parameters through online prediction of environmental information, so as to improve the stability of the control system [11]. Odhner L et al. solved the disturbance problem in dynamic grasping of dexterous hands based on the principle of dynamic constraints [12]. With the development of intelligent control theory, some intelligent control methods have been used on the basis of original impedance control. For example, Fusaomi et al. use neural network to estimate stiffness on the basis of impedance control to realize high quality machining of NC machine tools [13]. Yiting Dong et al. solved the problem of interactive control between uncertain robots and unknown environments by using interference estimators to estimate changes in impedance parameters

[14]. Wei He et al. proposed a fuzzy neural network learning algorithm to identify the uncertain object model and introduced impedance learning to deal with the interaction between the robot and the environment [15]. George S et al. designed a new continuous time controller capable of establishing and maintaining robot contact with a plane of unknown stiffness and position [16]. Friedrich Lange et al. studied the position-based parallel force control method, and considered the reference trajectory and the coupling of force and torque when controlling the force, thus realized the force and trajectory control in rigid contact [17].Loris Roveda et al. solved the problem of force control in deterministic interactive tasks of manipulator by online estimating the stiffness of interactive environment [18].

Based on the traditional induction control algorithm (position-based impedance control), this paper aims at the contact force control problem in the interaction process of dexterous hands. The following methods are adopted to achieve the tracking control of the contact force between the end of the fingers of dexterous hands and the grasped objects:

1. The hybrid dynamics model of unknown environment (captured objects) was established, and the model parameters were identified off-line based on recursive least square method.
2. The three parameters of the second-order admittance equation were adjusted online in real time according to the contact force error and the differential of the error.

2 Methodology

2.1 Admittance Control

The core idea of impedance control is to construct a virtual mass-damp-spring system between an actual physical system and an interactive environment, so as to simulate the dynamic relationship between the robot terminal position and the contact force. Because impedance control is to indirectly control the contact force between the robot by adjusting the dynamic relationship between the position of the robot end and the contact force, direct contact force control cannot be achieved. Impedance control algorithms can be divided into two types: force-based impedance control and position-based impedance control. The position-based impedance control is also called admittance control. For convenience of description, the admittance control shall prevail in the following descriptions in this paper.

The admittance control can control the contact force by adjusting the target admittance parameters according to the position, velocity, acceleration and force feedback data of the end of the multi-finger-dexterous hand. The model is shown in Eq. 1:

$$M_d\left(\ddot{X} - \ddot{X}_d\right) + B_d\left(\dot{X} - \dot{X}_d\right) + K_d(X - X_d) = E_f \qquad (1)$$

In the formula M_d, B_d, K_d is usually set as a semi-positive definite diagonal matrix of order n, where n is the dimension of the workspace of the robot multi-finger-dexterous hand. Since the forces, positions and admittance parameters in each direction of the admittance model in Cartesian space are independent of each other, the physical system is usually analyzed as a single degree of freedom system, and lowercase letters are used to represent each variable, Among them m_d, b_d, k_d are the inertia parameters, damping parameters and stiffness parameters of the admittance model, $e_f = f_d - f_e$, that is, as shown in Eq. 2:

$$m_d(\ddot{x} - \ddot{x}_d) + b_d(\dot{x} - \dot{x}_d) + k_d(x - x_d) = e_f \tag{2}$$

x_0, x_d, Δx, x are respectively the initial expected position of the finger end, the updated expected position, the updated value of the expected position and the actual position of the finger end, θ_d, θ are respectively the expected Angle of finger joint space and the actual Angle of finger joint space, F_e, F_d, e_f are the actual contact force of the finger end, the expected contact force of the finger end and the contact force error.

The initial position of the surface of the grasped object is x_e, After the fingers of the dexterous hand reach the initial position and touch the grasping object, if the fingers continue to close, the grasping object will be deformed and the contact force between the grasping object and the grasping object will be generated. In this constrained space, a controlled whole is formed between the fingers of the dexterous hand and the grasped object. Therefore, the dynamic model of the grasped object itself is bound to be involved in its theoretical analysis. In this section, it is assumed that the grasped object has spring characteristics (rigidity), as shown in Eq. 3. Among them k_e is the stiffness coefficient of the grasped object.

$$f_e = k_e(x - x_e) \tag{3}$$

The equivalent admittance model of the contact between the fingers of the multi-finger-dexterous hand and the grasping object is shown in Fig. 1, which can be divided into three stages. In the first stage, the dexterous hand moves in free space and does not touch the grasping object, and the contact force between them is always 0. In the second stage, the multi-fingered dexterous hand starts to contact with the grasping object, resulting in the effect of contact force. With the closure of the fingers, the contact force continues to increase. In the third stage, the dexterous hand stops moving, reaches the desired contact force, and enters the stable contact stage (Fig. 2).

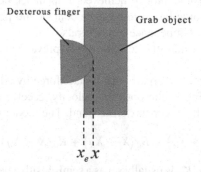

Fig. 1. Schematic diagram of hand object interaction

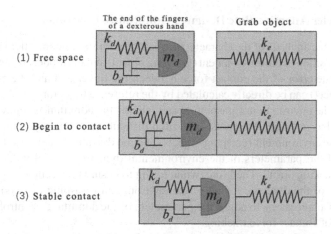

Fig. 2. Schematic diagram of contact between finger end of dexterous hand and grasping object

By substituting Eq. 3 into equation Eq. 2, the following equation can be obtained:

$$m_d\ddot{e}_f + b_d\dot{e}_f + (k_d + k_e)e_f = k_d(k_e x_e + f_d) - k_d k_e x_d \tag{4}$$

When the multi-fingered dexterous hand stops moving and grabs the object stably, the steady-state error of the expected contact force can be obtained as follows:

$$e_f = \frac{k_d k_e}{(k_e + k_d)}\left(x_e + \frac{f_d}{k_e} - x_d\right) \tag{5}$$

In order to make the steady-state error of the contact force between the end of the fingers of the multi-fingered dexterous hand and the grasping object 0, the initial expected trajectory of the dexterous hand should be set as:

$$x_d = x_e + \frac{f_d}{k_e} \tag{6}$$

It can be seen from Eq. 6,The initial surface position of the object when grasping x_e and stiffness coefficient k_e when is precisely known, the desired position of the fingers of the dexterous hand can be calculated directly according to Eq. 6, and the steady-state error of the contact force is 0. However, in the actual environment, the initial surface position and stiffness coefficient of the captured object can not be directly obtained very accurate results. As can be seen from Equation Eq. 5, there are two main factors affecting the steady-state error of the contact force: dynamic modeling of the environment (grasping objects) and stiffness parameters of the admittance controller. To accurately control the contact force between the end of the finger and the grasping object, it is necessary to adjust the control of these two factors. Next, this paper will achieve the tracking and control of the contact force between the finger end of the dexterous hand and the grasping object through the off-line parameter identification method of the environment (grasping object) dynamic model and the on-line adjustment method of the stiffness coefficient of the admission controller.

2.2 Parameter Adaptive Rate Design of Admittance Controller

According to the analysis of the characteristics of the admittance controller in this paper, if the initial position of the environment (grasping object) and the model are very accurate, the steady-state error of the contact force between the finger end and the environment (grasping object) can be directly calculated by the reference trajectory. In short, accurate modeling of the environment (grasping objects) helps the admittance controller to play a good role, but in actual situations, it is often difficult to accurately obtain the initial position of the environment (grasping objects) and the dynamics model, and insufficient estimation of the parameters of the environmental dynamics model will also lead to large force tracking errors. Therefore, while trying to ensure the accuracy of parameters identification of the dynamic model of the environment (grasping objects) mentioned above, it is also necessary to adjust the parameters of the admittance controller to solve the problem of contact force tracking.

The core idea of adaptive admittance control algorithm based on variable impedance parameters is simple and intuitive. The idea comes from the bionic process of human arm contact force control. Humans can adjust the stiffness coefficient of the arm to adapt to the required contact force during contact. In order to achieve accurate force tracking, the adjustment method of human arm contact force is extended to adaptive admittance control of multi-fingered dexterous hand. Equation (3–4) can be changed to the following Eq. 7:

$$m_d(t)(\ddot{x} - \ddot{x}_d) + b_d(t)(\dot{x} - \dot{x}_d) + k_d(t)(x - x_d) = e_f \qquad (7)$$

In the formula, $m_d(t)$, $b_d(t)$, $k_d(t)$ is a time-varying parameter, ideal stiffness coefficient $k_d(t)$ Adapt to different environments (grab objects).

Ideal stiffness coefficient $k_d(t)$ expression is as follows:

$$k_d(t) = \frac{k_f e_f + k_v \dot{e}_f}{\Delta x} \qquad (8)$$

In the formula, e_f is the expected contact force deviation, $\dot{e}_f$ is the differential of the expected contact force deviation, Δx is position deviation, k_f, k_v respectively are the proportional coefficient and differential coefficient of stiffness adaptive rate.

After determining the stiffness adaptive rate, we need to consider the adaptive parameters of the other two admittance controllers. For the second-order admittance system, the formula for calculating the second-order damping ratio is shown as follows:

$$\zeta_d = \frac{b_d}{2\sqrt{m_d(k_d + k_e)}} \qquad (9)$$

In practice, critical damping ratio is usually used as the damping ratio of second-order control system to achieve good control performance. After the system damping ratio is selected, the inertia parameters of the second order admittance controller need to be determined. Inertial parameter m_d It has great influence on the high speed movement, which is easy to produce large acceleration and impact. In practice, this parameter is usually set as a constant. In summary, the parameter adaptive rate of the adaptive admittance control algorithm designed in this chapter is shown as follows:

$$\begin{cases} m_d(t) = \text{constant} \\ b_d(t) = 2\zeta_d \sqrt{m_d(t)(k_d(t) + k_e)} \\ k_d(t) = \dfrac{k_f e_f + k_v \dot{e}_f}{\Delta x} \end{cases} \quad (10)$$

2.3 Stability Analysis

In this section, the steady-state error and stability of the adaptive admittance control algorithm proposed in this paper are analyzed strictly. Firstly, parameters of the unknown environment dynamics model are identified, and the obtained parameter identification results are sent to the controller together with the expected contact force. Then, the expected displacement is updated through the adaptive admittance control algorithm, and the control target is finally achieved.

The hybrid control model, is substituted into the second-order admittance controller. When the stable grasping stage is reached, it can be obtained:

$$k_d(t)\left[\left(\frac{f_d}{k_e}\right)^{\frac{1}{n}} + x_e - x_d\right] = e_f = f_d - f \quad (11)$$

$$x_d = \left(\frac{f_d}{k_e}\right)^{\frac{1}{n}} + x_e \quad (12)$$

As can be seen from the above equation, the expected position can be obtained when the expected contact force is given. However, due to the existence of model errors and parameter identification errors, this result is used as the reference (feedforward) input of the adaptive admittance controller.

By substituting the stiffness adaptive rate into the second-order admittance equation, Eq. (3–46) can be obtained as follows:

$$m_d(t)(\ddot{x} - \ddot{x}_d) + b_d(t)(\dot{x} - \dot{x}_d) + k_f e_f + k_v \dot{e}_f = e_f \quad (13)$$

When entering the stable grasping stage, the following Eq. (3–47) can be obtained:

$$k_f e_f = e_f \quad (14)$$

As can be seen from Eq. (14), as long as the proportional coefficient of stiffness adaptive rate k_f instead of setting it to 1, The steady-state error of the control system is always 0.

3 Experiment

Firstly, a hierarchical control system for dexterous hands is designed, and two groups of experiments are designed based on the control strategy and the control system. Are the motion control experiments of dexterous hands based on Angle feedback and the grasping force control experiments of objects with different dynamic characteristics.

3.1 Design of Experimental Platform for Dexterous Hand

The software design of the multi-finger dexterous hand control system needs to rely on the hardware system introduced in the previous two sections. The software design is the core part of the dexterous hand control system. The multi-finger dexterous hand control system designed in this paper is mainly composed of three parts: task planning layer, coordination control layer and motion control layer. Task planning layer is mainly realized by software in the upper computer PC, including the function modules of environmental dynamics parameter identification based on recursive least square method, multi-sensor real-time display, control instruction sending and so on. The software design of the lower computer motion control layer is based on the STM32F103C8T6 minimum system board, which mainly includes the sensor signal acquisition driver design, the position PID closed-loop realization, the adaptive admittance control algorithm realization and other functional modules. The three control layers cooperate to complete the control of the multi-finger dexterous hand. Figure 3 shows the software architecture of the multi-fingered dexterous hand control system.

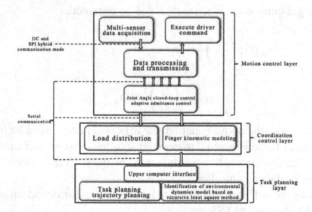

Fig. 3. Software system structure of multi fingered dexterous hand control system

Due to the decoupling characteristics of the mechanical structure of multi-fingered dexterous hands and the modular design of each finger, a single finger was taken as the data analysis object in this experiment to test and analyze the response of the expected Angle of single finger and single joint and the expected pose of the end of single finger. Figure 4 shows the single-finger experimental platform needed for this experiment.

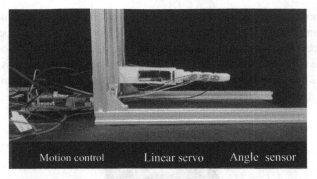

Fig. 4. Multi-fingered dexterous hand single finger experimental platform

3.2 Experiments on Grasping Force Control of Objects With Different Dynamic Characteristics

The grasping force control experiment based on objects with different dynamic characteristics is mainly to precisely control the grasping force of objects with different stiffness in order to achieve the effect of compliant control similar to that of human hand. In order to verify the application effect of the single-finger adaptive admittance control algorithm of multi-finger dexterous hand studied in this paper in the actual dexterous hand grasping task, a series of object grasping experiments were designed and conducted in this section for the purpose of the experiment.

In order to avoid the interference of other factors on the experimental results, a two-finger experimental platform is designed in this paper, as shown in Fig. 5. The platform consists of two dexterous fingers hanging upside down and facing each other, a frame made of 20 mm profiles, and wooden blocks used to place objects.

Fig. 5. Two finger experimental platform of multi-fingered dexterous hand

At the same time, in the planning of grasping task, the dexterous hand will generally default to have no obstacle in the whole process of movement, and the dexterous hand will directly contact the object to be grasped. However, in human-computer interaction and unstructured environment, due to the complexity of the application itself, it is difficult to fully analyze and plan the task space. Therefore, in order to prove the superiority of the adaptive admittance control algorithm studied in this paper in the process of hand-object interaction, the experiment is set into two scenarios, one is in the process of dexterous hand movement without obstacles. The other is when the dexterous hand encounters obstacles as it approaches an object.

Fig. 6. Two finger fine grasping experiment of multi fingered dexterous hand

As shown in Fig. 6, they are the two kinds of grasping objects used in this experiment. For different grasping objects, repeat the experimental steps. For the experiment in this paper, the stiffness threshold was set as 15 N/mm. Figure 7 shows the experimental results of flexible grasping of soft plastics, in which Fig. 7 (a) is the experimental effect of successful grasping of soft plastics, Fig. 7 (b) is the result of parameter identification.

Similarly, it can be seen from the figure that when off-line parameter identification is carried out for soft plastics, the stiffness obtained from the initial data is less than the stiffness threshold set. Therefore, the hybrid control model is adopted. After parameter identification of the dynamic model of soft plastics, the stiffness coefficient K is 0.5266 and the exponent n is 1.1232. The fitting curve is shown in Fig. 7 (b). It can be seen from the curve that the fitting curve will produce some errors with the increase of invasion depth, but the errors are also within the acceptable range. After receiving the contact force signal, it takes about 1.2 s to reach the steady state. Similarly, it can be seen that the steady state error is about 0.1 N, which can meet the control requirements.

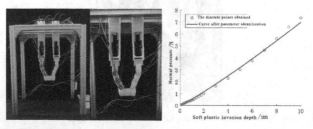

Fig. 7. Compliant grasp experiment of soft plastic based on adaptive admittance control. (a) grab results, (b) parameter identification results

In the above grasping force control experiments of two objects with different dynamic characteristics, it can be seen that the overshoot of the contact force curve of hardwood block is slightly larger, while that of soft plastic contact force curve is slightly smaller. There are mainly two reasons:

(1) Soft plastics are inherently soft and will absorb some of the finger impact.
(2) The physical properties of objects with different dynamic characteristics differ greatly, but due to the adaptability of the adaptive admittance algorithm to different environments, the dexterous hand can quickly realize the stable grasping control of objects with different dynamic characteristics.

4 Conclusion

Aiming at the contact force control problem of dexterous hands in the process of hand-object interaction, this paper designs an adaptive admittance control algorithm based on the basic principle of admittance control algorithm, takes the computational quantity of environment (grasping object) dynamic model as feedforward input, and takes variable parameter admittance controller as the main control ring. In order to realize the flexible grasp of objects with different dynamic characteristics, the dexterous hand can keep the compliance to the object in the grasp process. In addition, a hierarchical control system for the dexterous hand is designed based on the position perception and force perception of multiple fingers and joints. Finally, the experimental platform of dexterous hand was built, and the adaptive admittance control strategy was verified. For the position control strategy of multi-fingered dexterous hand, the step response test of the expected joint Angle and the expected pose step response and sinusoidal tracking response of the fingertip Cartesian space were respectively conducted on the single finger and single joint. The test results show that the inner loop of position control of multi-finger-dexterous hand has better control effect. Aiming at the grasping force control of objects with different dynamic characteristics, two-finger fine grasping experiments were carried out on two typical objects such as hardwood blocks and soft plastics under the scenario of unhindered task space. The experimental results show that the single-finger adaptive admittance control strategy proposed in this paper has good adaptability to grasping objects with different dynamic characteristics. A control experiment was conducted on a single finger in a task space obstruction scenario, and the experimental results demonstrated the active compliance of the finger ends.

Acknowledgments. This work was supported by the Key Research and Development Program of Zhejiang (Grand No. 2021C04015), Zhejiang Provincial Natural Science Foundation of China (Grand No. LZ23E050005, Q23E050071) and the Fundamental Research Funds for the Provincial Universities of Zhejiang (Grand No. RF-C2019004).

14   C. Wu et al.

References

1. Zheng, Y., Qian, W.: Improving grasp quality evaluation. Robot. Auton. Syst. **57**(6–7), 665–673 (2009)
2. Aleotti, J., Caselli, S.: Interactive teaching of task oriented robot grasps. Robot. Auton. Syst. **58**(5), 539–550 (2010)
3. Han, J., Chenghai, W.: Robot transition control based on states feedback. Robot **19**(6), 412–419 (1997)
4. Gu, H.: Research on Cross-coupled Control Scheme For Dexterous Hand Based on Neural Network. Heilongjiang: Harbin Institute of Technology 2011
5. Haiqiang, Q.: A Thesis Submitted to Chongqing University in Partial Fulfillment of the Requirement for the Master's Degree of Engineering. Chongqing University, Chongqing (2013)
6. Tondu, B., Lopez, P.: Modeling and control of McKibben artificial muscle robot actuators. Control Syst. IEEE **20**(2), 15–38 (2002)
7. Mills, J., Goldenberg, A.: Force and position control of manipulators during constrained motion tasks. IEEE Trans. Robot. Autom. **5**(1), 30–46 (1989)
8. Raibert, M., Craig, J.: Hybrid position/force control of manipulators. J. Dyn. Syst. Meas. Contr. **103**, 126 (1981)
9. Hogan, N.: Impedance control-an approach to manipulation. I-Theory. II-Implementation. III-Applications. ASME Trans. Dyn. Syst. Meas. Control **107** (1985)
10. Lasky, T.A., Hsia, T.C.: On force tracking impedance control of robot manipulators. In: Proceedings. 1991 IEEE International Conference on Robotics and Automation, pp. 274–275. IEEE Computer Society (1991)
11. Seraji, H., Colbaugh, R.: Force tracking in impedance control. IEEE. In: Proceedings of IEEE International Conference on Robotics and Automation, pp. 499–506 (1997)
12. Odhner, L.U., Jentoft, L.P., Claffee, M.R., et al.: A compliant, underactuated hand for robust manipulation. Int. J. Robot. Res. **33**(5), 736–752 (2014)
13. Fusaomi, N., Takanori, M., Shintaro, T., et al.: Impedance model force control using a neural network based effective stiffness estimator for a desktop nc machine tool. J. Manuf. Syst. **2010**(28), 78–87 (2009)
14. Dong, Y., Ren, B.: UDE based variable impedance control of uncertain robot systems. IEEE Trans. Syst. Man Cyber. Syst. **49**(12), 2487–2498 (2019)
15. He, W., Dong, Y.: Adaptive fuzzy neural network control for a constrained robot using impedance learning. IEEE Trans. Neural Netw. Learn. Syst. **29**(4), 1174–1186 (2017)
16. Kanakis, G.S., Dimeas, F., Rovithakis, G.A., Doulgeri, Z.: Prescribed contact establishment of a robot with a planar surface under position and stiffness uncertainties. Robot. Auton. Syst. **104**, 99–108 (2018)
17. Lange, F., Bertleff, W., Suppa, M.: Force and trajectory control of industrial robots in stiff contact. In: 2013 IEEE International Conference on Robotics and Automation, pp. 2927–2934. IEEE (2013)
18. Roveda, L., Pedrocchi, N., Tosatti, L.M.: Exploiting impedance shaping approaches to overcome force overshoots in delicate interaction tasks. Int. J. Adv. Robot. Syst. **13**(5), 24–35 (2016)

Design and Control of a Two-Segment Rotatable Wire-Driven Flexible Arm

Jun Guo, Haoyi Wu, Yuhao Liang, Yixin Li, Zhenfeng Wu, and Yong Zhong[✉]

Shien-Ming Wu School of Intelligent Engineering, South China University of Technology, Guangzhou 510640, China
zhongyong@scut.edu.cn

Abstract. This paper proposes a new design of a wire-driven flexible manipulator. The manipulator consists of rigid joints connected by internal linking loops and a flexible outer shell made of corrugated tubing. The design aims to provide higher flexibility and better adaptability, enabling the manipulator to cope with more complex working environments. The manipulator is controlled by stretching and retracting a line to bend it, and by driving the shell's rotation through the gears at the base to rotate the end effector. This two-segment design greatly increases the manipulator's flexibility, making it more adaptable to even more complex practical working environments. Furthermore, the rotating function on the outer surface of the design in conjunction with the corresponding end effector also greatly expands the range of applications for the flexible manipulator, with a promising future. In this paper, we performed kinematic modeling and control of the manipulator, achieved different trajectory movements, and obtained excellent experimental results of the manipulator's performance. This demonstrates the rationality of the manipulator's design, and enhances its control performance, providing a new approach for the development of flexible manipulators.

Keywords: wire-driven · Flexible robotic arm rotation · Motion control

1 Introduction

As a tool to replace humans in repetitive, dangerous and complicated work, robotic arms are being more and more widely used in various scenarios with the demand for productivity in social development. For example, machinery manufacturing [1], logistics handling [2], space exploration, medical rehabilitation [3] and other fields. The traditional robotic arm is a rigid robotic arm, driven by motors at the joint, which has the advantages of high speed, high precision and large load. However, for the operation of small and fragile objects and narrow and complex working environments, the application of rigid robotic arms has certain limitations. In order to compensate for these shortcomings, flexible robotic arms came into being.

The flexible robotic arm [4], being a bionic robot, draws inspiration from various biological features found in nature such as elephant trunks, octopus tentacles, snakes [5], and other species. It boasts of highly flexible movement characteristics that enable it to

© The Author(s), under exclusive license to Springer Nature Singapore Pte Ltd. 2023
H. Yang et al. (Eds.): ICIRA 2023, LNAI 14269, pp. 15–26, 2023.
https://doi.org/10.1007/978-981-99-6489-5_2

adapt to a variety of complex working environments. At present, the main driving forms of flexible manipulators are pneumatic driven [6, 7] and wire-driven, in which the wire-driven flexible manipulator has the characteristics of flexible structural arrangement, fast response speed and easy maintenance. By arranging the wire reasonably, the drive can be kept away from the main trunk of the robotic arm, which can effectively reduce the inertia of the end effector, improve dynamic performance, and save space. At the same time, the wire-driven is similar to a human tendon, which is more in line with the principle of bionics. Therefore, this article will mainly discuss flexible robotic arms based on the wire-driven form.

In recent years, many researchers have made fruitful efforts in the field of wire driven robotic arms, and proposed a series of significant innovations, which have continuously promoted the development of this field. Lin, W et al. propose a new modular locking mechanism that can be used to change the stiffness of wire-driven robotic arms. Locking and unlocking can be achieved with simple operations. This mechanism can make the flexible robotic arm have a certain stiffness under certain conditions and increase its load capacity [8, 9]. Wire-driven flexible robotic arms offer the advantage of being very flexible, and this advantage will undoubtedly continue to be amplified by the multi-stage design [10]. Bo Ouyang et al. [11] designed a flexible robotic arm with a three-stage type, using a super-elastic nitinol rod as the skeleton. The robot is operated by passing through twelve tendons of concentric disks. These tendons are divided into three groups. Each segment is driven by four tendons and controlled by two linear actuators. In order to realize the grasping ability of wire-driven robotic arms, Zhe Xu et al. [12] proposed a highly bionic humanoid robotic hand based on wire-driven for artificial limb regeneration. This manipulator has potential application prospects in a wider range of scenarios by placing the threads similar to the tendons of the human hand, so that it has flexibility and agility similar to the human hand in the process of operation. Jes´us M. G´omez-de-Gabriel et al. [13] also designed a multi-finger mechanism based on line drive, which can maintain the shape of the finger while generating active rolling on the surface, and realize the functions of grasping and material transfer through multi-finger cooperation, which is not enough for the limited degree of freedom of the finger, and can only be bent in one plane.

In this article, we introduce a two-segment wire-driven flexible robotic arm. It is characterized by a high degree of flexibility and the rotatable housing of the robotic arm, which further increases the degree of freedom of wire-driven flexible robotic arms. First, this two-segment design allows the robotic arm to easily access a space-tight, complex cavity. Secondly, the rotatable nature of the surface of the robotic arm can be transmitted to various actuators at the end, expanding the application scenarios of the robotic arm. For example, in minimally invasive surgery, robotic arms can easily adjust the angle and posture of endoscopes and surgical tools; Out of reach of humans, the robotic arm can pick up small, fragile items or manipulate connectors, such as screws. By installing a drill, the robot arm can also drill into complex spaces, clear obstacles, and more [14]. Therefore, this two-segment wire-driven flexible robotic arm has obvious advantages, and will be widely used in micro-operation, fine processing, medical surgery and other fields in the future.

2 Design and Manufacture

2.1 Robotic Arm

The flexible robotic arm design introduced in this article is a new type of two-segment rotatable robotic arm driven by wire, which differs from traditional robotic arm designs. Figure 1 shows the two-segment flexible structure used in the robotic arm and the rigid internal joints 3D printed with PLA material. Each segment of the robotic arm is composed of six rigid joints, which are connected to each other through connecting rings to form a structure similar to a universal joint. By controlling the wire, each segment of the robotic arm can independently bend in various spatial directions to achieve trajectories in various fields. Each segment of the robotic arm is controlled by two pairs of orthogonal wires, and each pair of wires is controlled by two servos. These servos can rotate to control the variation of the wire length, thereby causing the bending of the robotic arm in the plane, and the bending of the two pairs of wires can be superimposed to obtain the bending curve of the entire robotic arm in space. This design structure allows the flexible robotic arm to better adapt to different workspaces and working environments. The connecting ring is a key component of the robotic arm design, which can provide free rotation of the flexible robotic arm around the axis and bend in different directions. In addition, the connecting ring can also improve the reliability and stability of the robotic arm, as it can withstand and disperse the stress and impact generated in the robotic arm.

Moreover, the flexible robotic arm also has a unique feature in the design of its shell. The shell is 3D printed with flexible TPU material and has a corrugated tube-like shape with excellent deformation ability. The rotation of the rigid joint inside the shell can passively drive the bending of the shell. Tests have shown that the maximum deformation capacity of the shell is 30°, which is the angle between the two end planes in Fig. 2. This shell structure design can improve the applicability of the flexible robotic arm in specific workspaces and also improve its stability and control accuracy. The bottom of the shell is connected to the gear, which engages with the gear of the stepper motor, making the rotation of the flexible robotic arm more precise and controllable, as the stepper motor can accurately control the rotation of the gear. By connecting the shell to the stepper motor, the overall structure is more compact, saving valuable workspace and having more flexibility in the overall design. The gear is a key part of the entire structure, ensuring that the rotation of the stepper motor is accurately transmitted to the shell. Through this connection, the stepper motor can drive the entire robotic arm to rotate to the desired position, providing higher operation accuracy and control. The above design characteristics of the robotic arm enable it to better adapt to various working environments, with higher stability and reliability, and have broader application prospects.

2.2 Control System

TSFRA's control system consists mainly of four servos and a stepper motor, as shown in Fig. 3(a). The stepper motor is fixed on the other side of the base, and through gear transmission, the direction and speed of rotation of the robotic arm shell can be controlled. The gears have a 2:3 gear ratio, which allows more torque to be generated using smaller

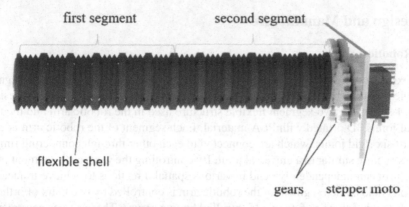

first segment   second segment

flexible shell

gears   stepper moto

Fig. 1. Design of the Two-Segment Rotatable wire-driven Flexible Arm (TSRFA)

30°

Fig. 2. Deformation of flexible shell

stepper motors. The formal arrangement of the line drive is more flexible, and pulleys are usually used to change the direction of the line. However, the increase in the number of pulleys often leads to an increase in friction, a decrease in transmission efficiency, and easy to lead to disconnection and control failure. So here we abandoned this method and used a Bowden cable to transmit the pull. Bowden cable is a mechanical servo drive consisting of a wire rope and a plastic casing, and its principle is based on the conversion of tension and pressure, as shown in Fig. 3(b). When an external pull force is applied, the wire rope is straightened and moved forward along the plastic casing, allowing the unit to be operated remotely. It is flexible because it does not require the transmission of tension to the other end of the line only when the line is straightened.

In the process of controlling the robotic arm, elastic deformation often occurs when the wire rope is subjected to tensile force, resulting in a decrease in control accuracy. Therefore, it is necessary to design a cable pretensioner. Azamat Yeshmukhamet et al. [15] have tried preloading using a combination of springs and pulleys. Since the use of pulleys mentioned above has certain defects, it is preloaded with only springs here, and the structural design is simple. As shown in Fig. 3(b), one end of the Bowden tube is fixed to the pretensioner, and the tensile end will move closer to the servo baffle and the other end away from the servo baffle. Therefore, the slack end of the line will obtain a relatively larger transition distance, so that the line at the slack end is also tensioned to a certain extent. Thanks to the 270-degree steering range, smaller servo reels can be designed. Combined with the use of pretensioning devices, the pull-in end and release end of the wire rope can be firmly wound on the servo reel.

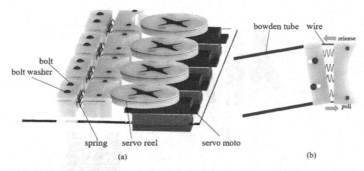

Fig. 3. (a) control system (b) Schematic diagram of a tensioning mechanism

2.3 Gripper Design

In order to make better use of the rotational characteristics of the robotic arm housing, we have developed a simple mechanical gripper, shown in the figure below, driven by a servo. Due to the different shapes and materials of the items that actually need to be gripped, the rigid structure of traditional mechanical grippers cannot fully meet the needs. Therefore, our mechanical grippers are made of flexible materials, and the distance between the three fingers can be adjusted according to the size of the item, which has good adaptability. This design enables the robotic arm to grasp items of all shapes and sizes. The working principle of the mechanical gripper is to drive the movement of the connecting rod by the rotation of the servo, and control the opening and closing degree of the mechanical gripper.

We designed the mechanical gripper to be directly connected to the flexible shell at the end, making it easy and quick to install and dismantle. By rotating the shell, the gripper can not only grasp items, but also screw them like a human hand. To prevent the wire from twisting badly while the gripper continuously rotates, we use an electrical slip ring to solve this problem. The electrical slip ring connects and secures the power supply and the rotating element, allowing the wire to follow the rotation while keeping the other end stationary. In the robotic arm, the wire on the rotating end of the electrical slip ring is connected to the servo motor to control the movement of the mechanical gripper. The wire on the stationary end passes through the connecting ring of the mechanical arm and is connected to the microcontroller and power source at the far end (Fig. 4).

3 Kinematic Modeling

In order to achieve high-precision control of the robotic arm, it is necessary to establish a kinematic model, and the theory in this regard is very mature [16, 17]. Theoretical modeling of wire-driven flexible robotic arms generally has two assumptions:

1. The whole of the robotic arm is normal curvature deformation, that is, the joint bending angle in each section of the robotic arm is the same, and the bending shape is similar to an arc.
2. The wire rope that controls the rotation of the joint of the robotic arm does not have elastic deformation, that is, the length will not change.

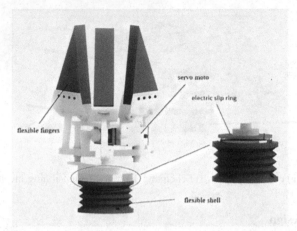

Fig. 4. Gripper structure

First, we build a model with a single-stage robotic arm as the object and analyze it. As shown in Fig. 6, a deflection angle φ and a bending angle θ determine the unique attitude of the robotic arm in the coordinate system. With the upper end face of the first section shell as the XOY plane, the X axis and the Y axis pass through two pairs of orthogonal line holes that control the bending of the first section of the robotic arm, and the center of the plane is the coordinate origin O. The positive direction of the Z axis is the extension direction of the joint of the robotic arm, and the positive direction is determined by the right-hand rule, and the counterclockwise is positive. The first coordinate system is the picker's reference frame. The second coordinate system is the rotation coordinate system $O_t\{X_t, Y_t, Z_t\}$, which corresponds to the angle at which the reference coordinate system rotates around the Z axis φ. Let the center of the terminal joint be point A, then OA is the translation vector of the curved coordinate system $O_b\{X_b, Y_b, Z_b\}$, and rotate θ around the Y_b. Finally, the coordinate system of the end joint is established $O_l\{X_l, Y_l, Z_l\}$, which is equivalent to the rotation of the bending coordinate system around the Z_b axis -φ angle, so that the X_l and Y_l axis still correspond to the initially set wire hole. Therefore, through the homogeneous transformation matrix, the transformation relationship between the end coordinate system and the reference coordinate system can be obtained.

$$T_o^l = \begin{pmatrix} R_{Z_t}(\theta) & 0 \\ 0 & 1 \end{pmatrix} \begin{pmatrix} R_{Y_b}(\varphi) & P_{OA} \\ 0 & 1 \end{pmatrix} \begin{pmatrix} R_{Z_l}(-\theta) & 0 \\ 0 & 1 \end{pmatrix} \tag{1}$$

The length remains unchanged after bending the neutral layer, and the center length of the first robotic arm is L. The radius of curvature of the robotic arm bending can be found:

$$L = \frac{R}{\theta} \tag{2}$$

The length of OA is:

$$OA = 2R * \sin\frac{\theta}{2} \tag{3}$$

Establish a cuboid space with OA as the diagonal, and find the coordinates of the x_A, y_A, z_A that is, the translation vector P_{OA}:

$$X_A = OA \cos(\frac{\pi - \theta}{2}) \cos\varphi = \frac{L(1 - \cos\theta) \cos\varphi}{\theta} \tag{4}$$

$$Y_A = OA \cos(\frac{\pi - \theta}{2}) \sin\varphi = \frac{L(1 - \cos\theta) \sin\varphi}{\theta} \tag{5}$$

$$Z_A = OA \sin(\frac{\pi - \theta}{2}) = \frac{L \sin\theta}{\theta} \tag{6}$$

Next, the relationship between the length of the wire rope and the attitude angle needs to be obtained, d is the distance from the center of the rigid joint to the wirehole, and the radius of curvature of each wire rope can be obtained from the top view of the robotic arm joint and the side view of the robotic arm shown in Fig. 5(a) and 5(b):

$$R_{l_1} = R - d \cos\varphi \tag{7}$$

$$R_{l_2} = R + d \cos\varphi \tag{8}$$

$$R_{l_3} = R - d \sin\varphi \tag{9}$$

$$R_{l_4} = R + d \sin\varphi \tag{10}$$

The change in the length of the wire rope can be obtained by changing the radius of curvature:

$$\Delta_{l_1} = R_{l_1}\theta - L = -d\theta \cos\varphi \tag{11}$$

$$\Delta_{l_2} = R_{l_2}\theta - L = d\theta \cos\varphi \tag{12}$$

$$\Delta_{l_3} = R_{l_3}\theta - L = -d\theta \sin\varphi \tag{13}$$

$$\Delta_{l_4} = R_{l_4}\theta - L = d\theta \sin\varphi \tag{14}$$

$\Delta_{l_1} = -\Delta_{l_2}$, $\Delta_{l_3} = -\Delta_{l_4}$. That is, a pair of lines controlled by the same servo control, the elongation length of one end is equal to the shortening length of the other end. The length change of the wire rope can calculate the angle at which the servo needs to rotate. The kinematic positive solution analysis can derive the relationship between the changes of two angles and line lengths:

$$\varphi = \tan^{-1} \frac{\Delta_{l_4}}{\Delta_{l_2}} \tag{15}$$

$$\theta = \frac{\sqrt{\Delta_{l_2}^2 + \Delta_{l_4}^2}}{d} \tag{16}$$

The analysis method of the two-stage robotic arm is the same as above, and each segment has its own bending angle and deflection angle. The homogeneous change matrix can be used to find the relationship between the end coordinate system and the reference coordinate system. However, because the wire rope that controls the second section of the manipulator passes through the first section, the problem of improving the accuracy coupling cannot be ignored. It is necessary to consider the effect of bending in the first section on the change in the line length of the second section of the robotic arm, as shown in Fig. 5(c).

The relationship between the passive length of the wire rope of the second robotic arm is as follows:

$$\Delta l_5{}' = -d\theta_1 \cos(\varphi_1 - \frac{\pi}{4}) \tag{17}$$

$$\Delta l_6{}' = d\theta_1 \cos(\varphi_1 - \frac{\pi}{4}) \tag{18}$$

$$\Delta l_7{}' = -d\theta_1 \sin(\varphi_1 - \frac{\pi}{4}) \tag{19}$$

$$\Delta l_8{}' = d\theta_1 \sin(\varphi_1 - \frac{\pi}{4}) \tag{20}$$

Since then, the accurate relationship between the movement of the robot arm and the length of the wire rope has been obtained, and precise control and trajectory planning can be carried out according to these formulas.

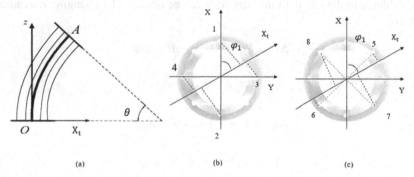

(a)   (b)   (c)

Fig. 5. (a)Robotic Arm side view(b)Top view(c) The effect of the bending of the second segment on the length of the first segment

4 Experiment and Results

To verify the bending performance of the robotic arm, we first need to introduce the concept of its workspace. The workspace refers to the spatial range that the robotic arm can reach, specifically, all the points that can be accessed by the arm. Traditional rigid

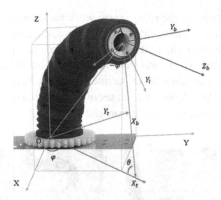

Fig. 6. Robotic Arm Bending

robotic arms have relatively small workspaces and are unable to adapt to complex environments and tasks due to the limitation of fixed joint angle combinations. In contrast, flexible robotic arms have greater degrees of freedom, making their workspaces broader. Furthermore, their flexibility also enables them to have more powerful gripping and handling abilities for difficult or irregularly shaped objects. However, due to the difficulty of obtaining geometric solutions for the trajectory of flexible robotic arms, the calculation and description of their workspaces have become more challenging. Therefore, we used the robot toolbox modeling method combined with the Monte Carlo method to calculate and analyze the workspace of the designed flexible robotic arm in this study, by simulating each angle in a random sample of joint angles. The obtained results can be seen in Fig. 7. Through this approach, we can gain a more comprehensive and accurate understanding of the workspace characteristics of the flexible robotic arm, providing more effective guidance and support for practical applications. Finally, we compared the obtained workspace with the experimental results to verify the bending performance of the robotic arm.

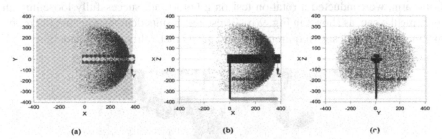

(a)   (b)   (c)

Fig. 7. (a) X-Y plane (b) X-Z plane (3) Y-Z plane

According to the design theory, the maximum bending angle for each section of the robotic arm is 180 degrees. Therefore, we first performed a maximum bending test on the first section of the robotic arm while keeping the second section stationary. As shown in Fig. 8(b), the result indicates that the test effect is very consistent with expectations.

Next, we let the two sections of the robotic arm work simultaneously, giving a deviation angle of 45 degrees and a bending angle of 90 degrees, making the robotic arm take an "S" shape. Finally, we kept the first section of the robotic arm stationary and let the second section bend. Figure (d) shows that the first section of the robotic arm remains relatively straight. Through practical experiments, it has been demonstrated that the robotic arm can bend independently in each section and can also be combined in various ways to form highly complex shapes, demonstrating its high flexibility.

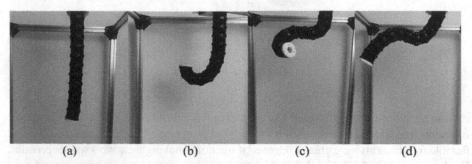

(a)   (b)   (c)   (d)

Fig. 8. (a) initial state of the robotic arm(b)first segment bending(c)both first and second segment bending(d)second segment bending

In the design of the robotic arm, not only flexibility and accuracy need to be considered, but also the load capacity and completeness of its functions. Therefore, we conducted load capacity tests by placing heavy objects on the first joint of the robotic arm and performing lifting and bending tests, as shown in Fig. 9(a). Additionally, the robotic arm has an end gripper and a housing rotation function, which can be used for grabbing, twisting and flexibly manipulating objects. Experimental results show that the robotic arm can successfully bear heavy loads under a certain bending angle and has appropriate structural strength. We also installed a flexible gripper and conducted object gripping tests in various bending states. Furthermore, to test the rotation function of the robotic arm, we conducted a rotation test on a bottle cap, successfully loosening and tightening the cap, as shown in Fig. 9(b). These test results demonstrate that the robotic arm functions meet design requirements, and have practicality and expandability.

(a)   (b)

Fig. 9. (a) load capacity test (b) rotation test

5 Discussions and Conclusion

In this paper, we show the design and features of TSFRA. It is composed of internal joints driven by wire ropes controlled by servos and flexible joints driven by stepper motors, with a very complete degree of freedom. We can draw the following conclusions: 1) The control accuracy of TSFRA is high, and the experimental results are in good agreement with the theoretical model, which can achieve the expected bending angle and deflection angle. 2) TSFRA has stable mechanical properties and a certain load capacity. 3) By cooperating with the end gripper can complete the expected goal, the function of turning the innovative point shell has great practical value and application prospects. Therefore, we believe that TSFRA will play an increasingly important role in the field of industrial automation and other related fields.

However, TSFRA still needs to be improved and improved. First of all, the accuracy of the theoretical model should be strengthened, the mechanical parameters and modeling skills should be improved, and the impact of unstable factors in the manufacturing process on the control of the robotic arm should be minimized. In the future, we will conduct more in-depth research and development on TSFRA, including optimization control algorithms and performance testing. We also plan to develop different types of end effector and conduct adaptability tests to explore more application scenarios and verify their practical value. In addition, we will explore autonomous decision-making and intelligence features, as well as the ability of multiple robotic arms to work together to achieve a level of intelligence, efficiency and ease of control. These efforts will promote the development of technology in the field of flexible robotic arms, bringing more technological innovation to the field of industrial manufacturing and automation.

References

1. Knight, G., Piotrowski, T., Shuford, J.: The role of robotics in manufacturing. Indust. Robot Int. J. **44**(2), 155–163 (2017)
2. Hulin, A., Souchet, S., Fromont, C.: Usage and benefits of robotics in logistics and warehousing activities. Int. J. Prod. Res. **56**(10), 3648–3668 (2018)
3. Kato, T., Okumura, I., Song, S.-E., Golby, A.J., Hata, N.: Tendon-Driven continuum robot for endoscopic surgery: preclinical development and validation of a tension propagation model. IEEE/ASME Trans. Mechatron. **20**(5), 2252–2263 (2015)
4. Zhong, Y., Du, R., Guo, P., Yu, H.: Investigation on a new approach for designing articulated soft robots with discrete variable stiffness. IEEE/ASME Trans. Mechatron. **26**(6), 2998–3009 (2021)
5. Simaan, N.: Snake-like units using flexible backbones and actuation redundancy for enhanced miniaturization. In: Proceedings of the 2005 IEEE International Conference on Robotics and Automation, pp. 3012–3017. Barcelona, Spain (2005)
6. Zhong, Y., Yu, B., Yu, H.: Design and study of scissor-mechanism-based pneumatic actuator with a characteristic of bidirectional contraction. IEEE/ASME Trans. Mechatron. **27**(4), 2080–2088 (2022)
7. Yu, B., Yang, J., Du, R., Zhong, Y.: A versatile pneumatic actuator based on scissor mechanisms: design, modeling, and experiments. IEEE Robot. Automa. Let. **6**(2), 1288–1295 (2021)

8. Lin, B., Wang, J., Song, S., Li, B., Meng, M.Q.-H.: A modular lockable mechanism for tendon-driven robots: design, modeling and characterization. IEEE Robot. Autom. Let. 7(2), 2023–2030 (2022). https://doi.org/10.1109/LRA.2022.3142907

9. Li, Z., Chiu, P., Du, R., Yu, H.: A novel constrained wire-driven flexible mechanism and its kinematic analysis. Mech. Mach. Theory 95, 59–75 (2016). https://doi.org/10.1016/j.mechmachtheory.2015.08.019

10. Clark, A.B., Mathivannan, V., Rojas, N.: A continuum manipulator for open-source surgical robotics research and shared development. IEEE Trans. Med. Robot. Bionics 3(1), 277–280 (2021)

11. Ouyang, B., Liu, Y., Sun, D.: Design of a three-segment continuum robot for minimally invasive surgery. Robot. Biomim. 3, 2 (2016)

12. Xu, Z., Todorov, E.: Design of a highly biomimetic anthropomorphic robotic hand towards artificial limb regeneration. In: 2016 IEEE International Conference on Robotics and Automation (ICRA), pp. 3485–3492. Stockholm (2016)

13. Gómez-de-Gabriel, J.M., Wurdemann, H.A.: Adaptive underactuated finger with active rolling surface. IEEE Robot. Autom. Let. 6(4), 8253–8260 (2021)

14. Zhao, Q., Lai, J., Hu, X., Chu, H.K.: Dual-segment continuum robot with continuous rotational motion along the deformable backbone. IEEE/ASME Trans. Mechatron. 27(6), 4994–5004 (2022)

15. Yeshmukhametov, A., Koganezawa, K., Seidakhmet, A., Yamamoto, Y.: A novel passive pretension mechanism for wire-driven discrete continuum manipulators. In: 2020 IEEE/SICE International Symposium on System Integration (SII), pp. 1168–1173. Honolulu, HI, USA (2020)

16. Ata, A.A., Haraz, E.H., Rizk, A.E.A., Hanna, S.N.: Kinematic analysis of a single link flexible manipulator. In: 2012 IEEE International Conference on Industrial Technology, pp. 852–857. Athens, Greece (2012)

17. Rao, P., Peyron, Q., Lilge, S., Burgner-Kahrs, J.: How to model tendon-driven continuum robots and benchmark modelling performance. Front. Robot. AI 7, 630245 (2021)

Design and Research of a New Underactuated Manipulator

Bo Wang, Zhen Wang, Tianya You, Ju Gao, and Xiangrong Xu[✉]

School of Mechanical Engineering, Anhui University of Technology, Ma'anshan 243002, Anhui, China
xuxr@ahut.edu.cn

Abstract. The manipulator is an important part of the robot to perform tasks efficiently, and the underactuated manipulator has attracted attention because of its low cost and easy maintenance. This paper mainly designs and analyzes the structure of the rod-wheel transmission coupled adaptive robot hand, and proposes the coupled adaptive grasping mode (CO-SA). This mode combines the functions of grasping and adaptive envelope, without the movement of the manipulator palm, the manipulator automatically rotates the second knuckle and wraps various objects of different sizes and shapes, expanding the range of objects that can be grasped. The grasping simulation of underactuated manipulator in Adams software, and the experiment proves that the designed robotic hand coupling adaptive grasping ability can perform the grasping task more efficiently and stably than the traditional manipulator.

Keywords: Robotic hand · Underdrive · Adaptive · Adams

1 Introduction

With the rapid development of robots today, as the end effector of robots, the robot hand is also one of its indispensable and important components. The robot hand has shown an extremely important role in various fields of various departments such as the medical industry, the automobile processing industry, the machinery industry, and the building materials industry. Underactuated manipulator is one of the research hotspots in the field of robotics. It achieves control with a higher degree of freedom through a driving method with less than one degree of freedom, exhibits flexibility and adaptability similar to that of a human arm, and has broad application prospects in industries, medical care, services and other fields. Rigid manipulators are generally composed of multiple rigid rods connected by hinges, which can complete precise and high speed positioning and handling tasks. Flexible manipulators use flexible materials or soft structures, which can be bent and deformed arbitrarily in space, and have better performance in terms of collaboration, grasping, and flexibility. The variable stiffness manipulator can freely switch between rigidity and flexibility according to the needs of different tasks, achieving more fine and detailed operations. Among them, the typical rigid manipulators in foreign countries include the humanoid hand of Korea University of Technology and Education [1] and

© The Author(s), under exclusive license to Springer Nature Singapore Pte Ltd. 2023
H. Yang et al. (Eds.): ICIRA 2023, LNAI 14269, pp. 27–40, 2023.
https://doi.org/10.1007/978-981-99-6489-5_3

the BLT gripper of IRIM Laboratory [2]; the typical rigid manipulators in China include the prosthetic hand of Harbin Institute of Technology The sorting manipulator designed based on the principle of soft coupling and screw transmission [4] and the bionic gripper based on the surface of beef tongue [5]. Typical flexible manipulators include the flexible humanoid hand of Ohio State University in the United States [6], the Octopus Gripper of Festo in Germany [7] and the three-finger pneumatic soft manipulator of Ritsumeikan University in Japan [8, 9]; domestic typical Soft manipulators include the pneumatic soft manipulator of Shanghai Jiao Tong University [10], the four-finger soft manipulator of Beihang University [11, 12] and the two-finger soft manipulator of National Cheng Kung University in Taiwan [13]. In terms of variable stiffness manipulators, typical cases include the variable stiffness manipulator developed by the University of Chicago based on the principle of particle clogging, the adjustable joint stiffness design of the under-actuated manipulator of the Swiss Federal Institute of Technology, and the Singapore University of Technology and Design based on shape memory polymers and 3D printing technology. Fabricated tunable stiffness manipulator. The typical domestic variable stiffness manipulators include Harbin Institute of Technology's variable stiffness soft hand based on low-melting point alloys, Yanshan University's three-finger variable stiffness soft manipulator based on pneumatic artificial muscle technology and bionics principles, and Hong Kong University based on shape memory polymer SMP. Two-finger soft hand with adjustable stiffness. In addition to the typical manipulators mentioned above, some new types of underactuated manipulators have emerged in recent years. For example, the soft hand of the ARMM-5 robotic arm developed by Purdue University in the United States has strong adaptive ability and local deformation function [14]; the Roboy robot of the Swiss Institute of Technology in Lausanne combines flexible structure and sensor technology to achieve a highly bionic motor and sensory abilities [15].

2   Adaptive Underactuated Robotic Hand

There are three single grasping modes of the underactuated robot hand, which are coupling, flat clamping and adaptive, and each mode has different emphases. Coupling mode is used for grasping thin-walled small objects, coupling mode is used for pinching objects, and self-adaptive mainly envelops objects according to the size, shape and size of objects, but for a single grasping mode, the function is too large single. Therefore, a composite grasping mode is proposed, that is, a coupled adaptive grasping mode. It can not only couple and bend multi-joints, but also adaptively envelope objects.

2.1   Force Analysis of Underactuated Hand Robot Grasping

The working principle of an adaptive robot finger is shown in Fig. 1, wherein the origin O is the joint below the first finger segment, the x-axis direction is the vertical upward direction passing through the point O, and the y-axis direction is the inverse direction of the x-axis direction passing through the point O. Rotate the direction of the hour hand by 90° to establish a Cartesian coordinate system, and the force on the object is shown in Fig. 2.

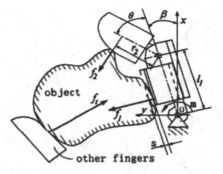

Fig. 1. Working principle of underactuated robotic finger

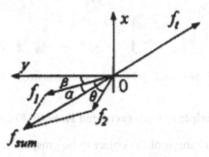

Fig. 2. Force diagram of an object

2.2 Underactuated Robotic Finger

The finger adopts a rod system and a wheel system, and is assembled according to a certain connection method and sequence, so that it can realize coupling and adaptive envelope grabbing functions. The finger device mainly adopts multi-stage belt transmission, and its purpose is to transmit motion and force from the motor to the kinematic joints. The robot hand in this paper contains two robot fingers, and the palm mechanism and the base are sequentially connected to the lower part of the palm mechanism.

The specific components used in this structural design include frame, finger segments (first finger segment, second finger segment), joint shafts (proximal joint shaft, distal joint shaft), transmission wheels (first pulley, second pulley, The third pulley, the fourth pulley, the fifth pulley, the sixth pulley), the spring, the belt (the first belt, the second belt, the third belt), the guide rod (the near guide rod, the far guide rod), guide sleeve, connecting rod (first connecting rod, second connecting rod, third connecting rod), shaft (first shaft, second shaft, third shaft), motor, synchronous belt mechanism. As shown in Fig. 3.

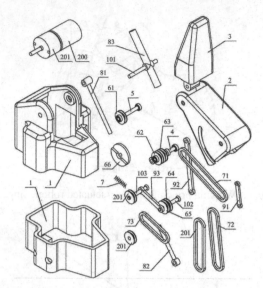

Fig. 3. Explosion diagram of the underactuated robot finger

2.3 The Working Principle of Underactuated Robotic Finger

According to the size and shape of the object to be grasped, it is decided whether the first finger segment or the second finger segment is to grasp the object. If it is the second finger contact, it is coupled pinching; if it is the first finger contact, it is adaptive grasping.

The working mechanism of the underactuated robot finger under coupled pinching is that the motor rotates first, and the third shaft is driven to rotate clockwise through the synchronous belt, and the first transmission wheel follows the third shaft to rotate clockwise. Connected by a spring, the third connecting rod rotates clockwise around the third axis at this time, and due to the joint action of the second connecting rod, the first connecting rod, the first finger segment, the axial guide sleeve, the first guide rod, and the second guide rod, Make the axis of the far joint move in a straight line. And the angle between the third connecting rod and the second connecting rod becomes smaller, this behavior will cause the fifth drive wheel to rotate clockwise relative to the proximal joint axis. Through the transmission action of the first transmission member, the sixth transmission wheel also rotates relative to the distal joint shaft. At this time, the axis of the distal joint moves closer to the grasped object, and the second finger segment will bend relative to the axis of the distal joint at the same time, that is, the linear coupling effect is achieved. As shown in Fig. 4.

The working principle of the underactuated robot finger under adaptive grasping is that the first finger segment is blocked after touching the object, so that it cannot continue to rotate. At this time, the motor continues to work, and the third shaft is driven to rotate through the action of the transmission member, so that the first transmission wheel rotates clockwise around the third shaft. Because connecting rod three can not move, this moment, spring part deforms, and the first drive wheel continues to rotate. Then by the first transmission wheel-the first transmission member-the second transmission wheel-the third transmission wheel-the second transmission member-the fourth transmission wheel-the fifth transmission wheel-the third transmission member-the sixth transmission wheel, so that The clockwise rotation of the far joint axis occurs. The second segment adaptive envelope captures the object, and the capture ends.

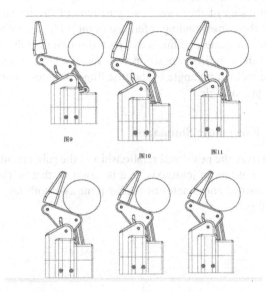

Fig. 4. The working principle of the underactuated robot finger

The robot finger designed in this paper uses the torsion spring to achieve the relative rotation of the second finger around the distal joint axis after the first finger touches the object, so as to achieve the purpose of grasping the object. According to the position, shape, and size of the object to be clamped, the robot finger can first move in a straight line to approach the object, and at the same time, the second finger segment rotates around the distal joint axis to grab the object; if the first finger segment touches the object, the second finger segment The finger segment rotates around the distal joint axis to achieve the purpose of adaptive grasping. The robot hand designed in this paper has the advantages of large grasping range and stable grasping; one motor is used to control two finger segments; the device is cheap and easy to assemble.

3   Kinematic Analysis and Simulation of Robot Finger

The purpose of the kinematics analysis of the driving robot finger is mainly to determine the positions of the near joint axis and the far joint axis, so as to draw the timeline diagram of displacement, velocity and acceleration. In general, in order to determine the direction of the coordinate system on each joint and the relative translation and rotation between two adjacent coordinate systems, the commonly used method is the D-H parameter method, but the D-H parameter method is mainly used to obtain the end joint The position and pose of, and it is suitable for tandem robots. The robot hand designed in this paper is a parallel robot. If the D-H parameter method is used, it will cause difficulty in calculation, and it can be seen from the structure diagram that the robot hand designed in this paper can be solved by using the knowledge of plane geometry in middle school. Set the coordinates of the origin through the knowledge of plane geometry in middle school, establish the corresponding coordinate system, and obtain the functional relationship of the coordinate positions of the proximal joint axis, the distal joint axis and the corresponding reference point with respect to the independent variable being the rotation angle of the active part, through matlab The software draws the change curve of the coordinate position with respect to the rotation angle and the change curve of the inclination angle of the first finger segment and the second finger segment with the rotation angle.

3.1 Robot Finger Kinematics Simulation

In order to better analyze the positional relationship of the robot hand, it is necessary to draw the plane figure of the far joint axis, that is, point D, that is, the change curve of the horizontal and vertical coordinates of the far joint axis with respect to the rotation angle, as shown in Fig. 5.

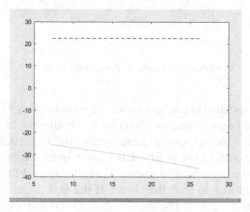

Fig. 5. The change curve of the distal joint with the rotation angle

The ordinate of the distal joint axis is approximately kept at about 25 mm, which is basically consistent with the theory in the previous section that the coupled adaptive robot hand designed in this paper moves approximately along the DK horizontal line, indicating that the end of the robot hand can approach in the form of a horizontal straight line. Object being grasped. And the value of the ordinate is 25 mm, which is a relatively large value, indicating that the second finger segment of the robot hand is far away from the position of the base during work, and interference will not occur during work. In order to better analyze the situation of the robot hand grasping the physical object, it is necessary to explain the change of the angle between the two finger segments and the horizontal direction. Therefore, the slope between the near-joint axis point C and the far-joint axis point D, and the slope between the far-joint axis point D and point H are drawn to illustrate the problem of the angle when the robot hand grasps the object.

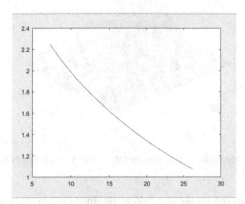

Fig. 6. Variation curve of distal joint axis with rotation angle

At the initial position, HD has a slope angle. As the rotation angle increases, the second finger segment rotates clockwise around the axis of the distal joint to achieve the purpose of continuously approaching and enveloping the object. As shown in Fig. 6, the line segment HD The slope angle of is decreasing, which is consistent with the fact. From the image of the tangent function, it can be seen that the function value is between 1–2.4 and the inclination angle is between 45°–67.38°, indicating that the bending of the second finger segment can well adapt to various objects of different sizes and shapes.

3.2   Kinematics Simulation of Underactuated Robot Finger

In order to better simulate the force of the object when the robot finger grasps the object, the following is divided into two segments: only the second finger segment holds the object in parallel and the first finger segment touches the object, and the second finger segment first couples and rotates to a certain According to the shape and size of the object, it will continue to rotate around the axis of the far joint, so as to achieve the force analysis and simulation of the two situations of adaptively enveloping the object. The contact force between the second finger segment and the object varies with the rotation angle of the first finger segment, the position of the contact point, and the relationship between the distal joint axis, as shown in Fig. 7.

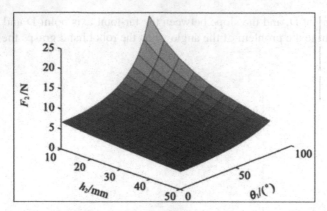

Fig. 7. Contact force and parameters of the second finger segment

It can be seen from the image that when the angle of the first joint is constant, the change of the distance between the force point and the axis of the far joint has little effect on the contact force of the second finger segment, which means that the robot finger designed in this paper is actually grasping the object, the stress on the second finger segment is relatively uniform.

Establish a mathematical model through matlab, that is, the image of the size of the grasping force changing with the angle of the first finger segment and the second finger segment, as shown in Fig. 8.

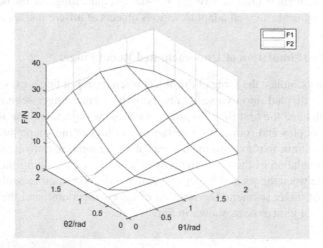

Fig. 8. Mathematical model diagram of contact force with respect to angle

When the relative rotation angles of the two finger segments increase, the contact force (F1) of the first finger segment tends to increase simultaneously. When using the robot hand to grab an object with a smaller size, the second relative rotation angle needs to be rotated by a larger value to achieve the purpose of enveloping the object. It can be seen from the image that the second finger contact force (F2) is greater than the first finger contact force (F1), which is in line with the basic common sense of human grasping. During this process, the force direction of the second finger segment will be towards the palm of the hand to firmly grasp the object, and the contact force of the two finger segments will be reasonably distributed on the grasped object to achieve a stable grasping effect. It can be seen from the graph that the curved surface is relatively smooth, and no matter how the distance (H1, H2) between the two contact points and the joint axis changes, the force exerted by the first finger segment on the object remains basically the same. The contact force of the second finger segment fluctuates slightly under the influence of H1, but fluctuates greatly under the influence of H2. With the increase of H1, the contact force of the second finger segment decreases, which is consistent with the situation in real life.

4 Grasping Simulation Experiment of Adaptive Robotic Hand

The work content of the robot hand is to locate the object through the visual recognition system first, then the three hands of the robot hand move closer to the direction of the object, and finally the fingers adapt to the object according to the shape and size of the object. When the object is fully grasped, Then move the object to the corresponding position according to the requirements. Therefore, it is particularly important to carry out grasping simulation experiments on the designed robot hand. On the one hand, the simulation method adopted in this paper is to analyze the image of the contact force between the robot hand and the object during the grasping process, and on the other hand, to observe the performance of the robot hand when grasping objects of different shapes and sizes. Difference to obtain simulation results. The simulation software used in this paper is Adams.

The simulation grasping experiment of the underactuated robot hand designed in this paper includes the following contents:

(1) Under the condition of using the same driving force, the adaptive robot hand grasps the spheres with different radii to obtain the simulation results;
(2) Under the condition of grabbing the same radius ball, give the robot hand different driving forces to obtain the simulation results;

4.1 Analysis of Simulation Results

Since the robot hand designed in this paper has a total of 3 fingers, which are arranged in a 120° ring with respect to the plane where the base is located, any two fingers are distributed symmetrically with respect to the remaining finger. Now it is necessary to study the relationship of the contact force on the relevant parts of each finger with respect to time. To simplify the model, two fingers of the robot hand are taken for research. The following are all such situations, so I won't repeat them here. The simulation diagram of the robot hand grabbing a sphere with a radius of 38 mm is shown in Fig. 9. Grab spheres with radii of 38 mm and 25 mm respectively, and the contact force between the finger segment and the sphere is shown in Figs. 10, 11, 12, and 13.

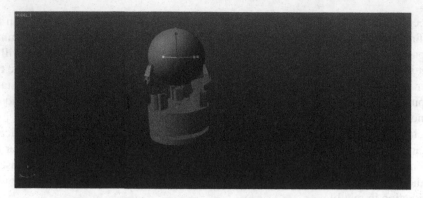

Fig. 9. Simulation diagram of robot hand grabbing a sphere

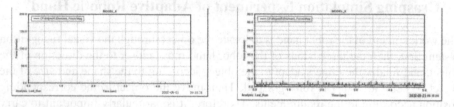

Fig. 10. The contact force-time diagram of the second segment of the first finger

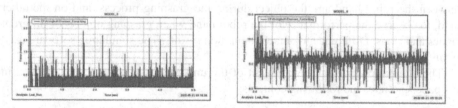

Fig. 11. Contact force-time diagram of the first segment of the first finger

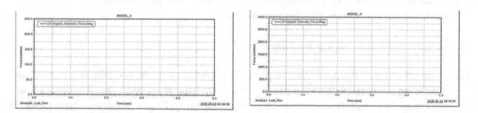

Fig. 12. Contact force-time diagram of the second segment of the second finger

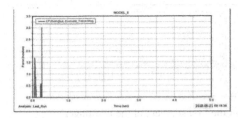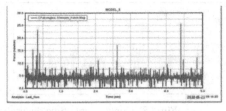

Fig. 13. Contact force-time diagram of the second segment of the second finger

From the image of the change of contact force on each segment of the robot finger with respect to time, it can be seen that when the robot hand is grabbing a sphere with a radius of 25 mm, the radius of the first segment and the second segment of the first finger is The contact forces of a 38 mm sphere are 0.6769N and 0.2292N, respectively, and the contact forces of the first and second finger segments of the second finger with a sphere with a radius of 38 mm are 0.9574N and 0.0351N, respectively. The contact force between the two finger segments of the first finger and the second finger and the sphere is too small, so the work of grasping the sphere with a radius of 38 mm cannot be done well. When the robot hand is grabbing a sphere with a radius of 25 mm, it can be seen from the contact force-time image that the contact forces of the second segment and the first segment of the first finger are 3.0308N and 5.6189N respectively, and the contact force of the second segment The contact forces of the second segment and the first segment of the finger are 5.5747N and 4.0224N respectively, which can adaptively grip a sphere with a radius of 25 mm. Therefore, the robot hand designed in this paper can stably grasp the sphere with a radius of 25 mm.

4.2 Analysis of Underactuated Robot Hand Grabbing a Sphere Under Different Driving Forces

The time-varying image of the contact force between robot fingers under the driving force of 15N and 20N. As shown in Figs. 14, 15, 16, and 17.

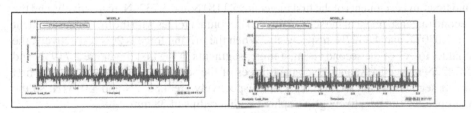

Fig. 14. Contact force-time diagram of the second segment of the first finger

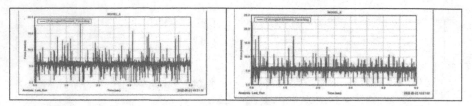

Fig. 15. Contact force-time diagram of the first segment of the first finger

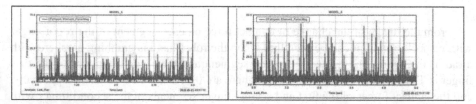

Fig. 16. Contact force-time diagram of the second segment of the second finger

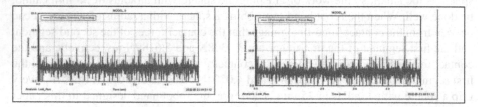

Fig. 17. Contact force-time diagram of the first finger segment of the second finger

From the time-varying image of the contact force of each finger segment on each finger when the driving forces of the robot hand are 15N and 20N respectively, when grasping a sphere with a radius of 38 mm, it can be seen that the robot hand designed in this paper can stably grasp a sphere with a radius of 38 mm. From the contact force-time graph, it can be seen that when the driving force is 15N, the contact forces of the second and first finger segments of the first finger are 5.1181N and 5.7326N, respectively, and the second finger segment of the second finger The contact forces with the first finger segment are 7.0307N and 4.1427N, respectively. When the driving force is 20N respectively, the contact forces of the second and first finger segments of the first finger are 2.7193N and 5.7222N respectively, and the contact forces of the second finger segment and the first finger segment of the second finger are respectively are 4.8022N and 4.0134N, so the manipulator can adaptively grip a sphere with a radius of 38 mm.

It can be seen from the simulation results that when the radius of the sphere is small, the radius in this paper is 25 mm, because the contact between the sphere and the finger is not sufficient, resulting in too small contact force and unable to achieve stable grasping. But when the radius of the sphere is 38 mm, the contact force between each finger segment and the sphere increases significantly, and the robot hand can stably adapt to the envelope grasping. Regarding the influence of the driving force on the grasping performance of the robot hand, when the driving force increases from 10N to 15N, the contact force of each finger segment increases and the envelope effect is better, and both of them can stably grasp a sphere with a radius of 38 mm. But when the driving force increased from 15N to 20N, the contact force decreased slightly.

5 Conclusion

In this paper, a rod-wheel transmission coupling adaptive robot finger mechanism and a rod-wheel transmission coupling adaptive robot hand mechanism are designed; the dynamic analysis of the robot hand designed in this paper is carried out using theoretical mechanics and the principle of virtual work, and the contact force of the finger segment is obtained -The change image of the rotation angle, analyzing the influence of the rotation angle and contact distance on the contact force of the corresponding finger segment; finally, using Adams to simulate the process of the robot hand grabbing the sphere, obtain the contact force-time graph of each finger segment, and analyze the sphere of different volumes and driving force on gripping performance. However, the shortcoming of this paper is that the designed rod-wheel transmission coupling robot finger mechanism uses a torsion spring damper, so that the contact force of the corresponding finger segment of the robot hand will not be stable at a certain value, but fluctuate within a certain range, which will affect the Fatigue damage is caused by each finger segment, which needs further improvement.

References

1. Kim, Y.J., Yoon, J., Sim, Y.W.: Fluid lubricated dexterous finger mechanism for human-like impact absorbing capability. IEEE Robot. Autom. Lett. **4**(4), 3971–3978 (2019)
2. Kim, Y.J., Song, H., Maengc, Y.: BLT gripper: an adaptive gripper with active transition capability between precise pinch and compliant grasp. IEEE Robot. Autom. Lett. **5**(4), 5518–5525 (2020)
3. Liu, Y., Feng, F., Gao, Y.: HIT prosthetic hand based on tendon-driven mechanism. J. Central South Univ. **21**(5), 1778–1791 (2014)
4. Zhi, W., Meng, N., Daqian, Y., et al.: Manipulator design and motion analysis. Mach. Des. Res. **38**(2), 97–100 (2022)
5. Yufeng, Z., Kun, W., Xuan, W., Bo, C., et al.: Design and experiment of a gripper with tongue-inspired surface structure. Mach. Des. Res. **38**(03), 70–74 (2022)
6. She, Y., Li, C., Cleary, J., et al.: Design and fabrication of a soft robotic hand with embedded actuators and sensors. J. Mech. Robot. **7**(2), 1–9 (2015)
7. Laschi, C., Cianchetti, M., Mazzolai, B., et al.: Soft robot arm inspired by the octopus. Adv. Robot. **26**(7), 709–727 (2012)
8. Wang, Z., Hirai, S.: Soft gripper dynamics using a line-segment model with an optimization-based parameter identification method. IEEE Robot. Autom. Lett. **2**(2), 624–631 (2017)
9. Wang, Z., Torigoe, Y., Hirai, S.: A prestressed soft gripper: design, modeling, fabrication, and tests for food handling. IEEE Robot. Autom. Lett. **2**(4), 1909–1916 (2017)
10. Shujun, W., Tianyu, W., Guoying, G.: Design of a soft pneumatic robotic gripper based on fiber-reinforced actuator. J. Mech. Eng. **53**(13), 29–38 (2017)

11. Hao, Y., Gong, Z., Xie, Z., et al.: Universal soft pneumatic robotic gripper with variable effective length. In: 2016 35th Chinese Control conference (CCC), pp. 6109–6114. IEEE (2016)
12. Hao, Y., Wang, T., Ren, Z., et al.: Modeling and experiments of a soft robotic gripper in amphibious environments. Int. J. Adv. Robot. Syst. **14**(3), 1729881417707148 (2017)
13. Liu, C.H., Chen, T.L., Chiu, C.H., et al.: Optimal design of a soft robotic gripper for grasping unknown objects. Soft Robot. **5**(4), 452–465 (2018)
14. Pal, A., Restrepo, V., Goswami, D., et al.: Exploiting mechanical instabilities in soft robotics: control, sensing, and actuation. Adv. Mater. **33**(19), 2006939 (2021)
15. Jia, H., Mailand, E., Zhou, J., et al.: Universal soft robotic microgripper. Small **15**(4), 1803870 (2019)

Medical Imaging for Biomedical Robotics

Accelerated Unfolding Network for Medical Image Reconstruction with Efficient Information Flow

Mengjie Qin[1,2], Rong Yang[1,2], Minhong Wan[1,2], Chunlong Zhang[1,2(✉)], and Te Li[1,2]

[1] Research Center for Intelligent Robotics, Research Institute of Interdisciplinary Innovation, Zhejiang Lab, Hangzhou 311100, China
{qmj,yang_rong,wanmh,zcl1515,lite}@zhejianglab.com
[2] Zhejiang Engineering Research Center for Intelligent Robotics, Hangzhou 311100, China

Abstract. Deep unfolding networks (DUNs) have become mainstream for many medical image reconstruction tasks due to their exceptional interpretability and high performance. Unlike black-box deep neural networks, DUNs can provide insight into the intermediary steps of the reconstruction process. Extensive work has been done to study classical optimization algorithms. However, there are several issues that still require further exploration, including the unfolding implications of accelerated optimization algorithms and the performance bottlenecks in unfolding algorithms. To tackle these two concerns, this paper initially validates the extent of performance enhancement achieved by accelerated variation of ADMM, as compared to the original method. As for the second issue, we point out that the coarse information fusion operations utilized in existing unfolding networks primarily impede their performance (e.g., simple addition and subtraction). Based on this, we design a simple, reasonable yet effective accelerated ADMM-based unfolding framework, which integrate multi-channel information into existing DUNs. Additionally, the developed efficient feature aggregation strategy can further enhance the performance of DUNs. We demonstrate, through MRI accelerated reconstruction experiments, that the proposed framework outperforms state-of-the-art DUNs while utilizing fewer parameters.

Keywords: accelerated unfolding network · MRI reconstruction · feature aggregation

1 Introduction

Medical computational imaging is not only one of the highly active fields in modern data science, but also an important subject in medical robotics, including X-ray computed tomography (CT), magnetic resonance imaging (MRI),

Supported by Key Research Project of Zhejiang Lab (No. G2021NB0AL03), Youth Foundation Project of Zhejiang Lab (No. K2023NB0AA03, No. K2023NB0AA04).

© The Author(s), under exclusive license to Springer Nature Singapore Pte Ltd. 2023
H. Yang et al. (Eds.): ICIRA 2023, LNAI 14269, pp. 43–54, 2023.
https://doi.org/10.1007/978-981-99-6489-5_4

and positron emission tomography (PET) [11]. Such applications try to deduce images inside the patient's body from the noise measurements acquired by the imaging device. However the most interesting features cannot be observed directly, but must be inferred from the samples. In many cases, the simplest approximation that accounts for the linear relationship between features and samples yields satisfactory results. A common technique for medical image reconstruction is to model it as a linear inverse problem to solve the linear relationship embedded in it. In general, the reconstruction problem can be defined as [1, 14]

$$\min_{x} F(x) \equiv f(x) + g(x) = ||y - \Phi(x)||_2^2 + \lambda R(x). \tag{1}$$

where $\Phi(\cdot)$ is a degradation operator, $x \in \mathbb{C}^N$ is an unknown signal constrained by the prior term $\lambda R(x)$ with regularization parameter $\lambda > 0$, and $y \in \mathbb{C}^M$ is the linear measurements. Equation(1) aims at recovering the N-dimensional signal x^* from the M measurements y and the operator Φ. Since $M \leq N$, the reconstruction process may be ill-posed and under-determined without the aid of prior knowledge $R(x)$. However, with certain regularization, such as the shape edges, the textures, and the local smoothness, the originally ill-posed problem could be converted to the well-posed one, which contributes significantly to solving the medical image reconstruction problem.

In the past, various traditional algorithms and their variants have been extensively developed to solve Eq. (1), such as alternating direction method of multipliers (ADMM) [8], half quadratic splitting (HQS) [15] and iterative shrinkage thresholding algorithm (ISTA) [19]. Recently, fueled by the powerful learning ability of deep networks, several deep network-based optimization methods have been proposed to learn the inverse mapping from y to x. Among these methods, deep unfolding network (DUN) [17, 20, 22] is a promising orientation due to its friendly interpretability and outstanding performance. Specifically, DUN attempts to construct interpretable deep neural networks by incorporating the framework of traditional iterative algorithms and have been empirically successful in solving optimization problems.

Typically, the integration of advanced network modules into the unfolding framework is a common practice to achieve superior performance. For instance, Aggarwal et al. proposed a recursive algorithm that alternates between CNN blocks and fidelity terms [1] in the image domain. And DuDoRNet [21] employs an augmented residual dense network to perform the reconstruction task, and achieves commendable results. To address the undersampling in the frequency domain, several cross-domain CNNs have been proposed, which incorporate not only the image domain but also more diverse and complex information sources [4,9]. By employing residual learning and the U-Net [2,3,7] architecture, MRI reconstruction has successfully learned to remove aliasing artifacts. Mardani et al. utilized generative adversarial networks (GANs) to model low-dimensional manifolds in high-quality magnetic resonance images [12]. Furthermore, the combination of U-Net and GANs has been proposed to further reduce aliasing artifacts [10,13,16].

Although remarkable achievements have been made, with a closer scrutiny of DUN, we find there are few works in the current DUN that discuss and analyze the following two issues. First, how effective is the unfolding of acceleration algorithms (e.g., accelerated ADMM)? Second, what are the main reasons limiting the performance of current unfolding networks? Since DUNs are mainly composed of two parts: model-based optimization methods and data-based neural networks. In fact, the above two questions correspond to two important perspectives for improving the performance of deep unfolding networks, i.e., the selection of optimization algorithms and the architecture of unfolding networks, respectively.

In this paper, we attempt to explore these two issues and offer a general, flexible and concise framework to guide the design of the DUNs. Our main contributions can be summarized as follows:

- An interpretable accelerated ADMM (AccADMM) iterations network is formed by unfolding optimization model. With the network's interpretability, the structure can be easily adjusted to the physical meaning, and some non-functional and redundant parts can be effectively removed.
- We point out the single-channel input and output at each stage and the insufficient information fusion mechanism as the main reasons for limiting the performance of the unfolding network. To break the bottleneck, we adopt a bi-attention approach for data enhancement during the transfer phase and a multi-channel attention fusion strategy during the information communication phase to enhance feature extraction.
- We propose a novel DUN based on accelerated efficient information flow network (AEIF-Net). Extensive experiments have demonstrated that the proposed scheme outperforms existing state-of-the-art DUNs by a significant margin, while maintaining a low number of parameters.

2   Proposed Method

2.1   AccADMM-Based Unfolding Framework

Rather than a black box, DUN frames the MRI reconstruction task as an optimization problem and incorporates learnable network blocks to handle the challenging components. DUN is typically constructed with a predetermined number of stages, with each stage being a direct representation of one iteration of the unfolded optimization algorithm. Additionally, all parameters, such as linear or nonlinear projections, shrinkage thresholds, and regularization parameters, can be trained end to-end utilizing back-propagation.

Previous unfolding frameworks ignored the impact of accelerated optimization algorithms, specifically failing to fully utilize second-order gradient information. To establish a connection between these sides, we extend the widely used ADMM algorithm in DUN to an accelerated version. To facilitate analysis, we directly present the iterative formulation of ADMM and AccADMM for solving problem (1) as follows:

$$\mathcal{L}_\rho(\boldsymbol{x}, \boldsymbol{z}, \boldsymbol{b}) = \frac{1}{2}\|\boldsymbol{y} - F\boldsymbol{x}\|_2^2 + \lambda R(\boldsymbol{z}) + \frac{\rho}{2}\|\boldsymbol{x} - \boldsymbol{z} + \frac{\boldsymbol{b}}{\rho}\|_2^2. \tag{2}$$

where F is obtained by multiplying the binary undersampling mask and the Fourier transform, $\boldsymbol{b}$ is Lagrangian multiplier, ρ is a penalty parameter.

In this case, update steps under the ADMM framework can be extended as:

$$\begin{cases} \boldsymbol{x}_{t+1} = \arg\min_x \frac{1}{2}\|\boldsymbol{y} - F\boldsymbol{x}_t\|_2^2 + \frac{\rho_{t+1}}{2}\|\boldsymbol{x}_t - \boldsymbol{z}_t + \frac{\boldsymbol{b}_t}{\rho_{t+1}}\|_2^2 \\ \boldsymbol{z}_{t+1} = \arg\min_z \text{proxNet}_{\mathcal{R},\tau}(\boldsymbol{x}_{t+1} + \frac{\boldsymbol{b}_t}{\rho_{t+1}}) \\ \boldsymbol{b}_{t+1} = \boldsymbol{b}_t + \beta_t(\boldsymbol{x}_{t+1} - \boldsymbol{z}_{t+1}), \end{cases} \tag{3}$$

where $\text{proxNet}_{\mathcal{R},\tau}(\boldsymbol{x}) = \arg\min_x \frac{1}{2}\|\boldsymbol{y} - F\boldsymbol{x}_t\|_2^2 + \tau\mathcal{R}(\boldsymbol{y})$, $t = \{1, \cdots, T\}$ denotes the iteration step.

In addition, the iterative formulation of AccADMM is constructed by introducing auxiliary variables $\hat{\boldsymbol{z}}$ and $\hat{\boldsymbol{b}}$. Specifically, we incorporate an acceleration strategy based on widely used first-order optimization algorithms, which could be regarded as a second-order differential equation with better convex approximation and $O(1/t^2)$-convergence rate, while the first-order convergence rate is $O(1/t)$. Then Eq. (3) is solved by carrying out the following iterative sub-problems:

$$\begin{cases} \boldsymbol{x}_{t+1} = \arg\min_x \frac{1}{2}\|\boldsymbol{y} - F\boldsymbol{x}_t\|_2^2 + \frac{\rho_{t+1}}{2}\|\boldsymbol{x}_t - \hat{\boldsymbol{z}}_t + \frac{\hat{\boldsymbol{b}}_t}{\rho_{t+1}}\|_2^2 \\ \boldsymbol{z}_{t+1} = \arg\min_z \text{proxNet}_{\mathcal{R},\tau}(\boldsymbol{x}_{t+1} + \frac{\hat{\boldsymbol{b}}_t}{\rho_{t+1}}) \\ \boldsymbol{b}_{t+1} = \hat{\boldsymbol{b}}_t + \beta_{t+1}(\boldsymbol{x}_{t+1} - \boldsymbol{z}_{t+1}) \\ \hat{\boldsymbol{z}}_{t+1} = \boldsymbol{z}_{t+1} + \beta_{t+1}(\boldsymbol{z}_{t+1} - \boldsymbol{z}_t) \\ \hat{\boldsymbol{b}}_{t+1} = \boldsymbol{b}_{t+1} + \beta_{t+1}(\boldsymbol{b}_{t+1} - \boldsymbol{b}_t) \end{cases} \tag{4}$$

To convert them into networks, the sub-problems of $\boldsymbol{x}_{t+1}$, $\boldsymbol{b}_{t+1}$, $\hat{\boldsymbol{z}}_{t+1}$ and $\hat{\boldsymbol{b}}_{t+1}$ in problem (4) are generally kept unchanged, with ρ_{t+1} and β_{t+1} set to trainable parameters. $\text{proxNet}_{\mathcal{R},\tau}$ can be treated as a denoising process with input $\boldsymbol{x}_{t+1} + \frac{\hat{\boldsymbol{b}}_t}{\rho_{t+1}}$. Obviously, the main change in the acceleration model lies in the acceleration variables $\hat{\boldsymbol{z}}$ and $\hat{\boldsymbol{b}}$, which in the framework is a second-order term of the ordinary differential equation and can be expressed in the neural network structure using skip connections.

For sub-problem $\boldsymbol{x}_{t+1}$, we can directly use the least square method to solve it, as follows:

$$\boldsymbol{x}_{t+1} = (F^T F + \rho_{t+1}I)^{-1}(F^T\boldsymbol{y} + \rho_{t+1}\hat{\boldsymbol{z}}_t - \hat{\boldsymbol{b}}_t) \tag{5}$$

where I is an identity matrix.

As previously analyzed, the intensive processing of DUN can be divided into two parts: image property enhancement (**IPE**), information flow fusion (**IFF**) and image calibration (**IC**). In this work, we argue that the pixel level processing in problem (4) is crude and limits the transmission of information. Therefore, by rethinking DUN, we propose a fine-modulated DUN based on accelerated

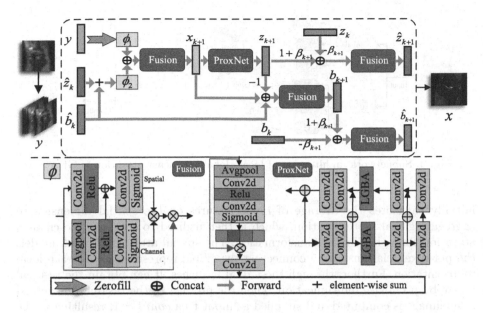

Fig. 1. Network architecture of our proposed AEIF-Net.

efficient information flow (AEIF-Net) to achieve more efficient information flow fusion. The iterative scheme of AEIF-Net is as follows:

$$\begin{cases} \boldsymbol{x}_{t+1} = \mathcal{C}_{att}(\phi_1(F^T\boldsymbol{y}) \oplus \phi_2(\hat{\boldsymbol{z}}_t - \hat{\boldsymbol{b}}_t)) \\ \boldsymbol{z}_{t+1} = \mathcal{D}_t(\boldsymbol{x}_{t+1} + \frac{\hat{\boldsymbol{b}}_t}{\rho_{t+1}}) \\ \boldsymbol{b}_{t+1} = \mathcal{C}_{att}(\hat{\boldsymbol{b}}_t \oplus \beta_{t+1}(\boldsymbol{x}_{t+1} \oplus (-\boldsymbol{z}_{t+1}))) \\ \hat{\boldsymbol{z}}_{t+1} = \mathcal{C}_{att}((1+\beta_{t+1})\boldsymbol{z}_{t+1} \oplus (-\boldsymbol{z}_t)) \\ \hat{\boldsymbol{b}}_{t+1} = \mathcal{C}_{att}((1+\beta_{t+1})\boldsymbol{b}_{t+1} \oplus (-\boldsymbol{b}_t)) \end{cases} \qquad (6)$$

where $\oplus$ is the concat operator, $\mathcal{C}_{att}(\cdot)$ represents the channel attention operator, $\mathcal{D}(\cdot)$ is the denoising module under the DUN framework, $\phi(\cdot)$ is a feature extractor that converts input variables from a single-channel image domain to a multi-channel feature domain.

2.2 Reconstruction Subnet

Our proposed model AEIF-Net consists of three modules: the image property enhancement module, the information flow fusion module and image calibration module. As shown in Fig. 1, to facilitate more comprehensive feature learning, we initially duplicate the input C times along the channel dimension.

IPE Module: Given input $\boldsymbol{y} \in \mathbb{R}^{C \times H \times W}$, the image property enhancement module $\phi(\cdot)$ is designed with dual branches to capture both the spatial and channel dependencies, and to refine the features. The channel attention branch

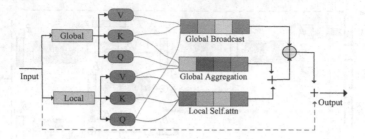

Fig. 2. Subnetwork architecture of local-global broadcast attention (LGBA).

initially calculates the average of input features on the spatial dimension to aggregate global representation, which is then utilized to compute the channel attention through a linear transformation. The spatial attention branch models the per-pixel relationship by connecting the global representation to each local representation. Further, through these dual branches, it can obtain the residual image by pixel-wise multiplication. Then the product of the residual image and input image is computed and supplied as input to a $conv1 \times 1$, resulting in the final output.

IFF Module: After obtaining the enhanced features, the image is further input into the information flow fusion module. Note that in order to better fuse contextual information, the element-wise addition is replaced with a channel attention module, denoted as $\mathcal{C}_{att}(\cdot)$. As in Eq. (6)

$$
\begin{aligned}
\boldsymbol{b}_{t+1} &= \mathcal{C}_{att}(\hat{\boldsymbol{b}}_t \oplus \beta_{t+1}(\boldsymbol{x}_{t+1} \oplus (-\boldsymbol{z}_{t+1}))) \\
&= \mathcal{C}_{att}(\hat{\boldsymbol{b}}_t \oplus \boldsymbol{x}_{t+1} \oplus \boldsymbol{z}_{t+1})
\end{aligned}
\tag{7}
$$

With $\hat{\boldsymbol{b}}_t$, $\boldsymbol{x}_{t+1}$ and $\boldsymbol{z}_{t+1}$ concatenated, the channel attention module, which is composed of 1×1 convolutions, is responsible for learning channel-wise weights in an adaptive manner to better fuse contextual information.

IC Module: In Eq. (6), proxNet$_{\mathcal{R},\tau}$ is a to-be-decided proximal operator. To devise a suitable unfolding strategy, it is essential to thoroughly examine the inherent meanings of the equation. Our main objective is to enhance features in both spatial and frequency domains. In the spatial domain, we have implemented a feature calibration module consisting of a typical 5-layer Unet structure to capture multi-scale information. As image calibration module "proxNet" shown in Fig. 1, the input is passed through an encoder and decoder to generate output with residual connections. Inspired by the LightViT model [6], in the process, we utilize a local-global broadcast attention (LGBA) module that plays a critical role in capturing local and non-local structural features at the spatial level. As shown in Fig. 2, LGAB mainly consists of three submodules, global broadcast, global aggregation, and local self-attention. To address the limitations of extensive receptive fields and long-range dependencies, this subnetwork leverages a lightweight approach to achieve local-global interactions. Specifically, it aggregates the global representation across the entire image feature map and broadcasts it into the feature map. Additionally, for local feature information, the subnetwork collects relevant global dependencies in a compact feature space and subsequently broadcasts the combined global information to the local feature. All information exchange is performed using a homogeneous transform attention mechanism.

3   Experiments

In this section, we conduct extensive experiments to evaluate the performance of the proposed algorithm. Specifically, the investigation experiments is conducted on MRI acceleration task.

Datasets: For MRI acceleration, two MRI datasets, the IXI and FastMRI are adopted to evaluate the clinical efficacy of the proposed method. The IXI dataset comprises 578 registered T2 images, each with a size of 256×256. For FastMRI dataset, 588 volumes of fat-suppressed proton density-weighted (FSPD) images are selected, each with a size of 320×320. We split these datasets into a ratio of $7 : 1 : 2$ for training, validation and testing. In addition, three different k-space undersampling masks (1d cartesian, including random and equispaced fraction and 2d radial) were employed in the experiments, with acceleration rates of $4\times$ and $8\times$.

Implementation Details: For both the two tasks, we implement our method in the Pytorch framework with an NVIDIA A100 S GPU. The settings for MRI acceleration is as follows:

   Loss: L_1, *Optimizer*: Adam(0.9,0.999), *Learning rate*: 10^{-4}, *Epoch*: 30, *batch size*: 1, *Stage number*: 18,

   Peak Signal-to-Noise Ratio (PSNR) and Structural Similarity Index (SSIM) serve as the evaluation metrices in all of our experiments.

Quantitative Comparisons: To objectively evaluate the validity of the proposed model, we selected the five state-of-the-art and representative methods employed for comparisons: including three learning-based methods, Unet [18], MICCAN [5] and DuDoRNet [21], and two deep unfolding methods, ISTA-Net [19] and HQS-Net [15]. For a fair comparison, the recommended parameter settings by the original authors were used for all the competitors, and the best performance is reported accordingly. Table 1 presents the quantitative results of the IXI dataset, where it is evident that AEIF-net outperforms most of its competitors in terms of parameter efficiency and only falls slightly behind DuDoRNet in a single instance with $8\times$ acceleration. As for effectiveness, AEIF-net exhibits remarkable performance in all cases. Table 2 presents the numerical results of image restoration of fastMRI data set, which are similar to the results of IXI data set, and the proposed model AEIF-net achieves optimal results in most cases. In the IXI dataset, AEIF-Net achieves impressive results PSNR of 49.235 and SSIM of 0.998 under $4\times$ radial acceleration. In comparison, the other two expansion methods, ISTA-Net and HQS-Net, have inferior performance and more parameters. As DuDoRNet, a purely learn-based approach, achieved the suboptimal results in all cases, highlighting the strong reconstruction ability of joint learning.

Table 1. Comparisons with SOTA methods using three masks on IXI dataset. Params, PSNR, and SSIM are reported. The best results are highlighted in bold.

Params			7.76M	1.19M	2.62M	1.23M	0.694M	2.12M
Acc	Masks	Metrics	Unet	ISTA-Net	MICCAN	HQS-Net	DuDoRNet	AEIF-Net
4×	radial	PSNR ↑	34.053	43.233	41.634	35.139	44.942	**46.245**
		SSIM ↑	0.967	0.992	0.991	0.969	0.995	**0.996**
	random	PSNR ↑	31.276	33.612	35.433	31.488	36.651	**37.077**
		SSIM ↑	0.954	0.960	0.973	0.948	0.980	**0.981**
	equispaced fraction	PSNR ↑	30.220	29.890	33.498	30.344	34.589	**35.470**
		SSIM ↑	0.946	0.921	0.965	0.942	0.972	**0.978**
8×	radial	PSNR ↑	29.752	31.976	32.830	29.017	**35.168**	34.129
		SSIM ↑	0.935	0.941	0.959	0.921	**0.972**	0.968
	random	PSNR ↑	29.057	28.329	31.687	28.697	32.984	**33.580**
		SSIM ↑	0.932	0.899	0.950	0.923	0.955	**0.962**
	equispaced fraction	PSNR ↑	27.905	26.833	29.987	27.401	30.945	**31.287**
		SSIM ↑	0.9220	0.886	0.940	0.909	0.947	**0.955**

Qualitative Comparisons: For visual comparison, Fig. 3 presents medical reconstructions of a bone marrow edema and a normal case from the fastMRI dataset. Generally, all algorithms can recover relatively clear bone and soft tissue structures. However, in order to distinguish the different reconstruction results more clearly, a part of the image was enlarged in the second row. Upon further observation, it can be seen that the structure of the bursae near the bone tissue in the reconstruction results of Unet and HQS-Net was blurry, while other comparison algorithms, such as DuDoRNet and AEIF-Net, retain the semantic details of the image more clearly. According to the results of the error map in the third row, roughly speaking, all the methods can process the reconstructed image well, yet the error map generated from AEIF-Net presents much bluer results (lower error). This further validates the superiority of the proposed AEIF-Net model based on the unfolding framework.

Ablation Studies: Our ablation analysis focused on three major components of AEIF-Net, i.e., acceleration strategy (AS), global-local fusion scheme (GFS), and optimized unfolding network (OUN). All experiments were performed on the fastMRI dataset using the radial mask for 4× accelerated reconstruction. For the acceleration strategy, subproblems $\hat{z}_{t+1}$ and $\hat{b}_{t+1}$ were removed from Eq. (6) as baseline-1 to conduct the ablation experiment. From Fig. 4 and Table 3, it can be observed that the convergence rate of the proposed AEIF-Net model is significantly faster than that of the baseline-1. Additionally, when the model tends

Table 2. Comparisons with SOTA methods using three masks on fastMRI dataset. Params, PSNR, and SSIM are reported. The best results are highlighted in bold.

Params			7.76M	1.19M	2.62M	1.23M	0.694M	2.12M
Acc	Masks	Metrics	Unet	ISTA-Net	MICCAN	HQS-Net	DuDoRNet	AEIF-Net
4×	radial	PSNR ↑	28.689	30.282	30.205	29.319	30.064	**30.376**
		SSIM ↑	0.830	0.867	0.865	0.839	**0.864**	0.854
	random	PSNR ↑	27.958	29.071	29.111	28.566	**29.163**	29.120
		SSIM ↑	0.811	0.834	0.835	0.819	**0.844**	0.812
	equispaced fraction	PSNR ↑	27.264	28.206	28.339	27.822	28.521	**28.641**
		SSIM ↑	0.780	0.797	0.802	0.787	0.804	**0.831**
8×	radial	PSNR ↑	26.424	27.259	27.414	27.818	27.832	**27.853**
		SSIM ↑	0.723	0.742	0.745	0.764	0.782	**0.784**
	random	PSNR ↑	26.375	27.028	27.374	26.636	27.376	**27.623**
		SSIM ↑	0.754	0.762	0.771	0.755	0.773	**0.781**
	equispaced fraction	PSNR ↑	26.212	26.580	26.963	26.416	26.815	**27.311**
		SSIM ↑	0.745	0.746	0.750	0.747	0.751	**0.782**

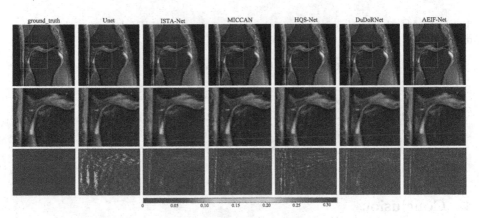

Fig. 3. Visual results and corresponding error map with 4× acceleration under *radial* mask for fastMRI dataset.

to converge, the proposed AEIF-Net model shows superior performance. This reveals that the corporation of second-order information is not only conducive to model convergence but also improves the performance of the model.

By replacing the IC module with Unet, a degraded version of AEIF-Net can be produced, which is named baseline-2. This approach can be employed to evaluate the importance of GFS. Further, in order to investigate the role of OUN, we employ baseline-3, which is obtained by excluding the information flow fusion module and can be considered as the solution of Eq. (4). As demonstrated in Table 3, the numerical results of baseline-2 and baseline-3 are inferior to those of our proposed model. This further confirms that GFS effectively fuses information

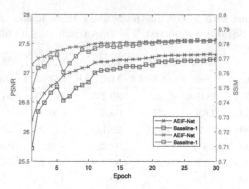

Fig. 4. Diagram of Convergence rates of baseline-1 and AEIF-Net with 8× acceleration under *equispaced fraction* mask for fastMRI dataset.

flows and that OUN has the capability to capture both local and non-local characteristics.

Table 3. Ablation study of three major components on fastMRI dataset with different masks.

	AS	GFS	OUN	*radial* 8×		*random* 8×		*equispaced* 8×	
				PSNR ↑	SSIM ↑	PSNR ↑	SSIM ↑	PSNR ↑	SSIM ↑
baseline-1	✗	✓	✓	27.652	0.768	27.635	0.768	27.280	0.779
baseline-2	✓	✗	✓	27.367	0.752	27.221	0.732	27.025	0.759
baseline-3	✓	✓	✗	27.156	0.712	26.635	0.701	26.471	0.721
Ours	✓	✓	✓	**27.853**	**0.784**	**27.623**	**0.781**	**27.311**	**0.782**

4   Conclusion

In this paper, we propose a novel DUN based on accelerated efficient information flow network (AEIF-Net), which improves the previous DUN method from three perspectives: image property enhancement, information flow fusion, and feature extraction scheme. Firstly, we have mathematically and empirically verified that the second-order gradient acceleration strategy leads to faster convergence and better approximation. Furthermore, we also designed a data property enhancement model based on bi-attention, and adopted a multi-channel information flow fusion scheme to alleviate the information loss and precision reduction caused by insufficient information flow of the current mainstream model in multi-stage operation. The MRI acceleration experiments conducted on two representative datasets show that our approach outperforms previous state-of-the-art methods. However, in medical image reconstruction, the model may have to process multiple invisible masks simultaneously, which necessitates further investigation on model generalization in future studies.

References

1. Aggarwal, H.K., Mani, M.P., Jacob, M.: MoDl: model-based deep learning architecture for inverse problems. IEEE Trans. Med. Imaging **38**(2), 394–405 (2018)
2. Beeche, C., et al.: Super U-Net: a modularized generalizable architecture. Pattern Recogn. **128**, 108669 (2022)
3. Du, G., Cao, X., Liang, J., Chen, X., Zhan, Y.: Medical image segmentation based on U-Net: a review. J. Imaging Sci. Technol. **64** (2020)
4. Eo, T., Jun, Y., Kim, T., Jang, J., Lee, H.J., Hwang, D.: KIKI-net: cross-domain convolutional neural networks for reconstructing undersampled magnetic resonance images. Magn. Reson. Med. **80**(5), 2188–2201 (2018)
5. Huang, Q., Yang, D., Wu, P., Qu, H., Yi, J., Metaxas, D.: MRI reconstruction via cascaded channel-wise attention network. In: 2019 IEEE 16th International Symposium on Biomedical Imaging (ISBI 2019), pp. 1622–1626. IEEE (2019)
6. Huang, T., Huang, L., You, S., Wang, F., Qian, C., Xu, C.: LightViT: towards light-weight convolution-free vision transformers. arXiv preprint arXiv:2207.05557 (2022)
7. Huang, Z., et al.: A novel tongue segmentation method based on improved U-Net. Neurocomputing **500**, 73–89 (2022)
8. Li, C., Yin, W., Jiang, H., Zhang, Y.: An efficient augmented Lagrangian method with applications to total variation minimization. Comput. Optim. Appl. **56**, 507–530 (2013)
9. Li, Z., et al.: Triple-d network for efficient undersampled magnetic resonance images reconstruction. Magn. Reson. Imaging **77**, 44–56 (2021)
10. Li, Z., Zhang, T., Wan, P., Zhang, D.: SEGAN: structure-enhanced generative adversarial network for compressed sensing MRI reconstruction. In: Proceedings of the AAAI Conference on Artificial Intelligence, vol. 33, pp. 1012–1019 (2019)
11. Lustig, M., Donoho, D., Pauly, J.M.: Sparse MRI: the application of compressed sensing for rapid MR imaging. Magn. Res. Med. Off. J. Int. Soc. Magn. Res. Med. **58**(6), 1182–1195 (2007)
12. Mardani, M., et al.: Deep generative adversarial neural networks for compressive sensing MRI. IEEE Trans. Med. Imaging **38**(1), 167–179 (2018)
13. Quan, T.M., Nguyen-Duc, T., Jeong, W.K.: Compressed sensing MRI reconstruction using a generative adversarial network with a cyclic loss. IEEE Trans. Med. Imaging **37**(6), 1488–1497 (2018)
14. Xie, J., Zhang, J., Zhang, Y., Ji, X.: PUERT: probabilistic under-sampling and explicable reconstruction network for CS-MRI. IEEE J. Sel. Top. Signal Processing **16**(4), 737–749 (2022)
15. Xin, B., Phan, T., Axel, L., Metaxas, D.: Learned half-quadratic splitting network for MR image reconstruction. In: International Conference on Medical Imaging with Deep Learning, pp. 1403–1412. PMLR (2022)
16. Yang, G., et al.: DAGAN: deep de-aliasing generative adversarial networks for fast compressed sensing MRI reconstruction. IEEE Trans. Med. Imaging **37**(6), 1310–1321 (2017)
17. Yuan, X., Brady, D.J., Suo, J., Arguello, H., Rodrigues, M., Katsaggelos, A.K.: Introduction to the special issue on deep learning for high-dimensional sensing. IEEE J. Sel. Top. Signal Process **16**(4), 603–607 (2022)
18. Zbontar, J., et al.: fastMRI: an open dataset and benchmarks for accelerated MRI. arXiv preprint arXiv:1811.08839 (2018)

19. Zhang, J., Ghanem, B.: ISTA-Net: interpretable optimization-inspired deep network for image compressive sensing. In: Proceedings of the IEEE Conference on Computer Vision and Pattern Recognition, pp. 1828–1837 (2018)
20. Zhang, J., Zhang, Z., Xie, J., Zhang, Y.: High-throughput deep unfolding network for compressive sensing MRI. IEEE J. Sel. Top Signal Process **16**(4), 750–761 (2022)
21. Zhou, B., Zhou, S.K.: DuDoRNet: learning a dual-domain recurrent network for fast MRI reconstruction with deep t1 prior. In: Proceedings of the IEEE/CVF Conference on Computer Vision and Pattern Recognition, pp. 4273–4282 (2020)
22. Zhou, M., Yan, K., Pan, J., Ren, W., Xie, Q., Cao, X.: Memory-augmented deep unfolding network for guided image super-resolution. Int. J. Comput. Vision **131**(1), 215–242 (2023)

Examining the Impact of Muscle-Electrode Distance in sEMG Based Hand Motion Recognition

Jinwei Shi[1], Mingchun Liu[2], Yinfeng Fang[2], Jiahui Yu[3,4], Hongwei Gao[1], and Zhaojie Ju[5(✉)]

[1] School of Automation and Electrical Engineering, Shenyang Ligong University, Shenyang 110159, China
{sjwdshyx2021,ghw1978}@sohu.com

[2] School of Telecommunication Engineering, Hangzhou Dianzi University, Hangzhou 310000, China
{222080240,yinfeng.fang}@hdu.edu.cn

[3] Department of Biomedical Engineering, Zhejiang University, Hangzhou 310027, China
Jiahui.yu@zju.edu.cn

[4] Innovation Center for Smart Medical Technologies & Devices, Binjiang Institute of Zhejiang University, Hangzhou 310053, China

[5] School of Computing, University of Portsmouth, Portsmouth PO13HE, UK
Zhaojie.Ju@port.ac.uk

Abstract. There are several factors that affect the sEMG signal during the process from its generation to its acquisition by sEMG devices. In this study, we tried to explain the physiological functional relationship between sEMG signals and muscles and between muscles and gestures in the human right forearm to increase confidence in the application of artificial intelligence in the medical field. For this purpose, we simulated the muscle and electrode positions with a 3D model to calculate their distance relationship, designed a cuff based on this model, and considered the effect of different distance solving methods on gesture recognition. The results showed that the highest accuracy of 93.95% was achieved for gesture recognition with the center of gravity method to find the electrode-to-muscle distance when the ratio of muscle electrode distance to the number of nerve muscle branches was 1:0.1. It is explained that the distance factor is the main factor affecting the recognition of sEMG signals, and an appropriate increase in the muscle length or neuromuscular branch number factor will play a positive role in the accuracy. The visualization of muscle activation further verifies and explains the relationship between sEMG signals and muscles, which makes the rehabilitation training more scientific and effective.

Keywords: sEMG · Biological relationship · Interpretability

© The Author(s), under exclusive license to Springer Nature Singapore Pte Ltd. 2023
H. Yang et al. (Eds.): ICIRA 2023, LNAI 14269, pp. 55–67, 2023.
https://doi.org/10.1007/978-981-99-6489-5_5

1   Introduction

In recent years, artificial intelligence technology has been applied to rehabilitation equipment, which has to some extent alleviated the shortage of existing rehabilitation trainers. At present, non-invasive sEMG (surface electromyogram) signals are mainly used by rehabilitation equipment to detect the muscles of patients with limb disabilities [1, 2]. Due to the large amount of information contained in sEMG signals [3], they have become the focus of many researchers and have been widely used in various fields such as prosthetics [4], robot control [5], and rehabilitation training [6]. Although the accuracy obtained through deep learning methods is high [7, 8], its interpretability is low and often questionable in the medical field. Therefore, endowing artificial intelligence with interpretability has become a current research hotspot.

Based on the relevant concepts of interpretability, research is mainly focused on the following two aspects: on the one hand, deconstruct as much knowledge as possible from the model for understanding, such as interpreting from the feature level, representing the model's knowledge in an interpretable manner, or judging the importance of features based on the impact of feature perturbations on model predictions [9]. Vijayvargiya et al. [10] introduced a method called interpretable artificial intelligence (XAI) to generate reliable predictive modeling results, explaining how the extracted features are expected or which features are most responsible for each action. On the other hand, visualization technology is used to achieve model transparency [11, 12], or modeling can generate understandable explanations, that is, using some essentially interpretable models to post interpret the prediction results of the black box model. As proposed by Jose et al. [13], combined with biomechanical simulations and using machine learning to classify 15 finger movements, the improved Opensim model can visualize the results of finger motion classification. Cheng et al. [14] proposed a muscle activity visualization system based on the HSV color gamut space to study the mapping relationship between hand movements and upper arm muscle activity regions. The interface of the system is very intuitive, and the muscle usage during hand movements can be explained.

In this study, a sleeve was designed by us, and a database was established based on this sleeve to study the transmission characteristics of electromyographic signals in the human body. In order to make the internal structure of the model more transparent and gain trust in the medical field, interpretable artificial intelligence has been adopted, and the relationship between electromyographic signals and single muscles and gestures has been verified. Finally, the accuracy of the relationship between sEMG signals and muscles is verified by visualization of single muscle activation, which improves the experience of human- computer interaction.

2   Methodology

2.1   Subjects

In the current database, 12 healthy subjects (2 females and 10 males, aged 23−27) participated in the experiment, with an average right forearm length (from the styloid process of the wrist to the olecranon of the elbow) of 22.33 ± 1.92 cm. All participants were informed of the experimental procedures and signed the informed consent form before the experiment, and the experimental protocol was done after the Declaration of Helsinki.

2.2 Experimental Protocol

Based on the average forearm length of the subjects, the position of the electrodes on the muscles was simulated using a three-dimensional graph. The average distribution of 32 electrodes was 8 layers, with staggered arrangement between each layer and an interval of 21 mm between each layer (see Fig. 1(b). Based on this three-dimensional model, an elastic electrode cuff (see Fig. 1(c)) was fabricated to fit the electrodes as closely as possible to the relevant muscles of different subjects. The electrodes are worn with the right elbow flexed and the palm facing upward. The radial and ulnar electrodes are distributed symmetrically on both sides of the thumb and little finger, and the columns of electrodes #3 and #7 are distributed along the middle finger to reduce the effect of bias.

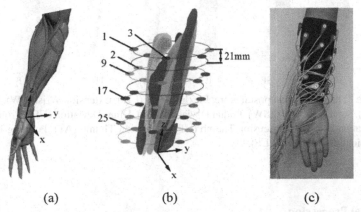

(a)   (b)   (c)

Fig. 1. 32 electrode positions. (a) The three-dimensional image simulated in the three-dimensional software, (b) the three-dimensional image of muscles and electrodes achieved in MATLAB using three-dimensional coordinates, with electrode positions arranged counterclockwise from top to bottom, and (c) the actual electrode positions.

During the collection process, efforts should be made to use force as evenly as possible, control the target muscles to the greatest extent, and relax other muscles. The duration of executing a complete action is about 20 s, and it must be ensured that the time under stable action is at least 10 s or more, with a 30 s rest after each action is completed.

2.3 Database

For each sEMG channel, the spectral components and 50 Hz power frequency noise in the frequency range of less than 20 Hz and greater than 500 Hz can be effectively suppressed, and the resolution and sampling frequency of the analog-to-digital converter are set to 24 bits and 1 kHz, respectively. The dataset recorded the sEMG signals of the right forearm muscle movement, including 12 different gesture operations from 12 subjects (see Fig. 2. The data was collected for a total of 20 days, and was collected every morning and afternoon.

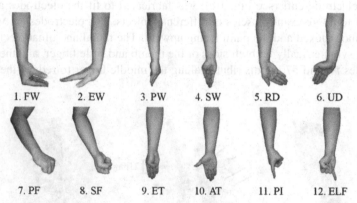

Fig. 2. The 12 hand and wrist postures are: Flexion Wrist (FW), Extension Wrist (EW), Pronation Wrist (PW), Supnation Wrist (SW), Radial Deviation (RD), Ulnar Deviation (UD), Pronation Fist (PF), Supnation Fist (SF), Extension Thumb (ET), Abduction Thumb (AT), Pointing Index (PI) and Extension Little Finger (ELF).

2.4 Signal Processing

In the database of this article, sEMG signals during gesture transformation are not considered, and only data in a stationary state is used to ensure correct sample labeling. The overlapping window segmentation method is used to process the collected electromyographic data, mainly using segmentation parameters such as window length and incremental segmentation length. These two parameters can effectively represent the relevant recognition accuracy and real-time performance of gestures. In this article, the feature data of each window is composed of 32 channels of sEMG signals, with a window length of 256 ms and an incremental segmentation length of 64 ms.

$$MAV = \frac{1}{N} \sum_{i=1}^{N} |X_i| \tag{1}$$

The commonly used features of EMG signals are time-domain, frequency-domain and time-frequency-domain features, and we have done experiments with MAV, RMS, SD, VAR and MPSD features respectively, and found that the accuracy obtained from MAV features is slightly higher than other features. Since the MAV features are relatively simple to calculate, meet the requirement of rapidity, can directly represent the amplitude of the original EMG signal, can intuitively display the envelope characteristics of the EMG signal, and can show the strength of muscle contraction to a certain extent, we extracted the MAV features with certain physiological interpretation for further study.

2.5 sEMG-Based Approach for Muscle Rehabilitation

In general, the smaller the distance between the electrode and the muscle, the greater the contribution of the muscle to the sEMG signal captured by the electrode, and there are other factors that can affect the signal collection, such as muscle length and the number of neuromuscular branches. Therefore, this article improves the neural network model by considering the transmission characteristics and physiological functions of myoelectric signals in the human body to explain the signal transmission process (see Fig. 3). The position errors caused while wearing are further corrected by updating $\omega_{i,j}^{(1)}$ and $\omega_{i,j}^{(2)}$ with a parametric constrained back-propagation algorithm.

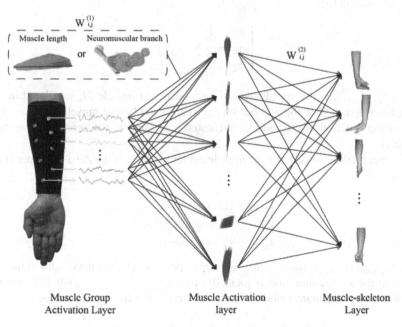

Muscle Group   Muscle Activation   Muscle-skeleton
Activation Layer   layer   Layer

Fig. 3. Bio-inspired Neural Network

Biological Characteristics Initialization $\omega_{i,j}^{(1)}$: If each muscle can be physically modeled in three-dimensional space and the position of the electrodes is fixed, the distance between the muscle and the electrode can be calculated using formula (2), and t biological weight $\omega_{i,j}^{(1)}$ can be derived.

$$d_{i,j} = \sqrt{(x_1 - x_2)^2 + (y_1 - y_2)^2 + (z_1 - z_2)^2} \tag{2}$$

where (x_1, y_1, z_1) represents the placement position of electrode, and (x_2, y_2, z_2) represents the center position of the muscle.

For muscle physical modeling in three-dimensional space, this article focuses on the right forearm (see Fig. 1). When the human body is in a standard anatomical orientation, we set the forearm position near the wrist joint as the origin. At this point, the palm direction is the positive direction of the X-axis, the ulnar direction is the positive direction of the Y-axis, and the direction from the wrist joint to the elbow joint is the positive direction of the Z-axis. Therefore, based on the three-dimensional data of each point, we can simulate the position of the cuff electrode and muscle in MATLAB software.

Due to the irregular shape of muscles and the close connection between different muscles, it is extremely important to find the accurate position of the muscle center for the initialization of in order to avoid confusion between muscles. Our research used two methods to solve the muscle center position, one is the center of gravity method, as shown in formula (3)

$$\begin{cases} x_2 = \frac{1}{N} \sum_{k=1}^{N} x_m^k \\ y_2 = \frac{1}{N} \sum_{k=1}^{N} y_m^k \\ z_2 = \frac{1}{N} \sum_{k=1}^{N} z_m^k \end{cases} \tag{3}$$

where (x_m^k, y_m^k, z_m^k) is the coordinates of each vertex of muscle M_i simulated in three-dimensional space, N is the number of vertices owned by the muscle, and (x_2, y_2, z_2) is the center position of the muscle calculated according to the center of gravity (see Fig. 4(a)).

Another method for solving the muscle center position is the Z-value center method (see Fig. 4(b)):

$$\begin{cases} x_2 = \frac{1}{2}(x_{z(max)} + x_{z(min)}) \\ y_2 = \frac{1}{2}(y_{z(max)} + y_{z(min)}) \\ z_2 = \frac{1}{2}(z_{max} + z_{min}) \end{cases} \tag{4}$$

where $(x_{z(max)}, y_{z(max)}, z_{max})$ is the coordinate point where the maximum value of the muscle in the Z-axis direction is located, and $(x_{z(min)}, y_{z(min)}, z_{min})$ is the coordinate point where the minimum value of the muscle in the Z-axis direction is located.

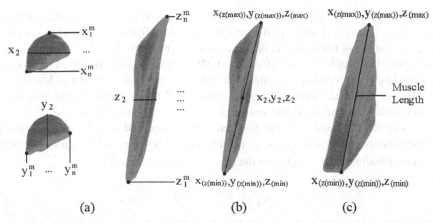

Fig. 4. Schematic diagram of muscle center of gravity and length, (a) solving the muscle center position using the center of gravity method. (b) Solve the muscle center position using the Z-value method. (c) Using the distance formula between two points to calculate muscle length.

Due to the greater contribution of muscles closer to the electrode, we have considered three weighting methods separately.

$$d_i^{(2)} = RCVR(S_{d_i^{(1)}} \times (0.98 - (i-1) \times 0.07)) \tag{5}$$

$$d_i^{(2)} = RCVR(S_{d_i^{(1)}} \times (RS(\frac{d_i^{(1)}}{max(d_i^{(1)})}))) \tag{6}$$

$$d_i^{(2)} = RCVR(S_{d_i^{(1)}} \times (RS(0.1 + \frac{LS - min(LS)}{max(LS) - min(LS)} \times 0.8))) \tag{7}$$

where $d_i^{(1)}$ is the original distance between electrode e_j and 14 muscles obtained from formula (2), i is an integer from 1 to 14, $S_{d_i^{(1)}}$ is the distance sorted from small to large, RS is the weight sorted from large to small, and $RCVR$ is the restoration of the original order, LS is $\log_{10} S_{d_i^{(1)}}$

Most common studies focus on the placement of electrodes in the forearm, ignoring the transmission characteristics of sEMG signals in the human body. There are many factors that affect sEMG signals, not only in terms of hardware. Therefore, in addition to considering the distance between the electrode and the muscle, we also considered two physiological factors: muscle length and the number of neuromuscular branches, in order to study the impact on signal acquisition.

We study muscle length by physically modeling each muscle in three-dimensional space. Due to individual and gender differences, some people have thick muscles while others have thin muscles. Here we take the average value and calculate the length of each muscle by converting the 3D model into 3D data that MATLAB can recognize (see Fig. 4).

sEMG signal is the superposition of motor unit action potential (MUAP) of many muscle fibers in time and space. Different muscles have different number of motor units, that is, the number of nerve muscle branches is different. Therefore, the number of nerve muscle branches may be a factor affecting sEMG signal acquisition. Based on anatomical knowledge, the number of neuromuscular branches can be roughly determined. Table 1 gives some information about the muscle and it was found that the number of neuromuscular branches (NB) was not related to the size of the muscle.

The experiment fused the Muscle-electrode distance and muscle length, Muscle-electrode distance and number of neuromuscular branches in proportion, thus obtaining a new contribution rate $d_{i,j}^{(3)}$ between the electrode and the muscle:

$$d_{i,j}^{(3)} = d_{i,j}^{(2)} + \beta \cdot f \tag{8}$$

where β is the proportion of the muscle length or the number of nerve muscle branches, and we performed the experiments with 0, 0.01, 0.1, 0.2, 0.5 and 1, respectively. And f is the matrix constructed by the muscle length factor or the number factor of nerve muscle branches. The last defined initialization formula is:

$$\omega_{i,j}^{(1)} = \alpha \cdot \frac{d_{i,j}^{(3)}}{\max\left(d_{i,j}^{(3)}\right)} - \frac{1}{2}\alpha \tag{9}$$

where α is the coefficient, set to 16, max is the maximum value of $d_{i,j}^{(3)}$.

Physiological Function Initialization $\omega_{i,j}^{(2)}$: The 12 wrist gestures used contain mainly 14 forearm muscles, which we classified according to their function in human anatomy. As can be seen in Table 1, each muscle is associated with one or more movements, so we initialized $\omega_{i,j}^{(2)}$ according to muscle physiology function:

$$\omega_{i,j}^{(2)} = \pm \frac{1}{k_i \sum_{s=1}^{n_j} \frac{1}{k_i}} \tag{10}$$

where k_i is the number of muscles involved, n_j is the number of muscles involved in the action, FW, PW, RD, PF, ET, PI are positive numbers, EW, SW, UD, SF, AT, and ELF are negative numbers.

Single Muscle Activation Visualization Model Initialization: According to the actual position of the forearm muscles, the pie chart is divided into 14 regions (see Fig. 5), with the outer side divided into 8 regions. Starting from the upper right side, it is counterclockwise divided into M1−M8, and the inner side is divided into 6 regions, M9−M14.

Table 1. Information about the parameters of the muscle.

Abb	Muscle Name	NB	Physiological Functions
M1	Flexor carpi ulnaris	102	Enables flexion of the wrist (FW) and pronation of the wrist (RD) and thumb (ET)
M2	Palmaris longus	36	Ability to flex the wrist (FW)
M3	Radial wrist flexor	38	Control of wrist flexion (FW) and ulnar lateral deviation (UD) and flexion of the elbow with fist rotation forward (PF)
M4	Pronator teres	87	Makes the forearm wrist internally rotated (PW) and the elbow bent and fist rotated forward (PF)
M5	Brachioradialis	60	Forward (PF) and backward (SF) rotation with bent elbow and clenched fist
M6	Extensor carpi radialis longus	68	Control of wrist extension (EW) and ulnar lateral deviation (UD)
M7	Extensor digitorum	113	For extending the four fingers except the thumb (ET) and extending the index finger (PI)
M8	Extensor carpi ulnaris	82	Control of radial wrist extension (EW) and wrist pronation (RD)
M9	Pronator quadratus	36	Anterior rotation of the forearm (PW), which is less pronounced due to the presence of the anterior rotation circular muscle
M10	Extensor carpi radialis brevis	38	For wrist extension (EW) and ulnar lateral deviation (UD)
M11	Abductor pollicis longus	46	Abduction of the thumb (AT)
M12	Extensor pollicis longus	43	Abduction of the thumb (AT)
M13	Supinator	105	For rotating the forearm to bring the palm forward (SW) and bending the elbow to make a fist to rotate back (SF)
M14	Extensor digiti minimi	41	Control the extension of the little finger (ELF)

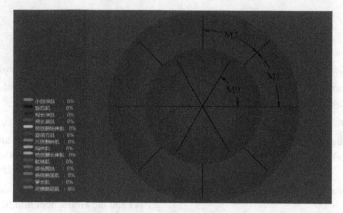

Fig. 5. 9 muscle activation initialization

The original color of the pie chart is blue, and a linear gradient function is used and the starting and ending angles of each loop are determined so that the color within each loop is linearly graded according to the value, with the higher the muscle activation, the more pronounced the red color is:

$$M_{act} = \frac{(E_{real} - E_{static}) \times \omega_{i,j}^{(1)}}{(E_{max} - E_{static}) \times \omega_{i,j}^{(1)}} \times 255 \tag{11}$$

where E_{real} is the real-time collected data, E_{static} is the collected sEMG signal under the relaxed gesture, E_{max} is the sEMG signal under the maximum force of the gesture, and M_{act} is the muscle activation degree.

3   Results

From the overall trends in Fig. 6 (a) and (b), it can be seen that increasing the muscle length or neuromuscular branch characteristics appropriately based on the Muscle-electrode distance will have a positive impact on accuracy. The distance factor is the main factor affecting the recognition of sEMG signals, and the accuracy decreases as the proportion of muscle length or neuromuscular branches increases. The distance between muscle and electrode was calculated by the center of gravity method, and the ratio with the nerve muscle branches was 1:0.1 was the highest accuracy, reaching 93.95%, indicating that it is very meaningful to consider the conduction characteristics of EMG signals in the human body.

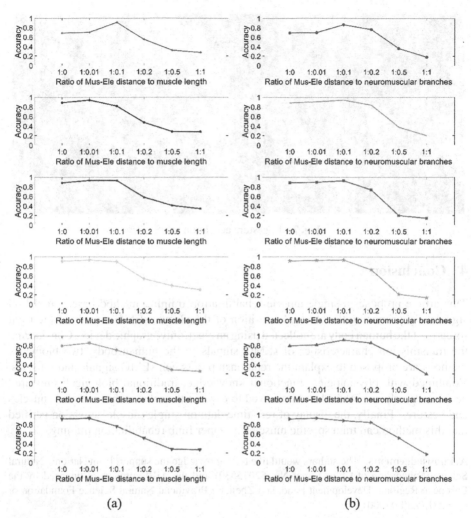

Fig. 6. (a) and (b) show the accuracy of the ratio of different Muscle-electrode distance to muscle length or nerve muscle branches, respectively

The single muscle activation experiment takes the MAV features of real-time collected data as input (see Fig. 7). In the case of combining only $\omega_{i,j}^{(2)}$, the target muscles can all be well activated when the corresponding gestures are made, verifying that the designed electrode patches are indeed positioned to record the activity of the corresponding muscles. At the same time, the visualization can reflect the real muscle activity state, when the force is not correct, the target muscle activation value will be smaller and the color tends to blue, when it is necessary to control the target muscle force.

Fig. 7. 12 gesture activation maps

4 Conclusion

This article proposes a single muscle rehabilitation training method based on sEMG signals. By proposing the electrode position of the sleeve, sEMG signals of the right forearm of the human body are collected using an electromyographic device. Considering the transmission characteristics of sEMG signals in the human body, two biometric methods are proposed to explain the relationship between sEMG signals and muscles. Combined with physiological functional knowledge, traditional biologically inspired neural networks are studied and improved to explain the relationship between muscles and gestures. Finally, the display of real-time data on single muscle activation verified that this method can train specific muscles in upper limb rehabilitation training.

Acknowledgements. The authors would like to acknowledge the support from National Natural Science Foundation of China (grant No. 52075530) and the AiBle project co-financed by the European Regional Development Fund, and Zhejiang Provincial Natural Science Foundation of China (LQ23F030001).

References

1. Maksymenko, K., Clarke, A.K., Mendez Guerra, I., Deslauriers-Gauthier, S., Farina, D.: A myoelectric digital twin for fast and realistic modelling in deep learning. Nat. Commun. **14**(1), 1600 (2023)
2. Zhao, J., Yu, Y., Sheng, X., Zhu, X.: Extracting stable control information from EMG signals to drive a musculoskeletal model - a preliminary study. In: Liu, H., et al (eds.). Intelligent Robotics and Applications. ICIRA 2022, vol. 13456. Lecture Notes in Computer Science. Springer, Cham (2022). https://doi.org/10.1007/978-3-031-13822-5_66
3. Roy, J., Ali, M.A., Ahmed, M.R., Sundaraj, K.: Machine learning techniques for predicting surface EMG activities on upper limb muscle: a systematic review. In: Bhuiyan, T., Rahman, MdMostafijur, Ali, M.A. (eds.) ICONCS 2020. LNICSSITE, vol. 325, pp. 330–339. Springer, Cham (2020). https://doi.org/10.1007/978-3-030-52856-0_26

4. Fang, B., et al.: Simultaneous semg recognition of gestures and force levels for interaction with prosthetic hand. IEEE Trans. Neural Syst. Rehabil. Eng. **30**, 2426–2436 (2022)
5. Zheng, J., Xie, C., Song, R., Xu, T.: A statistical learning approach for cable-driven robot in rehabilitation training. In: 2022 International Conference on Advanced Robotics and Mechatronics (ICARM), pp. 296−301. IEEE (2022)
6. Zhang, J., Liu, Y., Liu, J.: Wearable Sensing based virtual reality rehabilitation scheme for upper limb training. In: Liu, H., et al. (eds.). Intelligent Robotics and Applications. ICIRA 2022, vol. 13457. Lecture Notes in Computer Science(), Springer, Cham (2022). https://doi.org/10.1007/978-3-031-13835-5_3
7. Mukhopadhyay, A.K., Samui, S.: An experimental study on upper limb position invariant emg signal classification based on deep neural network. Biomed. Signal Process. Control **55**, 101669 (2020)
8. Yu, J., Gao, H., Zhou, D., Liu, J., Gao, Q., Ju, Z.: Deep temporal model-based identity-aware hand detection for space human–robot interaction. IEEE Trans. Cybern. **52**(12), 13738–13751 (2021)
9. Zhong, T., Li, D., Wang, J., Xu, J., An, Z., Zhu, Y.: Fusion learning for semg recognition of multiple upper-limb rehabilitation movements. Sensors **21**(16), 5385 (2021)
10. Vijayvargiya, A., Singh, P., Kumar, R., Dey, N.: Hardware implementation for lower limb surface emg measurement and analysis using explainable ai for activity recognition. IEEE Trans. Instrum. Meas. **71**, 1–9 (2022)
11. Yu, J., Gao, H., Chen, Y., Zhou, D., Liu, J., Ju, Z.: Adaptive spatiotemporal representation learning for skeleton-based human action recognition. IEEE Trans. Cogn. Dev. Syst. **14**(4), 1654–1665 (2021)
12. Yu, J., Xu, Y., Chen, H., Ju, Z.: Versatile graph neural networks toward intuitive human activity understanding. IEEE Trans. Neural Netw. Learn. Syst. (2022)
13. Amezquita-Garcia, J., Bravo-Zanoguera, M., Gonzalez-Navarro, F.F., Lopez-Avitia, R., Reyna, M.: Applying machine learning to finger movements using electromyography and visualization in opensim. Sensors **22**(10), 3737 (2022)
14. Cheng, Y., et al.: Visualization of activated muscle area based on semg. J. Intell. Fuzzy Syst. **38**(3), 2623–2634 (2020)

Fast Calibration for Ultrasound Imaging Guidance Based on Depth Camera

Fuqiang Zhao[1], Mingchang Li[2], Mengde Li[3], Zhongtao Fu[4], and Miao Li[1,3](✉)

[1] The School of Power and Mechanical Engineering, Wuhan University, Wuhan, China

[2] Department of Neurosurgery, Renmin Hospital of Wuhan University, Wuhan, China

[3] The Institute of Technological Sciences, Wuhan University, Wuhan, China
miao.li@whu.edu.cn

[4] School of Mechanical and Electrical Engineering, Wuhan Institute of Technology, Wuhan, China

Abstract. During the process of robot-assisted ultrasound (US) puncture, it is important to estimate the location of the puncture from the 2D US images. To this end, the calibration of the US image becomes an important issue. In this paper, we proposed a depth camera-based US calibration method, where an easy-to-deploy device is designed for the calibration. With this device, the coordinates of the puncture needle tip are collected respectively in US image and in the depth camera, upon which a correspondence matrix is built for calibration. Finally, a number of experiments are conducted to validate the effectiveness of our calibration method.

Keywords: Robot ultrasound · Robot calibration · Robot-assisted puncture

1 Introduction

With the fast development of ultrasound (US) imaging and medical robots [1], US-guided robotic puncture has been widely studied recently [2–7]. Compared with free-hand operation, US-guided robotic puncture can offer high accuracy and stability. In addition, the robots can achieve flexible control within a small surgical space and reduce surgical trauma. In general, ultrasound-guided robotic puncture can be classified into the following four categories: (1) Independent US robot with manual biopsy by a doctor. (2) Independent puncture robot with manual US scanning by a doctor. (3) Single-arm mechanical ultrasound-guided puncture robot. (4) Dual-arm ultrasound-guided robot puncture as shown in Fig. 1. For all of these four scenarios, it is necessary to estimate the location of the puncture needle from the pure 2D ultrasound imaging. Especially for the

This work was supported by Suzhou Key Industry Technology Innovation Project under the grant agreement number SYG202121.

© The Author(s), under exclusive license to Springer Nature Singapore Pte Ltd. 2023
H. Yang et al. (Eds.): ICIRA 2023, LNAI 14269, pp. 68–79, 2023.
https://doi.org/10.1007/978-981-99-6489-5_6

dual-arm robot system, with the US probe and puncture needle installed on two separated arms, it is more crucial to know the precise location of the puncture needle as shown in Fig. 2. In this work, we propose a new calibration method together with the auxiliary device for ultrasound imaging guidance task.

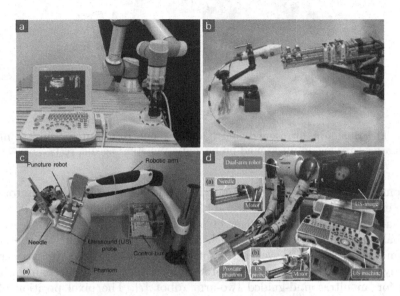

Fig. 1. US-guided robotic puncture classification: (a) Independent US robot with manual biopsy [8]. (b) Independent puncture robot with manual US scanning [9]. (c) Single-arm mechanical ultrasound-guided robotic puncture [10]. (d) Dual-arm ultrasound-guided robotic puncture [7].

1.1 Related Work

To meet the clinical requirements, many US image calibration methods have been developed, which can be roughly divided into two categories, mechanism-based calibration and image-based calibration [11–13]. The mechanism-based calibration method is mainly used for robotic system calibration [14], while The image-based calibration method is the mainly used for US probe calibration [15]. Traditional US calibration methods require a phantom to provide a set of fiducials, such as the N-wire phantom method [16]. Carbajal et al. proposed an improved N-wire phantom freehand US calibration method based on the middle wires to improve the calibration accuracy [16]. To reduce the isotropic fiducial localization errors in this method, Najafi et al. proposed a multiwedge phantom calibration method to achieve higher calibration accuracy [17]. In this method, the calibration matrix was solved with a closed-form solution, which enables easy and accurate US calibration. Afterward, Shen et al. proposed a new method considering the use of wires for US calibration [18]. However, these methods need external tracker and wire or wedge phantom, which also accumulate errors from

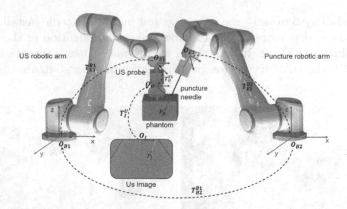

Fig. 2. The dual-arm ultrasound-guided robotic puncture system consists of two robotic arms carrying an ultrasound probe and a puncture needle, respectively.

phantom. Moreover, the process of mounting and dismounting the phantom will reduce efficiency, and increase the complexity of calibration process [19].

To address these issue, Hunger et al. attached a small rubber sleeve and a softball to the needle tip [20], which improved the positioning of the needle tip from the US images. However, the softball itself also resulted in extra errors. Recently, Xiong et al. proposed a calibration method based on mechanism-image fusion for an ultrasound-guided two-arm robot [7]. The pixel position of the needle tip in the US image is calculated by manual annotation, which also reduces the efficiency of registration. Due to the presence of US noise and artifacts, calibration accuracy and efficiency is still challenging in this approach.

In this paper, we proposed a fast calibration method based on depth camera. A puncture needle is used to replace the reference phantoms in previous works, which could reduce the extra errors from calibration model. A depth camera is used to annotation the needle tips automatically. The coordinate system transformation between the depth camera and the US images can be used to formulate the calibration process. Experimental results shows that our approach achieve better performance compared with previous methods [16,21].

2 Theory and Method

2.1 Calibration Setup

The US image calibration system is shown in Fig. 3, which consists of an US system, a depth camera, a puncture needle, a calibration sink, and a calibration phantom bracket. The medical US imaging uses the attenuation rate of sound waves to detect the internal structure of entities. Therefore, US imaging can be simplified as a linear model, and various parameters of US system can be obtained through calibration. The US image calibration system utilizes this linear model and coordinate system transformation, which means that every point in the US image has a corresponding point in the world coordinate system.

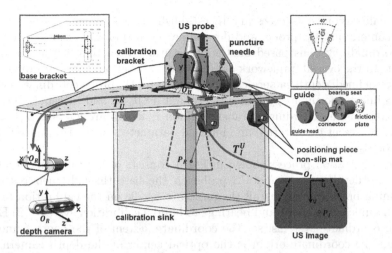

Fig. 3. US Calibration Setup. It consists of an US system, a depth camera, a puncture needle, a calibration sink, and a calibration phantom bracket. (Color figure online)

Before the calibration, the calibration bracket is placed on the calibration sink. The position can be adjusted with the positioning piece, as shown in Fig. 3. Multiple sets of positioning holes for the positioning bracket are designed on the base, and these evenly arranged positioning holes can adjust the position of the positioning bracket.

The coordinate system of the depth camera is defined as the world coordinate system, and the optical center of the depth camera is set as the origin of the actual coordinate system. The puncture needle moves along the guide, which is connected to the bearing and can rotate to adjust the puncture needle angle. In Fig. 3, the green arrow indicates the movable direction of the depth camera positioning bracket and purple arrow indicates the movable direction of the US probe positioning bracket. Note that if the probe is mounted on the robotic arm, these movement can be accomplished by the robotic arm.

2.2 Calibration Process

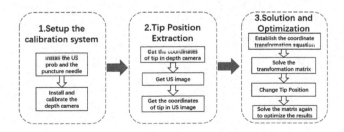

Fig. 4. US calibration process includes: system setup, date collection and optimization.

Before calibration, it is necessary to establish the coordinate systems for the depth camera and US probe, and determine the mapping relationship between the coordinate systems based on the structural parameters of the calibration bracket. In the overall framework of US image calibration, three coordinate systems are defined: depth camera coordinate system, US probe coordinate system, and US image coordinate system, represented by R, U, and I, respectively. The two corresponding coordinate transformation matrices are T_U^R and T_I^U, which actually represent the external and internal parameters in the US image calibration process.

The registration process shown in Fig. 4 consists of the following steps: (1) Install the depth camera and US probe on the base through their respective positioning brackets, and install the puncture needle on the calibration bracket through guide components and bearings to build a calibration system. (2) Establish the coordinate systems, set the coordinate system of the depth camera to O_R, and the coordinate origin is the optical center of the depth camera. The XOY plane is parallel to the imaging plane of the depth camera. The coordinate system of the US probe is O_U, and the origin of the coordinate is the center of the US probe. The XOY plane is parallel to the US imaging plane. The coordinate system of the US image is set to O_I, and the coordinate origin is the top-point of the center-line of the US image. The UOV plane coincides with the US image plane, as shown in Fig. 3.

2.3   Segmentation and Localization of Needle Tip

In order to accurately locate the needle tip position in US images, we use U-Net neural network to train the US images and to recognize the needle. U-Net neural network is a widely used image segmentation network framework for feature extraction from medical images [22]. In this work, we collect 200 US images of a puncture needle in water using an US system. The outline of the puncture needle in the images are annotated as the training set. After training the U-net network, we can extract the needle tip contour segmentation in the US images. Then, the needle is fitted into line segments and the end of the line segment that enters the image first according to the needle insertion direction is selected as the needle tip coordinate. The process of the needle tip segmentation and localization process is shown in Fig. 5.

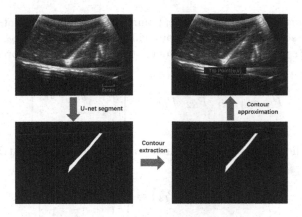

Fig. 5. Needle tip positioning process

2.4 Calibration Model

The spatial mapping of a point from an US image to a depth camera is represented as:

$$P_R = T \cdot P_I = T_U^R \cdot T_I^U \cdot P_I \tag{1}$$

P_I represents the position of a point in the US image, $P_I = [u,\ v,\ 1]^\mathrm{T}$. u and v are the coordinates of the point in the US image with the unit of pixel. P_R represents the position of the point in the depth camera, $P_R = [x_r,\ y_r,\ z_r,\ 1]^\mathrm{T}$, x_r, y_r, z_r are the coordinates of the point in the depth camera. In order to ensure the accuracy of calibration and reduce the requirements for calibration system, we use the needle tip coordinates of the puncture needle to calculate the transformation matrix T.

Transformation matrix T_U^R represents the transformation matrix between the depth camera and the US probe, which is also the extrinsic matrix of the US probe and determines the position of the US image imaging plane. Based on the structure of the designed calibration bracket, we can easily obtain the transformation matrix parameters x_u, y_u, z_u between the depth camera positioning bracket and the US probe positioning bracket. The transformation matrix is as follows:

$$T_U^R = \begin{bmatrix} 1 & 0 & 0 & x_u \\ 0 & 1 & 0 & y_u \\ 0 & 0 & 1 & z_u \\ 0 & 0 & 0 & 1 \end{bmatrix} \tag{2}$$

Transformation matrix $T_I^U = [I_x, I_y, I_0]$ represents the transformation matrix between the US probe and the US image, which is the intrinsic matrix of the US probe. The three vectors I_0, I_x and I_y here each contain four scalars to represent the main calibration parameters.

It should be noted that in order to solve T_I^U, we need to use the puncture needle guide on the calibration bracket to change the position of the needle tip multiple times to obtain a sufficient number of reference points. For ease of calculation, we select any three non-collinear points P_{R1}, P_{R2}, P_{R3}, and combine their coordinates under the depth camera into a matrix $P_{R'}$, represented as:

$$P_{R'} = \begin{bmatrix} P_{R1} & P_{R2} & P_{R3} \end{bmatrix} = \begin{bmatrix} x_{r1} & x_{r2} & x_{r3} \\ y_{r1} & y_{r2} & y_{r3} \\ z_{r1} & z_{r2} & z_{r3} \\ 1 & 1 & 1 \end{bmatrix} \tag{3}$$

Similarly, the coordinates in US images are combined as matrix $P_{I'}$, represented as:

$$P_{I'} = \begin{bmatrix} P_{I1} & P_{I2} & P_{I3} \end{bmatrix} = \begin{bmatrix} u_{i1} & u_{i2} & u_{i3} \\ v_{i1} & v_{i2} & v_{i3} \\ 1 & 1 & 1 \end{bmatrix} \tag{4}$$

The spatial mapping of US image to depth camera becomes:

$$P_{R'} = T \cdot P_{I'} = T_U^R \cdot T_I^U \cdot P_{I'} \tag{5}$$

Based on (1) (5) (6) (7), matrix operation T_I^U can be represented as follows and the inv represents the generalized inverse of the matrix.

$$T_I^U = inv(T_U^R) \cdot P_{R'} \cdot inv(P_{I'}) \tag{6}$$

3   Experiments and Results

3.1   Experiment Setup

In order to verify the accuracy of the US image calibration system, experiments were conducted on our proposed US calibration system as shown in Fig. 6. The base bracket in the calibration bracket is made of acrylic plate, and the positioning brackets for the depth camera and US probe, as well as the guide component for the puncture needle, are made of high-precision 3D printing and processing. We select Realsense-D435i for the depth camera, DW-580 for the US system, and the puncture needle diameter is of 0.8 mm.

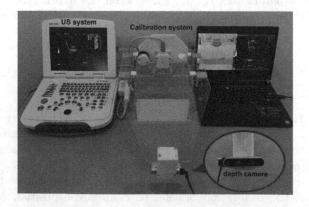

Fig. 6. US calibration experimental equipment

3.2   Position Extraction of Coordinate System and Needle Tip

We establish the coordinate system for the depth camera, US probe, and US image. The transformation matrix T_U^R between the depth camera and the US probe is given based on the structural parameters of the calibration bracket:

$$T_U^R = \begin{bmatrix} 1 & 0 & 0 & 35.31 \\ 0 & 1 & 0 & -50.24 \\ 0 & 0 & 1 & 349.00 \\ 0 & 0 & 0 & 1 \end{bmatrix}$$

Fig. 7. Needle tip in depth camera image (left) and in the US image (right)

For each set of needle coordinates, it is necessary to obtain the coordinates of the needle in the depth camera and the US image. According to the equation, at least three pairs of needle coordinates are needed to calculate the transformation matrix. To ensure accuracy and reduce errors, it is possible to collect more pairs of needle coordinates.

When obtaining the coordinates of the needle tip in the depth camera, painting fluorescent markers on the needle tip can increase localization accuracy, and also reduce the positioning error caused by the reflection of the puncture needle due to poor lighting condition.

Due to the severe attenuation of US in the air, it is necessary to fill the calibration sink with water when using the US system, the US probe can clearly obtain the image of the needle tip in the sink. By using the U-net network to segment the US image of the needle tip, the coordinates of the needle tip in the US image can be accurately located. The position of the needle tip in the US and depth camera is shown in Fig. 7.

Remarks: It should be noted that when using a depth camera to obtain the needle coordinates, the water in the sink needs to be extracted, as there will be obvious refraction phenomenon in the water. This can lead to significant positioning errors. We sampled 10 pairs of points, and their coordinate information in depth camera and US images, as shown in Fig. 8.

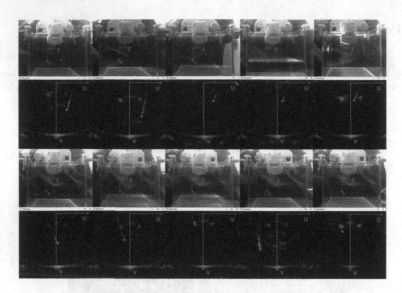

Fig. 8. Experimental collection of images

3.3   Calibration Results

Using the collected data points, the final solution of T_I^U is obtained using Eq. (6). After obtaining the US intrinsic matrix, the only corresponding point in the depth camera can be calculated through coordinate transformation for any point in any US image.

$$T_I^U = \begin{bmatrix} 0.3418 & 0.0074 & -0.6193 \\ -0.0025 & 0.3502 & 28.2740 \\ 0 & 0 & 0 \\ 0 & 0 & 1 \end{bmatrix}$$

The metric used to quantify the precision of a calibration method is the calibration reproducibility (CR) [16]

$$CR = \frac{1}{N} \sum_{n=0}^{N-1} |TP_{I,n} - P_{R,n}| \tag{7}$$

Target registration error (TRE) is also used to evaluate the accuracy of calibration [17]

$$TRE = \sqrt{\frac{1}{N} \sum_{n=0}^{N-1} (TP_{I,n} - P_{R,n})^2} \tag{8}$$

In the experiment, several sets of test points were selected from the collected images and needle coordinates, and the remaining points were used to calculate the transformation matrix T. The quantitative analysis of US image calibration is as shown in Table 1 and Fig. 9. Compared with other calibration methods, the comparison results are shown in the Table 2.

Table 1. Results of US image calibration.

No	P_I		Physical $P_W(mm)$			Calibration $P_R(mm)$			Errors(mm)
	u	v	x	y	z	x	y	z	$\lvert P_R - P_W \rvert$
1	88	234	66.40	59.94	349.0	66.488	59.764	349.0	0.1968
2	91	291	68.70	77.60	349.0	67.933	79.719	349.0	2.2535
3	79	153	62.18	33.07	349.0	62.817	31.420	349.0	1.7686
4	43	162	49.51	35.52	349.0	51.604	34.654	349.0	2.2660
5	28	155	44.14	33.45	349.0	45.400	32.247	349.0	1.7421
6	10	251	39.46	64.71	349.0	39.955	65.912	349.0	1.2999
7	−49	224	18.41	56.87	349.0	19.591	56.603	349.0	1.2108
8	−72	73	9.97	3.96	349.0	10.619	3.778	349.0	0.6740
9	−142	303	−11.91	84.29	349.0	−11.613	84.501	349.0	0.3643
10	−62	154	14.58	29.23	349.0	14.633	32.121	349.0	2.8915
								CR	1.4668
								TRE	1.6887

Table 2. Comparison with other calibration methods

Method	Precision and accuracy of calibration	
	CR (mm)	TRE (mm)
N-wire phantom	1.97	2.06
Multi-wedge phantom	1.58	1.80
proposed method	1.47	1.69

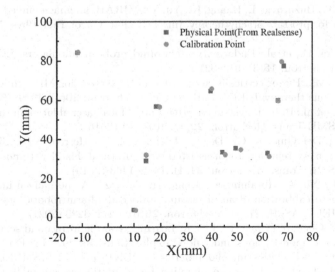

Fig. 9. Results between Physical Point and Calibration Point

4   Discussion and Conclusion

In this paper, we propose a fast calibration method for US images based on a depth camera that achieves an accuracy of within 2 mm. We completed the calibration on the designed experimental platform by solving the intrinsic matrix of the US system in conjunction with the conversion between coordinate systems.

In addition, the feasibility of the proposed method is discussed and verified through experiments. Specifically, in our proposed method, the CR and TRE of the whole system are only 1.4668 mm and 1.6887 mm, respectively. Those errors are smaller than the CR (1.97 mm) and TRE (2.06 mm) of the N-wire phantom calibration method [16] and the CR (1.58 mm) and TRE (1.80 mm) of the multi-wedge phantom calibration method in [17]. Our proposed calibration method is significantly better than the other two image-based methods in terms of the calibration accuracy of the whole system.

It should be noted that our method does not require additional calibration molds, but still requires a sufficiently high accuracy of the depth camera. Therefore, similar US calibration methods can be further developed to improve the flexibility and accuracy of US image calibration. For example, a higher precision positioning device could be used to locate the needle tip position, or the overall calibration device could be mounted on a robot to automate and streamline the calibration process in specialized application scenarios. This work provides a reference for the calibration of the US puncture robot as shown in Fig. 1.

References

1. Taylor, R.H., Simaan, N., Menciassi, A., Yang, G.-Z.: Surgical robotics and computer-integrated interventional medicine. Proc. IEEE **110**(7), 823–834 (2022)
2. Podder, T., Buzurovic, I., Huang, K., Yu, Y.: MIRAB: an image-guided multichannel robot for prostate brachytherapy. Int. J. Radiat. Oncol. Biol. Phys. **78**(3), S810 (2010)
3. Stoianovici, D., et al.: Endocavity ultrasound probe manipulators. IEEE/ASME Trans. Mechatron. **18**(3), 914–921 (2012)
4. Su, H., et al.: Piezoelectrically actuated robotic system for MRI-guided prostate percutaneous therapy. IEEE/ASME Trans. Mechatron. **20**(4), 1920–1932 (2014)
5. Chen, Y., et al.: Robotic system for MRI-guided focal laser ablation in the prostate. IEEE/ASME Trans. Mechatron. **22**(1), 107–114 (2016)
6. Sarli, N., Del Giudice, G., De, S., Dietrich, M.S., Herrell, S.D., Simaan, N.: TURBot: a system for robot-assisted transurethral bladder tumor resection. IEEE/ASME Trans. Mechatron. **24**(4), 1452–1463 (2019)
7. Xiong, J., Xu, C., Ibrahim, K., Deng, H., Xia, Z.: A mechanism-image fusion approach to calibration of an ultrasound-guided dual-arm robotic brachytherapy system. IEEE/ASME Trans. Mechatron. **26**(6), 3211–3220 (2021)
8. Deng, X., Chen, Y., Chen, F., Li, M.: Learning robotic ultrasound scanning skills via human demonstrations and guided explorations. In: 2021 IEEE International Conference on Robotics and Biomimetics (ROBIO), pp. 372–378. IEEE (2021)
9. Hoelscher, J., et al.: Backward planning for a multi-stage steerable needle lung robot. IEEE Robot. Autom. Lett. **6**(2), 3987–3994 (2021)

10. Chen, S., Wang, F., Lin, Y., Shi, Q., Wang, Y.: Ultrasound-guided needle insertion robotic system for percutaneous puncture. Int. J. Comput. Assist. Radiol. Surg. 16, 475–484 (2021)
11. Aalamifar, F., et al.: Robot-assisted automatic ultrasound calibration. Int. J. Comput. Assist. Radiol. Surg. 11, 1821–1829 (2016)
12. Huang, Q., Wu, B., Lan, J., Li, X.: Fully automatic three-dimensional ultrasound imaging based on conventional b-scan. IEEE Trans. Biomed. Circuits Syst. 12(2), 426–436 (2018)
13. Li, X., Kumar, D., Sarkar, S., Narayanan, R.: An image registration based ultrasound probe calibration. In: Medical Imaging 2012, Image Processing, vol. 8314, pp. 609–616. SPIE (2012)
14. Wang, J., Wu, L., Meng, M.Q.-H., Ren, H.: Towards simultaneous coordinate calibrations for cooperative multiple robots. In: 2014 IEEE/RSJ International Conference on Intelligent Robots and Systems, pp. 410–415. IEEE (2014)
15. Wang, L.: An automated calibration method of ultrasonic probe based on coherent point drift algorithm. IEEE Access 6, 8657–8665 (2018)
16. Carbajal, G., Lasso, A., Gómez, Á., Fichtinger, G.: Improving n-wire phantom-based freehand ultrasound calibration. Int. J. Comput. Assist. Radiol. Surg. 8, 1063–1072 (2013)
17. Najafi, M., Afsham, N., Abolmaesumi, P., Rohling, R.: A closed-form differential formulation for ultrasound spatial calibration: multi-wedge phantom. Ultrasound Med. Biol. 40(9), 2231–2243 (2014)
18. Shen, C., Lyu, L., Wang, G., Wu, J.: A method for ultrasound probe calibration based on arbitrary wire phantom. Cogent Eng. 6(1), 1592739 (2019)
19. Kim, C., Chang, D., Petrisor, D., Chirikjian, G., Han, M., Stoianovici, D.: Ultrasound probe and needle-guide calibration for robotic ultrasound scanning and needle targeting. IEEE Trans. Biomed. Eng. 60(6), 1728–1734 (2013)
20. Hungr, N., Baumann, M., Long, J.-A., Troccaz, J.: A 3-d ultrasound robotic prostate brachytherapy system with prostate motion tracking. IEEE Trans. Rob. 28(6), 1382–1397 (2012)
21. Pagoulatos, N., Haynor, D.R., Kim, Y.: A fast calibration method for 3-d tracking of ultrasound images using a spatial localizer. Ultrasound Med. Biol. 27(9), 1219–1229 (2001)
22. Ronneberger, O., Fischer, P., Brox, T.: U-Net: convolutional networks for biomedical image segmentation. In: Navab, N., Hornegger, J., Wells, W.M., Frangi, A.F. (eds.) MICCAI 2015, Part III. LNCS, vol. 9351, pp. 234–241. Springer, Cham (2015). https://doi.org/10.1007/978-3-319-24574-4_28

Zero-Shot Kidney Stone Segmentation Based on Segmentation Anything Model for Robotic-Assisted Endoscope Navigation

Hui Meng[1,2], Lingkai Chen[2], Shiqiang Zhu[2], Chentao Fei[3], Yong Zhang[1], Miaojuan Zheng[4], Jianda Han[2,5(✉)], and Wei Song[2(✉)]

[1] School of Intelligent Science and Technology, Hangzhou Institute for Advanced Study, University of Chinese Academy of Sciences, 1 Sub-lane Xiangshan, Hangzhou 310024, China
[2] Research Center for Intelligent Robotics, Research Institute of Interdisciplinary Innovation, Zhejiang Laboratory, Hangzhou 311100, China
weisong@zhejianglab.com
[3] Hangzhou ElephantChain Network Technology Co. Ltd., Hangzhou, China
[4] Faculty of Mechanical Engineering and Automation, Zhejiang Sci-Tech University, Hangzhou 310018, China
[5] College of Artificial Intelligence and Tianjin Key Laboratory of Intelligent Robotics, Institute of Robotics and Automatic Information Systems, Nankai University, Tianjin 300350, China
hanjianda@nankai.edu.cn

Abstract. Biomedical robotics has had a significant impact on flexible ureteroscopy (FURS) for the management of nephrolithiasis. The biomedical robots provide a suitable and safe platform for FURS. However, operating the robots expertly still represents a challenge for surgeons. Vision-based navigation is an effective means to simplify the operations of robots by surgeons, which has great potential to improve surgical efficiency. To achieve vision-based navigation, the localization of kidney stones in endoscopic images is the first step. In this paper, we propose a stone segmentation method (SSM) based on zero-shot learning, which consists of segmentation anything model (SAM), an image preprocessing module, and a mask postprocessing module. The SAM segments all objects in endoscopic images, which lack semantic information. The preprocessing module is designed to suppress interference of reflective area in endoscopic images, and the mask postprocessing module is used to filter noise masks. The experimental results on our collected endoscopic images indicate that our method achieves close accuracy on stone segmentation compared with supervised U-Net and VGG_U-Net, which significantly outperforms the Ostu and the SAM.

Keywords: Flexible ureteroscopy · Vision-based navigation · Stone segmentation · Zero-shot learning

---

H. Meng and L. Chen—Contributed equally to this work.

© The Author(s), under exclusive license to Springer Nature Singapore Pte Ltd. 2023
H. Yang et al. (Eds.): ICIRA 2023, LNAI 14269, pp. 80–90, 2023.
https://doi.org/10.1007/978-981-99-6489-5_7

1 Introduction

Urological stone is one of the common diseases of urology. In China, the incidence of kidney stone is 70% [10], and about 5.8% of adults suffer from urinary stone [11]. Currently, there are several treatment options available for kidney stones, including Extracorporeal Shock Wave Lithotripsy (ESWL), Percutaneous Nephrolithotomy (PCNL), and Flexible Ureteroscopy (FURS). ESWL is known to be relatively painful and may cause significant damage to the kidney, while PCNL carries the risk of postoperative infection. In comparison, FURS is a relatively mild treatment option and is the preferred choice for treating ureteral stones [16]. However, FURS represents a technically challenging procedure that requires specific endourologic skills [4,7,12]. During FURS, the endourologist needs assistance to insert and advance laser fibres or baskets and to start and maintain irrigation while holding the endoscope and focusing on the target. Additionally, the surgeon has to activate several devices by foot pedal, such as those for digital fluoroscopy, irrigation, or laser lithotripsy. Most surgeons accomplish this in a standing position, a suboptimal ergonomic posture that may result in orthopaedic complaints [5,6].

Robot-assisted surgery has dramatically influenced minimally invasive surgery with the introduction of console-based manipulators, such as the da Vinci robot (Intuitive Surgical, Sunnyvale, CA, USA) [13] or the Hansen device (Hansen Medical, Mountain View, CA, USA) [1–3]. Since 2012, ELMED (Ankara, Turkey) has been working on a robot specifically designed for FURS [15]. In 2014, Remzi Saglam et al. propose a robot (Roboflex Avicenna) for FURS, which provides a suitable and safe platform for robotic FURS with significant improvement of ergonomics [16]. The Roboflex Avicenna consists of a surgeon's console and a manipulator for the flexible ureterorenoscope. During surgery, the surgeon can sit before the Roboflex Avicenna and operate manipulator to control the endoscope and the laser fibres. Although the Roboflex Avicenna achieves precise control of the endoscope by the manipulator, the complex operations including rotating, warping, and advancing require surgeons to have rich experience. Additionally, it takes long time to focus on the target for intern doctors owing to the curved structure of the kidney. Therefore, automatic robotic-assisted endoscope navigation is urgently needed to improve surgical efficiency.

To achieve robotic-assisted endoscope navigation, we propose a vision-based navigation strategy. First, segment stones in the endoscopic images and calculate the location of the stone in the view based on segmentation results. Second, calculate the position offset between the stone and the endoscope. Last, adjust endoscope to make the stone in the center of the view based on the position offset. After the adjustment of the endoscope, the surgeon only need to control the advance of the endscope.

In this study, we propose a zero-shot kidney stone segmentation method (SSM) to segment stones in the endoscopic images. The SSM is designed based on segmentation anything model (SAM) [9], which is recently proposed for image segmentation in a wide range of applications. The SAM performs well in segmenting all objects in images, but the segmented objects lack semantic information. Therefore, we combine the SAM with image processing methods to achieve stone segmentation in endoscopic images under zero-shot learning. Based on characteristic of stones in endoscopic images, we design an image preprocessing module and a mask postprocessing module. The image preprocessing module aims to suppress interference of reflective area on stone segmentation, and the mask postprocessing module is used to filter noise masks. To assess the performance of the SSM, stone segmentation on endoscopic images of simulated model is implemented. Ostu [8], U-Net [14], the SAM [9], and VGG_U-Net [10] are used for comparisons. The SSM, the VGG_U-Net and the U-Net achieve accurate stone segmentation, which significantly outperform the Ostu and the SAM.

This paper is organized as follows: Sect. 2 introduces data acquisition method, the design of the SAM and the SSM, implementation details and evaluation metrics. Section 3 presents results of ablation studies and comparison studies. At last, Sect. 4 gives conclusion of our proposed method.

2   Methodology

2.1   Data Acquisition

To simulate kidney stone in real surgical environment, we purchase a 3D model of the ureteropelvis and place multiple balls with different shape in the model, as shown in Fig. 1. In this study, we record one video of soft ureteral endoscopy to simulate surgical procedures. All simulated stones in the model are recorded in the video. On the basis of ensuring that each image contains at least one simulated stone, 691 frames are extracted from the video in the principle of covering as many perspectives as possible, and 691 endoscopic images of 400 × 400 pixels are obtained. For each stone in endoscopic images, the ground truth outline is drawn by hand. As shown in Fig. 2, under different endoscopic perspectives, the reflective degree of different simulated stones is different. Additionally, liquid reflection on renal cavity wall presents similar characteristic to the simulated stones (Fig. 2(c)). The individual differences among different simulated stones and complex endoscopic imaging environment bring challenges to stone segmentation. To validate the performance of different methods, the data set is divided into three groups (i.e., training set, validation set and test set) in the ratio of 6:2:2.

2.2   Segment Anything Model

SAM is constructed by three interconnected components: an image encoder, a fast prompt encoder and a mask decoder. As shown in Fig. 3, the image encoder computes an image embedding, the prompt encoder embeds prompts, and then the two information sources are combined in a lightweight mask decoder that predicts segmentation masks. Under the design of network structure, the SAM achieves promptable segmentation task and goal of real-world use. Additionally,

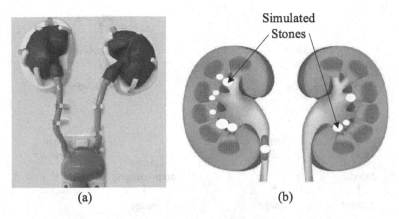

Fig. 1. 3D model of the ureteropelvis (a) and the placement of the simulated stones in the model (b). White balls indicate the simulated stones.

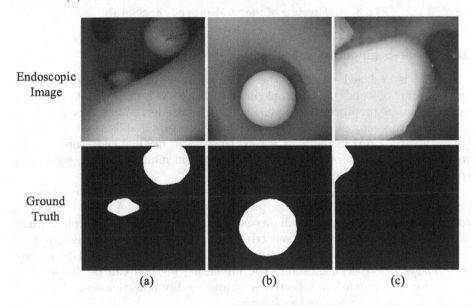

Fig. 2. Endoscopic images and the ground truth of stone segmentation. The simulated stones present different reflective degree under different endoscopic perspectives. The reflective area in (c) presents similar characteristic to the simulated stone.

a large segmentation dataset with over 1 billion masks on 11M licensed and privacy respecting images is built in [9]. The SAM is trained on the dataset and achieves strong generalization to new data distributions.

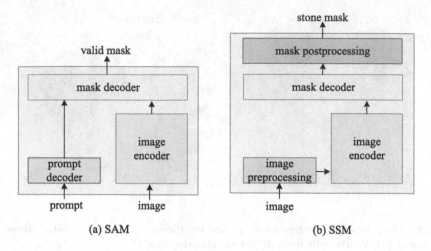

Fig. 3. Architecture of the SAM (a) and the SSM (b).

2.3 Stone Segmentation Model

The SSM is designed based on the SAM, which achieves zero-shot semantic segmentation of stones in endoscopic images. The SSM is built with four components: an image preprocessing module, an image encoder, a mask decoder, and a mask postprocessing module. The network architecture is shown in Fig. 3(b). In this study, the SAM in the SSM is used to segment original endoscopic images without prompt. The outputs of the SAM contain multiple masks, each mask corresponds to one object.

To achieve stone segmentation based on the SAM, we propose an image preprocessing module and a mask postprocessing module. As shown in Fig. 2, reflective area of renal cavity wall presents similar characteristic to stones, which make it difficult to filter the reflective area. To reduce the segmentation of reflective area in endoscopic images, we adopt inpainting method to preprocess images before segmentation. The inpainting method can be divided into two steps: extract mask of reflective area and modify reflective area. The mask of reflective area is calculated as follows:

$$M(i,j) = \begin{cases} 0, & I(i,j) < Thr \\ 1, & I(i,j) \geq Thr \end{cases} \quad (1)$$

where M and I indicate mask of reflective area and gray endoscopic image, respectively. (i,j) denotes pixel in the ith row and jth column. Thr is threshold value, which is set as 200 in this study. After extracting mask of the reflective area, inpainting method based on Navier-strokes is used to modify reflective area.

Besides the reflective area, dark region and speckle noise are also segmented by the SAM. Compared with stones, speckle noise has a much smaller size. In our method, the speckle noise masks are filtered out based on size of segmented objects. Additionally, threshold method is adopted to distinguish between stone and dark region. The threshold method is designed as follows:

$$Flag = \begin{cases} 1, & inten\_mean > Thr\_val \\ & and \quad inten\_var < Thr\_var \\ 0, & else \end{cases} \tag{2}$$

where $inten\_mean$ and $inten\_var$ are mean and variance of segmented object intensity in original images, respectively. Thr_val and Thr_var are threshold value of mean and variance, respectively. The Thr_val and Thr_var are set as 40 and 50, respectively. After filtering segmented masks, the remaining masks of one endoscopic image are merged into one mask. The stone segmentation method based on the SSM is summarized in Algorithm 1 (Table 1).

Table 1. Stone Segmentation Method

Algorithm 1 Stone Segmentation Method
Preprocess
1: Extracting mask of reflective area of renal cavity wall.
2: Modifying reflective area in original images based on inpainting method.
Segmentation
Implementing zero-shot segmentation based on the SAM.
Postprocess
1: Filtering segmented masks of speckle noise based on object size.
2: Removing segmented masks of dark region using threshold method.
3: Merging remaining masks into one mask for each endoscopic image.

2.4 Implementation Details and Evaluation Metrics

The test of the U-Net and the SAM are implemented using Pytorch and Python 3.8. All computer operation is performed on a personal computer with a RTX 2060 GPU and a 2.6 GHz Intel Core i7 CPU. The inference of the SAM is implemented based on ViT-B [9].

To quantitatively evaluate the performance of stone segmentation using different methods, Dice coefficient (denoted as Dice) and location error (LE) are used as the quantitative indexes. Dice measures the segmentation accuracy, which is defined as

$$Dice = \frac{2|X \cap Y|}{|X| + |Y|} \tag{3}$$

where X and Y denote pixel set of segmented stone region and actual stone region. Higher Dice index reveals a better similarity of the two regions.

The ultimate objective of stone segmentation is to provide location of stone center for navigation of robot for flexible ureteroscopy. LE measures the distance variation between the center of the actual stone region and the segmented stone region. For images containing more than one stones, the center location of the largest stone is used to calculate LE. The definition of LE is presented as follows:

$$LE = \|L_a - L_s\|_2 \tag{4}$$

where L_a and L_s denote the center coordinates of the actual stone region and the segmented stone region, respectively. $\|\cdot\|_2$ represents the operator of Euclidean distance.

3   Experiments

In this section, we evaluate the performance of the SSM using ablation studies and comparison experiments. This section is organized as follows: first, ablation studies are presented to verify the effectiveness of the image preprocessing module and the mask postprocessing module. Second, the performance of the SSM is compared with the Ostu, the SAM, the U-Net, and the VGG_U-Net. The VGG_U-Net is designed for endoscopic segmentation of kidney stone. The Ostu method achieves segmentation based on threshold, while the U-Net and the VGG_U-Net are data-driven methods. The U-Net and the VGG_U-Net are trained using the training set, while the SAM and the SSM are zero-shot learning models. The comparison experiments are implemented on the test set.

3.1   Ablation Studies

Figure 4 shows endoscopic images and segmentation results before and after image preprocessing. As shown in Fig. 4(c), the mask of reflective area of renal cavity wall is effectively extracted by the threshold method. Additionally, the inpainting method effectively restores the reflective area to normal renal cavity wall (Fig. 4(d)). Furthermore, the SSM model achieves more accurate segmentation on the preprocessed image (Fig. 4(d)) than the original image(Fig. 4(a)). These results demonstrate that the image preprocessing module can effectively reduce interference of reflective areas.

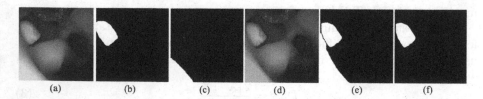

Fig. 4. Effectiveness of image preprocessing module. (a) Original image. (b) Ground truth of stone segmentation. (c) Extracted mask of reflective area. (d) Image after inpainting. (e) Segmentation mask of original image. (f) Segmentation mask of image after preprocessing.

Figure 5 shows segmentation results of ablation studies on the mask postprocessing module. As shown in Fig. 5(b), the tube embedded in the model and light spot are segmented while not using mask postprocessing. After mask postprocessing, the masks of the tube and the light spot are filtered and only the mask of stone is retained. These results verify the effectiveness of the mask postprocessing in the stone segmentation of the SSM.

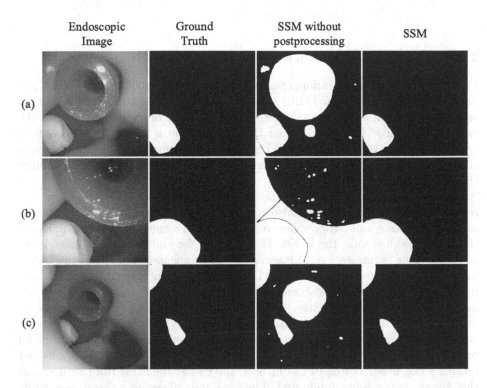

Fig. 5. Effectiveness of the mask postprocessing module. (a–c) present endoscopic images, ground truth, and segmentation results of three cases, respectively.

For quantitative analysis, mean and standard deviation (SD) of the Dice and the LE for different methods are calculated in ablation studies. As shown in Table 2, employing the image preprocessing and the mask postprocessing achieves the highest mean Dice (0.85) and the smallest mean LE (27.73). Compared with the SAM with the mask postprocessing module, employing image preprocessing yields a result of 27.73 in mean LE, which brings 1.66 improvement. Meanwhile, employing the mask postprocessing module individually outperforms the baseline by 0.37 in mean Dice. These results demonstrate that the image preprocessing module and the mask postprocessing module bring benefit to stone segmentation in endoscopic images.

Table 2. Quantitative Results of Dice and LE in Ablation Studies (Mean ± SD)

Method	Preprocessing	Postprocessing	Dice	LE
SAM			0.47 ± 0.28	124.01 ± 108.53
SAM	√		0.46 ± 0.27	129.51 ± 105.81
SAM		√	0.84 ± 0.27	29.39 ± 70.72
SAM	√	√	0.85 ± 0.26	27.73 ± 68.51

3.2   Comparison with Other Methods

Figure 6 presents segmentation results of five methods and Table 3 lists their quantifications of Dice and LE, respectively. The imaging environment of endoscopy is complex because of the lumen structure of the kidney. When the endoscope is close to the stone and the illumination is sufficient, the contour of the stone is clear (Fig. 6(a)). When the light source is far away from the stone, the stone is not fully illuminated and the contour of the stone is blurry (Fig. 6(b-c)).

As shown in Fig. 6(a), the stone is segmented by all methods. However, regions similar to the stone are also segmented by the Otsu method. Additionally, speckle noise and dark regions are segmented by the SAM. Compared with the above two methods, the U-Net, the VGG_U-Net and the SSM achieve more accurate stone segmentation. Furthermore, the segmentation mask of the U-Net has some speckle noise, while the SSM successfully filters noise masks. For cases in Fig. 6(b), the contours of segmented stones given by the Ostu and the U-Net are smaller than that of the stone in endoscopic image. Additionally, some background regions are incorrectly segmented as stone by the Ostu, the U-Net, and the VGG_U-Net. Furthermore, the segmentation results of the SAM contains all regions in the endoscopic image, while the SSM effectively filters noise masks and retains stone mask. For cases in Fig. 6(c), the endoscope is far from stones, and the stones are not fully illuminated. The Ostu fails to segment the stones, while the other methods achieves stone segmentation. All these results demonstrate that the SSM can achieve accurate stone segmentation in endoscopic images.

To quantitatively assess the performance of different methods, mean and SD of the Dice and the LE are calculated. As shown in Table 3, the Ostu method obtains the lowest mean Dice (0.28) and the largest mean LE (163.62). Additionally, the mean Dice given by the SAM is close to that of the Ostu, which is significantly smaller than that of the U-Net, the VGG_U-Net and the SSM, respectively. Furthermore, the mean LE of the SAM is about 14 times, 7 times, and 4 times of that of the U-Net, the VGG_U-Net and the SSM, respectively. Compared with the SAM, the SSM achieves significant improvement on Dice and LE, respectively. The U-Net achieves the highest mean Dice and the smallest mean LE, which is attributed to supervised learning. Although the SSM is based on zero-shot learning, the mean Dice and the mean LE given by the SSM are close to that of the U-Net. These results demonstrate that the SSM has potential to achieve accurate stone segmentation in endoscopic images.

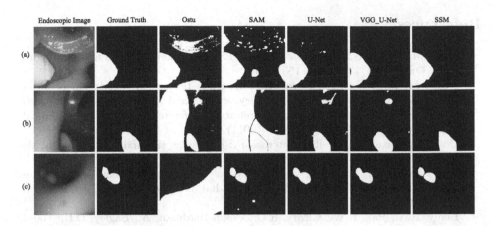

Fig. 6. Segmentation results of different methods. (a–c) present endoscopic images, ground truth, and segmentation results of different methods on three cases.

Table 3. Quantitative Results of Dice and LE for Different Methods (Mean ± SD)

Index	Ostu	SAM	U-Net	VGG_U-Net	SSM
Dice	0.28 ± 0.29	0.47 ± 0.28	0.92 ± 0.08	0.88 ± 0.14	0.85 ± 0.26
LE	163.62 ± 90.41	124.01 ± 108.53	8.81 ± 44.99	16.79 ± 62.48	27.73 ± 68.51

4 Conclusion

To achieve stone segmentation with zero-shot learning in robotic-assisted endoscope navigation, we propose the SSM based on the SAM. The SAM is recently proposed for image segmentation in a wide range of applications. The SAM performs well in segmenting objects in endoscopic images, but the segmented objects lack semantic information. To perform stone segmentation with the SAM, we propose the image preprocessing module and the mask postprocessing module according to the characteristic of stones and endoscopic images. With the help of the image preprocessing module and the mask postprocessing module, the SSM filters most of noise masks and retains stone masks.

To validate the performance of the SSM, we conduct stone segmentation on endoscopic images of the simulated model. Ostu, U-Net, VGG_U-Net and SAM are employed for qualitative and quantitative comparison. All results reveal that the SSM, the VGG_U-Net and the U-Net achieve accurate stone segmentation, which significantly outperform the Ostu and the SAM. Our work is a preliminary exploration of the SAM applied to the stone segmentation in endoscopic images. We hope that future work will maximize the advantages of the SAM in clinical data to achieve accurate stone segmentation for robotic-assisted endoscope navigation.

Acknowledgments. The authors would like to acknowledge the support from the Scientific Research Item of Zhejiang Lab under Grant No. 2022NB0AC01.

References

1. Aron, M., Haber, G.P., Desai, M.M., Gill, I.S.: Flexible robotics: a new paradigm. Curr. Opin. Urol. **17**(3), 151–155 (2007)
2. Desai, M.M., et al.: Flexible robotic retrograde renoscopy: description of novel robotic device and preliminary laboratory experience. Urology **72**(1), 42–46 (2008)
3. Desai, M.M., et al.: Robotic flexible ureteroscopy for renal calculi: initial clinical experience. J. Urol. **186**(2), 563–568 (2011)
4. Doizi, S., Traxer, O.: Flexible ureteroscopy: technique, tips and tricks. Urolithiasis **46**, 47–58 (2018)
5. Elkoushy, M.A., Andonian, S.: Prevalence of orthopedic complaints among endourologists and their compliance with radiation safety measures. J. Endourol. **25**(10), 1609–1613 (2011)
6. Healy, K.A., Pak, R.W., Cleary, R.C., Colon-Herdman, A., Bagley, D.H.: Hand problems among endourologists. J. Endourol. **25**(12), 1915–1920 (2011)
7. Holden, T., Pedro, R.N., Hendlin, K., Durfee, W., Monga, M.: Evidence-based instrumentation for flexible ureteroscopy: a review. J. Endourol. **22**(7), 1423–1426 (2008)
8. Jiao, S., Li, X., Lu, X.: An improved OSTU method for image segmentation. In: 2006 8th International Conference on Signal Processing, vol. 2. IEEE (2006)
9. Kirillov, A., et al.: Segment anything (2023). arXiv:2304.02643
10. Li, R., et al.: Endoscopic segmentation of kidney stone based on transfer learning. In: 2021 40th Chinese Control Conference (CCC), pp. 8145–8150 (2021). https://doi.org/10.23919/CCC52363.2021.9550652
11. Marien, T., Mass, A.Y., Shah, O.: Antimicrobial resistance patterns in cases of obstructive pyelonephritis secondary to stones. Urology **85**(1), 64–68 (2015). https://doi.org/10.1016/j.urology.2014.10.007
12. Monga, M., Dretler, S.P., Landman, J., Slaton, J.W., Conradie, M.C., Clayman, R.V.: Maximizing ureteroscope deflection: "play it straight". Urology **60**(5), 902–905 (2002)
13. Rassweiler, J., Safi, K., Subotic, S., Teber, D., Frede, T.: Robotics and telesurgery-an update on their position in laparoscopic radical prostatectomy. Minim. Invasive Ther. Allied Technol. **14**(2), 109–122 (2005)
14. Ronneberger, O., Fischer, P., Brox, T.: U-Net: convolutional networks for biomedical image segmentation. In: Navab, N., Hornegger, J., Wells, W.M., Frangi, A.F. (eds.) MICCAI 2015, Part III. LNCS, vol. 9351, pp. 234–241. Springer, Cham (2015). https://doi.org/10.1007/978-3-319-24574-4_28
15. Saglam, R., Kabakci, A.S., Koruk, E., Tokatli, Z.: How did we designed and improved a new Turkish robot for flexible ureterorenoscope. J. Endourol. **26**, A275–A275 (2012)
16. Saglam, R., et al.: A new robot for flexible ureteroscopy: development and early clinical results (IDEAL stage 1–2b). Eur. Urol. **66**(6), 1092–1100 (2014). https://doi.org/10.1016/j.eururo.2014.06.047

Sutures and Landmarks Joint Detection Method Based on Convolutional Neural Network for Rat Stereotactic Surgery

Bo Han, Hanwei Chen, Chao Liu$^{(\boxtimes)}$, and Xinjun Sheng

State Key Laboratory of Mechanical System and Vibration, School of Mechanical Engineering,
Shanghai Jiao Tong University, Shanghai, China
aalon@sjtu.edu.cn

Abstract. With the advantages of manual error reduction in manipulating instruments, surgical robots have shown great value in stereotactic surgery. Most of them require doctors to locate insertion sites manually, which introduces empirical errors. Some researchers have discussed deep-learning based methods to automatically segment medical images and locate targets. However, the existing studies mainly focus on the general-sized objects, while the landmarks of rat skull are a few pixels in size. Besides, the serious image noise produces further challenges. To solve the problems, we propose a sutures and landmarks joint detection method, which contains a two-branch framework, a hybrid loss and a class-specific pretraining method. The two-branch framework contains a shared encoder and two parallel decoders connected by feature fusion modules. The hybrid loss includes an intersection of union loss between different classes of landmarks and a contrastive feature loss to make the landmarks decoder extract more discriminative feature. The class-specific pretraining method supervise the two parallel decoders with boundary label and object label respectively, which makes the decoders learn related decoding processes in pretraining. A novel dataset containing sixty skull images of twenty Sprague Dawley rats is constructed for training and test. Experimental results show that the proposed method achieves 0.01 mean absolute error in sutures segmentation and over 80% correct rate in landmarks location.

Keywords: Rat stereotactic surgery · Sutures and landmarks detection ·
Two-branch framework · Hybrid loss · Pretraining method

1 Introduction

Surgical robots are widely used in human and animal stereotactic surgeries [1, 2], which reduce the manual error of moving and manipulating instruments and significantly improve surgery efficiency. ROSA robot [3] and NeuroMate robot [4] are able to complete the surgical task under MRI monitoring according to the preoperative surgical plan of doctors. NeuroArm [5] is an MRI-compatible robot that can be operated remotely to perform surgery. Ly *et al.* [6] design a three-dimensional (3D) skull profiler sub-system and a full six degree-of-freedom robotic platform to automatically insert

© The Author(s), under exclusive license to Springer Nature Singapore Pte Ltd. 2023
H. Yang et al. (Eds.): ICIRA 2023, LNAI 14269, pp. 91–104, 2023.
https://doi.org/10.1007/978-981-99-6489-5_8

probes into rat brain after the manual selection of landmarks in the point cloud. Liu *et al.* [7] design a digital stereotaxic instrument for pigeons, which reduces manual errors by displaying high-precision positional feedback of the end manipulator during surgery. However, the automatic landmarks detection methods are rarely mentioned in the above work, so the manual location error still exists.

In recent years, a large number of convolutional neural networks based on encoder-decoder architecture, such as U-Net [8] and its variants [9, 10], have been widely used in medical image segmentation task. Zhou *et al.* [11] adopted U-Net to locate landmarks in mice skull images, but the location error is a little large and doesn't meet the precision requirement of rat stereotactic surgery. Cai *et al.* [12] used densely connected convolutional layers as decoder blocks to reuse features and compensate for the resolution loss, which achieves high accuracy in cell segmentation tasks. Tong *et al.* [13] proposed a triple attention mechanism to make the decoder focus on more relevant target areas. Xie *et al.* [14] designed a context hierarchical integrated architecture, which extracted substantial complementary features hierarchically and integrated them to generate more discriminative features. The above studies mainly focus on the segmentation task of general-sized objects. However, in rat stereotactic surgery, the landmarks are only one pixel point. Besides, bloodstains and small skull burrs that cannot be removed cause serious image noise, which further increases the difficulty of landmarks location.

To address the above issues, we propose a sutures and landmarks joint detection method, which contains a two-branches framework, a hybrid loss and a class-specific pretraining method. The two-branches framework consists of a shared encoder and two parallel decoders, which are used to detect sutures and landmarks respectively. Feature fusion modules connect the two decoders and provide sutures information to the landmark decoder. The hybrid loss introduces a negative intersection of union loss and a contrastive feature loss, which enable the landmarks decoder to extract more discriminative feature. Boundary label and object label are used to supervise the sutures and landmarks decoders in pretraining, which makes the decoders learn related decoding processes. Sixty skull images of twenty Sprague Dawley (SD) rats make up a novel dataset for training and test. Ablation studies are implemented to verify the effectiveness of the proposed framework, hybrid loss and pretraining method.

The remainder of this paper are as follows: the methods for acquiring, annotating and preprocessing the rat skull image dataset are introduced in Sect. 2. In Sect. 3, we introduce the proposed sutures and landmarks joint detection method. Section 4 verifies the effectiveness of each part of the proposed method. The main contributions are summarized in Sect. 5.

2 Acquisition, Annotation and Preprocessing of Rat Skull Image Dataset

2.1 Image Acquisition

After the skull surface of a SD rat is exposed by a professional experimenter, a structured-light 3D camera is used to photograph the experimental area to obtain grayscale images and depth images, as is shown in Fig. 1. The imaging region is large enough that the relative position of the camera and rat can be set roughly. Three pictures are taken for each rat from three commonly used camera angles, as shown in Fig. 2. In all, the dataset contains 60 skull images of 20 rats.

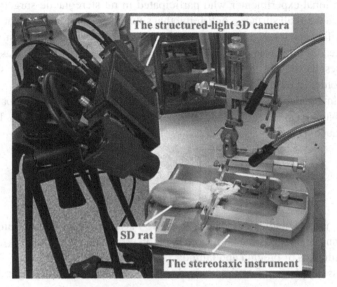

Fig. 1. Experimental scene of the work.

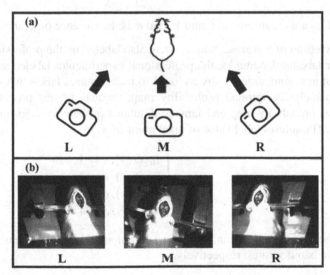

Fig. 2. Schematic diagram of three different camera angles. L, M and R represent left, middle and right camera angles. (a). The relative positions of camera and rat at the three different camera angles. (b). Grayscale images taken from the three different camera angles.

2.2 Annotation Method of Landmarks and Sutures

Annotation Method of Landmarks. The landmarks contain bregma and lambda (BL), which are the intersections of best-fit curves for sutures [15]. The annotator of landmarks is the professional experimenter who participated in rat stereotactic surgery and carefully observed the skull surface, confirming that sutures and landmarks of each rat can be clearly identified and located. In order to reduce random errors, the professional experimenter labeled for three rounds, and the average labeled positions are used as landmarks annotation results. Before the labeling start of each round, we randomly shuffled the appearance order of each rat.

The landmarks label includes three channels, namely background probability map, bregma probability map and lambda probability map, marked with $c = 1, 2, 3$. The landmarks label value of pixel point (c, x, y) is:

$$Label_{bl}(c, x, y) = \begin{cases} 1_{\alpha_1}(x, y), c = 1 \\ Gauss(x, y, x_b, y_b, \delta), c = 2 \\ Gauss(x, y, x_l, y_l, \delta), c = 3 \end{cases} \tag{1}$$

where $1_{\alpha_1}(x, y)$ is the indicator function, $Gauss(\cdot)$ is a gauss distribution function, α_1 is the background region, δ is the allowable location error, and (x_b, y_b) and (x_l, y_l) are the marked coordinates of bregma and lambda.

The gauss distribution function is used to smooth the gradient during training. It is:

$$Gauss(x, y, \mu_x, \mu_y, \sigma) = (2\pi\sigma^2)^{-1} \exp\left[-\frac{1}{2}\left(\frac{(x-\mu_x)^2}{\sigma^2} + \frac{(y-\mu_y)^2}{\sigma^2}\right)\right] \tag{2}$$

where μ_x and μ_y are the means of X and Y, and σ is the variance of X and Y.

Annotation Method of Sutures. Sutures were also labeled by the professional experimenter. After labeling landmarks, the professional experimenter labeled sutures for a round. The sutures annotation results are used to make sutures labels, which includes 4 channels, namely background probability map, coronal sutures probability map, sagittal sutures probability map and lambdoid sutures probability map, marked with $c = 1, 2, 3, 4$. The sutures label value of pixel point (c, x, y) is:

$$Label_s(c, x, y) = \begin{cases} 1_{\alpha_2}(x, y), c = 1 \\ 1_{co}(x, y), c = 2 \\ 1_{sa}(x, y), c = 3 \\ 1_{la}(x, y), c = 4 \end{cases} \tag{3}$$

where α_2 is the background region, and co, sa and la are the marked areas of coronal, sagittal and lambdoid sutures, respectively.

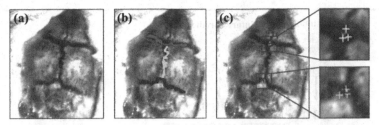

Fig. 3. The labels of sutures and landmarks in the preprocessed image.

2.3 Data Preprocessing

YOLO v5 [16] is adopted to automatically identify the skull region in images and remove other regions. Figure 3(a) shows a preprocessed skull image. The sutures label is shown in Fig. 3(b), where the red, green and blue curves are positions of coronal suture, sagittal suture, and lambdoid suture, respectively. The landmarks label is shown in Fig. 3(c), where the yellow and green pixel points are the labeled positions of bregma and lambda, and the red and blue pixel points are the average labeled positions.

3 Sutures and Landmarks Joint Detection Method

3.1 The Proposed Two-Branch Framework

The proposed two-branch framework consists of a shared encoder and two parallel decoders, which are used to predict sutures mask and landmarks mask respectively. The Fig. 4 illustrated the neural network architecture. The *DarkNet53* [16] are used as the encoder and is divided into six blocks to extract multi-level features from input images. The numbers of encoder blocks represent the downsampling rates of output features resolution relative to input image resolution. The output features resolutions of encoder blocks are:

$$(H_i, W_i) = \frac{1}{2^i}(H_{input}, W_{input}) \tag{4}$$

where H_i and W_i are height and width of output features of encoder block i, and H_{input} and W_{input} are height and width of input image.

Decoder Blocks Structure. The two parallel decoders contain six blocks correspondingly, which are simple feed-forward networks combined by convolution modules. The convolution modules consist of a convolution layer, a batch normalization and an activation function (ReLU). Figure 5 (a) and (b) shows the detailed structure of suture decoder blocks at highest level and other levels respectively. The structure of BL decoder blocks is the same as sutures decoder blocks at each level, but the input current-level encoded features are replaced by fused features. The sutures and BL decoder blocks are supervised by sutures and landmarks labels at each level.

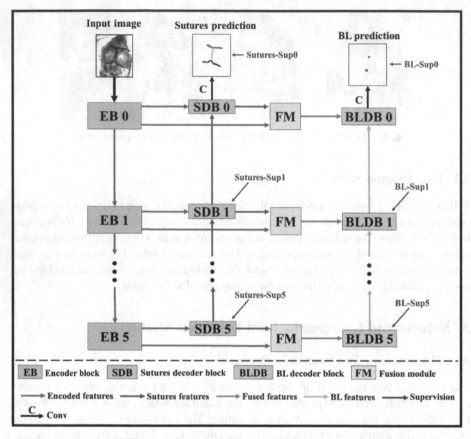

Fig. 4. The proposed two-branch framework.

Fusion Modules. The basic idea of fusion modules is to build a hierarchical decoding process, which obeys the hierarchical correlation of sutures and landmarks. Specifically, the fusion modules enable the BL decoders to utilize sutures features without interfering with sutures decoding process. Figure 5 (c) shows the detailed structure of fusion modules. We first concatenate encoded features and sutures features at each position since they are positionally aligned. Then, a 1×1 convolution module and 3×3 convolution module are used to fuse the concatenated features.

3.2 Loss Function

The training loss includes sutures prediction loss and the proposed hybrid landmarks loss. The total training loss is:

$$Loss_{total} = \sum_{i=0}^{5} loss_{s,i} + loss_{bl,i} \qquad (5)$$

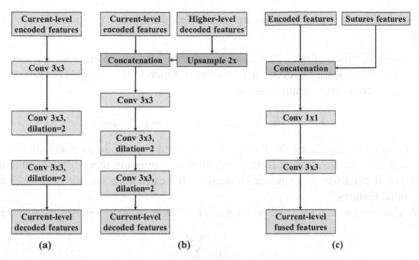

Fig. 5. The detailed structure of decoder blocks and fusion modules.

where $loss_{s,i}$ and $loss_{bl,i}$ represent the sutures prediction loss and the hybrid landmarks loss of i-th decoder block.

Sutures Prediction Loss. Qin *et al.* [17] proposed a hybrid loss to make the model more focus on the boundary of salient objects. Because the sutures are essentially the boundaries between different parts of skull, we use the same hybrid loss in [17] as the suture prediction loss, which consists of IoU loss, SSIM loss and BCE loss:

$$loss_s = l_{iou} + l_{ssim} + l_{bce} \qquad (6)$$

where l_{iou}, l_{ssim} and l_{bce} are the IoU loss, SSIM loss and BCE loss respectively.

The Proposed Hybrid Landmarks Loss. The proposed hybrid landmarks loss contains IoU loss, BCE loss, the negative intersection of union loss between bregma and lambda prediction mask (Neg-IoU-BL loss) and the contrastive feature loss:

$$loss_{bl} = l_{iou} + l_{bce} + l_{neg-iou-bl} + l_{cf} \qquad (7)$$

where $l_{neg-iou}$ and l_{cf} are the Neg-IoU-BL loss and the contrastive feature loss.

The Neg-IoU-BL loss. In our experiments, the landmarks decoder trained with only IoU loss and BCE loss locates bregma (lambda) to the nearby region of lambda (bregma) in some skull images. The main reason is that the local geometrical feature of bregma and lambda are similar. Thus, if one of BL is difficult to locate while another is easy, the landmarks decoder will incorrectly position the former near the latter. To solve this problem, we propose the Neg-IoU-BL loss:

$$l_{neg-iou-bl} = \frac{\sum_{x=1}^{W} \sum_{y=1}^{H} Pre_b(x,y)Pre_l(x,y)}{\sum_{x=1}^{W} \sum_{y=1}^{H} [Pre_b(x,y)+Pre_l(x,y)-Pre_b(x,y)Pre_l(x,y)]} \qquad (8)$$

where the $Pre_b(x, y)$ and $Pre_l(x, y)$ are the predicted bregma and lambda probability in the position of (x, y), and W and H are the width and height of the probability map.

The Neg-IoU-BL loss penalizes the landmarks decoder when it positions BL too close together.

The Contrastive Feature Loss. The contrastive feature loss is introduced to encourage the proposed model to learn landmark features that are more discriminative to background features. The contrastive feature loss is:

$$l_{cf} = CS\left(f_{b,avg}, f_{bg,avg}\right) + CS\left(f_{l,avg}, f_{bg,avg}\right) \tag{9}$$

where $f_{b,avg}, f_{l,avg}, f_{bg,avg}$ are the average bregma, lambda and background features, and $CS(\cdot)$ is the cosine similarity function, which is a commonly used distance function. Intuitively, it penalizes the landmarks decoder for extracting similar landmarks and background features.

We average the features at all positions in the feature map as the average feature:

$$f_{avg} = \frac{1}{W*H} \sum_{(x,y)}^{(W,H)} f_{(x,y)} \tag{10}$$

where $f_{(x,y)}$ is the features at the pixel point (x, y), W and H are the width and height of the feature map.

A common view is that high-level features contain more discriminative semantic information. We assume the same is true for landmarks features. Thus, the contrastive feature loss is only used in the highest three levels of supervision. We validate this assumption in the ablation experiments.

3.3 The Proposed Class-Specific Pretraining Method

According to the anatomical knowledge, the landmark feature includes suture information but not vice versa. Besides, the geometric feature difference between sutures and landmarks are huge. Thus, we suppose that making the two decoders learn related decoding processes in pretraining can improve the model performance. The boundary label and object label are used to supervise the sutures and landmarks decoder in pretraining, respectively. Figure 6 (a) illustrates the baseline class-independent pretraining method, which supervises the two decoders with object label. Figure 6 (b) illustrates the proposed class-specific pretraining method. It should be noted that the proposed pretraining method can also improve the performance of single-branch decoder framework, such as U-Net, which has been validated in the ablation experiments.

4   Experiments

4.1   Experimental Setup

The proposed model is firstly pretrained for 10 epochs by the proposed pretraining method. The *DUTS* [18] training set is used as the pretraining dataset. Then, the proposed model is initialized with the pretrained weights and trained until the training loss converges, which is typically after 300–400 epochs. In this paper, a 4-fold crossover

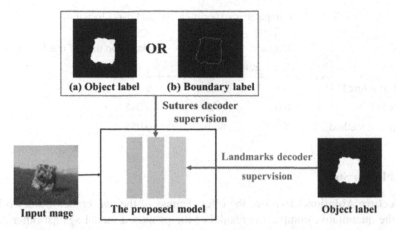

Fig. 6. Illustration of the baseline and proposed pretraining method.

experiment is implemented. The proposed model is carried out by using the PyTorch toolbox [19]. A computer with an Intel Core i9-13900 KF 3.00 GHz CPU (32 GB RAM) and an NVIDIA GeForce RTX 4090 GPU (24 GB RAM) is used for experiments. During the pretraining and training, input images are resized to 320×320. We use the Adam optimizer [20] with exponential decay rates of 0.9 and 0.999. The batch size is set to 2. The learning rate is initialized to 0.001 and halved every 100 epochs. During the test, images aren't resized.

The mean absolute error (MAE) and weighted F-measure (F_β^w) [21] are used to evaluate the sutures prediction performance of the proposed model. However, general evaluation metrics of segmentation tasks are not suitable for landmark segmentation, because they focus on general-sized objects, which are areas composed of many pixels, while landmarks are one pixel point. Therefore, we propose an evaluation metric for landmark segmentation based on anatomical knowledge. Watson and Paxinos [15] pointed out that the location error of BL should not exceed 0.5mm. In the skull images, the distance between adjacent pixels in the area around BL is about 0.1 mm. Thus, the allowable error is 5 pixels. If the distance between the predicted position and ground truth position is less than or equal to the allowable error, the prediction is correct. The average correct rates of landmarks prediction are used as the evaluation metric.

4.2   Comparative Experiment

To the best of our knowledge, the proposed method is the first to automatically detect sutures. Thus, we only compare the landmark location accuracy of the proposed method with other landmark location methods. One corresponding method is to fit manually marked sutures and use the intersections as landmarks. Another is to use a fully convolutional networks (FCN) to estimate the landmarks position. As shown in Table 1, the proposed method greatly outperforms other methods. A possible reason for the poor performance of the fitting suture method is that the method is only applicable to images from specific camera angles, while the images in our dataset are not taken from these camera angles.

Table 1. Comparative experiment on landmarks location.

Method	Bregma	Lambda	Detection time of one image (s)
	Correct rates (%)		
1. Fitting suture [11]	3.3	0.0	0.146
2. FCN [11]	30.0	1.7	0.046
3. Proposed method	85.0	80.0	0.055

4.3 Ablation Study

Architecture Ablation. To prove the effectiveness of the two-branch framework, we report the quantitative comparison results of the proposed model against other related architectures. The U-Net framework is used as the baseline architecture. Next, the single-branch decoder of the adopted U-Net is divided into two branches, both of which contain half channel number of the single-branch decoder. Finally, the two branches are connected by the feature fusion modules as described in Sect. 3.1. As Table 2 shows, the two-branches decoder structure not only improves the accuracy of landmarks location, but also reduces learning parameters. The feature fusion modules improve the model performance furthermore with modest parameter increase. There are two possible reasons. One is that the landmarks features contain sutures information. Another is that the sutures information is less susceptible to noise, and thus utilizing sutures information to detect landmarks improves the robustness to noise. Figure 7 and Fig. 8 show the segmentation results of different models (Table 3).

Table 2. The ablation study of architecture and loss.

Ablation	Configuration	Suture		Bregma	Lambda	Decoder parameter
		MAE	F_β^w	Correct rates %		
Architecture	U-Net framework	0.015	0.971	60.0	61.7	135.8M
	Two-branch	0.015	0.971	66.7	71.7	77.7M
	Two-branch + FM	0.010	0.981	78.3	76.7	93.1M
Hybrid landmarks loss	Two-branch + FM $+ l_{neg-iou-bl}$	0.010	0.980	81.7	76.7	93.1M
	Two-branch + FM $+ l_{neg-iou-bl} + l_{cf}^*$	0.010	0.980	36.7	30.0	93.1M
	Two-branch + FM $+ l_{neg-iou-bl} + l_{cf}$	0.010	0.980	85.0	80.0	93.1M

Table 3. The ablation study of pretraining method.

Configuration	Pretraining method	Suture		Bregma	Lambda
		MAE	F_β^w	Correct rates %	
U-Net framework	None	0.013	0.974	55.0	45.0
	Class-independent	0.013	0.974	56.7	60.0
	Class-specific	0.015	0.971	60.0	61.7
Two-branch + FM	None	0.011	0.979	70.0	73.3
	Class-independent	0.011	0.979	73.3	71.7
	Class-specific	0.010	0.981	78.3	76.7
Two-branch + FM $+ l_{neg-iou-bl} + l_{cf}$	None	0.011	0.979	81.7	66.7
	Class-independent	0.011	0.979	70.0	73.3
	Class-specific	0.010	0.980	85.0	80.0

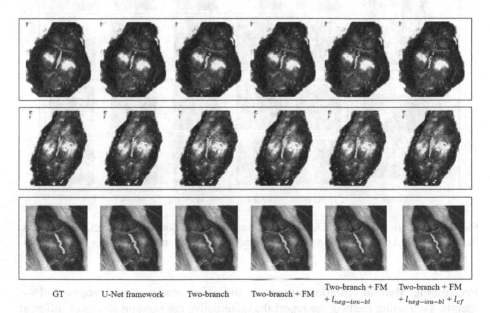

| GT | U-Net framework | Two-branch | Two-branch + FM | Two-branch + FM $+ l_{neg-iou-bl}$ | Two-branch + FM $+ l_{neg-iou-bl} + l_{cf}$ |

Fig. 7. Sutures prediction of different configurations in ablation study of architecture and loss. The red, green, blue lines represent coronal, sagittal and lambda sutures.

Hybrid Landmarks Loss Ablation. To prove the effectiveness of the proposed hybrid loss, we progressively introduce the Neg-IoU-BL loss and the contrastive feature loss into the hybrid landmarks loss. In Table 1, l_{cf}^* represents that the contrastive feature loss is used in all levels of the landmark decoder supervision, and l_{cf} represents that the contrastive feature loss is only used in the highest three levels. As Table 1 shows, the Neg-IoU-BL loss slightly improves the correct rate of bregma location. The contrastive feature loss used in the highest three levels further improves the landmark location accuracy, while the contrastive feature loss used in all levels damages the model performance. This result supports the assumption in Sect. 3.2.

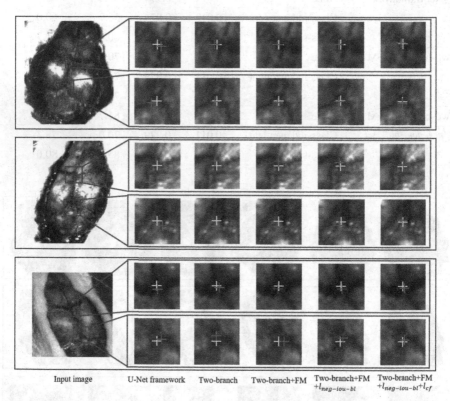

Input image   U-Net framework   Two-branch   Two-branch+FM   Two-branch+FM $+l_{neg-iou-bl}$ Two-branch+FM $+l_{neg-iou-bl}+l_{cf}$

Fig. 8. Landmarks prediction of different configurations in ablation study of architecture and loss. Red cross (+) and blue cross (+) represent the prediction and ground truth. (Color figure online)

Pretraining Method Ablation. To prove the effectiveness of the proposed class-specific pretraining method, we report the quantitative comparison results of different pretraining methods. Besides, to demonstrate that the proposed pre-training method can be used for single-branch framework and baseline loss function, the U-Net framework, the two-branch framework and the two-branch framework with the hybrid loss are used in this ablation study. As shown in Table 2, the proposed class-specific pre-training method improves the performance of all the three configurations compared to no pre-training.

5 Conclusion

In this paper, we propose a sutures and landmarks joint detection method for rat stereotactic surgery. The proposed method contains a two-branch framework, a hybrid loss and a class-specific pretraining method. The two-branch framework contains a shared encoder and two parallel decoders. Feature fusion modules are used to connect the two decoders, which make the landmarks decoder utilize sutures information. The proposed hybrid loss includes a negative intersection of union loss and a contrastive feature loss, which make the proposed model extract more discriminative landmarks features. In the proposed class-specific pretraining, the boundary label and object label are used to supervise the sutures decoder and landmarks decoder, respectively. The proposed pretraining method improves the model performance by enabling the two decoders to learn related decoding processes. Sixty images of twenty SD rats are used to construct a novel dataset for training and test. Experimental results show that the proposed method outperforms the baseline methods in every part. The proposed method achieves 0.01 mean absolute error in sutures segmentation and over 80% correct rate in landmarks location. In the view of the advantages, the sutures and landmarks joint detection method is hopeful to be applied to guide surgical robots in stereotactic surgeries.

Acknowledgments. This work was supported in part by the Natural Science Foundation of Shanghai (Grant No. Z1ZR1430700), China National Key Research and Development program (Grant No. 2020YFB1313500) and Natural Science and Technology Innovation 2030 Major Project (Grant No. 2022ZD0208601).

References

1. Elsabeh, R., et al.: Cranial neurosurgical robotics. Br. J. Neurosurg. **35**(5), 532–540 (2021)
2. Maarouf, M., Neudorf, C.: Robotics in stereotactic neurosurgery. In: Al-Salihi, M.M., et al. (eds.) Introduction to Robotics in Minimally Invasive Neurosurgery, pp. 25–38. Springer International Publishing, Cham (2022)
3. Alan, N., et al.: Intraparenchymal hematoma and intraventricular catheter placement using robotic stereotactic assistance (ROSA): a single center preliminary experience. J. Clin. Neurosci. **91**, 391–395 (2021)
4. Peciu-Florianu, I., et al.: Frameless robot-assisted stereotactic biopsies for lesions of the brainstem a series of 103 consecutive biopsies. J. Neurooncol **157**(1), 109–119 (2022). https://doi.org/10.1007/s11060-022-03952-6
5. Sutherland, G.R., et al.: The Evolution of neuroArm. Neurosurgery **72**(Supplement 1), A27–A32 (2013)
6. Ly, P.T., et al.: Robotic stereotaxic system based on 3D skull reconstruction to improve surgical accuracy and speed. J. Neurosci. Methods **347**, 108955 (2021)
7. Liu, X., et al.: Development of digital stereotaxic instrument for pigeons (Columba Livia). J. Bionic Eng. **19**(4), 1003–1013 (2022)
8. Navab, N., Hornegger, J., Wells, W.M., Frangi, A.F. (eds.): MICCAI 2015. LNCS, vol. 9349. Springer, Cham (2015). https://doi.org/10.1007/978-3-319-24553-9
9. Zhou, Z., Rahman Siddiquee, M.M., Tajbakhsh, N., Liang, J.: UNet++: a nested U-Net architecture for medical image segmentation. In: Stoyanov, D., Taylor, Z., Carneiro, G., Syeda-Mahmood, T., Martel, A., Maier-Hein, L., Tavares, J.M.R.S., Bradley, A., Papa, J.P., Belagiannis, V., Nascimento, J.C., Lu, Z., Conjeti, S., Moradi, M., Greenspan, H., Madabhushi, A.

(eds.) DLMIA/ML-CDS -2018. LNCS, vol. 11045, pp. 3–11. Springer, Cham (2018). https://doi.org/10.1007/978-3-030-00889-5_1

10. Guo, Y., et al.: Sau-net: a universal deep network for cell counting. In: Proceedings of the 10th ACM International Conference on Bioinformatics, Computational Biology and Health Informatics, pp. 299–306 (2019)

11. Zhou, P., et al.: Automatically detecting bregma and lambda points in rodent skull anatomy images. Plos One **15**(12) (2020)

12. Cai, S., et al.: Dense-UNet: a novel multiphoton in vivo cellular image segmentation model based on a convolutional neural network. Quant. Imaging Med. Surg. **10**(6), 1275–1285 (2020)

13. Tong, X., et al.: ASCU-Net: attention gate, spatial and channel attention u-net for skin lesion segmentation. Diagnostics **11**(3), 501 (2021)

14. Xie, X., et al.: A context hierarchical integrated network for medical image segmentation. Comput Electr. Eng. **101**, 108029 (2022)

15. Watson, C., Paxinos, G.: The Rat Brain in Stereotaxic Coordinates: Compact, 6th edn. Elsevier Science, San Diego (2007)

16. Redmon, J., Farhadi, A.: YOLOv3: an incremental improvement. arXiv preprint (2018)

17. Qin, X., et al.: Basnet: boundary aware salient object detection. In: Proceedings of the IEEE/CVF Conference on Computer Vision and Pattern Recognition, pp. 7479–7489 (2019)

18. Wang, L., et al., Learning to Detect Salient Objects with Image-Level Supervision. In: Proceedings of the IEEE Conference on Computer Vision and Pattern Recognition, p. 3796–3805 (2017)

19. Paszke, A., et al.: PyTorch: an imperative style, high-performance deep learning library. In: Advances in Neural Information Processing Systems 32, pp. 8024–8035. Curran Associates, Inc (2019)

20. Kingma, D.P., Ba, J.: Adam: a method for stochastic optimization. arXiv preprint (2014)

21. Margolin, R., Zelnik-Manor, L., Tal, A.: How to evaluate foreground maps. In: Proceedings of the IEEE Conference on Computer Vision and Pattern Recognition, pp. 248–255 (2014)

Prior Region Mask R-CNN for Thyroid Nodule Segmentation in Ultrasound Images

Chenzhuo Lu[1], Zhuang Fu[1(✉)], Zeyu Fu[1], and Jian Fei[2]

[1] Shanghai Jiao Tong University, Shanghai 200240, China
zhfu@sjtu.edu.cn

[2] Ruijin Hospital, Shanghai Jiao Tong University School of Medicine, Shanghai 200025, China

Abstract. The incidence of thyroid nodules has gradually increased in recent years, and its main detection method is ultrasonography. Segmentation of thyroid nodules in ultrasound images is important for the diagnosis of benign and malignant conditions. However, it is difficult and cumbersome to perform manual segmentation due to the speckle noise and low resolution of ultrasound images. Considering that the increasing number of cases now aggravates the work pressure of physicians, it is imminent to develop computer-aided thyroid nodule automatic segmentation algorithms. In this study, we find some misidentification and inaccurate segmentation problems when using Mask R-CNN for thyroid nodule segmentation. To solve these problems for better segmentation results, we propose Prior Region Mask R-CNN, which introduces the concept of the prior region. We incorporate the prediction of a prior region into the FPN and based on this performed spatial attention. In addition, a channel attention mechanism has been applied to screen for important features. Furthermore, RPN based on the prior region has also been proposed to reduce interference from surrounding tissues. In this paper, our data set has 1508 thyroid ultrasound images with nodule labels and thyroid labels, and 475 of them are used as a test set. According to our evaluation results, for the segmentation of thyroid nodules, we achieve a DSC of 87.32%, an IoU of 79.39%, and a precision of 90.39%, which is 3%, 3.41%, and 3.39% higher than Mask R-CNN respectively.

Keywords: Thyroid Nodules · Ultrasound Image · Image Segmentation · Deep Learning

1 Introduction

Thyroid cancer is a high-incidence disease worldwide in recent years [1] and it has been paid more and more attention. Medically, ultrasound is one of the most widely used methods at present in the diagnosis of thyroid nodules because of its safety, convenience, and low price. To standardize the evaluation criteria for malignant risk of thyroid nodules, the Thyroid Imaging Reporting and Data System (TI-RADS) [2] has been proposed and improved in recent years.

© The Author(s), under exclusive license to Springer Nature Singapore Pte Ltd. 2023
H. Yang et al. (Eds.): ICIRA 2023, LNAI 14269, pp. 105–116, 2023.
https://doi.org/10.1007/978-981-99-6489-5_9

However, in ultrasound images, thyroid nodules are varied in size, shape, cystic and solid, margins, and positions [3]. Therefore, it is difficult and cumbersome to identify and accurately segment them. What's more, the increasing number of cases leads to higher levels of stress for doctors. Manual drawing of nodules on ultrasound images will consume a lot of labor costs. Now, with the development and maturity of computer technology and image processing algorithms, computer-aided diagnosis is an important development trend in the medical field.

In order to realize the automation of thyroid nodule segmentation, researchers have done a lot of work on this issue. In the past few years, many models and methods have been proposed and applied [4]. For the conventional method, there are some segmentation algorithms based on active contour [5–7], such as the Level Set method. For the networks, the encoder-decoder structure model is the most used, mainly U-Net and optimized models based on U-Net [8–14]. Others, Webb et al. [15] and Han et al. [16] used DeepLabV3+ for the segmentation. Sun et al. [17] used FCN-AlexNet to segment images and adopted the transfer learning method to solve the problem of training data shortages. Ma et al. [18] proposed a Mul-DenseNet for automatically jointly segmenting lesions. Ma et al. [19] used a CNN-based method that formulates the thyroid nodule segmentation problem as a patch classification task. Kumar et al. [20] presented a multi-output CNN algorithm to segment thyroid nodules, cystic components inside the nodules, and normal thyroid glands from clinical ultrasound B-mode scans. Sun et al. [21] proposed TNSNet which has a shape-supervised path to enhance the identification and constraint of shape. Wu et al. [22] used ASPP fusion features to address the problem of difficult segmentation caused by complex tissue structures around the thyroid. Chen et al. [23] proposed a multi-branch two-stage model called MTN-Net to detect and segment thyroid nodules simultaneously. Although these methods have achieved reasonable results, there are still great challenges to improving the segmentation accuracy.

Considering the excellent performance of Mask R-CNN [24] in the field of image segmentation, in this paper, we try to apply it to the segmentation of thyroid nodules. Mask R-CNN was developed from RCNN [25] and matured after Fast RCNN [26] and Faster RCNN [27]. However, in the experiment, we find that the segmentation results of Mask R-CNN have some shortcomings. First, there are some cases of false recognition. In the ultrasound image, the tissue structure around the thyroid is complex and there are tissues similar to the nodules. The model sometimes identifies the surrounding thyroid tissue as nodules, especially arteria carotis communis. Second, there are some erroneous segmentations due to the indistinct boundary of thyroid nodules. This often occurs when the nodule is in contact with the surrounding tissue. It can be seen that Mask R-CNN lacks an understanding of anatomical structures in ultrasound images. Therefore, we modify it to make it more suitable for the thyroid nodule segmentation task.

In this study, we propose Prior Region Mask R-CNN (PR Mask R-CNN) to achieve better segmentation of thyroid nodules. To make up for the deficiency of Mask R-CNN, we have the idea of adding attention mechanisms to it. In the field of image processing, many attention models have been proposed and practiced [28–32], including spatial attention models and channel attention models. In our research, we creatively proposed the concept of a prior region as a spatial attention mechanism. And the structures of FPN and RPN are modified based on it. What's more, the channel attention model of the Convolutional Block Attention Module [28] is used to filter the features. Our model can achieve a DSC of 87.32%, an IOU of 79.39%, and a precision of 99% in the thyroid nodule segmentation task, which is 3%, 3.41%, and 3.39% higher than Mask R-CNN respectively.

2 Methods

2.1 Materials

In this study, we have 1508 thyroid ultrasound images with nodule labels and thyroid labels. All of them are marked with the help of professional physicians. And we crop all the images to remove irrelevant information around. These images vary in size and contrast, including transverse images and longitudinal images. Relevantly, the dataset contains nodules of various sizes, cystic and solid, benign and malignant, and various locations, basically covering all the characteristics of thyroid nodules. For training and testing, we divide it into a training set of 997 images, a validation set of 111 images, and a test set of 475 images.

2.2 Overall Architecture

In this section, the overall architecture of the proposed method is illustrated. We take ResNet101 as the backbone network, and then, via PR-FPN, generate the feature maps and prior region mask, as well as the spatial attention feature maps. In terms of generating ROIs, first, localized anchors are generated based on prior regions. Second, we use original feature maps and prior region masks as inputs of PR-RPN to acquire the bounding boxes offset and classification score. Therefore, compared with RPN, PR-RPN pays more attention to the understanding of the thyroid region and its surrounding environment, greatly reducing the interference and impact of irrelevant areas. Next, we will introduce the detailed structure of PR-FPN and PR-RPN.

2.3 PR- FPN

We all know that the FPN network consists of a bottom-up structure, a top-down architecture, and lateral connections. It combines low-resolution, semantically strong features with high-resolution, semantically weak features to get rich semantics at all levels [33]. Figure 2 explicates the structure of the PR-FPN. Considering that FPN is an encoder-decoder structure, we add convolution layers after the feature map P2 to predict the prior region. In our thyroid nodule segmentation task, the prior region is the thyroid gland. In order to reduce the amount of calculation, the size of the prior region mask in this structure is the same as that of feature map P2. When visualizing the segmentation result, we magnify it to the size of the original image to view it together with the nodule segmentation result.

To reinforce the network's ability to distinguish the targets from other objects, we use the channel attention module of CBAM to perform feature weighting on the feature maps [P2, P3, P4, P5] to obtain feature maps [P2', P3', P4', P5']. The channel attention module first generates two different spatial context descriptors using both average pooling and max-pooling operations. Then, both descriptors are forwarded to a shared network to produce the channel attention map. The shared network is composed of a multi-layer perceptron (MLP) with one hidden layer. After that, the output feature vectors are merged using element-wise summation [28]. Such a structure can enable the network to focus on important features for detecting the target object. In our task, this can make the network better distinguish thyroid nodules and surrounding easily confused tissues.

To enhance the attention of the network to the prior region, as well as reduce the interference of the surrounding confusing objects, we implemented a spatial attention mechanism on the feature maps [P2', P3', P4', P5'] to generate attention feature maps [Att_P2, Att_P3, Att_P4, Att_P5]. In detail, first, the prior region mask is resized to [PR2, PR3, PR4, PR5] using the bilinear interpolation method, corresponding to the shape of [P2', P3', P4', P5'] respectively. Then, based on [P2', P3', P4', P5'], we add their products with [PR2, PR3, PR4, PR5] to obtain the regional attention feature maps. In this way, the difference between the prior region and other regions can be enhanced, as well as the feature maps retain complete information. It is instrumental in solving the problem of poor segmentation effect caused by unclear boundaries when the nodule is connected with the surrounding tissue (Fig. 1).

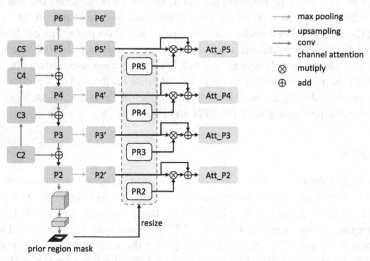

Fig. 1. The framework of PR-FPN. The prior region mask is calculated by three convolutions of P2. In our task, the size of P2 is (96, 96, 256), and we reduce the number of channels through convolution to 128, 64, and finally 1. So, the size of our prior region mask is (96, 96, 1). After channel attention and spatial attention, the 32 channels attention feature maps are generated.

2.4 PR-RPN

RPN takes an image as input and outputs a set of rectangular object proposals, each with a score for whether it is an object [27]. It generates anchors through sliding windows on the whole image. And then, it scores and warps them using shared fully-connected layers. However, for the segmentation of thyroid nodules, thyroid nodules must exist in the thyroid gland. Therefore, it is redundant to generate anchors and classify them on the whole feature map. Thus, in our PR-RPN, sliding windows generate anchors only on pixels of the prior region.

The structure of PR-RPN is shown in Fig. 3. First, we intercept the prior region feature on the feature map according to the prior region mask. Then, we reshape them to the shape of (1, N, depth). Finally, classes and bounding boxes are classified and regressed based on them. PR-RPN limits the generation range of bounding boxes, thereby, it reduces the introduction of irrelevant information, making the network focus on distinguishing between surrounding tissues and thyroid nodules.

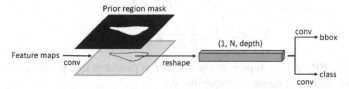

Fig. 2. The framework of PR-RPN. First, clipping feature maps based on [PR2, PR3, PR4, PR5]. Then, all of them are reshaped to (1, N, depth), from which the feature map with a normal shape can be obtained while maintaining the order of candidate frames.

2.5 Train

In the case of training, manually labeled thyroid nodule masks are used as the ground truth of the mask branches. The manually labeled thyroid masks are used as the ground truth of the prior region branch and taken as the input of PR-RPN. We generate anchors for training PR-RPN according to the ground truth of the prior region.

We use Dice Loss [34] as the loss function for the prior region branch of our model.

$$L_{pr} = 1 - \frac{2\sum_{i=1}^{N} p_i g_i}{\sum_{i=1}^{N} p_i + \sum_{i=1}^{N} g_i} \tag{1}$$

where L_{pr} represents the loss of the prior region branch, p represents the pixel value of the label, g represents the pixel value of the prediction, and N represents the total number of pixels.

Then we add it to the total loss of the network.

$$L = L_{pr} + L_{pr\_rpn} + L_{box} + L_{class} + L_{mask} \tag{2}$$

where L_{pr_rpn} represents the loss of the PR-RPN, L_{box} represents the loss of the bounding box prediction branch, L_{class} represents the loss of the class prediction branch, and L_{mask} represents the mask prediction branch.

2.6 Evaluation

For the evaluation of segmentation results of the prior region and thyroid nodules, we use some common evaluation indicators of biomedical image segmentation: dice similarity coefficient (DSC), intersection over union (IoU), precision, recall, and accuracy. They are defined as the following.

$$DSC = \frac{2TP}{FP + 2TP + FN} \tag{3}$$

$$IoU = \frac{TP}{FP + TP + FN} \tag{4}$$

$$Precision = \frac{TP}{TP + FP} \tag{5}$$

$$Recall = \frac{TP}{TP + FN} \tag{6}$$

$$Accuracy = \frac{TP + TN}{TP + FP + TN + FN} \tag{7}$$

where TP, TN, FP, and FN represent the number of pixels of true positive, true negative, false positive, and false negative respectively.

2.7 Experiments

We perform experiments based on Keras and Tensorflow frames using the GPU NVIDIA GeForce GTX 1060 6GB. Since the training is conducted on a small dataset, our model is fine-tuned from the pre-training results of Mask R-CNN on the COCO dataset [35]. After that, we evaluate the segmentation result of all epochs and chose the best one.

3 Results

3.1 Prior Region Results

For our PR Mask R-CNN, accurate prediction of the prior region is the basis for subsequent nodule detection and segmentation. Quantitatively, we evaluate the results of thyroid region segmentation and obtain a DSC of 83.60%, an IoU of 72.88%, a precision of 98.21%, a recall of 73.97%, and an accuracy of 94.40%. Such results can provide guarantees for subsequent nodule detection and segmentation.

3.2 Segmentation Results

To prove the progressiveness of our model, we compare our PR Mask R-CNN with Mask R-CNN and four commonly used networks in biomedical image segmentation: U-Net [36], Attention U-Net [29], U-Net + + [37], and FCN-8s [38]. All the models are trained and tested using the same dataset.

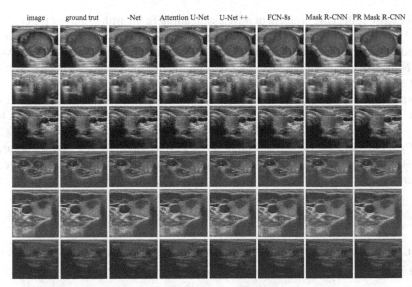

Fig. 3. Several examples of the thyroid nodule segmentation results. From left to right, the columns are the original ultrasound images, ground truth labels, U-Net segmentation results, Attention U-Net segmentation results, U-Net++ segmentation results, FCN-8s segmentation results, Mask R-CNN segmentation results, and PR Mask R-CNN segmentation results.

Figure 3 shows examples of the segmentation results of these models. Images in the first column are the original ultrasound image, the images in the second column are the ground truth of the nodule masks, and the following columns are the segmentation results of U-Net, Attention U-Net, U-Net++, FCN-8s, Mask R-CNN, and our PR Mask R-CNN respectively.

In the example in the first row, the nodule is complex in structure and large in size. For this nodule, the segmentation results of U-Net, Attention U-Net, U-Net++ and FCN-8s are incomplete, including multiple scattered areas. However, Mask R-CNN and PR Mask R-CNN can identify complete nodules, and the edges are also segmented perfectly. The second ultrasound image includes two nodules. One of them is located inside with a clear edge, and all the models segment it accurately. But the other nodule contacts with the common carotid artery, leading to an unclear edge. For this node, the segmentation result of U-Net is poor. Attention U-Net, U-Net++, and FCN-8s recognize the nodule area, but the edge segmentation results are not satisfactory. Mask R-CNN mistakenly divides part of the common carotid artery into the nodule, which represents that it lacks an understanding of thyroid structure. Compared with Mask R-CNN, our model can solve the segmentation error problem caused by the proximity of the nodule edge to the surrounding tissues. The third example is similar to the second one. Mask R-CNN mistakenly divides the common carotid artery into nodules, but our model does not. It shows that our model can better segment the nodule edge. The fourth example reflects the classification ability of our model. Because the shape and structure of the musculus longus colli in the figure are similar to that of nodules, Mask R-CNN wrongly identifies the musculus longus colli as a nodule. But other models do not. The fifth and sixth examples also reflect the problem of misclassification. In the fifth example, the common carotid artery is similar to a nodule, which is recognized as a nodule by Attention U-Net and Mask R-CNN. The sixth example is a longitudinal image of the thyroid, Mask R-CNN incorrectly identifies the tissues outside the thyroid gland as a nodule. But our model avoids such problems.

Quantitatively, we select the optimal results for each model and calculate the evaluation indicators. The evaluation results are listed in Table 1. Our model performs best among all models, followed by Mask R-CNN and U-Net++. We achieve a DSC of 83.60%, an IoU of 72.88%, a precision of 98.21%, a recall of 73.97%, and an accuracy of 94.40%. Compared with Mask R-CNN, the DSC, IoU, precision, accuracy, and recall are increased by 3%, 3.41%, 3.39%, 0.22%, and 1.17% respectively.

Table 1. Thyroid nodule segment evaluation results.

Models	DSC(%)	IoU(%)	Precision(%)	Accuracy(%)	Recall(%)
U-Net	81.11	71.83	84.97	98.60	82.61
Attention U-Net	81.62	72.30	85.03	98.60	82.79
U-Net++	82.84	73.61	87.55	98.69	82.88
FCN-8s	79.87	69.84	84.56	98.41	80.79
Mask R-CNN	84.32	75.98	87.00	98.81	85.78
PR Mask R-CNN	87.32	79.39	90.39	99.03	86.95

3.3 Ablation Studies

To prove the effectiveness of PR-RPN, we compare the ROIs outputted by PR-RPN and RPN. Some examples are shown in Fig. 4. Images in the first column are the original ultrasound images, and the second column shows the ground truth of the nodule boundary boxes. In the third and fourth columns, the dotted boxes with different colors show the ROIs given by RPN and PR-RPN. There are 5 boxes in each image. It is obvious that RPN often mistakenly identifies some surrounding tissues as thyroid nodules during inference. Although some wrong bounding boxes will be screened out in the subsequent classification stage, many will still be finally identified as nodules. However, in the PR-RPN stage, our model avoids many confusing regions, thus reducing the final false identification probability.

In addition, to better understand and analyze our model, we study the effects of PR-FPN and PR-RPN through experiments respectively. Both models have trained 200 epochs, and the training parameters are consistent with Mask R-CNN and PR Mask R-CNN mentioned above. The evaluation results are shown in Table 2. Compared with the results in Table 1, it can be seen that whether PR-FPN or PR-RPN is used, the segmentation effect can be significantly improved, and the effect is best when they are used at the same time. Therefore, it is proved that the PR-FPN and PR-RPN proposed in this paper are effective.

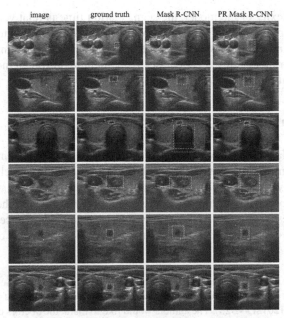

Fig. 4. Several examples of the ROIs outputted by PR-RPN and RPN. The dotted boxes with different colors show the ROIs given by RPN and PR-RPN.

Table 2. Effect of PR-FPN and PR-RPN

Models	DSC(%)	IoU(%)	Precision(%)	Accuracy(%)	Recall(%)
PR-FPN	86.98	78.98	88.82	99.00	88.07
PR-RPN	86.75	78.59	89.38	98.98	86.99

4 Discussion

After a series of experiments, we achieve some satisfactory results which are shown in the results section. Compared with Mask R-CNN, our model greatly reduces the possibility of mistaking surrounding tissues for nodules, the evaluation indicators have been significantly improved. And our model also has obvious advantages compared with other deep learning models. In the ablation studies, we compare the bounding boxes generated by PR-RPN and RPN respectively to confirm the advantages of PR-RPN. In addition, we explore the effects of PR-FPN and PR-RPN on the model respectively. All in all, our model has an excellent performance in this thyroid nodule segmentation task, and it can also be applied to other medical image processing tasks in the future.

Although our model performs well on our dataset, there are still some limitations. First of all, our model training requires a lot of data, but the data set is cumbersome to make. When labeling the data set, it needs to mark the position of the thyroid gland in addition to the thyroid nodule, which requires a lot of manpower and time. Secondly, due to the high complexity of the model, the segmentation time is relatively long. Finally, because the prior region size of each image is usually different, the batch size can only be taken as 1 during training, which makes the training time-consuming. In future, we will try to train our model on a larger dataset to obtain more universal model parameters and better segmentation results.

5   Conclusion

We propose PR Mask R-CNN to solve the problem of Mask R-CNN's misidentification and inaccurate segmentation in thyroid nodule segmentation. Our model has predictions of a prior region which is used for the spatial attention of feature maps. In addition, we generate anchors in the prior region and also make predictions of the candidate box based on it. The test results show that our model reduces the disturbance of surrounding tissues, and achieves better segmentation results than Mask R-CNN and other commonly used algorithms.

Acknowledgment. This work was greatly supported by the National Natural Science Foundation of China (Grant No. 61973210) and the Medical-engineering Cross Projects of SJTU (Grant No. YG2019ZDA17, ZH2018QNB23). The authors would like to thank the doctors of Ruijin Hospital afffliated to Shanghai Jiao Tong University for their helps, and all the authors of opensource codes and database used in this study.

References

1. Haymart, M.R., Banerjee, M., Reyes-Gastelum, D., Caoili, E., Norton, E.C.: Thyroid ultrasound and the increase in diagnosis of low-risk thyroid cancer. J. Clin. Endocrinol. Metab. **104**(3), 785–792 (2019)
2. Tessler, F.N., Middleton, W.D., Grant, E.G., Hoang, J.K., Berland, L.L., Teefey, S.A., et al.: ACR Thyroid Imaging, Reporting and Data System (TI-RADS): white paper of the ACR TI-RADS committee. J. Am. College Radiol. **14**(5), 587–595 (2017). https://doi.org/10.1016/j.jacr.2017.01.046
3. Dighe, M., Barr, R., Bojunga, J., Cantisani, V., Chammas, M.C., Cosgrove, D., et al.: Thyroid ultrasound: state of the art. Part 2 - focal thyroid lesions. Med. Ultrason. **19**(2), 195–210 (2017)
4. Chen, J., You, H., Li, K.: A review of thyroid gland segmentation and thyroid nodule segmentation methods for medical ultrasound images. Comput. Methods Programs Biomed. **185**, 105329 (2020)
5. Nugroho, H.A., Zulfanahri, E.L., Frannita, I.A., Choridah, L.: Computer aided diagnosis for thyroid cancer system based on internal and external characteristics. J. King Saud Univ. Comput. Inform. Sci. **33**(3), 329–339 (2021). https://doi.org/10.1016/j.jksuci.2019.01.007
6. Koundal, D., Sharma, B., Guo, Y.: Intuitionistic based segmentation of thyroid nodules in ultrasound images. Comput. Biol. Med. **121**, 103776 (2020)
7. Wang, Y., Mao, L., Yu, M.-A., Wei, Y., Hao, C., Dong, D.: Automatic recognition of parathyroid nodules in ultrasound images based on fused prior pathological knowledge features. IEEE Access **9**, 69626–69634 (2021)

8. Nugroho, H.A., Frannita, E.L., Nurfauzi, R.: An Automated Detection and Segmentation of Thyroid Nodules using Res-UNet. In: IOP Conference Series: Materials Science and Engineering, pp. 181–185 (2021)
9. Zhou, M., Wang, R., Fu, P., Bai, Y., Cui, L.: Automatic malignant thyroid nodule recognition in ultrasound images based on deep learning. In: E3S Web Conference (ICEEB), vol. 185, no. 03021 (2020)
10. Yang, Q., Geng, C., Chen, R., Pang, C., Han, R., Lyu, L., et al.: DMU-Net: dual-route mirroring U-Net with mutual learning for malignant thyroid nodule segmentation. Biomed. Signal Process. Control **77**, 103805 (2022)
11. Liao, X., Lin, K., Chen, D., Zhang, H., Li, Y., Jiang, B.: Image segmentation of thyroid nodule and capsule for diagnosing central compartment lymph node metastasis. In: Proceedings of the Annual International Conference of the IEEE Engineering in Medicine and Biology Society. EMBS, pp. 2765–2768 (2021)
12. Chen, C., Xu, B., Wu, Y., Wu, K., Tan, C.: Research on ultrasonic image segmentation of thyroid nodules based on improved U-net++. In: ACM International Conference Proceeding Series, pp. 532–536 (2022)
13. Ajilisa, O.A., Jagathy Raj, V.P., Sabu, M.K.: Segmentation of thyroid nodules from ultrasound images using convolutional neural network architectures. J. Intelligent Fuzzy Syst. **43**(1), 687–705 (2022)
14. Shahroudnejad, A., Vega, R., Forouzandeh, A., Balachandran, S., Jaremko, J., Noga, M., et al.: Thyroid nodule segmentation and classification using deep convolutional neural network and rule-based classifiers. In: Proceedings of the Annual International Conference of the IEEE Engineering in Medicine and Biology Society EMBS, pp. 3118–3121 (2021)
15. Webb, J.M., Meixner, D.D., Adusei, S.A., Polley, E.C., Fatemi, M., Alizad, A.: Automatic deep learning semantic segmentation of ultrasound thyroid cineclips using recurrent fully convolutional networks. IEEE Access **9**, 5119–5127 (2020)
16. Han, X., Chang, L., Song, K., Cheng, L., Li, M., Wei, X.: Multitask network for thyroid nodule diagnosis based on TI-RADS. Med. Phys. **49**(8), 5064–5080 (2022)
17. Sun, J., Sun, T., Yuan, Y., Zhang, X., Shi, Y., Lin, Y.: Automatic diagnosis of thyroid ultrasound image based on FCN-AlexNet and transfer learning. In: International Conference Digital Signal Processing DSP, pp. 1–5 (2018)
18. Ma, J., Bao, L., Lou, Q., Kong, D.: Transfer learning for automatic joint segmentation of thyroid and breast lesions from ultrasound images. Int. J. CARS **17**(2), 363–372 (2022)
19. Ma, J., Wu, F., Jiang, T., Zhao, Q., Kong, D.: Ultrasound image-based thyroid nodule automatic segmentation using convolutional neural networks. Int. J. CARS **12**(11), 1895–1910 (2017)
20. Kumar, V., Webb, J., Gregory, A., Meixner, D.D., Knudsen, J.M., Callstrom, M., et al.: Automated segmentation of thyroid nodule, gland, and cystic components from ultrasound images using deep learning. IEEE Access **8**, 63482–63496 (2020)
21. Sun, J., Li, C., Lu, Z., He, M., Zhao, T., Li, X., et al.: TNSNet: thyroid nodule segmentation in ultrasound imaging using soft shape supervision. Comput. Methods Programs Biomed. **215**, 106600 (2022)
22. Wu, Y., Shen, X., Bu, F., Tian, J.: Ultrasound image segmentation method for thyroid nodules using ASPP fusion features. IEEE Access **8**, 172457–172466 (2020)
23. Chen, L., Zheng, W., Hu, W.: MTN-Net: a multi-task network for detection and segmentation of thyroid nodules in ultrasound images. Lect. Notes Comput. Sci. **13370**, 219–232 (2022)
24. He, K., Gkioxari, G., Dollar, P., Girshick, R.: Mask R-CNN. In: Proceedings of IEEE International Conference on Computer Vision, pp. 2980–2988 (2017)
25. Girshick, R., Donahue, J., Darrell, T., Malik, J.: Rich feature hierarchies for accurate object detection and semantic segmentation. In: Proceedings of the IEEE Conference on Computer Vision and Pattern Recognition, pp.580–587 (2014)

26. Girshick, R.: Fast R-CNN. In: Proceedings of the IEEE Conference on Computer Vision, pp. 1440–1448 (2015)
27. Ren, S., He, K., Girshick, R., Sun, J.: Faster R-CNN: towards real-time object detection with region proposal networks. IEEE Trans. Pattern Anal. Mach. Intell. **39**(6), 1137–1149 (2017)
28. Woo, S., Park, J., Lee, J.-Y., Kweon, I.S.: CBAM: convolutional block attention module. Lect. Notes Comput. Sci. **11211**, 3–19 (2018)
29. Schlemper, J., Oktay, O., Schaap, M., Heinrich, M., Kainz, B., Glocker, B., et al.: Attention gated networks: learning to leverage salient regions in medical images. Med. Image Anal. **53**, 197–207 (2019)
30. Fu, J., Liu, J., Tian, H., Li, Y., Bao, Y., Fang, Z., et al.: Dual attention network for scene segmentation. In: Proceedings of the IEEE Conference on Computer Vision and Pattern Recognition, pp. 3141–3149 (2019)
31. Wang, X., Girshick, R., Gupta, A., He, K.: Non-local neural networks. In: Proceedings of the IEEE Conference on Computer Vision and Pattern Recognition, pp. 7794–7803 (2018)
32. Hu, J., Shen, L., Albanie, S., Sun, G., Wu, E.: Squeeze-and-excitation networks. IEEE Trans. Pattern Anal. Mach. Intell. **42**(8), 2011–2023 (2020)
33. Lin, T. -Y., Dollár, P., Girshick, R., He, H., Hariharan, B., Belongie, S.: Feature pyramid networks for object detection. In: Proceedings of the IEEE Conference on Computer Vision and Pattern Recognition, pp. 936–944 (2017)
34. Milletari, F., Navab, N., Ahmadi, S.-A.: V-Net: fully convolutional neural networks for volumetric medical image segmentation. In: Proceedings of the International Conference on 3D Vision. (3DV), pp. 565–571 (2016)
35. Lin, T.-Y., Maire, M., Belongie, S., Hays, J., Perona, P., Ramanan, D., et al.: Microsoft COCO: common objects in context. Lect. Notes Comput. Sci. **8693**, 740–755 (2014)
36. Ronneberger, O., Fischer, P., Brox, T.: U-net: Convolutional networks for biomedical image segmentation. Lect. Notes Comput. Sci. **9351**, 234–241 (2015)
37. Zhou, Z., Rahman Siddiquee, M.M., Tajbakhsh, N., Liang, J.: Unet++: a nested u-net architecture for medical image segmentation. In: Lecture Notes in Computer Science, vol. 11045, pp. 3–11 (2018)
38. Shelhamer, E., Long, J., Darrell, T.: Fully convolutional networks for semantic segmentation. IEEE Trans. Pattern Anal. Mach. Intell. **39**(4), 640–651 (2017)

Digital Twin Model Based Robot-Assisted Needle Insertion Navigation System with Visual and Force Feedback

Shilun Du[1], Zhen Wang[1], Murong Li[2], Yingda Hu[1], Mengruo Shen[1], Tian Xu[1], and Yong Lei[1(✉)]

[1] State Key Laboratory of Fliud Power and Mechatronics Systems, Zhejiang University, Hangzhou, Zhejiang, China
{shilundu,wangzhen97,yingda_hu,Shenmr,tianxu,ylei}@zju.edu.cn
[2] Zhejiang Lab, Hangzhou, Zhejiang, China
limurong@zhejianglab.com

Abstract. In needle insertion navigation, most researches focus on intraoperative images based navigation system that provides only visual feedback. Besides, few navigation systems are integrated with insertion robot. In this paper, we proposed a digital twin model based robot-assisted needle insertion navigation system with visual and force feedback. Our system can predict needle deflection, tissue deformation for visual feedback and interaction force for force feedback while insertion robot can help steering needle for accurate insertion. The proposed needle insertion navigation system integrates digital twin model and insertion-assisted robot. A digital twin model of target organ, which includes finite element model and visual model, can be generated based on preoperative CT image to predict needle deflection, tissue deformation and interaction force of planned needle path. Optic-based calibration method for our system is developed. A hybrid spring mapping method based on radial-basis function interpolation and spring-mass model is proposed as well for better visual feedback. The proposed navigation system can provide both visual feedback and force feedback in digital twin model for surgeons while robot can help steering needle to target position. Simulations and experiments are carried out for our navigation system and hybrid spring mapping method. Results show the calibrated system is accurate with 4mm targeting accuracy, which meets clinical accuracy requirements. Hybrid spring mapping method can update the visual model smoothly. Both force and visual feedback can be registered to the digital twin coordinate system, allowing for accurate and consistent feedback for navigation.

Keywords: Needle insertion navigation system · Needle-tissue interaction model · Digital twin model · Robot-assisted insertion

1 Introduction

Needle insertion is one of the most popular minimally invasive surgery with wide applications in the fields of tissue biopsy, local anesthesia, tumor ablation [1–

© The Author(s), under exclusive license to Springer Nature Singapore Pte Ltd. 2023
H. Yang et al. (Eds.): ICIRA 2023, LNAI 14269, pp. 117–131, 2023.
https://doi.org/10.1007/978-981-99-6489-5_10

4]. To accurately perform the needle insertion, navigation system and insertion robot are required, in which needle tip navigation and positioning are the key point.

For image guided navigation system, the imaging modalities currently available for navigation are X-ray, computed tomography (CT), magnetic resonance imaging (MRI), B-mode ultrasound, etc [5]. Glozman et al. [6] combined X-ray with 6-DOF parallel robot for needle insertion and proposed dual binomial correction algorithm to compensate system mechanical error and X-ray imaging error and improve insertion accuracy. Fichtinger et al. [7] developed CT image overlay system for the guidance of flexible needle. CT image can float in the patient's body with registered position to help surgeons improving insertion accuracy. Krieger et al [8,9] carried out prostate intervention surgery with MRI-guided navigation system. Tadayyon et al. [10] used multi-frame MRI images for 3D registration to compensate for the organ movement and needle deflection. Moreira et al. [11] combined MRI with fiber grating sensors. MRI can locate the target and obstacles preoperatively and the optical fiber sensor can calculates the position of the needle tip to form a closed-loop control of needle insertion. B-mode ultrasound is also feasible, with better economy and lower radioactivity. Various researches applied B-mode ultrasound for navigation [12–14]. However, all of them encounter challenges related to noise issues such as echo, air pockets, and speckles that occur during the imaging process.

Surgeons can complete needle insertion through assisted robot, which can effectively reduce the amount of radiation to which the physician is exposed and improve needle steering accuracy [15]. Glozman et al. [6] applied traditional PID algorithm to control insertion robot while compound force would disturb tissue. Duchemin et al. [16] uses hybrid position/force PI control and improve robot insertion performance. Reed et al. [17] proposed a rotation feedback compensation control strategy to maintain the target needle angle. Some researches also investigate the needle insertion control algorithm [18,19] and improve the insertion accuracy.

From the above research, most of the researches of navigation system focus on improving visualization with intraoperative image. Few researches pay attention to model based navigation to provide force and visual feedback [20] simultaneously. For image based needle insertion navigation system, either frequent image updates are required during the operation or only preoperative images without deformation can be visualized, which can lead to significant errors in surgeries involving highly deformable organs, and lack of force feedback is also a shortcoming of existing navigation systems. As for insertion robots, most studies have discussed flexible needle control algorithms, but have not addressed the integration to the navigation system. In conclusion. The current needle insertion navigation systems are mainly based on intraoperative image guidance, and few insertion robots are integrated with navigation systems.

In this work, we proposed a digital twin model-based robot-assist needle insertion navigation system. Our proposed navigation system can generate a digital twin model of the target organ, from which surgeon can obtain visual and force feedback of the organ along a specified virtual path while the insertion-assisted robot can steer the needle to the target position. Our contribution are three folds. First, we integrate needle-tissue interaction model with CT image to build navigation system, which can generate a digital twin model with visual and force feedback simultaneously for navigation. Second, we proposed a novel mapping method between surface mesh with partial FEM mesh for better visual feedback. Thirdly, we combine the navigation system with insertion robot, which can help surgeon to perform insertions accurately.

The paper is organized as follows. Section 2 presents the navigation system framework, registration method and proposed novel mapping method. Section 3 shows results of the mapping simulation and ex-vivo organ experiment of the navigation system, while Sect. 4 concludes the paper.

2   Material and Methods

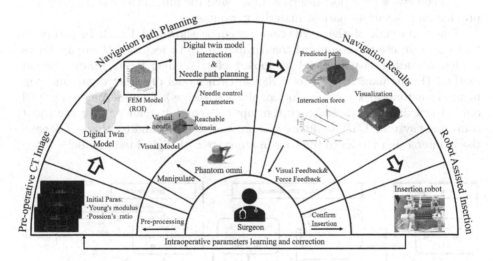

Fig. 1. Diagram of model-based needle insertion navigation system (Color figure online)

As shown in Fig. 1, we propose a novel needle insertion navigation system. The framework can be divided into four stages. Firstly, surgeons can obtain preoperative organ images through CT or other medical imaging modalities. Material parameters of the patient's tissue, such as Young's modulus and Poisson's ratio, are also given by the surgeon as input. Based on Mimics (a widely used medical image processing software), a 3D surface mesh for visualization and a tetrahedral mesh model for Finite Element Method (FEM) simulation can be obtained. Only the region of interests (ROI) will be reconstructed to tetrahedral mesh for improving calculation efficiency. Secondly, by combining the visual model with the FEM model, a digital twin model can be generated. The surgeon can manipulate a virtual needle using the Omni Phantom to visualize the virtual needle trajectory (reachable domains for flexible needles and needle trajectories for rigid needles) for planning in digital twin model. For flexible needle, the needle reachable domain (the red conical area in Fig. 1), which represents the area that the current virtual needle may reach, is calculated based on kinematics model. The third stage starts once a path is determined, the digital twin model will generate visual feedback through interface and force feedback through Phantom Omni. The force and deformation results are predicted by needle-tissue interaction model [21] and the mapping from the deformation of the FEM model to the deformation of the visual model is achieved through the hybrid spring mapping method. If the surgeon needs to select an alternative path, they can re-enter the second step. If the surgeon agrees to proceed with the chosen path, the 4th step starts. The robot will then manipulate the needle to the designated position for surgeon to perform the final insertion. After an insertion is completed, the system can perform tissue parameters learning and correction based on the difference between the post-insertion image and the model calculation results to provide more accurate patient material parameters.

The framework of the navigation system is shown in Fig. 2. In preoperative stage, we use the computed tomography (CT) to reconstruct pre-operative model, including visual model composed of triangular facets, finite element method (FEM) model to generate digital twin model of target organ and segmented anatomical structures (optional for surgeons). Calibration, using NDI optical tracking system and a custom optical template, can register the robot coordinate system, CT coordinate system, and the coordinate system of needle-tissue interaction model to the coordinate system of digital twin model.

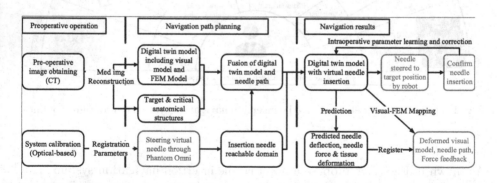

Fig. 2. Framework of model-based needle insertion navigation system. Blue block represents surgeon manipulate step. Red blocks represent navigation system output. (Color figure online)

In navigation path planning stage, surgeons can manipulate the proposed navigation system. With the assistance of fusion between the digital twin model and virtual needle, the surgeon can more effectively identify an optimal insertion path. In navigation results stage, digital twin model-based navigation starts once the path is selected. Needle tissue interaction model can predict needle deflection, tissue deformation and interaction force of selected path. Surgeons are provided with predicted force feedback and visual feedback of planned needle path in digital twin model. The needle insertion robot steers the posture of the insertion needle accordingly and insertion final confirmation should be completed by surgeon. After an insertion is completed, the system can perform intraoperative parameters learning and correction to provide more accurate patient material parameters for digital twin model.

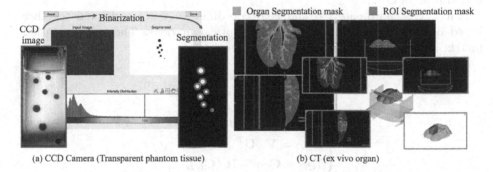

(a) CCD Camera (Transparent phantom tissue)   (b) CT (ex vivo organ)

Fig. 3. Preoperative imaging processing of CCD camera/CT

2.1   System Preoperative Processing and Calibration Method

Preoperative imaging evaluation can help surgeons confirm the insertion plan, and our navigation system similarly requires preoperative image to obtain the patient's anatomical structure for modeling and navigation. Preoperative optical calibration can align the coordinate systems of the needle insertion robot, CT images, Phantom Omni, and needle-tissue interaction model through an optical template.

Our navigation system is compatible with both CCD camera images and CT images. CCD camera images are suitable for laboratory environments and can be used in conjunction with transparent phantom tissue to validate the needle path planning algorithm. CT images are suitable for surgical scenarios, and without increasing the workload of the surgeons, we use the widely-applied preoperative processing method to generate both visual and force feedback based on model-based navigation system.

For image preprocessing of CCD camera shown in Fig. 3(a), transparent phantom tissues are used to mimic biomedical organs with anatomical structure. We perform binarization on the image first. For marker segmentation, which can be divided into obstacle markers and target markers, we conduct threshold segmentation and connectivity analysis to avoid capturing incorrect markers caused by image noise. For CT image preprocessing shown in Fig. 3(b), the threshold segmentation is applied to segment organ and ROI. Corresponding ROI tetrahedron mesh can be generated as well for FEM modeling. CCD camera-based reconstruction accuracy has been discussed in our previous research [22]. In this paper, CT images are used in following parts.

System calibration method is shown in Fig. 4. The calibration of the system ensures that the navigation system, surgeon's manipulation, and robot are all within the coordinate system of digital twin model. Results related to the robot and force feedback will be mapped back to their respective coordinate systems. In this study, the coordinate system of digital twin model C_D is the same as the visual model coordinate system C_V. In following text, we only state the registration of C_D.

First, CT coordinate C_C and NDI coordinate C_O are registered together based on a optical template with three optical markers. The transformation matrix is obtained by

$$
\begin{cases}
\mathbf{H} = \sum_{i=1}^{3}(p_{i_{NDIcen}} \cdot p_{i_{CTcen}}^{T}) \\
\mathbf{U}, \mathbf{S}, \mathbf{V}^{T} = SVD(\mathbf{H}) \\
\mathbf{R}_{CO} = \mathbf{V} \cdot \mathbf{U}^{T} \\
T_{CO} = \mathbf{C}_{CT} - \mathbf{R} \cdot \mathbf{C}_{NDI}
\end{cases}
\tag{1}
$$

where $p_{i_{NDIcen}} = p_{i_{NDI}} - C_{NDI}, p_{i_{CTcen}} = p_{i_{CT}} - C_{CT}$. $C_{NDI/CT}$ is the average coordinate of three markers in C_O/C_C. In CT, XY plane is parallel to the CT image plane. XY coordinates can be obtained through CT slice directly. Z-axis coordinate (D_t in Fig. 4) can be obtained by the interval between the number of markers in CT images and the distance interval between each layer of CT images. SVD represents SVD decomposition. $\mathbf{R}_{CO}, T_{CO}$ is 3×3 rotation matrix and 3×1 transformation vector respectively. Assemble $\mathbf{R}_{CO}\&T_{CO}$, the transformation matrix between $C_C\&C_O$ is

$$
\mathbf{T}_{CO} = \begin{bmatrix} & T_{CO1} \\ \mathbf{R}_{CO} & T_{CO2} \\ & T_{CO3} \\ 0\ 0\ 0 & 1 \end{bmatrix}
\tag{2}
$$

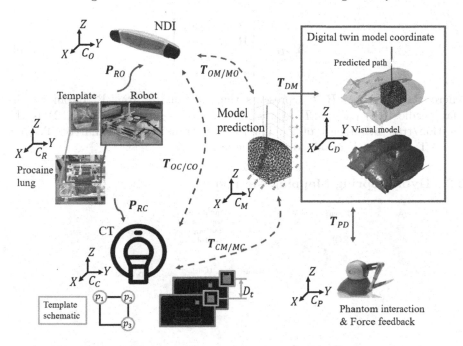

Fig. 4. System pre-calibration. The red box is the visual coordinate system, which is the main coordinate system of the system, and most of the system navigation results are displayed under this coordinate system (Color figure online)

After preprocessing the CT images, the digital twin model including the visual model and FEM model can be displayed for surgeons. The separated tetrahedral mesh will be transformed into the coordinate system of the needle-tissue interaction model C_M, and the transformation matrix between C_C and C_M is

$$\mathbf{T}_{CM} = \begin{bmatrix} & & T_{CM1} \\ \mathbf{R}_{CM} & T_{CM2} \\ & & T_{CM3} \\ 0\,0\,0 & 1 \end{bmatrix} \tag{3}$$

where $\mathbf{R}_{CM}$ causes the mesh to rotate, with its upper surface facing the positive Z-axis in C_M. $T_{CM1}, T_{CM2}, T_{CM3}$ translate the mesh to the origin of C_M.

Surgeon controls the virtual needle through Phantom Omni to input the expected needle posture. To register the Phantom Omni coordinate system C_P and digital twin model coordinate system C_D, the virtual needle is placed vertically downward first in the center of the ROI to output pose $\mathbf{P}_1$ in C_P, then place Phantom Omni haptic device in the same posture to output pose matrix $\mathbf{P}_2$ in C_D. Then, the transform matrix is

$$\mathbf{T}_{PD} = \begin{bmatrix} & & T_{PD1} \\ \mathbf{R}_{PD} & T_{PD2} \\ & & T_{PD3} \\ 0\ 0\ 0 & & 1 \end{bmatrix} \tag{4}$$

where $\mathbf{R}_{PD} = \mathbf{R}_2 \cdot \mathbf{R}_1^{-1}$ represents the rotation of from Phantom to virtual needle. $[T_{PD1}, T_{PD2}, T_{PD3}] = T_1 - \mathbf{R}_{PD} \cdot T_2$. $\mathbf{R}_i/\mathbf{T}_i(i = 1, 2)$ is the rotation/translation part of $\mathbf{P}_i$. For the rest transformation matrix, $\mathbf{T}_{OM} = \mathbf{T}_{OC} \cdot \mathbf{T}_{CM}, \mathbf{T}_{DM}$ is obtained from Mimics.

2.2 Hybrid Spring Mapping Method

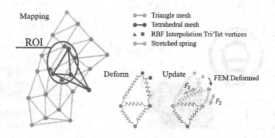

Fig. 5. Hybrid spring mapping update

Hybrid spring mapping (HSM) method can establish a correspondence between non-one-to-one vertex triangular mesh and tetrahedral mesh, thereby enabling the triangular mesh to deform along with the tetrahedral mesh. As shown in Fig. 5, HSM can be divided into two steps. In the first step, for the areas corresponding to the triangular mesh and tetrahedral mesh (usually ROI), we use RBF interpolation to assign the deformation from the sparse tetrahedral mesh vertices to the dense triangular mesh vertices (mapped vertices). As shown in Fig. 5, FEM mesh deforms first and in the triangular mesh modeled with a spring-mass model, the length of the spring changes due to the movement of the vertices, resulting in a spring force F_S. This force causes the unmapped vertices to move along, thereby deforming the entire triangular mesh.

Algorithm 1 Hybrid spring mapping method

Input: FEM Mesh M_{tet}, Visual triangle mesh M_{tri}, ROI
Output: deformed FEM mesh M'_{tet}, deformed visual mesh M'_{tri}
1: **function** HSM(M_{tet}, M_{tri})
2:     $\{V_{tetmap} \in \mathbf{P}_{FEM} | V_{tetmap} in ROI\}$
3:     $\{V_{trimap} \in \mathbf{P}_{SPR} | V_{trimap} in ROI\}$
4:     $M'_{tet} = FEMModel(M_{tet})$
5:     $\mathbf{P}'_{SPR} = RBFInter(\mathbf{P}_{FEM}, \mathbf{P}_{SPR})$
6:     $\{V'_{trimap} \in \mathbf{P}'_{SPR} | V'_{trimap} in ROI\}$
7:     $M'_{tri} = SpringMassModel(M_{tri}, V'_{trimap})$ **return** M'_{tri}, M'_{tet}
8: **end function**

---

a. V is a vertex in tetrahedron mesh/ triangle mesh.

b. $\mathbf{P}_{FEM}$&$\mathbf{P}_{SPR}$ are point sets of tetrahedron mesh and triangular mesh vertices belonging to ROI, and $\mathbf{P}_{SPR}$ will obtain the deformation of $\mathbf{P}_{FEM}$ through RBF interpolation.

c. In *SpringMassModel()*, only unmapped vertices ($V_{tri} \notin \mathbf{P}_{SPR}$) will be updated in Step.7.

Algorithm 1 shows the detail of HSM. Given a triangle mesh M_{tet} and a tetrahedral mesh M_{tri} and *ROI*. Firstly, RBF interpolation [23] is performed between $\mathbf{P}_{FEM}$&$\mathbf{P}_{SPR}$. V_{trimap} can follow the deformation of V_{tetmap}. Once all vertices in M_{tri} is in *ROI*, the spring mass model update (Step 6 & 7) can be skipped.

For FEM model [21], the needle tissue interaction model can predict M'_{tet} by inputting M_{tet} with essential boundary conditions. Then, the displacement of the mapped vertices V'_{trimap} will be assigned to be consistent with the corresponding finite element nodes V'_{tetmap}. The rest vertices are updated through mapped vertices and spring-mass model. Every vertex is updated through

$$\begin{cases} V'i_{tri} = Vi_{tri} + v_i \cdot \mathrm{dt} \\ Fi_v = \sum_{m=1}^{3} \Delta d_s \cdot K_s \cdot \mathbf{n}_{mi} + B_s \cdot v_{mi} \\ ai_v = Fi_v/m \\ v_i(t) = v_i(t-1) + ai_v \cdot \mathrm{dt} \end{cases} \tag{5}$$

where $V'i_{tri}$&Vi_{tri} are the vertices positions after and before time t respectively. Fi_v is the resultant force acting on the vertex, composed of the spring forces and damping forces of three adjacent springs. Δd_s is the length change of the spring. K_s is the spring stiffness coefficient, B_S is the damping coefficient, $\mathbf{n}_{mi}$ is the spring direction, and v_{mi} is the velocity difference between adjacent vertices. ai_v is the acceleration at t while velocity at time t can be obtained as $v_i(t)$.

2.3   Simulation and Experiment Setup

In order to validate the effectiveness of the aforementioned method and system, we first conducted simulations of a hemisphere and a cuboid to verify the effectiveness of HSM under full and partial mapping. Subsequently, we performed an ex vivo porcine lung insertion experiment guided by CT to validate the effectiveness and accuracy of the entire navigation system, including reachable domain generation, model prediction and visual & force feedback. The effectiveness of HSM in actual surgical scenarios is also validated.

In the HSM simulation, we first set up a simulation of a hemisphere-shaped deformable body under complete mapping. The shape of the visual model (triangular mesh) is consistent with that of the FEM model (tetrahedral mesh), with the visual model being more dense, i.e., the ROI covers the entire body. Secondly, we utilize a simulation of the deformable cuboid that partially maps the FEM model (tetrahedral mesh) to the visual model (triangular mesh), in which the ROI is part of the body. In both simulations, tensile/compressional forces are applied to the top of the deformable body. We evaluate the deformation effect of the visual model before and after mapping, and quantitatively analyze the smoothness of the visual model before and after deformation. Smoothness S_V is

$$
\begin{cases}
\mathbf{N}_i = normalize((V_{i2} - V_{i1}) \times (V_{i3} - V_{i1})) \\
\mathbf{N}_j = normalize(\sum(\mathbf{N}_i)) \\
\alpha_{ij} = \arccos(dot(\mathbf{N}_j, \mathbf{N}_i)) \\
\alpha_i = (\alpha_{i1} + \alpha_{i2} + \alpha_{i3})/3 \\
S_V = mean(\alpha_i)
\end{cases}
\tag{6}
$$

where $(\cdot)_i$ represents the vertices/normal vector of triangular face i. $\mathbf{N_j}$ is the vertex j. α_{ij} represents the angle between the normal vector of vertex j and the normal vector of the adjacent faces. α_i is the mean vertex angle for face i. S_V is the mean value of α_i for all faces to evaluate smoothness of a triangular mesh.

In ex vivo porcine lung insertion experiment, we performed insertion under CT guidance to validate the HSM, model-based navigation information prediction, registration based on the NDI optical tracking system, system positioning and insertion accuracy. The accuracy is defined by the Euclidean distance between the ideal needle tip point and the actual needle tip point. The porcine lung was placed flat on the CT scanning bed, and the insertion robot and optical templates were fixed to the robot. Before the operation, a CT scan was performed to obtain the preoperative state of the lung. Afterwards, the surgeon could interact with the navigation system through Phantom Omni for path planning. Predicted interactive force and needle deflection of the specified path are fed back when specific path is selected. The needle insertion robot can steer the needle to the target pose, and the final insertion is preformed by surgeon.

3   Results

3.1   HSM Simulation

Figure 6 shows the simulation results of HSM. The blue tetrahedron meshes are for FEM to calculate deformation based on boundary conditions. For the hemisphere, we adopted a complete mapping, in which visual model and FEM mesh share the same shape. The upper part of the hemisphere(red dot) experiences compression or tension, FEM mesh will depress or protrude. As can be seen from Fig. 6(a), visual models can accurately follow FEM deformations for both tension and compression. In non-stressed but still deformed area, the visual model also follows the deformation well.

For cuboid in Fig. 6(b), we adopted a partial mapping, only dividing the finite element mesh for ROI. Similarly, the top of the finite element mesh (red dot) experiences compression or tension, FEM mesh will depress or protrude. As can be seen from the simulation results, visual models can accurately follow FEM

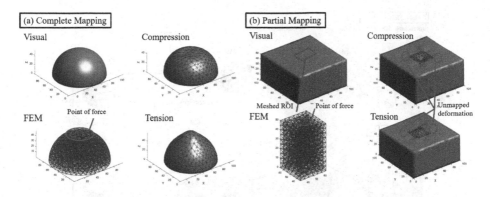

Fig. 6. Hybrid spring mapping update

Table 1. S_V for 4 cases in HSM simulations

Cases	S_V (Original)	S_V (Deformed)
HemispherePull	0.0740	0.0827
HemispherePush	0.0740	0.0854
CubePull	0.0750	0.0932
CubePush	0.0750	0.0942

deformations whether there are depressions or protrusions. In non-mapped areas, the visual model is also updated based on the spring-mass model to generate corresponding deformations, making the overall deformation more vivid.

As shown in Table 1, S_V before and after deformation keeps small with slight increase. Surface smoothness are guaranteed while visual model deformation is achieved based on proposed HSM method.

3.2 Ex Vivo Porcine Lung Experiment

As shown in Fig. 7, both flexible needle navigation (Case#1) and rigid needle navigation (Case#2) are performed. The reachable domain/needle path during the insertion during planning stage and the needle path and force feedback results during the navigation phase are all registered to the digital twin model and displayed. If a flexible needle is used, the reachable domain of the needle during insertion can be displayed as needed. After selecting the insertion path, the navigation system will display the path of the needle and the insertion force for force feedback during the insertion process as shown in Fig. 7(b). Once the insertion is confirmed, the navigation system send the necessary needle pose information to the needle insertion robot, which can steer the needle to move to the corresponding position to assist the surgeon for insertion. HSM method can also update the whole visual model based on mapped FEM deformation, which can help surgeon to have more realistic view of surgical scenes and have better sense of spatial view.

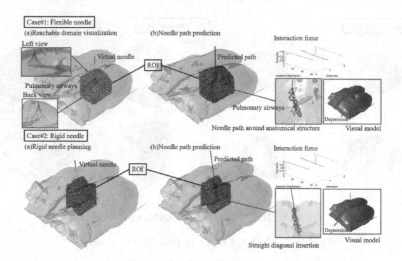

Fig. 7. Digital twin model based navigation results

As shown in Fig. 8, we not only tested registration the model-based augmented display of the navigation results, but also conducted 5 experiments on the system's localization and insertion accuracy. A rigid needle with straight path was used, and the localization accuracy was calculated based on the target needle pose and the real-time needle pose of the insertion needle. The results are shown in Table 2 with mean error 4.1442 mm, which is significantly smaller than the size of a small lung lesion (about 20 mm [24]), indicating that the entire system's accuracy is guaranteed, and accurate insertion can be preformed under system navigation.

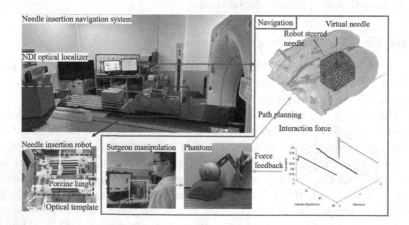

Fig. 8. Needle insertion navigation system experiment

Table 2. Target/Real needle tip position for 5 cases

Cases	P_{target}(mm)	P_{real}(mm)	Error(mm)
1	$(-55.6744, -54.4717, -564.909)$	$(-51.6452, -54.1554, -564.835)$	4.4020
2	$(-24.3210, -53.7394, -571.8420)$	$(-23.6418, -54.2291, -575.3740)$	3.6299
3	$(-11.4358, -53.4581, -572.9420)$	$(-16.0590, -51.6979, -573.1840)$	4.9530
4	$(-21.1258, -53.4894, -1061.9400)$	$(-24.3444, -52.0030, -1062.4400)$	3.5800
5	$(30.2313, -55.9735, -555.1180)$	$(26.3066, -56.0180, -556.4850)$	4.1563

4 Conclusion

In this paper, we proposed a digital twin model based robot-assisted needle insertion navigation system. The digital twin model contains visual model and needle-tissue interaction model. Needle-tissue interaction model can predict needle deflection, tissue deformation and interaction force based on preoperative CT images for planned needle path. These results are provided for surgeons with visual and corresponding force feedback, while the insertion robot can steer the needle to the target position. We also proposed a surface-to-volume mesh mapping method for navigation system visualization, which is applicable to both full and partial mapping and can provide surgeons with better visual feedback by updating deformed visual model. We conducted simulation and experimental validation for system and HSM method. Results showed that the proposed mapping method can deform the surface model without significantly increasing roughness. The navigation system can achieve visual and force feedback, with a insertion accuracy of about 4 mm, indicating guaranteed accuracy and effectiveness of the system in clinical scenarios. In the future, we will improve the registration method and integrate needle path planning method to improve targeting accuracy. Besides, the intraoperative parameter learning method and soft tissue damage prediction will be integrated to digital twin model.

Acknowledgments. This work was supported by the National Key Scientific Instrument and Equipment Development Project (Grant No. 81827804), Zhejiang Provincial Natural Science Foundation of China (Grant No. LSD19H180004), and Science Fund for Creative Groups of NSFC (Grant No. 51821903).

References

1. Ullrich, S., Grottke, O., Rossaint, R., Staat, M., Deserno, T.M., Kuhlen, T.: Virtual needle simulation with haptics for regional anaesthesia. IEEE Virtual Real. **52**(7), 1–3 (2010)
2. Marchal, M., Promayon, E., Troccaz, J.: Comparisons of needle insertion in brachytherapy protocols using a soft tissue discrete model. In: Pediatrics International, p. 153, September 2007
3. Hing, J.T., Brooks, A.D., Desai, J.P.: Reality-based needle insertion simulation for haptic feedback in prostate brachytherapy. In: IEEE International Conference on Robotics and Automation, pp. 619–624 (2006)

4. Moreta-Martínez, R., Rubio-Pérez, I., García-Sevilla, M., García-Elcano, L., Pascau, J.: Evaluation of optical tracking and augmented reality for needle navigation in sacral nerve stimulation. Comput. Methods Programs Biomed. **224**, 106991 (2022). https://doi.org/10.1016/j.cmpb.2022.106991

5. Wu, K., Li, B., Zhang, Y., Dai, X.: Review of research on path planning and control methods of flexible steerable needle puncture robot. Comput. Assist. Surg. **27**(1), 91–112 (2022). https://doi.org/10.1080/24699322.2021.2023647

6. Glozman, D., Shoham, M.: Image-guided robotic flexible needle steering. IEEE Trans. Rob. **23**(3), 459–467 (2007). https://doi.org/10.1109/TRO.2007.898972

7. Fichtinger, G., et al.: Image overlay guidance for needle insertion in CT scanner. IEEE Trans. Biomed. Eng. **52**(8), 1415–1424 (2005). https://doi.org/10.1109/TBME.2005.851493

8. Krieger, A., et al.: Design of a novel MRI compatible manipulator for image guided prostate interventions. IEEE Trans. Biomed. Eng. **52**(2), 306–313 (2005). https://doi.org/10.1109/TBME.2004.840497

9. Krieger, A., et al.: Development and evaluation of an actuated MRI-compatible robotic system for MRI-guided prostate intervention. IEEE/ASME Trans. Mechatron. Joint Publ. IEEE Industrial Electron. Soc. ASME Dyn. Syst. Control Div. **18**(1), 273–284 (2012). https://doi.org/10.1109/TMECH.2011.2163523

10. Tadayyon, H., Lasso, A., Kaushal, A., Guion, P., Fichtinger, G.: Target motion tracking in MRI-guided transrectal robotic prostate biopsy. IEEE Trans. Biomed. Eng. **58**(11), 3135–3142 (2011). https://doi.org/10.1109/TBME.2011.2163633

11. Moreira, P., Boskma, K.J., Misra, S.: Towards MRI-guided flexible needle steering using fiber Bragg grating-based tip tracking. In: 2017 IEEE International Conference on Robotics and Automation (ICRA), pp. 4849–4854 (2017). https://doi.org/10.1109/ICRA.2017.7989564

12. Aboofazeli, M., Abolmaesumi, P., Mousavi, P., Fichtinger, G.: A new scheme for curved needle segmentation in three-dimensional ultrasound images. In: 2009 IEEE International Symposium on Biomedical Imaging: From Nano to Macro, pp. 1067–1070 (2009). https://doi.org/10.1109/ISBI.2009.5193240

13. Zhu, M., Salcudean, S.E.: Real-time image-based b-mode ultrasound image simulation of needles using tensor-product interpolation. IEEE Trans. Med. Imaging **30**(7), 1391–1400 (2011). https://doi.org/10.1109/TMI.2011.2121091

14. Boctor, E.M., Choti, M.A., Burdette, E.C., Webster, R.J., III.: Three-dimensional ultrasound-guided robotic needle placement: an experimental evaluation. Int. J. Med. Robot. Comput. Assist. Surg. **4**(2), 180–191 (2008). https://doi.org/10.1002/rcs.184

15. Romano, J.M., Webster, R.J., Okamura, A.M.: Teleoperation of steerable needles. In: Proceedings 2007 IEEE International Conference on Robotics and Automation, pp. 934–939 (2007). https://doi.org/10.1109/ROBOT.2007.363105

16. Duchemin, G., Maillet, P., Poignet, P., Dombre, E., Pierrot, F.: A hybrid position/force control approach for identification of deformation models of skin and underlying tissues. IEEE Trans. Biomed. Eng. **52**(2), 160–170 (2005). https://doi.org/10.1109/TBME.2004.840505

17. Reed, K.B., Kallem, V., Alterovitz, R., Goldbergxz, K., Okamura, A.M., Cowan, N.J.: Integrated planning and image-guided control for planar needle steering. In: 2008 2nd IEEE RAS & EMBS International Conference on Biomedical Robotics and Biomechatronics, pp. 819–824 (2008). https://doi.org/10.1109/BIOROB.2008.4762833

18. Hauser, K., Alterovitz, R., Chentanez, N., Okamura, A., Goldberg, K.: Feedback control for steering needles through 3D deformable tissue using helical paths. Robot. Sci. Syst. Online Proc. **V**, 37 (2009). https://doi.org/10.15607/rss.2009. v.037

19. Zhao, X., Guo, H., Ye, D., Huo, B.: Comparison of estimation and control methods for flexible needle in 2D. In: 2016 Chinese Control and Decision Conference (CCDC), pp. 5444–5449 (2016). https://doi.org/10.1109/CCDC.2016.7531970

20. Aggravi, M., Estima, D.A.L., Krupa, A., Misra, S., Pacchierotti, C.: Haptic teleoperation of flexible needles combining 3D ultrasound guidance and needle tip force feedback. IEEE Robot. Autom. Lett. **6**(3), 4859–4866 (2021). https://doi.org/10. 1109/LRA.2021.3068635

21. Gao, D., Lei, Y., Lian, B., Yao, B.: Modeling and simulation of flexible needle insertion into soft tissue using modified local constraints. J. Manuf. Sci. Eng. **138**(12), 121012 (2016). https://doi.org/10.1115/1.4034134

22. Du, S., Li, M., Xu, T., Hu, Y., Wang, Z., Lei, Y.: Design and analysis of a novel experiment platform for 3D needle insertion based on orthogonally arranged dual camera. In: International Manufacturing Science and Engineering Conference, vol. Volume 1: Additive Manufacturing; Biomanufacturing; Life Cycle Engineering; Manufacturing Equipment and Automation; Nano/Micro/Meso Manufacturing (2022). https://doi.org/10.1115/MSEC2022-85764

23. Amidror, I.: Scattered data interpolation methods for electronic imaging systems: a survey. J. Electron. Imaging **11**(2), 157–176 (2002). https://doi.org/10.1117/1. 1455013

24. Guo, Y.Q., et al.: Ultrasound-guided percutaneous needle biopsy for peripheral pulmonary lesions: diagnostic accuracy and influencing factors. Ultrasound Med. Biol. **44**(5), 1003–1011 (2018). https://doi.org/10.1016/j.ultrasmedbio.2018.01.016

A Modified BiSeNet for Spinal Segmentation

Yunjiao Deng[1,2], Feng Gu[1], Shuai Wang[1], Daxing Zeng[1], Junyan Lu[5], Haitao Liu[2],
Yulei Hou[4], and Qinghua Zhang[3(✉)]

[1] School of Mechanical Engineering, Dongguan University of Technology, Dongguan 523015,
China
[2] School of Mechanical Engineering, Tianjin University, Tianjin 300072, China
[3] Department of Neurosurgery, Huazhong University of Science and Technology Union
Shenzhen Hospital, Shenzhen 518052, China
doctorzhangqinghua@163.com
[4] School of Mechanical Engineering, Yanshan University, Qinhuangdao 066004, China
[5] Department of Nursing, Dongguan Kanghua Hospital, Dongguan 523080, China

Abstract. Multi-class segmentation of vertebrae and intervertebral discs is of
paramount importance for accurate diagnosis and treatment of various spinal diseases. However, achieving precise segmentation remains a challenging task. In this
study, we propose a modified BiSeNet specifically designed for spine segmentation, aiming to address the limitations and improve the segmentation performance.
Our motivation behind modifying BiSeNet lies in fully leveraging the strengths
of both the context and spatial paths in feature extraction based on the BiSeNet.
To enhance segmentation effectiveness, we fuse the two paths, which consist of a
context extractor and a spatial extractor, using the feature fusion module (FFM)
in BiSeNet. We utilize a U-shaped architecture for the context path, incorporating
attention refinement modules (ARM) to leverage features from all encoder layers.
Additionally, a specific residual structure is introduced to enhance the context
extractor's effectiveness. For the spatial path, we introduce a novel multi-scale
convolution attention module based on the SegNext structure. These main contributions in our framework improve the segmentation effectiveness by capturing
long-range relationships among vertebrae and intervertebral discs while considering inter-class similarity and intra-class variation. Experimental results on an
MRI dataset comprising 172 subjects demonstrate impressive performance, with
a mean Dice similarity coefficient of 82.365% across all spinal structures. These
results indicate the considerable potential of our proposed method in aiding the
diagnosis and treatment of spinal diseases.

Keywords: Semantic segmentation · spine · vertebrae · intervertebral discs ·
MRI

1 Introduction

With the increasing impact of societal aging and shifts in people's lifestyles, the prevalence of spinal diseases is on the rise. Computed tomography (CT) and magnetic resonance imaging (MRI) play crucial roles in diagnosing and treating spinal conditions.

© The Author(s), under exclusive license to Springer Nature Singapore Pte Ltd. 2023
H. Yang et al. (Eds.): ICIRA 2023, LNAI 14269, pp. 132–144, 2023.
https://doi.org/10.1007/978-981-99-6489-5_11

Automatic segmentation of vertebrae and intervertebral discs is a vital step in spine image analysis and modeling, enabling the identification of spinal abnormalities, biomechanical modeling, vertebrae fracture detection, intervertebral disc protrusion assessment, and image-guided spine interventions. For instance, lumbar intervertebral disc radiofrequency ablation (RFA) is a commonly used minimally invasive procedure to alleviate lumbago and functional limitations caused by protruding lumbar intervertebral discs. CT is typically employed for precise guidance of the RFA needle tip to the accurate position, leveraging its high sensitivity to vertebrae. Meanwhile, MRI aids in locating the protrusion during RFA by providing enhanced visualization of the intervertebral discs. Hence, achieving precise segmentation of the spine is essential to ensure the successful execution of RFA.

Currently, there are two primary challenges in achieving accurate segmentation of the spine, specifically pertaining to vertebrae and intervertebral discs: inter-class similarity and intra-class variation. Inter-class similarity refers to the similarities in shapes and textures observed between intervertebral discs as well as between vertebrae. On the other hand, intra-class variation involves noticeable differences within the same class of intervertebral discs or vertebrae among different patients.

1.1 Related Works

Automated segmentation of vertebrae and intervertebral discs offers significant time-saving benefits for physicians and ensures a reproducible approach to spine diagnosis and treatment. As a result, it has garnered considerable interest among researchers. The available literatures on spine segmentation can be broadly classified into two approaches: separate segmentation for vertebrae and intervertebral discs, and simultaneous segmentation for both vertebrae and intervertebral discs.

Researches on the separate segmentation of vertebrae or intervertebral discs can be broadly classified into the following categories: threshold-based methods [1], active contours-based methods [2] and level-sets based methods [3], atlas-based methods [4], deformable shape-based methods [5], machine learning-based methods with handcrafted features [6], and deep learning-based methods [7–9]. For instance, Lee et al., proposed a multistep approach utilizing CT scans, which began with 2-D dynamic thresholding using local optimal thresholds, followed by procedures to recover the spine geometry in a high curvature environment [10]. Wang et al., developed a super-pixel mesh CT image improved segmentation algorithm using active contour, which improved the Mumford-Shah model in the active contour model and constructed the energy function [11]. Rehman et al., introduced a novel combination of traditional region-based level set and a deep learning framework to accurately predict the shape of vertebral bones [12]. Xie et al., designed a deep label fusion (DLF) segmentation model based on multi-atlas segmentation (MAS) and deep convolutional neural networks (DCNN). Their approach integrated the high accuracy of DCNN in segmenting various anatomical structures in medical images with the generalization capabilities of MAS on undiscovered datasets with different characteristics from training datasets [13]. Haq et al., proposed a shape-aware multi-surface simplex deformable model for the segmentation of both healthy and pathological lumbar spine in medical image data, enabling the identification of intervertebral disc protrusion [14]. Altini et al., developed a framework that combined deep learning and classical machine learning methodologies for vertebrae segmentation. They utilized a 3D convolutional neural network for automated segmentation of the whole spine and incorporated traditional machine learning algorithms to locate vertebrae centroids [15]. Moreover, Wang et al., introduced a multiscale large-kernel convolution U-Net (MLKCA-Unet) that employed large-kernel convolutions with different kernels for effective feature extraction [16]. Kim et al., designed a boundary-specific U-network (BSU-net) for fine-grain segmentation of intervertebral discs from MRI. They modified the convolutional and pooling layer scheme and applied a cascaded learning method to overcome limitations of the max-pooling layer in a conventional U-net [17]. Guinebert et al., trained two CNN networks, namely U-Net++ and Yolov5x, based on T2-weighted sagittal MRI scans. These networks were utilized for segmenting and detecting vertebrae and intervertebral discs, respectively [18].

Current researches on the simultaneous segmentation of vertebrae and intervertebral discs primarily focused on machine learning-based methods [19] and deep learning-based methods [20, 21]. Neubert et al., developed a fully automated 3D segmentation approach for MRI scans of the human spine, utilizing statistical shape analysis and template matching of grey level intensity profiles [22]. Oktay et al., applied support vector machines (SVM) to locate and label lumbar vertebrae and intervertebral discs in mid-sagittal MRI slices based on a Markov-chain-like graphical model of the ordered discs and vertebrae in the lumbar spine [23]. Lu et al., achieved accurate vertebrae segmentation and intervertebral disc-level localization using a combination of U-Net and a spine-curve fitting method [24]. Suri et al., proposed a deep learning system for multi-modality 2D segmentation of vertebrae and intervertebral discs, incorporating a feature generation network, a region recognition network, and a landmark detection network [25]. Wimmer et al., presented a cross-modality and fully automatic pipeline for labeling vertebrae and intervertebral discs in volumetric data of the lumbar and thoracolumbar spine by automatically localizing the sacral region, combining local entropy-optimized texture models with convolutional neural networks [26].

In summary, methods that segment vertebrae or intervertebral discs separately may not provide sufficient pathological features for doctors. Conversely, methods that segment vertebrae and intervertebral discs simultaneously can avoid overlapping and misjudgment, while extracting more accurate semantic features through their connection. However, in the aforementioned methods, all vertebrae or all intervertebral discs are assigned to a single class, and few researchers assign different vertebrae to different classes. The subdivision of intervertebral discs is also limited, which hampers precise positioning of vertebrae and intervertebral discs and the formulation of surgical plans. Pang et al., noted 'this limitation, but their proposed SpineParseNet, consisting of a 3D graph convolutional segmentation network for coarse segmentation and a 2D residual U-Net for segmentation refinement, is relatively complex and not easily applicable to clinical research [27, 28].

Overall, the current research landscape demonstrates a growing interest in the simultaneous segmentation of vertebrae and intervertebral discs. By advancing the field with improved methodologies and addressing the existing limitations, researchers can contribute to the development of robust and clinically relevant solutions for spine diagnosis and treatment.

1.2 Overview of the Proposed Method

BiSeNet [29] achieves a balance between speed and accuracy through a bidirectional segmentation network comprising a spatial path and a context path. In this study, we propose a modified version of BiSeNet specifically tailored for spine segmentation, aiming to fully leverage the advantages of both paths in feature extraction.

Our network architecture consists of two key components: a context extractor and a spatial extractor. The context extractor employs a U-shaped architecture and integrates attention refinement modules (ARM) to effectively utilize features from all encoder layers. Additionally, it incorporates a specific residual structure to ensure comprehensive feature extraction of vertebrae and intervertebral discs in MRI scans. On the other hand, the spatial extractor introduces a novel multi-scale convolution attention module based on the SegNext structure. This module captures long-range relationships among vertebrae and intervertebral discs, as well as the interconnections within the same class. By combining these two paths, we utilize the feature fusion module (FFM) from BiSeNet to maximize the synergistic effects of their complementary features.

The main contributions of this study can be summarized as follows:

1. We propose a modified BiSeNet framework for spine segmentation, specifically targeting the multi-class segmentation of vertebrae and intervertebral discs. In contrast to the original BiSeNet, our approach adopts a U-shaped architecture with encoder and decoder components for the context path, while utilizing a SegNext structure with depth-wise strip convolution (DWS Conv) for the spatial path.
2. To address challenges such as inter-class similarity and intra-class variation in fine segmentation of the spine, we introduce a modified multi-scale convolution attention module based on the SegNext structure in the spatial extractor. This module effectively captures long-range relationships among vertebrae and intervertebral discs, as well as the interconnections within the same class.

By incorporating these advancements into our modified BiSeNet framework, we aim to enhance the accuracy and performance of spine segmentation, thus contributing to the field of medical image analysis and facilitating improved diagnosis and treatment of spinal diseases.

2 Methods

Our proposed network as shown in Fig. 1, includes a context extractor and a spatial extractor.

2.1 Context Extractor

Given the remarkable performance of U-Net in medical image segmentation, our proposed network is built upon the standard U-Net architecture with several key modifications. Firstly, we replace the conventional convolution blocks in the encoder with a specific residual structure (Res Block). Secondly, in the decoder, we introduce a simplified channel adjustment structure (Head Block) as a replacement for the conventional convolution blocks. Additionally, to facilitate downsampling in the encoder, we modify the first convolution step size of each stage to 2, instead of employing maximum pooling operations.

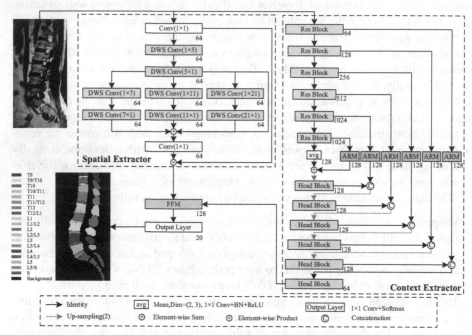

Fig. 1. The framework of our proposed network, which consists of a context extractor and a spatial extractor.

The Head Block consists of a 1×1 convolutions, batch normalization, and ReLU activation.

The Res Block is shown in Fig. 2. A given MR slice $F \in \mathbb{R}^{H \times W \times 3}$ is first fed to convolution layer and output $F' \in \mathbb{R}^{H \times W \times C}$, where H and W represent the height and width of the MR slice, respectively. The convolution layer consists of a convolution with a 5×5 kernel (with a stride of 1 in the first stage and a stride of 2 in subsequent stages), followed by batch normalization and ReLU activation. The output $F' \in \mathbb{R}^{H \times W \times C}$ is then fed into two parallel pathways. The first pathway comprises three convolutions with kernel sizes of 5×5 (for the first two) and 3×3 (for the last), respectively, accompanied by batch normalization and ReLU activation. The second pathway involves a single convolution with a 1×1 kernel. These pathways produce outputs $F_1 \in \mathbb{R}^{H \times W \times C}$ and $F_2 \in \mathbb{R}^{H \times W \times C}$. These two pathways are subsequently combined for further processing, yielding $y \in \mathbb{R}^{H \times W \times C}$:

$$\begin{cases} F' = f_5(F) \\ y = f_3\{f_5[f_5(F')]\} + C_1(F') \end{cases} \tag{1}$$

where C_1 is a convolutional layer with a 1×1 kernel, f_3, f_5 represent convolutional layers with kernel sizes of 3×3 and 5×5, respectively, followed by batch normalization and ReLU activation.

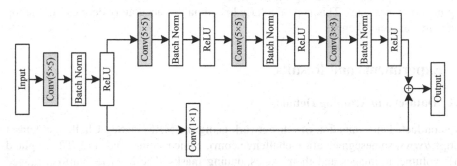

Fig. 2. The architecture of the Res Block.

2.2 Spatial Extractor

Given the elongated and fragmented nature of vertebrae and intervertebral discs, we have chosen the modified multi-scale convolution attention module with depth-wise strip convolution (DWS Conv) based on the SegNext structure. This module effectively captures the intricate details and fringe features in the spatial extractor.

The spatial extractor, illustrated in Fig. 1, begins with a given MR slice $F \in \mathbb{R}^{H \times W \times 3}$, which is initially processed by a convolutional layer to produce output $F_0 \in \mathbb{R}^{H \times W \times C}$, thereby expanding the channel's depth. The convolutional layer employs a 1×1 kernel. The output $F_0 \in \mathbb{R}^{H \times W \times C}$ is then passed through the DWS Conv, resulting in output $F_0' \in \mathbb{R}^{H \times W \times C}$. The DWS Conv consists of two convolutions with kernel sizes of 1×5 and 5×1, respectively. Subsequently, $F_0' \in \mathbb{R}^{H \times W \times C}$ is fed into three parallel pathways. The first pathway comprises two convolutions with kernel sizes of 1×7 and 7×1, respectively. The second pathway involves two convolutions with kernel sizes of 1×11 and 1×1, respectively. Lastly, the third pathway consists of two convolutions with kernel sizes of 1×21 and 21×1, respectively. These pathways produce outputs $F_1' \in \mathbb{R}^{H \times W \times C}$, $F_2' \in \mathbb{R}^{H \times W \times C}$, and $F_3' \in \mathbb{R}^{H \times W \times C}$, respectively. The three pathways are then combined using a convolutional layer with a 1×1 kernel, resulting in the output $F_a' \in \mathbb{R}^{H \times W \times C}$. Finally, the outputs $F_a' \in \mathbb{R}^{H \times W \times C}$ and $F_0 \in \mathbb{R}^{H \times W \times C}$ are combined using element-wise product to yield $y_s \in \mathbb{R}^{H \times W \times C}$:

$$\begin{cases} F_0' = C_{5 \times 1}\{C_{1 \times 5}[C_1(F)]\} \\ y_s = C_1\{C_{5 \times 1}[C_{1 \times 5}(F_0')] + C_{11 \times 1}[C_{1 \times 11}(F_0')] + C_{21 \times 1}[C_{1 \times 21}(F_0')]\} \otimes C_1(F) \end{cases}$$

(2)

where $C_{1 \times 5}, C_{5 \times 1}, C_{1 \times 11}, C_{11 \times 1}, C_{1 \times 21}, C_{21 \times 1}$ represent convolutional layers with kernel sizes of $1 \times 5, 5 \times 1, 1 \times 11, 11 \times 1, 1 \times 21$, and 21×1, respectively, $\otimes$ denotes the element-wise product operation.

From this, we can deduce that the resulting feature map encompasses both vertical and horizontal relationships at every point. Consequently, the modified multi-scale convolution attention module with depth-wise strip convolution enables the capture of long-range dependencies among vertebrae and intervertebral discs, thereby enhancing segmentation accuracy. This is particularly beneficial for accurately delineating the top structures and sacral crest.

3 Experiments and Results

3.1 Dataset and Training Details

We conducted an evaluation of our network using the MRSpineSeg Challenge dataset (https://www.spinesegmentation-challenge.com), which comprised 172 T2-weighted MR volumetric images and their corresponding masks. The MRI resolutions ranged from 512×512 to 1024×1024, with the number of slices varying from 12 to 18. The dataset consisted of 20 categories, including 10 vertebrae, 9 intervertebral discs, and the background. However, not all MR images contained all 20 categories.

To focus on the spinal region and reduce computational requirements, we cropped and resized all MRI slices to 128×256 and normalized them by gray level to 3 channels before feeding them into our network. For training and verification, 90% of the slices (1953) were used for training, while the remaining 10% (216) were used for verification.

We trained our proposed network for 500 epochs using the Adam optimizer, with a batch size of 20, a weight decay of 0.002, an initial learning rate of 1e−3, and a decay factor of 0.1 when the validation set's performance remained unchanged for 10 consecutive epochs. All networks were implemented using PyTorch and trained on a NVIDIA GeForce RTX 3090 GPU with 24 GB of memory.

To enhance the capabilities of our proposed network, we designed a new loss function called $DFKL$, which combines dice loss (DL), focal loss (FL), and KL divergence loss (KL) using exponential and logarithmic functions as follows:

$$L_{DFKL} = 3 \log DL^2 + \log FL^2 + 0.1 \log KL^2 \tag{3}$$

where the coefficients in the Eq. (3) were determined by considering importance of different loss functions.

We utilized a confusion matrix to evaluate the results, and the key parameters are presented in Table 1.

In Table 1, TP represents true positives, FN represents false negatives, FP represents false positives, and TN represents true negatives.

The dice coefficient was employed as the evaluation metric for spine segmentation, and it is calculated as follows:

$$Dice = \frac{2TP}{FP + 2TP + FN} \tag{4}$$

Table 1. Confusion matrix

Confusion matrix		True value	
		Positive	Negative
Predictive value	Positive	*TP*	*FP*
	Negative	*FN*	*TN*

3.2 Result

To validate the effectiveness of our proposed network and the combination of the new loss function, we quantitatively compared our networks (with cross-entropy loss *CE*, dice loss *DL*, and *DFKL*) with U-Net (VGG16 and ResNet34) and BiSeNet (ResNet34) based on the dice coefficients obtained from the MRSpineSeg Challenge spine validation dataset. The comparison results are presented in Table 2.

It is important to note that all the results were obtained directly from a single-model test without any reliance on post-processing tools. The input to our segmentation network was directly obtained from the extracted slices without any filtering or enhancement processing.

Table 2. Mean Dice (%) using different segmentation methods.

Method	*Dice*
U-Net (VGG16) [30]	64.595
U-Net (ResNet34) [31]	75.252
BiSeNet (ResNet34) [29]	69.737
Ours (*CE*)	80.964
Ours (*DL*)	82.203
Ours (*DFKL*)	**82.365**

As depicted in Table 2, our proposed network has achieved the highest dice coefficient, clearly demonstrating the superiority of our modified BiSeNet with its dual-path architecture. Figure 3 illustrates the impressive segmentation results obtained by our network, highlighting its exceptional capability to accurately segment various vertebrae and intervertebral discs with clear and well-defined edges Notably, our method excels in accurately identifying T9 and T9/T10, which pose significant challenges for other existing approaches. This achievement is particularly evident in the sixth and ninth cases, where our method demonstrates superior performance. In contrast, the original BiSeNet struggles to accurately identify these components, while U-Net achieves partial recognition, showing improved results when integrated with the ResNet34 framework. Additionally, our method outperforms others in capturing fine details. For instance, in the second case, our method accurately identifies the right half of L1 (highlighted in green),

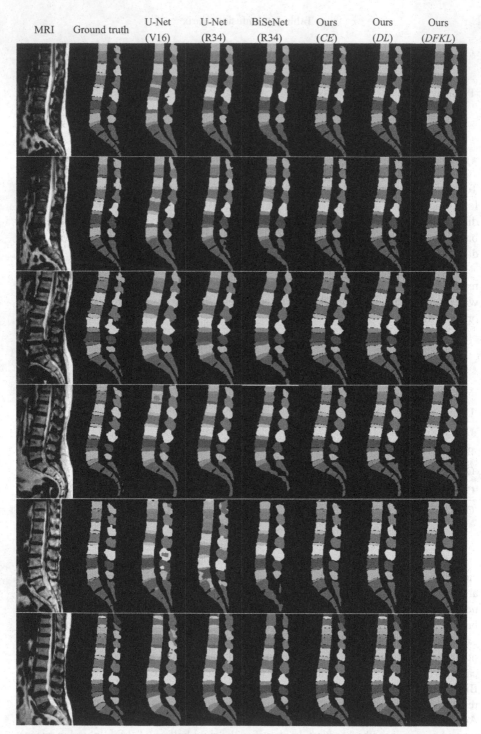

Fig. 3. The segmentation performance of some networks for the multi-class segmentation of spine. V is VGG and R is ResNet. (Color figure online)

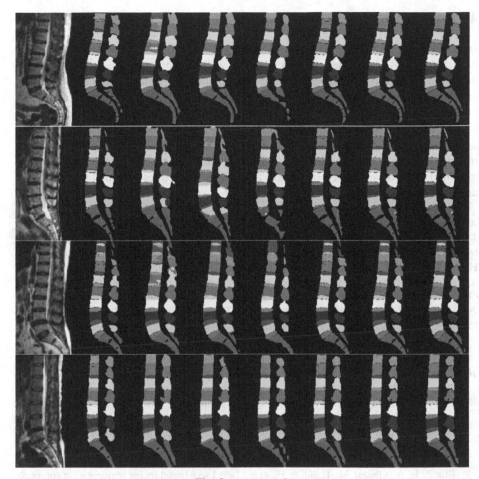

Fig. 3. (*continued*)

while BiSeNet fails to capture the edge information, and U-Net's edge recognition is limited. Furthermore, our method effectively addresses common issues in multi-class segmentation, such as misalignment and recognition errors. In the fourth case, when employing the U-Net model with the VGG16 framework, the left half of T12 is compressed, leading to incorrect recognition of structures above it. Similarly, in the sixth case, the segmentation results show some merging, with both L1 and T12 incorrectly identified as L1. Overall, our proposed method surpasses these challenges and achieves outstanding recognition accuracy.

Then, these results provide strong evidence that our designed *DFKL* loss surpasses conventional loss functions such as cross-entropy loss and dice loss in terms of network segmentation performance. For instance, in the first case, under the cross-entropy loss *CE*, the right edge segmentation of the right part of L3 appears notably sharp and prominent. With the dice loss *DL*, it is slightly more prominent, while under the *DFKL* loss, the segmentation exhibits a much smoother transition.

4 Conclusion

In conclusion, we have presented a modified BiSeNet that fully leverages the structural advantages of encoders and decoders, as well as the complementary benefits of dual-channel features, for the multi-class segmentation of vertebrae and intervertebral discs. To address challenges related to inter-class similarity and intra-class variation, we have incorporated a specific residual structure to extract detailed features, along with a modified multi-scale convolution attention module using depth-wise strip convolution to capture long-range relationships among vertebrae, intervertebral discs, and their interconnections within the same class. Our experimental results demonstrate that our modified BiSeNet effectively addresses the unique challenges in spinal segmentation and outperforms existing approaches.

Acknowledgment. This work was supported in part by the Project of Shenzhen Science and Technology Innovation Committee, China, under Grant KCXFZ20201221173202007; in part by the Key Scientific Research Platforms and Projects of Guangdong Regular Institutions of Higher Education, China, under Grant 2022KCXTD033; in part by the Scientific Research Capacity Improvement Project of Key Developing Disciplines in Guangdong Province, China, under Grant 2021ZDJS084; in part by the Guangdong Natural Science Foundation, China, under Grant 2023A1515012103; and in part by the Fundamental Public Welfare Research Project of Zhejiang Province, China, under Grant LGG21E050022.

References

1. Garg, S., Bhagyashree, S.R.: Spinal cord MRI segmentation techniques and algorithms: a survey. SN Comput. Sci. **2**(3), 229 (2021)
2. Fouladivanda, M., Kazemi, K., Helfroush, M.S., et al.: Morphological active contour driven by local and global intensity fitting for spinal cord segmentation from MR images. J. Neurosci. Methods **308**, 116–128 (2018)
3. Eltanboly, A., Ghazal, M., Hajjdiab, H., et al.: Level sets-based image segmentation approach using statistical shape priors. Appl. Math. Comput. **340**, 164–179 (2019)
4. Yu, W., Liu, W., Tan, L., Zhang, S., Zheng, G.: Multi-object model-based multi-atlas segmentation constrained grid cut for automatic segmentation of lumbar vertebrae from CT images. In: Zheng, G., Tian, W., Zhuang, X. (eds.) Intelligent Orthopaedics. AEMB, vol. 1093, pp. 65–71. Springer, Singapore (2018). https://doi.org/10.1007/978-981-13-1396-7_5
5. Hille, G., Saalfeld, S., Serowy, S., et al.: Vertebral body segmentation in wide range clinical routine spine MRI data. Comput. Methods Programs Biomed. **155**, 93–99 (2018)
6. Siemionow, K., Luciano, C., Forsthoefel, C., et al.: Autonomous image segmentation and identification of anatomical landmarks from lumbar spine intraoperative computed tomography scans using machine learning: a validation study. J. Craniovertebral Junction Spine **11**(2), 99 (2020)
7. Mushtaq, M., Akram, M.U., Alghamdi, N.S., et al.: Localization and edge-based segmentation of lumbar spine vertebrae to identify the deformities using deep learning models. Sensors **22**(4), 1547 (2022)
8. Chen, H., Dou, Q., Wang, X., Qin, J., Cheng, J.C.Y., Heng, P.A.: 3D fully convolutional networks for intervertebral disc localization and segmentation. In: Zheng, G., Liao, H., Jannin, P., Cattin, P., Lee, S.L. (eds.) MIAR 2016. LNCS, vol. 9805, pp. 375–382. Springer, Cham (2016). https://doi.org/10.1007/978-3-319-43775-0_34

9. Hutt, H., Everson, R., Meakin, J.: 3D Intervertebral Disc segmentation from MRI using supervoxel-based CRFs. In: Vrtovec, T., et al. (eds.) Computational Methods and Clinical Applications for Spine Imaging. CSI 2015. LNCS, vol. 9402, pp. 125–129. Springer, Cham (2016). https://doi.org/10.1007/978-3-319-41827-8_12

10. Lee, J., Kim, S., Kim, Y.S., et al.: Automated segmentation of the lumbar pedicle in CT images for spinal fusion surgery. IEEE Trans. Biomed. Eng. 58(7), 2051 (2011)

11. Wei, Y., Wang, X.: An improved image segmentation algorithm CT superpixel grid using active contour. Wirel. Commun. Mob. Comput. 2021, 1–9 (2021)

12. Rehman, F., Ali Shah, S.I., Riaz, M.N., et al.: A region-based deep level set formulation for vertebral bone segmentation of osteoporotic fractures. J. Digit. Imaging 33, 191–203 (2020)

13. Xie, L., Wisse, L.E.M., Wang, J., et al.: Deep label fusion: a generalizable hybrid multi-atlas and deep convolutional neural network for medical image segmentation. Med. Image Anal. 83, 102683 (2023)

14. Haq, R., Schmid, J., Borgie, R., et al.: Deformable multisurface segmentation of the spine for orthopedic surgery planning and simulation. J. Med. Imaging 7(1), 015002 (2020)

15. Altini, N., De Giosa, G., Fragasso, N., et al.: Segmentation and identification of vertebrae in CT scans using CNN, k-means clustering and k-NN. Informatics 8(2), 40 (2021)

16. Wang, B., Qin, J., Lv, L., et al.: MLKCA-Unet: multiscale large-kernel convolution and attention in Unet for spine MRI segmentation. Optik 272, 170277 (2023)

17. Kim, S., Bae, W.C., Masuda, K., et al.: Fine-grain segmentation of the intervertebral discs from MR spine images using deep convolutional neural networks: BSU-Net. Appl. Sci. 8(9), 1656 (2018)

18. Guinebert, S., Petit, E., Bousson, V., et al.: Automatic semantic segmentation and detection of vertebras and intervertebral discs by neural networks. Comput. Methods Programs Biomed. Update 2, 100055 (2022)

19. Fallah, F., Walter, S.S., Bamberg, F., et al.: Simultaneous volumetric segmentation of vertebral bodies and intervertebral discs on fat-water MR images. IEEE J. Biomed. Health Inform. 23(4), 1692–1701 (2018)

20. Huang, J., Shen, H., Wu, J., et al.: Spine explorer: a deep learning based fully automated program for efficient and reliable quantifications of the vertebrae and discs on sagittal lumbar spine MR images. Spine J. 20(4), 590–599 (2020)

21. Han, Z., Wei, B., Mercado, A., et al.: Spine-GAN: semantic segmentation of multiple spinal structures. Med. Image Anal. 50, 23–35 (2018)

22. Neubert, A., Fripp, J., Shen, K., et al.: Automated 3D segmentation of vertebral bodies and intervertebral discs from MRI. In: 2011 International Conference on Digital Image Computing: Techniques and Applications, pp. 19–24. IEEE (2011)

23. Oktay, A.B., Akgul, Y.S.: Simultaneous localization of lumbar vertebrae and intervertebral discs with SVM-based MRF. IEEE Trans. Biomed. Eng. 60(9), 2375–2383 (2013)

24. Lu J.T., Pedemonte S., Bizzo B., et al.: Deep spine: automated lumbar vertebral segmentation, disc-level designation, and spinal stenosis grading using deep learning. In: Finale, D., Jim, F., Ken, J., et al. (eds.) Machine Learning for Healthcare Conference, pp. 403–419. PMLR (2018)

25. Suri, A., Jones, B.C., Ng, G., et al.: A deep learning system for automated, multi-modality 2D segmentation of vertebral bodies and intervertebral discs. Bone 149, 15972 (2021)

26. Wimmer, M., Major, D., Novikov, A.A., et al.: Fully automatic cross-modality localization and labeling of vertebral bodies and intervertebral discs in 3D spinal images. Int. J. Comput. Assist. Radiol. Surg. 13, 1591–1603 (2018)

27. Pang, S., Pang, C., Zhao, L., et al.: SpineParseNet: spine parsing for volumetric MR image by a two-stage segmentation framework with semantic image representation. IEEE Trans. Med. Imaging 40(1), 262–273 (2020)

144   Y. Deng et al.

28. Li, C., Liu, T., Chen, Z., et al.: SPA-ResUNet: strip pooling attention resunet for multi-class segmentation of vertebrae and intervertebral discs. In: 2022 IEEE 19th International Symposium on Biomedical Imaging (ISBI), Kolkata, India, pp.1–5 (2022)
29. Yu, C., Wang, J., Peng, C., Gao, C., Yu, G., Sang, N.: BiSeNet: bilateral segmentation network for real-time semantic segmentation. In: Ferrari, V., Hebert, M., Sminchisescu, C., Weiss, Y. (eds.) ECCV 2018. LNCS, vol. 11217, pp. 334–349. Springer, Cham (2018). https://doi.org/10.1007/978-3-030-01261-8_20
30. Ronneberger, O., Fischer, P., Brox, T.: U-net: convolutional networks for biomedical image segmentation. In: Navab, N., Hornegger, J., Wells, W., Frangi, A. (eds.) MICCAI 2015. LNCS, vol. 9351, pp. 234–241. Springer, Cham (2015). https://doi.org/10.1007/978-3-319-24574-4_28
31. Rahman, H., Bukht, T.F.N., Imran, A., et al.: A deep learning approach for liver and tumor segmentation in CT images using ResUNet. Bioengineering **9**(8), 368 (2022)

Retinal Vascular Segmentation Based on Depth-Separable Convolution and Attention Mechanisms

Xiaopeng Liu[1], Dongxu Gao[2], Congyi Zhang[2], Hongwei Gao[1], and Zhaojie Ju[2(✉)]

[1] School of Automation and Electrical Engineering, Shenyang Ligong University,
Shenyang 110159, China
ghw1978@sohu.com

[2] School of Computing, University of Portsmouth, Portsmouth PO13HE, UK
{dongxu.gao,Congyi.zhang,Zhaojie.Ju}@port.ac.uk

Abstract. Retinal vascular segmentation is an important research direction in the field of medical image processing, its main purpose is to automatically segment the vascular area from the fundus image, and provide doctors with more accurate diagnosis results and treatment plans. In recent years, with the continuous development of deep learning technology, retinal vascular segmentation algorithm based on deep learning has gradually become a research hotspot. In this paper, the retinal vascular segmentation algorithm based on deep learning is mainly improved, and the retinal vascular segmentation algorithm based on IPN-V2 is improved, in an attempt to make new explorations.

The retinal vascular segmentation algorithm based on IPN-V2 provides global information, but requires a large amount of image data and label information, the image size is different, and most importantly, the accuracy of the model for the segmentation of the original image is not enough. Therefore, this paper improves the retinal vascular segmentation algorithm based on IPN-V2, introduces the attention mechanism, and constructs a retinal vascular segmentation model based on ASR-IPN-V2, which enables the model to extract more image details from the original image through the depth-separable convolution and convolutional block attention mechanisms.

Experiments show that the retinal vascular segmentation model based on ASR-IPN-V2 greatly improves the efficiency of retinal vascular segmentation.

Keywords: IPN-V2 model · Segmentation of retinal blood vessels · Attention mechanism

1 Introduction

Retinal vascular segmentation refers to the segmentation of retinal blood vessels in fundus images, which plays an important role in the early diagnosis, treatment and evaluation of ophthalmic diseases. Optical coherence tomography angiography (OCTA)

The authors would like to acknowledge the support from the National Natural Science Foundation of China (52075530).

© The Author(s), under exclusive license to Springer Nature Singapore Pte Ltd. 2023
H. Yang et al. (Eds.): ICIRA 2023, LNAI 14269, pp. 145–160, 2023.
https://doi.org/10.1007/978-981-99-6489-5_12

is a non-invasive test that enables high-resolution imaging of ocular blood vessels. The combination of OCTA technology and retinal vascular segmentation technology can realize accurate and non-invasive imaging and segmentation of ocular blood vessels, further improving the effect of diagnosis and treatment. In the traditional retinal vascular segmentation method, image processing and machine learning technology are mainly used, but due to the noise in the image, the complex morphology of blood vessels and the differences in different pathological conditions, the segmentation effect of these methods is often unsatisfactory.

In recent years, with the rapid development of deep learning technology, retinal vascular segmentation methods based on deep learning have attracted more and more attention. Deep learning is a machine learning technology that can automatically learn feature representation, which has strong expression ability and generalization ability, and can effectively solve some problems in traditional methods. Among them, the Convolutional Neural Network (CNN) is a deep learning model with powerful feature extraction and classification capabilities. CNN-based retinal vascular segmentation methods mainly include FCN network, U-Net network, Seg Net network, etc., which can automatically learn feature representation and improve the segmentation effect.

Deep learning is a hot technology in the field of artificial intelligence, with a wide range of application prospects and trends. The following are the application prospects and trends of deep learning:

(1) Computer vision: Deep learning is widely used in computer vision, including image recognition, object detection, face recognition, image segmentation and other fields [1]. Object detection and image classification have always been the focus of deep learning applications in the field of computer vision. Through the training and optimization of deep learning algorithms, the recognition and classification of objects can be achieved, which supports applications such as image retrieval and object tracking. Deep learning also plays an important role in video analytics. Through the training and optimization of deep learning algorithms, applications such as object tracking and action recognition in video can be realized, so as to provide support for video surveillance, video analysis and other fields [2]. Deep learning also has a wide range of applications in 3D reconstruction. Through the training and optimization of deep learning algorithms, the reconstruction and recognition of three-dimensional space can be realized, so as to provide support for architecture, engineering, geology and other fields. With the continuous optimization and performance improvement of deep learning algorithms, the application field of computer vision will be more extensive.

(2) Natural language processing: Deep learning also has a wide range of applications in natural language processing, including speech recognition, machine translation, sentiment analysis and other fields [3]. Deep learning also has a wide range of applications in text classification and information extraction. Through the training and optimization of deep learning algorithms, the classification of text and information extraction can be realized, so as to provide support for text mining, intelligence analysis and other fields [4]. Deep learning is also becoming more widely used in automated question answering and knowledge graphs. Through the training and optimization of deep learning algorithms, the understanding and answering of natural

language problems can be realized, which provides support for the question answering system and knowledge graph construction. Deep learning is also becoming more widely used in emotion recognition and text generation. Through the training and optimization of deep learning algorithms, the recognition and expression of emotions can be realized, which can support applications such as sentiment analysis and text generation. With the continuous improvement and optimization of deep learning algorithms, the application of natural language processing will become more popular and mature [5].

(3) Speech recognition: Speech recognition is a technology that converts human speech into computer-readable text, and it has a wide range of applications in artificial intelligence, smart home, intelligent customer service and other fields [6]. The development of deep learning technology has greatly improved the accuracy of speech recognition, making the application of speech recognition in real life more popular [7]. Deep learning technology can provide powerful support for the training of speech recognition models. Through the training and optimization of deep learning algorithms, the feature extraction of speech signals and the training of speech recognition models can be realized, so as to improve the accuracy and stability of speech recognition. Deep learning technology also has a wide range of applications in multilingual speech recognition. Through the training and optimization of deep learning algorithms, the recognition and conversion of multilingual speech signals can be realized, so as to provide support for multinational enterprises and international conferences.

At present, deep learning has shown excellent results in the fields of speech recognition, natural language processing, and computer vision. There are many kinds of deep learning algorithm models, including automatic coding machines, restricted Boltzmann machines, deep neural networks, convolutional neural networks, recurrent neural networks, and neural networks with multi-network model fusion, among which there are both traditional algorithms and the latest algorithm models [8]. When applying deep learning technology, it is necessary to reasonably select algorithm models according to the characteristics of different fields, and cannot abandon the use because the models are old. Specific analysis of specific problems, reasonable selection of deep learning models is crucial. Although deep learning technology is still evolving, it will still be full of opportunities and challenges in the future.

The retinal vascular segmentation method based on deep learning has the advantages of high precision, high efficiency and automation, and has been widely used in the diagnosis and treatment of many ophthalmic diseases. However, there is still some room for development in OCTA reconstruction using deep learning methods. For example, methods and bases based on convolutional neural networks require a large amount of labeled data to train the model, and have high requirements for the quality and quantity of data. The instability of GAN model training and the possible distortion of the generated image may occur. With the continuous development and improvement of deep learning technology, retinal vascular segmentation method based on deep learning will have wider application prospects.

The IPN-V2 model successfully overcomes the "checkerboard effect" by introducing attention mechanisms and residual blocks, improving the accuracy and robustness of segmentation. Since the IPN-V2 model is a graph-to-graph method, it needs to be trained with complete image information, which requires a large amount of labeled data to train the model. In practice, obtaining sufficient labeled data is a very time-consuming and difficult task, especially for some rare cases or diseases that require a high degree of expertise. This study has conducted an in-depth study on retinal vascular segmentation based on deep learning, and proposed a new method to improve the IPN-V2 model for retinal vascular segmentation, which has important theoretical and practical significance.

In theory, although the IPN-V2 model performs well in the retinal vascular segmentation algorithm, it still has some limitations, such as insufficient capture of detailed information and insufficient processing of edge information. Therefore, this paper improves the IPN-V2 model to improve the performance and stability of the IPN-V2 model. This improvement provides a theoretical basis for the further development of IPN-V2 model, and enriches the research results of IPN-V2 model and retinal vascular segmentation algorithm.

In practice, the study of retinal vascular segmentation based on deep learning has become a hot area of current research. Through the improvement and application of IPN-V2 model in practice, this paper provides a practical reference for the retinal vascular segmentation method based on deep learning. At the same time, the improved IPN-V2 model proposed in this paper has achieved good results in practice, which verifies the effectiveness and practicability of the model. Therefore, the practical research in this paper provides an important reference and reference value for the application and promotion of retinal vascular segmentation algorithm based on deep learning.

The main contribution of this paper is the following improvements to the IPN-V2 model:

1. The amount of parameters in the network and the resources consumed during calculation are reduced with deep separable convolution.
2. The introduction of attention mechanism can effectively improve the accuracy of network segmentation.

The rest of this article is organized as follows. In the second part, we reviewed the work related to retinal vascular segmentation from the segmentation method. The third part introduces our methodology, and then the results and analysis of the experiment are presented in the fourth section. The final part is the summary.

2   Related Work

2.1   Retinal Vascular Segmentation Method Based on Machine Learning

For retinal vascular segmentation tasks, the usual segmentation methods include Bayesian method, K-nearest neighbor method, support vector machine, random forest, Ada Boost, etc., all of which are typical supervised machine learning algorithms. For example, Wu Kui et al. (2016) consider that when the 2DGabor wavelet algorithm is used alone, the vascular morphology and structural information will be ignored, and the 2DGabor wavelet transform is no longer used alone, but a combined line detection operator is introduced into the algorithm, which first uses wavelet changes and detection operators to process the fundus image, and after processing, a six-dimensional pixel feature vector is obtained, and finally a Bayesian Gaussian mixture model is adopted to classify all pixels in the fundus image. The final segmentation result is superior to the 2DGabor wavelet algorithm alone [9]. In general, retinal vascular segmentation methods based on traditional supervised machine learning are based on the premise of feature extraction, and the quality of the extracted features determines the performance of subsequent classifier classification. However, determining which features to extract requires a certain amount of accumulated experience, which leads to segmentation results that are largely influenced by personal experience.

The principle of unsupervised machine learning is to self-summarize and summarize the knowledge contained in unlabeled data, and use this knowledge to categorize new things. Commonly used unsupervised machine learning methods include K-means clustering algorithm, EM algorithm (GMM-expectation maximization), FCM clustering algorithm, etc. For example, Roychowdhury et al. (2014) implemented a three-step retinal vascular segmentation algorithm: first acquire a binary image; for the extracted binary images, the EM algorithm is selected as the classifier to determine the category of the pixels inside. Finally, by flattening the main part of the blood vessel and the divided blood vessel pixels, the algorithm can reduce the dependence on the training data and achieve consistent segmentation accuracy on healthy pictures and pathological pictures [10]. Jia Hong et al. (2020) consider that the previous retinal vascular segmentation algorithm based on spatial FCM clustering only focuses on the clustering characteristics of pixels in feature space, but ignores the structural coherence information of the domain in pixel space, so the algorithm combines the local linear structure constraints of blood vessels in the pixel spatial domain to solve the above problems, compared with the feature-space FCM clustering algorithm, the retinal vascular segmentation results constructed in this way have better continuity and higher sensitivity to microscopic blood vessels [11]. In summary, the unsupervised machine learning method achieves the goal of training classification algorithms using no labeled data or less labeled data, and solves the problem of insufficient labeled data. However, since the data of unsupervised learning is not labeled, the evaluation of the effectiveness of such algorithms is still a problem to be solved.

2.2   Retinal Vascular Segmentation Method Based on Deep Learning

With the continuous improvement of deep learning technology, its application in computer vision is becoming more and more extensive. In the field of medical image processing, new deep learning models and auxiliary modules have been introduced one after another, continuously improving and improving the continuity and accuracy of retinal vascular segmentation.

The U-NET model was originally proposed to be used to segment the cells in the electron microscope image, which is composed of two parts: encoder and decoder, the shallow semantic information of the image is obtained in the coding stage, the high-level semantic information of the image is extracted in the decoding stage, and the image size is restored, and the proposed cascade structure can realize the fusion of the shallow feature map and the deeper feature map obtained in the coding stage, so as to obtain more comprehensive context information. Lu Huihui (2018) analyzed the network structure of U-net, built a U-net network model, and realized fundus image vascular segmentation based on convolutional neural network. Gao Dongxu (2019) proposed a U-net-based fringe noise removal framework [12], which is able to remove fringe noise in OCTA images, leaving a clean image. Dali Chen (2020) proposes a semi-supervised learning method for vascular segmentation with limited labeled data. In this method, they use an improved U-Net deep learning network to segment the vascular tree. On this basis, the authors implement the training dataset update strategy based on U-Net network. In order to analyze the segmentation performance of the semi-supervised learning method proposed in this paper, a large number of experiments are carried out. Experimental results show that the proposed method can avoid the problem of insufficient manual labeling and achieve satisfactory performance [13]. Sun Ying (2022) proposes a U-shaped network that fuses rough neurons and channel attention mechanisms. The network first introduces the concept of upper and lower approximation in rough set theory to design rough neurons. Then, based on rough neurons, the rough channel attention module is constructed, which adopts global maximum pooling and global average pooling to construct approximate neurons in the U-Net jump connection, and performs weighted summation between neurons to reasonably roughen the established channel dependency, which not only contains global information but also has local characteristics, which can effectively realize the accurate recalibration of extracted retinal vascular features. Then, residual connections are added to transfer features directly from the lower layer to the higher layer, which helps to solve the problem of network performance degradation and effectively extract richer retinal vascular features [14].

In summary, compared with traditional supervised machine learning methods, the deep learning-based method does not need to manually extract features, but the model independently learns the information contained in the data, avoiding the influence of human subjective factors. Compared with unsupervised machine learning methods, although deep learning requires more labeled data, it is more accurate than unsupervised machine learning methods. Although the emergence of deep learning technology has greatly helped to improve the segmentation of retinal blood vessels, the segmentation of tiny blood vessels is still a major challenge, and the continuity of segmented blood vessels is also an urgent problem to be solved. At the same time, there are relatively few studies on improving the sensitivity of vascular segmentation. All in all, there are still many areas for improvement in the task of automatic division of retinal blood vessels by deep learning methods.

2.3 Dataset

The retinal vascular image public dataset is a collection of public data integrated by some medical institutions or scientific research organizations after collecting and processing retinal vascular images [15]. These datasets consist of two parts, one of which is a color image of retinal blood vessels, and the other part is a corresponding image of retinal blood vessels manually labeled by experts [16]. In this paper, the OCTA-500 dataset is mainly used to train and test the proposed network model.

3 Retinal Vascular Segmentation Based on Attention Mechanism

Retinal vascular segmentation is difficult to accurately segment because the ends of the vessels are small and easily confused with the background. As a result, the blood vessels at the image border may be misdivided into backgrounds or blood vessels may be broken. The image projection network (IPN-V2) enables micro-resolution to visualize the three-dimensional structure of retinal blood vessels, which can realize 3D-2D RV segmentation and FAZ segmentation, and solve the problem of weak recognition ability and "checkerboard effect" in the horizontal direction. In order to further improve the segmentation accuracy of retinal blood vessels, this paper proposes a retinal vascular segmentation algorithm based on improved IPN-V2, which optimizes the IPN-V2 network structure and improves the block processing effect of raw data images.

3.1 IPN-V2-Based Retinal Vascular Segmentation

Retinal vascular density is used to diagnose the health of the retinal vascular system, which provides a basis for clinical diagnosis of retinal diseases and significantly improves the decision-making efficiency of doctors. Both OCT and OCTA can provide 3D data, but most retinal metrics, such as blood vessel density and FAZ area, are quantified on projection maps rather than in 3D space. Moreover, the failure of layer segmentation makes the index difficult to quantify, which has become a bottleneck in the field of retinal disease analysis. To this end, Ming chao Li (2020) proposes an image projection network (IPN), a novel end-to-end architecture that enables 3D to 2D image segmentation in optical coherence tomography angiography (OCTA) images. IPN uses the original 3D volume as input instead of a projection map, avoiding the use of retinal layer segmentation, thus overcoming the negative effects of false layer segmentation. In addition, using volume information can help the network better distinguish similar areas in the projection map, such as non-perfusion areas and FAZ regions. However, IPN still has some limitations. For example, the lack of downsampling in the horizontal direction makes the IPN lack a wide range of receptive fields in the horizontal plane, which leads to weak recognition in the horizontal direction. In addition, because 3D networks are computationally intensive, raw data needs to be cut into small pieces when computing resources are limited. In the stitching process of the segmentation results, the segmentation results have a "checkerboard effect".

To this end, Mingchao Li (2020) further proposed image projection network-V2 (IPN-V2) [17]. IPN-V2 introduces planar perceptrons to enhance perceptron capabilities in the horizontal direction. At the same time, in order to overcome the "checkerboard effect" during splicing, a global retraining process, called IPN-V2+, is added to IPN-V2, which stitches the 2D feature map output by the network and then trains a global network. This process not only overcomes the "checkerboard effect", but also provides global information that compensates for the limitations of patch training. The IPN-V2 network architecture is shown in Fig. 1.

IPN-V2 expands the IPN and adds a flat fluoroscope, which strengthens the perspective capability in the lateral direction. At the same time, a global retraining process was introduced, overcoming the "checkerboard effect". Experimental results show that

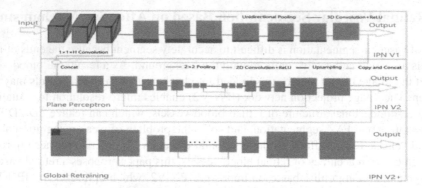

Fig. 1. IPN-V2 network architecture

IPN-V2 has better performance than IPN and other deep learning methods in segmentation tasks. However, although IPN-V2 provides global information and contains complete image information every time training, this graph-to-graph method requires a large amount of image data and label information, and the dataset of medical images, especially the dataset of fundus images, is often relatively small, and at the same time, fundus images often contain a large number of vascular modalities, if the complete image is used every time training, it is not conducive to the convergence of the network, but also occupies a lot of memory space. For the image, the original image data is chunked, and the problem is to select different tiling schemes considering the specific characteristics of the vascular map. The segmentation method based on image blocks can not only enhance the data by chunking, increase the data set, but also reduce the memory occupation by reducing the number of vascular modalities. Therefore, in the task of retinal vascular segmentation, the segmentation method based on image blocks is adopted to improve the retinal vascular segmentation algorithm based on IPN-V2.

3.2   Attention Mechanism

The Attention Mechanism has been widely used in various research fields of deep learning. The attention mechanism allows neural networks to reallocate computing resources and focus on key areas to highlight important local information. The attention mechanism often used in the field of computer vision mainly includes channel attention mechanism and spatial attention mechanism.

Channel Attention Mechanism
Convolutional neural networks can rely on convolution operations and use local receptive field ideas to fuse spatial domain information with channel domain information for feature extraction [18]. The Channel Attention (CA) mechanism, as the name implies, strengthens the network model from the channel dimension to improve its performance. In 2017, SENet [19], which used the channel attention mechanism, won first place in the ILSVRC 2017 classification task. For convolutional neural networks, the most important core computation is the convolution operation, through which new features are learned from the input feature map. Therefore, for convolutional neural networks, the process

of learning features is to fuse the features of local regions, which can be divided into spatial features and channel features.

The innovation of SENet is to focus on the relationship between different channels, hoping to improve the branching structure of the model, so that the network model can learn the importance of different channels during the training process. SENet presents a channel attention module SE, which hopes to enhance the performance of the network model from the channel dimension. In order to obtain the importance of the feature map, the SE module uses the Squeeze operation to process the original multi-channel feature map, compress it into a one-dimensional vector according to each channel, and also learn the weight features of each channel, and then strengthen the original feature map with the learned feature vector. The SE structure is essentially similar to the Inception structure, except that the Inception structure adopted no longer focuses on the integration of features at different scales, but more on the importance between different channels. Therefore, the SE module mainly considers the dependence of different channels of neural network on feature selection in feature selection, and improves the segmentation accuracy through the strengthening of channel features.

Spatial Attention Mechanisms
The Spatial Attention mechanism focuses attention on an important part of the spatial dimension, so that the network model can simultaneously suppress the expression of other location information, so as to achieve the purpose of improving the segmentation results. Due to the complex features of retinal vascular images and the existence of noise problems, false positive predictions are difficult to reduce. Different from channel attention, the spatial attention mechanism can enhance the local feature extraction ability of the network model to a certain extent.

The CBAM module [20] is proposed by Woo et al., similar to the channel attention SE module proposed by Hu et al., and is a simple channel spatial attention module suitable for convolutional neural networks. Although the SE module is effective in enhancing model performance, the location information in the feature map is generally ignored, which is critical for generating spatially selective feature maps. CBAM extracts and combines important information in space and channel, and proposes that given intermediate feature mapping, two independent dimensions of attention mapping are deduced along the channel and space, and then the attention map is multiplied by the input feature map to achieve adaptive feature refinement. CBAM module is also suitable for segmentation tasks, the module can adaptively refine the mapping of feature maps, pay attention to important feature information and suppress unimportant feature information, improve segmentation performance, its structure is shown in Fig. 2:

The CBAM module is a lightweight general-purpose module that combines two attention mechanisms and can be added behind the convolutional layer of any network [21]. The specific calculation process of this module is shown in the following formula:

$$F' = M_c(F) \otimes F \tag{1}$$

$$F'' = M_s(F') \otimes F' \tag{2}$$

$$M_c(F) = \sigma(MLP(AvgPool(F)) + MLP(MaxPool(F))) \tag{3}$$

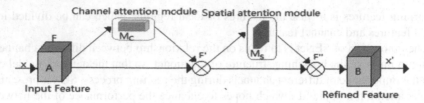

Fig. 2. CBAM block structure diagram

$$\mathbf{M}_s(F) = \sigma\left(f^{7\times7}([\mathrm{AvgPool}(F); \mathrm{MaxPool}(F)])\right) \tag{4}$$

where F represents the input of feature Figure (C × H × W), M_c is a channel attention map of one-dimensional (C × 1 × 1), M_s is a spatial attention map of 2D (1 × H × W), ⊗ indicates multiplication operation, F is the intermediate output (C × H × W), F is the final output (C × H × W), MLP is a multilayer perceptron, AvgPool is an average pooling operation, and MaxPool is a maximum pooling operation, σ is the sigmoid activation function, $f^{7\times7}$ is a convolution operation with a convolution kernel size of 7 × 7, [;] is the splicing operation of the channel dimension.

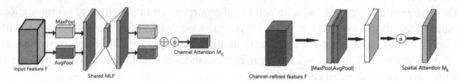

Fig. 3. Channel attention block   **Fig. 4.** Spatial attention block

Figure 3 is the operation process of the channel attention submodule, which has one more global maximum pooling than the SE module, and the pooling operation itself is to extract high-level features, and different pooling means that the extracted high-level features are richer. Firstly, the average pooling and maximum pooling operations are used to aggregate the spatial information of a feature map to produce two spatial context descriptors: AvgPool(F) and MaxPool(F), which represent the features after average pooling and the features after maximum pooling, respectively. Then, both descriptors are fed forward into a network shared by both to produce a channel attention map. There are hidden layers of multi-layer sensing mechanisms into that shared network. After each spatial context descriptor is processed by the shared network, Mc(F) is obtained by using bitwise addition fusion output feature vector activated by sigmoid, and it is multiplied by the original input feature map to generate channel attention feature F' as the output of the channel attention submodule.

Figure 4 shows the operation process of the spatial attention submodule. The submodule takes the output feature map of the channel attention submodule as input, first completes the channel-based global maximum pooling and global average pooling operations, and then realizes the splicing of the two results according to the channel, merges into the feature map of channel number 2, and then becomes 1 channel through the convolution kernel size 7 × 7 standard convolutional layer. Then, the spatial attention feature is generated by sigmoid activation, and finally the feature is multiplied by the input feature of the spatial attention submodule, and the generated feature Figure F" is used as the output of the spatial attention submodule, which is also the final output of the CBAM module.

3.3   Retinal Vascular Segmentation Model Based on ASR-IPN-V2

IPN and IPN-V2 are used for effective feature selection and dimensionality reduction to achieve OCTA vascular segmentation of end-to-end structures with 3D output to 2D. However, IPN and its improvements increase the complexity of the model while also adding additional computation, which consumes higher computer resources and relatively long segmentation time. In view of the above problems, this paper introduces the attention mechanism, improves the retinal vascular segmentation algorithm based on IPN-V2, and proposes a retinal vascular segmentation algorithm based on ASR-IPN-V2. On the one hand, in each sampling layer, the deep separable convolution is used instead of the conventional convolution for feature learning while reducing the amount of parameters. On the other hand, a lightweight and efficient convolutional block attention-weighted module is added to obtain the importance of channel information and spatial information in the feature map by learning, and the weight of each feature map is adaptively adjusted according to the learned importance to complete the recalibration of the feature map. The retinal vascular segmentation algorithm based on ASR-IPN-V2 pays more attention to subtle segmentation, improves the accuracy of segmentation, and occupies less computing resources.

Depth Separable Convolution
In IPN and IPN-V2, PLM consists of three 3D convolutional layers and a unidirectional pooling layer. The convolutional layer is used to extract image features, and the unidirectional pooling layer is used to select valid features along the projection direction. At the end of the network, convolutional layers are used to reduce the number of channels to aggregate the 2D planar information obtained by the PLM module. The main role of convolution is feature extraction. A regular convolution operation is a joint mapping that implements channel and spatial dependencies. Depthwise separable convolutions [22] are a method of convolution proposed by Chollet et al. Deep separable convolution operation is the process of decomposing a conventional convolution operation into a deep convolution plus a point-by-point convolution, so that it performs spatial convolution while keeping channels separated, and then convolutes in the direction of depth. Compared with conventional convolution operations, deep separable convolution operations have the advantages of reducing computational complexity and reducing the number of parameters. The deeply separable convolutional structure is shown in Fig. 5:

Compared with conventional convolution operations, deep separable convolution broadens the width of the network, while greatly reducing the number of parameters in the network and reducing the resources consumed during calculation. Existing experiments have verified that deep separable convolution can reduce the number of parameters while ensuring task accuracy. Since the OCTA-500 segmentation dataset has the problem of small sample size, the deep separable convolution operation is compared with the conventional convolution operation, which will inevitably reduce the number of network

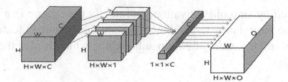

Fig. 5. Depth separable convolutional structure diagram

parameters, reduce the computational complexity, and achieve better learning results. Therefore, this paper proposes to replace the conventional convolution operation in each sampling layer of IPN-V2 with a deep separable convolution operation, and replace the two conventional convolution operations used for feature extraction in each layer with a deep separable convolutional block.

Convolutional Block Attention Mechanism

The CBAM module can achieve the parameter weights that are conducive to model training on the enlarged feature map at the minimum computational cost, reduce the weights of parameters that are unfavorable to the model, extract spatial and channel important information and combine them [23]. Due to the widespread phenomenon of small vascular ends and easy to be confused by the background in the images of OCTA-500 retinal blood vessels, some areas have missing vascular ends and small vascular parts are mistakenly divided into backgrounds when segmentation is used with IPN-V2. Therefore, this paper adds a CBAM module after each depth separable convolutional block (Previousconvblock) and before the next convolution block (Nextconvblock) to continue to learn the spatial information and channel information of the feature map and improve the accuracy of network segmentation. A schematic diagram of inserting a CBAM module into two adjacent convolutional blocks is shown in Fig. 6 below:

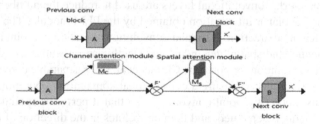

Fig. 6. CBAM inserted into two adjacent convolutional blocks

The model uses deep separable convolution instead of regular convolution to reduce the number of parameters and computational complexity. At the same time, a lightweight and efficient convolutional block attention-weighted module is added, which can learn the importance of channel information and spatial information in the feature map, so as to better calibrate the feature map. Eventually, the model can complete the task of segmenting retinal blood vessels.

The final retinal vascular segmentation model of ASR-IPN-V2 is shown in Fig. 7:

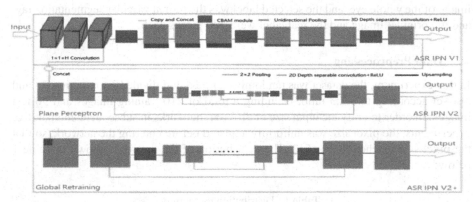

Fig. 7. ASR-IPN-V2 network architecture

4   Experiments and Discussion

The proposed methods and baselines are all implemented with PyTorch on 1 NVIDIA GeForce RTX 3090 GPU. The batch size is set as 4, the learning rate is 5×10^{-4}, epochs is 300, Adam is used as the optimizer.

4.1   Experimental Datasets

The dataset used in this experiment is the 20th version of the retinal vascular dataset OCTA-500 published by Professor Chen Qiang and his team on IEEE-Data Port, which is currently the largest OCTA image dataset. The OCTA-500 dataset contains optical coherence tomography angiography data from 500 individuals. Each eye contains one OCTA image, a total of 1,000 OCTA images, including information such as age, gender, and ophthalmic history, which can be used to study the impact of these factors on ophthalmic diseases. In addition to being divided into two subsets, OCTA_6M and OCTA_3M by field of view, the OCTA-500 dataset can also be classified based on factors such as data source, image quality, and more. Among them, OCTA_6M dataset includes OCTA images with a 6x6mm field of view, which is suitable for studying changes in blood flow in large areas of retina, such as diabetic retinopathy, venous obstructive retinopathy and other diseases. The OCTA_3M dataset includes OCTA images with a 3x3mm field of view, which is suitable for studying small local retinal blood flow changes, such as retinal aneurysm, prominent vitreoretinopathy and other diseases. In addition, the OCTA-500 dataset is categorized according to the source of the data, including multi-center datasets and single-center datasets. The multi-center dataset includes data from different medical institutions, covering different eye disease types and different patient populations, with high representativeness and universality. The single-center dataset, on the other hand, only includes data from a single medical institution, and the data source is relatively single. In this experiment, only the dataset used for segmentation in the OCTA_6M subset was selected, in which the original image selected was the OCTA image of the whole eye, and the selected label was the retinal vascular segmentation tag, and the original image and the real label were 300 pieces each.

4.2　Data Preprocessing

In this experiment, the dataset was randomly sampled and divided into training set and test set according to a 7:3 ratio, including a total of 210 training images and 90 test images. In order to unify the input size of different networks in subsequent comparative experiments, the pixel size was uniformly adjusted before entering the network, so that the pixel size reached 512×512. The distribution of the dataset is shown in Table 1 below:

Table 1. Distribution of datasets

Data set	Training set	Test set
Number of samples	210	90
Sample dimension	512 * 512 * 3	512 * 512 * 3

In the training process, the small amount of data is one of the main reasons for model underfitting. The relative scarcity of OCTA images results in a small amount of data in the OCTA-500 retinal vascular segmentation dataset. Therefore, in order to reduce the impact of underfitting, this paper adopts the method of random cropping, flipping, scaling, and panning of the input image to enhance the online data of the input image, making the data richer and more diverse.

4.3　Analysis of Experimental Results

In order to verify the rationality of various improvement measures of the algorithm in this paper, the method of ablation experiment is adopted to verify the OCTA-500 dataset. The results are shown in Table 2.

Table 2. Ablation test results

Model	Acc(%)	Sn(%)	Sp(%)	F1(%)
U-Net	94.36	72.4	94.3	76.2
IPN	95.3	74.8	**95.1**	80.3
IPN-V2	96.5	78.3	93.6	82.0
IPN-V2+	96.7	78.4	93.5	82.1
Ours	**96.9**	**80.1**	93.2	**82.5**

4.4 Discussion

It can be seen from Table 2 that IPN-V2 has a certain improvement in the comprehensive performance of IPN, ACC has increased to 0.965, Sn and F1 values have also increased relatively little, and Sp values have decreased, because the global retraining process has improved the performance of the network, but it will also increase a large number of parameters to a certain extent, resulting in overfitting. Compared with IPN and IPN-V2, the ASR-IPN-V2 algorithm has better performance in various indicators, although the performance in Sp is slightly worse, but compared with IPN and IPN-V2, the proposed algorithm has a great improvement in other indicators. Overall, the ASR-IPN-V2 algorithm proposed in this paper has excellent performance on the OCTA-500 dataset.

5 Conclusion

Retinal vascular segmentation based on deep learning has great practical significance in the field of medical image processing, which can be used for disease monitoring and prediction, through the analysis and processing of fundus images, it can timely detect and monitor changes in diseases, provide more accurate data support for the treatment and management of diseases, help doctors better analyze and identify pathological features in fundus images, and provide more accurate reference for disease diagnosis and treatment. Combined with the current research status and development trend of retinal vascular segmentation based on deep learning, this paper improves the retinal vascular segmentation based on IPN-V2 according to the IPN-V2 network structure, and the main conclusions are as follows:

Retinal vascular segmentation algorithm based on ASR-IPN-V2. In the IPN-V2-based retinal vascular segmentation model, the attention mechanism is introduced to improve the IPN-V2-based retinal vascular segmentation algorithm. The retinal vascular segmentation algorithm based on ASR-IPN-V2 uses deep separable convolution instead of conventional convolution, which can greatly reduce the amount of network parameters, improve the computational efficiency of the network, and maintain good segmentation effect. Adding the CBAM module after each deep separable convolutional block can further improve the segmentation accuracy of the network, because the CBAM module can learn the spatial information and channel information of the feature map, so as to better capture the semantic information of the image.

Through experimental analysis, it is found that compared with the IPN model and IPN-V2 model, the ASR-IPN-V2 model proposed in this paper has significantly improved the efficiency of retinal vascular segmentation, which has important practical significance for the early diagnosis, treatment and evaluation of ophthalmic diseases. At the same time, the research ideas and methods of this paper also provide reference for other studies of retinal vascular segmentation based on deep learning.

References

1. Xu, W.J.: Application of deep learning in the field of computer vision. Electron. Technol. **5**, 20–21 (2021)

2. Sun, Y.: Application analysis of deep learning in computer vision analysis. China New Commun. **23**, 169–171 (2018)
3. Wang, J.P.: Development analysis of natural language processing technology based on deep learning. China Secur. **12**, 40–43 (2022)
4. Ye, F.: Research on the application of deep learning in natural language processing NLP. Inf. Record. Mater. **11**, 148–149 (2021)
5. Yoav, G., Che, W.X., Guo, J., Zhang, W., Liu, M.: Natural language processing based on deep learning. J. Chin. Inf. Technol. **8**, 145 (2021)
6. Guo, B.B., Yang, Z.Y., Zhang, Z.X., Zhang, J.: Research on the application of deep learning technology in assisted decision-making. Sci. Technol. Innov. Appl. **22**, 175–176 (2020)
7. Fang, Y., Ma, L.Z.: Deep learning technology and its application. Comput. Knowl. Technol. **5**, 190–193 (2020)
8. Wang, Y., Zhu, J., Song, Q.: Retinal vascular image segmentation based on improved R2U-Net network. Radio Eng. **5**, 814–823 (2022)
9. Wu, K., Cai, D.M., Jia, P., et al.: Retinal vascular segmentation based on 2DGabor wavelet and combination line detection operator. Sci. Technol. Eng. **16**(12), 106–112 (2016)
10. Roychowdhury, S., Koozekanani, D.D., Parhi, K.K.: Blood vessel segmentation of fundus images by major vessel extraction and subimage classification. IEEE J. Biomed. Health Inform. **19**(3), 1118–1128 (2014)
11. Jia, H., Zheng, C.J., Li, C.B., et al.: FCM clustering retinal vascular segmentation based on local line structure constraints. Acta Opt. Sin. **40**(9), 40–49 (2020)
12. Gao, D.X., Celik, N., Wu, X.Y., Williams, B.M., Stylianides, A., Zheng, Y.: A novel deep learning based OCTA de-striping method. In: Zheng, Y., Williams, B.M., Chen, K. (eds.) MIUA 2019. CCIS, vol. 1065, pp. 189–197. Springer, Cham (2020). https://doi.org/10.1007/978-3-030-39343-4_16
13. Chen, D., Ao, Y.Y., Liu, S.X.: Semi-supervised learning method of u-net deep learning network for blood vessel segmentation in retinal images. Symmetry **12**(7), 1067 (2020). https://doi.org/10.3390/sym12071067
14. Sun, Y., Ding, W.P., Huang, J.H., Ju, H.R., Li, M., Geng, Y.: RCAR-UNet: retinal vascular segmentation network based on rough attention mechanism. Comput. Res. Dev. 1–15 (2022)
15. Wang, C.Y., Guan, Z.Y., Wu, X., Yao, C.: Retinal vascular image segmentation algorithm based on multi-directional filtering. Prog. Laser Optoelectron. **8**, 463–469 (2022)
16. Zhang, L.J., Mei, C., Li, C.R., Zhang, R.: Retinal vascular image segmentation based on RAU-net. Infrared Technol. **12**, 1222–1227 (2021)
17. Li, M., Zhang, Y., Ji, Z., et al.: IPN-V2 and OCTA-500: Methodology and Dataset for Retinal Image Segmentation (2020)
18. Zhang, J., Zhang, L.H.: Text generation image method based on conditional enhancement and attention mechanism. J. Test. Technol. **2**, 112–119 (2023)
19. Hu, J., Li, S., Albanie, S., Sun, G., Wu, E.: Squeeze-and-Excitation Networks. arXiv preprint arXiv:1709.01507 (2017)
20. Woo, S.Y., Park, J.C., Lee, J.-Y., In, S.K.: CBAM: Convolutional Block Attention Module. arXiv preprint arXiv:1807.06521 (2018)
21. Jiang, Y., Liu, W.H., Liang, J.: Retinal vascular segmentation network of joint attention and transformer. Comput. Eng. Sci. **11**, 2037–2047 (2022)
22. Nithin Rao, K., Park, T., Boris, G.: TitaNet: Neural Model for Speaker Representation with 1D Depth-Wise Separable Convolutions and Global Context. arXiv preprint arXiv:2110.04410 (2021)
23. Jiang, L., Li, S., Cao, J., Sun, S., Feng, R., Zou, H.: Retinal vascular segmentation based on multi-scale high-order attention mechanism. Comput. Syst. Appl. **10**, 368–374 (2022)

SW-YOLO: Improved YOLOv5s Algorithm for Blood Cell Detection

Yonglin Wu[1], Yinfeng Fang[2], Dongxu Gao[3], Hongwei Gao[1], and Zhaojie Ju[3](✉)

[1] School of Automation and Electrical Engineering, Shenyang Ligong University,
Shenyang 110158, China
ghw1978@sohu.com
[2] School of Telecommunication Engineering, Hangzhou Dianzi University, Hangzhou 310000,
China
yinfeng.fang@hdu.eud.cn
[3] School of Computing, University of Portsmouth, Portsmouth PO13HE, UK
{dongxu.gao,Zhaojie.Ju}@port.ac.uk

Abstract. This paper proposes an improved target detection algorithm SW-YOLO based on the YOLOv5s framework to solve the problems of low detection accuracy, wrong detection and missed detection in blood cell detection tasks. To begin with, the end of the backbone network is fused with Swin Transformer to improve network feature extraction. Next, since blood cells are mostly small and medium-sized targets, resulting in poor detection of large cells, the network layer that identifies large cells is removed. In addition, the normal convolution in the PANet network is replaced with depth-separable convolution during the feature fusion process to ensure the accuracy and real-time detection while having better detection results for small targets. At last, the loss function of the prediction layer uses EIOU to solve the positive and negative sample imbalance problem of CIOU. Compared with existing target detection algorithms such as Faster-RCNN, YOLOv4 and YOLOv5s, SW-YOLO improves to 99.5%, 95.3% and 93.3% mAP on the blood cell dataset BCCD for white blood cells, red blood cells and platelets respectively. The experimental results are eximious and the algorithm is highly practical for blood cell detection.

Keywords: Blood Cells Testing · Swin Transformer · PAN · EIOU

1 Introduction

Blood cell testing is a technique that analyses the cellular components of blood by means of specialist instruments. In medicine, the cells circulating in the blood are divided into three categories: white blood cells, red blood cells and platelets [1]. When the results of these three types of cell count are abnormally high or low, the body may already be suffering from certain diseases. Accurate and efficient identification of these three types of cells can provide an overview of a patient's overall health status [1].

Previously, blood cell testing mainly used traditional image processing techniques, most classically manual photography and staining, followed by manual observation

© The Author(s), under exclusive license to Springer Nature Singapore Pte Ltd. 2023
H. Yang et al. (Eds.): ICIRA 2023, LNAI 14269, pp. 161–172, 2023.
https://doi.org/10.1007/978-981-99-6489-5_13

and classification with microscope [3], which required the testers to have extensive basic knowledge of cell morphology and to be skilled in morphological observation and discrimination through continuous study and repeated practice.

In recent years, as many efficient deep learning-based target detection algorithms have been proposed, they have also been widely applied to blood cell detection tasks. Current deep learning-based target detection algorithms can be broadly classified into two main categories. Two-stage algorithms, represented by Faster R-CNN [4], extract regions of interest (ROI) through a region proposal network (RPN) and then classify the regions of interest. This type of algorithm usually has high detection accuracy, but the detection speed is slow. Single-stage algorithms, represented by the SSD [5], RetinaNet [6] and YOLO [7, 8] series, treat localisation and classification as a regression problem and achieve end-to-end detection. This class of algorithms is fast in detection, but low in detection accuracy. From Fig. 1, we can see that the detection results with Faster R-CNN, SSD, and YOLO algorithms do have the problem of wrong detection and missed detection.

Fig. 1. Comparison of blood cells in target detection algorithms

This paper introduces SW-YOLO small target detection algorithm to address the issues of inadequate detection accuracy, incorrect detection and missed detection which are common in target detection algorithms for blood cell detection tasks. The precision of small-target blood cell identification is enhanced while maintaining real-time. This paper focuses on the following tasks:

(1) Enhancing feature extraction for small targets by connecting the end of the backbone network to the Swin Transformer [9].
(2) By removing the large target detection layer, the number of parameters in the network can be reduced, while improving detection performance.
(3) Replacing the normal convolution in the PANet network with depth-separable convolution, the detection accuracy and real-time performance are guaranteed while the detection of small targets is more effective.
(4) Replacing the loss function CIOU with the loss function EIOU [10] can solve the problem of positive and negative sample imbalance.

2   Related Work

2.1   YOLOv5s Model

YOLOv5 is divided into four models: s, m, l and x by varying the depth and width of the model to obtain different numbers of convolution kernels [11], thus choosing the appropriate model according to one's needs. To facilitate the detection of small and medium-sized models such as blood cells, YOLOv5s, which has the smallest model, is used as the base framework in this paper. As shown in Fig. 2, the network structure is divided into four main parts: input, backbone, neck and prediction.

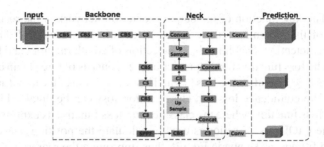

Fig. 2. YOLOv5s network architecture

Input. The role of the input is to scale, colour change and data enhancement of the input image. The processed image on the input side then enters the backbone network for feature information extraction. The current backbone networks in the field of target detection are generally ResNet [12], AmoebaNet [13], Xception [14] and other networks.

Backbone. The backbone network in YOLOv5s is mainly composed of the CBS module, C3 module and SPPF modules, as shown in Fig. 3(a). The CBS is to speed up the inference of the model, the C3 module makes full use of the geometric information and resolution of the shallow features, the perceptual field and semantic information of the deep features. The SPPF module is able to convert feature maps into fixed size feature vectors regardless of the size of the input feature map, and it serves to improve the speed of generating candidate frames and reduce overfitting.

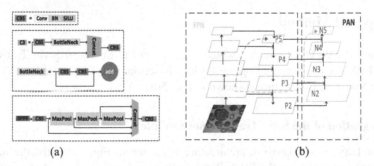

(a)   (b)

Fig. 3. (a) Represents the main modules of YOLOv5s backbone network, (b) Representing the structure of the neck network

Neck. After the feature map is extracted, it enters the neck network, which is composed of FPN [15] (feature pyramid network) and PANet [16] (path aggregation network). The network structure is shown in Fig. 3(b). The semantic features of the feature map are first passed from the top down by the FPN layer, and then the localization features are passed from the bottom up by the PANet, so that the shallow semantic features and the deep localization features can be fused and the feature fusion capability of the model can be improved.

Prediction. The key function of the output prediction network is the recognition and classification of the incoming feature maps. YOLOv5s uses a total of three different sizes for image detection, enabling object detection of small, medium and large targets respectively. The loss function for the prediction part consists of three main components: confidence loss L_{obj}, classification loss L_{cls} and loss of position of the target and predicted frames L_{box}. The confidence loss and classification loss can be obtained by using the cross-entropy loss function, where the classification loss function is expressed as shown in Eq. (1). The CIOU loss function is used to calculate the position loss of the target and prediction frames, as shown in Eq. (2), thus improving the regression speed of the prediction frame and the convergence speed of the network, and solving the bounding box overlap problem of YOLOv4. The total loss function is the sum of the three components of confidence loss, classification loss and position loss of the target and prediction frames. The expression is shown in Eq. (3).

$$L_{cls}(p, y) = -\frac{1}{N} \sum_{i=1}^{N} [y \log p + (1 - y)\log(1 - p)] \tag{1}$$

$$\begin{cases} L_{obj} = 1 - IoU + \frac{\rho^2(b, b^{gt})}{c^2} + \alpha v \\ v = \frac{4}{\pi^2}\left(\arctan\frac{w^{gt}}{h^{gt}} - \arctan\frac{w}{h}\right) \\ \alpha = \frac{v}{1-IoU(b, b^{gt})+v} \end{cases} \tag{2}$$

$$L_{total} = L_{obj} + L_{cls} + L_{box} \tag{3}$$

3 Proposed Method

The proposed SW-YOLO model, which focuses on the fusion of Swin Transformer, improved PANet structure and optimised loss function, is mainly based on YOLOv5s [11]. The SW-YOLO structure is shown in Fig. 5(a).

3.1 Integration of the Swin Transformer module

The Swin Transformer network architecture is shown in Fig. 4. Firstly, the input [H, W, 3] image is passed into the Patch Partition layer, where every 4 × 4 adjacent pixels are chunked into a patch and expanded along the channel direction, making the image dimension into [H/4, W/4, 48], and then the channel data of each pixel is linearly transformed through the Linear Merging layer, making the image dimension becomes [H/4, W/4, C], while each sample is normalised in the feature dimension.

The Swin Transformer employs a window-based MSA module in lieu of the standard Multi-head self-attention module (MSA) in the conventional Transformer module, a window-based MSA is composed of a combination of window multi-head self-attention layers (W-MSA) and sliding window multi-head self-attention layers (SW-MSA). This technique splits the input image into multiple segments that do not overlap and limits the attention computation to each separate window. The backbone network with two Swin Transformer modules in the first, second and fourth stages and six Swin Transformer modules in the third stage, with the feature maps of the second, third, fourth and fourth stages being fused together. The output feature maps are extracted for 3 distinct grid sizes. This technology is capable of identifying targets of varying sizes within blood cells.

YOLOv5s can leverage Swin Transformer as its core network to gain more accurate image feature extraction.

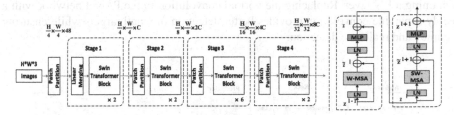

Fig. 4. Swin Transformer Network Architecture

3.2 Improved the PANet Network Architecture

Since the PANet network outputs predictions at three different scales for small, medium and large targets through $8\times$, $16\times$ and $32\times$ down-sampling respectively. In the BCCD dataset, for example, the image size is 1024×1024. If the image size is 640×640, the output prediction layer is 80×80, 40×40 and 20×20 after $8\times$, $16\times$ and $32\times$ down-sampling respectively. However, in the BCCD dataset, the target size is between 8×9 and 285×442, and small and medium-sized cells account for 95% of the total blood cells. When the image is down-sampled by 32 times, the target size of blood cells smaller than 102×102 in the image will be compressed into one pixel, resulting in low efficiency of the network in detecting small-sized cells. In order to reduce the number of network model parameters while improving the efficiency of target detection, this paper does not use the 32-fold down-sampling correlation network layer for network redundancy, thus improving the efficiency of detection of small-sized cells.

3.3 Improved Convolutional Structures in PAN

The top diagram in Fig. 5(b) is a normal Conv-BN-SiLu module, where SiLu is the activation function. The lower diagram in Fig. 5(b) is an over-parameterised schematic, which uses M identical parallel branches and then sums the outputs of all branches before feeding them into the activation function. Over-parameterisation methods can increase the complexity of the model at training time while maintaining the same inference structure.

The depth-separable convolution is a method of over-parameterisation. As shown in Fig. 5(c), it consists of two parts, the upper part based on Depthwise Convolution and the lower part on Pointwise Convolution. Depthwise Convolution is essentially a grouped convolution with the same number of groups g as the input channels. Pointwise Convolution, on the other hand, is a 1 × 1 convolution. The depth convolution module in the figure consists of three branches. The leftmost branch is a 1 × 1 convolution, the middle branch is an over-parameterised 3 × 3 convolution, i.e. k 3 × 3 convolutions, and the right-hand part is a jump connection containing the BN layer. Here both the 1 × 1 convolution and the 3 × 3 convolution are deep convolutions (the number of groupings g is equal to the number of input channels). The dot-convolution module in the figure consists of two branches. The left branch is an over-parameterised 1 × 1 convolution, consisting of k 1 × 1 convolutions. The right branch is a jump connection containing a BN layer. Replacing the normal convolution in the PANet network with a deeply separable convolution provides better detection of small targets while ensuring accuracy and real-time detection.

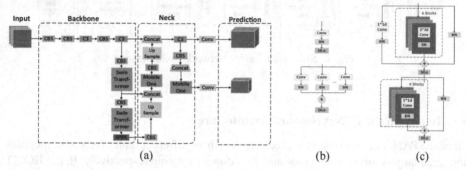

Fig. 5. (a) Representing the SW-YOLO structure, (b) Representing over-parameterised structures, (c) Representing depth-separable convolutional structure

3.4 Improved IOU Loss Function

As can be seen from the classification loss function in Eq. (1), when the prediction probability value (p ≥ 0.5) is larger, the loss value of positive samples is smaller than that of negative samples, making it difficult for positive samples to affect the training parameters, thus affecting the detection accuracy. In order to solve the above problem, this paper adopts EIOU based on the cross-entropy loss function, the expression is shown in Eq. (4), the penalty term of EIOU is based on the penalty term of CIOU to split the influence factor of aspect ratio to calculate the length and width of target frame and anchor frame respectively, the loss function contains three parts: overlap loss, centre distance loss, width and height loss. The first two parts continue the approach in CIOU, but the width-height loss directly minimises the difference between the width and height of the target and anchor boxes, allowing for faster convergence. The regression accuracy is higher and can solve the positive and negative sample imbalance problem. Therefore,

EIOU Loss is chosen to replace CIOU Loss in this paper.

$$L_{EIOU} = L_{IOU} + L_{dis} + L_{asp} = 1 - IOU + \frac{\rho^2(b, b^{gt})}{c^2} + \frac{\rho^2(w, w^{gt})}{c_w^2} + \frac{\rho^2(h, h^{gt})}{c_h^2}$$

(4)

4 Experiments

4.1 Dataset

In this paper, we use the BCCD public dataset [17], which is a small-scale dataset of relatively homogeneous blood shapes for cell detection with 768 train images and 106 test images, generated by annotating the images in the dataset. The BCCD dataset contains a small number of white blood cells (WBC), platelets and a large number of red blood cells (RBC).

4.2 Experimental Configuration

The experimental configuration: Ubuntu 9.4.0 as the operating system, Pytorch 1.7.1 as the deep learning framework, E-2136 as the CPU, 16 GB as the RAM, and Quadro P5000 as the GPU with 16 G of video memory.

The details regarding the training parameters for this paper are provided in Table 1.

Table 1. Training parameter settings for the BCCD dataset

Parameter Name	Parameter values	Parameter Name	Parameter values
Batch size	16	Epoch	133
Learning rate	0.01	Momentum	0.937
Box loss	0.05	Cls loss	0.5
Anchors	(10,13), (16,30), (33,23), (30,61), (62,45), (59,119)	Obj loss	1.0

4.3 Evaluation Indicators

To verify the effectiveness of the proposed SW-YOLO blood cell detection algorithm, the SW-YOLO algorithm in this paper is compared with Faster R-CNN, YOLOv3, YOLOv4 and YOLOv5 networks to evaluate the algorithm detection performance in terms of experimental detection accuracy (Precision), recall and mean average precision (mAP). This is shown in Eqs. (5)–(7).

$$Precision = \frac{TP}{TP + FP}$$

(5)

$$\text{Recall} = \frac{TP}{TP + FN} \qquad (6)$$

$$mAP = \frac{1}{N} \int_0^1 P_i(R)dR \qquad (7)$$

TP denotes the number of correctly identified blood cell classes, FP denotes the number of incorrectly identified blood cell classes, FN denotes the number of incorrectly identified non-blood cell classes, and TN denotes the number of correctly identified non-blood cell classes. Therefore, Precision is the probability of correctly predicting blood cell classes as a percentage of predicted blood cell classes, and Recall is the probability of correctly predicting blood cell classes as a percentage of true blood cell classes. N in Eq. (7) represents the number of total blood cell categories, so mAP is the mean value of the average accuracy of all categories.

4.4 Results

The P-R curves of the SW-YOLO algorithm for the three classes of blood cells are shown in Fig. 6(a), and the mAP values for these classes of blood cells can be obtained by calculating the area under the P-R curve.

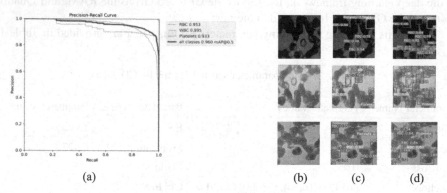

(a)   (b)   (c)   (d)

Fig. 6. (a) Representing the P-R curves of SW-YOLO, (b) Original image of blood cells, (c) Blood cell images under other detection algorithms, (d) Blood cell images under SW-YOLO detection algorithm

Figure 6(c) and (d) represent the detection results of blood cells under the other algorithms and the SW-YOLO algorithm respectively. From the figures, we can see that our proposed SW-YOLO does solve the problem of missed detection of other algorithms. Preliminary proof that our algorithm is effective.

This paper evaluates the performance of the SW-YOLO model in comparison to the traditional single-stage and two-stage target detection models, and the results of the comparison are illustrated in Table 2.

Table 2 provides the detection speed as FPS (frames per second), which represents the amount of images that the algorithm can process in one second. Examining Table 2,

Table 2. Comparative analysis experiments

Method	Input size	WBCS	RBCS	Platelets	mAP	FPS
Faster-RCNN [4]	1000 × 600	0.803	0.722	0.770	0.765	9.2
YOLOv3 [7]	608608	0.914	0.829	0.774	0.839	34.5
YOLOv4 [8]	640 × 640	0.930	0.798	0.813	0.847	36.1
TE-YOLOF-B3 [19]	416 × 416	0.987	0.873	0.898	0.919	43
ISE-YOLO [20]	416 × 416	0.965	0.927	0.896	0.857	34.5
YOLOv5 [11]	640 × 640	0.977	0.838	0.873	0.896	56.7
SW-YOLO	640 × 640	0.995	0.953	0.933	0.960	43.4

it is clear that the SW-YOLO not only has reduced complexity but also has significant advantages in precision compared to the majority of target detection networks. The mAP metric showed that the SW-YOLO network model is 19.5, 12.1, 11.3, 4.1, 10.3 and 6.4 percentage points better than Faster-R-CNN [4], YOLOv3 [7], YOLOv4 [8], TE-YOLOF-B3 [18], ISE-YOLO [19] and YOLOv5 [13] respectively. The results of the comparative analysis demonstrate that this algorithm outperforms all the other models in terms of the mAP metric. The SW-YOLO have a higher detection rate and are faster by 0.4 and 9 FPS than the TE-YOLOF-B3 and ISE-YOLO algorithms, which are utilized to carry out detection on the publicly accessible blood cell dataset BCCD. The SW-YOLO show an increase in both speed and accuracy of detection on the blood cell data set compared to the prior two network models. The algorithm is not as speedy as YOLOv5, and the processing time of a single image increases by 0.07 s with a frame rate of 43.4, which is sufficient to support real-time detection needs on hardware terminals while still improving the false and missed detections issue in the original network. The results of the experiment suggest that this algorithm has the best overall performance compared to other models, as it is able to increase the mAP while maintaining the detection speed.

The performance of the SW-YOLO model is compared with the latest YOLO detection model and the comparative results are shown in Table 3.

Table 3. Comparative experiments with the latest technology

Method	Input size	WBCS	RBCS	Platelets	mAP	FPS	F1_curve	Precision
YOLOv7	640 × 640	0.995	0.954	0.928	0.959	9.1	0.92	0.864
YOLOv8	640 × 640	0.995	0.960	0.945	0.967	54.8	0.93	0.807
SW-YOLO	640 × 640	0.995	0.953	0.933	0.960	43.4	0.92	0.851

SW-YOLO compared to YOLOv7, although the precision is 1.3% lower than YOLOv7, its F1_curve is the same as YOLOv7 and the map is 0.1% higher than YOLOv7, and the detection speed is 31.3 FPS higher than YOLOv7.

SW-YOLO compared to YOLOv8, although F1_curve is 0.01% lower than YOLOv8, map is 0.7% lower than YOLOv8 and detection speed is 11.4 FPS lower than YOLOv8, SW-YOLO has a 4.4% higher precision than YOLOv8.

In summary, our improved SW-YOLO compares favourably with the most advanced YOLO technology, although some of its performances are inferior to theirs, some are better than YOLOv7 and YOLOv8, so it is further proof that SW-YOLO can meet the current requirements in terms of detection accuracy and real-time performance.

5   Comparison with Other Datasets

To determine the generality of the SW-YOLO algorithm, other datasets are tested in this paper. Firstly, the LIDC-IDRI dataset [20], which is the same medically relevant lung CT dataset. The annotation of the images result in 3144 train set images and 349 test set images. The another is dataset is TT100K [21], which is also a small to medium sized target dataset. The TT100K dataset is dedicated to the recognition of traffic signs and after annotating the images contained in the dataset, we have 8816 images in the train set and 1712 images in the test set. The performance metrics under both datasets are shown in Fig. 7.

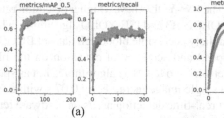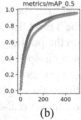

(a)   (b)

Fig. 7. (a) Comparison of the YOLOv5s algorithm and the SW-YOLO algorithm on the LIDC-IDRI dataset, (b) Comparison of the YOLOv5s algorithm and the SW-YOLO algorithm on the TT100K dataset. Where the blue line represents the original YOLOv5s algorithm and the orange line represents the SW-YOLO algorithm.

From Fig. 7(a) we can see that the SW-YOLO algorithm is significantly more effective on the LIDC-IDRI dataset than YOLOv5s, and the experiments also show that SW-YOLO yields the mAP of 72%, which is higher than the 70% mAP of YOLOv5s. From Fig. 7(b), we can see that the SW-YOLO algorithm does not work as well as YOLOv5s on the TT100K dataset, but it is not very bad either, and the experiments also show that the mAP of SW-YOLO is similar to that of YOLOv5s, both reaching 96%, so our proposed SW-YOLO is still effective.

6   Ablation Studies

In order to verify the effectiveness of each module and to analyze the impact of each module on the accuracy of the SW-YOLO algorithm, we conducted an ablation experiment, using YOLOv5s is used as the base network to gradually add improvement points, setting the fuse Swin Transformer as A, only small and medium target blocks are detected as B, Replacing the ordinary convolution in PAN with the depth-separable convolution as C, and replacing CIOU loss function with EIOU loss function as D. The experimental results are shown in Table 4. According to the data from the ablation experiments in Table 4, the improvement of either module resulted in 4.1% mAP to 7.5% mAP increase over the YOLOv5s algorithm, F1_curve increased by 0.1% to 0.3% and precision increased by 0.3% to 6.4%. SW-YOLO show an average accuracy improvement of 6% over the original YOLOv5s network for the detection of 3 types of blood cells. It is highly practical.

Table 4. Ablation studies

Method	Input size	WBCS	RBCS	Platelets	mAP	F1_curve	Precision
YOLOv5s [13]	640 × 640	0.977	0.838	0.873	0.896	0.90	0.858
0.93YOLOv5s + A	640 × 640	0.995	0.949	0.959	0.968	0.93	0.922
YOLOv5s + B	640 × 640	0.991	0.938	0.953	0.961	0.92	0.892
YOLOv5s + C	640 × 640	0.995	0.959	0.945	0.966	0.92	0.865
YOLOv5s + D	640 × 640	0.995	0.950	0.967	0.971	0.93	0.888
YOLOv5s + A + B + C	640 × 640	0.995	0.948	0.953	0.965	0.92	0.862
YOLOv5s + A + C + D	640 × 640	0.995	0.948	0.955	0.966	0.93	0.909
YOLOv5s + B + C + D	640 × 640	0.995	0.939	0.958	0.964	0.92	0.904
SW-YOLO	640 × 640	0.995	0.953	0.933	0.960	0.92	0.902

7 Conclusion

This paper proposes a SW-YOLO network model for BCCD blood cell detection. This paper first introduces the structure of YOLOv5s, followed by the SW-YOLO network structure, which includes fusing Swin Transformer, removing the large target detection structure, replacing the ordinary convolution in PAN with depth-separable convolution, and replacing the CIOU loss function with the EIOU loss function. In this paper, comparison experiments with other mainstream detection algorithms, comparison experiments with other datasets and ablation experiments are conducted respectively. The experimental results demonstrate that the SW-YOLO algorithm has excellent detection accuracy and real-time detection effect.

Acknowledgement. The authors would like to acknowledge the support from the National Natural Science Foundation of China (52075530).

References

1. Chen, Y.: Study on the value of blood smear analysis in routine blood tests. China Pharm. Guide **16**(1), 118–119 (2018)
2. Chan, L., Laverty, D., Smith, T.: Accurate measurement of peripheral blood mononuclear cell concentration using image cytometry to eliminate RBC-induced counting error. J. Immunol. Methods **388**(1), 25–32 (2013)
3. Lehmann, T.M., Guld, M.O., Thies, C.: Content-based image retrieval in medical applications. Methods Inf. Med. **43**(4), 354–361 (2004)
4. Ren, S.Q., He, K., Girshick, R.: Faster R-CNN: towards real-time object detection with region proposal networks. IEEE Trans. Pattern Anal. Mach. Intell. **39**(6), 1137–1149 (2017)
5. Chen, D.H., Sun, S.R., Wang, Y.C.: Research on improved SSD algorithm for small target detection. Sensors Microsyst. **42**(3), 65–68 (2023)
6. Liu, J.C., Li, X.F., Liu, A.X.: Improved RetinaNet for UAV small target detection. Sci. Technol. Eng. **23**(1), 274–282 (2023)
7. Yan, W.J., Dai, J.H.: Traffic sign recognition based on improved YOLOv3. J. Wuhan Eng. Vocation. Technol. Coll. **35**(1), 31–35 (2023)
8. Chen, Y.F., Yan, C.C., Zhou, C.: Improved YOLOv4-based vehicle detection for autonomous driving scenarios. Autom. Instrum. **38**(1), 59–63 (2023)
9. Zheng, C.W., Lin, H.: A YOLOv5 helmet wearing detection method based on Swin Transformer. Comput. Meas. Control **31**(3), 15–21 (2023)
10. Zhang, Y.F., Ren, W., Zhang, Z.: Focal and efficient IOU loss for accurate bounding box regression. Neurocomputing **506**, 146–157 (2022)
11. Ouyang, D., Huang, H., Li, J.: Improved yolov5s model for aerial image target detection algorithm. Fujian Comput. **39**(5), 7–15 (2023)
12. He, K., Zhang, X., Ren, S.: Deep residual learning for image recognition. In: Proceedings of the IEEE Conference on Computer Vision and Pattern Recognition, pp. 770–778 (2016)
13. Shah, S.A.R., Wu, W., Lu, Q.: AmoebaNet: an SDN-enabled network service for big data science. J. Netw. Comput. Appl. **119**, 70–82 (2018)
14. Chollet, F.: Xception: deep learning with depthwise separable convolutions. In: Proceedings of the IEEE Conference on Computer Vision and Pattern Recognition, pp. 1251–1258 (2017)
15. Lin, T.Y., Dollar, P., Girshick, R.: Feature pyramid networks for object detection. In: Proceedings of the IEEE Conference on Computer Vision and Pattern Recognition, pp. 2117–2125 (2017)
16. Liu, S., Qi, L., Qin, H.: Path aggregation network for instance segmentation. In: Proceedings of the IEEE Conference on Computer Vision and Pattern Recognition, pp. 8759–8768 (2018)
17. https://github.com/Shenggan/BCCD_Dataset. Accessed 24 Feb 2018
18. Xu, F., Li, X., Yang, H.: TE-YOLOF: tiny and efficient YOLOF for blood cell detection. Biomed. Signal Process. Control **73**, 103416 (2022)
19. Liu, C., Li, D., Huang, P.: ISE-YOLO: Improved squeeze-and-excitation attention module based YOLO for blood cells detection. In: 2021 IEEE International Conference on Big Data, pp. 3911–3916 (2021)
20. Lung Nodule Analysis 2016. https://luna16.grand-challenge.org. Accessed 20 Oct 2020
21. Huang, S.A.: Traffic sign detection based on improved YOLO model. Sci. Technol. Innov. **18**, 194–196 (2021)

A Novel Full Prediction Model of 3D Needle Insertion Procedures

Murong Li[1], Yong Lei[2], Shilun Du[2], Yingda Hu[2], Zhen Wang[2], Tian Xu[2], and Wei Song[1(✉)]

[1] Zhejiang Lab, Hangzhou, Zhejiang, China
weisong@zhejianglab.com
[2] State Key Laboratory of Fluid Power and Mechatronic Systems, Zhejiang University, Hangzhou, China

Abstract. Needle-tissue interaction deformation model can provide the future interaction deformation prediction which can be used to establish the virtual surgery training platform. The prediction information can be used to assist needle path planning scheme. However, existing models either only model the global coupled deformation without force prediction module or model the local contact mechanism between the needle and tissue. The calculation efficiency of the contact mechanism based model limits its application in needle path planning task. In this paper, a novel full prediction model of 3D needle insertion procedures was proposed. The Kriging model can realize fast calculation of the friction force, which is coupled to the 3D needle-tissue coupled deformation model. The local constraint method is applied to avoid the reconstruction of stiffness matrix in each step. The model can simultaneously predict tissue deformation, needle deflection and the interaction force with an acceptable calculation efficiency. The simulation results demonstrate the accuracy of the Kriging based friction force model. The visual simulation results of needle insertion process was also given in this paper. The simulation calculation speed (with an average run time of 30 s) demonstrates the feasibility of its application to needle path planning schemes.

Keywords: needle insertion · full prediction model · Kriging model · local constrained method

1 Introduction

Minimally invasive surgery has the advantages of small wound size, mild patient pain, fewer complications, good prognosis, and fast patient recovery [7]. Needle insertion, as a common minimally invasive surgery, refers to use a long needle into the patient's tissues and organs in different scenarios, extract the histiocyte inside the human body, or drain specific drugs within the target cells of viscera tissue to achieve medical diagnosis or disease treatment [11,19], which is commonly used in tissue biopsy local anesthesia and brachytherapy, etc. [17,21]. However, the interaction between the needle and tissue would cause the needle

© The Author(s), under exclusive license to Springer Nature Singapore Pte Ltd. 2023
H. Yang et al. (Eds.): ICIRA 2023, LNAI 14269, pp. 173–186, 2023.
https://doi.org/10.1007/978-981-99-6489-5_14

deflection and tissue deformation [16], leading to a lower targeting accuracy. The needle deflection and tissue deformation can be modeled and predicted by the needle-tissue interaction model, which can be used to assist needle path planning system [6,15].

The difficulty in mechanism of needle insertion lies in how to construct a needle-tissue interaction model. A simple coupled model only models the compress process [4], which only involves the compression deformation and relaxation of the tissue, not the fragmentation of the tissue or the cutting deformation of the needle. Some researcher study on the puncture process which is modeled by using the energy based method [2,19]. Due the computation limitation, the above model only focused on the force simulation of piercing process without considering the needle deflection deep in the tissue.

To assist the needle path planning, the model is needed to predict the needle-tissue coupled deformation with acceptable calculation efficiency [6,15]. Early models used the spring mass method to model the deformation of soft tissue, where the mass were connected to each other through spring actuators and dampers, which can provide real-time tissue deformation [3,9]. To take physical equilibrium equations and the true mechanical properties of materials into account, most scholars use FEM to model the needle-tissue interaction mechanism. Existing coupling methods include mesh adaptation, fast low rank updates, mesh reconstruction, etc. Tanaka et al. proposed a binary refinement algorithm for cutting process simulation, which improves computational efficiency compared to traditional mesh partitioning schemes [20]. Phuoc et al. [5] proposed a robust and fast local grid repartition method from the perspective of improving economic grids, which can achieve realistic and real-time computation. Alterovitz et al. [1] adopted grid dynamic reconstruction method to keep the needle tip at the tissue node during the whole insertion process.

In our previous work, we proposed two kinds of needle-tissue interaction model. In [8], needle-tissue interaction is modeled based on the local constraint method, the stiffness and interaction force of the needle is mapping to the tissue nodes, which can improve the efficiency of the model [8]. However, the model is established on the 2D plane. The friction force comes from experimental data and lacks quantitative relationships between different tissue material parameters, needle parameters and friction forces. In [12], the contact algorithm based on CFEMP established the relationship between the friction force and the material parameters. However, it lacks the prediction module of the needle deflection and the running time of the model is 13 h, which limits its application into the needle path planning.

In summary, the existing research only model the global coupled deformation without force prediction module or model the local contact mechanism between the needle and tissue. The calculation efficiency of the contact mechanism based model limits its application in needle path planning scheme. In this paper, based on the prior two works, we proposed a novel full prediction model of 3D needle insertion procedures. The contribution are twofolds: first, the original 2D needle-tissue interaction model based on the local constraint method is expanded to 3D scenes. second, a Kriging based friction prediction model are coupled into the 3D needle-tissue interaction model. The innovation lays on that the model can realize simultaneous prediction of friction force, needle deformation and tissue deformation with an acceptable calculation efficiency. The proposed model can be used to build a high-precision needle insertion virtual training platform and navigate needle path planning.

The rest of this paper is organized as follows: The Kriging based friction force fast prediction model is shown in the following section. Section 3 introduced the needle-tissue coupled deformation model and how the friction prediction model was integrated into it based on the local constraint method. Subsequently, simulation results are described in Sect. 4. A summary of the work close the paper.

2   Material and Methods

2.1   Kriging Based Friction Fast Prediction Model

Kriging model is an approximate simplified model of computer simulation model (including finite element model) without affecting the accuracy. The dataset is generated by high-precision model. The Kriging model can be regarded as an interpolation of the input/output of the calculation and simulation model and can effectively reduce the number of simulations of the original model and reduce the consumption of computing resources. The mean squared error on the training dataset is guaranteed to be 0. In this section, the Kriging based model was used to predict the friction force given the basic information in the current insertion case. The schematic process was shown in Fig. 1. The dataset was generated from MPM based needle-tissue interaction model [12]. The parameters in Kriging model were trained and optimized offline.

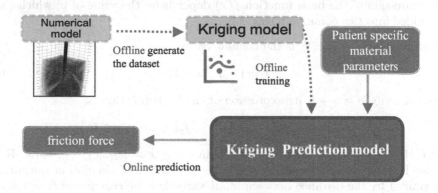

Fig. 1. Kriging-based friction prediction model

The basic principles of Kriging model was introduced as follows:

The expression of the Kriging model is the sum of the polynomial and its deviation, which can be written as:

$$\hat{y}(x) = f^T(x)\beta^* + r^T(x)\gamma^* \tag{1}$$

where $f(x)$ is a polynomial basis function which is also termed as regression function. $r(x)$ is the column vector which was formed by the correlation matrix $\mathcal{R}_{m \times m}$:

$$\mathcal{R}_{m \times m} = [R(x_i, x_1), R(x_i, x_2), \cdots, R(x_i, x_m)]^T \quad i = 1, 2, \cdots, m \tag{2}$$

The coefficient of the polynomial basis function and correlation matrix can be calculated as $\beta^* = \left(F^T R^{-1} F\right)^{-1} F^T R^{-1} Y$, $\gamma^* = R^{-1}(Y - F\beta^*)$, where F is the design matrix which can be calculated as:

$$F_{m \times p} = [f(x_1), f(x_2), \cdots, f(x_m)]^T \tag{3}$$

where m is the running times of the numerical model. p is the order of the basis function. The formula for calculating the mean square deviation of Kriging prediction model is [14]:

$$\varphi(x) = \sigma^2 \left(1 + u^T (F^T R^{-1} F)^{-1} u - r^T R^{-1} r\right) \tag{4}$$

where $u = F^T R^{-1} r - f$, $\sigma^2 = \frac{1}{m}(Y - F\beta^*)^2 R^{-1}(Y - F\beta^*)$ is the maximum likelihood estimation of variance. The design matrix $F_{m \times p}$ consists of basis function:

$$F_{m \times p} = \begin{bmatrix} f_1(x_1) & \cdots & f_p(x_1) \\ \vdots & \ddots & \vdots \\ f_1(x_m) & \cdots & f_p(x_m) \end{bmatrix}_{m \times p} \tag{5}$$

The expression of the basis function $f(x)$ depends on the value of p, which can be divided into two common forms [14]:

– constant form, $p = 1$, F is the column vector.

$$f_1(x) = 1 \quad x \in \mathbf{R}^n \tag{6}$$

– linear form, $p = n + 1$, its expression of the basis function is:

$$f_1(x) = 1, f_2(x) = w_1, \cdots, f_p(x) = w_n \quad x \in \mathbf{R}^n \tag{7}$$

where the component form of the test points x is $x = [w_1, w_2, \cdots, w_n] \in \mathbf{R}^n$. In the Kriging model, assuming that the correlation of simulation output is determined by the distance between input variables, the correlation function of input variables can be expressed as the product of none-dimensional correlation equations:

$$R(w, x) = R(\theta, w, x) = \prod_{j=1}^{n} R_j(\theta, d_j) \tag{8}$$

where $d_j = w_j - x_j$, θ is the correlation coefficient. In the Kriging model, the most widely used correlation model is that shown in Eq. 9:

$$R(\theta, w, x) = \prod_{j=1}^{n} \exp\left(-\theta_j \|d_j\|^n\right) \tag{9}$$

where $\|\cdot\|$ denotes the Euclidean distance of d_j. When $n = 2$, the form of the correlation function is Gaussian, as shown in Eq. 11.

$$R_j(\theta, d_j) = \exp\left(-\theta_j \|d_j\|\right) \tag{10}$$
$$R_j(\theta, d_j) = \exp\left(-\theta_j \|d_j\|^2\right) \tag{11}$$

The correlation function decreases with the increase in the Euclidean distance d_j, and a larger correlation coefficient leads to a rapid decline of the correlation function. Substituting the correlation function into 4, the mean square error is a function of the covariance σ^2 and the correlation coefficient θ. The optimal solution to the correlation coefficient θ^* is converted into an unconstrained global optimization problem [18], as shown in Eq. 12

$$\theta^* = \arg\min_{\theta} \left[\psi(\theta) \equiv |R|^{\frac{1}{m}} \sigma^2\right] \tag{12}$$

where $|R|$ is the determinant value of the correlation matrix R.

2.2 Dataset Generation of Friction Force

The CFEMP based needle-tissue interaction model can produce the compression force data [12], which is the important part of the friction force calculation. However, the computation efficiency limits its application in needle navigation and path planning. In this section, Kriging based model is applied to compression force calculation. The dataset is generated from CFEMP model by varying the needle type, tissue material properties and insertion velocity. The compression force per unit length F_{cp} as the characteristic value of compression force which is the division of the integral of the force on the finite element node along the radial direction and the contact length L, as shown in Eq. 13:

$$F_{cp} = \int_L \sqrt{F_x^2 + F_y^2} \tag{13}$$

The friction per unit length F_{fp} is calculated as the product of the compression force per unit length F_{cp} and the semiempirical friction coefficient formula in [13]:

$$F_{fp} = F_{cp} f \tag{14}$$

Four variables including the Young's modulus of the soft tissue, needle diameter, needle tip bevelled angle and insertion velocity are utilized as the input in the simulation, and the range is shown in the Table 1.

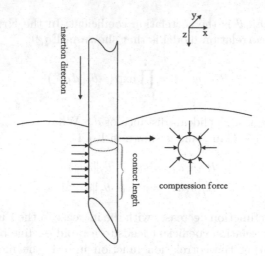

Fig. 2. Direction of the compression force

Table 1. Input variables and its range

variables	factor name	range	
		minimum value x_L	maximum value x_U
x_1	Young's modulus of the soft tissue	10 kPa	50 kPa
x_2	needle diameter	30G(d = 0.31 mm)	14G(d = 2.11 mm)
x_3	needle tip bevelled angle	10°	50°
x_4	insertion velocity	2 mm/s	18 mm/s

The input variables are defined as $X = [x_1, x_2, x_3, x_4]$, which is utilized for established the design matrix of the Kriging model. The input parameters are first normalized to the interval $[0, 1]$ as calculated as Eq. 15

$$\tilde{x}_i = \frac{x_i - x_L}{x_U - x_L}, \quad \tilde{x}_i \in [0, 1] \tag{15}$$

where $\tilde{x}_i$ is the normalized results of x_i, x_L and x_U are maximum and minimum value of variables x_i. Due to the good edge characteristics of Latin Hypercube Sampling (LHS), it can uniformly fill in each factor x_i. Therefore, this sampling method is applied to randomly generate the sample space, ensuring that variables can fill all parts of the vector space.

Based on the CFEMP model, an interactive force dataset was generated offline for different material parameters, needle geometry parameters, and insertion speed. The program was carried out for 25 times, and the compression force per unit length during the insertion process was extracted as the output of the Kriging model. This process does not require computational efficiency, and the simulation parameters and generated compression force data are used as input and output datasets for the Kriging model, respectively. The input dataset and output dataset are used to train the Kriging model. The process of training the Kriging model is essentially the process of optimizing the parameters of the Kriging model.

2.3   Needle-Tissue Coupled Deformation Model Based on the Local Constraint Method

To avoid the redrawing or repositioning of interaction nodes of tissue and needle, the local constraint method is applied to establish the needle-tissue interaction model. In the local constraint method, the whole stiffness of the tissue is not rebuilt during the insertion step, and the contact force between the needle and tissue is mapped on the tissue nodes. By overlaying the needle stiffness with the original tissue stiffness, the solution of deflection and force is completely controlled by the tissue model. The methods may sacrifice some accuracy but reduce the difficulty of grid division, significantly improving computational efficiency. Compared to the local constraint method based needle-tissue interaction model in [10], we extended the this work into 3D case.

The process that needle insertion into the soft tissue changes the stiffness of the system, as shown in Fig. 3. The nodes of the red grids through which the needle path was passed by are marked by the triangular and the stiffness of these nodes are strengthened. By transforming the system stiffness into the global coordinate, the stiffness matrix and global control equation can be written as:

$$
\begin{aligned}
K_{\text{global}} &= K_{\text{needle}} + K_{\text{tissue}} \\
K_{\text{global}} \cdot u_{\text{global}} &= F_{\text{global}}
\end{aligned}
\tag{16}
$$

The method of friction assignment is shown in Fig. 4: As the needle nodes penetrate into the inside of the tissue, the friction force will assigned onto the tissue nodes of the grid that the needle nodes passed by. As shown in 18, needle passed by the two faces (face ABC and face BCD) of the tetrahedron ABCD, and the intersection of the needle segment and the faces are H1 and H2. As for the needle segment H1H2, the friction force can be calculated as product of the friction force per unit length and the length of H1H2. That is, $F^{H1H2} = F_{fp}L_{H1H2}$, where F_{fp} is the friction force per unit length and L_{H1H2} is the vector of the needle segment inside the current grid. The friction of the needle segment H1H2 assigned onto the nodes A, B and C according to the area ratio. Assume that the nodal force of face ABC is $F_{ABC} = [F^A, F^B, F^C]^T$, F^A, F^B, F^C are the assigned friction force on the nodes A, B and C, which can be expressed as the production of friction on the needle segment F^{H1H2} and mapping function N_f, as shown in Eq. 17.

$$
F_{ABC} = N_f F^{H1H2}
\tag{17}
$$

where $\boldsymbol{N}_f = [\lambda_a \boldsymbol{I} | \lambda_b \boldsymbol{I} | \lambda_c \boldsymbol{I}]^T$ is the mapping function from the needle nodes to tissue nodes, $\boldsymbol{I}$ is the unit matrix, λ_a, λ_b and λ_c can be calculated as

$$\begin{cases} \lambda_a + \lambda_b + \lambda_c = 1 \\ \lambda_a = \frac{S_{\triangle H_1 BC}}{2 S_{\triangle ABC}} \\ \lambda_b = \frac{S_{\triangle H_1 AC}}{2 S_{\triangle ABC}} \\ \lambda_c = \frac{S_{\triangle H_1 AB}}{2 S_{\triangle ABC}} \end{cases} \tag{18}$$

where $S_{\triangle H_1 BC}, S_{\triangle H_1 AC}, S_{\triangle H_1 AB}$ and $S_{\triangle ABC}$ are the area of the corresponding triangle. The principle of force assignment of BCD is the same as ABC.

As the compression force and friction coefficient are both material-related. Therefore, the friction force along the insertion needle path is dependent on the contact tissue's material, as calculated as Eq. 19.

$$\boldsymbol{F}^{H1H2}(Ei) = F_{fp}(Ei) \boldsymbol{L}_{H1H2} \tag{19}$$

where F_{fp} is the friction force per unit length with the Young's modulus of Ei. In this model, the friction force is the function of insertion length, material parameters of the tissue, insertion velocity, normal pressure and the needle diameter.

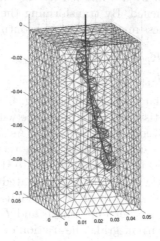

Fig. 3. Strengthen the local stiffness that the needle passed by

The cutting force acting on the needle tip is also assigned on the tissue nodes, as shown in Fig. 5.

When needle tip is in the tetrahedron ABCD, the cutting force is assigned according to the volume ratio of the tetrahedron divided by the needle tip. Assume the cutting force is $\boldsymbol{F}^T$, the assigned cutting force nodes A, B, C and D can be expressed as $\boldsymbol{F}_{ABCD} = [\boldsymbol{F}^A, \boldsymbol{F}^B, \boldsymbol{F}^C, \boldsymbol{F}^D]^T$ and satisfies the following relationship:

$$\boldsymbol{F}_{ABCD} = \boldsymbol{N}_c \boldsymbol{F}^T \tag{20}$$

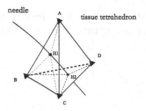

Fig. 4. Friction assignment

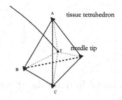

Fig. 5. Cutting force assignment

where $N_c = [L_a I | L_b I | L_c I | L_d I]^T$ is the mapping function from the needle nodes to the tissue nodes. I is the unit matrix and L_a, L_b, L_c and L_d satisfy that:

$$\begin{cases} L_a + L_b + L_c + L_d = 1 \\ L_a = \frac{V_{TBCD}}{V_{ABCD}} \\ L_b = \frac{V_{TACD}}{V_{ABCD}} \\ L_c = \frac{V_{TABD}}{V_{ABCD}} \\ L_d = \frac{V_{TABC}}{V_{ABCD}} \end{cases} \quad (21)$$

where V is the corresponding volume of the tetrahedron.

3   Simulation Results

3.1   Kriging Based Friction Force Fast Prediction Model

The CFEMP model was running 25 times to generate the dataset. The Kriging model is built in Matlab by using the DACE Toolkit. The correlation coefficient of Kriging is θ, and the initial value of θ is $\theta_0 = [1.0, 1.0, 1.0, 1.0]$. The upper bound of θ is $\theta_{ub} = [10.0, 10.0, 10.0, 10.0]$ and the lower bound is $\theta_{lb} = [0.1, 0.1, 0.1, 0.1]$. Extract 24 groups of data $([X_{in}(1,:), \cdots, X_{in}(i-1,:), X_{in}(i+1,:), \cdots, X_{in}(25,:)])$ as the training data to construct the design matrix, and $X_{in}(i,:)$ is left as the test data. To ensure the accuracy of the results, traverse each group as test data. A total of 25 sets of Kriging models were constructed to determine the regression function, correlation function, and coefficients of the Kriging model, and analyze their errors. There are four types of Kriging models, namely zero-order Gaussian, zero-order exponential, first-order Gaussian, and first-order exponential Kriging models. Compared with the original numerical model, Kriging based model accelerate the running time from 13 h to within 0.03 s.

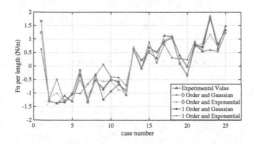

Fig. 6. Prediction results of four kinds of Kriging based models

The results are shown in Fig. 6. In this figure, the horizontal axis represents the data group number. The vertical axis represents the model prediction results. The blue marked data represents the calculation results of the numerical calculation model (CFEMP numerical model), which can be regarded as the ground truth. As can be seen from the figure, four Kriging models can all effectively predict the compression force. Define residual between the numerical model y and Kriging prediction model $\hat{y}$, namely $\mathbf{e} = \hat{y} - y$. The maximum residual values of the Kriging model for zero-order Gaussian, zero-order exponential, first-order Gaussian, and first-order exponential are 1.2955 N/m, 0.6751 N/m, 0.4332 N/m, and 0.4601 N/m, respectively. The mean residual values of the Kriging model for zero-order Gaussian, zero-order exponential, first-order Gaussian, and first-order exponential are 0.3952 N/m, 0.2123 N/m, 0.1902 N/m, 0.1829 N/m, respectively. The residual curve is shown in Fig. 7. It can be obtained that in terms of prediction model accuracy, the first-order Gaussian model has a similar accuracy to the first-order exponential model and is greater than the zero-order exponential model. The worst prediction accuracy is the zero-order Gaussian model.

Table 2. Correlation coefficient of four kinds of Kriging model

type	0-order Gaussian	0-order exponential	1-order Gaussian	1-order exponential
θ_1	0.5946	0.4719	3.7755	2.1497
θ_2	1.1554	0.1245	10.0000	8.0289
θ_3	0.1403	0.1000	6.4375	10.0000
θ_4	0.1146	0.1000	0.1168	0.1071

Table 2 shows the correlation coefficient of the four Kriging models. where β of zero-order Gaussian and zero-order exponential are 0.1368 and 0.0517, respectively. $\beta \in R^5$ of the first-order Gaussian and first-order exponential are [0.0110,0.9310,−0.2827,0.1469,0.0144] and [0.0084,0.9318,-0.2816,0.1483,0.0113], respectively.

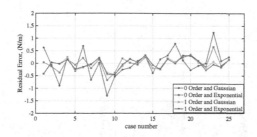

Fig. 7. Residual of four kinds of Kriging based model

3.2   Visual Simulation Results of Needle Insertion Process

The needle-tissue interaction full prediction model is deployed on Macbook Pro (13-inch, M1, 8 GB) with MATLAB 2019b. The mean running time is within 30 s that is acceptable for needle path planning.

As shown in Fig. 8, the tissue is set as a cuboid as 50 mm × 50 mm × 100 mm. The fixed constraints are loaded on the bottom surface of the soft tissue. Apply xy constraint front, back, left and right surface of the tissue, while the needle insertion direction (z) can deform freely. The needle length is 150 mm with the diameter of 1 mm. The inclined angle of the needle tip is 20°. The Young's modulus and Poisson's ratio are 10 kPa and 0.49, respectively. The insertion velocity is 6 mm/s and the cutting force is set as 0.15 N (average experimental experience). There are 3 visual results of the three cases:

Case 1: Insertion depth is 80 mm without the rotation (a and c).
Case 2: Rotate the needle base of 180° in the insertion depth of 40 mm (b and c).
Case 3: Rotate the needle base of 90° in the insertion depth of 40 mm (d and e).

As can be seen from the figure, in the case of insertion with a fixed angel, the needle trajectory is approximately an arc, where the arc plane is aligned with the angle direction of the needle inclined plane. The direction of arc deflection is consistent with the direction of the needle tip slope.

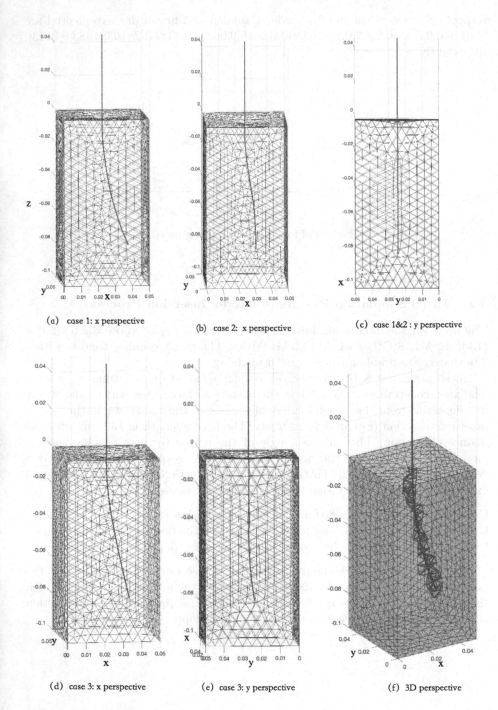

(a) case 1: x perspective

(b) case 2: x perspective

(c) case 1&2 : y perspective

(d) case 3: x perspective

(e) case 3: y perspective

(f) 3D perspective

Fig. 8. Visual results of the 3D full prediction model

4 Conclusion

In this paper, a novel full prediction model of 3D needle insertion procedures is proposed. The Kriging based friction prediction model is integrated into the 3D needle insertion model based on the local constraint method. The proposed model can avoid the reconstruction of stiffness matrix in each step to improve the calculation efficiency. The simulation results demonstrate the accuracy of the Kriging based friction force model. The simulation model shows that tissue deformation, needle deflection and the interaction force can be simultaneously predicted, given the tissue material parameters. The calculation speed (with an average run time of 30 s) demonstrates the feasibility of its application to needle path planning schemes.

Acknowledgments. This work was supported by Key Research Project of Zhejiang Lab (No. G2021NB0AL03), the National Natural Science Foundation of China Grant (Grant No. U21A20488) and Zhejiang Provincial Natural Science Foundation of China (Grant No. LSD19H180004).

References

1. Alterovitz, R., Goldberg, K.Y., Pouliot, J., Hsu, I.: Sensorless motion planning for medical needle insertion in deformable tissues. IEEE Trans. Inf. Technol. Biomed. Publ. IEEE Eng. Med. Biol. Soc. **13**(2), 217–25 (2009)
2. Azar, T., Hayward, V.: Estimation of the fracture toughness of soft tissue from needle insertion. In: Biomedical Simulation. pp. 166–175. Berlin, Heidelberg (2008)
3. Basafa, E., Farahmand, F., Vossoughi, G.: A non-linear mass-spring model for more realistic and efficient simulation of soft tissues surgery. Stud. Health Technol. Inf. **132**, 23–25 (2008)
4. Bojairami, I.E., Hamedzadeh, A., Driscoll, M.: Feasibility of extracting tissue material properties via cohesive elements: a finite element approach to probe insertion procedures in non-invasive spine surgeries. Med. Biol. Eng. Comput. **59**(10), 2051–2061 (2021)
5. Bui, H.P., Tomar, S., Courtecuisse, H., Cotin, S., Bordas, S.P.A.: Real-time error control for surgical simulation. IEEE Trans. Biomed. Eng. **65**(3), 596–607 (2018)
6. Cueto, E., Chinesta, F.: Real time simulation for computational surgery: a review. Adv. Model. Simul. Eng. Sci. **1**(1), 11 (2014)
7. Fuchs, K.: Minimally invasive surgery. Endoscopy **34**(2), 154–159 (2002)
8. Gao, D., Lei, Y., Lian, B., Yao, B.: Modeling and simulation of flexible needle insertion into soft tissue using modified local constraints. J. Manuf. Sci. Eng. **138**(12), 121012 (2016)
9. Hammer, P.E., Sacks, M.S., Nido, P.J.D., Howe, R.D.: Mass-spring model for simulation of heart valve tissue mechanical behavior. Ann. Biomed. Eng. **39**(6), 1668–1679 (2011)
10. Lei, Y., Lian, B.: Modeling and simulation of flexible needle insertion into soft tissue using modified local constraint method. In: ASME 2014 International Manufacturing Science Conference, p. V002T02A031 (2014)
11. Li, H., Wang, Y., Li, Y., Zhang, J.: A novel manipulator with needle insertion forces feedback for robot-assisted lumbar puncture. Int. J. Med. Robot. Comput. Assist. Surg. **17**(2), e2226 (2021)

12. Li, M., Lei, Y., Gao, D., Hu, Y., Zhang, X.: A novel material point method (MPM) based needle-tissue interaction model. Comput. Methods Biomech. Biomed. Eng. **24**(12), 1393–1407 (2021)
13. Li, M., et al.: A novel semiemperical friction coefficient model between needle and PVA tissue phantom and its validation by using computational inverse technique. J. Tribol. **144**(8), 081203 (2022)
14. Lophaven, S.N., Nielsen, H.B., Sondergaard, J.: Dace - a matlab kriging toolbox - version 2.0. Technical Report, Technical University of Denmark, Denmark (2002)
15. Misra, S., Ramesh, K.T., Okamura, A.M.: Modeling of tool-tissue interactions for computer-based surgical simulation: a literature review. Presence **17**(5), 463–491 (2008)
16. Podder, T., Clark, D., Fuller, D.: Effects of coating on friction force during needle insertion in soft materials. Med. Phys. **32**(7), 2421 (2005)
17. Ra, J., et al.: Biomedical paper spine needle biopsy simulator using visual and force feedback. Comput. Aided Surg. **07**, 317–370 (2002)
18. Sacks, J., Welch, W.J., Mitchell, T.J., Wynn, H.P.: Design and analysis of computer experiments. Statistical Science, pp. 409–423 (1989)
19. Takabi, B., Tai, B.: A review of cutting mechanics and modeling techniques for biological materials. Med. Eng. Phys. **45**, 1–14 (2017)
20. Tanaka, H.T., Tsujino, Y., Kamada, T., Viet, H.Q.H.: Bisection refinement-based real-time adaptive mesh model for deformation and cutting of soft objects. In: 2006 9th International Conference on Control, Automation, Robotics and Vision, pp. 1–8 (2006)
21. Ullrich, S., Grottke, O., Rossaint, R., Staat, M., Deserno, T.M., Kuhlen, T.: Virtual needle simulation with haptics for regional anaesthesia. IEEE Virtual Reality **52**(7), 1–3 (2010)

Autofocusing for Cleavage-stage Embryos in Brightfield Microscopy: Towards Automated Preimplantation Genetic Testing

Sheng Yao[1,2,3], Kairui Wu[1,2,3], Li Qi[1,2,3], Feng Yang[1,2,3]([✉]), and Qianjin Feng[1,2,3]([✉])

[1] School of Biomedical Engineering, Southern Medical University, Guangzhou, China
{yangf,fengqj}@smu.edu.cn
[2] Guangdong Provincial Key Laboratory of Medical Image Processing, Southern Medical University, Guangzhou, China
[3] Guangdong Province Engineering Laboratory for Medical Imaging and Diagnostic Technology, Southern Medical University, Guangzhou, China

Abstract. Autofocusing is essential and serves as a prerequisite for the automation of embryo biopsy in preimplantation genetic testing (PGT) using robotics. Despite the existence of numerous autofocus algorithms, achieving accurate autofocusing for cleavage-stage embryos in brightfield microscopy remains challenging due to their non-unimodal nature. Thus, an adaptive and robust autofocusing method is required. This paper presents an autofocusing method based on an adaptive focus measure. The proposed method employs an adaptive focus measure selection approach and incorporates a coarse-to-fine strategy for autofocusing cleavage-stage embryos in brightfield microscopy. Experimental results demonstrate that the proposed autofocusing method achieves superior performance compared to other regular autofocus algorithms in brightfield microscopy for cleavage-stage embryos. This advancement marks a significant step forward in the automation development of PGT.

Keywords: Autofocusing · Focus measure · Embryo biopsy · Preimplantation genetic testing

1 Instruction

Preimplantation genetic testing (PGT) [1] is one of the assisted reproductive technology that extracts blastomeres or trophectoderm from the early-stage embryos for diagnosis. Although PGT is prominent to reduce a specific genetic condition or certain types of chromosome abnormalities in embryos created with in vitro fertilization (IVF), the popularity of PGT is still relatively low as well as the biochemical pregnancy rate [2, 3]. The primary obstacles to the clinical advancement of PGT are the high costs associated with the limited precision of manual embryo biopsy.

S. Yao and K. Wu—These authors contributed equally to this work.

© The Author(s), under exclusive license to Springer Nature Singapore Pte Ltd. 2023
H. Yang et al. (Eds.): ICIRA 2023, LNAI 14269, pp. 187–198, 2023.
https://doi.org/10.1007/978-981-99-6489-5_15

Automation of IVF through biomedical robotics has emerged as a promising solution for enhancing the efficiency and precision of PGT [4–6], which has the potentials to lower the medical service cost. To enable automated embryo biopsy, the development of machine vision and medical imaging techniques is crucial to facilitate the necessary procedures [7]. Visual sensing plays a vital role in automated micromanipulation, necessitating clear visual feedback for robotic systems [8, 9]. Consequently, achieving robust autofocusing is essential and serves as a prerequisite for automated PGT.

Numerous scholars have conducted research on autofocusing algorithms for automated biological and biomedical applications. For instance, Sun et al. [10] conducted a comparative study of 18 focus measures across different microscopy techniques, including brightfield, phase contrast, and differential interference contrast microscopy. Ang et al. [11] compared various focus measures specifically in brightfield microscopy, which remains the most prevalent setup in biomedical robotics. Pertuz et al. [12] provided a comprehensive evaluation and analysis of different focus measures under broader conditions, offering a comprehensive review. In the field of cell manipulation, Zhang et al. [13] developed an autofocusing strategy for fully automated cell microinjection, encompassing both macro and micro field of view. Wang et al. [14] proposed an autofocusing algorithm based on edge detection for automated oocyte manipulation, achieving a high success rate. Luo et al. [15] employed a deep learning-based method to generate virtually focused images from a single defocused image.

Despite numerous proposed focus algorithms, the focus measures of a cleavage-stage embryos are not unimodal, which requires an adaptive and robust method for autofocusing cleavage-stage embryos under brightfield microscopy. As a result, this paper presents an autofocusing method as a prerequisite for automated PGT. An adaptive focus measure selection approach is proposed, and a coarse-to-fine strategy based on region-of-interest localization is applied to achieve accurate autofocusing of cleavage-stage embryos in brightfield microscopy.

2 System Design

2.1 System Architecture

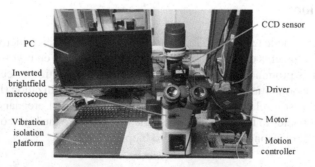

Fig. 1. Autofocusing system setup based on brightfield microscopy for cleavage-stage embryos.

As shown in Fig. 1, the autofocusing system is established based on a standard inverted brightfield microscope, a CCD sensor, a motion control card, a servo motor and a personal computer. As the preliminary to the autofocusing method design, the dataset of the cleavage-stage embryos from the University of Toronto is used [16]. All algorithms were implemented in Python.

2.2 Overall Sequence

Blastomeres and zona pellucida need to be recognized and located in 3D during embryo biopsy, which requires a robust autofocusing method. Therefore, an autofocusing method is proposed in this paper, which is essential towards automated PGT. Figure 2 summarizes the overall sequence of the proposed method. Several focus measures are firstly evaluated on the cleavage-stage embryo images under brightfield microscopy, where an adaptive method is designed. Then, region-of-interest localization is conducted, where the zona pellucida and blastomeres are located for autofocusing based on a coarse-to-fine strategy.

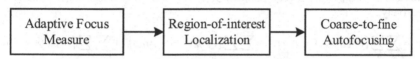

Fig. 2. Overall flowchart of the proposed autofocusing method for cleavage-stage embryos in brightfield microscopy.

3 Methods

3.1 Design of the Adaptive Focus Measure

An optimal focus measure should exhibit a peak at the focusing position while demonstrating a decline when the microscopic image is out-of-focus. Despite the existence of numerous focus measures, their efficacy in the context of cleavage-stage embryos under brightfield microscopy remains to be assessed. Those focus measures include:

Sum of Absolute Difference (SAD). *SAD* is a gradient-based focus measure that calculates the absolute difference in the vertical direction and sums up these differences to obtain the pixel's gradient. The focus measure value is then computed as the sum of the gradient values of all pixels. This can be mathematically formulated as follows:

$$f_{SMD} = \sum_x \sum_y \left[|i(x+1, y) - i(x, y)| + |i(x, y+1) - i(x, y)| \right] \tag{1}$$

Normalized Variance (Variance). *Variance* is a statistics-based focus measure that characterizes the image's focus quality using statistical parameters. It computes the gray level variations between pixels and enhances the difference between each pixel value and the average pixel value μ using a power function.

$$f_{Varance} = \frac{1}{MN} \sum_x \sum_y \left[i(x, y) - \mu \right]^2 \tag{2}$$

Auto Correlation (Vollath). As depicted in Eq. (3), *Vollath* examines the correlation among pixels to differentiate between clear and blurred images. A higher autocorrelation coefficient indicates a clearer image with greater contrast.

$$f_{Vollath} = \sum_x \sum_y i(x,y)i(x+1,y) - \sum_x \sum_y i(x,y)i(x+2,y) \tag{3}$$

Tenegrad. *Tenegrad* employs S_x and S_y as the image gradients computed by convolving the given image i with the Sobel operator. It then determines the focus measure value by summing the squares of all pixels.

$$f_{Tenegrad} = \sum_x \sum_y \left\{ [S_x * i(x,y)]^2 + [S_y * i(x,y)]^2 \right\} \tag{4}$$

Wavelet Variance (WAVV). *WAVV* is a wavelet-based focus measure that reconstructs four sub-images *LL*, *HL*, *LH* and *HH* from the discrete wavelet transform, which represent the image components in low frequency, horizontal, vertical and diagonal directions respectively:

$$f_{WAVV} = \sum_x \sum_y [(W_{LH}(x,y) - \mu_{LH})]^2 + \sum_x \sum_y [(W_{HL}(x,y) - \mu_{HL})]^2 + \sum_x \sum_y [(W_{HH}(x,y) - \mu_{HH})]^2 \tag{5}$$

Wavelet Ratio (WAVR). *WAVR* utilized the ratio between the high and low frequency coefficients M_H and M_L of the wavelet transform as a focus measure:

$$f_{WAVR} = \frac{M_H^2}{M_L^2}$$

$$M_H^2 = \sum_k \sum_{(i,j) \in \Omega_D} W_{LHk}(i,j)^2 + W_{HLk}(i,j)^2 + W_{HHk}(i,j)^2 \tag{6}$$

$$M_L^2 = \sum_k \sum_{(i,j) \in \Omega_D} W_{LLk}(i,j)^2$$

where k indicates that the k-th level wavelet is used to compute the coefficients.

Then an adaptive method is designed based on five quantitative evaluation metrics: Width of Steep Zone (W), Sharpness Ratio (R), Steepness (S), Sensitivity (SE) and the Number of Local Peaks (p), which can be defined as:

$$W = x_{rp} - x_{lp} \tag{7}$$

$$R = \frac{1}{2}\left(\frac{f_{max}}{f_{lp}} + \frac{f_{max}}{f_{rp}} \right) \tag{8}$$

$$S = \frac{2f_{max} - f_{lp} - f_{rp}}{W} \tag{9}$$

$$SE = \frac{f_{max} - f(x_{max} + \Delta)}{f(x_{max} + \Delta)} \tag{10}$$

where f_{max} is the maximum value of the focus measures, x_{lp} and x_{rp} are left and right limit points respectively, Δ is the sensitive threshold, as illustrated in Fig. 3. While W, R, S, SE the higher the better, fewer p would be preferable.

To obtain the optimal focus measure, the overall-score is designed for the adaptive focus measure selection approach:

$$Overall - Score = \beta_1 \times Rank_W + \beta_2 \times Rank_R + \beta_3 \times Rank_S + \beta_4 \times Rank_{SE} + \beta_5 \times Rank_p \quad (11)$$

where β is the weight of each metric and $Rank$ is the ranking of the focus measure candidates according to each metric. After the $Overall$-$Score$ for all focus measure candidates is calculated, the highest-score focus measure is chosen as the optimal focus measure for the following autofocusing procedures.

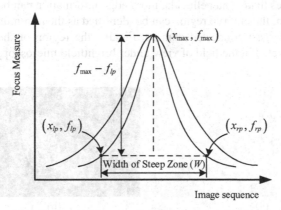

Fig. 3. Metrics for adaptive focus measure selection.

Pseudocode 1: Adaptive focus measure
Input: Z-stack images of the cleavage-stage embryos I
Output: Optimal focus measure $f_{adaptive}$
1. **Procedure** metric calculation of focus measures
2. calculate metrics W, R, S, SE for all focus measure candidates
3. **Procedure** $Overall$-$Score$ calculation
4. Sort and obtain the $Rank$ for all metrics
5. Set the weights β
6. $Overall$-$Score$ for all focus measure candidates
7. Sort and select the optimal focus measure $f_{adaptive}$ according to $Overall$-$Score$
8. **Return** $f_{adaptive}$

3.2 Region-of-Interest Localization

Cleavage-Stage Embryo Localization. Region-of-interest localization plays a pivotal role in achieving accurate autofocusing, as it directly impacts the performances. By

192   S. Yao et al.

identifying a suitable region within the cleavage-stage embryos, the adverse effects of image noise and environmental fluctuations can be effectively mitigated. Consequently, in this paper a specific approach is devised for localizing the region of interest intended for autofocusing, and the corresponding procedure is depicted visually in Fig. 4.

The Sobel edge detector, known for its robust noise reduction capabilities, is employed to extract edge details from the image. These edges are then added back to the original image to enhance its sharpness. To accommodate varying light intensities, we utilize the adaptive local threshold segmentation method. This technique involves calculating the mean value of the pixel neighborhood and setting a cutoff value, with the difference between the two serving as the segmentation threshold for the neighborhood. To ensure connectivity and filter out extraneous regions, morphological operations such as dilation, erosion, and hole filling are applied to the binary image. Since blastomeres have richer textures than zona pellucida, more edge information can be detected inside the embryos. Then, the embryo region can be identified as the minimum circumscribed rectangle of the largest connected domain. Finally, the region of the cleavage-stage embryo can be located in the field of view under brightfield microscopy.

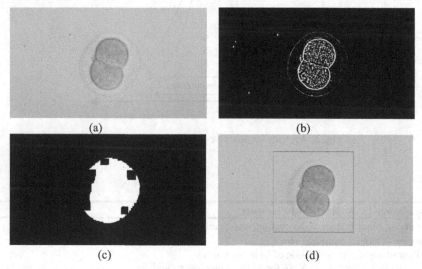

(a)   (b)

(c)   (d)

Fig. 4. Automatic Region-of-interest localization. (a) Brightfield microscopic image. (b) Adaptive local thresholding. (c) Morphological processing. (d) Final result.

Segmentation of Zona Pellucida. The zona pellucida holds significant importance as a distinguishing feature of early embryos, directly impacting the focus measure of embryo images. In well-focused embryo images, the zona pellucida exhibits a distinct and clear appearance. However, in defocused images, the transparent area of the zona pellucida gradually becomes blurry, resulting in an expanding halo. Thus, the edge sharpness of the zona pellucida serves as a discerning factor for distinguishing varying degrees of focus and can be employed as a straightforward metric for assessing image quality.

Due to the relatively low edge sharpness exhibited by the zona pellucida, the effectiveness of the adaptive local threshold segmentation method in accurately segmenting its boundary is limited. Custom threshold segmentation approaches require precise threshold determination, which proves challenging in the presence of non-uniform illumination across different image regions. In order to mitigate noise interference from the image background, we employ the minimum circumcircle of the focusing window as the designated image processing area. Recognizing the higher sensitivity of edge detection operators to horizontal and vertical directions, we transform the inner region of the circle into polar coordinates. Subsequently, the Sobel operator is applied to extract the edges, followed by enhancement through the LOG operator. Threshold segmentation is then performed on the polar coordinate image, as presented in the Fig. 5.

By means of the threshold segmentation, binary images of the zona pellucida and partial blastomeres are generated. The binary mask is subsequently converted back to the Cartesian coordinate system. Discrete points within the image are expanded using a closed operation, enabling the depiction of the outer boundary of the zona pellucida through ellipse fitting. In contrast to the outer boundary, the inner boundary of the zona pellucida contains more background and neighboring interference information. Thus, we extend the contour of the outer boundary to form an elliptical ring and eliminate the edge information within this ring from the binary mask. An image opening operation is employed to enhance the contour of the embryo in the image, followed by re-performing ellipse fitting to acquire the inner boundary. Considering the assumption that the thickness of the zona pellucida remains relatively uniform, the elliptical angle of the fitted inner boundary is expected to align with that of the outer boundary.

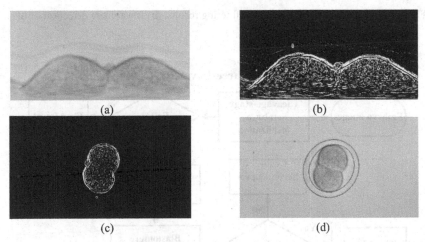

Fig. 5. Segmentation of zona pellucida. (a) Polar coordinate transformation. (b) Sobel edge detection. (c) Zona pellucida estimation. (d) Final result.

Blastomere Detection. As the primary subject of observation, the blastomere exhibits a complex spatial distribution within the zona pellucida. In a well-focused image, the edge of the blastomere appears sharp, while the cellular content remains clear and discernible.

Conversely, in progressively defocused images, the blastomere gradually transforms into a halo with an expanded radius. Thus, by detecting and quantifying the number of blastomeres present in the image, it becomes possible to analyze the degree of focus.

The blastomere exhibits a rich texture and intricate internal details, which can potentially interfere with its detection. To address this issue, we apply an edge-preserving filter to the image within the focused window area. This filtering procedure helps neutralize the internal grayscale and smooth out color details, as shown in the Fig. 6(a). However, the edge sharpness of the blastomere might be reduced during the filtering process, necessitating subsequent edge enhancement. To detect the circular shape of the blastomere, we employ the Hough transform. Various parameters such as the minimum and maximum circle sizes, as well as the number of votes, are set to optimize the filtering process. The detection results are shown in Fig. 6(b). Although slight distortion and deformation may occur between blastomeres, there is no overlap, eliminating the possibility of concentric circles.

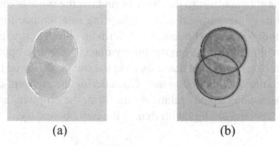

(a)   (b)

Fig. 6. Blastomere detection. (a) Edge filtering results. (b) Blastomere detection results.

3.3 Coarse-to-Fine Autofocusing (Three-Level Strategy)

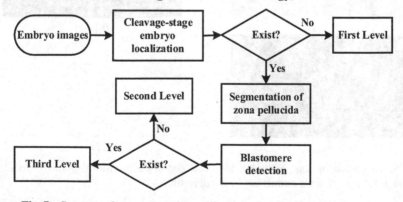

Fig. 7. Coarse-to-fine autofocusing method based on the three-level strategy

A coarse-to-fine strategy is designed based on the provided approaches in the preceding sections and named three-level autofocusing method, as presented in Fig. 7.

Blastomere detection is chosen as an indicator, since blastomeres have rich textures for autofocusing. Therefore, the final focus measure by the coarse-to-fine method is categorized into three levels: 1) blur, 2) coarse focusing, and 3) fine focusing. Initially, the presence of a focusing window in the image determines whether it falls within the blurring or coarse focusing period. Subsequently, based on whether the focusing window can detect blastomeres, it is further categorized into coarse focusing or the fine. The definition of the focus measure of the image is calculated according to the corresponding definition as outlined in the Table 1, where f is the adaptive focus measure using the adaptive approach in Sect. 3.1, I_{full} is the full-resolution image, $Width$ is the width of the zona pellucida, I_{embryo} is the embryo region, and $I_{blastomere}$ is the blastomere region, and v is the final focus measure values of autofocusing.

By cumulatively summing the focus measure values, the higher level surpasses the lower level. This accumulation ensures a positive correlation between image quality and focus measure value, as the high level incorporates the value derived from lower-level calculation. Simultaneously, images at the same level are differentiated based on their multivariate evaluation, including zona pellucida width and the number of blastomeres.

Table 1. Focus measure v from coarse to fine in different levels

First level	Second level	Third level
$v_1 = f_{adaptive}\left(I_{full}\right)$	$v_2 = v_1 + \frac{f_{adaptive}\left(I_{embryo}\right)}{Width}$	$v_3 = v_2 + \sum_{blastomeres} f_{adaptive}\left(I_{blastomere}\right)$

Pseudocode 2: Three-level strategy for coarse-to-fine autofocusing

Input: Z-stack images of the cleavage-stage embryos I
Output: Coarse-to-fine focus measure v
1. **Initialization** Adaptive focus measure
2. Obtain the optimal focus measure $f_{adaptive}$;
3. **Procedure** Coarse-to-fine autofocusing
4. First level: full field-of-view image under brightfield microscopy, calculate v_1;
5. Second level: cleavage-stage embryo localization, calculate v_2;
6. Third level: zona pellucida segmentation and blastomere detection, calculate v_3;
7. **Return** v

---

4 Experiment Results

In the experiments, 2-cell embryo z-stack images under brightfield microscopy were used. Daubechies (DB), Coiflets (COIF), Symlets (SYM), and Harr wavelet bases were evaluated and compared on the cleavage-stage embryo images under brightfield microscopy for the wavelet-based focus measures. In general, Harr showed better performances and was selected as the wavelet bases for processing cleavage-stage embryo images. Δ was set as 2 for the SE metric, x_{lp} and x_{rp} were obtained by $f_n/\bar{f}_{n-1} > 1.1$ where f_n and $\bar{f}_{n-1}$ were the focus measure value on the current image and average focus measure value of previous n-1 images in the image sequence I respectively, the weights for $Overall\text{-}Score$ β_1, β_2, β_3, β_4, β_5 were set as 0.35, 0.15, 0.15, 0.2, 0.15 respectively.

The experimental results of the adaptive focus measure are listed in Table 2. Particularly, $Variance$ shows poor performances and fails to obtain the overall-score. The local peak fluctuations of SMD and $Vollaths$ curves are relatively large, making them easy to be disturbed and regard a local peak p as a steep zone, thereby affecting the width of the steep zone W. $Tenegard$ shows better performances in R and SE compared to $WAVV$. Although SE of $Tenegrad$ is lower compared to $WAVR$, R is still higher in $Tenegrad$. Therefore, in this case $Tenegrad$ is chosen as the optimal focus measure according to the adaptive approach.

Table 2. Experimental results of the adaptive focus measure.

Metric	W (Rank)	R (Rank)	S (Rank)	SE (Rank)	p (Rank)	Overall-Score (Rank)
SMD	9(4)	2.550(4)	0.134(2)	0.601(5)	5(3)	2.25(5)
Variance	NA					
Vollaths	15(1)	1.827(5)	0.060(5)	0.842(4)	3(1)	3.2(2)
Tenegrad	15(1)	15.678(2)	0.115(4)	1.306(2)	4(2)	4.05(1)
WAVV	9(4)	4.764(3)	0.175(1)	1.679(1)	11(4)	3.2(2)
WAVR	14(3)	34.610(1)	0.130(3)	1.201(3)	11(4)	2.55(4)

Coarse-to-fine autofocusing method based on the three-level strategy was also validated in the experiments, as shown in Fig. 8. Table 3 lists the experimental results compared with regular focus measure on the full field-of-view images under bright-field microscopy. It can be seen that the overall performance of the proposed three-level method is superior to other traditional focus measure. The width of steep zone W, sharpness ratio R, and sensitivity SE have been improved by 20%, 133.27%, and 142.96% compared to the original $Tenegrad$. Due to the proposed three-level method, as the coarse-to-fine process and its level increases, the visualized curve also experiences a sharp increase, resulting in the best $Overall\text{-}Score$ by increasing 28.6% compared to $Tenegrad$. It also proves that the autofocusing algorithms are highly sensitive to variations of region selection, which indicates the necessity of the proposed coarse-to-fine method.

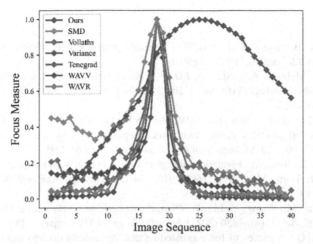

Fig. 8. Experimental Results of the proposed autofocusing method compared to the regular focus measures.

Table 3. Experimental results of autofocusing based on the three-level method

Metric	W (Rank)	R (Rank)	S (Rank)	SE (Rank)	p (Rank)	Overall-Score (Rank)
Three-level (Ours)	18(1)	36.572(1)	0.101(5)	3.173(1)	3(1)	5.4(1)
SMD	9(5)	2.550(5)	0.134(2)	0.601(6)	5(4)	2.4(6)
Vollaths	15(2)	1.827(6)	0.060(6)	0.842(5)	3(1)	3.35(3)
Tenegrad	15(2)	15.678(3)	0.115(4)	1.306(3)	4(3)	4.2(2)
WAVV	9(5)	4.764(4)	0.175(1)	1.679(2)	11(5)	3.35(3)
WAVR	14(4)	34.610(2)	0.130(3)	1.201(4)	11(5)	3.3(5)

5 Conclusion

This paper introduces an autofocusing method for cleavage-stage embryos under bright-field microscopy. A scoring approach is designed based on multiple metrics for adaptive focus measure selection, and a region-of-interest localization approach is proposed for coarse-to-fine autofocusing. Experimental results show that the proposed autofocusing method based on the three-level strategy outperforms regular focus measures and shows strong robustness under brightfield microscopy. The study can contribute to analysis of cleavage-stage embryos and paly an essential role for automated embryo biopsy in the robotic systems.

Acknowledgments. This work was supported in part by Science and Technology Program of Guangzhou under Grant 2023A04J2039 and National Training Program of Innovation and Entrepreneurship for Undergraduates under Grant 202212121051.

References

1. Brezina, P.R., Brezina, D.S., Kearns, W.G.: Preimplantation genetic testing. BMJ **345**, e5908 (2012). https://doi.org/10.1136/bmj.e5908
2. Kang, H.-J., Melnick, A.P., Stewart, J.D., Xu, K., Rosenwaks, Z.: Preimplantation genetic screening: who benefits? Fertil. Steril. **106**(3), 597–602 (2016). https://doi.org/10.1016/j.fer tnstert.2016.04.027
3. Won, S.Y., Kim, H., Lee, W.S., Kim, J.W., Shim, S.H.: Pre-implantation genetic diagnosis and pre-implantation genetic screening: two years experience at a single center. Obstet. Gynecol. Sci. **61**(1), 95–101 (2018). https://doi.org/10.5468/ogs.2018.61.1.95
4. Liu, X., Lu, Z., Sun, Y.: Orientation control of biological cells under inverted microscopy. IEEE/ASME Trans. Mechatron. **16**(5), 918–924 (2011). https://doi.org/10.1109/TMECH. 2010.2056380
5. Zhao, X., Cui, M., Zhang, Y., Liu, Y., Zhao, X.: Robotic precisely oocyte blind enucleation method. Appl. Sci. **11**(4), 1850 (2021). https://doi.org/10.3390/app11041850
6. Wei, Y., Xu, Q.: A survey of force-assisted robotic cell microinjection technologies. IEEE Trans. Autom. Sci. Eng. **16**(2), 931–945 (2019). https://doi.org/10.1109/TASE.2018.2878867
7. Shan, G., et al.: 3D morphology measurement for blastocyst evaluation from 'all angles'. IEEE Trans. Biomed. Eng. 1–10 (2022). https://doi.org/10.1109/TBME.2022.3232068
8. Yao, S., Li, H., Pang, S., Zhu, B., Zhang, X., Fatikow, S.: A review of computer microvision-based precision motion measurement: principles, characteristics, and applications. IEEE Trans. Instrum. Meas. **70**, 1–28 (2021). https://doi.org/10.1109/TIM.2021.3065436
9. Zhang, Z., Wang, X., Liu, J., Dai, C., Sun, Y.: Robotic micromanipulation: fundamentals and applications. Annu. Rev. Control Robot. Auton. Syst. **2**(1), 181–203 (2019). https://doi.org/ 10.1146/annurev-control-053018-023755
10. Sun, Y., Duthaler, S., Nelson, B.J.: Autofocusing in computer microscopy: selecting the optimal focus algorithm. Microsc. Res. Tech. **65**(3), 139–149 (2004). https://doi.org/10.1002/ jemt.20118
11. Yu, M.Y., Han, M.L., Shee, C.Y., Ang, W.T.: Autofocusing algorithm comparison in bright field microscopy for automatic vision aided cell micromanipulation. In: 2010 IEEE International Conference on Nano/Molecular Medicine and Engineering, Hung Hom, China, pp. 88–92. IEEE (2010). https://doi.org/10.1109/NANOMED.2010.5749811
12. Pertuz, S., Puig, D., Garcia, M.A.: Analysis of focus measure operators for shape-from-focus. Pattern Recogn. **46**(5), 1415–1432 (2013). https://doi.org/10.1016/j.patcog.2012.11.011
13. Su, L., et al.: Macro-to-micro positioning and auto focusing for fully automated single cell microinjection. Microsyst. Technol. **27**(1), 11–21 (2021). https://doi.org/10.1007/s00542-020-04891-w
14. Wang, Z., Feng, C., Ang, W.T., Tan, S.Y.M., Latt, W.T.: Autofocusing and polar body detection in automated cell manipulation. IEEE Trans. Biomed. Eng. **64**(5), 1099–1105 (2017). https:// doi.org/10.1109/TBME.2016.2590995
15. Luo, Y., Huang, L., Rivenson, Y., Ozcan, A.: Single-shot autofocusing of microscopy images using deep learning. ACS Photon. **8**(2), 625–638 (2021). https://doi.org/10.1021/acsphoton ics.0c01774
16. Yao, S., Mills, J.K., Ajamieh, I.A., Li, H., Zhang, X.M.: Automatic three-dimensional imaging for blastomere identification in early-stage embryos based on brightfield microscopy. Opt. Lasers Eng. **130**, 106093 (2020). https://doi.org/10.1016/j.optlaseng.2020.106093

Advanced Underwater Robot Technologies

Cooperative Pursuit-Evasion Game for Multi-AUVs in the Ocean Current and Obstacle Environment

Xiao Sun, Bing Sun$^{(\boxtimes)}$ ⓘ, and Zinan Su

Shanghai Maritime University, Shanghai 201306, China
hmsunbing@163.com

Abstract. In future ocean battlefields, cooperative pursuit and confrontation using Autonomous Underwater Vehicles (AUVs) will emerge as a crucial combat method. This paper presents a cooperative pursuit-evasion game strategy algorithm, utilizing multi-step Q-learning, to address the challenges posed by ocean currents and obstacles in complex underwater environments. The algorithm enables multiple AUVs to perform cooperative operations and jointly hunt down evading AUVs. By integrating optimal control and game theory, we enhance the learning capabilities of reinforcement learning for discrete behaviors. Through numerical example simulations, we validate the effectiveness of the proposed method. This research marks an important step towards enabling AUVs to operate collaboratively and effectively in future ocean battlefields.

Keywords: Pursuit-evasion game strategy · Multi-step reinforcement learning · Nash equilibrium

1 Introduction

The pursuit-evasion game strategy has broad applications in various domains, such as military operations, autonomous systems, and target tracking. However, there are several challenges in applying this strategy to AUVs for pursuit-evasion scenarios:

1. Limited research on multi-to-one pursuit-evasion game strategy: The current focus of research is primarily on one-to-one pursuit-evasion games, with less investigation into multi-to-one scenarios.
2. Lack of research on underwater AUV pursuit-evasion game strategy: Most research in pursuit-evasion game strategy revolves around mobile robots, unmanned vehicles, and similar systems, with limited consideration of underwater AUV scenarios that involve ocean currents and obstacles.

Supported in part by the National Natural Science Foundation of China under Grant 52271321, 61873161, Shanghai Rising-Star Program under Grant 20QA1404200 and Natural Science Foundation of Shanghai under Grant 22ZR1426700.

© The Author(s), under exclusive license to Springer Nature Singapore Pte Ltd. 2023
H. Yang et al. (Eds.): ICIRA 2023, LNAI 14269, pp. 201–213, 2023.
https://doi.org/10.1007/978-981-99-6489-5_16

3. Training complexity of reinforcement learning algorithms: Existing reinforcement learning algorithms require extensive model training when dealing with pursuit-evasion game strategies, resulting in time-consuming and error-prone processes.

The pursuit-evasion game strategy is akin to a path optimization problem. Extensive research has been conducted in this area, yielding various applicable results [1]. In real-world scenarios, reinforcement learning [2,3], especially Q-learning [4], has addressed the challenge of increased model uncertainty in designing pursuit-evasion strategies. However, Q-learning has limitations due to the expanding state space, leading to longer learning times and resource costs. To overcome these challenges, the Deep Q-Network (DQN) method [5] was introduced. DQN utilizes deep neural networks to approximate the Q function, enabling it to handle complex environments. Xu et al. [6] improved action learning efficiency in unknown environments using a DQN method with two experience pools for drone-based target monitoring.

However, the convergence theory of Q-learning, guaranteed in single-agent trajectory planning, is not assured in multi-agent scenarios. The independent Q-learning algorithm exacerbates the exploration-exploitation dilemma, particularly in the multi-AUV pursuit-escape game [7]. Training becomes challenging due to an unstable environment.

The subsequent sections of this article are organized as follows: Sect. 2 presents the modeling of AUV pursuit-evasion strategies. Section 3 introduces the improved multi-step Q-learning pursuit-evasion strategy. Section 4 discusses the multi-to-one AUV pursuit-evasion strategy based on reinforcement learning. Finally, Sect. 5 concludes the research.

2   Modeling of AUV Pursuit-Evasion Game Strategy

This article mainly uses the OpenAI Gym API [8] library to build a simulation model for analyzing AUV pursuit-evasion game strategies. By using the environments provided in the Gym library, we can establish an AUV pursuit-evasion strategy simulation model and design a certain AUV action space and observation space, as well as define a certain reward to assist in completing the AUV training and achieving the preset goals.

2.1   Simulating Interference in Ocean Current Environments

Establishing Irregular Obstacles. In the experiments in this paper, the map is set to a small scale of 25*25. In order to simulate the real ocean environment, irregular obstacles are randomly set in the initial construction of the environment. These obstacles are generated by random distribution on the map, making them closer to the real ocean environment. Through reinforcement learning in this environment, a more robust and adaptive AUV model can be trained to provide strong support for practical applications. The environment image is shown in the Fig. 1.

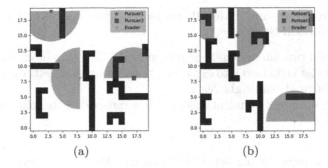

Fig. 1. Randomly generated two sets of underwater obstacle interference simulation images

Setting Random Flow Disturbance. Ocean currents can cause significant disturbances to the motion trajectory and attitude of an AUV, posing challenges to its control and navigation. Ocean currents may cause AUV drift, turning, and shaking, and may even lead to AUV loss of control or collision. Therefore, this simulation includes horizontal and vertical random ocean current disturbances. The implementation process of the random ocean current disturbance used in this paper can be intuitively understood through Fig. 2. When the AUV is affected by ocean current disturbances, it will also be recorded in the reward function for reinforcement learning.

Parameter a indicates whether the intensity of random water currents can affect the direction changes of the AUV, while parameter b represents that the direction of random water currents causes the AUV to change in different directions. x, y specifies the positive direction of the environmental interface.

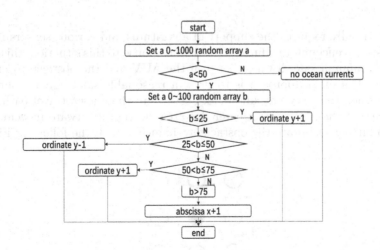

Fig. 2. Diagram of simulating water flow disturbance

2.2 Action Space and Safe Obstacle Avoidance of AUV Pursuit and Evasion Strategy

In the case of a two-dimensional environment, the direction of movement of the AUV underwater is divided into eight directions: front, rear, left, right, left front, left rear, right front, and right rear.

For an AUV, the environment space can be expressed by the following formula:

$$X = \{x_i, y_i, \theta, \zeta\} \tag{1}$$

where (x_i, y_i) represents the action node of the AUV at a certain moment, θ represents its action angle and ζ represents the environmental information.

The map mentioned above is a 25*25 square grid map, combined with the action space A_i of each AUV, so Table 1 can be obtained:

Table 1. AUV action, linear component, angular component

Action	Linear component	Angular component
Stop	0	0
Forward	1	0
Turn Left	0	1
Turn Right	0	−1
Forward Turn Left	1	1
Forward Turn Right	1	−1
step back	−1	0
Back and turn Left	−1	1
Back and turn Right	−1	−1

AUV usually requires the support of algorithms and various sensors to deal with obstacles encountered during travel. In response to this situation, this paper sets the minimum safe distance between the AUV and the obstacle to prevent collisions. The main approach is to draw a reasonable safety area around the obstacle when the AUV encounters an obstacle in the known travel path, so as to ensure that the AUV cannot enter this area during the forward movement. In order to further elaborate the obstacle avoidance model, the following Fig. 3 is

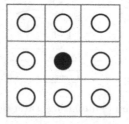

Fig. 3. Obstacle avoidance model

designed for display. Assuming that the solid point represents the position of the known obstacle, with the position of the known obstacle as the center, and the surrounding area can be divided into eight points around this obstacle. These eight points correspond to eight discrete coordinates, the AUV is required to avoid entering these eight points as a safety buffer zone to ensure obstacle avoidance. In this process, the reward and punishment mechanism in the Q-Learning algorithm model is further introduced. When the AUV enters the hollow point area during the movement, points will be deducted in the Q-Table, so that can make AUV learn to avoid hitting obstacles in iterative learning.

2.3 Two-to-One AUV Cooperative Pursuit Model

Introducing multiple pursuit AUVs into the pursuit-evasion game strategy model, assuming that each player does not have any information about its default strategy or the strategies of other players, each pursuer can know the instantaneous position of the escaper within the monitoring range, and vice versa The same is true. The goal is to allow AUVs to work together and approach the escapee at different locations. The following is the PE differential game model of two pursuers and one runner, as shown in Fig. 4.

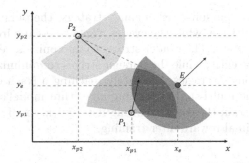

Fig. 4. Diagram of Q-Learning algorithm model

In order to obtain a balanced state, we expand the monitoring range of the escaper, This enables the escaper to accurately detect the instant positions of the two pursuing AUVs when they enter the detection range. When one of the pursuing AUVs senses the escapee within the detection range, the other pursuing AUV can also obtain the instant location information of the evading AUV.

In this game, both the pursuing AUVs and the evading AUV self-learn their control strategies online by interacting with each other.

2.4 Nash Equilibrium Theory

Nash equilibrium theory [9] refers to a state in the game, in which the decision made by each participant is optimal. And these decisions are coordinated with each other, and no participant can obtain better benefits by changing his own decisions. In the Nash equilibrium theory, the decision-making of participants not only depends on their own interests, but also is affected by the decisions of other participants.

In the game model, let $G = \{S_1, \cdots, S_n; u_1, \cdots, u_n\}$. Assuming that for each strategy composition $(s_1^*, \cdots, s_n^*)$ of the objects participating in the game, any strategy s_i^*, the participating player i is the best response to the remaining strategy composition $(s_1^*, \cdots, s_n^*)$,i.e., $u_i(s_1^*, \cdots, s_n^*) \geq u_j(s_1^* \cdots, s_n^*)$. For any $s_{ij} \in S_i$, then this strategy composition is called a Nash equilibrium of G. The following equation can be obtained:

$$p_i(s) = \max_{r_i}[p_i(s, r_i)] \tag{2}$$

The ultimate training goal of the pursuit-evasion game model for AUV is to achieve a Nash equilibrium state. In the competitive game between the pursuer and the evader, reaching a balanced state will realize the Nash equilibrium of the AUV pursuit-evasion strategy.

3   Improved Multi-step Q-Learning Pursuit-Evasion Strategy

In the scenario of the pursuit-evasion game strategy, the pursuer wants to catch the evader in a short time, while the evader wants to escape from the pursuer or prolong the pursuit time. The evader strives to maximize a certain payoff value through various strategies, while the pursuer strives to minimize the same payoff value through various strategies, ultimately reaching a Nash equilibrium point. This article uses the multi-step Q-learning algorithm model's Markov Decision Process (MDP) to train the AUV, allowing it to quickly make the best decision and obtain the optimal reward after training.

3.1   Optimal Strategy

In the Markov decision-making process, the agent will consider that different actions in a certain environment will generate completely different rewards, so there is an optimal situation among many choices. The decision-making process to solve the highest reward is called the optimal strategy. For policies π and π', if $\forall s \in v_\pi(s)$ and there exists $\exists v_\pi(s) \geq v_{\pi'}(s)$, then π is said to be better than π', denoted as $\pi \geq \pi'$. If there exists at least one policy whose return is better than that of any other policy, it is called the optimal policy, denoted as π^*.

$$\forall s, v^*(s) = \max v_\pi(s) \tag{3}$$

$$\forall s, q^*(s, a) = \max q_\pi(s, a) \tag{4}$$

Combining the relationship between $v_\pi(s)$ and $s - a$ for the value function mentioned earlier, we can derive:

$$q^*(s, a) = E[r_{t+1} + \gamma v^*(s+1)|s_t = s, a_t = a] \tag{5}$$

Combining the Bellman equation, we can obtain the Q-value function under the optimal policy:

$$v^* = \max_a \sum_{s',r} p(s',r|s,a)[r + \gamma v^*(s')] \tag{6}$$

As shown above, the $s - a$ value function in the optimal strategy and the Bellman equation combined with the Q-value function can be used to perform real-time evaluation of the current strategy based on the reward value.

3.2   The Multi-step Q-Learning Algorithm

Q-Learning Model and Q-value Table. Using the features of autonomous learning, recursive update, and autonomous adaptation of MDP, combined with the Q-Learning algorithm in reinforcement learning, the AUV can autonomously select actions to obtain the best reward. The following Q table is established, where the reward obtained within an action cycle (T) of the agent is influenced by the state s and action a, especially in this paper, unless otherwise stated, S, A, and R refer to random variables. Combining Q, s, and a, a corresponding Q-value table can be obtained for producing a certain action in a certain state.

Q-Learning Overall Algorithm and Update. In order to illustrate the Q-Learning algorithm model, this article focuses on the pursuer's behavior logic in the AUV pursuit-evasion game strategy. Assuming that the pursuer can only perceive the evader when they are within each other's field of view, nine different decision problems for pursuit direction are considered based on the relative positions. Each pursuit-evasion decision made by the AUV is recorded in the Q-Table and influences the selection of the next decision. The Q-Learning algorithm model updates the Q-Table based on the rewards received, guiding the pursuer's future actions. The ϵ-greedy approach determines the agent's decision-making strategy, allowing a certain percentage of random actions for further learning. Overall, the Q-Learning algorithm model is an iterative process for updating Q-values (Fig. 5).

TD objective function:

$$y_t = r_t + r^n * \max Q^*(S_{t+1}, a) \tag{7}$$

TD error function:

$$\delta_t = \gamma \max_a Q^*(S_{t+1}, a_t) + r_t - Q^*(S_t, A_t) \tag{8}$$

The overall algorithm of this model is as follows:

$$Q^*(S_t, A_t) \leftarrow Q^*(S_t, A_t) - \alpha[r_t + \gamma \max_a Q^*(S_{t+1}, a_t) - Q^*(S_t, A_t)] \tag{9}$$

Here are the tree diagram of the Q-learning algorithm:

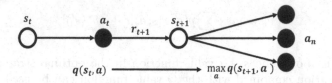

Fig. 5. Q-Learning Algorithm Model Tree Diagram

The Multi-step Q-Learning. Q-learning and a series of TD algorithms are usually used and trained in a single-step situation. Extending Q-learning to multiple time steps can achieve better performance. As shown in the figure below, the shorter box represents single-step Q-learning, and the longer box represents multi-step reinforcement learning with a step length of 2.

In this article, multiple iterations are used to sum and analyze the multi-step rewards to improve the stability of the algorithm's reward data, so that the rewards for chasing and evading the AUV can reach a balance more quickly (Fig. 6).

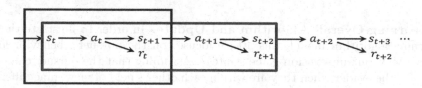

Fig. 6. Multi-step Q-learning Algorithm Model Chain Diagram

The n-step reward value of multi-step reinforcement learning can be transformed using the following formula:

$$G_{t:t+n} = R_{t+1} + \gamma R_{t+2} + \gamma^2 R_{t+3} + \cdots + \gamma^{n-1} R_{t+n} + \gamma^n Q_{t+n-1}(S_{t+n}, A_{t+n}) \quad (10)$$

$$G_{t:t+n} = \sum_{i=0}^{n-1} \gamma^i R_{t+i+1} + \gamma^n Q_{t+n-1}(S_{t+n}, A_{t+n}) \quad (11)$$

With the above definition, the TD target function for the improved n-step Q-learning algorithm can be obtained as follows:

$$y_t = \sum_{i=0}^{n-1} \gamma^i * r_{t+1} + \gamma^n * \max_a Q^*(S_{t+n}, a) \quad (12)$$

The overall algorithm of this model is as follows:

$$Q^*(S_t, A_t) \leftarrow Q^*(S_t, A_t) - \alpha[\sum_{i=0}^{n-1} \gamma^i * r_{t+1} + \gamma^n * \max_a Q^*(S_{t+n}, a) - Q^*(S_t, A_t)] \quad (13)$$

The main advantages of multi-step reinforcement learning over single-step reinforcement learning include:

1. Reduced variance: Multi-step reinforcement learning allows for controlling the number of updates using the discount factor, thereby reducing the variance of updates and accelerating the convergence of the model.
2. Better estimation of long-term rewards: Multi-step reinforcement learning can better estimate long-term rewards by accumulating multi-step rewards, thereby improving the quality of the model's decisions.
3. Better state estimation: Multi-step reinforcement learning can better estimate the value of the current state through multi-step transitions, thereby improving the learning efficiency and accuracy of the model.

4 Multi-to-One AUV Pursuit-Evasion Strategy Based on Reinforcement Learning

4.1 Principle and Model Training of Two-Dimensional AUV Pursuit and Evasion Simulation

We use the Q-Learning algorithm model's MDP to train the AUV, so that it can quickly make the best decision and get the optimal reward after training. To illustrate this more clearly, refer to Fig. 8 below. When the AUV generates an initial state, it will initially choose a random policy and take the first action, receiving a reward that will be stored in the Q-Table. The AUV will perform the action pairing when making the next decision (Fig. 7).

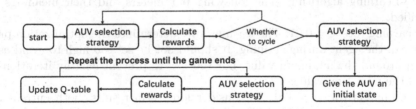

Fig. 7. Q-Learning applied to AUV pursuit-evasion Strategy model

At the same time, for this game process, the two sides involved in the pursuit-evasion are in an adversarial state, and their Q-Tables will be updated after each step. The ultimate training goal in the game process is to achieve a Nash equilibrium, and in this process, the AUV will seek the optimal strategy described earlier. This optimal strategy is actually the Hamilton-Jacobi equation:

$$\min_{u \in U(x)} \max_{v \in V(x)} \left[l(x, e, p, t) + \frac{\partial G^*}{\partial x_i} + \sum_{i=1}^{n} \frac{\partial G^*}{\partial x_i} f_i(x, u, v, t) \right] = 0 \qquad (14)$$

The variables in the equation are as follows: e represents the evader, p represents the pursuer, x is the state space S, t represents time, and $l(x, e, p, t)$ is the reward function for the evader and pursuer in a certain state space. G^* is the optimal strategy to be solved.

Based on the theory of optimal strategy, in order to make the pursuit-evasion game model based on the Q-Learning algorithm model continue to train and achieve good training results, it is necessary to design a suitable reward function, as shown in Table 2.

Table 2. Reward

R_{AUV}	R_{p1}	R_{p2}	R_e
Uncaptured	−1	−1	+2
Observation object	+2	+2	−4
Evader captured	+100	+100	−200
Colliding with obstacles	−5	−5	−5
Ocean current influence	−5	−5	−5
Collision with same−team	−10	−10	0

4.2 2v1 Pursuit-Evasion Strategy Based on Multi-step Reinforcement Learning

Selection of Hyperparameters. In the real underwater environment with obstacles, this paper focuses on analyzing the pursuit-evasion strategy using the Q-Learning algorithm. The following parameters and their meanings are specified:

Learning rate: $\epsilon = 0.01$. The learning rate determines the optimization probability of the agent during training. It should not be set too high to avoid oscillation around the minimum value, nor too low to prevent lengthy iterations to reach the minimum value.

Discount factor: $\gamma = 0.9$. To consider long-term results, both current and future rewards are important. The discount factor, γ, ranges between 0 and 1, and it determines the frequency of the agent choosing rewards in the future. A good strategy encourages the agent to select actions with maximum future rewards.

2D Obstacle-Based AUV Pursuit-Evasion Strategy Simulation. In this section, a water environment map with obstacles of size 25*25 is used. In order to obtain a more intuitive training result, the following indicators are set:

1. Reward and penalty situation for pursuing AUV 1;
2. Reward and penalty situation for pursuing AUV 2;
3. Reward and penalty situation for evading AUV;

All parameters are set, and the training process of AUV's pursuit-evasion strategy is shown below for part of the training process:

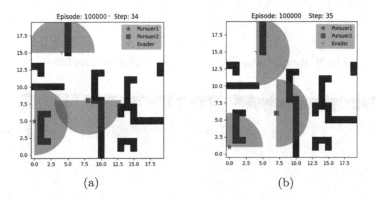

(a)   (b)

Fig. 8. Simulation of a certain pursuit-evasion game scenario (including 2 steps)

In the program, to account for randomness, a step limit is set to prevent episodes from getting stuck in loops. When the participating agents reach 1000 steps, the episode is considered over. If the pursuer fails to capture the evader within 1000 steps, it is marked as a capture failure, resulting in point deductions in the Q-Table. Training then proceeds to the next episode.

After each training episode, the values of these three metrics are recorded and stored in the Q-Table. These data metrics are plotted to visualize the training results and observe the training progress. This approach allows us to analyze the training situation of the intelligent agent at different iteration times, track data trends, determine if the AUV's training is converging, and make real-time updates to parameter settings for desired training outcomes. This method also enables real-time data export, providing quick access to training effects at any given training set number.

Multi-step Q-Learning for Pursuit-Evasion Strategy Model. We set the step parameter of n-step Q-learning to $w = 10$. To make a comparison, we also included the result of single-step Q-learning as a gray line in the graph. Since directly exporting raw data cannot reflect the training effect intuitively, we applied a median filter to calculate the average value of the data. The results of the processing are shown in Fig. 9, 10 and 11.

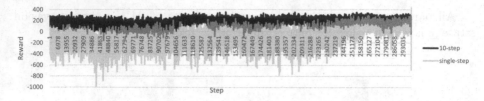

Fig. 9. Reward situation of Pursuer 1 after median filtering

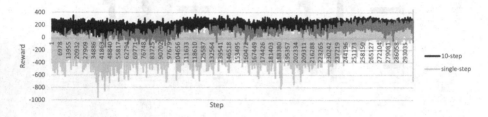

Fig. 10. Reward situation of Pursuer 2 after median filtering

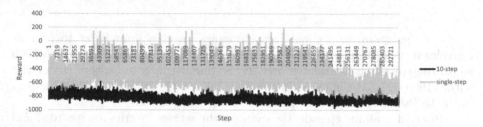

Fig. 11. Rewards for the Evader after median filterin

After analyzing the data, we can see that in the scenario of seeking the optimal strategy for the multi-to-one pursuit-evasion at Nash equilibrium in the pursuit-evasion game, enhancing single-step Q-learning to multi-step Q-learning can make the reward value of the Q-table grow more steadily, and the data fluctuations are relatively mild compared to before. After 120,000 training sessions, the reward fluctuation gradually decreased and eventually became stable. On the other hand, single-step Q-learning only showed a relatively stable reward situation after 250,000 training sessions, indicating that multi-step Q-learning greatly shortened the required training time.

Comparing the results, we can see that even after stabilizing, single-step Q-learning still exhibits fluctuations in reward values, with differences of over 400 between maximum and minimum values, while multi-step Q-learning can effectively control reward errors to within 100, making it relatively more stable. Therefore, based on the results of this experiment, we can conclude that multi-step Q-learning has higher stability and better performance in seeking the optimal strategy for pursuit and evasion in the pursuit-evasion game one-on-one scenario, compared to single-step Q-learning.

5   Conclusion

This paper has developed a multi-AUV multi-player pursuit-evasion motion model that simulates an underwater environment with irregular obstacles and random ocean currents. To address the pursuit-evasion strategy problem, we utilized the Multi-step Q-learning algorithm as the training agent algorithm, transforming it into a differential game problem. By designing a suitable and effective Q-Table with reward and punishment allocation, and supplementing the training with sensors of a certain specification. Eventually, we achieved Nash equilibrium in the confrontation between pursuers and evaders. The proposed Multi-step Q-learning algorithm effectively solves the shortcomings of Q-learning such as poor stability and large data fluctuations.

References

1. De Souza, C., Newbury, R., Cosgun, A., Castillo, P., Vidolov, B., Kulić, D.: Decentralized multi-agent pursuit using deep reinforcement learning. IEEE Robot. Autom. Lett. **6**(3), 4552–4559 (2021)
2. Zhu, K., Zhang, T.: Deep reinforcement learning based mobile robot navigation: a review. Tsinghua Sci. Technol. **26**(5), 674–691 (2021)
3. Fang, Y., Huang, Z.W., Pu, J.Y., Zhang, J.S.: AUV position tracking and trajectory control based on fast-deployed deep reinforcement learning method. Ocean Eng. **24514**, 110452 (2022)
4. Xi, M., Yang, J., Wen, J., Liu, H., Li, Y., Song, H.H.: Comprehensive ocean information-enabled AUV path planning via reinforcement learning. IEEE Internet Things J. **9**(18), 17440–17451 (2022)
5. Liu, L., Tian, B., Zhao, X., Zong, Q.: UAV autonomous trajectory planning in target tracking tasks via a DQN approach. In: 2019 IEEE International Conference on Real-time Computing and Robotics (RCAR), pp. 277–282 (2019)
6. Xu, G., Wang, Y., Liu, H.: UAV multi-target surveillance cruise trajectory planning based on DQN algorithm. In: 2022 China Automation Congress (CAC), pp. 851–856 (2022)
7. Wang, Z., Sui, Y., Qin, H., Lu, H.: State super sampling soft actor-critic algorithm for multi-AUV hunting in 3D underwater environment. J. Mar. Sci. Eng. **11**(7), 1257 (2023)
8. Setiaji, B., Pujastuti, E., Filza, M.F., Masruro, A., Pradana, Y.A.: Implementation of reinforcement learning in 2d based games using open AI gym. In: 2022 International Conference on Informatics, Multimedia, Cyber and Information System (ICIMCIS), pp. 293–297 (2022)
9. Frihauf, P., Krstic, M., Basar, T.: Nash equilibrium seeking in noncooperative games. IEEE Trans. Autom. Control **57**(5), 1192–1207 (2012)
10. Feinberg, E.A.: Continuous time discounted jump markov decision processes: a discrete-event approach. Math. Oper. Res. **29**(3), 492–524 (2004)
11. Feng, Y., Dai, L., Gao, J., Cheng, G.: Uncertain pursuit-evasion game. Soft. Comput. **24**(4), 2425–2429 (2020)

Rock-Climbing Fish Inspired Skeleton-Embedded Rigid-Flexible Coupling Suction Disc Design for Adhesion Enhancement

Wenjun Tan[1,2,3] ⓘ, Hengshen Qin[1,2,3] ⓘ, Chuang Zhang[1,2(✉)] ⓘ,
Ruiqian Wang[1,2,3] ⓘ, Yiwei Zhang[1,2,3] ⓘ, Lianchao Yang[1,2,3] ⓘ, Qin Chen[4] ⓘ,
Feifei Wang[5] ⓘ, Ning Xi[6] ⓘ, and Lianqing Liu[1,2] ⓘ

[1] State Key Laboratory of Robotics, Shenyang Institute of Automation, Chinese Academy of Sciences, Shenyang 110016, China
zhangchuang@sia.cn
[2] Institutes for Robotics and Intelligent Manufacturing, Chinese Academy of Sciences, Shenyang 110169, China
[3] University of Chinese Academy of Sciences, Beijing 100049, China
[4] Chengdu Institute of Biology, Chinese Academy of Sciences, Chengdu 610042, Sichuan, China
[5] Department of Electrical and Electronic Engineering, University of Hong Kong, Hong Kong 999077, China
[6] Emerging Technologies Institute, Department of Industrial and Manufacturing Systems Engineering, University of Hong Kong, Pokfulam, Hong Kong 999077, China

Abstract. Underwater high-performance biological adhesion systems have attracted increasing research interest to inspire engineered adhesion systems. Switchable underwater adhesion systems typically employ suction adhesion. However, achieving low pre-pressure negative pressure adhesion is still a challenge. An inspiring nature mode is provided by the rock-climbing fish, which needs little preload and can resist a pull-off force of 1000 times its own body weight. The pectoral and abdominal fins of rock-climbing fish have evolved to almost a flat suction cup. Through micro CT, we found that a unique skeletal network is embedded in the suction cup. This unique structure increases the stiffness of the suction cup and enhances its adhesion performance. Through numerical simulation, it was revealed that this rigid, flexible coupling structure enhances the ability of the suction cup to resist lateral pressure and increases the energy dissipation of the edge detachment of the suction cup. This work can shed light on the design of novel underwater adhesion systems and inspire underwater adhesion crawling robots.

Keywords: Suction · Bioinspired · Underwater Adhesion · Skeleton-Flesh · Adhesion-Enhancement

© The Author(s), under exclusive license to Springer Nature Singapore Pte Ltd. 2023
H. Yang et al. (Eds.): ICIRA 2023, LNAI 14269, pp. 214–225, 2023.
https://doi.org/10.1007/978-981-99-6489-5_17

1   Introduction

Underwater adhesion systems are receiving increasing attention due to their potential applications in ocean exploration, underwater operations, and underwater grasping. Recently rock-climbing fish have broken into people's vision due to their excellent adhesion-crawling ability. The rock-climbing fish (Beaufortia kweichowensis) can attach itself to the rock in the current with strong water impact [1], uses the entire body as a suction cup [2], has an adhesion capacity of 1000 times its own body weight and can adhere and slide on the wall surface [3]. This fish requires less preload to achieve suction adhesion. The adhesion performance and mechanism of the fish have been discussed, and the main contribution of adhesion force is provided by negative pressure [1, 4]. Based on its adhesion locomotion model, a climbing robot is designed that is able to crawl on walls in a gait manner [3, 5]. However, there have been few reports on the mechanism of the low preload demand of rock-climbing fish.

Underwater switchable biological adhesion systems mainly employ suction force to adhere and require a large pre-pressure to maintain attachment [6–9]. However, the high pre-pressure required for negative pressure adhesion is a challenge, as it requires an elaborate process to provide pre-pressure and considerable force to achieve detachment [10]. Biological suction cups are composite materials with specially oriented internal structures in most cases. For example, octopus suction cups consist of a well-aligned three-dimensional array of muscle fibers. The crossed connective tissue fibers may store elastic energy, providing an economical mechanism for maintaining attachment [11, 12]. Remora suction discs have vertically oriented collagen fibers, which enable anisotropic mechanical properties and can enhance the adhesion performance of suction discs [13]. In the adhesion pad of tree frogs, hexagonal arrays of (soft) epithelial cells are crossed by densely packed and oriented (hard) keratin nanofibrils. The presence of hard nano fibrils alters the stress distribution at the contact interface of micropillars and therefore enhances the adhesion and friction of the composite micropattern [14]. The adhesion systems of sea urchins and sea stars also have the ability to deform viscoelastically to enhance adaptability to the substrate [15].

As a typical surface effect, surface adhesion has become the frontier of surface mechanics [16, 17]. The skeletal muscle coupling model is used to enhance the mechanical performance of the structure [18–21]. The contact failure process of these composite biological structure suction cups can be analyzed based on the interface failure model of the soft material bonding structure [22, 23]. The peeling model has been developed to describe the surface adhesion of flies [24], geckos [25], frogs [26], spiders [27], ants, bees [28], and so on. The contact and peeling process between the suction cup lip and the substrate affects the suction cup adhesion and detachment phenomena. Therefore, studying the peeling process of the skeleton-embedded rigid, flexible coupling suction disc of the rock-climbing fish is of great significance for understanding the adhesion of the fish, but it is ignored.

In this article, a unique skeletal network image of rock-climbing fish was obtained by micro CT; the Young's modulus of the fish skeleton and flesh were measured using AFM; and the four main failure modes of negative pressure suction cups were analyzed. Through a theoretical model based on the principle of minimum potential energy for adhesive contact between thin elastic films and rigid substrates, the mechanical process of suction cup edge peeling from the substrate was analyzed.

Using Abaqus numerical simulation software, the deformation and failure process of suction cups with and without a skeleton under detachment force was analyzed. The mechanism by which the skeleton structure enhances the adhesion performance has been revealed: the skeleton network embedded in the edge of the suction cup can enhance the edge stiffness, store elastic potential energy, and consume more energy to peel off the edge of the suction cup, thereby reducing the demand for pre-pressure when the suction cup adheres and maintains adhesion; At the same time, the skeleton network can also enhance the stiffness of the cavity, withstand large lateral force, and resist the failure caused by the inward contraction of the suction cup edge, thereby enhancing the adhesion performance. The rigid, flexible coupling suction cup model with the embedded bone network can achieve low pre-pressure adhesion, providing inspiration for the design of novel underwater adhesion systems and adhesion-crawling robots.

2 Method and Materials

2.1 Sample Preparation

All experiments and surgical procedures were approved by the Animal Use and Care Committee at Chengdu Institute of Biology, Chinese Academy of Sciences, which complies with the National Institutes of Health Guide for the Care and Use of Laboratory Animals (AUCC number: CIBDWLL2022032). All efforts were made to minimize the number of animals used and their suffering.

We collected 10 rock-climbing fish (*B. kweichowensis*) in the field and raised them in a $60 \times 100 \times 50$ cm fish tank. The fish tank was equipped with a filter device, an air pump, and a thermostat. The temperature was maintained at 22 ± 1 °C, and the fish were fed every day with multiple algae wafers.

2.2 Measurement of Young's Modulus of the Skeleton and Flesh of Rock-Climbing Fish

An adult rock-climbing fish (*B. kweichowensis*), with a length of 6.5 cm and a weight of 3.2g was used, and anesthetized to death with 0.5 g/L MS-222 (Sigma Chemical, USA) for 15 min, cut off the skull, pectoral fin section, pelvic fin section, caudal fin bone section, and backbone section of rock-climbing fish, washed with phosphate buffer solution (PBS) (Sigma Chemical, USA) three times, every time 10 min. Rinse off the mucus and secretions on the surface of the tissue, and glue the cut tissue section onto a slide with ultraviolet curable glue (NOA63, Edmund Optics). The force curve of the skeleton was measured by using a TESP-V2 probe (spring constant of 42 N/m) in the AFM (Dimension Icon, Bruker Corporation, USA) contact in air mode. Measurement of flesh Young's modulus: dissect and cut off the sections of the pectoral fin, pelvic fin, abdomen, back, and tail of rock-climbing fish with a scalpel, wash them with PBS three times, 20 min each time, and glue the cleaned tissues to the bottom of the culture dish with light curing adhesive, and soak them in PBS. The force curve was measured by using the MLCT-C probe (spring constant of 0.01 N/m) in the AFM (Dimension Icon, Bruker Corporation, USA) contact in fluid mode. NanoScope Analysis 1.8 software is used to fit the retrace curve of the obtained force curves, and the Hertzian model is used to fit force–displacement curves, ensure that the fitting goodness R2 > 99%, and read the value of Young's modulus.

2.3 Micro CT Scanning of the Skeleton

An adult rock-climbing fish (B. kweichowensis), with a length of 6.2 cm and a weight of 3.1g was used and, anesthetized to death with 0.5 g/L MS-222 (Sigma Chemical, USA) for 15 min. The attached state was maintained, and the fish was fixed with 2.5% glutaraldehyde (EM Grade) (Solarbio, Beijing Co. Ltd.) for 48 h. To reduce the damage of glutaraldehyde to the enzyme activity of tissue cells, fixation was carried out at 4 °C. After fixing the sample, SkyScan2211 (Bruker Corporation, USA) was used for micro CT scanning and 3D reconstruction to obtain the skeleton of the rock-climbing fish.

2.4 Suction Cup Dynamic Simulation

The simulation was performed using Abaqus/CAE 2021 software. Two suction cup models were built: a soft suction cup and a skeleton embedded inside the suction cup. The Young's modulus and Poisson's ratio of the soft cup ($E_1 = 40$ kPa, $v_1 = 0.45$) and the skeleton ($E_2 = 2.5$ GPa, $v_2 = 0.3$), respectively, along with a density of 1 g/cm^3 for the sucker and 1.138 g/cm^3 for the rigid support. Rigid constraints are applied to the pulling surface of the suction cup to prevent rapid local deformation caused by excessive concentrated forces during the pulling process. A face-to-face tie constraint is applied to the rigid body support and the suction cup cavity to achieve insertion. Set the tangential behavior (frictionless) and the normal behavior (hard contact, the rest by default) as contact properties for the general contact of the whole model. A concentrated force load of 0.24 N is applied to the rigidized pulling surface, and a pressure load of 3 Pa is applied to the lip ring of the suction cup to constrain the displacement of the outer ring of the suction cup so that it slides only in the plane. Additionally, because suction cups are axisymmetric shapes, symmetry constraints are imposed on the suction cup model tangents.

3   Results and Discussion

3.1 Morphology and Skeleton Structure of the Rock-Climbing Fish

The pectoral and pelvic fins of the rock-climbing fish have evolved into a nearly flat suction cup, as shown in Fig. 1A. The cavity structure of the suction cup is not obvious. From the top view of the rock-climbing fish in Fig. 1B, it can be seen that its trunk width accounts for approximately one-third of the entire body width, and the outer edge of the suction cup formed by the pectoral and pelvic fins accounts for two-thirds of the entire body width. The skeletal network of the rock-climbing fish is shown in Fig. 1C, with the pectoral and pelvic fins densely arranged to form a flat outer edge of the suction cup. The diameter of the pectoral and pelvic fins is approximately 0.3 to 0.4 mm, and the length is approximately 2.5 to 5 mm. The pectoral fins are connected to the skull, and the pelvic fin bones are not connected to the pectoral fins or the skull and exist independently. The spine is connected to the skull and disconnected from the pectoral and abdominal fins. The backbone is 0.8 to 1.2 mm wide, with a fin diameter of 0.2 mm, and bends inward.

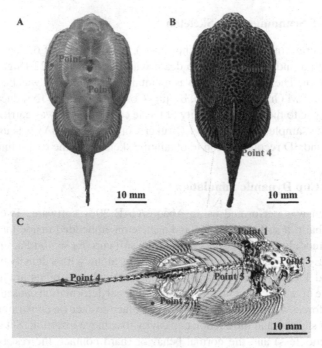

Fig. 1. The rock-climbing fish and its skeleton network. (A) Bottom view of the rock-climbing fish; (B) Top view of the rock-climbing fish; (C) The skeletal network structure of the rock-climbing fish, obtained through micro CT.

3.2 Young's Modulus of the Skeleton and Flesh of the Rock-Climbing Fish

To investigate the mechanical properties of rock-climbing fish sucker, the Young's modulus of skeleton and flesh were measured by atomic force microscopy. The positions of the test points are shown in the marks in Fig. 1. The Young's modulus is shown in Fig. 2, with an average skeletal Young's modulus of 2661.28 ± 226.58 MPa and a flesh of 39.12 ± 7.07 kPa. The skull is harder than other skeletons, and the abdominal flesh is softer than other parts of the flesh. The difference in Young's modulus between the skeleton and the flesh is nearly five orders of magnitude.

3.3 Failure Forms of Suction Cups

Negative pressure adhesion can be reducible to the axisymmetric model shown in Fig. 3A. When the pull-off force and negative pressure reach an equilibrium state,

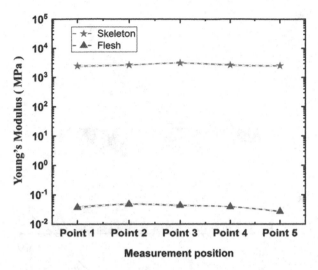

Fig. 2. Young's modulus of skeletons and flesh in different points of the rock-climbing fish

$F_{pull} = (P_o - P_{in}) * \pi * R^2$, F_{-ad} is the adhesion force at the edge of the suction cup, and F_1 is the internal force of the suction cup, which affects the failure form of the suction cup. The main forms of negative pressure adhesion failure include the following:

- $F_1 \sin\theta > F_{-ad}$, the suction cup falls off the surface
- $F_1 \cos\theta > F_{-f}$, the suction cup edge contracts inward
- Under the action of F_1, the suction cup edge peels off, and the contact line expands
- $\Delta P > P_{max}$, the medium is pressed into the cavity, damaging the seal, or the pressure inside the underwater suction cup reaches the cavitation pressure.

In the first case, F_{-ad} is provided by pre-pressure or interfacial adhesion force. When the vertical component of the cup's internal force under the pull-off force is greater than the adhesion force at the edge of the suction cup, it will cause the entire suction cup to detach from the substrate. In the second case, the horizontal component of the internal force of the cup is greater than the sliding friction force between the suction cup and the base, causing the edge of the suction cup to slip toward the center and collapse. In the third case, under the internal force of the cup, the contact line between the edge of the suction cup and the substrate gradually expands outward, ultimately causing the suction cup to peel from the substrate. In the fourth case, when the pressure difference between the inside and outside of the suction cup is too large, the external medium of the suction cup is pressed into the suction cup, balancing the pressure difference and causing the suction cup to fail. In addition, during underwater adhesion, there is another situation: the volume expansion of vapor or dissolved gas inside the liquid or at the liquid-solid interface forms cavities (bubbles) due to the decrease in the pressure inside the liquid, leading to the failure of the suction cup. For the first case, to enhance adhesion, an increase in the adhesion force can be achieved by increasing the pre-pressure, and the fourth case is the limit case of the suction cup. The main failure modes of suction cups are the second and third cases, which are related to the stress-strain and energy dissipation

220   W. Tan et al.

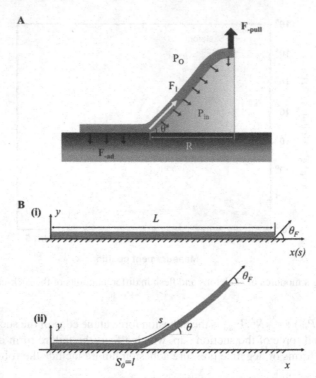

Fig. 3. Schematic diagram of a suction cup. (A) Force analysis diagram of an axisymmetric sucker; (B) Schematic diagram of the film peeling process from initial to steady state on a flat substrate.

of soft materials and can be simplified as the process of film peeling (Fig. 3B). The pre-pressure at the edge of the suction cup can be regarded as the adhesion force between the film and the substrate.

3.4   Failure Model for the Bonding Interface of Rigid Flexible Coupled Composite Materials

A theoretical model for adhesive contact between elastic thin films and rigid sub-strates was established based on the principle of minimum potential energy [17]. Based on this model, the entire process of thin film from initial debonding to steady-state debonding is described. At the initial moment (Fig. 3B-i), the film adheres to the sub-strate. The interfacial force is represented by the Lennard–Jones potential function $V(r) = W\left[\left(\sigma/_r\right)^{12} - \left(\sigma/_r\right)^6\right]$, where W is the depth of the potential well, σ is the length parameter that determines the equilibrium position of two atoms, and γ is the distance between the two atoms. The right end of the film is subjected to an external force F, and the tearing angle is θ_F. At any stage during the film peeling process (Fig. 3B-ii), the total potential energy of the system can be expressed as:

$$G = \int_0^L \frac{1}{2} D\{\theta'^2 ds + \int_0^L \frac{F^2}{2Eh} \cos^2(\theta - \theta_F) ds - \int_0^L \frac{F^2}{Eh} \cos(\theta - \theta_F) \cos(\theta_L - \theta_F) ds$$

$$- \int_0^L F \cos(\theta - \theta_F) ds + \int_0^L W\left[\left(\frac{\sigma}{y}\right)^9 - \left(\frac{\sigma}{y}\right)^3\right] ds + \int_0^L \lambda_1(y' - \sin\theta) ds$$

$$+ \int_0^L \lambda_2(x' - \cos\theta) ds \tag{1}$$

where E and h represent the Young's modulus and thickness of the thin film, respectively, $D = h^3/12$ represents the bending stiffness of the membrane, θ is the tangential angle at any point on the film, s is the arc length of the film starting from the origin, and λ_1 and λ_2 represent two Lagrange multipliers.

The control equation for the film peeling process can be obtained by minimizing the total potential energy of the system and combining it with the corresponding boundary conditions:

$$F\sin(\theta - \theta_F) - \frac{F^2}{Eh}\sin(\theta - \theta_F)\cos(\theta_L - \theta_F) = 0 \tag{2}$$

$$\lambda'_1 = -\frac{\partial V}{\partial y}, \lambda_2 = 0 \tag{3}$$

$$x' = \cos\theta, y' = \sin\theta \tag{4}$$

$$\lambda_1(L) = 0, \theta'(0) = 0, \theta'(L) = 0 \tag{5}$$

From this peeling-off model, the peel-off angle and bending stiffness have important effects on the peel-off behavior of films. In the initial debonding stage, the peel-off force monotonically increases with increasing peel distance. After the film reaches the steady-state peel-off stage, the pell-off force remains unchanged. Bending stiffness mainly affects the initial stage of film peel-off, and the peel force increases with increasing bending stiffness.

For the skeleton-embedded rigid-flexible coupling suction disc, the effective elastic modulus of the composite cup E_{comp} can be estimated as [14]:

$$E_{comp} = V_{skeleton}E_{skeleton} + V_{flesh}E_{Flesh} \tag{6}$$

where V is the volume fraction for each material, and E is Young's modulus. Taking $E_{skeleton}$, E_{flesh}, and $V_{skeleton}$ to be 2661 MPa, 39 kPa, and 0.33, respectively, the estimated Ecomp is 878.16 MPa, which is 2×10^4 times higher than flesh.

The enhanced stiffness of the composite cup has significant effects on the peeling-off process in the beginning. The peel force increases with increasing bending stiffness. Therefore, it enhances the adhesion performance of the rigid-flexible coupling suction disc.

3.5 Numerical Simulation of Rigid-Flexible Coupling Negative Pressure Suction Cup

To analyze the failure process of suction cups under the action of pull-off force, the failure process of vacuum suction cups with and without a skeleton is analyzed through dynamic simulation, as shown in Fig. 4. It can be seen that the suction cup without a skeleton exhibits a phenomenon of peeking at the edge of the suction cup and inward sliding between 0–1 ms. The suction cup with an embedded skeleton structure showed almost no change in the angle between the inner wall of the suction cup and the base within 0–1 ms, indicating that there was almost no peeling process.

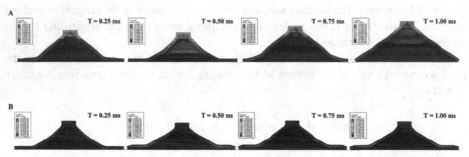

Fig. 4. Dynamic simulation of a suction cup under a pull-off force. (A)The deformation process of the pure soft cup. (B) The deformation process of the cup with an embedded skeleton.

The outer side of the suction cup was selected as point P1 (Fig. 5A-C) and its displacement along the X direction under the pulling force (Fig. 5D). Select the critical contact point (near the inside of the suction cup) between the suction cup and the substrate surface P2 was selected and its displacement along the Y direction under the pulling force was plotted (Fig. 5E). The center of mass of the tetrahedral grid close to the substrate surface where the critical contact point between the two types of suction cups and the substrate surface is located is selected separately, and the stress changes under the pulling force are analyzed (Fig. 5A-F).

From Fig. 5D, it can be seen that compared to the pure soft suction cup, the inward sliding displacement of the suction cup lip in the x-axis direction is smaller, and the peeling amplitude of the suction cup is also smaller (Fig. 5F). To investigate the causes of deformation differences, we analyzed the changes in stress on the inner side of the suction cup. From the stress result (Fig. 5A-F), it can be seen that at 0.35 ms, the force is transmitted to the skeleton, which is absorbed and stored as elastic potential energy by the rigid skeleton, weakening further deformation of the soft cup (red line). As a comparison, the suction cup without a rigid skeleton continued to increase after 0.35ms, ultimately leading to greater deformation and displacement of the suction cup edge (blue line). The skeleton structure can reduce the suction cup's deformation and enhance the suction cup's adhesion performance.

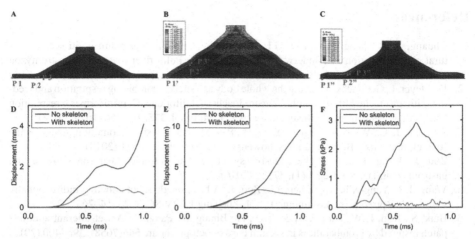

Fig. 5. The analysis of dynamic simulation. (A)The point selected for analysis. (B) The final deformation of the soft cup. (C) The final deformation of the cup with an embedded skeleton. (D) Displacement in the x-direction of point P1. (E) Displacement in the y-direction of point P2. (F) Stress changes at point P3.

4 Conclusion

In this article, we conducted a mechanical analysis of the unique skeletal muscle suction cup structure of rock-climbing fish and analyzed the process of detachment failure caused by deformation of the suction cup edge based on the thin film peeling model. We compared the failure forms of suction cups with and without skeletal networks. Through numerical simulation, the deformation process and stress transfer process of composite materials were analyzed, revealing the reason why the skeleton network structure enhances the suction cup adhesion force. On the one hand, edge toughening requires more energy to peel off the edge of the suction cup, reducing the demand for F-ad and achieving low pre-pressure negative pressure adsorption. On the other hand, the small angle between the substrate and the suction cup of the rock-climbing fish reduces the vertical component of the internal force of the suction cup, resulting in a smaller demand for F_{ad} at the edge of the suction cup and reducing the demand for preload. At the same time, the embedded skeleton network can enhance the stiffness of the cavity and withstand significant lateral pressure. This work can shed light on the design of novel underwater adhesion systems and inspire underwater adhesion crawling robots.

Funding. This work was supported by National Key R&D Program of China [2020YFB1313100]; National Natural Science Foundation of China [62003338]; National Natural Science Foundation of China [61925307]; National Defense Science and Technology Innovation Key deployment project of Chinese Academy of Sciences [JCPYJJ-22020]; Youth Innovation Promotion Association, Chinese Academy of Science [2023210].

224   W. Tan et al.

References

1. Chuang, Y.C., Chang, H.K., Liu, G.L., Chen, P.Y.: Climbing upstream: multi-scale structural characterization and underwater adhesion of the Pulin river loach (Sinogastromyzon puliensis). J. Mech. Behav. Biomed. **73**, 76–85 (2017)
2. De Meyer, J., Geerinckx, T.: Using the whole body as a sucker: combining respiration and feeding with an attached lifestyle in hill stream loaches (Balitoridae, Cypriniformes): respiration and feeding mechanism in hill stream loaches. J. Morphol. **275**(9), 1066–1079 (2014)
3. Wang, J., Ji, C., Wang, W., Zou, J., Yang, H., Pan, M.: An adhesive locomotion model for the rock-climbing fish. Beaufortia kweichowensis. Sci. Rep. **9**(1), 16571 (2019)
4. Zou, J., Wang, J., Ji, C.: The adhesive system and anisotropic shear force of guizhou gastromyzontidae. Sci. Rep. **6**(1), 37221 (2016)
5. Wang, J.R., Yong-Xin, X.I., Chen, J.I., Zou, J.: A biomimetic robot crawling bidirectionally with load inspired by rock-climbing fish. J. Zhejiang UNIV-SC A. **23**, 14–26 (2022)
6. Baik, S., Kim, D.W., Park, Y., Lee, T.-J., Ho Bhang, S., Pang, C.: A wet-tolerant adhesive patch inspired by protuberances in suction cups of octopi. Nature **546**(7658), 396–400 (2017)
7. Wang, Y., et al.: A biorobotic adhesive disc for underwater hitchhiking inspired by the remora suckerfish. Sci. Robot. **2**(10), eaan8072 (2017)
8. Lee, H., Um, D.-S., Lee, Y., Lim, S., Kim, H., Ko, H.: Octopus-inspired smart adhesive pads for transfer printing of semiconducting nanomembranes. Adv. Mater. **28**(34), 7457–7465 (2016)
9. Wainwright, D.K., Kleinteich, T., Kleinteich, A., Gorb, S.N., Summers, A.P.: Stick tight: suction adhesion on irregular surfaces in the northern clingfish. Biol. Lett. **9**(3), 20130234 (2013)
10. Ditsche, P., Summers, A.P.: Aquatic versus terrestrial attachment: Water makes a difference. Beilstein J. Nanotechnol. **5**, 2424–2439 (2014)
11. Kier, W.M.: The structure and adhesive mechanism of octopus suckers. Integr. Comp. Biol. **42**(6), 1146–1153 (2002)
12. Tramacere, F., Beccai, L., Kuba, M., Gozzi, A., Bifone, A., Mazzolai, B.: The morphology and adhesion mechanism of octopus vulgaris suckers. PLoS One **8**(6), e65074 (2013)
13. Su, S., et al.: Vertical fibrous morphology and structure-function relationship in natural and biomimetic suction-based adhesion discs. Matter **2**(5), 1207–1221 (2020)
14. Xue, L., et al.: Hybrid surface patterns mimicking the design of the adhesive toe pad of tree frog. ACS Nano **11**(10), 9711–9719 (2017)
15. Dodou, D., Breedveld, P., de Winter, J.C.F., Dankelman, J., van Leeuwen, J.L.: Mechanisms of temporary adhesion in benthic animals. Biol. Rev. **86**(1), 15–32 (2011)
16. Majumder, A., Ghatak, A., Sharma, A.: Microfluidic adhesion induced by subsurface microstructures. Science **318**(5848), 258–261 (2007)
17. Peng, Z., Chen, S.: Effect of bending stiffness on the peeling behavior of an elastic thin film on a rigid substrate. Phys. Rev. E. **91**(4), 042401 (2015)
18. Britz, R., Johnson, G.D.: Ontogeny and homology of the skeletal elements that form the sucking disc of remoras (Teleostei, Echeneoidei, Echeneidae). J. Morphol. **273**(12), 1353–1366 (2012)
19. Meyers, M.A., Chen, P.-Y., Lin, A.Y.-M., Seki, Y.: Biological materials: structure and mechanical properties. Prog. Mater. Sci. **53**(1), 1–206 (2008)
20. Sander, I.L., Dvorak, N., Stebbins, J.A., Carr, A.J., Mouthuy, P.-A.: Advanced robotics to address the translational gap in tendon engineering. Cyborg Bionic Syst. **2022**, 9842169 (2022)
21. Perez-Guagnelli, E., Jones, J., D Damian, D.: Hyperelastic membrane actuators: analysis of toroidal and helical multifunctional configurations. Cyborg Bionic Syst. **2022**, 9786864 (2022)

22. Gu, Z., Li, S., Zhang, F., Wang, S.: Understanding surface adhesion in nature: a peeling model. Adv. Sci. **3**(7), 1500327 (2016)
23. Chen, Y., Meng, J., Gu, Z., Wan, X., Jiang, L., Wang, S.: Bioinspired multiscale wet adhesive surfaces: structures and controlled adhesion. Adv. Funct. Mater. **30**(5), 1905287 (2020)
24. Niederegger, S., Gorb, S., Jiao, Y.K.: Contact behaviour of tenent setae in attachment pads of the blowfly Calliphora vicina (Diptera, Calliphoridae). J. Comp. Physiol. A -Neuroethol. Sens. Neural Behav. Physiol. **187**(12), 961–970 (2002)
25. Pesika, N.S., et al.: Peel-zone model of tape peeling based on the gecko adhesive system. J. Adhes. **83**(4), 383–401 (2007)
26. Hanna, B.W.J.P.: Adhesion and detachment of the toe pads of tree frogs. J. Exp. Biol. **155**, 103–125 (1991)
27. Skopic, B.H., Schniepp, H.C.: Peeling in biological and bioinspired adhesive systems. JOM **72**(4), 1509–1522 (2020). https://doi.org/10.1007/s11837-020-04037-3
28. Federle, W., Brainerd, E.L., McMahon, T.A., Holldobler, B.: Biomechanics of the movable pretarsal adhesive organ in ants and bees. Proc. Natl. Acad. Sci. U.S.A. **98**(11), 6215–6220 (2001)

An Underwater Inductively Coupled Power Transfer System with a Ring-Shaped Coupler for ROV Charging

Yurui Zhang, Bohao He, Anzhe Yi, and Yanhu Chen[✉]

State Key Laboratory of Fluid Power and Mechatronic Systems, Department of Mechanical Engineering, Zhejiang University, Hangzhou 310000, China
yanhuchen@zju.edu.cn

Abstract. The wireless charging of underwater vehicles by underwater docking stations is an important application of Inductively Coupled Power Transfer (ICPT) technology. At present, most of the underwater docking stations are designed for rotary structures and suitable for single-direction docking. Aiming at the underwater docking and charging of Remote Operated Vehicle (ROV), a ring-shaped coupler mechanism is proposed in this paper. The charging station adopts a cylindrical ring structure, on which coil segments of the primary side are evenly distributed. The bottom of the ROV is equipped with a multi-joint mechanical claw, on which coil segments of the secondary side are wound. Through the action of ROV mechanical claw, ring-coupling is realized between coils on two sides for wireless power transfer. Such docking system supports omnidirectional docking in the horizontal direction. A prototype is established and experiments are carried out in a water tank. It is proven that the system is able to achieve 45 W wireless power transmission, of which maximum efficiency is 57%.

Keywords: Inductively Coupled Power Transfer · Remote Operated Vehicle · Ring-shaped Coupler

1 Introduction

Based on the phenomenon of electromagnetic induction, ICPT technology has been applied for underwater power transfer. The wireless charging of underwater vehicles by docking stations is an important application of ICPT technology [1, 2]. Most of the present underwater docking stations adopt the passive docking method of bell mouth, and often designed for the rotary structures like AUVs [3]. But its versatility is limited, since a single docking station can only satisfy the docking of single outer-diameter vehicle [4]. In addition, most underwater docking systems can only adapt to one-direction docking, unable to support omnidirectional docking. Faced with the complex underwater currents in the ocean, the fault tolerance of the docking position is valued.

    With the development of underwater unmanned vehicles, structures of them have gradually diversified, partly no longer suitable for traditional docking systems. For example, ROV operating in shallow water, usually does not have a torpedo-like appearance

© The Author(s), under exclusive license to Springer Nature Singapore Pte Ltd. 2023
H. Yang et al. (Eds.): ICIRA 2023, LNAI 14269, pp. 226–234, 2023.
https://doi.org/10.1007/978-981-99-6489-5_18

that can be adapted to the bell mouth. So the corresponding docking system needs redesigning. Wang et al. installed a planar dual-coil on the bottom of the ROV and an inverter chamber [5]. And the proposed method of reducing eddy current loss is verified by electromagnetic field simulation. Such coil structure can be adapted to a platform docking station. Ahluwalia et al. proposed a power transfer system, utilizing ROVs to wirelessly charge underwater sensor networks. The coil on the ROV side is installed at the bottom, and coupled with the coil of the underwater sensor node through docking. The coupler adopts a planar spiral coil and magnetic core. The prototype has an optimal efficiency of 90% when operating at an output power of 50 W and an output voltage of 15.6 V [6].

This paper proposes a ring-shaped coupler mechanism for ROV docking. The charging station on the primary side has a cylindrical structure, which is designed to be installed on the embedded cable of the submarine observation network [7]. Through ROV operating its mechanical claw, the coupling between the secondary coil on the ROV and the primary side on the charging station can be realized, both mechanically and electromagnetically, conducting underwater inductively power transmission. This solution keeps the magnetic field generated by the coil away from the ROV circuit cavity, reducing the electromagnetic interference to the ROV internal circuit. The ring-shaped coupler is to make the docking omnidirectional in the horizontal direction. The prototype of the designed system the 45W wireless power transfer and maximum efficiency 57%, limited by the electromagnetic coupling coefficient.

2 Design of Ring-Shaped Coupler

2.1 Mechanical Design

The primary charging station is designed in a cylindrical shape with primary side coil segments evenly distributed for a more uniform magnetic field distribution, allowing ROV omnidirectionally docking horizontally. The bottom of the ROV is equipped with a single-degree-of-freedom multi-joint mechanical claw, each side connected to a linkage driven by a waterproof steering gear. The two steering gears are installed on the bottom frame of the ROV, drive the upper mechanical claw through the linkage. The unilateral gripper has two joints and three contact surfaces. Each contact surface is reserved a space for coil winding.

When needs charging, ROV adjusts its sailing attitude to approach the ring-shaped charging station. Then the mechanical claw is driven to close, to hold the charging station tightly, completing the coupling of the primary and secondary coils and perform wireless power transmission. The schematic diagram of the ROV docking process is shown in Fig. 1.

The detailed mechanical design of the mechanical claw is shown in Fig. 2. When the ROV is carrying out daily work, the mechanical arm is in the open state. In this situation, the outer two mechanical claw surfaces on each side fit each other to achieve the maximum opening. When the ROV is charging, the mechanical claw is in the closed state. The angle between the claw surfaces of each mechanical claw is 120°, embracing the primary side charge station.

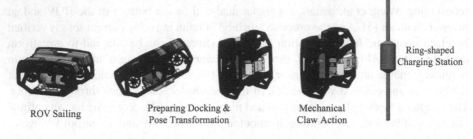

ROV Sailing

Preparing Docking &
Pose Transformation

Mechanical
Claw Action

Ring-shaped
Charging Station

Fig. 1. The Schematic Diagram of the ROV Docking Process

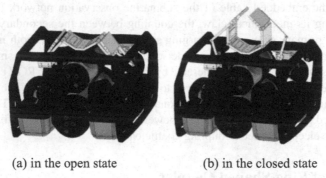

(a) in the open state   (b) in the closed state

Fig. 2. The Detailed mechanical design of the mechanical claw.

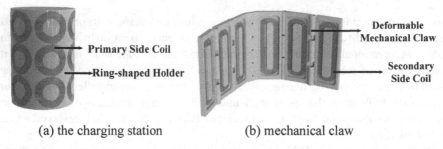

Primary Side Coil

Ring-shaped Holder

Deformable
Mechanical Claw

Secondary
Side Coil

(a) the charging station   (b) mechanical claw

Fig. 3. Schematic diagrams of (a) the primary side charging station and (b) mechanical claw.

The charging station acts as the primary side electromagnetic coupler, and the ROV mechanical claw acts as the secondary side coupler. The schematic diagram of the coupler is shown in Fig. 3. The charging station on the primary side is cylindrical, also serves as a holder for the coil. A total of 6 rows of coil segments are evenly distributed in the radial direction. And 3 coil segments in each row are equally spaced in the axial direction, totally 18 coil segments. The coil segments are connected, namely, there is only one path for the current of the entire primary side. So the current flows in the same direction in each coil segment. The coil on the secondary side is wound on the surface of the mechanical claw. After the coupling is completed, the 6 claw surfaces are evenly distributed radially every 60°. The potting of the coil adopts epoxy resin glue.

The schematic diagram of the coupling is shown in Fig. 4. The height of the charging station is H_1. The height of the mechanical claw is H_2. And the height position difference between the coupler is represented by Δh, and the relative axial rotation angle is represented by $\Delta \theta$.

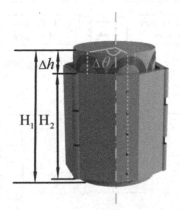

Fig. 4. Schematic diagram of coupling.

2.2 Electrical Design

The flow chart of ICPT charging process is shown in Fig. 5. The battery of the charging station works as a DC power source, which is then converted into the required DC voltage level by the DC/DC module. After the DC/AC inverter, the coil on the primary side converts the electric field energy into magnetic field energy and emits it. In order to improve the power transmission efficiency, the LCC-S compensation circuit is adopted. The coil on the secondary side completes the conversion of magnetic field energy to electric field energy. After secondary side resonance compensation, the rectifier module converts AC power into DC power. Through the power management module, the charging of the ROV battery is realized.

The circuit diagram of ICPT charging system is shown in Fig. 6. RC snubber circuits are connected in parallel between the MOS transistor DS poles to reduce spikes. L_p and L_S are self-inductances of the primary side and secondary side coils, respectively. M is the mutual inductance of the electromagnetic coupler. L_{f1} is the primary side series compensation inductor, C_{f1} is the primary side parallel compensation capacitor, and C_P is the primary side series compensation capacitor. C_S is the secondary side series compensation capacitor. V_{in} and I_{f1} are the input voltage and current of the primary compensation circuit respectively. I_P, I_S are the coil currents of two sides respectively. To simplify the analysis, the output load of the rectifier bridge is simplified as a resistive load R_L. r_p, r_s are the internal resistance of two coils respectively.

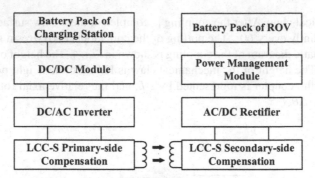

Fig. 5. The flow chart of ICPT charging process.

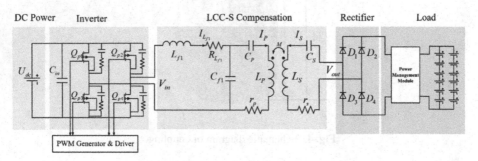

Fig. 6. Circuit diagram of ICPT charging system.

For a full-bridge rectifier circuit with a load resistance of R_L, the equivalent load resistance seen from the rectification input end is,

$$R_{eq} = \frac{8}{\pi^2} R_L \tag{1}$$

In order to make the system resonant, the circuit parameters are determined by:

$$\omega^2 L_{f1} C_{f1} = 1 \tag{2}$$

$$\omega^2 L_S C_S = 1 \tag{3}$$

$$L_p - L_{f1} = \frac{1}{\omega^2 C_p} \tag{4}$$

The ratio of the output voltage to the input voltage, that is, the voltage gain G_v, can be expressed as

$$G_v = \frac{V_{\text{out}}}{V_{\text{in}}} = \frac{MR_{eq}}{L_{f1}(R_{eq} + r_2)} \tag{5}$$

Given the primary side supply voltage and ROV battery voltage, the corresponding LCC-S compensation parameters can be determined [8].

The transmission efficiency η of the ICPT system is

$$\eta = \frac{P_{out}}{P_{in}} = \frac{I_2^2 R_{eq}}{V_{in} I_{f1}} = \frac{\omega^2 M^2 R_{eq}}{\left(Z_{ref} + r_1\right)\left(R_{eq} + r_2\right)^2} \tag{6}$$

Z_{ref} is the equivalent reflected impedance generated by the secondary side on the primary side. Assuming that r_p, r_s is ideal enough, the power supply is a constant voltage power supply. And the parameters of the circuit components are considered fixed, then the output voltage of the secondary side is constant, which can satisfy the charging need of ROV.

3 Experiments

The prototype established is shown in Fig. 7. Both the charging station holder and the mechanical claw are 3D printed. There are threaded holes on the side of the charging station for connection to the waterproof cover. And there exist threaded holes on the side of the mechanical claw for connection with the linkage. The claw surfaces are connected by pins. The coil is wound by litz wire in the previously reserved depression on the surface. The potting is completed with epoxy resin glue.

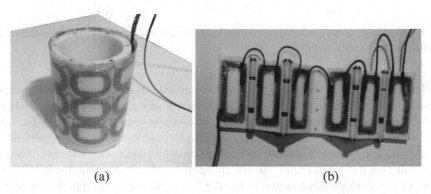

(a)   (b)

Fig. 7. Prototype of (a) primary side charging station and (b) secondary side mechanical claw.

The prototype parameter table is shown in Table 1.

The curves of the measured coupler mutual inductance M versus height difference Δh and relative rotation angle $\Delta\theta$ are shown in Fig. 8. It can be seen that when the relative position of the coupler changes, the mutual inductance value fluctuates, leading to a change in the coupling coefficient.

Table 1. The parameters of the prototype.

Parameter	Symbol	Value
Charging station height	H_1	150 mm
Claw height	H_2	130 mm
Primary self-inductance	L_p	43 μH
Primary side internal resistance	r_p	0.59 Ω
Secondary self-inductance	L_s	102 μH
Secondary side internal resistance	r_s	0.26 Ω

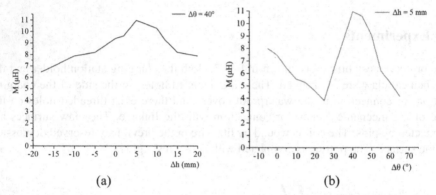

(a)   (b)

Fig. 8. The curves of the measured coupler mutual inductance M versus (a) height difference Δh and (b) relative rotation angle $\Delta \theta$.

The ICPT wireless charging experiment is carried out in a water tank. The experimental settings are shown in Fig. 9. The secondary side circuit load is an electronic load. The primary side is powered by a 48 V constant voltage power supply. The operating frequency of the system is 56 kHz. The coupler position is set with highest mutual inductance. The curves of electric energy transmission power and efficiency changing with load were measured as Fig. 10. The changing trend is in line with the ICPT theory of the LCC-S compensation network. The ICPT system proposed supports a maximum power transmission of 45 W and a maximum transmission efficiency of 57%. The power transfer power of the system is limited by coupling coefficient, which can be further improved through coupler structure enhancement.

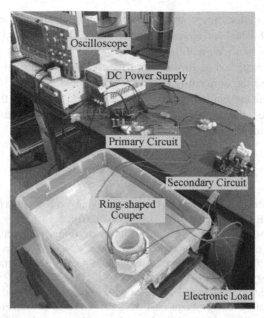

Fig. 9. The settings of ICPT experiments.

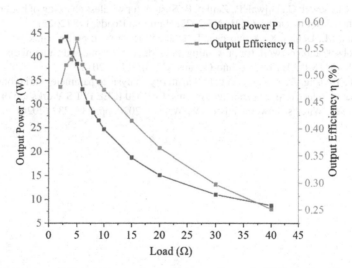

Fig. 10. The curves of electric energy transmission power and efficiency changing with load.

4   Conclusions

Based on the underwater docking and charging needs of ROV, this article designs an ICPT system equipped with a ring-shaped coupler. A cylindrical charging station is adopted in the primary side, while a transformable mechanical claw is utilized in the secondary side, aiming at horizontal omnidirectional ROV docking. After the mechanical claw holds the charging station, non-contact transmission of electrical energy is carried out. A prototype is established and tested in a water tank. The system achieved a maximum power transmission of 45 W, with a maximum power transmission efficiency of 57%. In the future, it is expected to further improve the shape and distribution of the coil segments to improve the uniformity of the magnetic field, to adapt to docking position changes under ocean current interference. It is expected that under the relative rotation of two coupler sides, the mutual inductance changes inconspicuously and maintain a high value, improving the efficiency of power transmission.

References

1. Mcewen, R.S., Hobson, B.W., Mcbride, L., et al.: Docking control system for a 54-cm-diameter (21-in) AUV. IEEE J. Oceanic Eng. **33**(4), 550–562 (2019)
2. Haibing, W., Baowei, S., Kehan, Z., et al.: A novel electromagnetic actuator in an inductive power transmission system for autonomous underwater vehicle. Adv. Mech. Eng. **10**(9) (2018)
3. Allen, B., Austin, T., Forrester, N., et al.: Autonomous docking demonstrations with enhanced REMUS technology. OCEANS-IEEE, Singapore: OCEANS **2006**, 1539 (2016)
4. Mingwei, L., Canjun, Y., Dejun, L., et al.: Design and analysis of the load adaptive IPT system applied to underwater docking system. OCEANS 2016 MTS/IEEE Monterey. IEEE, 1–7 (2016)
5. Wang, J., Song, B., Wang, Y.: A method to reduce eddy current loss of underwater wireless power transmission by current control. Appl. Sci. **12**(5), 2435 (2022)
6. Urvi, A., Chenevert, G., Ujjwal, P., Zeljko, P.: System for wireless charging of battery-powered underwater sensor networks. OCEANS 2022, Hampton Roads, 1–8 (2022)
7. Mochizuki, M., Uehira, K., Kanazawa, T., et al.: S-net project: performance of a large-scale seafloor observation network for preventing and reducing seismic and tsunami disasters. 2018 OCEANS - MTS/IEEE Kobe Techno-Oceans (OTO). IEEE, 2018
8. Qiang, B., Yuwang, Z., Yanjie, G., et al.: Sensitivity analysis to parameter variations in LCC-S compensated inductive power transfer systems. In: 2020 IEEE PELS Workshop on Emerging Technologies: Wireless Power Transfer (WoW), vol. 2020, pp. 233–237 (2020)

Micro-needle Dynamic Anchoring Foot Design for Underwater Drilling Robot

Xu Wang, Demin Zhang, Qi Lan, Cong Wang, Junpeng Zhang, Mengruo Shen, and Yong Lei[✉]

State Key Laboratory of Fluid Power and Mechatronic Systems, Zhejiang University, Hangzhou, China

{awangxu,17799854531,lanqi,22125204,22125214,shenmr, ylei}@zju.edu.cn

Abstract. Aiming repairing underwater concrete structural defects in hydraulic structures, this paper proposes and designs a micro-needle dynamic anchoring foot which can provide stable adsorption and friction for underwater drilling robots. Firstly, the structural design and workflow of the anchoring foot are explained. According to its functions, the dynamic anchoring foot can be divided into two modules: the swirling sucker module and the micro-needle array module, which provide normal adsorption force and friction force respectively. Then, the friction performance of the micro-needle array composed of multiple microneedles is simulated and analyzed and the parameters are optimized. Finally, the adsorption and friction performance of the micro-needle anchoring foot prototype were tested experimentally to verify its design rationality. Based on the micro-needle anchoring foot prototype, a drilling experiment platform was designed and built, and multi-angle inclined drilling experiments were carried out. The results showed that the micro-needle anchoring foot can be applied to underwater robots with high reaction force operations such as drilling.

Keywords: Underwater Robot · Anchoring Foot · Swirling Sucker · Micro-needle Array · Experimental Test

1 Introduction

Traditional maintenance and repair of underwater concrete structures is based on manual restoration, which has certain safety risks and high operational skill requirements. At the same time, the harsh environment and complicated operation also bring great challenges to the construction [1, ?] With the continuous development of underwater robot technology, using underwater robots to repair underwater concrete buildings can improve the repair efficiency, improve the quality of work, ensure the safety of operators and reduce the cost, which has a good market and application prospect, so more and more research began to explore the concrete building repair technology based on underwater robots [3]. However, there is little research on underwater robot equipment for drilling at home and abroad, and the existing underwater robots are also difficult to adapt to drilling on a

© The Author(s), under exclusive license to Springer Nature Singapore Pte Ltd. 2023
H. Yang et al. (Eds.): ICIRA 2023, LNAI 14269, pp. 235–246, 2023.
https://doi.org/10.1007/978-981-99-6489-5_19

small inclined dam surface with a certain angle. In the process of drilling inclined holes, it is required that the operating robots can adjust the drilling angle underwater and resist the drilling reaction force during drilling process [4].

Aaron Parness [5] designed a robot to grab huge stones. The way of grabbing is mainly to surround the huge stones with external claws, and each claw has a micro-needle structure close to the inside of the stones, and the final anchorage of the huge stones is realized through the drill bit in the middle of the claws. Xi'an University of Technology has conducted bionic research on the wall-climbing mechanism of inchworm, and designed and developed a bionic crawler-type wall-climbing robot, which can crawl on the vertical concrete wall and rough ceiling by needling the claw [6]; Researchers at the University of California have designed and developed a six-legged wall-climbing robot [7], whose feet adopt a needle-like structure and can crawl vertically on the rough tree surface. In actual operation, the acupuncture of the foot hooks into the ravine on the rough surface of the tree, forming a limit and improving the friction. Researchers at Stanford University have developed a multi-legged robot [8, 9] that can climb on the concrete wall, and its feet adopt a micro-needling structure. Liu Jinfu of China University of Science and Technology [10] took the foot characteristics of flies and geckos as bionic objects, and developed a wall-climbing robot prototype with a combined structure of "adhesion-grasping-adsorption" by using the mechanism configuration synthesis method.

Most of the research on underwater operation robots is currently at the theoretical design stage, and the practical applicability is poor. For heavy operations such as drilling, especially oblique drilling, the existing adsorption device cannot provide enough adsorption force and friction force to resist the working reaction at the same time. Few drilling mechanisms are directly applied to underwater concrete structures, and an important reason for this is the lack of an adsorption device that can sustain the robot for stable vertical and oblique drilling operations on underwater concrete surfaces. In this paper, we propose and design a micro-needle dynamic anchoring foot based on needle anchoring and swirling adsorption technology, which can provide stable adsorption and friction for the operation of underwater robots.

The rest of the paper is organized as follows. Section 2 mainly introduces the overall structure of the microneedle anchoring foot, including the design and optimization of the swirling sucker and microneedle array. In Sect. 3, the adsorption performance and friction performance of the microneedle anchoring foot are tested experimentally, and a drilling platform is built to simulate the actual drilling operation scene. Section 4 summarizes this paper and looks forward to the future work focus.

2   Design of Micro-needle Dynamic Anchoring Foot

For underwater operation robots, the existing way to maintain stability is mainly to install adsorption devices for the equipment, which generate a large friction force to resist the operational reaction force through a large adsorption force. However, when the operational reaction force is very high, the adsorption environment of the adsorption device will be difficult to maintain thus causing adsorption failure. In this paper, an adsorption mechanism based on micro-needle array is conceived by combining the respective characteristics of needle anchoring and swirling sucker, and its principle is schematically shown in Fig. 1. On the premise of determining the design requirements of drilling reaction, the force of drilling robot is simulated and analyzed, and the requirements of adsorption force and friction force of adsorption foot are 500N and 350N respectively.

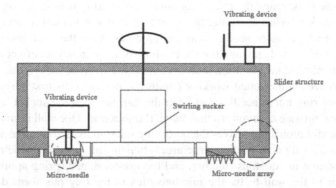

Fig. 1. Schematic of the principle of adsorption mechanism based on microneedle array

2.1 Overall Structural Design of Micro-needle Adsorption Foot

The micro-needle dynamic anchoring foot is mainly provided by the normal adsorption force by the cyclonic negative pressure sucker, which generate a local negative pressure inside the sucker housing by the high-speed rotation of the blades, and the adsorption force is generated by the external waters pressing the sucker on the wall. The friction force of the micro-needle anchoring foot is mainly provided by the contact between the peripheral parts of the sucker and the wall, relying on the larger friction coefficient and the adsorption force provided by the sucker to produce a larger friction force to resist the operational reaction force to which the robot is subjected.

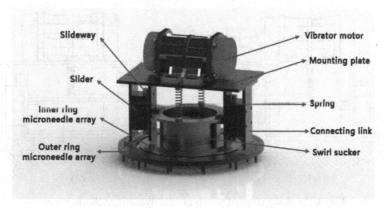

Fig. 2. Micro-needle dynamic anchoring foot model

As can be seen from Fig. 2, in the structure of micro-needle anchoring foot, the parts that provide friction mainly include vibration motor, slide rail, slider, outer ring micro-needle array and inner ring micro-needle array. The vibration motor is placed on the mounting plate, the connecting link is arranged between the mounting plate and the outer ring microneedle array, two sliders are installed on the connecting link, two slideways are installed on the sucker, and the inner ring microneedle array is installed on the bottom edge of the sucker. When working, the vibration motor generates a large amplitude of vibration, and the micro-needle array reciprocates along the slide rail through the limiting effect of the slide rail and the slider, thus forming an impact effect on the wall. The mounting plate of the vibration motor is connected with the suction cup by a spring and pre-tightened. In the actual working condition, the sucker is first adsorbed on the wall, the inner ring micro-needles can keep the gap between the sucker and the wall unchanged and provide a certain friction force, the sucker and the wall remain relatively fixed, and the vibration motor drives the outer ring micro-needle array to reciprocate the wall, forming a local micro-drilling structure. When the microneedles penetrate into the wall, the vibration motor stops running, and the pre-tensioned spring applies pressure perpendicular to the wall to fix the microneedles in the tiny pits formed by impact vibration, thus forming mechanical limit and providing greater friction. The working steps of micro-needle dynamic anchoring foot are shown in Fig. 3.

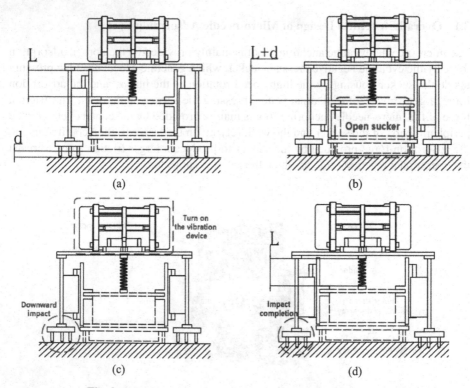

Fig. 3. Working steps of micro-needle dynamic anchoring foot

The process from the anchoring foot of the microneedle just touching the wall to stable adsorption can be described as follows: when the anchoring foot of the microneedle just touches the wall, the original length of the spring is L, and the distance between the bottom surface of the sucker and the needle tip of the outer ring is D, as shown in Fig. 3 (a); Then open the sucker to generate adsorption force, which will make the sucker move to the wall surface along the slide rail and stick to the wall surface, and at the same time stretch the spring to change the length to L + D; Then turn on the vibration device (at this time, the sucker is in a stable adsorption state), so that the microneedle array generates reciprocating vibration perpendicular to the wall surface, which impacts the wall surface, and microneedles penetrate into the wall surface, as shown in Fig. 3(c); When the impact is completed, the microneedle penetrates into the wall to a certain depth, and the vibration device is turned off. Due to the limit of the spring, the microneedle stays in the generated cone pit, and finally forms a lateral limit, as shown in Fig. 3(d).

2.2 Design and Optimization of Swirling Sucker

The part of the microneedle anchoring foot that provides adsorption is the swirling sucker, and its structure and principle are shown in Fig. 4. The sucker structure consists of a shell, blades and a waterproof DC motor.

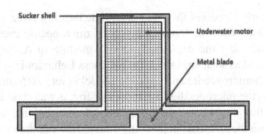

Fig. 4. Schematic diagram of swirl sucker

In actual work, there is a certain gap between the bottom surface of the sucker blade and the wall surface. The waterproof motor drives the blades to rotate at a high speed, so that the fluid in the cavity of the sucker generates centrifugal effect due to the rotation, and flows out of the cavity from the lower gap, and at the same time, the external water flows into the cavity through the lower gap to form dynamic balance. The pressure inside the sucker cavity presents an annular distribution, and its radial pressure distribution presents a parabolic shape. The equation of motion of the fluid in the sucker can be expressed as:

$$\frac{\rho \mu_\alpha^2}{r} = \frac{\partial P}{\partial r} \tag{1}$$

where ρ is fluid density, μ_α is tangential velocity, r is radial position and P is fluid pressure. The fluid is driven by the high-speed rotating blades, so the tangential speed of the fluid $\mu_\alpha = \omega \cdot r$, and ω is the rotating speed of the blades, so the formula (1) can be expressed as follows, and the pressure distribution inside the sucker can be obtained by further integrating it as follows:

$$\rho\omega^2 r = \frac{\partial P}{\partial r} \Rightarrow P = \frac{1}{2}\rho\omega^2 r^2 + P_0 \tag{2}$$

Especially, when the gap between the bottom surface and the wall surface of the sucker is small and the outer diameter of the sucker is R, the pressure P is integrated with the area of the blade surface, and the adsorption force can be obtained as follows:

$$F = \frac{1}{4}\pi\rho\omega^2 R_2^4 \tag{3}$$

According to the formula of adsorption force, the adsorption force of sucker is related to the rotation speed and blade diameter of sucker blade. From this formula, it can be concluded that the adsorption force of the sucker is proportional to the square of the blade rotation speed and the fourth square of the blade diameter, and increasing the blade rotation speed and blade diameter can significantly increase the adsorption force of the sucker.

2.3   Microneedle Array Design and Simulation Optimization

In order to more clearly represent the process and the limiting effect of the microneedle array piercing the wall, the simulation analysis of microneedle piercing the concrete wall was carried out using the explicit dynamics module in Ansys. The material of microneedle is selected as structural steel, the Stiffness Behavior is selected as rigid, the Element Size of both microneedle and concrete model is set to 0.5 mm, a constant force of 10N is applied to the microneedle perpendicular to the wall, and a Fixed Support is set on the lower surface of the concrete model, and the simulation analysis time is set to 0.002 s, we can obtain the size and shape of the damage area of the surrounding concrete wall during the lateral movement of a single microneedle. The stress and shape of the area damaged by the microneedle are shown in Fig. 5.

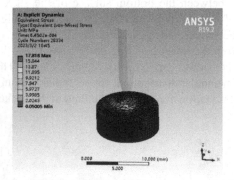

(a) Stress nephogram of micro-needle damage area   (b) Micro-needle damage area

Fig. 5. Simulation analysis results

In order to explore the relationship between the overall limiting friction and the arrangement of microneedles, the installation and arrangement of microneedles array are designed and analyzed. As shown in Fig. 5(b), the irregular damage area on the wall is simplified to approximate a red circular area with a radius of 8 mm, and at the same time, in order to avoid the interaction between microneedles in actual work, the safety area between microneedles is designed to be a circle with a radius of 10 mm, that is, a circle with a radius of 10mm is made with each microneedle installation position as the center.

The shape of the microneedle mounting plate is ring-shaped, and its size is determined by the overall size of the drilling robot and the design requirement of the drilling reaction. It is known above that our design requirement for the adsorption force of a single adsorption foot is 500N. The overall size of the designed drilling robot are 780 mm, 580 mm, and 650 mm in length, width, and height, respectively, so it can be tentatively decided that the inner circle diameter of the ring-shaped microneedle mounting plate is 185 mm and the outer circle diameter is 255 mm. The installation mode of microneedles is annular, as shown in Fig. 6. According to the description of the damaged area of microneedles above, the number of layers of microneedles is three, and the installation positions of the first, second and third layers of microneedles are on circles with diameters of 190 mm, 220 mm and 250 mm respectively. See Fig. 7 for the parameters involved in the arrangement of microneedles. According to the size of the mounting plate, the maximum number of microneedles in each layer is 24.

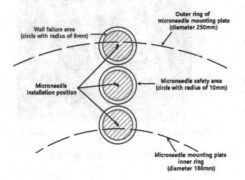
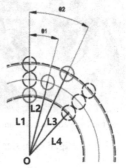

Fig. 6. A partial schematic diagram of an arrangement

Fig. 7. Different arrangements of microneedle arrays

Because there are many variables, the orthogonal experiment is used to study the influence of the arrangement of micro-needles on the limiting friction [11], and the primary and secondary factors are analyzed to select the appropriate parameter range to optimize the overall friction. The orthogonal experiment table selects five factors and four levels [12], that is, L16(45). When the number of microneedle cone angle is too large, the penetration depth of microneedle will be reduced, and when the cone angle is too small, the stiffness of microneedle will be reduced, so we choose a microneedle cone angle of 45° and a penetration depth of 1 mm in the simulation process, and use Ls-dyna for simulation experiments. In the post-processing, the maximum limiting friction provided by microneedle array is obtained by analyzing the reaction force on the wall.

The simulation results show that the number of microneedles in each layer has a great influence on the total limiting friction by the way the microneedles are arranged, and the included angle of microneedles between different layers has little influence on the total limiting friction.

3 Experiment of Micro-needle Dynamic Anchoring Foot and Adjustable Angle Drilling Platform

3.1 Experiment on Adsorption Performance of Micro-needle Anchoring Foot

The key components of micro-needle adsorption foot are micro-needle, vibration motor and swirling sucker. The selection of micro-needle includes the shape parameters of single micro-needle and the arrangement of micro-needle array. According to the conclusion of the above simulation analysis, the final choice is that the taper angle of microneedles is 45, the total number of microneedles in the microneedle array is 24, and the number of layers is 3. The circular arrangement mode is adopted, and the microneedles can absorb enough objects, as shown in Fig. 8.

(a) The micro-needle adsorption foot in kind   (b) The pool experiment of micro-needle adsorption foot

Fig. 8. Physical diagram of micro-needle dynamic anchoring foot

In the experiment, the rotation speed of the sucker is controlled to be 500 rpm ~ 2000 rpm, the interval is 250 rpm, and the suction cup gap is selected to be 2 mm ~ 9 mm, and the interval is 1 mm. After the sucker is stably adsorbed, a dynamometer is used to apply tension to the sucker. When the clearance between the sucker and the wall changes, the applied force minus the gravity of the adsorption foot in the water is the adsorption force generated by the sucker. The experimental data obtained by repeated experiments are shown in Fig. 9.

The experimental results show that when the clearance between the sucker and the ground is kept constant, the suction force of the sucker is approximately proportional to the second power of the rotation speed. At the rotation speed of 2000 rpm, the maximum suction force can reach 600 N, which meets the design requirements of a single micro-needle anchoring foot and the underwater drilling robot. With the increase of the clearance, the suction force of the sucker gradually decreases, which is the same as the conclusion of simulation analysis.

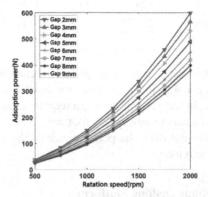

Fig. 9. Relationship curve of adsorption force with rotation speed and ground clearance

3.2 Experiment on Friction Performance of Micro-needle Anchoring Foot

Place the micro-needle adsorption foot on the concrete plate, turn on the sucker motor, and adjust the rotation speed to 1500 rpm to make the adsorption foot stably adsorb on the concrete plate. Then, the vibration motor is turned on to drive the microneedle array to impact the wall, so that the microneedle array pierces the wall and waits for 30 s. Then adjust the rotation speed of the sucker to 500 rpm, and then apply a pulling force parallel to the wall surface of the concrete slab with a dynamometer. When the microneedle moves out of the cone pit, read the dynamometer to get the maximum limiting friction force that can be generated by the microneedle suction foot. Adjust the governor of the vibration motor to change the parameters of vibration force. The vibration force is selected to be 100 N ~ 200 N at intervals of 20 N, and the friction force of the adsorption foot is measured. The friction data of the inner ring "micro-needle" array measured experimentally are shown in Table 1. The friction data of the outer ring microneedle array are shown in Table 2.

Table 1. Experimental data of friction force of micro-needle array in the inner ring of dynamic anchoring foot

Blade speed (rpm)	500	1000	1500	1750	2000
Friction (N)	12.4	52.4	108.5	144.9	187.0

According to the experiment of adsorption force and friction force, it can be concluded that when the rotation speed of the sucker motor is adjusted to 2000 rpm, the gap is set to 2 mm, and the vibration force of the vibration motor is adjusted to 200 N,

Table 2. Experimental data of friction force of micro-needle array in the outer ring of dynamic anchoring foot

Vibration force (N)	100	120	140	160	180	200
Friction (N)	208.5	246.5	291.2	330.5	371.4	409.3

the adsorption force of the micro-needle adsorption foot can reach 598 N, and the total limiting friction force is equal to the sum of the friction forces of the inner and outer rings of the micro-needle. In this paper, the design requirements of adsorption force and friction force of the micro-needle adsorption foot are 500 N and 350 N respectively. According to the experimental data, the performance of the micro-needle adsorption foot meets the design requirements.

3.3 Experiment of Oblique Drilling Platform

In the actual drilling operation, the micro-needle dynamic anchoring foot may also be affected by environmental factors, and torque may also be generated during drilling to make the adsorption foot unstable. Therefore, it is necessary to simulate the actual drilling operation scene and test the performance of micro-needle anchoring foot against the reaction force of drilling operation. A prototype of the drilling test rig was built to carry out multi-angle drilling experiments, and the stability of the micro-needle adsorption foot during drilling operation was observed, and whether there was a large vibration and lateral displacement. Before starting the experiment, the experimental platform is placed in the engineering test pool, the sucker of the micro-needle anchoring foot is connected with the underwater motor, the vibration motor is connected with the governor, and the stepping motor is connected with the driver, so that the drilling rig can feed and drill C40 concrete slab at a speed of 2 mm/s. The experimental site and drilling results are shown in Fig. 10.

(a) 30-degree drilling experiment

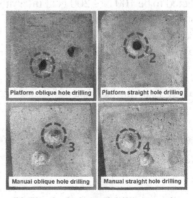

(b) Physical view of drilling results

Fig. 10. Field Diagram of Drilling Platform Experiment

The experimental results show that when drilling is carried out, the experimental platform can adsorb stably, and the anchoring foot will not vibrate or slip greatly because of the reaction force of drilling. The friction and adsorption stability of the experimental platform are sufficient, the sliding distance is less than 2 mm, and the experimental platform will not overturn, which shows that the adsorption force and friction performance of the dynamic anchoring foot can meet the requirements of drilling operation.

4   Summary and Outlook

Aiming at the technical challenge of repairing deep-water concrete structural defects, in this paper, a kind of micro-needle dynamic anchoring foot for underwater drilling robot is designed by combining swirling adsorption with micro-needle array. The anchoring foot can provide large adsorption force and friction force, so that the underwater robot can resist large drilling reaction force in many directions. A prototype of the micro-needle anchoring foot was built, and on this basis, a drilling experiment platform was designed and built. The multi-angle drilling experiment proved that it can be applied to drilling operations with large reaction force. However, the micro-needle anchoring foot designed in this paper only considers the case that the working surface is flat. In the actual working environment, the working wall may be curved or defective. In the future, we will consider changing the shape parameters and layout of micro-needles, designing the anti-interference control algorithm of suction force, or adding adaptive structure to improve the adaptability of micro-needle anchoring foot to complex walls.

References

1. Tengxiao, Z., Guipeng, Y.: Construction technology of high-speed underwater concrete revetment restoration. Yunnan Hydropower **37**(10), 33–35 (2021)
2. Zhang, H., Li, J., Kang, F., Zhang, J.: Monitoring depth and width of cracks in underwater concrete structures using embedded smart aggregates. Measurement **204**, 112078 (2022)
3. Hotta, S., Mitsui, Y., Suka, M., Sakagami, N., Kawamura, S.: Lightweight underwater robot developed for archaeological surveys and excavations. ROBOMECH J. **10**(1) (2023)
4. Keita, I., et al.: Development of underwater drilling robot based on earthworm locomotion. IEEE Access **7** (2019)
5. Parness, A., Willig, A., Berg, A., et al.: [IEEE 2017 IEEE Aerospace Conference - Big Sky, MT, USA (2017.3.4–2017.3.11)] 2017 IEEE Aerospace Conference - A microspine tool: Grabbing and anchoring to boulders on the Asteroid Redirect Mission, pp. 1–10 (2017)
6. Yanwei, L., Limeng, W., Sanwa, L., et al.: Design and analysis of bionic claw-piercing crawler wall-climbing robot. Mech. Sci. Technol. **38**(11), 1689–1694 (2019)
7. Saunders, A., Goldman, D.I., Full, R.J., et al.: The rise climbing robot: body and leg design. In: SPIE Defense & Security Symposium, Unmanned Systems Technology. International Society for Optics and Photonics (2006)
8. Kim, S., Asbeck, A.T., Cutkosky, M.R., et al.: SpinybotII: climbing hard walls with compliant microspines. In: International Conference on Advanced Robotics. IEEE (2005)
9. Asbeck, A.T., et al.: Scaling hard vertical surfaces with compliant microspine arrays. Int. J. Robot. Res. (2006)
10. Liu, J.: Research on key technologies of multi-mode wheeled bionic wall-climbing robot. China University of Science and Technology (2020)

11. Ruijiang, L., Yewang, Z., Chongwei, W., et al.: Research on orthogonal experimental design and analysis method. Experimental Technol. Manag. **27**(9), 4 (2010)
12. Hao, L., Yu, H.: Analysis of the use of orthogonal test design table. Acta Editologic **17**(5), 2 (2005)

Adaptive Control for Compact Vector-Propelled ROVs in Underwater Detection: Enhancing Stability and Maneuverability

Qi Lan[1], Bonan Chen[1], Xu Wang[1], Tian Xu[1], Wensheng Wang[2], and Yong Lei[1(✉)]

[1] State Key Laboratory of Fluid Power and Mechatronic Systems,
Zhejiang University, Hangzhou, China
{lanqi,bnchen,awangxu,tianxu,ylei}@zju.edu.cn
[2] Hangzhou HuaNeng Engineering Safety Technology Co., Ltd., Hangzhou, China
Wang_ws@hn-safety.com

Abstract. Regular underwater inspections are crucial for ensuring the safety and maintenance of underwater structures. However, using a compact remotely operated vehicle (ROV) with inspection modules poses a significant challenge in maintaining stable control due to changes in system parameters. This paper proposes an attitude adaptive control system for vector-propelled ROVs to achieve attitude stabilization equipped with inspection modules for underwater detection. Firstly, the configuration and discrete dynamics model of the ROV are presented. Secondly, a double closed-loop attitude controller is introduced, which is integration of dynamic closed loop with the Model Prediction Controller (MPC) through online identification. Additionally, the control distribution of the vector thruster is optimized, considering angular accessibility. Finally, underwater manipulation experiments are conducted, demonstrating the system's quick adaptation to changes in angular velocity and its ability to maintain stability when equipped with the inspection module.

Keywords: Underwater detection · ROV · Vector propulsion · Adaptive control

1 Introduction

By the end of 2014, there were 4,496 large and medium-sized reservoirs in China, with a total capacity of 769.5 billion m^3 [1]. However, some underwater structures become safety critical due to its aging effects over low construction standard and poor maintenance. Therefore, it is necessary to detect and evaluate the damage

This work supported in part by National Key R&D Program of China Grant No. 2022YFC3005405 and the National Natural Science Foundation of China under Grant 52072341.

© The Author(s), under exclusive license to Springer Nature Singapore Pte Ltd. 2023
H. Yang et al. (Eds.): ICIRA 2023, LNAI 14269, pp. 247–260, 2023.
https://doi.org/10.1007/978-981-99-6489-5_20

of these underwater structures. Currently, underwater testing mainly relies on divers, which are timing consuming and dangerous tasks with limited operation ranges. In recent years, ROVs (remotely operate vehicles) are widely used in underwater detection which offer lower risks and greater flexibility [2]. However, existing underwater detection ROVs are often large and heavy, requiring the assistance of cranes and other equipment for deployment, making the operation complicated [3]. Hence, there is a need to develop compact and lightweight underwater vehicles equipped with inspection modules to enable stable underwater detection operations.

In the literature, commonly used control algorithms for underwater robots include PID control, fuzzy or neural network control, adaptive control, etc. Shang et al. [4] used a fuzzy logic PID controller to realize the navigation speed and yaw control of the bionic robot, but due to the lack of a precise control model, the trajectory following effect was poor in different environments. Ma et al. [4] used ant colony algorithm to optimize the positioning, depth fixation and orientation control of PID controller parameters for underwater robots, but there was a problem of slow convergence. Rodrigo et al. [5] designed a neural network-based autotuning PID controller and experimented on ROV, but it is difficult to have enough data to train the controller in practical applications. Kim et al. [6] used synovial controller to control the submersion and steering of the robot, but there was a certain steady-state error in using the measured speed and acceleration to produce the best prediction, which could not guarantee the accuracy of the system. Bing et al. [7] replaced the switching term with an adaptive continuum, eliminating jitter when using sliding mode control, but did not take into account the variation in parameters. Chatchanayuenyong et al. [8] used neural networks to solve the switching of sliding mode controllers based on the Pontryagin time optimal principle, but ignored the dynamic model of the robot, and the controller was prone to oscillation when switching at the sliding surface. Guo et al. [9] used the sliding mode fuzzy logic controller for motion control of underwater vehicles, but due to the uncertainty and external interference of the given model, there is a trade-off between tracking accuracy and stability.

As it can be seen from literature, the aforementioned algorithms cannot solve the nonlinearity and physical limitation control problems caused by the variation of system model parameters when the vector thruster ROV is equipped with the inspection module. In this work, a new attitude control algorithm is developed for compact vector propulsion detection ROV is proposed to distribute thruster thrusts and provide stable attitude for detection ROVs. The rest of this article is below. In Sect. 2, a prototype of a compact detection vector-propelled ROV is introduced. In Sect. 3, a mathematical model of the ROV system is established. In Sect. 4, a dual closed-loop adaptive attitude control system is proposed, including a full-angle PI control using SO(3) logarithmic mapping, an adaptive angular velocity follower constructed using online identification and MPC methods and a control distribution method for vector thrusters. In Sect. 5, a laboratory experiment was carried out to verify the proposed control system.

2 Designed Vector Thruster ROV

In order to carry out underwater detection in a limited space with fast deployment time, a compact prototype detection vector propulsion ROV was designed and built, as shown in Fig. 1. The prototype is an underwater mobile platform with camera functions, light detection equipment, and variable direction thrusters. The structure of the compact vector propulsion ROV is PA nylon plate. It has a total length of 450 mm, maximum width of 410 mm, overall height of 120 mm, and a total mass of 6.7 kg. It is designed to withstand a maximum underwater pressure depth of 300 m. The control section mainly consists of electronic equipment composed of MPU (Microprocessor Unit), MCU (Microcontroller Unit), and IMU (Inertial Measurement Unit) and the power system is composed of four brushless motors and two servos, brushless motor controller, servo controller, lithium battery, ESC, plastic propeller, and buoyant materials.

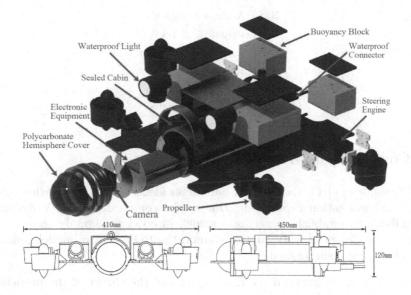

Fig. 1. Configuration of vector-propelled ROVs for underwater detection.

The two thrusters on the front side of ROV are fixed thrusters, and the two thrusters on the rear side are vector thrusters. For vector thrusters, the servo is connected to the thruster by a rotating axis, and by adjusting the servo angle, the thruster thrust axis direction can be manipulated. The combination of 2 fixed thrusters and 2 vector thrusters realizes the ROV's 5° of freedom control. By controlling the thrust and servo angle, the ROV's three-degree-of-freedom rotation (pitch, roll, yaw) can be realized; It can also realize the ROV's two-degree-of-freedom movement (front, back, up and down). The parameters for the underwater motor used for the thruster and the underwater servo motor employed for the rotational control of the vectored thruster are presented in Table 1 and Table 2.

Table 1. Underwater motor (Rovmaker)'s parameters.

Parameter	Value
Rated Voltage	24 V
Maximum Power	300 W
Maximum Forward Thrust (24 V)	20 N
Maximum Reverse Thrust (24 V)	18 N
Operating Depth	300 m
KV Rating	350
Weight	80 g

Table 2. Underwater servo motor (Rovmaker)'s parameters.

Parameter	Value
Rated Voltage	24 V
Peak current	4.3 A
Operating torque	1.5 Nm
Angle range	359°
Operating Depth	300 m
Weight	360 g

3   Control System Modeling

ROV dynamic model is the basis for parameter identification, navigation control design and navigation experiment. Due to the complexity of ROV dynamics, it is difficult to establish an accurate model, in order to simplify the model to facilitate the design of ROV control system, the ROV control model is derived in the following assumptions:

1. The relationship between the ESC signal and the thrust of the propeller is linear and inertial.
2. The relationship between the servo signal and the servo angle is linear, saturated, and inertia-free.
3. We believe that the actual torque thrust of the ROV can be obtained by several actuators associated with it, and the driving signal is mapped by a function.
4. The buoyancy module of the ROV provides buoyant force equal to its weight. When establishing the control model, the influence of buoyancy and gravity is disregarded.

First, the spatial coordinate system is defined as follows. The body coordinate system $B(x, y, z)$ and the geodetic coordinate system $E(x, y, z)$ of the ROV are shown in Fig. 2(a). For the two vector thrusters on the ROV, as shown in

Fig. 2(b), F_v and F_h are projections of vector thruster thrust F in the vertical and horizontal directions, respectively.

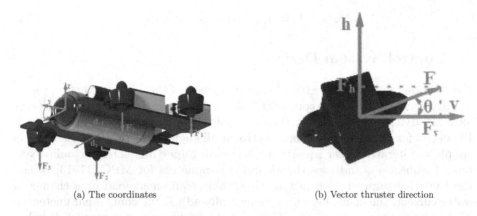

(a) The coordinates   (b) Vector thruster direction

Fig. 2. The coordinate system of the ROV and the vector thruster direction.

d_x and d_y represent the transverse and longitudinal distances from the propeller to the center of mass, respectively, and the total torque caused by the propeller rotor at $B(x, y, z)$ can be obtained (1).

$$\begin{bmatrix} M_x \\ M_y \\ M_z \end{bmatrix} = \begin{bmatrix} F_0 d_{y1} - F_{1v} d_{y2} - F_{2v} d_{y2} + F_3 d_{y1} \\ F_0 d_x + F_{1v} d_x - F_{2v} d_x - F_3 d_x \\ -F_{1h} d_x + F_{2h} d_x \end{bmatrix} \tag{1}$$

Then, set the sampling interval to Δt. $K_\omega = \begin{bmatrix} K_{\omega x}, K_{\omega y}, K_{\omega z} \end{bmatrix}^T$ represents the damping coefficients of the three channels. Then the attitude discrete dynamics model of ROV under $B(x, y, z)$ is (2).

$$\begin{cases} \omega_x(k+1) = (1 - K_{\omega x} \Delta t)\omega_x(k) + \dfrac{I_y - I_z}{I_x} \Delta t \omega_y \omega_z + \dfrac{\Delta t}{I_x} M_x \\[2mm] \omega_y(k+1) = (1 - K_{\omega y} \Delta t)\omega_y(k) + \dfrac{I_z - I_x}{I_y} \Delta t \omega_z \omega_x + \dfrac{\Delta t}{I_y} M_y \\[2mm] \omega_z(k+1) = (1 - K_{\omega z} \Delta t)\omega_z(k) + \dfrac{I_x - I_y}{I_z} \Delta t \omega_x \omega_y + \dfrac{\Delta t}{I_z} M_z \end{cases} \tag{2}$$

According to the ROV dynamic model, The angular velocity channels, denoted as x, y, and z, exhibit similar structural characteristics. Taking the x-channel model as an example, its dynamic model is represented by (3).

$$\omega_x(k+1) = a_{x1}\omega_x(k) + a_{x2}M_x(k) + a_{x3} + a_{x4}\omega_y(k)\omega_z(k) \tag{3}$$

The right-hand side of the equation consists of the update term for the current angular velocity channel, input term, disturbance term, and coupling term with other angular velocity channels. Therefore, the simplified dynamic model (4) is obtained by ignoring other angular velocity channel coupling terms. Where, $a = \begin{bmatrix} a_1, a_2, a_3 \end{bmatrix}^T$ is the system parameter.

$$\omega(k+1) = a_1\omega(k) + a_2M(k) + a_3 \tag{4}$$

4   Control System Design

This section introduces the attitude control system of the compact vector propulsion ROV in Fig. 3, and the controller is divided into two parts: kinematic closed-loop and dynamic closed-loop. The kinematics closed-loop adopts $SO(3)$ [10] + PI control for attitude closed-loop control at all angles. The dynamic closed-loop adopts the iterative least squares method with forgetting factor for online system identification, and uses the identified parameters for MPC [11–13]. When the ROV is equipped with new or changeable equipment load or a change in water current, the controller can automatically adjust the control parameters to adapt to the change of inertia. Then, for the vector thruster control distribution nonlinearity problem, linearizing and constraining it to obtain the optimal thrust distribution method.

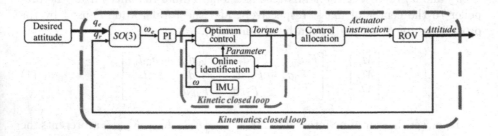

Fig. 3. Attitude control block diagram.

    First, a full-angle mapping of the kinematic closed loop is performed, and the desired angular velocity is outputted via the PI controller. Here, q_e represents the desired pose quaternion, and q_r represents the actual pose quaternion. R_e and R_r correspond to rotation matrices, and the error direction cosine matrix is given by $R_d = R_e R_r^{-1}$. The mapping from $SO(3)$ to $so(3)$ is performed to obtain the desired angular velocity ω_e (5).

$$\begin{cases} \omega_e = \log(R_d)^\vee \\ \theta = \arccos \dfrac{\text{tr}(R_d) - 1}{2} \end{cases} \tag{5}$$

where, $\log()$ is a logarithmic mapping function that uses the logarithmic mapping function to map elements of $SO(3)$ to elements of $so(3)$. R_d is the $SO(3)$ element, and then the desired angular velocity vector is obtained by the $\vee$ operation.

Second, input and output data are collected for online identification in order to generate system parameters for updating the model. The dynamic closed loop utilizes the parameters identified by the online system for model predictive control. Taking into account the significant change in moment of inertia after equipping the ROV with equipment, this paper employs the iterative least squares method (6) with a forgetting factor to achieve online identification of ROV parameters.

$$\begin{cases} K(k) = \dfrac{P(k-1)\varphi(k)}{\lambda + \varphi^T(k)P(k-1)\varphi(k)} \\[2mm] P(k) = \dfrac{1}{\lambda}[I - K(k)\varphi^T(k)]P(k-1) \\[2mm] \theta(k) = \hat{\theta}(k-1) + K(k)[y(k) - \varphi^T(k)\hat{\theta}(k-1)] \end{cases} \quad (6)$$

The calculated desired angular velocity is substituted into the online identification system (6). Here, $K(k)$ is the gain vector at k, P is the covariance matrix, φ is the system input data vector, λ is the forgetting factor (recommended value range $0.9 < \lambda < 1$), $\hat{\theta}$ is the estimated system parameter, and y is the system output. When the algorithm is initialized, it is recommended to take $\hat{\theta}(k) = \begin{bmatrix} 1\ 0.5\ 0 \end{bmatrix}^T$, $P(0) = 10000I$, $\lambda = 0.999$, and take $\varphi(k) = \begin{bmatrix} \omega(k-1)\ M(k-1)\ 1 \end{bmatrix}^T$ and $y(k) = \omega(k)$ at k. The resulting vector $\varphi(k)$ is the system parameter $a = \begin{bmatrix} a_1\ a_2\ a_3 \end{bmatrix}^T$.

Then, the model predictive control (MPC) is employed to achieve optimal control by generating a new predictive torque output.

$$e(k) = \omega_d(k) - \omega(k) \quad (7)$$

$$e(k+1) = a_1 e(k) - a_2 M(k) + (1 - a_1)\omega_d(k) - a_3 \quad (8)$$

Set the target to be followed to $\omega_d(k)$, and the tracking error $e(k)$ represents the difference between $\omega_d(k)$ and $\omega(k)$ (7). The state-space model of state ω (5) can be rewritten as a state-space model (8) by state error e.

$$\min_{U(k)} \tfrac{1}{2}U^T(k)HU(k) + (\omega(k)E)U(k) \quad (9)$$

Constructing the cost function formula (9), which can obtain the optimal solution $U(k)$. Where, $U(k)$ is the predictive control vector. $H = C^T\overline{Q}C + \overline{R}$, and $E = M^T\overline{Q}C$. M and C are the system parameter matrixes. $\overline{Q}$ and $\overline{R}$ are both cost weight matrices, and Q,R,F are cost weights. Based on (8), it can be concluded that the output of the controller is $M(k)$ (10).

$$M(k) = u_m(k) + a_2^{-1}\left((1 - a_1)\omega_d(k) - a_3\right) \quad (10)$$

where $U(k)$ is the first term in the optimal solution $U(k)$ used as the control quantity for this control period in the actual case of this article $u_m(k)$, $\omega_d(k)$ is the target that the controller needs to follow. Lars [14] et al. proved the stability of MPC.

At last, as shown in Fig. 4, a control distribution method for vector thrusters is proposed, which maps the required torque and thrust to the actual feasible thrust and angle of each thruster to drive the ROV.

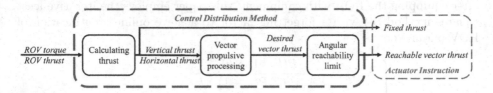

Fig. 4. Vector thrusters control the distribution process.

Inverse solution to the mechanism constraint equation for vector thruster ROV (11).

$$F_t = \bar{C}_F^{-1} \left[0 \; T_y \; T_z \; M_x \; M_y \; M_z\right]^T \tag{11}$$

where $F_t = \left[F_0 \; F_{1v} \; F_{1h} \; F_{2v} \; F_{2h} \; F_3\right]^T$ is the thrust of thruster decomposition. F_θ and F_3 are the thrust of the two stationary thrusters, F_{1v}, F_{1h} and F_{2v}, F_{2h} are the horizontal and vertical components of the two vector thrusters, respectively. $\bar{C}_F \in \mathbb{R}^{6 \times 6}$ is a 6th-order constraint matrix, depending on the ROV mechanism constraints. In order to avoid the influence of the motor torsion torque on the M_z, this paper adds a constraint: $\theta = F_\theta - F_{1v} + F_{2v} - F_3$.

According to the coordinate system established by Fig. 2.(b), the angle $\theta = \text{atan2}(F_h, F_v)$ and the resultant force $F = \sqrt{F_h^2 + F_v^2}$. Assuming that the servo angle at k time is $\theta(k)$, the expected thrust $F(k+1)$ and the desired angle $\theta(k+1)$ of the vector thruster at $k+1$ are due to the servo angle limitation:

1. When $\theta(k+1) > 135°$, take $\theta(k+1) = \theta(k+1) - 180°$, $F(k+1) = -F(k+1)$;
2. When $\theta(k+1) < -135°$, take $\theta(k+1]) = \theta(k+1) + 180°$, $F(k+1) = -F(k+1)$;
3. When $45° < \theta(k+1) \leqslant 135°$ and $(\theta(k+1) - \theta(k))^2 > (\theta(k+1) - \theta(k) - 180°)^2$, take $\theta(k+1) = \theta(k+1) - 180°$, $F(k+1) = -F(k+1)$;
4. When $-135° \leqslant \theta(k+1) < -45°$ and $(\theta(k+1) - \theta(k))^2 > (\theta(k+1) - \theta(k) + 180°)^2$, take $\theta(k+1) = \theta(k+1) + 180°$ and $F(k+1) = -F(k+1)$.

Considering servo angle reachability. Among them, the no-load speed of the vector propeller servo proposed in this paper is $150°/s$, the operating frequency of the controller is $50\,\text{Hz}$, and the maximum rotation angle $\theta_{\max} = 2°$ of the servo in a single iteration. θ_r is the actual reachable angle of the servo (12).

$$\theta_r(k+1) = \begin{cases} \theta(k+1), & |\theta(k+1) - \theta(k)| \leqslant \theta_{\max} \\ \theta(k) + \theta_{\max}\text{sig}(\theta(k+1) - \theta(k)), & |\theta(k+1) - \theta(k)| > \theta_{\max} \end{cases} \tag{12}$$

At the actual reachability angle, calculate the optimal thrust. Let the actual thrust be f_r and construct a cost function (13).

$$J = q_v(f_e \cos(\theta_e) - f_r \cos(\theta_e))^2 + q_h(f_e \sin(\theta_e) - f_r \sin(\theta_e))^2 \tag{13}$$

Among them, the q_v and q_h are the cost weights of the vertical and horizontal forces, respectively, and the optimal solution is the optimal thrust f_r (14).

$$f_r = \frac{q_v f_e \cos(\theta_e) \cos(\theta_r) + q_h f_e \sin(\theta_e) \sin(\theta_r)}{q_v \cos^2(\theta_r) + q_h \sin^2(\theta_r)} \qquad (14)$$

5   Experiments and Results

In this section, the control model and the full-angle adaptive attitude controller are experimentally verified in laboratory environment. The experimental environment includes a water-filled tank, the ROV, and the ground station. The ground station comprises a boost power supply and a control computer. Power and signals are connected to the robot's control cabin through a neutrally buoyant tether. Firstly, the tracking performance of the attitude controller to the desired angle is verified. Then a mobile platform (considered as a inspection module) with a total mass of 4.5 kg (equivalent to 67% of the ROV's own weight) was installed on the ROV, and the ROV with the mobile platform conduct experiments again to verify the adaptive performance of the algorithm and estimate the system parameters. The components of the robotic experimental system are shown in Fig. 5.

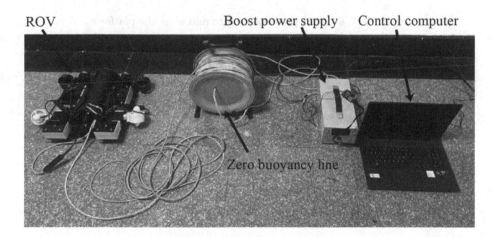

Fig. 5. Components of a robotic experimental system.

The ROV was positioned in a pool for experimentation. Figure 6 shows the experimental picture of the ROV equipped with a mobile chassis, and the ROV can achieve a cruise motion with stable attitude (a), a pitch motion at a large angle (b), and a roll motion at a large angle (c) driven by a fixed thruster and a vector thruster. Similarly, a mobile platform (the red circle in Fig. 6) is mounted on the ROV, and the mobile platform allows the ROV to move using wheels. The ROV weighs about 6.7 kg and the mobile platform on board weighs about 4.5 kg. The mass of the ROV has increased by 67% since the mobile platform was installed, and the characteristics of the attitude system have changed significantly. It can also achieve a cruise motion with stable attitude (d), a pitch movement at a large angle (e), and a roll motion at a large angle (f).

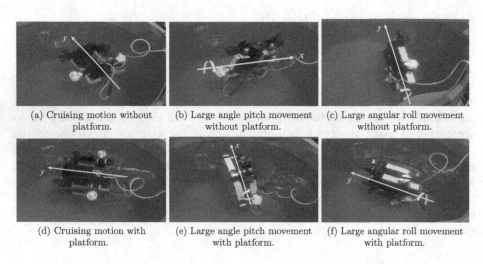

(a) Cruising motion without platform.   (b) Large angle pitch movement without platform.   (c) Large angular roll movement without platform.

(d) Cruising motion with platform.   (e) Large angle pitch movement with platform.   (f) Large angular roll movement with platform.

Fig. 6. ROV attitude pool test before and after the platform.

The closed-loop control of attitude kinematics uses the $SO(3)$ + PI controller. $SO(3)$ algorithm such as (4), PI controller parameters such as Table 3.

Table 3. Attitude kinematics closed-loop PI controller parameters.

Closed-loop	K_p	K_i	MO	MO_i
x-axis angular velocity	6.5	1	20	8
y-axis angular velocity	2.5	1	20	8
z-axis angular velocity	8.0	1	20	8

Pose dynamics in closed-loop control uses iterative least squares online identification method with MPC with forgetting factor. The online identification method is shown in (6), the identification model is (5). The MPC cost function is shown in (9), the controller output is (10), and the output upper and lower limits are $\pm MO$. The initialization parameters of the three channels and the controller parameters are the same as shown in Table 4.

Table 4. Initialization parameters of online identification and MPC parameters.

Parameter	$\varphi(0)$	$P(0)$	λ	N	Q	R	F	MO
Value	$\begin{bmatrix} 1 & 0.5 & 0 \end{bmatrix}^T$	$10000I$	0.999	10	1	2	2	10

Use the same controller structure and parameters as in the previous section. The change of ROV attitude Euler angle before the mobile platform mounting is shown in Fig. 7 (a), and the change of ROV attitude Euler angle after the mobile platform mounting is shown in Fig. 7 (b). Its control performance quantitative indicators: attitude adjustment speed and oscillation amplitude are shown in Table 5.

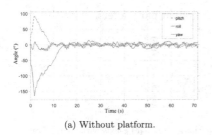
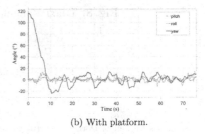

(a) Without platform.   (b) With platform.

Fig. 7. ROV attitude Euler angle error.

Table 5. MPC attitude controller performance specifications.

Closed-loop	Speed of adjustment ($°/s$)		Oscillation amplitude ($°$)	
	Without platform	With platform	Without platform	With platform
x-axis angular velocity	13.0	8.6	9.5	6.2
y-axis angular velocity	12.1	8.5	11.5	12.3
z-axis angular velocity	13.1	15.6	14.3	15.4

The parameters of the triaxial angular velocity system identified online are shown in Fig. 8. The model adopts (5), and the parameters uniformly select the data at the 50 s of the system operation, and the accuracy is retained to four decimal places. It can be seen that compared with the previous ROV, the x-axis moment of inertia of the ROV equipped with the mobile platform is increased by 92%, the y-axis moment of inertia is increased by 84%, and the z-axis moment of inertia is increased by 8%. When maintaining the cruising motion, the ROV body is subject to the head-up torque, and the right side has a tendency to sink, plus the chassis is affected by the head-down torque as a whole, and the left and right basic levels. The angular velocity following effect of the dynamic closed-loop controller is shown in Fig. 9.

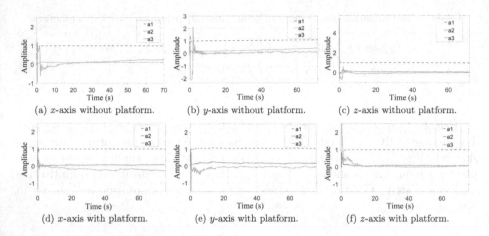

Fig. 8. Triaxial angular velocity system parameters.

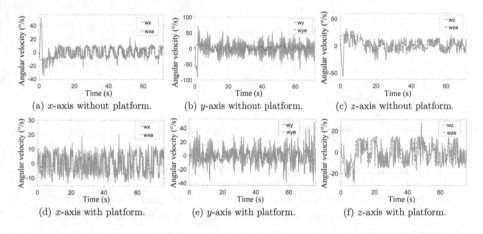

Fig. 9. The MPC controller follows the three-axis angular velocity.

The experimental results show that the controller can automatically identify the system parameters according to the past input and output, and then use the identified parameters to predict the future response, and use the prediction results to optimally control the output. The controller works well, and there are very few parameters that need to be adjusted, which greatly reduces the workload of manual parameter adjustment. After the large change of system properties, the proposed control system can still maintain good control performance, which demonstrated the adaptive ability of the proposed control algorithm.

6   Conclusion

This article proposes a compact vector-propelled detection ROV control system to control the attitude of the ROV equipped with detection equipment to maintain the stability of the ROV. This system utilizes two vector thrusters, two fixed thrusters, and data collected from an inertial measurement unit (IMU) to control the attitude of the ROV. The control system include $SO(3)$ mapping for generating the desired angular velocity, real-time update of inertia parameters using online system identification, and angle follower designed by MPC method. Additionally, a control distribution algorithm for the vector thruster ROV is designed, establishing a mapping relationship between thrust, torque, and control signals of each thruster, considering physical limitations. This experimental results show that the control system achieves rapid tracking of angular velocity changes, and automatic adjustment of controller parameters after equipped with the mobile platform, ensuring ROV stability.

Future work will focus on improving the current control system considering the nonlinear dynamic model for ROVs attitude adjustment, and developing a high-speed maneuvering control system for underwater moderate propulsion of ROVs.

References

1. Peng, C., Qian, G.: Prospect of hydropower development in China in the 21st century. Water Power **32**(2), 6 (2006)
2. Kramar, V., Kabanov, A., Kramar, O., Fatcev, S., Karapetian, V.: Detection and recognition of the underwater object with designated features using the technical stereo vision system. Fluids **3** (2023). https://doi.org/10.3390/FLUIDS8030092
3. Dai, Y., Su, Q., Zhang, Y.: A new dynamic model and trajectory tracking control strategy for deep ocean mining vehicle. Ocean Eng. **216**, 108162 (2020)
4. Ma, W., Pang, Y., Jiang, C., et al.: Research on the optimization of PID control of remotely operated underwater vehicle, IEEE (2011)
5. Rodrigo, H.A., Luis, G.V., Tomás, S., et al.: Neural network-based self-tuning PID control for underwater vehicles. Sensors **16**(9), 1429 (2016)
6. Kim, J., Kim, K., Choi, H.S., et al.: Estimation of hydrodynamic coefficients for an AUV using nonlinear observers. IEEE J. Oceanic Eng. **27**(4), 830–840 (2002)
7. Bing, S., Zhu, D.: A chattering-free sliding-mode control design and simulation of remotely operated vehicles. In: Proceedings of the 2011 Chinese Control and Decision Conference (CCDC) (2011)
8. Chatchanayuenyong, T., Parnichkun, M.: Neural network based-time optimal sliding mode control for an autonomous underwater robot. Mechatronics **16**(8), 471–478 (2006)
9. Guo, J., Chiu, F.C., Huang, C.C.: Design of a sliding mode fuzzy controller for the guidance and control of an autonomous underwater vehicle. Ocean Eng. **30**(16), 2137–2155 (2003)
10. Yun, Y., Yang, S., Wang, M., et al.: High performance full attitude control of a quadrotor on SO(3), IEEE (2015)
11. Daoud, M.A., Osman, M., Mehrez, M.W., Melek, W.W.: Path-following and adjustable driving behavior of autonomous vehicles using dual-objective nonlinear MPC. In: IEEE International Conference on Vehicular Electronics and Safety (ICVES), pp. 1–6 (2019)
12. Verschueren, R., De Bruyne, S., Zanon, M., Frasch, J. V., Diehl, M.: Towards time-optimal race car driving using nonlinear MPC in real-time. In 53rd IEEE Conference on Decision and Control, pp. 2505–2510 (2014)

13. Ye, H., Jiang, H., Ma, S., Tang, B., Wahab, L.: Linear model predictive control of automatic parking path tracking with soft constraints. Int. J. Adv. Rob. Syst. **16**(3), 1729881419852201 (2019)
14. Grune, L., Rantzer, A.: On the infinite horizon performance of receding horizon controllers. IEEE Trans. Autom. Control **53**(9), 2100–2111 (2008)

Dual-Arm Dynamic Planning with Considering Arm Reachability Constraint in Task Space

Xin Shu, Xinyang Fan, Kang Min, Zhu Ji, Fenglei Ni[(✉)], and Hong Liu

State Key Laboratory of Robotics and System, Harbin Institute of Technology, Harbin, China
flni@hit.edu.cn

Abstract. This paper aims to address the issue of planning dual-arm motions in scenarios involving tracking dynamic desired pose and obstacle avoidance. In situations where dual-arm motion requires synchronous behavior, inflexible planning, encountering obstacles, and beyond-the-arm motion capability may lead to task failure. To overcome these issues, we propose a dynamic-system-based method for dual-arm collaborative planning. The method can coordinate the motions of dual arms while keeping synchronous behavior in tracking the moving target and avoiding obstacles. Meanwhile, we incorporate the reachability by modeling the motion boundary to ensure that the arms moving within the reachable space. The experiment successfully verified the above scenarios, showcasing its adaptability in dual-arm planning and its potential applicability in dual-arm applications such as transportation.

Keywords: Dual-Arm Motion · Collaborative Planning · Moving Target · Dynamic Tracking

1 Introduction

In the face of some complex manipulation tasks, such as carrying large and heavy objects that are beyond the capabilities of a single arm, the advantages of dual-arm become evident. Dual-arm robotic systems expand the workspace and allow highly complex manipulation that would otherwise be infeasible for single-arm systems. Consequently, considerable attention has been directed toward the research of planning and control techniques for dual-arm manipulation.

Most efforts in the field of dual-arm research have focused on developing strategies for manipulating static objects. Few works have focused on dual-arm planning to track moving desired poses while maintaining synchronous behavior. Instances, where this type of planning is pertinent, include the flexible transportation or placement of objects, repositioning of desired targets during transportation, obstacle avoidance in dynamic environments, and other similar applications.

Extensive research has been conducted in the field of robotics to explore the coordination of dual arms for object manipulation and synchronous motions. These can be briefly divided into the following three categories: 1) RRT-based algorithms. This approach ensures feasible grasping with both arms while also considering self-collision

© The Author(s), under exclusive license to Springer Nature Singapore Pte Ltd. 2023
H. Yang et al. (Eds.): ICIRA 2023, LNAI 14269, pp. 261–273, 2023.
https://doi.org/10.1007/978-981-99-6489-5_21

avoidance, e.g., [1, 2]. However, due to its inherent computational complexity, real-time performance and adaptability may be compromised, particularly when attempting to track moving targets. 2) Master-slave strategies. The motion of one arm is known, and the other arm follows to satisfy the closed-chain constraints of both arms, such as [3]. While this strategy offers computational efficiency, it can be susceptible to performance degradation if communication delays. Furthermore, problems arise when assigning the master-slave roles to the arms, particularly when dealing with moving targets. 3) Centralized control strategy. Treating the arms as symmetrical without distinguishing between master and slave, a motion-synchronous controller can be used to coordinate two arms, as explored in works such as [4–6]. This method exhibits favorable effects. Building upon this concept, Ref [7] proposes a reach-to-grasp strategy specifically tailored for moving objects. However, to the best of the authors' knowledge, seldom work has focused on developing strategy for tracking dynamic desired poses under dual-arm synchronous behaviors.

Apart from dynamically tracking the desire and avoiding obstacles, it is also necessary to ensure synchronous constraints between two arms. Therefore, dual-arm needs to be within their respective reachable space. Until now, the establishment of the arm's reachable space includes: 1) generating a geometric model of the reachable space, such as polynomial discriminant and classical geometric methods [8, 9]; 2) Approximating reachable space using density functions, as demonstrated in [10, 11]; 3) Reachable spaces are represented by constructing a comprehensive database in Cartesian space, as showcased in studies [12–14]. Here, a combination of methods 3) and 2) is applied to establish boundary constraints in dual-arm planning.

In this paper, we propose a dynamic system (DS) based method to coordinate dual-arm motion, which can enable the tracking of a moving desired pose while ensuring obstacle avoidance. The method integrates task and coordination constraints, ensuring synchronous behavior and asymptotic convergence. Additionally, to avoid task failure due to unreachability, we establish motion boundary constraints utilizing a Gaussian mixture model (GMM). The main contributions of this paper are as follows:

- Proposal of a dual-arm dynamic planning strategy capable of real-time tracking of moving desired poses and obstacle avoidance.
- Establishment of a dual-arm motion boundary to confine the arm's motion within its reachable space.
- Empirical validation showcasing the performance of the proposed strategy through a series of experiments, demonstrating its adaptability in dual-arm planning.

This paper concentrates on dual-arm dynamic planning. It begins with modeling dual-arm manipulation in Sect. 2, proposes a DS-based dual-arm planning method in Sect. 3, considers arm reachability constraints in Sect. 4, conducts empirical validation in Sect. 5 and concludes in Sect. 6.

2 Dual-Arm Modeling

Consider a system of two manipulators that firmly grasp a shared rigid object, illustrated in Fig. 1. Each arm is fully actuated with n_i DOFs, where $i = [l, r]$ is the index for the left and right arm, respectively. $x = [x_l, x_r]^T$ is the generalized coordinates for Tool Center Point (TCP) frame expressed in the base frame $\sum$ base.

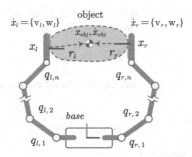

Fig. 1. The model of dual-arm cooperative manipulation.

In dual-arm synchronous motions, such as transportation, synchronous constraints must be satisfied in both the position and velocity levels. The position-level constraint is expressed as

$$T_{obj} = T_l T_l^{obj} = T_r T_r^{obj} \tag{1}$$

where T_{obj} is the pose of the object, expressed in $\sum$ base. T_l^{obj}, T_r^{obj} are the transformations of the object relative to the left and right arm frame, respectively.

As defined in [17], the grasp matrix for a dual-arm system can be expressed as

$$G = \begin{bmatrix} G_l & G_r \end{bmatrix} = \begin{bmatrix} I_3 & O_3 & I_3 & O_3 \\ S(r_l)^T & I_3 & S(r_r)^T & I_3 \end{bmatrix} \tag{2}$$

where $G = \begin{bmatrix} G_l & G_r \end{bmatrix} \in \mathbb{R}^{12}$ is the grasp matrix. I_3, O_3 are 3-dimensional identity and zero matrices, respectively. $S(.)$ is the skew-symmetric operator, and r_l, r_r are the position vectors (3×1) from the left and right end-effector to the contact point on the object shown in Fig. 1. It can be easily derived from synchronous motion that the velocity-level constraint holds,

$$\dot{x} = J\dot{q} = G^T t_{obj} \tag{3}$$

where $J = \begin{bmatrix} J_l \\ J_r \end{bmatrix} \in \mathbb{R}^{12}$ is the Jacobian matrix, $\dot{x}, \dot{q} \in \mathbb{R}^{12}$ are the vectors expressing the twist (linear and angular velocity) and joint velocity of arms. $t_{obj} \in \mathbb{R}^6$ are the twist of the object. The matrix G is full-row rank.

Equation (3) gives the velocity coupling relationship of the closed chain. By utilizing formulas (1) and (3), the dual-arm trajectory that fulfills the synchronous constraints can be obtained when the desired motion of the object in the task space is known. Subsequently, the joint motion of the arms can be solved via centralized inverse kinematics.

3 Dynamic-System Based Dual-Arm Planning

3.1 Dynamic-System Related Formulation

Dynamic-System. Define that the state of a robot during autonomous motion is x, and the time-invariant dynamic system can be described as

$$\dot{x} = f(x) \tag{4}$$

where $f(.)$ is continuous. Given the initial robot state x_0, the robot state at the moment of t can be iterated as

$$\{x\}_t = \{x\}_{t-1} + f(x).\delta t \tag{5}$$

where δt is the integration time step.

   In order to realize the autonomous motion, $f(.)$ should be an asymptotic system that continually drives the robot towards the target, satisfying $\lim_{t \to \infty} f(x) = 0$. A straightforward system that satisfies this requirement is a linear dynamical system of the form

$$\dot{x} = f(x) = -k(x - x^a) \tag{6}$$

where, k is the proportional coefficient, and x^a is the target state, which is the attractor of the dynamic system.

Obstacle Avoidance. Assume the obstacles are convex, and define each obstacle to have a continuous boundary function $\Gamma(x)$, at least C^1 smooth. According to the distance, the following types of points can be distinguished, as illustrated in Fig. 2a.

   free point: $x^{\{} = \{x \in \mathbb{R}^d : \Gamma(x) > 1\}$
   boundary point: $x^{\lfloor} = \{x \in \mathbb{R}^d : \Gamma(x) = 1\}$
   interior point: $x^{\rangle} = \{x \in \mathbb{R}^d : \Gamma(x) < 1\}$
   where $\Gamma(x)$ increases monotonically with the distance from the obstacle center point or reference point. The reference direction r_i between the robot and the obstacle is defined as.

$$r_i(x) = (x - x_i^r)/\|x - x_i^r\|. \tag{7}$$

   The real-time obstacle avoidance of the robot is realized based on the flow around a circular cylinder, by applying a modulation matrix [15] to the dynamical system,

$$\dot{x} = M(x)f(x) \text{ with } M(x) = E(x)D(x)E(x)^{-1} \tag{8}$$

   $E(x)$ is the basis matrix, expressed as

$$E(x) = \begin{bmatrix} n(x) \, e_1(x) \, \cdots e_{d-1}(x) \end{bmatrix} \tag{9}$$

where n is the normal vector at the boundary point, and e_i are the orthonormal tangent vectors evaluated at the boundary point, and $\mathbf{D}(x)$ is the diagonal eigenvalue matrix, which defines the stretch length in each basis direction.

Note that, any motions should start outside the obstacle, and the modulated $\dot{x}$ via (8) ensures that there is no penetration into the obstacle (Proof could be found in [15]). Thus, formula (8) can realize dynamic obstacle avoidance, as depicted in Fig. 2b, where all streamlines converge towards the attractor.

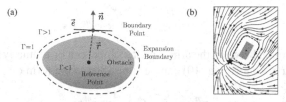

Fig. 2. Illustration of obstacle avoidance based on dynamic systems. (a) the obstacle definition, and (b) obstacle avoidance.

3.2 Dual-Arm Planning with Synchronous Behaviors

The synchronous behaviors of dual-arm manipulation encompass both position and orientation constraints, making it more complex than simple point motion. Furthermore, during the motions, both arms must also navigate around obstacles. To extend the dynamic planning algorithm to accommodate the synchronous motion of two arms, we introduce control points x_i, coupled with a w_i for each point, as shown in Fig. 3. Each control point serves the purpose of resisting external disturbances, such as obstacle avoidance.

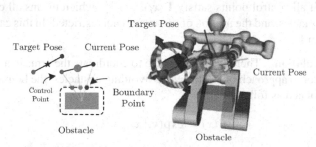

Fig. 3. Illustration of Distance calculation, taking 2D as an example, and three control points, x_l, x_r, x_{obj}, are demonstrated.

Velocity Composition of Control Points. In this paper, the proposed method follows the centralized control concept, where the synchronous motion of the arms x_i is dictated by the desired motion of the object x_{obj}, that is, $\dot{x}_{obj}$ can be mapped to the arms $\dot{x}_i$

through centralized control, and $\dot{x}_i$ serves as the velocity input for each control point. Subsequently, the modulated motion $\dot{x}_i^m$ of the arms can reverse-mapped back after planning, yielding the desired motion of the object $\dot{x}_{obj}^m$ integrating target tracking and obstacle avoidance.

Each control point obtains the modulated motion through formula (8). To fulfill the synchronous constraints of the arms, the velocity of each control point needs to be synthesized to the object, as follows

$$\mathbf{v}_{obj} = \sum w_i \mathbf{v}_i^m$$
$$\mathbf{w}_{obj} = \sum w_i (x_{obj} - x_i) \times (\mathbf{v}_i^m - \mathbf{v}_{obj}) \tag{10}$$

In fact, the motion between the arms and the object can be mutually mapped through the grasping matrix, so formula (10) can be simplified to the form of

$$\dot{x}_{obj}^m = \sum (G_i^{T^{-1}} w_i \dot{x}_i^m) \tag{11}$$

where, $\dot{x}_{obj}^m$ is the modulated object velocity, $\dot{x}_i^m$ is the output of each control point after modulation, and w_i is assigned by the distance between the point and the obstacle, which satisfies the following

$$w_i = \begin{cases} (\Gamma^{cut} - \Gamma^{min})/(\Gamma x_i - \Gamma^{min}) - 1 & \text{if } \Gamma x_i \le \Gamma^{cut} \\ 0 & \text{if } \Gamma x_i > \Gamma^{cut} \end{cases} \tag{12}$$

Then normalize the weights,

$$w_i = w_i / \sum_i w_i \tag{13}$$

where, Γ^{cut} is the boundary value for judging whether it is close to the obstacle, and Γ^{min} is the boundary value threshold ($\Gamma^{min} \ge 1$).

Note that if all control points satisfy $\Gamma(x_i) > \Gamma^{cut}$, which means all control points are far from obstacles, and the motion of the arms is not restricted. In this case, all weight w_i can be set to 1.

Distance Calculation. There is limited space to coordinate the arms in a synchronized manner. In order to approach obstacles while avoiding obstacles, the boundary function we use is calculated as follows

$$\Gamma(x) = \exp(\kappa . \|x - x_i^b\|) \tag{14}$$

where, κ is the distance magnification factor, and x_i^b is the boundary point at obstacle i, satisfying

$$x_i^b = b r_i(x_i) + x_r, \text{ where } b > 0, \text{ and } x_i^b \in x^{\llcorner} \tag{15}$$

4 GMM-Based Arm Reachability Prediction

4.1 Arm Capability Map

Robot reachable space helps to guide robot planning and operation, and can measure the robot's ability to move in a specific location. Before initiating any motion, it is necessary to determine whether the object's grasping pose falls within the reachable space. Traditional geometric descriptions of the reachable space provide limited information, lacking orientation considerations and intuitive guidance. Some approaches generate a Cartesian space database through forward kinematics by sampling the joint space, also lacking intuitiveness. Therefore, we adopt the method in [16], which involves uniformly dividing the geometric workspace into 3D cells. Then, a capability map is established, with a reachability score for each cell.

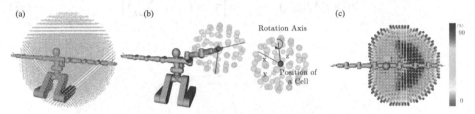

Fig. 4. Modeling arm capability map. (a) Mesh workspace into cells, (b) generate the pose on each cell, inverse solution and recording, and (c) generate the capability map.

The capability map of the arm is visualized in Fig. 4, and the implementation steps include: 1) Grid the workspace into 3D cells, and calculate the center of the inscribed sphere of each cell (see Fig. 4a). 2) Generate n_p discrete points on each sphere surface, and create z-axis from the sphere center to each surface point, and using the angular-axis method generates m_o poses (see Fig. 4b). For instance, 12 poses can be obtained by rotating at 30 degrees. 3) Calculate all poses via inverse kinematics and record the number of available solutions $R_o(g)$. 4) Calculate the reachability score $D_o(g)$ at each sphere via formula (16), and draw the capability map (see Fig. 4c).

$$D_o(g) = R_o(g)/(n_p.m_o).100\% \tag{16}$$

The capability map utilizes color gradients and scores to visually represent the distribution of available solutions in the reachable space. This map provides an intuitive demonstration of the robot's dexterous space, where regions with higher scores indicate higher dexterity.

4.2 GMM-Based Reachability Prediction

Although the capability map provides visualized guidance, it only offers a score indicating a relative dexterity of a particular position. This discrete representation may not be convenient for digital guidance. Therefore, we utilize GMM to model the capability map, and use the model to predict whether the target pose is reachable or not, providing a continuous and convenient representation.

We define $\eta = [\eta_{pos}; \eta_{ori}]$ to express pose, where $\eta_{pos} \in \mathbb{R}^3$ represents the position and $\eta_{ori} \in \mathbb{R}^6$ represents the orientation of the end effector, which consists of the first two columns of the rotation matrix, corresponding to the x and y axes. The rotation matrix can also represent the similarity between orientations more accurately than the Euler angle or quaternion representation.

The dataset of reachable poses is obtained from the arm capability map, and all poses are stored in the base coordinate system. The trained reachable space model $\mathcal{M}_{reach}$ consists of k Gaussian models, which are represented as $\{\pi_k, \mu_k, \sum_k\}_{k=1:K}$. $\pi_k, \mu_k, \sum_k$ are corresponding to the prior, mean, and covariance matrix, respectively.

Given a target pose $\eta \in \mathbb{R}^9$, the likelihood probability density is

$$\ln \mathcal{P}(\eta|\mathcal{M}_{reach}) = \sum_{k=1}^{K} \ln\left\{\pi_k \mathcal{N}(\eta|\mu_k, \sum_k)\right\} \tag{17}$$

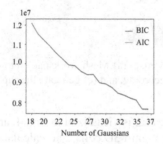

Fig. 5. AIC and BIC curves to model the reachable space.

If the target pose is valid, its score needs to exceed the likelihood threshold ρ_{reach}. The threshold is determined such that the likelihoods of 99% of all reachable poses are higher than it. The number of Gaussians $K = 36$ is determined using the Akaike and Bayesian information criterion (AIC, BIC), shown in Fig. 5.

4.3 Dual-Arm Motion Boundary Constraints

In order to ensure synchronous motion between two arms and within their reachable spaces, we employ the GMM model and likelihood threshold ρ_{reach} to estimate the motion boundary for each arm.

Take 2D as an example, and assume that the orientation does not change much. Figure 6a presents the likelihood probability distribution of a fixed orientation on $x = 1.0$ plane. The motion boundary can be roughly approximated by the probability density contour, and the regions over than ρ_{reach} can be roughly estimated as the motion boundary on $x = 1.0$ (see Fig. 6b), which will be imposed on dual-arm motions.

It should be noted that the representation of 3D motion boundaries is more complicated that continues to be a subject of ongoing research.

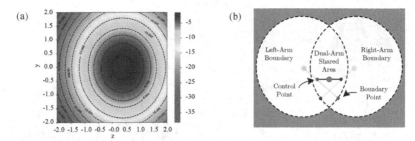

Fig. 6. Modeling the motion boundary. (a) Likelihood probability density distribution on $x = 1.0$ with a fixed orientation. (b) motion boundary approximated by probabilistic contour.

5 Empirical Validation

In the experiment, we conduct three validations to verify the performance of the proposed method: (1) dual-arm dynamic planning for tracking a moving desired pose; (2) dual-arm synchronous motion considering the reachable boundary constraint; (3) dual-arm cooperative obstacle avoidance. All validations were performed in the task space, and the robot's joint angles were computed using damped least square pseudo-inverse kinematics.

The robot used in our experiments is Dexbot, a track-legged humanoid robot equipped with two symmetrical arms, each having 7 DOFs. In the experiment, 2D motion information $[p_y, p_z, \theta_x]$ is demonstrated.

5.1 Dual-Arm Dynamic Collaborative Planning

The first experiment is to track a moving desired pose in a synchronous manner. A box is grasped by dual-arm, and its length, width, and height are 0.3, 0.2, and 0.15, respectively. The desired pose is specified by the RViz Marker. In this experiment, we continuously change the pose of the marker to evaluate the adaptability of the method.

Figure 7 illustrates the tracking process, where Fig. 7a depicts the motion sequence, and Fig. 7b-7c is the evolution of the target and object motions over time. As demonstrated in Fig. 7a and 7b, the dynamic system's asymptotic stability ensures that the planner can adjust its motion to follow the desired pose. Meanwhile, the velocity vector depicted in Fig. 7a-i to a-iv, closely aligns with the marker's moving trend throughout the motion, and thus, the adaptability of this method get well reflected.

Figure 7c shows the dual-arm synchronous constraints in terms of position and orientation during the motion, where Δp, Δq are the relative distance (Euclidean norm) and relative orientation (the angle between two quaternions) between the left arm x_l and right arm x_r, respectively. The data reveals that the relative distance between two arms is within 0.3m $\pm$ 2% (Fig. 7c-i), and the relative orientation between two arms nearly coincides (Fig. 7c-ii). These results indicate that the dual-arm synchronous constraints are maintained throughout the motion without being violated.

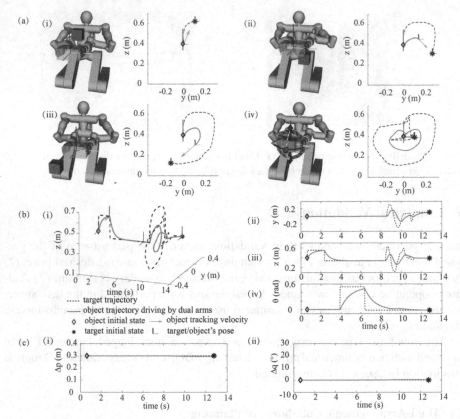

Fig. 7. Illustration of dual-arm tracking a moving target. (a) motion sequences, (b) evolution of the target and object motions along time, and (c) dual-arm synchronous constraint in position and orientation.

5.2 Considering Motion Boundary

If the pose of either side is unreachable during motion, the synchronization constraint of dual-arm is likely to be broken, at which point it can result in the object falling and the task is considered failed. Therefore, in this experiment, we test the effectiveness of the boundary constraints, given the desired pose that is intentionally set outside the boundary, making it unreachable for one side.

Figure 8 illustrates the results of the tracking process with the proposed method. Despite the desired markers being positioned outside the bounds in both Fig. 8a-i and 8a-ii, the control points are effectively constrained within their respective bounds. The evolution of target and object motion over time, shown in Fig. 8b, confirms that the object does not fully reach the desired pose due to motion boundary constraints. Nevertheless, the arms' synchronized behavior should be prioritized to prevent object slippage. Then, it can be fed back to the controller for further optimal planning.

As a comparison, Fig. 9 illustrates the process of both arms without considering the boundaries. Similar to Fig. 8, the scene remains the same, but in this case, the dual-arm motions violate the synchronous constraint, particularly evident in Fig. 9a-ii. Additionally, the data in Fig. 9b clearly shows the significant changes in position and orientation between two arms. These deviations from synchronization would lead to task failure and should be avoided.

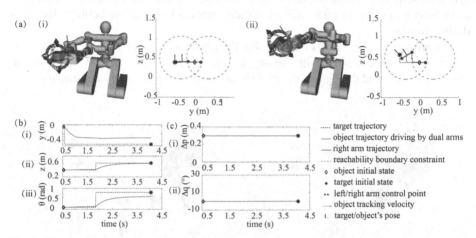

Fig. 8. Illustration of dual-arm planning with reachability boundary. (a) motion sequences, (b) evolution of the target and object motions along time, and (c) dual-arm synchronous constraint in position and orientation.

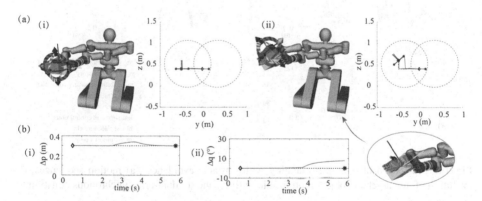

Fig. 9. Illustration of dual-arm planning without boundary constraint. (a) motion sequences, and (b) dual-arm synchronous constraint in position and orientation.

5.3 Obstacle Avoidance

To further verify the adaptability of the method, we place an obstacle (a box with $0.3 \times 0.2 \times 0.15$ m) within the motion boundary between the object's initial and desired state. This task requires both arms to avoid obstacles in synchrony.

Figure 10 shows the process of obstacle avoidance. Figure 10a shows the motion sequence. The weight strategy indicates that the control point on the right side has a larger weight. Following the principle of obstacle avoidance, the control point on the right generates circumnavigation motion (see Fig. 10a-ii and 10a-iii), and the arms rotate synchronously to avoid the obstacle. Figure 10b and 10c show the evolution of the target and object motions over time, as well as the synchronous behaviors between the arms during motion.

As anticipated, the results indicate that the object successfully reaches the desired pose without any collisions with the obstacle, and the synchronous constraints of the arms are maintained throughout the motion, also within the boundary constraints.

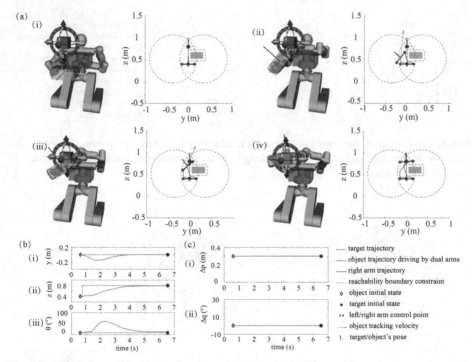

Fig. 10. Illustration of dual-arm planning with obstacle avoidance. (a) motion sequences, (b) evolution of the target and object motions along time, and (c) dual-arm synchronous constraint.

6 Conclusion

This paper proposes a novel dual-arm dynamic planning method based on a dynamic system framework. The proposed method enables dual-arm tracking of moving desired poses and obstacle avoidance with synchronous behaviors, and incorporates motion boundary constraints to ensure reachability. The experimental results validate the effectiveness and flexibility of the method in three different scenarios: tracking dynamic desired poses, motion under boundary constraints, and obstacle avoidance. The results demonstrate the flexibility and adaptability of the proposed method, which offers a favorable solution to issue of the collaborative planning for dual-arm systems.

There is some work remained to be explored. This paper presents preliminary verification in simplified scenarios, and future work will focus on addressing more complex scenarios and situations to enhance its applicability.

Acknowledgment. The research supported by the National Natural Science Foundation of China [Grant numbers 51875114], and Self-Planned Task [NO.SKLRS202204B] of State Key Laboratory of Robotics and System (HIT).

References

1. Kim, D.H., et al.: A RRT-based motion planning of dual-arm robot for (Dis) assembly tasks. IEEE ISR 2013. IEEE (2013)
2. Vahrenkamp, N., et al.: Simultaneous grasp and motion planning: humanoid robot ARMAR-III. IEEE Robot. Autom. Mag. **19**(2), 43–57 (2012)
3. Huang, Y., et al.: Peg-in-hole assembly based on master-slave coordination for a compliant dual-arm robot. Assembly Autom. **40**(2), 189–198 (2020)
4. Likar, N., Bojan, N., Leon, Ž.: Virtual mechanism approach for dual-arm manipulation. Robotica **32**(6) (2014)
5. Shahbazi, M., et al.: Inverse dynamics control of bimanual object manipulation using orthogonal decomposition: an analytic approach. In: 2017 IEEE/RSJ International Conference on Intelligent Robots and Systems (IROS). IEEE (2017)
6. Ren, Y., et al.: Adaptive hybrid position/force control of dual-arm cooperative manipulators with uncertain dynamics and closed-chain kinematics. J. Franklin Inst. **354**(17), 7767–7793 (2017)
7. Salehian, S.S.M., et al.: Coordinated multi-arm motion planning: Reaching for moving objects in the face of uncertainty. Robot.: Sci. Syst. (2016)
8. Guan, Y., Yokoi, K., Zhang, X.: Numerical methods for reachable space generation of humanoid robots. Int. J. Robot. Res. **27**(8), 935–950 (2008)
9. Lagriffoul, F., et al.: Efficiently combining task and motion planning using geometric constraints. Int. J. Robot. Res. **33**(14), 1726–1747 (2014)
10. Detry, R., et al.: Learning grasp affordance densities. Paladyn 2, 1–17 (2011)
11. Kim, S., Shukla, A., Billard, A.: Catching objects in flight. IEEE Trans. Rob. **30**(5), 1049–1065 (2014)
12. Vahrenkamp, N., Tamim, A., et al.: Robot placement based on reachability inversion. In: 2013 IEEE International Conference on Robotics and Automation. IEEE (2013)
13. Zacharias, F., Borst, C., Hirzinger, G.: Capturing robot workspace structure: representing robot capabilities. In: 2007 IEEE/RSJ International Conference on Intelligent Robots and Systems. IEEE (2007)
14. Zhang, H., et al.: A novel coordinated motion planner based on capability map for autonomous mobile manipulator. Robot. Auton. Syst. **129**, 103554 (2020)
15. Khansari-Zadeh, S.M., Aude, B.: A dynamical system approach to realtime obstacle avoidance. Auton. Robots **32**, 433–454 (2012)
16. Zacharias, F.: Knowledge representations for planning manipulation tasks. vol. 16. Springer Science & Business Media (2012)
17. Caccavale, F., et al.: Six-DOF impedance control of dual-arm cooperative manipulators. IEEE/ASME Trans. Mechatron. **13**(5), 576–586 (2008)

SLAM Algorithm of Underwater Vehicle Based on Multi-beam Sonar

Yangming Zhang[1], Zheng Yang[2], Rongxin Cui[1(✉)], Xiaofei Song[1], and Ye Li[1]

[1] School of Marine Science and Technology, Northwestern Polytechnical University,
Xi'an 710072, China
`r.cui@nwpu.edu.cn`
[2] Xi'an Precision Machinery Research Institute, Xi'an 710075, China

Abstract. Due to insufficient underwater illumination and serious electromagnetic signal attenuation, the use of cameras, lidars and satellite positioning and navigation systems in the underwater environment is greatly limited. In this paper, an underwater robot simultaneous localization and mapping (SLAM) algorithm based on multi-beam forward looking sonar is proposed. First of all, on the basis of the cell average constant false alarm rate (CA-CFAR) detection algorithm, the feature constraints of the plane line model are added to optimize the sonar data filtering effect; Then provide reliable initial values for point cloud precise registration by performing correlation scanning matching in advance to ensure the accuracy of inter-frame registration; Then, the factor graph is constructed based on the constraint relationship generated by the inter-frame registration to realize the SLAM back-end optimization; Finally, the effectiveness of the algorithm is verified by the pool experiment.

Keywords: Multi-beam Forward-looking Sonar · Underwater Robot · Simultaneous Localization And Mapping · Interframe Registration · Factor Graph Optimization

1 Introduction

Due to the inability to receive satellite positioning signals underwater, precise underwater navigation and positioning have always been essential factors restricting autonomous underwater vehicles (AUVs) from operating independently for long distances underwater. The commonly used underwater navigation methods can be divided into three types: inertial navigation, acoustic navigation, and geophysical field navigation. However, the errors of the inertial navigation system will gradually accumulate and require external reference information to assist in correction. Although acoustic navigation has no cumulative error, it involves the deployment of a transponder array in advance and is limited by

This work was supported by the National Natural Science Foundation of China under Grant U22A2066.

© The Author(s), under exclusive license to Springer Nature Singapore Pte Ltd. 2023
H. Yang et al. (Eds.): ICIRA 2023, LNAI 14269, pp. 274–286, 2023.
https://doi.org/10.1007/978-981-99-6489-5_22

the baseline length and positioning range. Geophysical field navigation requires accurate prior knowledge of geomagnetic, gravity, and terrain environments.

As an autonomous navigation and mapping method for robots in unknown environments, Simultaneous Localization and Mapping (SLAM) technology enables robots to achieve autonomous perception and planning in unknown environments without prior map, and correct navigation and positioning errors at the same time. The propagation characteristics of sound waves that are not easily attenuated in water make acoustic sensors the optimal choice for underwater detection and perception. The sonar-based SLAM method has also become an important research direction for underwater SLAM algorithms. Based on the dataset of the port of Girona, Spain, Burguera [1] and Mallios [2] proposed SLAM solution using mechanical scanning sonar as sensor to perceive the artificial structured environment. But this method uses artificial environments such as embankments as information sources and is only applicable to structured scenarios such as ports. Maurice et al. [3] designed a SLAM algorithm based on multi-beam forward-looking sonar to enable AUVs to locate underwater targets of interest accurately. This algorithm introduces negative information into the matching process, enhancing the robustness of feature matching. Hurtos [4] proposed a feature registration technique based on the Fourier transform, which can handle issues such as low resolution, noise, and artifacts in sonar images. The results of pool experiments and ship detection experiments have demonstrated that this method has high robustness in the registration of continuous and discontinuous views. However, there are significant differences in the observation results of the same feature by sonar at different heading angles, which requires AUVs to observe the same area twice with similar heading angles in order to construct data correlation. The above harsh conditions make the closed-loop detection process of forward-looking sonar SLAM extremely difficult.

Therefore, based on the threshold segmentation of sonar data, geometric modeling feature constraints are added to extract feature points; At the same time, the constraint relationship generated by inter-frame registration is used to construct a factor graph, and the global optimization of the system is realized by optimizing the factor graph.

2 Feature Extraction for Multi-beam Forward Looking Sonar

2.1 Principle of Multi Beam Forward-Looking Sonar Imaging

When the multi-beam sonar is working, its scanning range is the cone area with the sonar center as the coordinate origin, as shown in Fig. 1, where D_1, D_2, D_3, and D_4 are the four boundary point of the sonar field of view, R is the sonar effective detection distance, α is the horizontal open angle of the sonar transmitting beam, and ϕ is the vertical open angle of the sonar beam.

Although the field of view of a multi-beam forward-looking sonar is a sector-shaped cone in space when imaging the target information within the detection

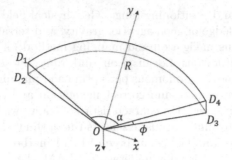

Fig. 1. Multi-beam forward-looking sonar 3D field of view range.

range of the field of view, the sonar system uses a projection method to perform two-dimensional projection mapping of the target in the three-dimensional sector shaped cone space and stores the original echo data in the form of distance angle in the two-dimensional matrix $N_r \times N_b$ in a polar coordinate system, i.e., $\{(r_i, b_j), 0 \le i \le N_r, 0 \le j \le N_b\}$, where N_r represents the number of sampling points on a beam, which is related to the detection distance setting of the sonar, N_b represents the number of beams, as shown in Fig. 2. Each matrix column represents an independent beam data, with the same angular resolution between each column [5]. Each row of the matrix represents the sampling points on each beam at an equal radius distance from the center of the sonar, with the same distance resolution between each row.

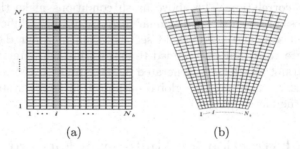

(a)   (b)

Fig. 2. (a) Original polar acoustic image. (b) Cartesian fan-shaped acoustic image.

2.2 Threshold Segmentation Processing

Considering the complexity of underwater scene noise, to determine whether the sonar echo data is background noise or potential target signal, this paper adopts the Cell Average Constant False Alarm Rate (CA-CFAR) detection algorithm, adaptively calculates the detection threshold based on the statistical characteristics of the target background clutter, compares the detected pixel with the adaptive threshold, and determines whether it is a target point. The adaptive detection of all pixels is realized by sliding the reference window, and its work flow is shown in Fig. 3.

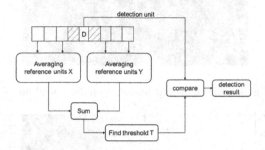

Fig. 3. CA-CFAR adaptive threshold detection process.

D represents the strength value of the unit to be tested, x_i $(i = 1, 2, ..., n)$ and y_i $(i = 1, 2, ..., n)$ represent the reference units on both sides of the unit to be tested (also known as the leading edge and trailing edge reference sliding windows), with the reference sliding window length $R = 2n$, n being the leading edge and trailing edge reference sliding window lengths, and X and Y being the local estimates of clutter intensity by the leading edge and trailing edge sliding windows, respectively. In the CA-CFAR detector, the background clutter intensity Z is estimated based on the sampling values in reference units x_i and y_i.

$$Z = \frac{1}{2n} \sum_{i=1}^{n} x_i + \frac{1}{2n} \sum_{i=1}^{n} y_i \tag{1}$$

The threshold segmentation results of the fixed threshold method and the CA-CFAR detection method for the original sonar image (see Fig. 4) are shown in Fig. 5. This article conducts CA-CFAR detection on each beam of a multi-beam forward-looking sonar separately. Figure 5c shows the adaptive change of the detection threshold with echo intensity values on the 100th beam. The experimental results show that a single threshold cannot effectively and clearly segment the target points, especially in situations with background water waves. The detection threshold of the CA-CFAR method will adaptively change with the beam echo intensity value, and it performs better in target detection and extraction.

2.3 Feature Extraction of CA-CFAR Sonar Data Based on Line Features

In scenes with obvious linear structural features such as ports, embankments, or water pools, this paper uses the Random Sample Consensus (RANSAC) algorithm to apply line feature constraints to the filtered sonar point cloud, eliminate

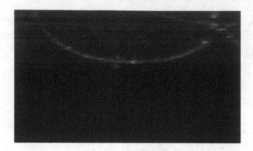

Fig. 4. Original sonar images in polar coordinates.

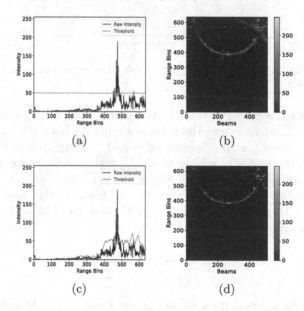

Fig. 5. (a) Change in echo intensity at each sampling point on the 100th beam. (b) Fixed threshold segmentation effect. (c) Echo intensity and threshold changes at each sampling point on the 100th beam. (d) The segmentation effect of CA-CFAR threshold method.

clutter interference, and further optimize the extraction effect of sonar data feature points. The effect of the pool experiment is shown in Fig. 6. Figure 6a shows the sonar image obtained by scanning the corner of the pool wall with multibeam forward-looking sonar. In Fig. 6b, the green dots are the sonar feature points after CA-CFAR threshold segmentation. The red dots are two straight lines extracted after adding line feature constraints based on threshold segmentation, corresponding to two pool walls respectively. The outlier green dots in Fig. 6b indicate that the threshold segmentation process has limited effectiveness in extracting sonar point cloud data and cannot fully restore the structural features of the underwater environment. After adding model constraints for line features, it can effectively eliminate "outliers" that do not conform to the linear structural feature model, reduce the interference of clutter noise, and provide clear and easily distinguishable geometric features for subsequent inter-frame matching.

3 Inter-frame Registration and Factor Graph Optimization

3.1 Improved Inter-frame Registration Method

The most commonly used method for inter-frame registration of spatial points is the Iterative Closest Point (ICP) algorithm, which establishes correspondence between spatial point sets and iteratively solves relative transformation relationships to minimize the sum of squares of distances between points in the corresponding point sets, ultimately completing registration. However, the registration effect of the ICP algorithm depends on the initial value. When there is a significant difference between the scene dataset and the model dataset (there is a large translation or rotation), and the effective initial value cannot be provided (at this time, the initial value will be set as identity matrix I), the ICP method will often fall into the local area of non-global optimization, and eventually lead to wrong convergence results [6]. The ground SLAM system can use encoders or GPS information data to obtain the robot's motion transformation and use it as the initial value for ICP registration. Still, in underwater environments, GPS information cannot be used. This paper proposes an ICP matching algorithm based on Correlation Scan Matching (CSM) initial values to address the issues of significant errors and insufficient accuracy in point cloud registration between two frames using robot motion information obtained from DVL and IMU dead reckoning in underwater environments, as well as the situation where sonar point cloud data is sparse and prone to mismatches.

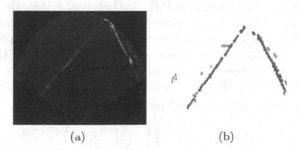

           (a)   (b)

Fig. 6. (a) Sonar image in the corner of the pool wall. (b) Effect of extracting feature points from pool wall corners. (Color figure online)

The correlation scanning matching algorithm uses probability model search to obtain the rigid body transformation that maximizes the probability of observation data and has the advantages of strong initial error robustness and high computational efficiency [7]. As shown in Fig. 7, u represents the motion transformation between adjacent poses, while x_i and x_{i-1} represent the pose of the robot in the current keyframe and the previous keyframe, respectively. z_i represents the multi-beam sonar observation data of the current frame, and z_{i-1} or m represents the observation data of the previous frame or historical cumulative observation data.

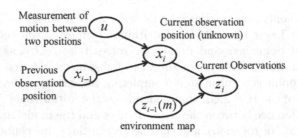

Fig. 7. Probability scan matching model.

To calculate the posterior probability distribution $p(x_i|x_{i-1}, u, m, z_i)$ of robot pose, according to the Bayesian rule and removing irrelevant conditions, we can get:

$$p\left(x_i|x_{i-1}, u, m, z_i\right) \propto p\left(x_i|x_{i-1}, u\right) p\left(z_i|x_i, m\right) \tag{2}$$

where $p\left(x_i|x_{i-1}, u\right)$ represents the motion model, and $p\left(z_i|x_i, m\right)$ represents the observation model. The motion model can be obtained from the odometer. In some cases, such as when there is no motion observation, the motion model can be omitted, and only the observation model can be considered; in other cases, such as when the accuracy of IMU or DVL is not high, the weight of the motion model can be lowered to reduce its impact on the overall probability distribution. This article assumes that the pose is uniformly distributed around the initial guess provided by the odometer, so it only focuses on the probability formula of the second observation model.

Assuming that the probability distribution of the positions of point cloud $z_i^{(k)}$ in the observation data z_i is independent of each other, then:

$$p\left(z_i|x_i, m\right) = \prod_k p\left(z_i^{(k)}|x_i, m\right) \tag{3}$$

Take the logarithm on both sides of the above formula to change multiplication into addition, as follows:

$$p_{\log}\left(z_i|x_i, m\right) = \sum_k p_{\log}\left(z_i^{(k)}|x_i, m\right) \tag{4}$$

In order to increase the robustness of scan matching, this article adopts the Multiple CSM method, which utilizes multiple historical point clouds to construct a query table. In order to obtain the relative transformation relationship T_i between the robot's current pose x_i and the previous pose x_{i-1}, it is necessary to transform the existing point cloud P_i into the query table $M\left(P_{i-1}\right)$ obtained by rasterizing the last point cloud P_{i-1} and determine the optimal transformation parameter T^* based on the principle of the highest score. The innovation of Multiple-CSM lies in the fact that the generation of raster query tables not only relies on the previous point cloud information but also relies on historical multi-frame point cloud information, which can be obtained from the following equation:

$$M\left(P_{i-k}, P_{i-k-1}, \ldots, P_{i-1}\right) = \overset{N_{ssm}}{\underset{k=1}{\cup}} T_{i-1,i-k} P_{i-1} \qquad (5)$$

where $T_{i-1,i-k}$ represents the transformation matrix that transforms the historical point cloud P_{i-k} from frame $i-k$ of the point cloud to frame $i-1$ of the point cloud P_{i-1}. Traverse the search within the confidence region and select the corresponding pose $\tilde{x}_i$ with the highest degree of overlap as the optimal estimate of x_i. Use $T_0 = x_{i-1}{}^{-1}\tilde{x}_i$ as the initial value for subsequent ICP matching.

Figure 8 shows the scores of 19 ICP registrations performed by two registration methods that provide initial values for ICP registration during an 8-min experimental process. The registration scores of the methods proposed in this paper are not lower than that of the whole section, and the scores of 9 times are higher than that of the method that provides the initial ICP registration value by dead reckoning. The method proposed in this paper is superior to the method which provides initial ICP registration value from dead reckoning in point cloud registration overlap score.

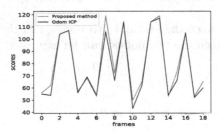

Fig. 8. Comparison of ICP registration scores under different initial values.

3.2 Factor Graph Optimization

The SLAM algorithm based on filters only considers the mobile robot's current pose state and environmental observation information. It does not have loop detection ability, which has problems such as linearization and low update efficiency. This article uses registration information between adjacent frames and loop detection results to construct a SLAM factor graph based on keyframes, as shown in Fig. 9. The robot poses variables for each keyframe are represented as black squares, green circles represent the constraint factors generated by matching between adjacent frames, and red circles represent the loop detection constraint factors. Adjusting the relationship between nodes and edges allows each node in the graph to meet the constraints as much as possible, resulting in the minimum overall error.

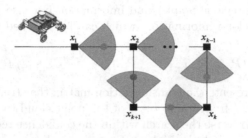

Fig. 9. Factor graph model.

To distinguish the pose state at the time i from the x-coordinate in the pose, in this section, the node pose vector is represented by c_i, and a set $C = (c_1, c_2, ..., c_n)$ can represent all nodes. Because sonar is a two-dimensional mapping, this article only considers the robot's motion in a fixed depth state. Therefore, there are:

$$c_i = \left[t_i^{\mathrm{T}}, \theta_i \right]^{\mathrm{T}} = [x_i, y_i, \theta_i]^{\mathrm{T}} \tag{6}$$

where t_i is the position coordinate of the robot, and θ_i is the heading angle of the robot.

The constraint between the i-th and j-th nodes, i.e., the relative transformation relationship between the two nodes, can be expressed as:

$$\hat{z}_{ij}(c_i, c_j) = \begin{bmatrix} R_i^{\mathrm{T}}(t_j - t_i) \\ \theta_j - \theta_i \end{bmatrix} \tag{7}$$

where R_i is the cosine matrix related to θ_i.

$$R_i = \begin{bmatrix} \cos \theta_i & -\sin \theta_i \\ \sin \theta_i & \cos \theta_i \end{bmatrix} \tag{8}$$

The error function of this edge, that is, the error of the two nodes inter observation measurement z_{ij} and the expected value $\hat{z}_{ij}$, can be expressed as:

$$e_{ij}(c_i, c_j) = z_{ij} - \hat{z}_{ij}(c_i, c_j) \tag{9}$$

The total error function of all edges can be expressed as:

$$F(c) = \sum_{ij} e_{ij}^{\mathrm{T}} \Omega_{ij} e_{ij} = \sum_{ij} F_{ij} \tag{10}$$

where Ω_{ij} is the information matrix, which represents the size of the component weight in the error.

The objective of the optimization is to find the optimal pose configuration to minimize the overall error function $F(c)$:

$$c^* = \arg \min F(c) = \arg \min \sum_{ij} e_{ij}{}^{\mathrm{T}} \Omega_{ij} e_{ij} \tag{11}$$

The above equation can be solved using the open-source optimization library Georgia Tech Smoothing And Mapping(GTSAM) [8].

4 Experimental Result

To verify the performance of the algorithm in natural underwater environments, this paper uses an amphibious robot equipped with M750d multi-beam dual frequency forward-looking sonar and Doppler velocimeter, as shown in Fig. 10, to scan the walls of an experimental water tank that is 24 m long, 22 m wide, and 8 m deep, and then outline the water tank, as shown in Fig. 11.

Fig. 10. Amphibious robot.

The experimental results of the algorithm are shown in Fig. 12. The gray part represents the accessible area for detecting obstacles, while the black region represents the pool wall. The white scatter points represent the robot motion trajectory calculated by the fusion of DVL and IMU data, the green lines represent the robot trajectory obtained by the algorithm in this paper, and the red lines represent the detected loop. The specific trajectory comparison is shown in Fig. 13. The robot starts from the coordinate origin, and during the second circle of motion along the pool, the trajectory obtained from the dead reckoning has undergone significant drift. However, the trajectory obtained by the SLAM algorithm in this paper is closer to the actual motion situation and exhibits good positioning performance.

Fig. 11. Experimental pool.

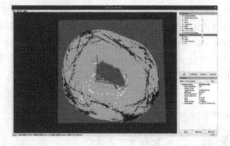

Fig. 12. Effect of pool experiment.

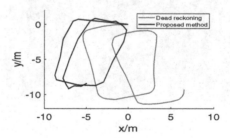

Fig. 13. Robot trajectory.

The map construction effects of the algorithm in this article and the filtering-based Gmapping algorithm are shown in Fig. 14 and Fig. 15, respectively. The Gmapping algorithm based on filtering is recursive and heavily relies on odometers. In the case of significant trajectory errors in dead reckoning, once there is a deviation in the estimation at the current time, it cannot be corrected, failing the constructed map to achieve closure and the failure of mapping. To quantify the mapping accuracy of the SLAM algorithm in this article, the map contour was measured using the Measure tool in Rviz and compared with the actual length of the pool wall. The measurement data is shown in Table 1. Due to the aliasing of multi-frame point cloud data, the constructed map is slightly smaller than the actual pool size.

Fig. 14. Proposed algorithm for mapping effect.

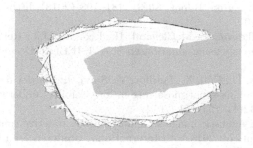

Fig. 15. Gmapping algorithm for mapping effects.

Table 1. Map Size Data

Wall	Length(m)	Mapping length (m)	Error (m)	Error percentage
East	24	21.96	−2.04	8.5
West	24	22.52	−1.48	6.17
South	22.	19.86	−2.14	9.73
North	22	20.20	−1.8	8.18

5   Conclusion

This article proposes a SLAM algorithm for underwater robots based on multi-beam forward-looking sonar, which can achieve simultaneous localization and mapping of robots in scenarios with sparse sonar data and high noise. Firstly, combined with the principle of multi-beam forward-looking sonar imaging, the feature extraction effect of sonar data is optimized by adding the feature constraint of the plane line model based on the CA-CFAR detection algorithm; And providing reliable initial values for ICP point cloud precise registration by pre executing correlation scanning matching, ensuring inter-frame registration accuracy; Simultaneously utilizing the constraint relationships generated by inter-frame registration to construct factor graphs, achieving SLAM backend optimization; Finally, the effectiveness of our algorithm in underwater robot navigation and environmental map construction was verified through pool experiments.

References

1. Burguera, A., Oliver, G., Gonzàlez, Y.: Scan-based SLAM with trajectory correction in underwater environments. In: 2010 IEEE/RSJ International Conference on Intelligent Robots and Systems, October 2010. IEEE (2010)
2. Mallios, A., Ridao, P., Ribas, D., Hernández, E.: Scan matching SLAM in underwater environments. Auton. Robot. **36**(3), 181–198 (2013). https://doi.org/10.1007/s10514-013-9345-0
3. Fallon, M.F., Folkesson, J., McClelland, H., Leonard, J.J.: Relocating underwater features autonomously using sonar-based SLAM. IEEE J. Oceanic Eng. **38**(3), 500–513 (2013)
4. Hurtós, N., Ribas, D., Cufí, X., Petillot, Y., Salvi, J.: Fourier-based registration for robust forward-looking sonar mosaicing in low-visibility underwater environments. J. Field Robot. **32**(1), 123–151 (2014)
5. Mai, N.T., et al.: Acoustic image simulator based on active sonar model in underwater environment. In: 2018 15th International Conference on Ubiquitous Robots (UR), June 2018. IEEE (2018)
6. Salvi, J., Matabosch, C., Fofi, D., Forest, J.: A review of recent range image registration methods with accuracy evaluation. Image Vis. Comput. **25**(5), 578–596 (2007)
7. Olson, E.: Real-time correlative scan matching. In: 2009 IEEE International Conference on Robotics and Automation, May 2009. IEEE (2009)
8. Forster, C., Carlone, L., Dellaert, F., Scaramuzza, D.: IMU preintegration on manifold for efficient visual-inertial maximum-a-posteriori estimation. In: Robotics: Science and Systems XI. Robotics: Science and Systems Foundation, July 2015

Design and Development of ROV for Ship Hull Inspection Using ADRC

Yuan Liu[1](✉), Mingzhi Chen[2](✉), and Daqi Zhu[2]

[1] Merchant Marine College, Shanghai Maritime University, Shanghai 201306, China
202230110162@stu.shmtu.edu.cn
[2] School of Mechanical Engineering, University of Shanghai for Science and Technology, Shanghai 200093, China
mingzhichen2008@163.com

Abstract. Remote Operated Vehicles (ROVs) have been widely used in complex underwater environments. One important application of ROVs is in the inspection of underwater ship hulls. This article describes the design and development of an ROV to assist in this task. The ROV is designed as an open-frame type, with many sensors installed to detect the condition of the ship's submerged structures. The article presents the design of the ROV's power and control compartments, as well as the control program. The ROV has two modes of operation: manual and automatic. In manual mode, the ROV is operated using a joystick. In automatic mode, it can run at a fixed position, depth and direction. Experimental results show that the use of the Active Disturbance Rejection Control (ADRC) algorithm is effective and can assist in underwater inspections. Underwater detection experiments were also conducted.

Keywords: Remote Operated Vehicle (ROV) · Hull Inspection · ADRC · Design

1 Introduction

The ocean contains abundant resources, providing people with a wealth of marine biological resources, mineral resources, ocean power resources, and more. At the same time, it provides an economic and convenient way for communication and trade between countries. Therefore, fully utilizing marine resources and mastering various information about the ocean is an important step for countries to develop their marine strategies. In the past, due to various reasons, people's understanding and control of the ocean were at a relatively low level. However, with the continuous development of marine resources, in order to further strengthen the control of marine information, the demand for marine engineering equipment is increasing. Remote Operated Vehicle (ROV) is the main equipment for current marine exploration and research, and it has the advantages of long underwater working time, timely data transmission and reception, and can play an important role in many aspects. At the same time, with the rapid development of China's shipbuilding industry in recent years, the demand for underwater fault detection, maintenance, and repair technology of ships is increasing. The complex underwater situation

© The Author(s), under exclusive license to Springer Nature Singapore Pte Ltd. 2023
H. Yang et al. (Eds.): ICIRA 2023, LNAI 14269, pp. 287–296, 2023.
https://doi.org/10.1007/978-981-99-6489-5_23

may affect the judgment of divers on ship faults, and the safety of divers cannot be guaranteed. The emergence of underwater robots can to some extent reduce the difficulty of underwater work [1].

Unmanned underwater vehicles are usually divided into two categories: remotely operated vehicles (ROVs) and autonomous underwater vehicles (AUVs). As a device that can move underwater, has visual and sensing systems, and can detect the submerged parts of a ship through remote control or autonomous operation, ROVs have significant advantages in underwater operations. The power of the remotely operated vehicle comes from the mother ship, which can carry more equipment and work for a longer time. This project relies on the technical advantages of the "Shanghai Submarine Engineering Detection Professional Technical Service Platform" to research the application of underwater robots in ship detection, explore the feasibility of their application in underwater ship detection, and develop an engineering prototype that meets the requirements of ship detection applications, thus improving the integration capabilities of maritime "land, sea, air, and space". This article designs and produces a remotely operated submersible that meets the requirements of underwater ship detection. The ROV typically completes three steps for inspecting the ship's hull in the port. (1) General visual inspection to assess the integrity of the structure. (2) Detailed visual inspection to examine the underwater structure in detail. (3) Non-destructive testing, which is conducted on the selected suspicious areas based on the first two steps [10].

There are many studies on underwater hull inspection [6, 7]. Hong et al. designed an autonomous underwater visual inspection system [2]. Ozog et al. designed a system to perform in situ, multiple-session hull inspection using long-term simultaneous localization and mapping (SLAM) with an autonomous underwater vehicle [3]. Negahdaripour designed a vision system for automated hull inspection [4]. These studies focus on underwater visual systems. This article focuses on the design and development of the platform and adopts the Active Disturbance Rejection Control (ADRC) algorithm in attitude control. The robot is lightweight, small in size, easy to operate, and can be used for fast inspection of the underwater parts of the hull. Harbin Engineering University studied the control system architecture of a remote-controlled underwater robot for hull inspection [5]. Aguirre-Castro et al. designed a ship detection robot that utilizes Raspberry Pi 3 and performs parallel computing using thread libraries. They achieved processing up to 42 frames per second during the video capture stage [9].

In this article, the ADRC (Active Disturbance Rejection Control) algorithm was used to optimize the attitude control of the ROV. ADRC is a control method that is highly robust to system disturbances. Its main idea is to regard system disturbances as an additional unknown input, and to estimate and compensate for them in order to control the system. It is mainly composed of a tracking differentiator (TD), an extended state observer (ESO), and an error compensation controller. The tracking differentiator is responsible for pre-arranging the transition process, extracting input signals containing random noise and their differential signals, and solving the contradiction between PID overshoot and fast response. The extended state observer is the core of this algorithm, responsible for estimating the real-time effect of internal and external disturbances in the system and providing compensation in feedback to eliminate the influence of disturbances, thus having an anti-interference effect. The error compensation controller has the function of disturbance suppression and reduction. It controls and compensates for disturbances based on the given signal and its differential signal obtained by TD, and the error between the system output and its derivative observed by ESO [8]. The reason for choosing ADRC in this article is because ADRC has the following advantages: 1) Easy parameter tuning, compared to PID, ADRC parameters are less sensitive. As long as they are within a certain range, the effect is good, and adjusting a single parameter will not cause the system to be unstable. 2) Better robustness compared to PID. 3) Low computational complexity, which is a great advantage for high-speed systems. It can also compensate for disturbances affecting the ROV during ship hull inspection, such as external factors like waves.

According to the actual situation of hull inspection, the external main frame of the ROV is designed, and the main parameters are shown in Table 1.. The ROV is designed for a working depth range of 200 m.

Table 1. Technical performance of ROV

Working depth	200 m
Speed	3 nautical mile/h (nm/h)
Sensor configuration	Camera, Depth gauge, Sonar, Inertial navigation

This paper is organized as follows: The mechanical design is presented in Sect. 2. The electrical design is presented in Sect. 3. The control program design is presented in Sect. 4. The experiments are shown in Sect. 5. Finally, the conclusion is given in Sect. 6.

2 Mechanical Design

The ROV system consists of an external frame, umbilical cable, shore power supply, and shore-based computer. The ROV must be able to adapt to various complex situations in the water, so its mechanical design is crucial. The ROV is designed as an open-frame type, and the frame is made of high molecular weight polyethylene (UPE). The entire ROV includes thrusters, a control cabin, a power cabin, buoyancy materials, an optoelectronic composite cable, and sensors. The overall structure is shown in Fig. 1.

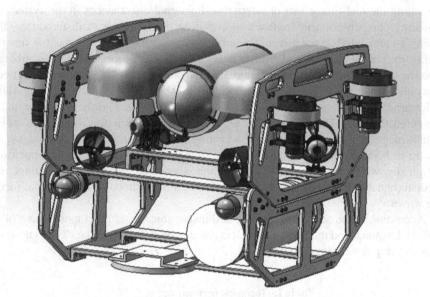

Fig. 1. Overall structure of ROV

The thruster used in the ROV is the T60–30 model produced by C-HEX. It can provide 3.8 kgf of forward thrust and 2.5 kgf of backward thrust. The horizontal thrusters are tilted about 45° to the x-axis. Equation (1) is the power parameter layout matrix for the underwater robot, and by matrix calculation, the forces and moments generated in each degree of freedom direction under the relevant layout of the eight thrusters can be calculated. X, Y, and Z represent the forces in three directions, and K, M, and N represent the moments in three directions. a represents the angle at which the horizontal thruster tilts towards the x-axis, and L_1, L_2, and L_3 represent the moments of force on the X, Y, and Z axes, respectively.

$$
\begin{bmatrix} X \\ Y \\ Z \\ K \\ M \\ N \end{bmatrix} = \begin{bmatrix} 0 & 0 & 0 & 0 & \cos a & \cos a & \cos a & \cos a \\ 0 & 0 & 0 & 0 & \sin a & -\sin a & \sin a & -\sin a \\ 1 & 1 & 1 & 1 & 0 & 0 & 0 & 0 \\ -L_1 & -L_1 & L_1 & L_1 & 0 & 0 & 0 & 0 \\ -L_2 & L_2 & L_2 & -L_2 & 0 & 0 & 0 & 0 \\ 0 & 0 & 0 & 0 & L_3 & -L_3 & -L_3 & L_3 \end{bmatrix} \begin{bmatrix} T_1 \\ T_2 \\ T_3 \\ T_4 \\ T_5 \\ T_6 \\ T_7 \\ T_8 \end{bmatrix} \tag{1}
$$

3 Electrical Design

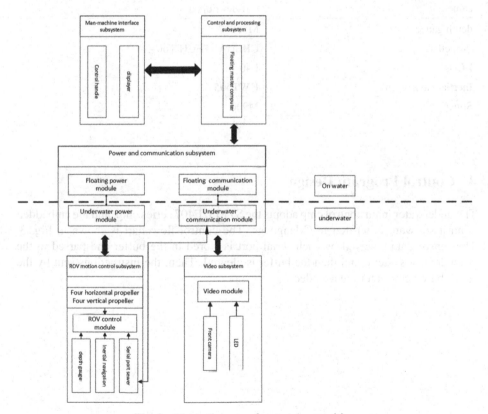

Fig. 2. Block diagram of system composition

The electrical design includes the design of the power compartment and the control compartment. The shore power supply is AC 220 V converted to DC 150 V. At the same time, to reduce the current from the ground to the underwater device, power conversion is performed underwater through a power converter. The power supply of the power compartment is converted from 150 V to 24 V and 12 V to supply the normal operation of various equipment. The sensor configuration in the control compartment is shown in Table 2. Most sensors send data to the main control board via RS232, and the decoding program in the main control board decodes the data to obtain the sensor values. The decoded data is transmitted to the shore-based computer via Ethernet protocol through fiber optics. The ROV is operated by a joystick, and the thrust command of the thrusters is generated by the joystick. The composition diagram of the entire system is shown in Fig. 2.

Table 2. Configurations of sensors

camera	self-developed
depth gauge	MS5837
Propeller	CHEHAI TECH T60–30
LEDs	L40
Inertial navigation	HWT605
Sonar	M900

4 Control Program Design

The underwater main control chip adopts the STM32F407 series chip, and the embedded control software is written in C language. The control flowchart is shown in Fig. 3. The sensor data received by each serial port is stored in the buffer and parsed in the main control system, and then the buffer is cleared. Then, the instructions sent by the shore-based computer are decoded.

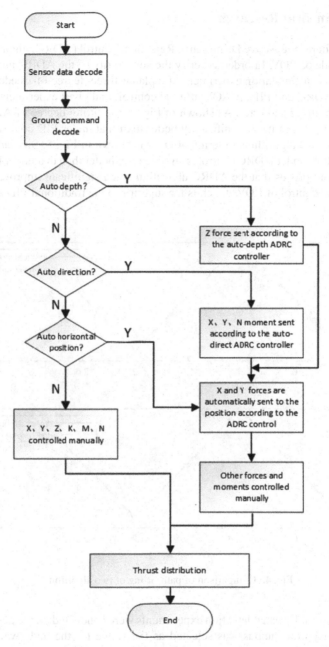

Fig. 3. Control program flow chart

5 Experimental Research

This article adopts the Active Disturbance Rejection Control (ADRC) algorithm to control the attitude of ROV. In order to verify the superiority of the ADRC algorithm, this article conducts a simulation experiment of a planar three-degree-of-freedom with two algorithms, ADRC and PID, in ROV attitude control, and gives experimental results in terms of path fitting and error. As shown in Fig. 4, the fitting degree of ADRC in two directions to the set route is significantly better than that under PID control. The comparison of the two algorithms in terms of error is shown in Fig. 5. Similarly, the error situation of ROV under ADRC control is significantly better than that under PID control. The experiment proves that the ADRC algorithm has a significant improvement effect on the attitude control of ROV, which is far superior to the traditional PID algorithm.

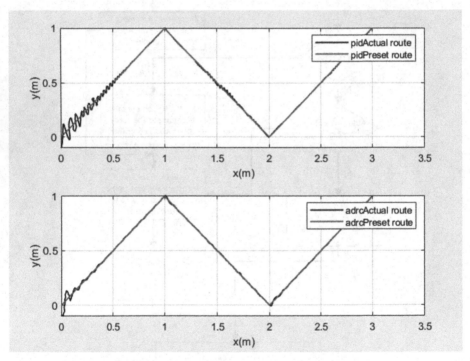

Fig. 4. Comparison of path fitting of two algorithms

In addition, underwater detection experiments were conducted on the designed ROV. An artificial lake on campus was selected as the venue for the underwater detection experiment. Experiments were conducted on self-depth, self-direction, and horizontal motion, and the parameters of the ADRC control were adjusted. Manual control tests were also conducted by operating the ROV with a joystick. Real-time underwater images were collected through the M900 sonar carried by the ROV. The experiment proved that the ROV could clearly observe the underwater situation through the M900 sonar, as shown in Fig. 6.

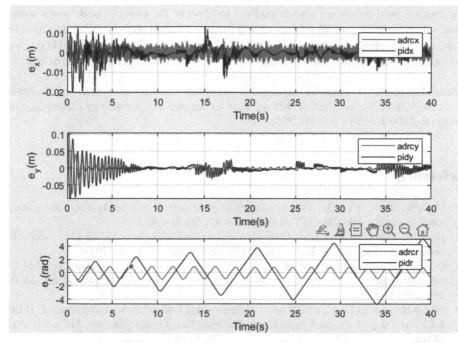

Fig. 5. Comparison of the errors of the two algorithms

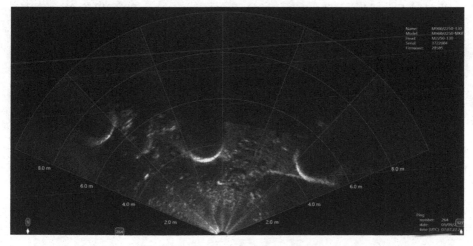

Fig. 6. Underwater detection experiment

6   Conclusion

This article introduces the design of an ROV for underwater ship detection, including its mechanical and electrical design, as well as control program design. Simulation experiments were conducted on the attitude control using both ADRC and PID algorithms.

Preliminary pool tests were also carried out to observe the effect of underwater sonar observation. In the future, further research will be conducted on the ADRC algorithm to make it more suitable for the developed ROV. Experiments will be conducted in deeper river areas or ship berths to further adjust the ROV to assist in underwater ship detection.

Acknowledgment. This work was supported in part by the National Natural Science Foundation of China (52001195), and Creative Activity Plan for Science and Technology Commission of Shanghai (21DZ2293500, 20510712300) .

References

1. Chen, S., Liu, X., Wang, L., et al.: Application of multi-sensor combined system of underwater robot in ship detection. Mach. Tool Hydraulics **47**(23), 61–63 (2019)
2. Hong, S., Chung, D., Kim, J., et al.: In-water visual ship hull inspection using a hover-capable underwater vehicle with stereo vision. J. Field Robot. **36**(3), 531–546 (2019)
3. Ozog, P., Carlevaris-Bianco, N., Kim, A., et al.: Long-term mapping techniques for ship hull inspection and surveillance using an autonomous underwater vehicle. J. Field Robot. **33**(3), 265–289 (2016)
4. Negahdaripour, S., Firoozfam, P.: An ROV stereovision system for ship-hull inspection. IEEE J. Oceanic Eng.: J. Devoted Appl. Electr. Electron. Eng. Oceanic Environ. **31**(3), 551–564 (2006)
5. Huang, H., Wan, L., Pang, Y., et al.: Control system structure of remote-controlled underwater robot for ship detection. In: Chinese Society of Ocean Engineering (COES), Proceedings of the 15th China Marine (Shore) Engineering Symposium (on), pp.206–210. TaiYuan (2011)
6. Chen, M., Zhu, D., Pang, W., et al.: Design and development of an underwater search and rescue vehicle. In: Northeastern University, Professional Committee of Information Physical System Control and Decision of Chinese Association of Automation (CCDC), Proceedings of the 33rd Chinese Control and Decision Conference, no. 12, pp.3389–3393. KunMing (2021)
7. Anonymous.: New underwater hull inspection system by remote operated vehicles. Mater. Perform. **59**(11), 11–12 (2020)
8. Han, J.: From PID technology to self-disturbance rejection control technology. Control. Eng. **03**, 13–18 (2002)
9. Aguirre-Castro, O.A., Inzunza-González, E., et al.: Design and construction of an ROV for underwater exploration. Sensors **19**(24), 5387–5387 (2019)
10. Sun, B., Han, Y., Tang, L.: Nondestructive testing methods and point selection for large LNG carriers. Ship Sea Eng. **49**(02), 98–101 (2020)

Research on Structure Design and Drive Control of Soft Joint on Underwater Snake-Like Robot

Yinglong Chen[1,2(✉)], Fei Gao[1], and Shuangxi Yang[1]

[1] Naval Architecture and Ocean Engineering College, Dalian Maritime University, Dalian 116026, China
chenyinglong@dlmu.edu.cn

[2] Key Laboratory of Rescue and Salvage Engineering Liaoning Province, Dalian 116026, China

Abstract. Compared with the snake-like underwater vehicle with steering gear, the snake-like underwater vehicle with soft joint connection is more flexible and compliant, and it also provides the possibility for the robot to contact with the environment. In this paper, a soft joint for underwater snake-like robot is innovatively proposed, and a test prototype of soft joint is developed. A soft joint attitude control strategy based on feedforward and feedback is proposed to realize high-precision pressure control of soft unit and underwater attitude control of soft joint. Based on the software and hardware control system of the developed soft joint, a test platform for soft joint control is established to verify the feasibility of the proposed soft joint and its attitude control algorithm.

Keywords: Underwater snake-like robot · Soft joint · Attitude Control

1 Introduction

With the increasing investment of human beings in ocean exploration, the development of underwater robots is also very rapid [1, 2]. However, most underwater robots have low working efficiency, which is mainly manifested as large turning radius and slow speed [3, 4]. Snake-like robot is gradually applied to the field of underwater operation because of its multi-degree of freedom, strong coupling, high redundancy and ability to adapt to various complex and changeable environments. Compared with traditional ROVs, AUVs and other underwater robots, snake-like underwater robots can adapt to more complex and rugged environments, and play an important role in oil pipeline inspection, submarine cable inspection, structural maintenance of underwater equipment and exploration of submarine mining areas.

Scholars at home and abroad have carried out a lot of research on underwater snake robots. In 2017, Eelume [5] underwater snake-like robot was jointly developed by Norwegian University of Science and Technology and several maritime technology companies.

This research was funded by the National Natural Science Foundation of China (NSFC) under Grant 52275053, in part by Fundamental Research Funds for the Central Universities under Grant 3132022352, and in part by the Open Foundation of the State Key Laboratory of Fluid Power and Mechatronic Systems under Grant GZKF-202112.

© The Author(s), under exclusive license to Springer Nature Singapore Pte Ltd. 2023
H. Yang et al. (Eds.): ICIRA 2023, LNAI 14269, pp. 297–308, 2023.
https://doi.org/10.1007/978-981-99-6489-5_24

The robot connection module has two degrees of freedom of yaw and pitch, and can bend ±90° around each joint axis. In 2021, CHOSET from Carnegie Mellon University proposed a new type of underwater robot HUMRS [6]. All the propellers are placed inside the body, and the connection module has two degrees of freedom of yaw and pitch, which makes the robot pass through a narrower area. The above snake-like robots are connected by rigid joints, which lack pliability, flexibility and environmental contact. Zhang [7] developed a dynamic model of underwater snake-like robot with rigid propulsion and soft joint hybrid drive control. The simulation verifies that the robot includes forward and backward linear motion, yaw turning, pitch motion and spiral ascending motion multimodal swimming behavior. In this paper, the soft joint is one of the important components of the robot.

Compared with traditional rigid robots composed of connecting rods and rotating joints, soft robots made of elastic materials show higher flexibility and pliability. In recent years, soft robots have been explored and various soft arms have been studied. In 2006, the University of Pennsylvania and the University of Clemson designed the OctArm series of soft manipulators based on pneumatic artificial muscles [8]. The series of manipulators consists of three independent soft arms. Each independent soft arm has two degrees of freedom of bending and elongation around the axis, and all muscles are driven by air pressure. In 2013, the STIFF-FLOP robotic arm for minimally invasive surgery was designed by the Santa Ana Bio-Robot Institute in Italy, which combined flexible fluid actuators and chambers using particle interference mechanism [9, 10]. The robotic arm can provide nearly 260° bending and up to 62% extension. The performance of the robotic arm in terms of workspace, reinforcement and force generation was tested experimentally. In 2017, Zhang Linfei of University of Science and Technology of China proposed a soft arm based on shape memory alloy spring [11]. It is equipped with a memory alloy spring to drive. According to the characteristics of the memory alloy, a feedback system is established. The spring can be controlled to achieve a wide range of motion in the soft body space to complete the heavy object grasping action in different positions.

Most of the underwater snake-like robot connection modules are rigid structures with only one or two degrees of freedom, which limits the motion flexibility of the snake-like robot. This paper presents a rigid-flexible coupling underwater snake-like robot. As shown in Fig. 1, the soft arm is used as a turning and reversing joint, which has flexibility and more degrees of freedom, making the snake-like robot have higher turning efficiency, motion flexibility and environmental accessibility. This paper mainly focuses on the control of the soft joint of the robot.

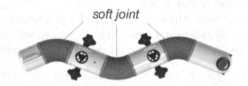

Fig. 1. Underwater snake-like robot with soft joints

2 Design and Control Principles of Soft Joint

In this paper, a fabric enhanced hydraulic drive soft joint is designed. The steering of the soft joint is controlled by configuring the pressure in the cavity of three soft units. The overall structure of the soft body joint is shown in Fig. 2, including two parts: the flexible structure on the left side and the sealed chamber on the right side.

The key components in the flexible structure include the soft units, cages and bellows. The silicone body in the soft unit can generate elastic deformation, and the outer layer is wrapped with spiral wires and woven fabrics, which is used to limit the radial deformation of the silicone matrix. The soft units can provide driving forces for soft joint rotation by pressurizing and stretching. Several cages are equidistantly installed on the three soft elements, which are mainly used to maintain the balance of the three soft elements, and can better control the bending attitude and stiffness of the joints. The bellows are installed on the outermost side of the soft joint to protect the internal structure and aesthetics.

Various electrical components are mainly placed in the sealed cabin, including water hydraulic pump, throttle valve, pressure sensor, controller, etc., which are mainly used for pressure monitoring and control of the soft unit.

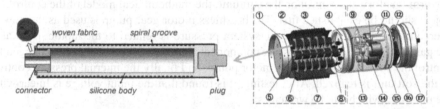

Fig. 2. Structure composition of soft joint.

In order to achieve attitude control of the soft joint, individual pressure control is used for each soft unit. The principle of soft joint hydraulic drive system is shown in Fig. 3. In the figure, n1 ~ n3 are brushless motor gear pumps, P1 ~ P3 are pressure sensors, R1 ~ R3 are soft units, and V1 ~ V3 are electric proportional hydraulic throttle valves. When the pump is working normally, there is a mapping relationship between the speed and the maximum pressure it can provide. Due to the minimum stable speed limit of the brushless motor gear pump, the full range pressure control of the soft unit cannot be realized. Therefore, the pressure control method of pump valve combination is innovatively adopted. For example, when the desired pressure is lower than the pressure corresponding to the lowest stable speed of the pump, a lower pressure control can be achieved by the pressure relief of the throttle valve. The research on the control of the whole soft joint will be elaborated in the following chapters.

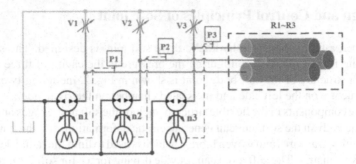

Fig. 3. Soft joint water hydraulic system principle

3 Pressure Control of Soft Robotic Units Based Feedforward/Feedback

3.1 Feedforward/Feedback Control Strategy

Feedforward Model. Feedforward control is predictive of the entire output. In order to perform feedforward control on the soft unit, the mathematical model of the controlled object should be established first. The brushless motor gear pump is used as the power source of the hydraulic system, the system pressure is related to the motor speed and the parameters of the water pressure component. The input signal voltage is changed to control the speed of the brushless motor pump, and finally the internal pressure control of the soft unit is realized. After testing, it is found that the input voltage is linear with the pressure, which can be written as:

$$P_\omega = K_1\omega_{P_\omega} = K_2 U_{P_\omega} \tag{1}$$

where ω_{P_ω} is the speed of the brushless motor when the pressure is equal to P_ω, U is the input voltage of the motor when the pressure is equal to P_ω, K_1 is the speed-pressure gain coefficient, and K_2 is the voltage-speed ratio gain coefficient. The gain coefficient is related to the pressure, and it can be obtained by experimental test fitting.

Combined Feedforward/Feedback Strategy. Even if the feedforward model is very close to the system, if there are other external interferences, the system error cannot be eliminated. Feedback control can make the system realize closed-loop to achieve better control performance. This article utilizes a combination of feedforward and PID feedback control to effectively mitigate system deviations, improve response speed, control accuracy, and stability. The compound control strategy of feedforward and feedback is shown in Fig. 4.

3.2 Soft Unit Pressure Control Experiment

Pump-Controlled Pressure Experiments with Different P Values. Since the soft body pressure at the lowest speed of the water pressure pump is 0.16 MPa, a pressure control test with a desired pressure of 0.2 MPa is conducted with the throttle valve in

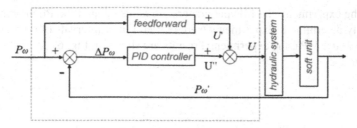

Fig. 4. Feed-forward/PID feedback control framework

the closed state and the P-value inputs in the PID are 0, 1, 5, 10, 15 and 20, respectively, and the soft body unit pressure changes as shown in Fig. 5.

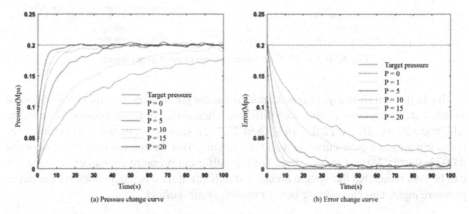

(a) Pressure change curve   (b) Error change curve

Fig. 5. 0.2 MPa pressure pump control experiment at different P values

From the Fig. 5(a), we can learn that when P = 0, the feedback model did not work, due to the elasticity of the soft unit, and as the pressure rises, the pump leakage increases, and the pressure increment gradually decreases in the same time, and at the 100th s, the pressure reaches 0.1774 MPa. When the P value is equal to 1, the pressure reaches 0.1873 MPa at the 100th s. The pressure approaches the target input when the P values are 5, 10, 15 and 20 and reaches 0.2 MPa at 67.07 s, 42.05 s, 23.39 s, 38 s and 17.87 s, respectively.

The system pressure error variation is shown in Fig. 5(b), from which it can be seen that the error decreases more rapidly with increasing P value. At the 100th s, the soft body pressure errors are 0.0226 MPa, 0.0127 MPa, 0.0064 MPa, 0.006 MPa, 0.0024 MPa, and 0.0017 MPa, respectively, and the overall error of adding feedback regulation is less than 10%.

Pressure Pump Control Experiment with Different Targets. Through the 0.2 MPa pressure experiment, it can be seen that the increase of P value obviously shortens the time of pressure change inside the software unit and improves the system response.

Through the experiment, the PID parameters are adjusted, and the PID parameter P =
20 is finally determined. Experiments were carried out at intervals of 0.05 MPa in the
range of 0.2~0.4 MPa, the experimental results are shown in Fig. 6.

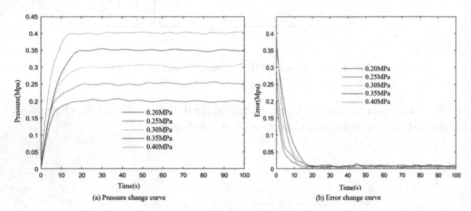

(a) Pressure change curve   (b) Error change curve

Fig. 6. 0.2~0.4 MPa pressure pump control experiment

It can be seen from Fig. 6(a) that under the same parameters, the time for the system
to reach stable pressure is not much different when different target pressures are input,
which are 20.9 s, 20.7 s, 22.8 s, 19.9 s and 22.7 s, respectively. Figure 6(b) is the corresponding pressure error curve, and all the pressure error fluctuation ranges are between
0.0023~0.0148 MPa at steady state. Through different pressure control experiments, it
can be concluded that the system pressure stabilization time is independent of the target
pressure input, and can achieve better pressure control effect.

4   Attitude Control Based on Pump-Valve Combination

4.1   Kinematics Model of Soft Joint

In this paper, the kinematic modeling of the soft joint is carried out based on the piecewise
constant curvature model [12–14]. Figure 7 shows the bending model of the soft joint.
The center of the contact circle between the front end cover and the software unit is
taken as the origin O of the coordinate axis. Through the origin of the axis, the axis
perpendicular to the contact circle is the η axis, and the line to the center of the software
unit 1 and the center of the software unit 2 is ξ, Determine the ζ axis according to the
right hand rule. The central Angle corresponding to the bending arc of the soft joint is
bending angle α. The Angle between the curved plane of the flexible structure and the
$\eta O \xi$ plane is the deflection Angle θ.

Through the spatial geometric relationship, the expressions of soft joint length l,
deflection angle θ and bending angle α can be calculated.

The length l of the soft joint can be expressed as:

$$l = \frac{l_1 + l_2 + l_3}{3} \tag{2}$$

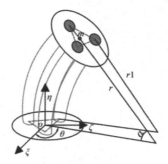

Fig. 7. Kinematic schematic diagram of soft flexible structures.

where l_1, l_2 and l_3 are the lengths of the three soft units.

The deflection angle θ is:

$$\theta = \arctan\left(\frac{\sqrt{3}(l_2 + l_3 - 2l_1)}{3(l_2 - l_3)}\right) \tag{7}$$

The bending angle α is:

$$\alpha = \frac{2\sqrt{l_1^2 + l_2^2 + l_3^2 - l_1 l_2 - l_1 l_3 - l_3 l_2}}{3m} \tag{3}$$

where m is the distance between the axis of the soft driving unit and the axis of the soft joint.

When three soft units are filled with the same pressure to produce the same length, the flexible structure only forms axial elongation at this time, the bending angle is zero, and the deflection angle direction cannot be defined. And the length of soft unit can be calculated according to Hooke's law, as shown in the following equation.

$$l_i = \frac{P_{\omega i} A_0 l_0}{EA} + l_0 \tag{4}$$

where $P_{\omega i}$ is the driving pressure of the driving unit i, A_0 is the cavity cross-sectional area of the soft unit, A is the cross-sectional area of the soft element soft material and E is the elastic modulus of soft material.

4.2   Pump-Valve Combination Pressure Control Strategy

Pressure Valve Control Experiments with Different P Values. In order to compare with the pump control pressure, the valve control test is carried out under the pressure of 0.2 MPa. When the valve control is adopted, the system water pressure pump maintains a constant speed of 1500 r/min, and the given signal is input at the 7 s time. The pressure change curves with P values of 0, 1, 5, 10 and 20 are shown in Fig. 8.

It can be seen from Fig. 8 that when P is equal to 0, the stable pressure of the system is about 0.1932 MPa, and the pressure reaches stability at 99.8 s. As the P value increases,

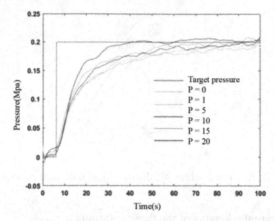

Fig. 8. 0.2 MPa valve control pressure change curve

the time for the system to reach the input pressure gradually decreases. Comparing and analyzing the two different ways of pump control and valve control under 0.2 MPa input pressure, the valve control has high control accuracy and shortens the pressure change time, but the pressure adjustment time of pump control is obviously less than that of valve control.

Combined Control Strategy. The minimum stable speed of the hydraulic pump is 500 r/min. When the throttle valve port is fully closed, the internal pressure of the corresponding soft unit is 0.16 MPa. Therefore, in order to achieve full-range pressure control, a pump-valve combined control mode is adopted. The control strategy is shown in Fig. 9. When the expected pressure of the system is greater than 0.16 MPa, the pump control mode is adopted, and the throttle valve port is closed at this time. When the expected pressure of the system is less than 0.16 MPa, the control mode of pump valve combination is adopted, the pump maintains the minimum speed of 500 r/min, and the throttle valve port is in an adjustable state.

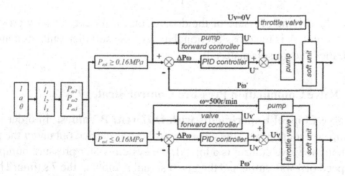

Fig. 9. Pump-valve combination pressure control framework

In order to verify the built pump-valve combination control model, the pump-valve combination control experiment is carried out. During the experiment, the pressure signal input was continuously changed from 0 to 0.3 MPa within 10 s, and finally stabilized at 0.3 MPa. The feasibility of the control model was verified by the feedback of pressure and pump and valve input voltage changes. The experimental results are shown in Fig. 10.

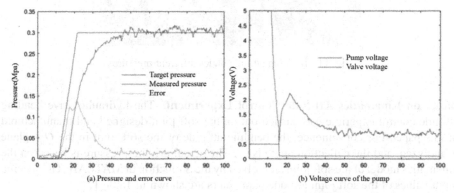

(a) Pressure and error curve   (b) Voltage curve of the pump

Fig. 10. 0~0.3 MPa pump-valve combination control experiment

From Fig. 10, it can be seen that the initial input pressure is 0 MPa, the water pump works under a constant input voltage, and the throttle valve spool is in a fully open position. As the input pressure continues to increase, the input voltage of the throttle valve decreases, and the valve port is gradually closed. At this time, it is PID valve control mode. When the pressure input is higher than 0.16 MPa, the input voltage of the throttle valve is 0.05 V, and the valve port is fully closed. At this time, it is changed to PID pump control mode. During the whole process, the pressure error increases first and then decreases, and finally stabilizes between 0.0068~0.0231 MPa, which is 2.27~7.7% of the expected input.

4.3 Soft Joint Attitude Control Experiment

Joint Posture Under Different Pressures. The main function of the soft joint is to realize the change of multiple degrees of freedom. The hydraulic pressure control test is carried out on the designed soft joint, and the soft joint is fixed in the test pool. The water pump can directly obtain the water source from the environment. The attitude of the soft joint under different pressure driving is shown in Fig. 11.

From the previous section, it can be seen that the soft body joint will only produce axial elongation when the driving pressure of the three soft body units is the same. Figures 11(a) to (c) show the three soft bodies are charged with 0.1 MPa, 0.2 MPa, and 0.3 MPa simultaneously, and the joint realizes the elongation function; Figs. 11(d) to (f) show only the soft body No. 3 is charged with 0.1 MPa, 0.2 MPa, and 0.3 MPa, respectively, and the joint $O_{\eta\zeta}$ plane achieves bending. It can be seen from the figures that the soft body joint bends almost close to 90°when the pressure is 0.3 MPa.

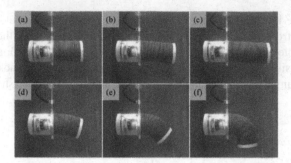

Fig. 11. Bending attitude under different pressures

Based on Kinematics Attitude Control Experiment. The hydraulic drive bending attitude control experiment is carried out on the soft joint designed and manufactured in this paper. For convenience, the bending attitude of the soft joint in the $O_{\eta\zeta}$ plane is analyzed, and the deflection angle is $0°$. The actual driving pressure is based on the kinematics model of the soft joint and solved by the S function in MATLAB. The specific input values of the soft joint attitude parameters are shown in Table 1.

Table 1. Underwater attitude control parameters for soft joint

Parameter	l/mm	α/°	l_1/mm	l_2/mm	l_3/mm
Value	285	30	309	251	251
	320	60	351	257	257
	350	90	397	256	256

Figure 12 shows the underwater attitude of the soft joint under the input of l and α. The target inputs of Figs. 12(a) to (d) are the initial state of $0°$, $30°$, $60°$and $90°$respectively, and the actual underwater bending angles are $30.85°$, $61.18°$and $89.26°$respectively. It can be seen from Fig. 12 that the bending attitude of the soft joint is in good agreement with the target attitude.

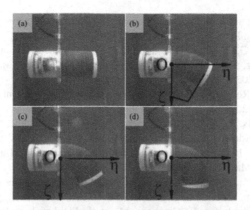

Fig. 12. Attitude control experiment

5 Conclusion

In this paper, a soft joint for underwater rigid-flexible coupling is designed, and the precise kinematics control of the soft joint is realized. The composite control strategy based on pressure feedforward/feedback is studied. The software unit control experiments under different P values and expected pressures are carried out. Under different P values, the pressure change time decreases with the increase of P value, and the target pressure error is less than 10%. Under different target input pressures, the pressure stability change time is basically the same, and the pressure error fluctuation range is small, which is between 0.0023 and 0.0148 MPa. The composite control strategy shortens the pressure change time of the software unit and improves the pressure control accuracy. The kinematics model of the soft joint is established, and the relationship between the three-dimensional space posture of the soft joint and the pressure of the soft unit is analyzed. A pump-valve combined control model based on feedforward/feedback composite control strategy is established, and underwater attitude control experiments are carried out. The actual bending angles corresponding to the expected bending angles of 30°, 60°and 90°are 30.85°, 61.18°and 89.26°, respectively. The effectiveness of the control strategy is verified by underwater attitude control experiments.

This paper has conducted relevant work on the design of soft joint structures and driving control, but further research is needed to apply it to underwater snake-like robots. In the follow-up work, we will use water hydraulic components with better performance, optimize the control algorithm for soft joints, and improve the response speed and flexibility of soft joints. Our robot design is intended to add contact functionality with the environment, so we also need to study the dynamic characteristics of soft joints when they collide with structures.

References

1. Tran, C., et al.: Operability analysis of control system for ROV launch-and-recovery from autonomous surface vessel. Ocean Eng. **12**(5), 277–283 (2023)

308   Y. Chen et al.

2. De Oliveira Éverton, L., et al.: Station-keeping of a ROV under wave disturbance: modeling and control design. Proc. Instit. Mech. Eng. **237**(2), 455–477 (2023)
3. Abdulshaheed, A.G., Hussein, M.B., Dzahir, M.A.M., et al.: A review on snake robot locomotion, modelling, and controlling in challenging environment. J. Comput. Theor. Nanosci. **17**(2), 558–569 (2020)
4. Liu, J., Tong, Y.: Review of snake robots in constrained environments. Robot. Auton. Syst. **43**(141), 103785 (2021)
5. Liljebäck, P., Mills, R.: A flexible and subsea resident IMR vehicle. In: Proceedings of the Oceans 2017-Aberdeen, F. IEEE **15**(124), 234–246 (2017)
6. CMU Homepage: https://www.cmu.edu/news/stories/archives/2021/april/snake-robot.html. Last accessed 30 May 2023
7. Zhang, J., Chen, Y., Liu, Y., et al.: Dynamic modeling of underwater snake robot by hybrid rigid-soft actuation. J. Mar. Sci. Eng **10**(12), 1914(2022)
8. Mcmahan, W., Chitrakaran, V., Csencsits, M., et al.: Field trials and testing of the OctArm continuum manipulator. In: Proceedings. 2006 IEEE International Conference on Robotics and Automation, pp. 1403–1406. IEEE (2006)
9. Ranzani, T., Gerboni, G., Cianchetti, M., et al.: A bioinspired soft manipulator for minimally invasive surgery. Bioinspir. Biomim. **10**(3), 108–115 (2015)
10. Cianchetti, M., Ranzani, T., Gerboni, G., et al.: STIFF-FLOP surgical manipulator: mechanical design and experimental characterization of the single module. In: Proceedings 2013 IEEE/RSJ International Conference on Intelligent Robots & Systems, pp. 1214–1216 (2013)
11. Zhang, L., Xu, M., Yang, H.: Research on soft manipulator actuated by shape memory alloy (SMA) springs. In: Proceedings 2017 IEEE International Conference on Real-time Computing and Robotics (RCAR), pp. 200–206 (2017)
12. Jones, B.A., Walker, I.D.: Kinematics for multisection continuum robots. IEEE Trans. Rob. **22**(1), 43–55 (2006)
13. Iii, R., Jones, B.A.: Design and kinematic modeling of constant curvature continuum robots: a review. Int. J. Robot. Res. **29**(13), 1661–1683 (2010)
14. Ding, H., Zhao, J.: Performance analysis of variable speed hydraulic systems with large power in valve-pump parallel variable structure control. J. Vibroeng. **16**(2), 1042–1062 (2014)

Reconfigurable Torso-Based Quadruped Robot for Post-tilt Recovery

Yuhang Liu and Chunyan Zhang[✉]

Shanghai University of Engineering Science, Shanghai 201620, China
1300094862@qq.com

Abstract. When working in a complex and unmanned environment, a quadruped robot is likely to lose motion when tilted by external interference; therefore, the robot must be able to recover from tilting. The conventional recovery solution can only rely on the movement of the legs, whereas the reconfigurable quadruped robot can accomplish self-recovery of the quadruped robot after capsizing through the coordinated movement of the torso and legs. In this paper, based on the configurational variability of the reconfigurable torso, a variety of bionic forms are obtained, and a variety of post-tip recovery schemes are planned, and four post-tip recovery schemes are compared and analyzed from the perspective of force and energy. Simulation of each scheme is carried out to verify the feasibility of the implementation of each scheme, and the data of each scheme are analyzed to arrive at a better post-collapse recovery scheme, and finally a theoretical prototype is fabricated.

Keywords: reconfigurable torso · quadruped robot · overturning · recovery

1 Introduction

In complex environments, quadriped bionic robots can explore, rescue, monitor, inspect, and provide care for a variety of duties [1, 2]. Quadruped robots are an essential direction for the development of intelligent robots; they are widely used in industry, life, and other fields [3–5]; and their research value and future development prospects are of the utmost importance [6–8]. Currently, representative quadruped robots include Boston Dynamics' BigDog, WildCat, and SpotMini robots [9], MIT's Cheetah robot, which has developed three generations [10], the Italian Institute of Technology's HyQ robot [11], Zhejiang University's Jedi Shadow and Red Rabbit robots, and others.

When robots work in complex and changing environments, tipping is inevitable, which may lead to structural damage, system loss and recovery difficulties. In some areas that are inaccessible to humans, if the robot does not automatically recover its attitude when it is working, it will lead to mission failure, so it is necessary to study the rapid recovery of attitude after capsizing. NASA's jumping robot can recoup by flipping its body 90° after tipping over. Boston Dynamics' RHex robot relies on dynamic feedback for self-recovery by controlling the robot's dynamic performance. Diansheng Chen et al. proposed a robot flip mechanism based on the triangular center of gravity

© The Author(s), under exclusive license to Springer Nature Singapore Pte Ltd. 2023
H. Yang et al. (Eds.): ICIRA 2023, LNAI 14269, pp. 309–320, 2023.
https://doi.org/10.1007/978-981-99-6489-5_25

theory and demonstrated the feasibility of the mechanism. Xilun Ding proposed a method of self-recovery relying on the coordinated movement of the six legs.

The above methods are mostly based on torso flipping by additional mechanism, relying on closed-loop control to make the torso swing by inertia, etc. The torso is rigid and does not participate in the motion during the flipping process, while the variable cell quadruped robot designed by Shengjie Wang has a variable torso and an innovative recovery strategy after tipping. Inspired by the movable torso of quadruped robot and multimodal mobile robot, this paper designs a bionic quadruped robot based on reconfigurable theory, proposes two new recovery schemes for the robot after tipping, and compares them with the traditional recovery scheme, and analyzes the different characteristics of the new recovery scheme and the traditional scheme through simulation to obtain a better recovery scheme.

2   Overview of Reconfigurable Quadruped Robot Bionics

The torso of the reconfigurable quadruped robot uses a 12-rod mechanism evolved from the 4R mechanism with a square shape, and the morphological transformation of the torso is achieved by changing and locking the axis relationship of the rotation subsets in the torso. The reconfigurable torso can be transformed into two main types of torsos, plane torso and space torso, through rotation and deformation, and each torso can be subdivided into fixed torso and continuous torso, fixed torso can be equated to rigid torso and continuous torso can be equated to single degree of freedom torso. The morphology of each trunk is shown in Fig. 1, and the red axis indicates that it is active at this time.

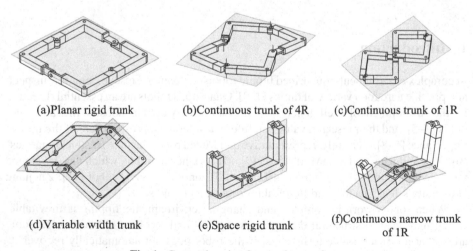

(a)Planar rigid trunk   (b)Continuous trunk of 4R   (c)Continuous trunk of 1R

(d)Variable width trunk   (e)Space rigid trunk   (f)Continuous narrow trunk of 1R

Fig. 1. Comprehensive figure of torso shape

Based on the above-mentioned reconfigurable torso, the leg joints are added, and the theoretical dimensions between the joint points are preset. As shown in Table 1, the unilateral section size of the platform is 20×20 mm, and the leg section size is 20

× 10 mm. Modeling, the overall model is shown in Fig. 2. Reconfigurable robots can realize six different postures. According to the principle of bionics, they can be divided into turtles, spiders, lizards, tiger weasels, stick insects and dogs, as shown in Figs. 3, 4.

Table 1. Theoretical size between joint points.

Parameter	Length/mm
$B_i D_i$	110
$D_i E_i$	40
$E_i F_i$	100
$FiGi$	100

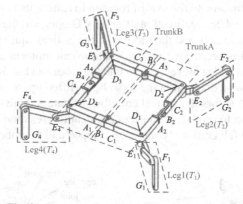

Fig. 2. The overall model of the quadruped robot

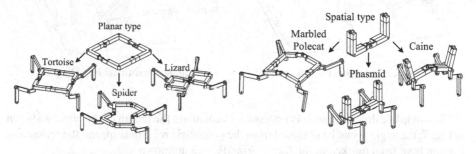

Fig. 3. Planar Bionics   **Fig. 4.** Bionic space form

3 Analysis of the Recovery Characteristics After Overturning

When the robot is in the tilted posture, it cannot continue to move, and if it wants to restore the normal posture, it needs to turn its body 180° in the vertical plane in order to restore its movement ability. When a footed animal lies on the ground after tipping and needs to roll over, it can twist its body to turn over. The force arm of the animal with the longitudinal axis of rotation of the torso is smaller than the force arm with the horizontal axis of rotation of the torso. Since the mass of the torso remains the same, a shorter force arm can effectively reduce the torque required for flipping. The animal tends to rotate around the longitudinal line of the body and adjust the position of the center of gravity to flip by gravity, which can reduce the energy consumption. Based on the analysis of the animal flipping process, the recovery of the robot after tipping is analyzed based on the position of the change of the center of gravity.

3.1   Restoration Process and Analysis of Traditional Robots

The traditional robot is mostly a rigid torso, which relies entirely on the leg activity to recover during the flipping process, and is divided into three main stages as shown in Fig. 5. 1 state is the robot in the tilted attitude, which loses the ability to move and requires the robot to flip around the axis of rotation to restore its normal attitude. 2 state is the critical attitude, when the direction of gravity G points to the axis of rotation and the gravitational moment is 0, and the robot is in the critical equilibrium. State 3 is the normal posture, and it is necessary to provide a transient moment after state 2 to break the critical equilibrium by leg movement, so that the robot can fall freely by gravity. The left side of Fig. 6 shows a diagram of the torso being lifted up by the leg motion, while the right side of Fig. 6 shows the critical equilibrium state required for flipping, which requires the leg motion to provide a transient moment to break the equilibrium, so that the robot continues to fall until it is completely flipped and the robot recovers.

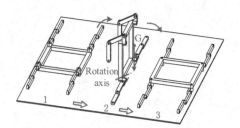
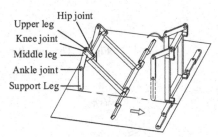

Fig. 5. Traditional Flip Diagram   **Fig. 6.** Traditional Flip Diagram

To complete this process, it is necessary to calculate the length of the legs, as shown in Fig. 7, the angle γ can be obtained from the geometric relationship, and the remaining lengths have been marked in the figure, h_1 and h_3 are unknown

$$\begin{cases} h_1 = a \sin \alpha + b \cos \alpha + c \sin \alpha = e + d \sin \beta \\ \pi = \alpha + \beta + \gamma \end{cases} \tag{1}$$

By solving α and β first, the size of h_1 can be obtained.

$$h_3 = h_2 - d \cos \gamma - e \tag{2}$$

If the robot is to be flipped to the right side of Fig. 7, the calculated value for h_3 must be less than or equal to 0, i.e., the support legs must be lengthened to the dotted line after achieving equilibrium in Fig. 7, which will increase the load on the actuators at each joint and have a significant effect on the robot's performance. This also confirms that the turtle's rigid torso and short legs prevent it from turning over after being lifted, whereas the locust's long and thin legs allow it to flip easily. After reaching equilibrium, the torso center-of-mass flip trajectory is shown in Fig. 8.

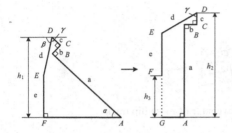
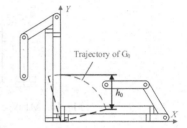

Fig. 7. Dimensions

Fig. 8. Traditional torso center of mass flip trajectory

3.2 Trunk Reconfigurable Recovery Process and Analysis

The robot relies on the degrees of freedom of the legs for motion recovery when the torso is rigid, which has certain requirements for the length of the robot legs, thus increasing the requirements of the joint actuators. After the robot is in critical equilibrium, the robot falls freely and the high impact force when touching the ground may cause damage to the mechanical structure and key hardware structures. Therefore, we hope to use the reconfigurability of the torso to solve these problems encountered in the traditional rigid torso in the flipping, reduce the requirements for joint actuators, and reduce the impact in the flipping process.

3.2.1 Trunk Arch Recovery Program

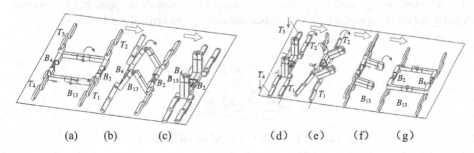

(a)   (b)   (c)   (d)   (e)   (f)   (g)

Fig. 9. Trunk Arch Recovery

The initial overturning shape of the robot is shown in Fig. 9 (a). The trunk arch recovery scheme proposed by Wang Shengjie, hereinafter referred to as M1, the turning trajectory of the center of mass of the torso is shown in Fig. 10. Compared with the action of the non-mutant mode, the M1 overturning mode, There are no special requirements for the size of the legs, and the posture of the robot is symmetrical during the recovery process, and a stable isosceles triangle support relationship is always maintained at any time, which greatly improves the stability of the recovery, but the robot still has a certain impact on the torso during the recovery process.

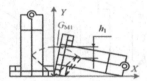

Fig. 10. M1 type torso center of mass flip track

3.2.2   Recovery Plan for Unilateral Torso Upturn

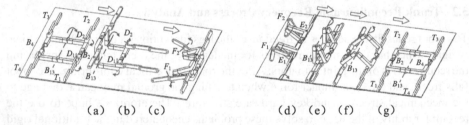

(a) (b) (c)   (d) (e) (f)   (g)

Fig. 11. Recovery Analysis of Unilateral Trunk Upturn

T This paper proposes an overturning recovery scheme for unilateral torso upturning, referred to as M2 in the following text. Figure 11(a) depicts the robot's initial overturned configuration. Figure 12 depicts the turning trajectory of the center of mass of the torso. The M2 overturning method has impacts during the recovery process, but it does not directly act on the torso, which can reduce the damage to critical hardware.

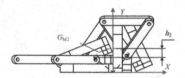

Fig. 12. M2 Trunk Center of Mass Flip Trajectory

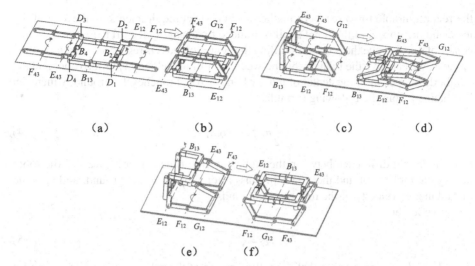

Fig. 13. Rollover recovery analysis

3.2.3 Rolling Flip Recovery Scheme

This paper proposes the overturning recovery of the overall rolling and flipping of the robot, hereinafter referred to as the M3. The initial overturning shape of the robot is shown in Fig. 13 (a), the final shape is shown in Fig. 13 (f). The position of the center of mass of the key attitude in the recovery process of M3 is shown in Fig. 14.

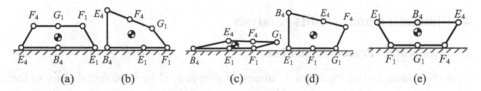

Fig. 14. M3 Flip Centroid Map

3.3 Principle of Reconfigurable Recovery Shock Absorption

Since the overall structure of the robot torso is approximately symmetrical, its center of mass can be integrated into a plane for calculation. The formula for calculating the center of mass is:

$$\begin{cases} X_G = \dfrac{\sum m_i x_i}{\sum m_i} \\ Y_G = \dfrac{\sum m_i y_i}{\sum m_i} \end{cases} \quad (3)$$

After calculation, we know: $h_0 > h_1 > h_2$, where h_0 is much larger than h_1 and h_2, while h_1 and h_2 are relatively close. Compared with the traditional method, using the reconfigurable torso recovery method has no strict requirements on the size of the legs, and the impact of the robot's fall is reduced by changing the lift height of the torso center of mass. Since the process of falling the center of mass is regarded as a quasi-static process, we can give the relationship between the falling velocity v_i of the robot and the height difference h_i of the center of mass when the robot touches the ground, which can be obtained from the following formula

$$\frac{1}{2}mv_i^2 = mgh_i \tag{4}$$

h_i is the height difference between the highest point of the center of mass of the robot during the movement and the center of mass after flipping to the ground, and v_i is the instantaneous velocity of the robot when it lands.

solve it, get

$$v_i = \sqrt{2gh_i} \tag{5}$$

$h_0 > h_1 > h_2$, It can be seen that the falling speed of the robot *is* $v_0 > v_1 > v_2$, and it can be obtained from the momentum theorem,

$$F_i t = mv_i \tag{6}$$

In the formula, F is the impact force suffered by the robot when it decelerates to zero when it lands, and t is the time required for the robot to decelerate to zero when it lands.

It can be seen from the above formula that within the same time t, $F_0 > F_1 > F_2$, the greater the landing speed of the robot, the greater the impact force it receives.

4   Simulation and Results Analysis

4.1   Restoration Process Simulation

Using Solidworks to establish three-dimensional models of the three initial states of the virtual prototype of the reconfigurable torso quadruped robot after overturning, import it into ADAMS software for dynamic simulation, add parameters such as part material, rotation joint constraints, drive, gravity and contact, and verify these three The feasibility and rationality of this recovery strategy. Figures 15, 16, 17, 18, 19, 20 are the simulation process and input angle-time curves of M1 to M3 types respectively.

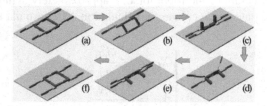

Fig. 15. Resuming the simulation process after the M1 overturned

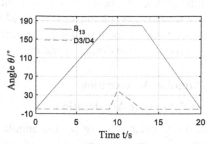

Fig. 16. M1 driving joint input angle-time curve

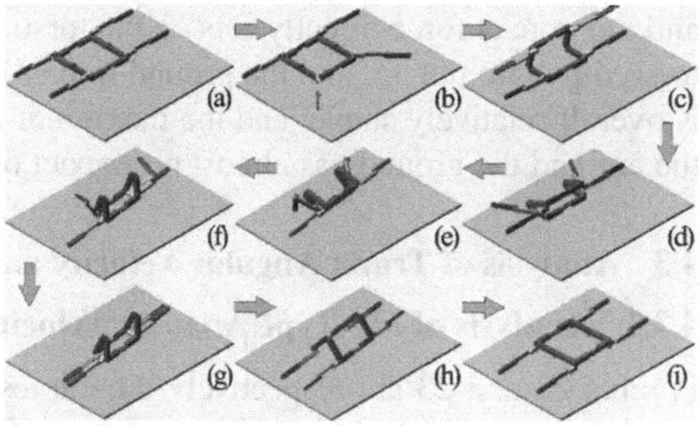

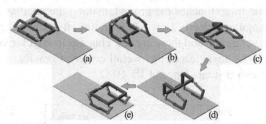

Fig. 17. Resuming the simulation process after the M 2 overturned

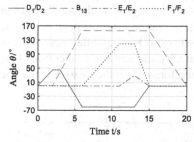

Fig. 18. M2 drive joint input angle-time curve

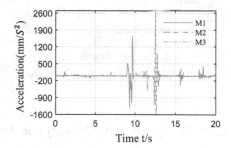

Fig. 19. Resuming the simulation process after the M3 overturned

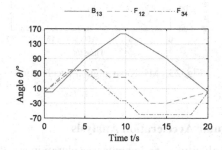

Fig. 20. M3 driving joint input angle-time curve

Fig. 21. M1-M3 Center of mass acceleration

4.2 Analysis of the Acceleration of the Center of Mass of the Trunk

Figure 21 shows the mass center accelerations of the three types of overturning recovery. The mass center acceleration of the M1 type is a max at 9~10 s, $a_{max} = 1.65$ m/s², when the acceleration of the center of mass of M2 type is 11~13 s, $a_{max} = 2.65$ m/s², when the acceleration of the center of mass of M3 type is 11~12 s, $a_{max} = 0.61$ m/s², the maximum acceleration of the center of mass of the M3 type is much smaller than that of the M1 and M2. At the maximum acceleration of M1, the torso falls to the ground, and the impact force directly acts on the torso; at the maximum acceleration of M2, the torso flips into the air, and the ground impact force directly acts on the legs; while M3 is overall relatively stable, and the maximum acceleration occurs at the torso flips into the air, and the ground has almost no impact on the robot's torso during operation.

4.3   Analysis of Trunk Angular Velocity and Angular Acceleration

4.3.1   Analysis of M1-Type Angular Velocity and Angular Acceleration

Figures 22 and 23 are respectively the curves of the angular velocity ω_1 and angular acceleration α_1 of the M1-type torso center of mass with time t. It can be seen from the figure that within 0 to 9 s, since the center of mass of the trunk only changes in the vertical direction, the angular velocity and angular acceleration does not change much, but at 9 to 10 s, both the angular velocity and the angular acceleration peak. At this time, the torso falls to the ground by gravity, and the peak value appears at the moment when the torso touches the ground, making the angular acceleration reach its peak, while the angular velocity is at After landing, it gradually returns to zero, and the torso A turns over again, and there are still changes in angular velocity and angular acceleration. Due to the deviation of the overall center of gravity of the torso when the torso A lands, the torso B jumps once at 18–19 s.

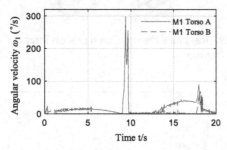

Fig. 22. M1 torso angular velocity

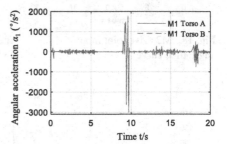

Fig. 23. M1 Torso angular acceleration

4.3.2   M2 Type Angular Velocity and Angular Acceleration Analysis

Figures 24, 25 are the curves of the angular velocity ω_2 and angular acceleration α_2 of the center of mass of the M2 torso with time t. It can be seen from the figure that within 2 to 6 s, the torso A turns upwards, and the torso B does not move, 6 to 12 s Within 12–14 s, both the angular velocity and the angular acceleration have peak values, and the robot will automatically turn over by gravity. The peak value appears at the moment when the torso A touches the ground, making the angular acceleration after reaching the peak, the angular velocity gradually returns to zero after falling to the ground. At this time, the torso A touches the ground on one side. After 15–16 s, the whole torso opens, and the torso B touches the ground instantaneously, so that the angular velocity and angular acceleration reach a local peak, finally, the center of mass of the torso changes only in the vertical direction, and the angular velocity and angular acceleration change little.

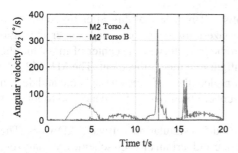

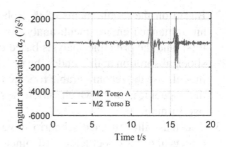

Fig. 24. M2 torso angular velocity   **Fig. 25.** M2 Torso angular acceleration

4.3.3 Analysis of M-3 Angular Velocity and Angular Acceleration

Figures 26, 27 are respectively the curves of the angular velocity ω_3 and angular acceleration α_3 of the center of mass of the M3 trunk with time t. It can be seen from the figure that the overall range of the angular velocity and angular acceleration curves of the M3 type is smaller than that of the M1 and M2 types. The movement process is relatively gentle, and the instantaneous peak value of angular velocity and angular acceleration appears at 11–12 s. At this time, the torso turns upward as a whole, and the robot jumps slightly due to the gravity imbalance between the trunk and legs, but the peak value of angular velocity and angular acceleration Smaller, the momentary peak can be eliminated by optimizing the gravity ratio of the torso and legs in the later stage.

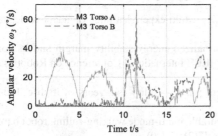

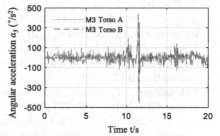

Fig. 26. M3 Torso angular velocity   **Fig. 27.** M3 Torso angular acceleration

4.4 Theoretical Prototyping

Based on the theoretical prototype of the reconfigurable robot, we apply its bionic strategy to obtain various bionic poses, as shown in Fig. 28. The theoretical prototype is used to test the feasibility of each mechanism and provide an effective reference for subsequent research.

5 In conclusion

1. According to the reconfigurable characteristics of the robot, six bionic quadruped robots are obtained, which have strong flexibility and environmental adaptability.

2. Based on the requirements of the robot's self-recovery ability after overturning in an unmanned environment, analyze the size parameter constraints under the rigid torso and the principle analysis based on the trajectory of the center of mass and the shock absorption ability under the reconfigurable torso movement. The M1, M2, M3 models use the reconfigurable torso to complete the self-recovery scheme and design their specific actions, which enrich the recovery methods of the quadruped robot after overturning.

3. The feasibility of each scenario is verified by simulation software ADAMS. The effects of friction coefficient and joint torque and terrain on each scheme are analyzed. M1 and M2 are less affected by friction coefficient but limited by terrain, while M3 type is not limited by terrain and each joint torque is relatively small. Finally, the M3 model was concluded as the best solution and a theoretical prototype was fabricated.

References

1. Niquille, SC.: Regarding the pain of SpotMini: or what a robot's struggle to learn reveals about the built environment. Architect. Des. **89**(1) 2019
2. Hutter, M., Remy, C.D., Höpflinger, M.A., et al.: ScarlETH: design and control of a planar running robot. In: IEEE/RSJ International Conference on Intelligent Robots & Systems. IEEE (2011)
3. Hutter, M.C., et al.: ANYmal – toward legged robots for harsh environments. Adv. Robot. **31**(17) 2017
4. Yang, C., Yuan, K., Zhu, Q., Yu, W., Li, Z.: Multi-expert learning of adaptive legged locomotion. Sci. Robot. **5**(49), 2020
5. Hirose, S., Tsukagoshi, H., Yoneda, K.: Normalized energy stability margin and its contour of walking vehicles on rough terrain. In: IEEE International Conference on Robotics & Automation. IEEE (2001)
6. Vukobratovic, M., Borovac, B.: Zero-moment point — thirty five years of its life. Int. J. Humanoid Rob. **1**(1), 157–173 (2004)
7. Liu, X., Zhang, C., Ni, C., Lu, C.: A reconfigurable multi-mode walking-rolling robot based on motor time-sharing control. Industr. Robot **47**(2), (2020)
8. Messuri, D., Klein, C., et al.: Automatic body regulation for maintaining stability of a legged vehicle during rough-terrain locomotion. Robot. Autom. IEEE J. **1**(3), 132–141 (1985)
9. Raibert, M., Blankespoor, K., Nelson, G., Playter, R.: BigDog, the rough-terrain quadruped robot. In: IFAC Proc. Volumes **41**(2) (2008)
10. Hyun, D.J., Lee, J., Park, S., Kim, S.: Implementation of trot-to-gallop transition and subsequent gallop on the MIT Cheetah I. Int. J. Robot. Res. **35**(13) (2016)
11. Semini, C., Tsagarakis, N.G., Guglielmino, E., Focchi, M., Cannella, F., Caldwell, D.G.: Design of HyQ – a hydraulically and electrically actuated quadruped robot. In: Proceedings of the Institution of Mechanical Engineers, Part I: J. Syst. Control Eng. **225**(6) (2011)

Innovative Design and Performance Evaluation of Robot Mechanisms

Kinematics Analysis of a New Parallel Mechanism with Complete Separation of Constraints and Drives

Can Qiu[1], Yu Wang[1], Jiabin Wu[1], Xiaoyu He[1], Xuejian Ma[1], Yundou Xu[1,2(✉)], and Yongsheng Zhao[1,2]

[1] Parallel Robot and Mechatronic System Laboratory of Hebei Province, Yanshan University, Qinhuangdao 066004, China
ydxu@ysu.edu.cn
[2] Key Laboratory of Advanced Forging and Stamping Technology and Science of Ministry of National Education, Yanshan University, Qinhuangdao 066004, China

Abstract. At present, there is a growing demand for parallel mechanisms with fewer inputs and more outputs. These mechanisms are highly sought after in industries such as aerospace, antenna, and entertainment facilities, among others. Therefore, this paper proposes a new parallel mechanism (PM) that utilizes separation of constraints and drives, resulting in centralized drive management. Thereby achieving a small amount of driving to drive multiple parallel moving platforms. For example, 3nRRS/PPPS parallel mechanism. In this study, we utilize the closed-loop vector method to obtain the inverse solution for the 3RRS/PPPS parallel mechanism. To perform a static analysis, we construct a complete Jacobian matrix for the mechanism. Under the premise of satisfying the workspace, the key dimensional parameters of the mechanism were optimized with the objective of improving the load-carrying capacity of the mechanism and minimizing the driving force. The method of complete separation of constraints and drives is easier to centrally manage drives, greatly improving energy utilization and work efficiency, and having a wide range of application scenarios in antenna, entertainment facilities, and other situations.

Keywords: parallel mechanism · fewer inputs and multiple outputs · scale optimization

1 Introduction

Parallel mechanisms (PMs) are increasingly used in many fields such as machining, packaging and assembly, aerospace, and medical treatment. Among them, successful applications include motion simulators [1], fast grasping and handling robots [2], entertainment equipment, multi-axis processing equipment for large structural components [3], satellite radar docking, and aircraft component assembly [4–6], Parallel mechanisms with relatively mature applications (normal drive) include a 3-DOFs parallel mechanism DELTA, a 3-DOFs PM H4, and a 2-DOFs mechanism 3-PRS, 3-UPS/UP, and 2-UPR/SPR. Note that in this paper P, R, S, U and C represent prismatic, revolute, spherical, universal and cylindrical joints, respectively.

© The Author(s), under exclusive license to Springer Nature Singapore Pte Ltd. 2023
H. Yang et al. (Eds.): ICIRA 2023, LNAI 14269, pp. 323–336, 2023.
https://doi.org/10.1007/978-981-99-6489-5_26

Currently, the driving forms of parallel mechanisms include normal driving [7–9], redundant driving [10], and underactuated [11–15]. Other scholars have also proposed parallel mechanisms with single passive constraint branches and multiple drive branches. Reference [16] proposes the 3UPS-PU motion simulation platform, which includes three unconstrained branch UPS and passive constrained branch PU. Reference [17] proposes a class of six-limbs five degree of freedom (5-DOF) parallel machining robots with high stiffness and flexibility such as 5UPS-PRPU which includes five unconstrained branch UPS and passive constrained branch PRPU and 5UPS-UPU which includes five unconstrained branch UPS and passive constrained branch UPU. Compared to just constrained branches 3UPS-RRP PM, 3RRS/PPPS is more convenient for driver management to achieve array output. However, in the scenario of synchronous driving of multi output PMs, although the above methods separate the constraints and driving properties of the branches, they cannot achieve simultaneous driving of multiple outputs with fewer driving.

With the rise of emerging industries, solar trackers [18], antennas, entertainment facilities [19], and synchronous control of attitude angles of up to upper shutter/blade outputs in aeroengines require the use of few inputs array output drive forms. By separating the constraints and drives of PM branches, and centralizing the management of the drive branches of each mechanism, it is possible to achieve the goal of using fewer drives to drive multiple platforms to synchronize array output, achieving manufacturing convenience, reducing costs, and energy conservation and emission reduction.

This research creatively proposes a new PM with separation of drives and constraints. Compared with traditional PMs, this new mechanism achieves separation of drives and constraints, making it easier to centrally manage drives and has better motion/force transmission performance, allowing multiple outputs, greatly improving energy utilization and work efficiency.

2   Kinematics Analysis of 3RRS/PPPS PMs

The 3RRS/PPPS parallel mechanism is shown in Fig. 1(a). $3n$RRS/PPPS PM is composed of n 3RRS/PPPS PM and shares a PPPS drive branch as shown in Fig. 1(b). The fixed platform and the moving platform are connected by three RRS branches with the same structure and one PPPS branch through the center points of the moving and fixed platforms. The fixed platform $B_1B_2B_3$ is connected to the rods of three RRS branches through revolute joint, the moving platform $A_1A_2A_3$ is connected to the rods of three identical RRS branch through spherical joint, and the two rods are directly connected through revolute joint. The 3RRS PM is connected to the fixed platform 1, and the PPPS branch is connected to the fixed platform 2. There is a PPPS branch as shown in the figure between the center of the fixed platform and the center of the moving platform. The center of the moving platform is directly connected to the rod of the branch, and the side near the moving platform is a vertically upward prismatic joint. The prismatic joint is connected to the spherical joint through another rod, and below the moving platform are two prismatic joints that are 90° each other.

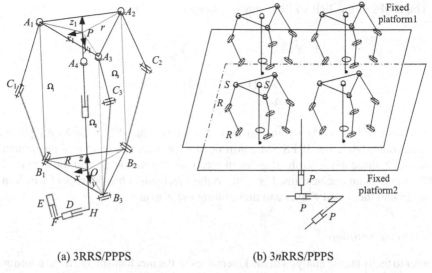

(a) 3RRS/PPPS   (b) 3nRRS/PPPS

Fig. 1. PM with fewer inputs and more outputs

From the modified G-K formula [20], it can be obtained:

$$K = d(n - g - 1) + \sum_{i=1}^{g} f_i + v \tag{1}$$

where:

d——The order of the PM, $d = 6 - \lambda$

n——Number of PM components

g——The number of joints in the PM

f_i——Number of DOF of the i-th joint

v——Number of redundant constraints for PMs

The expression for the redundant constraint v is

$$v = l - k \tag{2}$$

where, l is the number of remaining screws after removing the common constraints of the mechanism, and k is the screw composed of the remaining screws after removing the common constraints of the mechanism the rank of a rotational system.

The DOFs of the 3RRS/PPPS parallel mechanism can be obtained:

$$K = d(n - g - 1) + \sum_{i=1}^{g} f_i + v$$
$$= 6 \times (11 - 13 - 1) + 21 + 0$$
$$= 3$$

Based on the screw theory analysis, it is known that the RPS branch only provides one constraint, while the 3RPS PM constrains the degrees of freedom of movement in the X and Y directions and the degrees of freedom of rotation around the Z axis. The PPPS branch is an unconstrained branch, so the mechanism has degrees of freedom to rotate around the X and Y axes and move along the Z axis.

2.1 Inverse Solution

In order to facilitate the analysis of the kinematics of the mechanism, the fixed coordinate system $O - xyz$ is established at the center of the fixed platform $B_1B_2B_3$, and the moving coordinate system $P - x_1y_1z_1$ is established at the center of the moving platform $A_1A_2A_3$.

The attitude of the moving coordinate system relative to the fixed coordinate system can be transformed through the Z-Y-X Euler angle (α, β, γ), and the resultant rotation transformation matrix can be described as:

$$_P^O R = R(z, \alpha)R(y, \beta)R(x, \gamma) = \begin{bmatrix} c\alpha c\beta & c\alpha s\beta s\gamma - s\alpha c\gamma & c\alpha s\beta c\gamma + s\alpha s\gamma \\ s\alpha c\beta & s\alpha s\beta s\gamma + c\alpha c\gamma & s\alpha s\beta c\gamma - c\alpha s\gamma \\ -s\beta & c\beta s\gamma & c\beta c\gamma \end{bmatrix} \quad (3)$$

where, c represents cos and s represents sin.

The coordinate points A_i and B_i relative to the coordinate systems P and O can be expressed as: $^P A_i$ and B_i $(i = 1,2,3)$.

$$^P A_1 = [\tfrac{\sqrt{3}}{2}r, -\tfrac{r}{2}, 0]^T \quad ^P A_2 = [-\tfrac{\sqrt{3}}{2}r, -\tfrac{r}{2}, 0]^T \quad ^P A_3 = [0, r, 0]^T$$
$$B_1 = [\tfrac{\sqrt{3}}{2}R, -\tfrac{R}{2}, 0]^T \quad B_2 = [-\tfrac{\sqrt{3}}{2}R, -\tfrac{R}{2}, 0]^T \quad B_3 = [0, R, 0]^T \quad (4)$$
$$P = [x, y, z]^T$$

The above formula (3) is expressed as

$$_p^O R = \begin{bmatrix} T_{11} & T_{12} & T_{13} \\ T_{21} & T_{22} & T_{23} \\ T_{31} & T_{32} & T_{33} \end{bmatrix} \quad (5)$$

The A_i coordinates in a fixed coordinate system can be expressed as:

$$q_i = {}^O A_i = {}_p^O R\, {}^P A_i + P \quad (6)$$

Substituting formulas (4) and (5) into (6):

$$q_i = \begin{bmatrix} T_{11}S_{ix} + T_{12}S_{iy} + T_{13}S_{iz} + P_x \\ T_{21}S_{ix} + T_{22}S_{iy} + T_{23}S_{iz} + P_Y \\ T_{31}S_{ix} + T_{32}S_{iy} + T_{33}S_{iz} + P_Z \end{bmatrix} \qquad (7)$$

Considering the constraints of the revolute joints of the three RRS branches, the A_1B_1, A_2B_2 and A_3B_3 branches can only move in the Ω_1, Ω_2 and Ω_3 planes, as shown in Fig. 1(a).

Therefore, the following constraint relationships exist:

$$q_{1y} = -\frac{\sqrt{3}}{3}q_{1x}$$
$$q_{2y} = \frac{\sqrt{3}}{3}q_{2x} \qquad (8)$$
$$q_{3x} = 0$$

Obtained from the above formula (5), (7) and (8):

$$x = -r(\cos\alpha\sin\beta\sin\gamma - \sin\alpha\cos\gamma)$$
$$y = -\frac{r}{2}(\sin\alpha\sin\beta\sin\gamma) \qquad (9)$$
$$\alpha = -\arctan(\frac{\sin\beta\sin\gamma}{\cos\beta + \cos\gamma})$$

Therefore, formula (9) are three constraints imposed on the moving platform. When the moving platform moves, it will generate adjoint motion in the x, y, and around the z axis directions.

The position analysis of PM is to solve the position relationship between the input and output components of the mechanism. For the 3RRS/PPPS PM, when the driver pushes the prismatic joint to different distances, the corresponding moving platform of the PM will change its pose in space. If the posture of the moving platform in space is known, calculate the displacement of each prismatic joint, and the resulting value is the inverse solution of the position of the moving platform of the mechanism in the current posture.

As shown in Fig. 1(a), taking PE as the research object, it can be obtained from Fig. 2:

$$\vec{FF} + \vec{FH} + \vec{HA_4} - \vec{EA_4} \qquad (10)$$

where, $\vec{x}$, $\vec{y}$, $\vec{z}$ are the unit direction vectors of each branch of the PPPS branch, which always maintain a mutually perpendicular relationship during movement. $\vec{x} = L(1, 0, 0)^T$, $\vec{y} = L(0, 1, 0)^T$, $\vec{z} = L(0, 0, 1)^T$. Let the left and right sides of formula (10) be dot multiplied $\vec{x}$, $\vec{y}$, $\vec{z}$ at the same time. Where, l_x, l_y and l_z is the module length of the branch in (x, y, z) three directions, and its absolute value represents the length.

$$\vec{EF} = l_y \cdot \vec{y}$$

$$\vec{FH} = l_x \cdot \vec{x}$$

$$\vec{HA_4} = l_z \cdot \vec{z}$$

$$\vec{EA_4} = \vec{OP} + \vec{PA_4} - \vec{OE}$$

The variation of the $\vec{EA_4}$ branch on the l_x, l_y and l_z prismatic joint can be expressed as:

$$\begin{bmatrix} \Delta l_x \\ \Delta l_y \\ \Delta l_z \end{bmatrix} = \begin{bmatrix} l_x - l_{x0} \\ l_y - l_{z0} \\ l_z - l_{z0} \end{bmatrix} \tag{11}$$

When the pose of the moving platform including the position $[P_x, P_y, P_z]^T$ and orientation expressed by ZYX Euler angles (α, β, γ) are known, the displacement distance variation of driving branch l_x, l_y and l_z prismatic joint can be obtained by using formula (11).

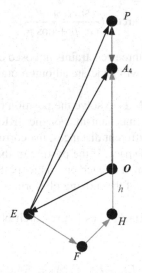

Fig. 2. Closed loop vector method

2.2 Velocity Analysis of 3RRS/PPPS PMs

Establish the speed relationship of each point of the moving platform as shown in Fig. 1 (a):

$$v_{A_4} = v_p + \omega \times {}_P^O R \cdot \vec{pA_4} \tag{12}$$

where, v_{A_4} is the linear velocity of the moving platform A_4 point; v_p is the linear velocity of the moving platform reference point P; ω is the angular velocity of the moving platform; $\vec{pA_4}$ is a vector of a moving platform reference point to A_4 point.

The unit direction vectors n_1, n_2, n_3 of the coordinate system x-axis, y-axis, and z-axis are determined by dot product at both ends of formula (12):

$$\dot{q}_i = v_{A_4} \cdot n_i = v_p \cdot n_i + \omega \times {}_P^O R \cdot \vec{pA_4} \cdot n_i = v_p \cdot n_i + {}_P^O R \cdot \vec{pA_4} \times n_i \cdot \omega (i = 1, 2, 3) \tag{13}$$

where, $n_1 = \begin{bmatrix} 1 & 0 & 0 \end{bmatrix}^T, n_2 = \begin{bmatrix} 0 & 1 & 0 \end{bmatrix}^T, n_3 = \begin{bmatrix} 0 & 0 & 1 \end{bmatrix}^T$.

Compile the above formula into a matrix:

$$\begin{pmatrix} \dot{q}_1 \\ \dot{q}_2 \\ \dot{q}_3 \end{pmatrix} = \begin{pmatrix} n_1^T \left({}_P^O R \cdot \vec{pA_4} \times n_1 \right)^T \\ n_2^T \left({}_P^O R \cdot \vec{pA_4} \times n_2 \right)^T \\ n_3^T \left({}_P^O R \cdot \vec{pA_4} \times n_3 \right)^T \end{pmatrix} \cdot \begin{pmatrix} v_p \\ \omega \end{pmatrix} \tag{14}$$

Fohrmula (14) can be obtained

$$\dot{q} = J_a \cdot V \tag{15}$$

where, $v_p = \begin{bmatrix} v_{p_x} & v_{p_y} & v_{p_z} \end{bmatrix}^T$, $\omega = \begin{bmatrix} \omega_x & \omega_y & \omega_z \end{bmatrix}^T$; $\dot{q}$ represents a generalized driving speed that includes the input speeds $\dot{q}_1, \dot{q}_2, \dot{q}_3$ of the drive branch PPPS; V represents the generalized velocity of the moving platform, J_a representing the driving Jacobian matrix of 3×6 [21].

The instantaneous motion screw system of the moving platform is represented in the moving coordinate P-xyz as:

$$\$_p = \sum_{j=1}^{3} \omega_{j,i} \$_{j,i} \quad (i = 1, 2, 3) \tag{16}$$

where, $\omega_{j,i}$ represents the angular velocity of the jth revolute joint of the ith branch; $\$_{j,i}$ represents the unit screw of the jth revolute joint of the ith branch; ω represents the angular velocity of the moving platform; v_p represents the linear speed of the reference point of the moving platform.

$$\$_{1,i} = \begin{bmatrix} s_{1,i} \\ s_{1,i} \times \overrightarrow{B_ip} \end{bmatrix}^T \quad \$_{1,i} = \begin{bmatrix} s_{2,i} \\ s_{2,i} \times \overrightarrow{C_ip} \end{bmatrix}^T \quad \$_{3,i} = \begin{bmatrix} s_{3,i} \\ s_{3,i} \times \overrightarrow{A_ip} \end{bmatrix}^T$$

$$\$_{4,i} = \begin{bmatrix} s_{4,i} \\ s_{4,i} \times \overrightarrow{A_ip} \end{bmatrix}^T \quad \$_{5,i} = \begin{bmatrix} s_{5,i} \\ s_{5,i} \times \overrightarrow{A_ip} \end{bmatrix}^T \quad \$_p = \begin{bmatrix} \omega \\ v_p \end{bmatrix}^T$$

According to the screw theory, the constraint anti-screw of a single constraint branch i is calculated as:

$$\$_i^r = \begin{bmatrix} s_{1,i} \\ s_{1,i} \times \overrightarrow{A_ip} \end{bmatrix}^T \tag{17}$$

Perform reciprocal product on both ends of formula (16) and formula (17), respectively, to obtain:

$$\begin{pmatrix} s_{1,1}^T \left(s_{1,1} \times \overrightarrow{A_1p} \right)^T \\ s_{2,1}^T \left(s_{2,1} \times \overrightarrow{A_2p} \right)^T \\ s_{3,1}^T \left(s_{3,1} \times \overrightarrow{A_3p} \right)^T \end{pmatrix} \cdot \begin{pmatrix} v_p \\ \omega \end{pmatrix} = \begin{pmatrix} 0 \\ 0 \\ 0 \end{pmatrix} \tag{18}$$

It can be obtained from formula (18).

$$J_c \cdot V = 0 \tag{19}$$

where, J_c representing the constraint Jacobian matrix of 3×6, V represents the generalized velocity of a moving platform.

Combining formula (15) with formula (19) can obtain a complete Jacobian matrix

$$J \cdot \begin{pmatrix} v_p \\ \omega \end{pmatrix} = V_l \tag{20}$$

where, $V_l = \begin{bmatrix} \dot{q}_1 & \dot{q}_2 & \dot{q}_3 & 0 & 0 & 0 \end{bmatrix}^T$, J represents a total Jacobian matrix.

$$J = \begin{pmatrix} J_a \\ J_c \end{pmatrix}$$

Therefore, the mapping of speed from drive joint to the output of the moving platform can be obtained.

2.3 Static Analysis

Taking a moving platform as the research object, ignoring the inertia of the legs and the friction between the joints, the static balance equation can be obtained based on the virtual work principle:

$$\begin{pmatrix} F_a \\ F_q \end{pmatrix}^T \cdot V_l + \begin{pmatrix} F \\ T \end{pmatrix}^T \cdot \begin{pmatrix} v_p \\ w \end{pmatrix} = 0 \tag{21}$$

where, $F_a = \begin{bmatrix} F_{a1} & F_{a2} & F_{a3} \end{bmatrix}^T$ is expressed as a driving force vector, and F_{a1}, F_{a2}, F_{a3} respectively represent the input driving force sizes of the three drives on the driving branch PPPS; $F_q = \begin{bmatrix} F_{q1} & F_{q2} & F_{q3} \end{bmatrix}^T$ represented as a constraint vector, and F_{q1}, F_{q2}, F_{q3} respectively represent the constraint sizes of the three constraint branches RRS. $F = \begin{bmatrix} F_x & F_y & F_z \end{bmatrix}^T$ represents the external force acting on the moving platform, with the point of action at the reference point P of the moving platform, and $T = \begin{bmatrix} T_x & T_y & T_z \end{bmatrix}^T$ represents the external torque acting on the moving platform.

By $W = \begin{bmatrix} F \\ T \end{bmatrix}$ introducing formula (20) into formula (21), it is concluded that:

$$\begin{pmatrix} F_a \\ F_q \end{pmatrix} = -\left(J^T\right)^{-1} W \tag{22}$$

The mapping relationship between the external force on the moving platform and the driving force in the branch PPPS can be obtained.

2.4 Scale Optimization

Scale optimization [22–24] of PMs is one of the most important parts of the mechanism design process. Based on the characteristics of the 3RRS/PPPS mechanism, this paper optimizes the key dimensional parameters of the mechanism with the objective of improving the load-carrying capacity and minimizing the driving force while satisfying the workspace.

The configuration parameters of the 3RRS/PPPS mechanism include the radius R of the circle where the center of the revolute joint of the fixed platform is located, the radius r of the circle where the center of the spherical joint of the moving platform is located, the position $(x1, y1, z1)$ of the PPPS spherical joint center A_4 of the driving branch PPPS relative to the coordinate system of the moving platform at the initial moment, and the size of the constrained branch RRS. Compared to traditional 3-RRS PMs, the driving force of this mechanism is independent of the size of the moving and fixed platform and the size of the constraint branch, but is related to the driving branch. Therefore, the selection of optimization objects is different. The optimization object selected in this paper is the position $(x1, y1, z1)$ of the spherical joint center A_4 of the driving branch PPPS relative to the coordinate system of the moving platform.

To optimize the dimensions of a mechanism, first of all, it is necessary to analyze the movement of the moving platform within the preset workspace under a certain configuration size, calculate the movement range of the driving branch through inverse solution, and consider whether the driving branch will interfere with structures such as revolute joints on the fixed platform. On this basis, set the external force on the moving platform as a vertical downward gravity, and calculate the driving force corresponding to each posture under this configuration size through formula (22). The configuration parameters $x1$, $y1$, and $z1$ were optimized with the objective of minimizing the driving forces F_{a1}, F_{a2}, and F_{a3} of the drive joints FH, EF, and HA_4.

The specific process (as shown Fig. 3):

(1) Initialize the mechanism parameters. Set the radius R of the circle where the center of the revolute joint of the fixed platform is located and the radius r of the circle where the center of the spherical joint of the moving platform is located to be 200mm. Set the range of parameters to be optimized to be $x1 \in [-100, 100]$ mm, $y1 \in [-100, 100]$ mm, and $z1 \in [200, 400]$ [200, 400] mm, respectively;

(2) The workspace of the moving platform is required to meet the rotation angle $\alpha \in [-10°, 10°]$ around the x-axis and the rotation angle $\beta \in [-10°, 10°]$ around the y-axis, as the height of the moving platform does not affect the magnitude of the driving force in the branch, so it is set to a fixed value $z_0 = 500$ in the scale optimization;

(3) Under the initial configuration parameters, calculate the activity range of the drive branch PPPS in the required workspace through inverse solution to determine whether the drive branch will interfere with the revolute joint and other structures on the fixed platform;

(4) Calculate the driving force magnitude F_{1i} (or F_{2i}, F_{3i}) corresponding to all positions and postures of the mechanism in the required workspace under this configuration parameter, find out the maximum value F_{1imax} (or F_{2imax}, F_{3imax}), and save it;

(5) Increase the configuration parameters by appropriate steps and return to step (3);

(6) Find the minimum value of all obtained F_{1imax} (or F_{2imax}, F_{3imax}), and the corresponding configuration parameter is the optimization result.

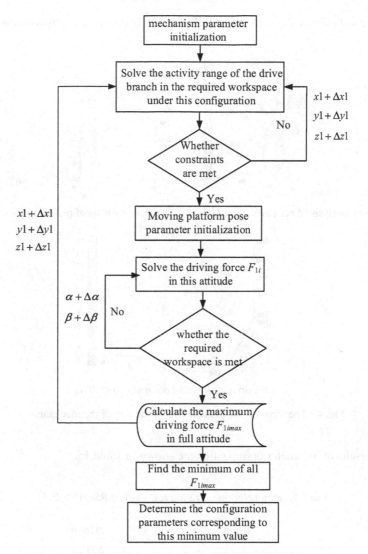

Fig. 3. Scale optimization of 3RRS/PPPS PM

Figure 4 shows the drive forces of PPPS branch in different configurations.

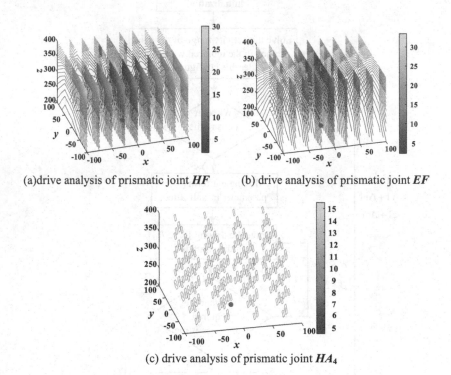

(a)drive analysis of prismatic joint *HF*   (b) drive analysis of prismatic joint *EF*

(c) drive analysis of prismatic joint *HA₄*

Fig. 4. The force on the branches under the size of the mechanism

The results of parameter optimization are shown in Table 1:

Table 1. Parameter optimization results of 3RRS/PPPS PM

$x1$(mm)	$y1$(mm)	$z1$(mm)
0	0	200

3   Conclusions and Future Works

In this paper, the 3RRS/PPPS PM with drive and constraint separation is proposed. The adjoint motion of 2R1T PM 3RRS/PPPS with three DOFs is analyzed. The closed-loop vector method is used to solve the motion of linear actuator. Jacobian matrix method is used to analyze the mapping relationship between input velocity and output velocity. And the mapping relationship between the external force on the moving platform and the driving force in the branch PPPS is analyzed. According to the characteristics of

3RRS/PPPS mechanism, the key dimension parameters of the mechanism were optimized to improve the bearing capacity of the mechanism and minimize the driving force under the premise of satisfying the working space.

In a word, we separate the drive and constraint of the PM, and the drive is easier to be centrally managed, which greatly improves the utilization rate of energy and work efficiency. Thus, we propose a new PM with fewer inputs and more outputs, which has a wide range of application scenarios in antenna, entertainment facilities and other occasions. However, in this work, no corresponding prototype has been made, so the experiment has not been realized. We will make a prototype and carry out experimental verification in the future work.

References

1. Petrasinovic, M.D., Grbovic, A.M., Petrasinovic, D.M., Petrovic, M.G., Raicevic, N.G.: Real coded mixed integer genetic algorithm for geometry optimization of flight simulator mechanism based on rotary stewart platform. Appl. Sci.-Basel 12(14), 7085 (2022)
2. Pillai, R.R., Ganesan, M.: Intelligent controller for robust orientation control of smart actuator based parallel manipulator. Proc. Inst. Mech. Eng. Part C-J. Mech. Eng. Sci. 236(20), 10573–10588 (2022)
3. Huang, T., Dong, C., Liu, H., Sun, T., Chetwynd, D.G.: A simple and visually orientated approach for type synthesis of overconstrained 1T2R parallel mechanisms. Robotica 37(07), 1161–1173 (2019)
4. Li, S.G., Deng, Z.P., Zeng, Q., Huang, X.: A coaxial alignment method for large aircraft component assembly using distributed monocular vision. Assem. Autom. 38(4), 437–449 (2018)
5. Jin, J.: Inverse and forward kinematics analysis of 6 DOF multi axis simulation table and verification. Trans. Korean Soc. Mech. Eng. 32(2), 202–208 (2008)
6. Chu, W.M., Huang, X.: Posture adjustment method for large components of aircraft based on hybrid force-position control. Ind. Robot Int. J. Robot. Res. Appl. 47(3), 381–393 (2020)
7. Zhang, D.S., Xu, Y.D., Yao, J.T., Zhao, Y.S.: Kinematics modelling and optimization design of a 5-dof hybrid manipulator. Int. J. Robot. Autom. 33(4), 407–417 (2018)
8. Shi, H.Q., Zhang, J.Z., Wang, T., Li, R., Huang, Q.X.: Mechanism design and kinematic analysis of a bioinspired 5-DOF parallel driving mechanism. Mech. Mach. Theory 181, 105178 (2023)
9. Gallardo-Alvarado, J.: Kinematics of a three-legged 1R2T decoupled parallel manipulator. J. Braz. Soc. Mech. Sci. Eng. 45(2), 109 (2023)
10. Liu, Z.Y., Tao, R., Fan, J.F., Wang, Z., Jing, F.S., Tan, M.: Kinematics, dynamics, and load distribution analysis of a 4-PPPS redundantly actuated parallel manipulator. Mech. Mach. Theory 167, 104494 (2022)
11. Moosavian, A., Xi, F., Hashemi, S.: Optimal configuration design for the variable geometry wingbox. AIAA J. Aircr. 51(03), 811–823 (2014)
12. Wang, J., Zhao, Y.J., Xi, F.F., Tian, Y.Z.: Design and analysis of a configuration-based lengthwise morphing structure. Mech. Mach. Theory 147, 103767 (2020)
13. Xi, F.F., Zhao, Y.J., Wang, J.Y., Wang, W.B., Tian, Y.Z.: Two actuation methods for a complete morphing system composed of a VGTM and a compliant parallel mechanism. J. Mech. Robot.-Trans. ASME 13(02), 021020 (2021)
14. Idà, E., Bruckmann, T., Carricato, M.: Rest-to-rest trajectory planning for underactuated cable-driven parallel robots. IEEE Trans. Rob. 35(06), 1338–1351 (2019)

15. Shen, H.P., Zhu, X.R.: The design methodology for fewer input-more output parallel mechanisms. Mech. Mach. Theory **104**, 43–58 (2016)
16. Blanco, J.C., Rodriguez, C.F.: Configuration optimization of a boat simulation platform for a mobile user. Proc. Asme Int. Mech. Eng. Congr. Exposition **8**, 625–631 (2012)
17. Chen, K.X., Wang, R.Y., Niu, Z.L., Wang, P.F., Sun, T.: Topology design and performance optimization of six-limbs 5-DOF parallel machining robots. Mech. Mach. Theory **185**, 105333 (2023)
18. Wu, C.H., Wang, H.C., Chang, H.Y.: Dual-axis solar tracker with satellite compass and inclinometer for automatic positioning and tracking. Energy Sustain. Dev. **66**, 308–318 (2022)
19. Chen, Z.M., Chen, X.C., Gao, M., Zhao, C., Zhao, K., Li, Y.W.: Motion characteristics analysis of a novel spherical two-degree-of-freedom parallel mechanism. Chin. J. Mech. Eng. **35**(1), 29 (2022)
20. Zhang, H.Q., Fang, H.R., Fang, Y.F., Jiang, B.S.: Workspace analysis of a hybrid kinematic machine tool with high rotational applications. Math. Probl. Eng. **2018**, 2607497 (2018)
21. Wang, M.X., Chen, Q.S., Liu, H.T., Huang, T., Feng, H.T., Tian, W.J.: Evaluation of the kinematic performance of a 3-RRS parallel mechanism. Robotica **39**(04), 606–617 (2021)
22. Ren, J., Li, Q.L., Wu, H.H., Cao, Q.Y.: Optimal design for 3-PSS flexible parallel micromanipulator based on kinematic and dynamic characteristics. Micromachines **13**(09), 1457 (2022)
23. Xie, F.G., Liu, X.J., Wang, J.S., Wabner, M.: Kinematic optimization of a five degrees-of-freedom spatial parallel mechanism with large orientational workspace. J. Mech. Robot.-Trans. ASME **9**(05), 051005 (2017)
24. Wang, Y.H., Tang, X.Q., Xiang, C.Y., Hou, S.H.: Force sensitivity analysis and scale design of Stewart parallel manipulator. Adv. Mech. Eng. **13**(07), 168781402110359 (2021)

Design of Flexure Hinges Using Topology Optimization Based on Isogeometric Analysis

Jinqing Zhan, Jiakun Yan, Xinfeng Yang, and Min Liu[✉]

School of Mechanotronics and Vehicle Engineering, East China Jiaotong University, Nanchang, China
lmin2016@foxmail.com

Abstract. A novel method for design of flexure hinges using topology optimization based on isogeometric analysis is presented in this paper. The NURBS curve is employed to express geometric model and analysis model. The density distribution function is used to describe the material distribution and the weighted form of the compliance is developed as the objective function. The volume fraction and the position of rotational center are used as the constraints. The model for topological design of flexure hinges based on isogeometric analysis is established. Numerical examples are presented to demonstrate the validity of the proposed design method. The configurations of flexure hinge obtained by topology optimization are different under different spring stiffness conditions. As the spring stiffness value continues to increase, the thickness of the straight line in the middle gradually becomes thicker and the length becomes shorter, and the compliance of rotational direction gradually decreases. In addition, the influence of the position of the rotational center on topological design results is also investigated.

Keywords: Flexure hinges · Topology optimization · Isogeometric analysis

1 Introduction

The flexure hinge is the key component of the flexure-based compliant mechanism, which can transmit rotation, translation and force through its own elastic deformation between two adjacent rigid links. Compared with traditional rigid hinges, flexure hinges have the advantages of compact structure, no gap, no lubrication and low assembly cost, so they have been widely used in the design of precision instruments [1]. Thorp et al. [2] proposed the flexure hinge with a leaf-shaped flexible element. Subsequently, Smith et al. [3] designed and analyzed the elliptical flexure hinge based on the research of the straight circular hinge. Tseytlin [4] presented the calculation equations for the compliance of straight circular and elliptical flexure hinges. It can be seen that the traditional design method is to derive the calculation formulas of various performance indicators of the flexure hinge by determining the geometric parameters of the flexure hinge from the above-mentioned. In contrast, the corresponding geometric parameters can be calculated by the certain specific performance of the flexure hinge. However, if one wants to design flexible hinges with multiple performance parameters, the traditional design methods are no longer applicable. But topology optimization design methods are up to the job and can design flexible hinges with the desired parameters.

© The Author(s), under exclusive license to Springer Nature Singapore Pte Ltd. 2023
H. Yang et al. (Eds.): ICIRA 2023, LNAI 14269, pp. 337–347, 2023.
https://doi.org/10.1007/978-981-99-6489-5_27

The basic idea of topology optimization is to seek the best layout of a structure or mechanism under the condition of satisfying certain constraints, and to optimize a certain performance [5]. Recently, the design of flexure hinge using topology optimization has been put forward one after another. Zhu et al. [6] first used the topology optimization method of continuum structure to design a translational flexible hinge and a rotational flexible hinge from the topological point of view, the research shows that the performance of these two hinges is better than that of traditional hinges. Liu et al. [7] designed a high-precision flexure hinge based on the SIMP method, but the hinge has obvious stress concentration. Therefore, a stress-constrained topology optimization method for flexure hinges is proposed [8]. Pinskier et al. [9] developed a new topology optimization method for the design of flexure hinge with stiffness constraint, resulting the flexure hinge gained has greater stiffness and precision.

The above topology optimization of flexure hinges is designed and analyzed based on finite element analysis, but as we all know, finite element analysis has certain defects in numerical analysis. Hughes et al. [10] presented the concept of isogeometric analysis for the first time, and used non-uniform rational B-spline (NURBS) basis function as the shape function to express the geometric model and analysis model, realizing the seamless integration between geometric modeling and structural analytics. Seo et al. [11] used the coordinates of the control points as the design variables to realize the topology optimization design using isogeometric analysis based on spline surfaces with equal clipping. Subsequently, more and more scholars have carried out research on topology optimization design based on isogeometric analysis. Gao et al. [12] put forward a multi-material structural topology optimization method based on isogeometric analysis. Xu et al. [13] carried out the isogeometric topology optimization based parametric level set. At present, there are seldom studies on the topology optimization of flexure hinges using isogeometric analysis.

An approach for design of flexure hinges using topology optimization based on isogeometric analysis is proposed in this paper. The NURBS curve is employed to express geometric model and analysis model. The density distribution function is used to describe the material distribution. The model for topological design of flexure hinges with the constraints of volume fraction and the position of rotational center is established. The remainder of the paper is organized as follow. In Sect. 2, the relevant concepts of NURBS basis functions and isogeometric analysis are introduced. Section 3 presented the model of flexure hinges, the compliance of flexure hinges and the position constraint of rotational center, and established the model for topological design of flexure hinges based on isogeometric analysis. In Sect. 4, the sensitivities of objective function and constraint functions are computed. Numerical examples and discussion are shown in Sect. 5 and conclusions are given in Sect. 6.

2   Isogeometric Analysis Theory

The core concept of isogeometric analysis is that the basis functions of geometric modelling are consistent with the shape functions of structural analysis, and are both based on NURBS basis functions [14].

First of all, the monotonous non-decreasing node vector including some one-dimensional univariate B-spline functions is given as follow:

$$\Xi = \left\{ \xi_1, \xi_2, \cdots, \xi_i, \cdots, \xi_{n+p+1} \right\} \tag{1}$$

where $\xi_i \in R$ is the i_{th} node, i denotes the index coordinate of the node, and $\xi_i \leq \xi_{i+1}$. p and n indicate the order of spline and the number of all control points, respectively. Then, the i_{th} p- order spline basis function can be deducted by the Cox-de-Boor formula [15] iteratively:

$$N_{i,0}(\xi) = \begin{cases} 1, & \xi_i \leq \xi < \xi_{i+1} \\ 0, & \text{otherwise} \end{cases} \tag{2}$$

and if $p \geq 1$, the basis functions are given in the follow form:

$$N_{i,p}(\xi) = \frac{\xi - \xi_i}{\xi_{i+p} - \xi_i} N_{i,p-1}(\xi) + \frac{\xi_{i+p+1} - \xi}{\xi_{i+p+1} - \xi_{i+1}} N_{i+1,p-1}(\xi) \tag{3}$$

It is a remarkable fact that the fractions with the form 0/0 are equal to zeros in Eq. (3).

In isogeometric analysis, refinement is performed directly on the existing mesh model, avoiding the most time-consuming mesh division in finite element analysis. For two-dimensional planar problems, the geometric functions represented by NURBS surfaces are defined by the tensor product form [16] as follow:

$$S(\xi, \eta) = \sum_{i=1}^{n} \sum_{j=1}^{m} R_{i,j}^{p,q}(\xi, \eta) \boldsymbol{P}_{i,j} \tag{4}$$

where ξ and η are the parameter coordinates, $\boldsymbol{P}_{i,j}$ denotes the control grid formed by the control points. n and m mean the number of control points in the two parameter directions respectively, p and q indicate the order of the basis functions in the two parameter directions respectively, $R_{i,j}^{p,q}(\xi, \eta)$ is the NURBS basis function, and a detailed form is given by

$$R_{i,j}^{p,q}(\xi, \eta) = \frac{N_{i,p}(\xi) M_{j,q}(\eta) \omega_{ij}}{\sum_{\hat{i}=1}^{n} \sum_{\hat{j}=1}^{m} N_{\hat{i},p}(\xi) M_{\hat{j},q}(\eta) \omega_{\hat{i}\hat{j}}} \tag{5}$$

where ω_{ij} denote the weight of the control point $\boldsymbol{P}_{i,j}$, $N_{i,p}$ and $M_{j,q}$ represents the univariate basis functions in the two parameter directions respectively.

According to the concept of isoparameters, the structural displacement can be expressed as

$$U = \sum_{i=1}^{n} \sum_{j=1}^{m} R_{i,j}^{p,q}(\xi, \eta) \boldsymbol{U}_{i,j} \tag{6}$$

where U and $\boldsymbol{U}_{i,j}$ mean the displacement field of the design domain and the vector of displacement about the control point, respectively.

Isogeometric analysis can maintain high-order continuity on the interface because the NURBS basis functions possess a great deal of advantages such as non-negativity, partition, local support and smoothness [17]. Since bi-quadratic NURBS elements have C^1 continuity which improves the calculation accuracy, the bi-quadratic NURBS elements in the isogeometric analysis are adopted in this paper.

3 Problem Formulation for Flexure Hinges Design

3.1 Objective for Generic Flexure Hinges

Generally, we give a regular design domain shown in Fig. 1 to facilitate the implementation for the topological design of flexure hinges. The left end of the design domain Ω_D is fixed with the Dirichlet condition Γ_d, and Ω_R means the rigid link which belongs to the non-design domain with length L. The general design domain and non-design domain need to satisfy the relationship $L \geq 3l$, this paper takes $L = 3l$. The points O and O' indicate the actual rotational center of flexure hinge and the geometric center of design domain with length l respectively. Points A and B are the right midpoint of the design domain and the rigid link respectively. In order to calculate the flexibility of the flexure hinge in the direction of rotation, a concentrated load F_y is applied in the y-direction at point B. At the same time, a concentrated load F_x is applied in the x-direction at point B to calculate the compliance in the direction of the parasitic motion. Usually, it is necessary to add an artificial spring k_s with constant stiffness in the y-direction of point B.

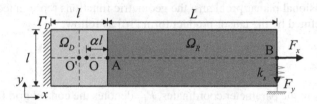

Fig. 1. Design domain, boundary conditions and loads of flexure hinges.

To make the flexible hinge designed possess specific performance within the design domain, it is of requisite to construct an appropriate objective function. In general, the compliance of point A is used to represent the compliance of a flexure hinge. The flexure hinge needs to produce greater compliance in the y-direction of point A which is denoted as C_y, and in the x-direction at point A will produce the smaller compliance which is called as C_x. Therefore, the objective function that needs to be set in this optimization problem is to minimize C_x while maximizing C_y. The objective function can be expressed in weighted form as follow:

$$\min : \omega C_x - (1 - \omega) C_y \tag{7}$$

where $\omega(0 < \omega < 1)$ means the weighting factor.

The force F_x and F_y at point B are equivalent to the force and moment at point A. Therefore, the relationship between the forces at point B and the displacements and compliance C_x and C_y at point A can be stated as follow:

$$C_x = \frac{u_x^A}{F_x} \tag{8}$$

$$C_y = \frac{u_y^{\mathrm{A}}}{F_y} \frac{\alpha l}{\alpha l + L} \tag{9}$$

where u_x^{A} indicates the displacement in the x-direction generated by exerting a separate force F_x while u_y^{A} is the displacement with an artificial spring k_s in the y-direction generated by imposing a separate force F_y. u_x^{A} and u_y^{A} can be gained by calculating the follow equation:

$$u_x^{\mathrm{A}} = L_x^{\mathrm{T}} U_x \tag{10}$$

$$u_y^{\mathrm{A}} = L_y^{\mathrm{T}} U_y \tag{11}$$

where L_x and L_y denote the unit vectors, theirs magnitude in the direction of the degree of freedom of the output displacement is 1, and the direction of other degrees of freedom is 0. U_x and U_y represent the displacement vector about control points due to F_x and F_y, respectively.

3.2 Position Constraint of the Rotation Center

The position of rotational center is set as a constraint to preinstall the position of rotational center for topological optimization of flexure hinges. As shown in Fig. 1, the distance from point A to rotation center point O is set to be αl. In order to ensure high precision, the extension of the line segment AB must pass through the preset rotational center point O as much as possible when the flexure hinges rotate at a certain angle, that is the flexure hinge always deforms around the rotational center point O. As a result, on the basis of geometric relation, the position constraint of rotation center can be written as follow formula:

$$\left(\frac{u_y^{\mathrm{A}}}{u_y^{\mathrm{B}}} - \frac{\alpha l}{\alpha l + L} \right) \leq \xi \tag{12}$$

where u_y^{B} represents the displacement in the y-direction generated by exerting a separate force F_y. ξ is a very small positive number which is utilized to command the position of rotational center of flexure hinge. It is simple to see from Fig. 1 that the position of rotational center is within the design domain when $\alpha \leq 0.5$, the position of rotational center is outside the design domain when $\alpha > 0.5$, and when $\alpha = 0.5$, the position of rotational center just falls on the geometric center point O′.

3.3 Density Distribution Function

In order to make the topological boundary smoother, the density distribution function (DDF) is used to describe the material distribution [18]. Adopting the Shepard function to smooth the control point density, and using the NURBS basis function to linearly combine the smoothed control point density to construct the density distribution function [19], so the density value at any point in the design domain can be obtained as

$$\Phi(\xi, \eta) = \sum_{i=1}^{n} \sum_{j=1}^{m} R_{i,j}^{p,q}(\xi, \eta) \tilde{\phi}_{i,j} \tag{13}$$

where Φ denotes the density distribution, $\tilde{\phi}_{i,j}$ is the density of the smoothed control point which can be expressed as follow:

$$\tilde{\phi}_{i,j}(\xi, \eta) = \sum_{i=1}^{n} \sum_{j=1}^{m} \varphi(\phi_{i,j}) \phi_{i,j} \tag{14}$$

where $\phi_{i,j}$ represents the density of control point, and $\varphi(\phi_{i,j})$ indicates the Shepard function which can improve the smoothness between the control points.

Combining the foregoing analysis, the objective is to maximize the compliance C_y in the y-direction and minimize the compliance C_x in the x-direction of point A. Meanwhile, the position of rotational center and volume fraction are used as the constraints. The model for the design of flexure hinges using topology optimization based on isogeometric analysis can be established as follow:

$$\min : f(\tilde{\boldsymbol{\phi}}) = \omega C_x - (1 - \omega) C_y$$
$$\text{s.t.} : \boldsymbol{F}_x = \boldsymbol{K} \boldsymbol{U}_x$$
$$\boldsymbol{F}_y = \boldsymbol{K} \boldsymbol{U}_y$$
$$f_r(\tilde{\boldsymbol{\phi}}) = \left(\frac{u_y^A}{u_y^B} - \frac{\alpha l}{\alpha l + L} \right) \leq \xi \tag{15}$$
$$V = \frac{1}{|\Omega_D|} \int_{\Omega_D} \Phi(\xi, \eta) v_0 \mathrm{d}\Omega_D \leq f^* V_0$$
$$0 \leq \tilde{\phi}_{i,j} \leq 1 (i = 1, \ldots, n; j = 1, \ldots, m)$$

where $\tilde{\boldsymbol{\phi}}$ is the control point vector. $\boldsymbol{F}_x$ and $\boldsymbol{F}_y$ are the force vector with the value of F_x and F_y at the position of the input degree of freedom, zeros at positions of the other degrees of freedom, respectively. $\boldsymbol{K}$ denotes the global stiffness matrix with the artificial spring. v_0 is the element volume filled with solid material, V_0 and V indicate are the volume before and after optimization respectively, and f^* is the allowable volume ratio.

4   Sensitivity Analysis for Topology Optimization

The method of moving asymptotes (MMA) algorithm is applicable to copy with the multiple constraints optimization problems [20]. Hence, the MMA algorithm is applied to solve problem for topological design of flexure hinges in this work.

The derivative of objective function $f(\tilde{\boldsymbol{\phi}})$ with respect to the density $\phi_{i,j}$ of control point can be obtained by the chain rule, and a detailed form is given by:

$$\frac{\partial f(\tilde{\boldsymbol{\phi}})}{\partial \phi_{i,j}} = \frac{\partial f(\tilde{\boldsymbol{\phi}})}{\partial \Phi} \frac{\partial \Phi}{\partial \tilde{\phi}_{i,j}} \frac{\partial \tilde{\phi}_{i,j}}{\partial \phi_{i,j}} \tag{16}$$

where the first-order derivative of $f(\tilde{\boldsymbol{\phi}})$ with respect to the density distribution function can be calculated by Eq. (8) and Eq. (9), a detailed form is stated as follow:

$$\frac{\partial f(\tilde{\boldsymbol{\phi}})}{\partial \Phi} = \omega \frac{C_x}{\partial \Phi} - (1 - \omega) \frac{C_y}{\partial \Phi} = \frac{\omega}{F_x} \frac{\partial u_x^{\mathrm{A}}}{\partial \Phi} - \frac{\alpha l(1 - \omega)}{F_y(\alpha l + L)} \frac{\partial u_y^{\mathrm{A}}}{\partial \Phi} \tag{17}$$

where $\partial u_y^{\mathrm{A}}/\partial \Phi$ can be obtained by adjoint matrix equation as follow:

$$\frac{\partial u_x^{\mathrm{A}}}{\partial \Phi} = -\tilde{\boldsymbol{U}}_x^{\mathrm{T}} \frac{\partial \boldsymbol{K}}{\partial \Phi} \boldsymbol{U}_x \tag{18}$$

where the vector $\tilde{\boldsymbol{U}}_x^{\mathrm{T}}$ can be obtained by solving the adjoint matrix equation $\boldsymbol{L}_x = \boldsymbol{K}\tilde{\boldsymbol{U}}_x$.

According to Eq. (13) and Eq. (14), the derivatives of the DDF with respect to the smoothed control point after threshold projection and smoothed control point densities with respect to control point can be achieved respectively as follow:

$$\frac{\partial \Phi(\xi, \eta)}{\partial \tilde{\phi}_{i,j}} = R_{i,j}^{p,q}(\xi, \eta) \tag{19}$$

$$\frac{\partial \tilde{\phi}_{i,j}}{\partial \phi_{i,j}} = \varphi(\phi_{i,j}) \tag{20}$$

Similarly, the derivative of the position constraint of rotational center with respect to the density of control point can be derived by the chain rule, and a detailed form is given by:

$$\frac{\partial f_r(\tilde{\boldsymbol{\phi}})}{\partial \phi_{i,j}} = \frac{\partial f_r(\tilde{\boldsymbol{\phi}})}{\partial \Phi} \frac{\partial \Phi}{\partial \tilde{\phi}_{i,j}} \frac{\partial \tilde{\phi}_{i,j}}{\partial \phi_{i,j}} \tag{21}$$

The first term of the above equation can be calculated, and expressed by:

$$\frac{\partial f_r(\tilde{\boldsymbol{\phi}})}{\partial \Phi} = 2 \left(\frac{u_y^{\mathrm{A}}}{u_y^{\mathrm{B}}} - \frac{\alpha l}{\alpha l + L} \right) \frac{\frac{\partial u_y^{\mathrm{A}}}{\partial \Phi} u_y^{\mathrm{B}} - \frac{\partial u_y^{\mathrm{B}}}{\partial \Phi} u_y^{\mathrm{A}}}{\left(u_y^{\mathrm{B}} \right)^2} \tag{22}$$

where the part $\partial u_y^{\mathrm{B}}/\partial \Phi$ can be derived by using the same method above:

$$\frac{\partial u_y^{\mathrm{B}}}{\partial \Phi} = -\tilde{\boldsymbol{U}}_{y,\mathrm{B}}^{\mathrm{T}} \frac{\partial \boldsymbol{K}}{\partial \Phi} \boldsymbol{U}_y \tag{23}$$

where $\tilde{\boldsymbol{U}}_{y,\mathrm{B}}$ can be obtained by calculating the adjoint matrix equation $\boldsymbol{L}_{y,\mathrm{B}} = \boldsymbol{K}\tilde{\boldsymbol{U}}_y$, where the $\boldsymbol{L}_{y,\mathrm{B}}$ is also the unit vector, its magnitude of the degree of freedom in the y-direction of point B is 1, and the direction of other degrees of freedom is 0.

The derivative of volume constraint with respect to the density of control point is calculated by chain rule as follow:

$$\frac{\partial V}{\partial \phi_{i,j}} = \frac{\partial V}{\partial \Phi} \frac{\partial \Phi}{\partial \tilde{\phi}_{i,j}} \frac{\partial \tilde{\phi}_{i,j}}{\partial \phi_{i,j}} = \frac{1}{|\Omega_D|} \int_{\Omega_D} R_{i,j}^{p,q}(\xi, \eta) \varphi(\phi_{i,j}) v_0 \mathrm{d}\Omega_D \tag{24}$$

5   Numerical Examples and Discussions

In the section, several numerical examples for the topological design of flexure hinges based on isogeometric analysis are presented to demonstrate the validity of the topology optimization method proposed in this paper. The numerical examples are all 2D structures and the geometrical parameters are all taken as dimensionless quantities. Supposing that the isotropic material has a Young's modulus $E = 1$ and a Poisson's ratio $\mu = 0.3$. The allowable volume fraction f^* is set as 30% and the penalty factor p is 3 for all cases. The domain with a length $l = 5$ and the rigid link with a length $L = 15$ are discredited into 45×45 and 135×45 bi-quadratic NURBS elements. The parameter ω of the objective function is set as 0.5 and the position constraint ξ of rotational center is set as 1×10^{-3}. The force F_x and F_y are 10 and 1 respectively.

The optimal topological configuration of the flexure hinge with the artificial spring $k_s = 1.5 \times 10^{-3}$ and $\alpha = 0.5$ is shown in Fig. 2(a). It can be seen that the optimal contour line of the hinge obtained by topology optimization design is convex curves. Figure 2(b) indicates the topology optimization iterative convergence diagram of C_x and C_y of the objective function. It can be clearly observed that the rotational compliance C_y gradually increases from the initial value and gradually tends to a stable value of 9.151 after 40 iterations of optimization, while the axial compliance C_x gradually decreases from the initial value and finally tends to a stable value of 1.402.

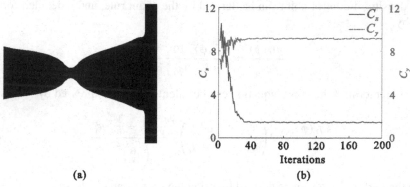

(a)   (b)

Fig. 2. The topology optimization results with $k_s = 1.5 \times 10^{-3}$ and $\alpha = 0.5$: (a) the topological configuration and (b) topology optimization iterative histories of C_x and C_y.

To research the influence of the artificial spring k_s on the results, the topological design of flexure hinges with $\alpha = 0.5$ based on isogeometric analysis is carried out under the conditions of different artificial spring stifff k_s of 1×10^{-3}, 2×10^{-3}, 3×10^{-3}, 4×10^{-3}, 5×10^{-3} and 0.01. The configuration of flexure hinges are displayed in Fig. 3. The structures of the flexure hinges with different spring stiffness are roughly the same, only the straight-line section of the middle connection part subtle changes. As the spring stiffness value continues to increase, the thickness of the straight line in the middle gradually becomes thicker and the length becomes shorter. Table 1 shows the comparison of the compliance C_x and C_y of the hinges obtained by topology optimization under different spring stiffness. It can be seen that the compliance C_y gradually decreases as the spring stiffness increases, indicating that the hinges are not easy to rotate, which also verifies the trend of the topological configuration of flexure hinges change numerically.

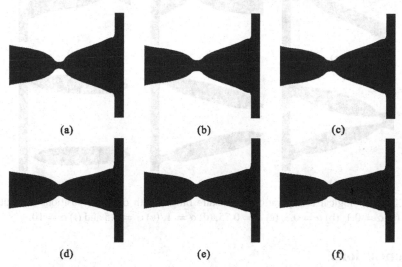

Fig. 3. Topological configuration of flexure hinges with different artificial spring stiffness: (a) $k_s = 1 \times 10^{-3}$, (b) $k_s = 2 \times 10^{-3}$, (c) $k_s = 3 \times 10^{-3}$, (d) $k_s = 4 \times 10^{-3}$, (e) $k_s = 5 \times 10^{-3}$, and (f) $k_s = 0.01$.

Table 1. The comparison for the compliance of the hinges obtained by topology optimization under different spring stiffness.

k_s	0.001	0.002	0.003	0.004	0.005	0.01
C_x	1.571	1.276	1.550	4.522	1.595	1.536
C_y	13.781	6.777	4.525	3.412	2.754	1.370

To further investigate the influence of the rotational center position on the results, several different rotational center positions are considered to design flexure hinges with $k_s = 1 \times 10^{-3}$. Figure 4 displays the topological configurations of flexure hinges with different positions of rotational center, i.e., $\alpha = 0.1, 0.3, 0.75, 1, 1.5$ and 10. It can be seen that when the rotational center is located in the right half of the design domain, that is, $\alpha = 0.1$ and 0.3, the distribution of materials in the design domain shows a phenomenon that the left side is more and the right side is less. The material distribution in the design domain manifests a phenomenon of more right and less left when the rotational center is located in the left half of the design domain, that is, $\alpha = 0.75$ and 1. The flexure hinge is composed of two rods that are symmetrical about the horizontal axis when $\alpha = 1.5$ and 10, and as the value of α increases, the two rods gradually tend to be parallel. The flexure hinge with the value of α equals to 10 becomes a translational hinge, which does not have the ability to rotate, thus the value of α should not be too large.

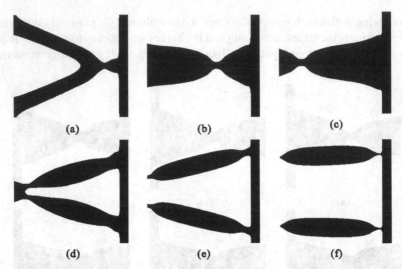

Fig. 4. The topological configurations of flexure hinges with different positions of rotational center: (a) $\alpha = 0.1$, (b) $\alpha = 0.3$, (c) $\alpha = 0.75$, (d) $\alpha = 1$, (e) $\alpha = 1.5$ and (f) $\alpha = 10$.

6 Conclusions

In this paper, a novel method for design of flexure hinges using topology optimization based on isogeometric analysis is proposed. Numerical examples verify the effectiveness of the proposed method. The configurations of flexure hinge obtained by topology optimization are different under different spring stiffness conditions, and they all satisfy the rotation center constraint. As the spring stiffness value continues to increase, the thickness of the straight line in the middle gradually becomes thicker and the length becomes shorter, and the compliance C_y gradually decreases. In addition, the influence of the position of the rotational center on topological design results is also investigated.

References

1. Zhan, J., Li, Y., Luo, Z., Liu, M.: Topological design of multi-material compliant mechanisms with global stress constraints. Micromechines **12**(11), 1397 (2021)
2. Thorpe, A.G.: Flexure pivots-design formulas and charts. Prod. Eng. **24**(2), 192–200 (1953)
3. Smith, S.T., Badami, V.G., Dale, J.S., et al.: Elliptical flexure hinges. Rev. Sci. Instrum. **68**(3), 1474–1483 (1997)
4. Tseytlin, Y.M.: Notch flexure hinges: an effective theory. Rev. Sci. Instrum. **73**(9), 3363–3368 (2002)
5. Lu, Y., Tong, L.: Topology optimization of compliant mechanisms and structures subjected to design-dependent pressure loadings. Struct. Multidiscip. Optim. **63**(4), 1889–1906 (2021)
6. Zhu, B., Zhang, X., Fatikow, S.: Design of single-axis flexure hinges using continuum topology optimization method. Sci. China Technol. Sci. **57**(3), 560–567 (2014)
7. Liu, M., Zhang, X., Fatikow, S.: Design and analysis of a high-accuracy flexure hinge. Rev. Sci. Instrum. **87**(5), 055106 (2016)
8. Liu, M., Zhang, X., Fatikow, S.: Design of flexure hinges based on stress-constrained topology optimization. Proc. Inst. Mech. Eng., Part C: J Mech. Eng. Sci. **231**(24), 4635–4645 (2017)

9. Pinskier, J., Shirinzadeh, B., Ghafarian, M., et al.: Topology optimization of stiffness constrained flexure-hinges for precision and range maximization. Mech. Mach. Theory **150**, 103874 (2020)
10. Hughes, T.J.R., Cottrell, J.A., Bazilevs, Y.: Isogeometric analysis: CAD, finite elements, NURBS, exact geometry and mesh refinement. Comput. Methods Appl. Mech. Eng. **194**(39–41), 4135–4195 (2005)
11. Seo, Y.D., Kim, H.J., Youn, S.K.: Shape optimization and its extension to topological design based on isogeometric analysis. Int. J. Solids Struct. **47**(11–12), 1618–1640 (2010)
12. Gao, J., Luo, Z., Xiao, M., Gao, L., Li, P.: A NURBS-based multi-material interpolation(N-MMI) for isogeometric topology optimization of structures. Appl. Math. Model. **81**, 818–843 (2020)
13. Xu, M., Wang, S., Xie, X.: Level set-based isogeometric topology optimization for maximizing fundamental eigenfrequency. Front. Mech. Eng. **14**, 222–234 (2019)
14. Qian, X.: Topology optimization in B-spline space. Comput. Methods Appl. Mech. Eng. **265**, 15–35 (2013)
15. Boor, C.D.: A Practical Guide to Splines. Springer-Verlag, New York (1987)
16. Wang, Y., Benson, D.J.: Isogeometric analysis for parameterized LSM-based structural topology optimization. Comput. Mech. **57**, 19–35 (2016)
17. Wang, Y., Liao, Z., Ye, M., Zhang, Y., Li, W., Xia, Z.: An efficient isogeometric topology optimization using multilevel mesh, MGCG and local-update strategy. Adv. Eng. Softw. **139**, 102733 (2010)
18. Gao, J., Gao, L., Luo, Z., Li, P.: Isogeometric topology optimization for continuum structures using density distribution function. Int. J. Numer. Meth. Eng. **118**(10), 991–1017 (2019)
19. Wu, X., Zhang, Y., Gao, L., Gao, J.: On the indispensability of isogeometric analysis in topology optimization for smooth or binary designs. Symmetry-Basel **14**(5), 845 (2022)
20. Liu, M., Zhan, J., Zhang, X.: Topology optimization of compliant mechanism considering actual output displacement using adaptive output spring stiffness. Mech. Mach. Theory **143**(4), 103728 (2020)

Design and Workspace Evaluation of a Novel Parallel Grasping Manipulator with Configurable Platform

Fuqun Zhao[1], Donglai Xu[2], Xiaodong Jin[2]([✉]), Sheng Guo[2], and Kun Xu[1]

[1] Institute of Robotics, Beihang University, Beijing, China
[2] Department of Mechanical Engineering, Beijing Jiaotong University, Beijing, China
xdjin@bjtu.edu.cn

Abstract. To solve the lack of grasping performance caused by separate driven device installed at the end-effector of parallel grasping manipulator, a novel parallel grasping manipulator with configurable platform is presented in this paper. Firstly, the modified Grübler-Kutzbach equation is utilized to verify that the parallel grasping manipulator has 4 degree-of-freedom (DOF), including 3-DOF for plane motion and 1-DOF for grasping. Based on the link constraint equation, the input-output velocity relationship and Jacobian matrix are obtained. The workspace performance of the parallel grasping manipulator under the coupled DOFs is evaluated. Singularity analysis is studied to demonstrate the manipulator can produce ±90° large rotation angle due to kinematical redundancy. The optimum structure dimension parameters are determined by comparing workspace performance under the constraint range of each link. At last, a prototype is constructed based on the determined dimension parameters, and the experiment of motion DOFs and grasping ability are carried out. The results show that the proposed parallel grasping manipulator has good motion ability and grasping performance.

Keywords: parallel manipulator · configurable platform · grasping · kinematics · workspace evaluation

1 Introduction

Grasping robots can replace or assist human working on industrial production and package sorting, which are indispensable technical equipment in industry, transportation and other fields. From the view of structure, grasping robots can be divided into serial structure [1] and parallel structure [2]. Parallel structure has the advantages of high speed, high stiffness and high precision, which can overcome the shortcomings of series ones in response speed, grasping stiffness and motion accuracy.

Parallel grasping robots such as Delta [3] and H4 [4] have been used in logistics sorting, food packaging and other fields. These robots usually need to equip with vacuum cups, electromagnets or mechanical grippers in the end-effector to grasp the target object. However, these methods make robots need to be actuated by additional motors, which increases the inertia of motion and the difficulty of control when performing the grasping

© The Author(s), under exclusive license to Springer Nature Singapore Pte Ltd. 2023
H. Yang et al. (Eds.): ICIRA 2023, LNAI 14269, pp. 348–360, 2023.
https://doi.org/10.1007/978-981-99-6489-5_28

task. To solve the above problems, some scholars proposed a class of parallel mechanisms with configurable platforms. The moving platforms of these parallel mechanisms are no longer as fixed structures, but kinematic chains composed of several links and joints. Based on this design method, different links in the configuration platforms can realize relative motion through connect with different limbs of the mechanism. The generated relative motion can be used to complete high performance operation tasks.

Gosselin [5, 6] first proposed the design idea by using configurable platforms in both planar and spatial redundant parallel mechanisms. Such designs can be used as a grasping device especially for irregular or large objects or even as a micro-positioning device after grasping the object. Wen [7] presents methods to exploit the redundancy of a kinematically redundant spatial parallel mechanism with three redundant DOFs. Jin [8] studied the synthesis method for a new class of 4-DOF generalized parallel mechanisms with the integrated 1-DOF end-effectors. Each degree of freedom of rotation is independent, and it can produce a very large rotation angle. Tian [9] also constructed a class of reconfigurable generalized parallel mechanisms with remotely operated grippers, and evaluated the workspace.

It can be concluded from the above research that workspace performance with large rotation angle is a worth issue for parallel grasping mechanisms. Indeed, the structure of mechanism depends on workspace performance. However, the workspace of parallel grasping mechanism is restricted by its structural characteristics.

In recent years, by introducing redundant design into parallel mechanism to avoid singularity, scholars have improved the kinematic performance [10–12]. Nouri [13] presented a novel class of kinematically redundant parallel mechanisms with a reconfigurable platform. The proposed mechanisms can be used for grasping irregular objects and avoiding singularity. Schreiber [14] presents a novel passive redundant spherical joint with a very large range of motion. The proposed joint does not require any active component, so as to avoid singular configuration. Experimental prototypes are demonstrated that can obtain a large range of tilt angle.

By combining configurable platform design with kinematical redundancy, this paper presents a novel parallel grasping mechanism with configurable platform, which can actuate the two grippers of moving platform to realize grasping in the plane. This mechanism has the characteristic of kinematical redundancy and a large rotation range. Mechanism design and workspace evaluation are the focus of this work.

The research content of this paper is as follows: the structure of parallel grasping mechanism is introduced in Sect. 2. The kinematic model is established in Sect. 3. Workspace evaluation is presented under different structure parameter, and singularity analysis is studied to prove the high workspace performance in Sect. 4. Prototype experiments including motion verification and grasping performance are carried out in Sect. 5. Finally, the result is concluded in Sect. 6.

2 Design of The Novel Grasping Manipulator

2.1 Structure Description

The 3D model diagram of the parallel grasping manipulator is shown in Fig. 1. Limb 1 and Limb 2 are connected to the moving platform by the revolute joints B_1 and B_2. Limb 3 and Limb 4 are connected by the revolute joint C and can form a redundant limb. The redundant limb is connected with two grippers and sliders of the moving platform respectively by revolute joint B_3. Based on the above structure, the manipulator can realize the movement of the slider along the guide rail in the moving platform, and the opening and closing movement of the two grippers along the guide rail, so as to carry out the grasping operation. According to the connection of each joint, the manipulator can be referred to as a 2$\underline{P}$R-2$\underline{P}$R (R)/RP manipulator, where $\underline{P}$ represents the actuated joint, the others represent the passive joints, and (R) represents the compound revolute joint. The 2$\underline{P}$R-2$\underline{P}$R (R)/RP manipulator has four DOFs, including two translation DOFs in x-y plane and the rotation DOF around z-axis, and the grasping DOF. The manipulator has the following characteristics: (1) The actuated joints of the manipulator are all installed in the base, and the grasping device is no longer configured with a separate actuated device. Therefore, the motion output of the slider can serve as the actuation of the gripper. (2) It can improve the grasping speed and perform a stable grasping process. (3) The redundant limb can effectively avoid the singular configuration and improve the performances of motion and workspace.

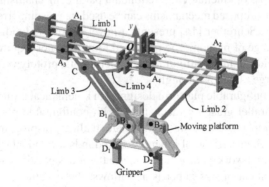

Fig. 1. 2PR-2PR (R)/RP manipulator

2.2 DOF Verification

The modified Grübler-Kutzbach equation [15] is used to find 2PRR-2PR(R)/RP manipulator:

$$M = d(n - g - 1) + \sum_{i=1}^{g} f_i + v$$

$$= 3 \times (13 - 16 - 1) + 16 + 0 = 4$$

(1)

where M is the number of DOF of the manipulator, d is the order of the manipulator, $d = 6 - \lambda$, λ is the number of common constraints on the manipulator, for plane manipulator $\lambda = 3$, n is the number of all links of the manipulator, g is the number of all joints of the manipulator, f_i is the number of DOF of the i-th joint, v is the number of redundant constraints of the manipulator.

According to Eq. (1), the 2PR-2PR(R)/RP manipulator has 4 DOFs, which can realize the two-dimensional movement and rotation in the plane and perform the grasping manipulation.

3   Kinematics Analysis

Figure 2 shows the schematic diagram of the 2PR-2PR (R)/RP manipulator. The base coordinate system O-xyz is established at the center point of the frame. The moving coordinate system P-uvw is established at the center point of line B_1B_2 of the moving platform. In initial configuration, the axes of the moving coordinate system P-uvw are parallel with the base coordinate system O-xyz.

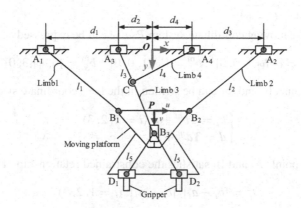

Fig. 2. Schematic diagram of the 2PR-2PR(R)/RP manipulator

d_i represents the displacement of actuated joint A_i ($i = 1,2,3,4$) in the base coordinate system O-xyz, which are the input parameters of the manipulator. The distance of the grippers moves relative to its initial position is expressed as g. The length of link A_iB_i is denoted by l_i ($i = 1,2,3$). The length of link A_4C is denoted by l_4. The lengths of link B_3D_1 and link B_3D_2 are denoted by l_5.

Based on DOF analysis, it can be assumed that the distance of the moving coordinate system moves relative to base coordinate system along x-axis and y-axis is x_0 and y_0 respectively, and the angle of rotation about the z axis is α. Then the transformation matrix $\mathbf{T}$ of the moving coordinate system relative to the base coordinate system can be expressed as:

$$\mathbf{T} = \mathbf{T}_x(x_0)\mathbf{T}_y(y_0)\mathbf{R}_z(\alpha) \tag{2}$$

3.1 Inverse Kinematics

The inverse kinematics is to solve the output parameters x_0, y_0, g, α of the moving platform by given the actuated input parameters d_1, d_2, d_3, d_4 through the constraints of the structure.

The center point P of the moving coordinate system in the base coordinate system. $O\text{-}xyz$ can be expressed as:

$$p = [x_0, y_0, 0]^T$$

The coordinates of the actuated joint point A_i are represented in the base coordinate system $O\text{-}xyz$:

$$a_1 = [d_1, 0, 0]^T, a_2 = [d_2, 0, 0]^T, a_3 = [d_3, 0, 0]^T, a_4 = [d_4, 0, 0]^T$$

Point D_1 can be expressed in the moving coordinate system $P\text{-}uvw$:

$$d^m = [g, h, 0]^T$$

where $h = l_{PB3} + \sqrt{l_5^2 - g^2}$.

Point B_i in the moving coordinate system $P\text{-}uvw$ can be expressed:

$$b_1^m = [-l_{PB}1, 0, 0]^T, b_2^m = [l_{PB}1, 0, 0]^T, b_3^m = [0, l_{PB}3, 0]^T$$

Therefore, points B_i and D_1 can be written in the base coordinate system $O\text{-}xyz$ as:

$$\begin{cases} b_i = Tb_i^m + p \ (i = 1, 2, 3) \\ d = Td^m + p \end{cases} \tag{3}$$

In limb 1–3, points A_i and B_i satisfies the constrained relationship of the link A_iB_i:

$$l_i^2 = [b_i - a_i]^T[b_i - a_i], (i = 1, 2, 3) \tag{4}$$

According to Eq. (4), d_1, d_2 and d_3 can be obtained.

For limb 4, assuming that the coordinate of point C in the base coordinate system is $c = [C_x, C_y, 0]^T$, the distance between points A_3, B_3 and C satisfies the following relationship:

$$\begin{cases} C_x = l_{B3C}/l_3 \times (d_3 - B_{3x}) + B_{3x} \\ C_y = -l_{B3C}/l_3 \times B_{3y} + B_{3y} \end{cases} \tag{5}$$

where B_{3x} and B_{3y} represent the coordinates of x and y of point B_3 respectively.

In limb 4, points A_4 and C satisfies the constrained relationship of the link A_4C:

$$l_4^2 = (A_{4x} - C_x)^2 + (A_{4y} - C_y)^2 \tag{6}$$

where A_{4x} and A_{4y} represent the coordinates of x and y of point A_4, C_x and C_y represent the coordinates of x and y of point C respectively.

Based on Eq. (6), d_4 can be obtained.

According to the inverse kinematics solution, the trajectory of the moving platform is given as Eq. (7) to solve the values of each input actuation:

$$\begin{cases} x_0 = 5 \cdot \sin[t], \, y_0 = 5 \cdot \cos[t] - 5 \\ \alpha = \frac{\pi}{4} \cdot \sin[t], \, g = -93.7 \end{cases} \tag{7}$$

The dimension parameters of the manipulator are shown in Table 1. Here, we set value $t \in (0,15)$. By substituting these parameters into Eqs. (4) and (6), the variation curves of d_1, d_2, d_3 and d_4 are obtained as shown in Fig. 3.

Table 1. Dimension parameters

parameter	value/mm	parameter	value/mm	parameter	value/mm
l_1, l_2, l_3	300	l_{PB1}, l_{PB2}	50	l_{A3C}	100
l_{B3C}	200	l_4	260	l_5	142

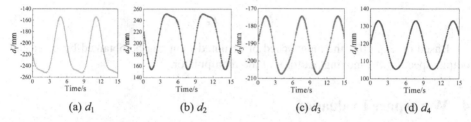

(a) d_1 (b) d_2 (c) d_3 (d) d_4

Fig. 3. Variation curves of actuation joints

In Fig. 3, the variation curves of the parallel grasping manipulator are smooth within 0–15 s. There is no sharp point and singularity appear in the movement process, which verifies the correctness of the inverse kinematics solution.

3.2 Jacobian Matrix

The relationship between the actuated joint velocity and the moving platform velocity can be obtained by calculating the Jacobian matrix. Assume that the output speed of the moving platform is $\dot{x} = [\dot{x}_0, \dot{y}_0, \dot{\alpha}, \dot{g}]^T$, the input speed of actuated joint is $\dot{q} = [\dot{d}_1, \dot{d}_2, \dot{d}_3, \dot{d}_4]^T$.

The output speed and input speed meet the following calculation form:

$$J_x \dot{x} = J_q \dot{q} \tag{8}$$

where J_x is the constrained Jacobian matrix, J_q is the actuated Jacobian matrix.

By differentiating the position constraint Eqs. (4) and (6) with respect to time, the velocity constraint equations are obtained:

$$\begin{cases} a_{11}\dot{x}_0 + a_{12}\dot{y}_0 + a_{13}\dot{\alpha} + a_{14}\dot{g} - r_{11}\dot{d}_1 = 0 \\ a_{21}\dot{x}_0 + a_{22}\dot{y}_0 + a_{23}\dot{\alpha} + a_{24}\dot{g} - r_{22}\dot{d}_2 = 0 \\ a_{31}\dot{x}_0 + a_{32}\dot{y}_0 + a_{33}\dot{\alpha} + a_{34}\dot{g} - r_{33}\dot{d}_3 = 0 \\ a_{41}\dot{x}_0 + a_{42}\dot{y}_0 + a_{43}\dot{\alpha} + a_{44}\dot{g} - r_{44}\dot{d}_4 = 0 \end{cases} \tag{9}$$

By sorting out the equations of actuated values and motion parameters of the moving platform in Eq. (9), the constrained Jacobian matrix J_x and the actuated Jacobian matrix J_q can be obtained:

$$J_x = \begin{pmatrix} a_{11} & a_{12} & a_{13} & a_{14} \\ a_{21} & a_{22} & a_{23} & a_{24} \\ a_{31} & a_{32} & a_{33} & a_{34} \\ a_{41} & a_{42} & a_{43} & a_{44} \end{pmatrix} \quad J_q = \begin{pmatrix} r_{11} & 0 & 0 & 0 \\ 0 & r_{22} & 0 & 0 \\ 0 & 0 & r_{33} & 0 \\ 0 & 0 & 0 & r_{44} \end{pmatrix}$$

Therefore, the whole Jacobian matrix of the manipulator can be obtained as J:

$$J = J_q^{-1} \cdot J_x \tag{10}$$

Based on Eq. (10), the input speed of actuated joint can be obtained by given the output-speed of the moving platform of the manipulator.

4 Workspace Evaluation

4.1 Workspace Analysis

To evaluate the workspace performance of the parallel grasping manipulator under the coupled DOFs, the workspace performance of the manipulator under three conditions will be studied in this section: (1) Two-dimensional workspace when position is fixed; (2) Two-dimensional workspace when orientation is fixed; (3) Three-dimensional workspace when one of DOFs is fixed. According to the structure parameters of the manipulator in Table 1, the projection of link l_i onto the x-axis can be expressed as:

$$\begin{cases} Q_i = |A_{ix} - B_{ix}| (i = 1, 2, 3) \\ Q_4 = |A_{4x} - C_{4x}| \end{cases} \tag{11}$$

where A_{ix} and B_{ix} represent the x coordinates of points A_i and B_i respectively, A_{4x} and C_{4x} represent the x coordinates of points A_4 and C_4 respectively.

Then, the angle between link l_i and the x-axis positive direction is expressed by θ_i:

$$\theta_i = \arccos(Q_i / l_i) \quad (i = 1, 2, 3, 4) \tag{12}$$

The variation range of input parameter d_i and joint angle θ_i is set as: $d_i \in [20, 40]$, unit: mm, $\theta_i \in [0, 160]$, unit: Degree.

Condition 1: When the position value of the moving platform is fixed, that is, $x_0 = 0$, $y_0 = -50$ mm, the orientation workspace as shown in Fig. 4(a). The value range of the orientation angle α is $[-180, 180]$, unit: Degree, and the value range of the displacement g is $[-150, 150]$, unit: mm.

Condition 2: When the orientation value of the moving platform is fixed, that is, $\alpha = 0$, $g = 0$, the position workspace as shown in Fig. 4(b). The reachable position range of x_0 is $[-100, 100]$, and the reachable position range of y_0 is $[-400, -50]$, unit: mm.

As shown in Fig. 4, with reachable position range of the parallel grasping manipulator $d_i \in [20,40]$, unit: mm, the moving platform can produce a $180°$ rotation and can grasp objects up to 300 mm in size, which demonstrates it possess an excellent workspace performance.

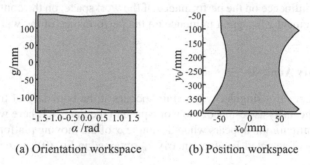

(a) Orientation workspace   (b) Position workspace

Fig. 4. Two-dimensional workspace

Condition 3: The values of x_0, y_0, g and α are given to obtain three-dimensional workspace of the manipulator. To analyze the influence of different parameters on the workspace, here we set the values of structure parameters under the same conditions, and fixed four parameters in turn to measure the reachable range of the remaining three parameters. The parameter values of each group are listed in Table 2. The solution of workspace is shown in Fig. 4.

Table 2. The values for each workspace

	x_0/mm	y_0/mm	g_0/mm	α/degree
WS(a)	0	$[-1000,1000]$	$[-150,150]$	$[-180,180]$
WS(b)	$[-500,500]$	0	$[-150,150]$	$[-180,180]$
WS(c)	$[-500,500]$	$[-1000,1000]$	$[-150,150]$	0
WS(d)	$[-500,500]$	$[-1000,1000]$	0	$[-180,180]$

As can be seen from Fig. 5, under given structural parameters and constraints, the moving platform of the manipulator can realize $180°$ rotation without singularity, and

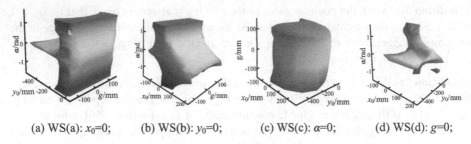

(a) WS(a): $x_0=0$;   (b) WS(b): $y_0=0$;   (c) WS(c): $\alpha=0$;   (d) WS(d): $g=0$;

Fig. 5. Three-dimensional workspace

has a certain motion performance and grasping performance. Further, the fixed rotation angle has little influence on the performance of the workspace, on the contrary, the fixed gripper displacement g has great influence on the performance of the workspace.

4.2 Singularity Analysis

The inverse kinematics singularity generally occurs at the boundary of the workspace. According to the analysis results of the workspace in the Sect. 4.1, here we assume that the singular configuration appears when the angle α of the moving platform is in $\pm90°$. The parameters of actuated Jacobian matrix J_q obtained in Eq. (9) can be written as:

$$\begin{cases} r_{11} = x_0 - d_1 - l_{PB_1} \cos[\alpha] \\ r_{22} = x_0 - d_2 + l_{PB_1} \cos[\alpha] \\ r_{33} = x_0 - d_3 + (\sqrt{-g^2 + l_5^2} - h) \sin[\alpha] \\ r_{44} = x_0 - d_4 - \frac{l_{B_3C}}{l_3} \varphi(\cos(\alpha)) + (\sqrt{-g^2 + l_5^2} - h) \sin[\alpha] \end{cases} \tag{13}$$

where r_{ij} represents the parameter of i-th row and j-th column of J_q, $\varphi(\cos(\alpha))$ is the function of $\cos(\alpha)$, when $\alpha = \pm90°$, $\varphi(\cos(\alpha))$ is equal to 0, d_i is the function of x_0, y_0, α and g.

When $|J_q|=0$, that is, the singular configuration occurs when one or more of the parameters of J_q equals to 0, the manipulator is in singular configuration. Taking special cases to calculate, when $r_{11} = r_{22} = 0$, it can obtain $y_0 = -247$ mm, that is, when the moving platform angle $\alpha = \pm90°$, the inverse kinematic singularity will occur when the moving platform moves to the position with $y_0 = -247$ mm. However, it can be seen from Fig. 5(a) that the manipulator is in the position with $y_0 = -50$ mm at this moment, which is inconsistent with $y_0 = -247$ mm. Therefore, the singular position is no longer in the actual reachable workspace of the manipulator.

When $r_{33} = r_{44} = 0$, we can obtain $y_0 = 533$ mm or $y_0 = -1027$ mm through the same method to represent the manipulator will occur inverse kinematic singularity. Similarly, the two singular positions are not in the actual reachable workspace of the grasping manipulator, so the inverse kinematics singularity will not occur in the normal motion process of the manipulator, which demonstrate the motion performance is well.

4.3 Dimension Determination Based on Workspace Maximization

To determine the dimensions that satisfy the maximum workspace for practical application, this section will study the influence of parameters on the size and shape of the workspace of the manipulator according to different dimension values of links.

According to Sect. 3.1, when the dimension of the link is less than 300 mm, there is no solution in the inverse kinematic of the manipulator. Therefore, we set the initial link dimension $l_1 = l_2 = l_3 = 300$, the increment of link dimension is 100, the range of the value is [300, 700], unit: mm. Utilizing the same method in Sect. 4.1, Then, we can analyze the influence of the change of link dimension on the size and shape of the workspace. The results under different dimension values can be obtained as shown in Fig. 6.

Considering practical processing and application, the selected structural parameters should have a large workspace on the basis of relatively small link dimension. By comparing the results in Fig. 6, it can be seen that the best structure scheme is when link dimension taking $l_1 = l_2 = l_3 = 400$ mm.

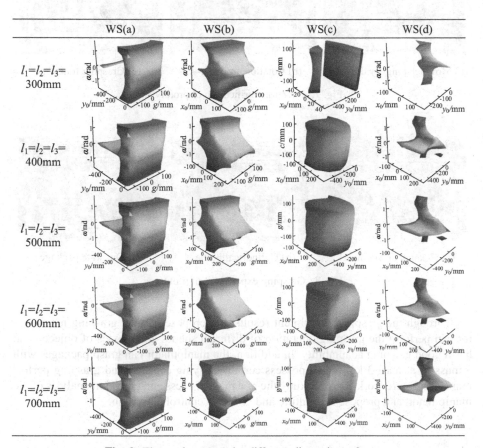

Fig. 6. The workspace under different dimension values

5   Prototype Experiment

Based on the obtained link dimension, the prototype of the parallel grasping manipulator is designed as shown in Fig. 7. Adjusting the prototype to the initial position, the motion ability of the moving platform moving along the horizontal direction x, vertical direction y and rotation around the z-axis is verified respectively. Finally, the grasping function of the manipulator is verified as shown in Fig. 7.

After verifying the correctness of the actuation control, motion performance and the motion DOF of the manipulator, the grasping experiment is carried out to verify the grasping performance of the manipulator. The grasping ability of the manipulator is verified by grasping objects of different masses and shapes as shown in Fig. 8.

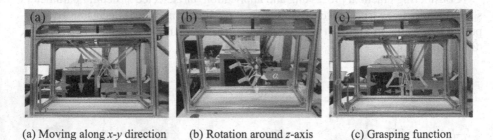

(a) Moving along x-y direction   (b) Rotation around z-axis   (c) Grasping function

Fig. 7. Function verification of prototype

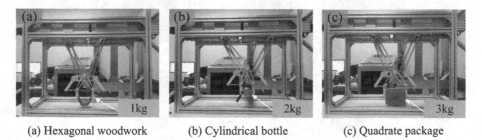

(a) Hexagonal woodwork   (b) Cylindrical bottle   (c) Quadrate package

Fig. 8. Grasping experiment of prototype

Through the grasping experiment results, the propose parallel grasping manipulator can perform the grasping operation of different shapes and masses of objects, and has a good grasping adaptability. In addition, the manipulator can grasp packages with a mass of at least 3 kg, which possess certain carrying capacity and grasping performance. In future work, we will study the grasping stiffness and precision analysis of the manipulator, and propose a scientific and effective control algorithm.

6 Conclusion

A novel parallel grasping manipulator with configurable platform is proposed. By using the output motion of the slider on the moving platform as the driving force of the gripper, there is no additional driven motor which is required to the grippers of the manipulator, avoiding the impact of separate driven device installed at the end of the manipulator on grasping performance. The redundant structure ensures that the manipulator doesn't occur singularity and mechanical interference in the desired workspace. The workspace performance of the parallel grasping manipulator is evaluated and the manipulator has the largest workspace when link dimension taking $l_1 = l_2 = l_3 = 400$ mm. The results of the prototype experiment show that the manipulator can flexibly realize $\pm 90°$ large rotation angle and has good grasping adaptability.

Acknowledgements. This work was supported by the National Natural Science Foundation of China (Grant No. 52205006).

References

1. Hua, H.L., Liao, Z.Q., Hao, J.B.: Design, analysis, and experiment of an underactuated robotic gripper actuated by linear series elastic actuator. J. Mech. Rob.-Trans. ASME **15**(2), 021002 (2022)
2. Choi, H., Konno, A., Uchiyama, M.: Singularity analysis of a novel 4-DOFs parallel robot H4 by using screw theory. In: Proceedings of the ASME 2003 International Design Engineering Technical Conferences and Computers and Information in Engineering Conference, pp. 1125–1133. Chicago, Illinois, USA (2003)
3. Sterheim, F.: Computation of the direct and inverse geometric-models of the delta-4 parallel robot. Robotersysteme **3**(4), 199–203 (1987)
4. Liu, Y., Kong, M., Wan, N., et al.: A geometric approach to obtain the closed-form forward kinematics of H4 parallel robot. J. Mech. Robot.-Trans. ASME **10**(5), 051013 (2018)
5. Mohamed, M., Gosselin, C.M.: Design and analysis of kinematically redundant parallel manipulators with configurable platforms. IEEE Trans. Robot. **21**(3), 277–287 (2005)
6. Wang, J., Gosselin, C.M.: Kinematic analysis and design of kinematically redundant parallel mechanisms. J. Mech. Design-Trans. ASME **126**(1), 109–118 (2004)
7. Wen, K.F., Nguyen, T.S., Harton, D., et al.: Exploiting the kinematic redundancy of a (6+3) degrees-of-freedom parallel mechanism. J. Mech. Robot.-Trans. ASME **11**(2), 021005 (2019)
8. Jin, X.D., Fang, Y.F., Zhang, D.: Design of a class of generalized parallel mechanisms with large rotational angles and integrated end-effectors. Mech. Mach. Theory **134**, 117–134 (2019)
9. Tian, C.X., Zhang, D.: Design and analysis of novel kinematically redundant reconfigurable generalized parallel manipulators. Mech. Mach. Theory **166**, 104481 (2021)
10. Yao, J., Li, T.M., Wang, L.P.: Dynamic modeling and redundant force optimization of a 2-DOF parallel kinematic machine with kinematic redundancy. Robot. Comput.-Integrated Manuf. **32**, 1–10 (2015)
11. Shin, H., Kim, S., Jeong, J., et al.: Stiffness enhancement of a redundantly actuated parallel machine tool by dual support rims. Int. J. Precis. Eng. Manuf. **13**, 1539–1547 (2012)
12. Zhao, F.Q., Guo, S., Zhang, C.Y., et al.: Singularity analysis and dexterity performance on a novel parallel mechanism with kinematic redundancy. Int. J. Adv. Rob. Syst. **16**(5), 1–15 (2019)

13. Nouri, R.A., Carretero, J.A.: Modeling and real-time motion planning of a class of kinematically redundant parallel mechanisms with reconfigurable platform. J. Mech. Robot. **15**(2), 021004 (2023)
14. Schreiber, L.T., Gosselin, C.M.: Passively driven redundant spherical joint with very large range of motion. J. Mech. Robot.-Trans. ASME **9**(3), 031014 (2017)
15. Li, Y.W., Wang, L.M., Liu, J.F., et al.: Applicability and generality of the modified Grübler-Kutzbach criterion. Chinese J. Mech. Eng. **26**(2), 257–263 (2013)

Research on Forward Kinematics Solutions of 3RPUPc-UPS Parallel Mechanism Based on Particle-Artificial Bee Colony Algorithm

Zhenzhen Chang, Yanbin Zhang[✉], and Yaoguang Li

Henan University of Science and Technology, Luoyang 471003, China
yanbin_zh@163.com

Abstract. Aim to solve the numerical forward solutions of 3RPUPc-UPS parallel mechanism, the particle-artificial bee colony algorithm is proposed. By analyzing the topological characteristics of the mechanism, the position and orientation characteristics sets, degrees of freedom and coupling degrees are obtained. According to the geometric characteristics of the mechanism, the inverse kinematics equations and the forward kinematics solutions model are established. Through a forward solution software of the mechanism, which is developed based on the particle swarm optimization, the artificial bee colony and the particle-artificial bee colony algorithm, the numerical solutions of the mechanism are obtained. The results show that the running time of the particle-artificial bee colony algorithm is shortened 47.46% than the artificial bee colony algorithm, and the accuracy of the solution is improved 10 orders of magnitude compared with the particle swarm optimization algorithm. The particle-artificial bee colony algorithm has fast calculation and high precision. This work provides a new method for studying the forward kinematics of parallel mechanisms.

Keywords: Parallel mechanism · Forward kinematics solution · Position and orientation characteristics · Particle-artificial bee colony algorithm

1 Introduction

The parallel mechanisms has been widely used in medical rehabilitation, aerospace, industrial production and other fields since the high precision, small error accumulation, strong bearing capacity and compact structure [1, 2]. However, due to the strong coupling, the popularization and application of parallel mechanisms are restricted.

Kinematics analysis includes inverse kinematics and forward kinematics analysis, which is the basis of theoretical research on structure optimization, performance analysis and precise control. Compared with the inverse kinematics solutions, the forward kinematics solutions (FKS) of parallel mechanisms are much more complicated. Numerical [3] and analytical methods [4] are commonly used to solve the forward kinematics. According to the geometric characteristics of a 3-CRRR parallel mechanism, NAZARI [5] transformed the spatial expression into a planer expression, which reduced the complexity of forward kinematics equations. HAN [6] analyzed the forward kinematics of a

© The Author(s), under exclusive license to Springer Nature Singapore Pte Ltd. 2023
H. Yang et al. (Eds.): ICIRA 2023, LNAI 14269, pp. 361–373, 2023.
https://doi.org/10.1007/978-981-99-6489-5_29

6SPS parallel mechanism by the fixed-point iteration method, and this method is proved that more advantageous than the Newton iteration method.

In recent years, the intelligent algorithms have been applied by many scholars to solve the FKS of parallel mechanisms [7–9], such as the neural network algorithm (NN) [10], the genetic algorithm (GA) [11], and the particle swarm optimization algorithm (PSO) [12]. The NN algorithm has superior performance but needs a large number of training samples. The GA algorithm is extensible and easy to combine with other algorithms, but the local search ability is poor. The PSO algorithm has fast convergence speed, but the global optimization is weak. The artificial bee colony (ABC) algorithm [13] has less parameter and superior search characteristics for global optimization of continuous functions, but the convergence rate is slow in the later stage.

In this paper, the forward kinematics of the novel 3RPUPc-UPS parallel mechanism is analyzed. In Sect. 2, the single-open chains (SOC), degrees of freedom (DOFs) and coupling degrees are obtained by analyzing the topological characteristics of the mechanism. In Sect. 3, according to the geometric characteristics of the mechanism, the inverse kinematics solutions are established. In Sect. 4, the FKS model is constructed and the particle-artificial bee colony algorithm (P-ABC) algorithm is proposed for solving the forward solutions. The forward solution software of the mechanism is developed by the GUI module of MATLAB, and the effectiveness of the P-ABC algorithm is verified by the example analysis.

2 Kinematics Characteristics Analysis of the Mechanism

2.1 Structure Design

The structural diagram of the 3RPUPc-UPS parallel mechanism is shown as Fig. 1. The moving platform and the fixed base are connected by two different structure limbs.

The first structure limb is RPUPc (L_i, $i = 1$–3), which is composed of revolute joint R_i, prismatic joint P_i, universal joint U_i and annular prismatic joint P_{ci}. The P_{ci} is connected to the moving platform, and R_i is connected to the fixed base. For the convenience of expression, U_i is replaced by two vertically intersecting revolute joints R_{i1} and R_{i2}. The axis of R_i is parallel to the axis of R_{i1} and perpendicular to the moving direction of P_i. The axis of R_{i2} through the center point Q of the moving platform in the moving platform plane and is perpendicular to the motion direction of P_{ci}. The P_{ci} and U_i are always located in the moving platform plane.

The second structure limb is UPS (L_4), which is composed of universal joint U_4, prismatic joint P_4 and spherical joint S. U_4 is represented by revolute joints R_{41} and R_{42} with two axes perpendicular to each other, and S is represented by revolute joints R_{S41}, R_{S42} and R_{S43} with three axes intersecting at one point and perpendicular to each other. The axis of R_{41} is perpendicular to the fixed base. The axis of R_{42} and R_{S41} are perpendicular to the moving direction of P_4 respectively, and the axis of R_{S42} through the point Q in the moving platform.

The centers of P_{ci} are defined points A_i, the centers of U_i ($i = 1$–3) and S are defined points C_i. The points A_i and C_i are on the circle Q_r with radius r and the circle Q_c with radius c respectively, and circles Q_r and Q_c have the same center Q. The centers of R_i and U_4 are defined points B_i. The points B_i are evenly distributed on the circle O_R with

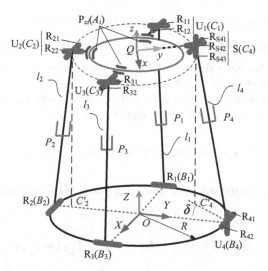

Fig. 1. Structural diagram of 3RPUPc-UPS parallel mechanism

the center point O and radius R, and the axis of R_i tangents to circle O_R. The axis of R_2 is perpendicular to the axis of R_1 and R_3. At the initial position, the axis of R_2 parallels to the axis of R_{42}.

2.2 Degrees of Freedom

The topological characteristics of the RPUPc limb is denoted as $\{-R_i(\perp P_i) //R_{i1}(\perp R_{i2})//P_{ci}-\}$, and the UPS limb is denoted as $\{-R_{41}\perp R_{42}(\perp P_4) //R_{S41}\perp R_{S42}\perp R_{S43}\}$. The motion effect of P_{ci} can be equivalent to a revolute joint R_{ci} whose rotational axis coincides with the center line of the moving platform. Therefore, the position and orientation characteristics (POC) sets [14] of the end of limbs can be expressed as Eqs. (1) and (2).

$$M_{bi} = \left[_{r^2//(R_{i1}, R_{i2}) \cup r^1//R_{ci}}^{t^2} \right] (i = 1, 2, 3) \tag{1}$$

$$M_{b4} = \left[_{r^3//(R_{S41}, R_{S42}, R_{ci})}^{t^3} \right] \tag{2}$$

The DOFs of the mechanism based on the POC set is Eq. (3).

$$F = \sum_{k=1}^{g} f_k - \sum_{j=1}^{v} \xi_{Lj} \tag{3}$$

where F is the DOFs of the mechanism, $\xi_{Lj} = \dim.\{(\overset{j}{\underset{i=1}{\cap}} M_{bi}) \cup M_{b(j+1)}\}$, $v = g - n + 1$, f_k is the number of DOFs of the kth joint, n is the number of components, g is the total number of the joints, v is the number of independent loop, ξ_{Lj} is the number of independent displacement equations of the jth independent loop, $\overset{j}{\underset{i=1}{\cap}} M_{bi}$ is the POC set of the sub-parallel mechanism composed of the first j limbs, $M_{b(j+1)}$ is the POC set of the end components of the $(j+1)$th limb.

The first independent loop is constituted by the L_1 and L_2, the number of the independent displacement Eq. can be computed via Eq. (4).

$$\xi_{L1} = \dim.\{M_{b1} \cup M_{b2}\} = \dim.\{\begin{bmatrix} t^3 \\ r^3 \end{bmatrix}\} = 6 \tag{4}$$

The POC set of the first sub-parallel mechanism (PM1) composed of the L_1 and L_2 is Eq. (5).

$$M_{S(1-2)} = M_{b1} \cap M_{b2} = \begin{bmatrix} t^2 \\ r^3 \end{bmatrix} \cap \begin{bmatrix} t^2 \\ r^3 \end{bmatrix} = \begin{bmatrix} t^1 \\ r^3 \end{bmatrix} \tag{5}$$

The second independent loop is constituted by PM1 and the L_3, the number of the independent displacement Eq. is Eq. (6).

$$\xi_{L2} = \dim.\{M_{S(1-2)} \cup M_{b3}\} = \dim.\{\begin{bmatrix} t^2 \\ r^3 \end{bmatrix}\} = 5 \tag{6}$$

The POC set of the second sub-parallel mechanism (PM2) is Eq. (7).

$$M_{S(1-3)} = M_{S(1-2)} \cap M_{b3} = \begin{bmatrix} t^1 \\ r^3 \end{bmatrix} \cap \begin{bmatrix} t^2 \\ r^3 \end{bmatrix} = \begin{bmatrix} t^1 \\ r^3 \end{bmatrix} \tag{7}$$

The third independent loop is constituted by PM2 and the L_4, the number of the independent displacement Eq. is Eq. (8).

$$\xi_{L3} = \dim.\{M_{S(1-3)} \cup M_{b4}\} = \dim.\{\begin{bmatrix} t^3 \\ r^3 \end{bmatrix}\} = 6 \tag{8}$$

The DOFs and POC sets of the mechanism are Eqs. (9) and (10).

$$F = \sum_{k=1}^{g} f_k - \sum_{j=1}^{v} \xi_{Lj} = 21 - (6 + 5 + 6) = 4 \tag{9}$$

$$M_{S(1-4)} = M_{S(1-3)} \cap M_{b4} = \begin{bmatrix} t^1 \\ r^3 \end{bmatrix} \cap \begin{bmatrix} t^3 \\ r^3 \end{bmatrix} = \begin{bmatrix} t^1 \\ r^3 \end{bmatrix} \tag{10}$$

The Eqs. (9) and (10) illustrate that the mechanism has 4 output DOFs, correspond to the Flexion/ Extension, Radial/ Ulnar, Pronation/ Supination and Traction/ Extrusion motions in the process of wrist rehabilitation. Therefore, the mechanism can be used as a wrist rehabilitation mechanism. The linear displacement of the P_i $(i = 1, 2, 3)$ and the angle displacement of the R_{41} are selected as the actuated input of the mechanism.

2.3 Coupling Degrees

According to the principle of mechanism composition based on the SOC [15], any mechanism can be decomposed into several basic chains, and the basic chains with v independent loops can be decomposed into v ordered SOC_i ($i = 1 \sim v$). The constraint degrees Δ of the jth SOC_j is defined as Eq. (11).

$$\Delta_j = \sum_{k=1}^{g_j} f_k - I_j - \xi_{Lj} \tag{11}$$

where g_j represents the number of kinematic joints of the jth SOC_j, I_j represents the number of actuated joints of the jth SOC_j.

The coupling degrees can be calculated via Eq. (12).

$$k = \frac{1}{2}\min\{\sum_{j=1}^{v} |\Delta_j|\} \tag{12}$$

The constraint degrees of each SOC of the mechanism is respectively Eqs. (13), (14) and (15).

$$\Delta_1 = \sum_{k=1}^{g_1} f_k - I_1 - \xi_{L1} = 10 - 2 - 6 = 2 \tag{13}$$

$$\Delta_2 = \sum_{k=1}^{g_2} f_k - I_2 - \xi_{L2} = 5 - 1 - 5 = -1 \tag{14}$$

$$\Delta_3 = \sum_{k=1}^{g_3} f_k - I_3 - \xi_{L3} = 6 - 1 - 6 = -1 \tag{15}$$

The coupling degrees of the mechanism is Eq. (16).

$$k = \frac{1}{2}\sum_{j=1}^{v} |\Delta_j| = \frac{1}{2}(2 + 1 + 1) = 2 \tag{16}$$

Due to the coupling degrees of the mechanism is greater than 1, it is very complicated to directly establish the analytical expression of forward solutions [14], it is necessary to construct the forward solution model according to the inverse kinematic solution.

3 Inverse Kinematics

The coordinate system Q-xyz is established with the point Q as the origin, the y-axis passes through the point C_4, the z-axis is perpendicular to the moving platform, and the x-axis is determined by the right-hand rule. The coordinate system O-XYZ is established with the center point O of the fixed base as the origin, that the X-axis passes through the point B_3, the Y-axis passes through the point B_4, and the Z-axis is perpendicular to the fixed base.

3.1 Solution of Inverse Kinematics

The l_i denotes the lengths of the actuated rods of the first three limbs and δ represents the rotational angle of the R_{41} from the initial position, as show in Fig. 1. The inverse kinematics solutions of the mechanism refers to solve l_i and δ when the attitude parameters α, β, γ and z of the moving platform are known.

In the xQy plane, the coordinates of any point on circle Q_c is defined $C_Q (x, y, 0)$, the Eq. of circle Q_c is Eq. (17).

$$x^2 + y^2 = c^2 \tag{17}$$

The coordinate transformation matrix of the moving platform relates to the fixed base can be expressed as Eq. (18).

$$\boldsymbol{R} = \boldsymbol{R}_x(\alpha)\boldsymbol{R}_y(\beta)\boldsymbol{R}_z(\gamma) = \begin{bmatrix} c\beta c\gamma & -c\beta s\gamma & s\beta \\ s\alpha s\beta c\gamma + c\alpha s\gamma & c\alpha c\gamma - s\alpha s\beta s\gamma & -s\alpha c\beta \\ c\alpha s\beta c\gamma - s\alpha s\gamma & -c\alpha s\beta s\gamma - s\alpha c\gamma & c\alpha c\beta \end{bmatrix} \tag{18}$$

where $\boldsymbol{R}_x(\alpha), \boldsymbol{R}_y(\beta)$ and $\boldsymbol{R}_z(\gamma)$ are the coordinate transformation matrices of the moving platform around axes x, y and z, respectively. The c and s represent "cos" and "sin", respectively.

The coordinates vector $\boldsymbol{C}_O$ of the point C_Q in $O\text{-}XYZ$ can be evaluated via Eq. (19).

$$\boldsymbol{C}_O = \boldsymbol{R}\boldsymbol{C}_Q + \boldsymbol{Q} \tag{19}$$

where $\boldsymbol{C}_Q$ represents the coordinate vector of the point C_Q in $Q\text{-}xyz$, $\boldsymbol{Q}$ is the coordinate vector $(0\ 0\ z)$.

Due to the rotation around the z-axis of the moving platform not affects the shape of the projection of circle Q_c on plane XOY. The projection coordinate (x_O, y_O) of the point C_Q on the plane XOY can be obtained by substituting $\gamma = 0$ into the Eq. (19), and it is Eq. (20).

$$x_O = c\beta x \quad y_O = s\alpha s\beta x + c\alpha y \tag{20}$$

Substituting the Eq. (20) into the Eq. (17), the formula of the projection of the circle Q_c on plane XOY is Eq. (21).

$$\left(\frac{x_O}{c\beta}\right)^2 + \left(\frac{y_O}{c\alpha} - t\alpha t\beta x_O\right)^2 = c^2 \tag{21}$$

where t represents "tan".

According to the Eq. (21), the coordinate of projections points $C'_i (x_{COi}, y_{COi})$ of the points $C_i (i = 1, 2, 3)$ on the plane XOY are Eq. (22).

$$x_{CO1} = -x_{CO3} = -c\frac{c\alpha c\beta}{\sqrt{1 - c^2\beta s^2\alpha}} \quad y_{CO1} = y_{CO3} = 0 \quad y_{CO2} = -cc\alpha \quad x_{CO2} = 0 \tag{22}$$

The angles between QC_i and the horizontal plane are defined θ_i ($i = 1, 2, 3$), and $\theta_2 = \alpha$, $\theta_1 = \theta_3$, Fig. 2 is the instantaneous configuration of θ_3. Let $\theta_1 = \theta_3 = \theta$, the Eq. (23) can be obtained Eq. (23).

$$\cos\theta = \frac{c\alpha c\beta}{\sqrt{1 - c^2\beta s^2\alpha}} \tag{23}$$

According to the geometric constraints of the mechanism, the l_i can be obtained via Eq. (24), (25) and (26).

$$l_1^2 = (R - c\cos\theta)^2 + (z - c\sin\theta)^2 \tag{24}$$

$$l_2^2 = (R - c\cos\alpha)^2 + (z + c\sin\alpha)^2 \tag{25}$$

$$l_3^2 = (R - c\cos\theta)^2 + (z + c\sin\theta)^2 \tag{26}$$

According to the Eq. (19), the coordinate of the point C_4 $(0, c, 0)^T$ on $O\text{-}XYZ$ is Eq. (27).

$$x_{CO4} = -cc\beta s\gamma \quad y_{CO4} = c(c\alpha s\gamma - s\alpha s\beta s\gamma) \quad z_{CO4} = -c(c\alpha s\beta s\gamma + s\alpha c\gamma) + z \tag{27}$$

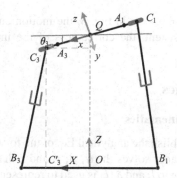

Fig. 2. Instantaneous configuration of angular θ_3

The projection of the point C_4 on plane XOY is defined the point C'_4, the angle δ between the vector $B_4C'_4$ $(x_{B4C'4}, y_{B4C'4})$ and B_4O $(0, -R)$ can be expressed as Eq. (28).

$$\cos\delta = \frac{B_4C'_4 \cdot B_4O}{|B_4C'_4||B_4O|} \tag{28}$$

When the Eq. (28) is solved, the Eq. (29) can be obtained via Eq. (29).

$$\delta = \arccos\frac{y_{B4C'4}}{\sqrt{x_{B4C'4}^2 + y_{B4C'4}^2}} \tag{29}$$

where $x_{B4C'4} = x_{CO4}$, $y_{B4C'4} = y_{CO4} - R$.

3.2   Verification of the Inverse Solution

When the structural parameters of the mechanism are defined $c = 60\,\text{mm}$ and $R = 120\,\text{mm}$, according to the Eqs. (24), (25), (26) and (29), the inverse solution is numerically simulated by MATLAB, and the motion curves of the actuated joints of each limb are drawn. At the same time, SOLIDWORKS is used for virtual prototype modeling and inverse kinematics simulation. The simulation results are shown in Fig. 3, and the simulation time t is 20 s.

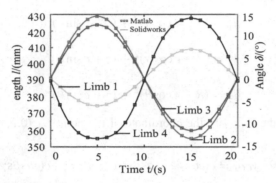

Fig. 3.   Simulation of inverse solution

Compared the simulation results in Fig. 3, the motion curve of the two simulation results are completely consistent, the correctness of the inverse solution analysis is verified.

4   Forward Kinematics

4.1   Model of Forward Kinematics

Because it is difficult to establish the analytical Eq. of the forward kinematics of parallel mechanisms directly, this paper solves the α, β, γ and z that satisfying the Eqs. (24), (25), (26) and (29) according to l_i and δ (l_4 is used to represent δ for convenience) of the mechanism. Namely, the numerical solution of the mechanism is obtained. The inverse solution of the mechanism can be rewritten as Eq. (30).

$$l_i - f_i(\alpha, \beta, \gamma, z) = 0(i = 1 \sim 4) \tag{30}$$

Transforming the Eq. (30) into a constrained multi-objective nonlinear Eq. Minimization problem, the numerical forward solution model of the mechanism can be established as Eq. (31).

$$f_{PS} = \sum_{i=1}^{4} [l_i - f_i(\alpha, \beta, \gamma, z)]^2 \quad -\frac{\pi}{2} \le \alpha, \beta, \gamma \le \frac{\pi}{2} \quad 300\,\text{mm} \le z \le 400\,\text{mm} \tag{31}$$

where the f_{PS} refers to the fitness of algorithm, represents the overall error of the forward solution, and the smaller the value, the higher the solution accuracy.

4.2 Construction of P-ABC Algorithm

In practical applications, the fast and accurate control of parallel mechanisms depends on the accuracy and response time of the FKS. In this paper, a P-ABC algorithm based on ABC and PSO algorithm is proposed to solve the FKS of the 3RPUPc-UPS parallel mechanism.

The ABC Algorithm. The ABC algorithm comes from the process of bees find nectar source and collect honey, is shown as Fig. 4. The algorithm model includes nectar source, leader bees, observer bees and scout bees. After leader bees find nectar source, they return to the hive and exchange nectar source information with other bees in the dance area. Leader bees have a certain probability to hire other bees to explore the current nectar source or be hired to explore other nectar sources. The probability is determined by the quality of nectar source. After the current nectar source is explored, leader bees will give up it and convert themselves into scout bees to reconnoitre new nectar source near the hive.

A) The PSO algorithm.

The PSO algorithm is derived from the research of the foraging behavior of birds, and the individuals in birds colonies are simplified as particles with position and velocity, and the foraging process of birds is shown as Fig. 5. The foraging direction of birds is affected by two factors. One is the place P_{pbest} where they once found the most foods, and the other is the place P_{gbest} where other individuals once found the most foods.

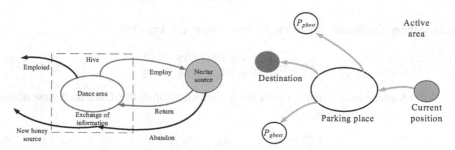

Fig. 4. The process of bees collecting nectar   **Fig. 5.** The process of birds foraging

The P-ABC Algorithm. The PSO algorithm has fast iteration speed, but lacks dynamic adjustment of the speed, which leads to easy to fall into local optimum, low accuracy and difficulty in convergence, and its results will be affected by the parameters. Although the iteration speed of ABC algorithm is slow, the searching of global and local optimal solution will be carried out in each iteration, so the probability of finding the optimal solution is higher. In order to improve the speed and accuracy of solving FKS of the mechanism, the P-ABC algorithm is proposed, which takes into account the characteristics of fast of PSO algorithm and high accuracy of ABC algorithm.

In the above three algorithms, the nectar source and Pg correspond to the leader bees and particles one by one, which represent the possible solutions of the optimization problem. The P-ABC algorithm has two stages. Firstly, in a D dimensional search space with N particles, the position and velocity update formulas of the ith particle are Eq. (32).

$$X_{id}^{p+1} = X_{id}^p + V_{id}^p \quad V_{id}^{p+1} = \omega V_{id}^p + c_1 r(P_{id,pbest}^p - X_{id}) + c_2 r(P_{id,gbest}^p - X_{id}^p) \quad (32)$$

where ω represents the inertia weight, c_1 represents the individual learning factor, the larger the value, the direction of birds foraging is more biased towards P_{pbest}, c_2 represents the group learning factor, the larger the value, the direction of birds foraging is more biased towards P_{gbest}, r represents the random number between $0 \sim 1$, V_{id}^k represents the dth dimensional velocity vector of the ith particle in the kth iteration, X_{id}^k represents the dth dimensional position vector of the ith particle in the kth iteration, $P_{id,pbest}^k$ represents the current optimal position of the ith particle, $P_{id,gbest}^k$ represents the current optimal position of the birds colonies.

Secondly, the optimal position after p iterations of PSO algorithm is taken as the initial nectar source information of the first iteration of ABC algorithm. The nectar source information M_i obtained by leader bee are Eq. (33).

$$M_i = P_{i,gbest}^p = \{ x_{i,1}, x_{i,2}, ..., x_{i,D} \} \quad (33)$$

where $x_{i,j}$ denotes the jth dimension value of the ith nectar source, $i = 1 \sim N$.

Observer bees obtain all nectar source information in the dance area, and the probability of selecting a new nectar source is Eq. (34).

$$p_i = \frac{fit_{Mi}}{\sum_{i=1}^{S_N} fit_{Mi}} \quad (34)$$

among them, the fitness fit_{Mi} of the ith nectar source is Eq. (35).

$$fit_{Mi} = \begin{cases} 1/(1 + f_{PS_i}) & (f_{PS_i} \geq 0) \\ 1 + |f_{PS_i}| & (f_{PS_i} < 0) \end{cases} \quad (35)$$

After leader bees exchange nectar source information in the dance area, new nectar sources are obtained via Eq. (36).

$$x_{i,j}^{new} = x_{i,j} + \varphi_{i,j}(x_{i,j} - x_{k,j})(k \neq i) \quad (36)$$

where $\varphi_{i,j}$ is a random number on the interval $[-1,1]$.

After leader bees become scout bees, new nectar sources are obtained according to the Eq. (37)

$$x_{i,j} = x_j^{min} + r(x_j^{max} - x_j^{min})(j = 1 \sim D) \quad (37)$$

where r is a random number in the interval $[0,1]$, x_j^{max} and x_j^{min} represent the upper and lower boundaries of the search range respectively.

Each bee will compare the fitness f_{PS} of the new and old nectar sources through the greedy method, and select the dominant solution as new nectar source. After the end of the algorithm running, the nectar source corresponding to the minimum fitness f_{PS} is the optimal solution.

4.3   Example Analysis

In this section, the ABC, PSO and P-ABC algorithms are used to solve the FKS to verify the superiority of the P-ABC algorithm. The maximum iterations of three algorithms is 300, p is half of the total iterations, the number of leader bees and particles are all 100, $\omega = 0.8$, $c_1 = c_2 = 2$, the other algorithm parameters are common values. In order to facilitate the calculation and compare the performance of three algorithms, the GUI module in MATLAB is used to develop a forward solution software based on them, the interface is shown as Fig. 6.

Taking the solution of the moving platform attitude $\alpha = 24°$, $\beta = 32°$, $\gamma = 20°$ and $z = 350mm$ as an example. The structure parameters are $R = 120$ mm, $c = 60$ mm, and the inverse kinematics solutions $l_1 = 323.887$ mm, $l_2 = 380.037$ mm, $l_3 = 390.29$ mm and $l_4 = -13.4237°$. Input all above parameters into the corresponding input box of the interface. The running time, solution error, fitness and fitness curve of three algorithms can be obtained, the fitness curve is shown as Fig. 7.

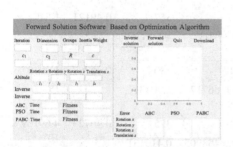

Fig. 6. Initial interface of software

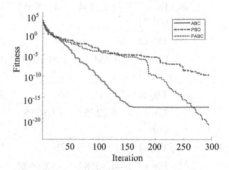

Fig. 7. Fitness curve

Figure 7 shows that the convergence speed of ABC algorithm is faster than PSO and P-ABC algorithm in the first 150 iterations. After that, the fitness curve of ABC algorithm keeps in a stable state, and PSO converges slowly. While the fitness curve of P-ABC algorithm accelerates to converge, and deviates from the PSO algorithm. After 300 iterations, the fitness of P-ABC algorithm is much smaller than that of ABC and PSO algorithms, which overcomes the defects not iterating after 150 iterations of ABC algorithm and low accuracy of PSO algorithm.

After the software operating 30 times independently, the average error of the results is recorded in Table 1. Compared with the ABC algorithm, the running time of P-ABC algorithm is shortened 47.46%, and the overall error level is changed from 10^{-18} to 10^{-20}. Compared with the PSO algorithm, although the running time is long, the error level is reduced from 10^{-10} to 10^{-20}, which reduces 10 orders of magnitude.

In order to verify the applicability of the P-ABC algorithm, 30 groups of different attitudes are selected to solve forward solution, after 300 iterations the results of 5 groups are recorded in Table 2. The calculation results show that the single solution time of the P-ABC algorithm is within 0.5 s, and the solution error level is 10^{-20}, which can effectively meet the practical application.

Table 1. The average error of P-ABC running 30 times independently

Algorithm	Average error (10^{-4})				Time t/(s)	Fitness
	α/(°)	β/(°)	γ/(°)	z/(mm)		
ABC	1.25033	-2.29573	-1.32003	1.8755	0.90337	2.72×10^{-18}
PSO	1.13344	-2.27477	-1.26569	1.94536	0.02085	5.89×10^{-10}
P-ABC	1.25034	-2.26266	-1.32003	1.87548	0.47466	1.04×10^{-20}

Table 2. The forward results of P-ABC in different attitudes

Numbers	Parameters					Time t/(s)	Fitness
		α/(°)	β/(°)	γ/(°)	z/(mm)		
1	Target	25	30	40	360	0.49229	7.08319×10^{-22}
	Error (10^{-4})	-2.22834	-0.25264	-0.40138	-2.06653		
2	Target	32	24	34	357	0.49121	1.5702×10^{-21}
	Error (10^{-4})	1.9764	0.501095	2.39203	-1.63769		
3	Target	28	28	38	380	0.46767	1.09307×10^{-20}
	Error (10^{-4})	-6.22757	-1.8615	-6.66717	1.70431		
4	Target	31	29	10	375	0.46723	4.69169×10^{-21}
	Error (10^{-4})	-4.30584	-1.08608	-0.458905	0.416131		
5	Target	10	9	15	345	0.46406	2.72921×10^{-22}
	Error (10^{-4})	5.14469	-2.34221	0.154985	-1.55105		

5   Conclusion

In this paper, the output characteristics of the 3RPUPc-UPS parallel mechanism are analyzed, and the P-ABC algorithm is proposed, which provides a new way for solving the forward kinematics of parallel mechanisms. The mechanism has 4 DOFs including three rotations and one translation, and the 2 coupling degrees indicate that the mechanism has strong kinematic coupling. The numerical FKS model of the mechanism is established depend on the inverse kinematics equations, and the FKS is transformed into a minimization problem of multi-objective nonlinear equations with constraints. The results of the example analysis show that compared with the ABC algorithm, the running time of the P-ABC algorithm is shortened 47.46%, and the solution accuracy is improved 10 orders of magnitude compared with the POS algorithm. The P-ABC algorithm has fast operation and high accuracy.

References

1. Gallapdo-alvarado, J.: A Gough-stewart parallel manipulator with configurable platform and multiple end-effectors. Meccanica **55**(3), 597–613 (2020)
2. Zhu, W., Liu, J.H., Li, H.B., et al.: Design and analysis of a compliant polishing manipulator with tensegrity-based parallel mechanism. Aust. J. Mech. Eng. **19**(4), 414–422 (2021)
3. Jaime, G.A., Jose, M.R.-M., Gurse, A.: Kinematics and singularity analyses of a 4-dof parallel manipulator using screw theory. Mech. Mach. Theor. **41**(9), 1048–1061 (2006). https://doi.org/10.1016/j.mechmachtheory.2005.10.012
4. Gao, L.Y., Wu, W.G.: Forward kinematics modeling of spatial parallel linkage mechanisms based on constraint equations and the numerical solving method. Robotica **35**(2), 293–309 (2015)
5. Ali, A.N., Ayyub, H., Majid, B.: Screw theory-based mobility analysis and projection-based kinematic modeling of a 3-CRRR parallel manipulator. J. Braz. Soc. Mech. Sci. Eng. **40**(7), 1–15 (2018)
6. Han, X.G., Zhang, J.: A method to get the forward kinematics of parallel kinematics mechanisms based on the fixed point iteration. Advanced Materials Research **753–755**, 2949–2953 (2013)
7. Zhang, H.Q., Fang, H.R., Jiang, B.S., et al.: A newton-raphson and BP neural network hybrid algorithm for forward kinematics of parallel manipulator. In: 2019 WRC Symposium on Advanced Robotics and Automation (WRC SARA), pp. 122–127. IEEE, Beijing (2019)
8. Wu, S.L., Liang, X.M., Liu, L., et al.: Bacterial foraging optimization algorithm based on normal cloud model for forward kinematics of a 4-dof parallel manipulator. Ferroelectrics **594**(1), 175–188 (2022)
9. Ghorbani, L., Omurlu, V.E.: Forward kinematics of a 6 × 6 UPU parallel mechanism by ANFIS method. In: 2018 6th International Conference on Control Engineering & Information Technology (CEIT), pp. 1–6. IEEE, Turkey (2018)
10. Tavassolian, F., Khotanlou, H., Varshovi-Jaghargh, P.: Forward kinematic analysis of spatial parallel robots using a parallel evolutionary neural networks. Iran. J. Sci. Technol. Trans. Mech. Eng. **47**, 1079–1092 (2022)
11. Wang, X.S., Hao, M.L., Cheng, Y.H.: On the use of differential evolution for forward kinematics of parallel manipulators. Appl. Math. Comput. **205**(2), 760–769 (2008)
12. Zhang, S.Z., Yuan, X.L., Docherty, P.D., et al.: An improved particle swarm optimization algorithm and its application in solving forward kinematics of a 3-dof parallel manipulator. Proc. Inst. Mech. Eng. C J. Mech. Eng. Sci. **235**(5), 896–907 (2021)
13. Gao, W.F., Liu, S.Y.: A modified artificial bee colony algorithm. Comput. Oper. Res. **39**(3), 687–697 (2012)
14. Yang, T.L., Liu, A.X., Luo, Y.F.: Theory and Application of Robot Mechanism Topology, 1st edn. Science Press, Beijing (2012)
15. Shen, H.P., Zhu, X.R., Yin, H.B.: Principle and design method for structure coupling-reducing of parallel mechanisms. J. Mech. Eng. **52**(23), 102–113 (2016)

Stiffness Calculation Method and Deformation Energy of Lattice Filled Structure

Sai Wang and Wei Song[✉]

Zhejianglab, Hangzhou 311121, Zhejiang, People's Republic of China
weisong@zhejianglab.com

Abstract. With the appearance of additive manufacturing processing technology, lattice structures exhibit a variety of novel properties, such as thermal conductivity, weight reduction, magnetic conductivity. In view of its effect on structural weight reduction, some scholars try to apply it to the design of bionic robot structure. There are specific conditions for its application, as lattice structure could reduce stiffness. In this paper, the stiffness of the lattice structure is studied by taking plate and pipe as the research content. At first, the influence of relative density and diameter of lattice rod on the stiffness of lattice packed plate under vertical force is studied. A mechanical model is established, and the optimal selection principle of relative density of lattice is proposed. Then, the stiffness variation of lattice filled pipe under vertical force and three-point bending condition is studied. It is found that lattice filling can be used to release stress in the structure, which will improve the energy absorption, and the suitable application scenario of lattice structure is given.

Keywords: lattice structure · mechanical · gradient structure

1 Introduction

In the bionic robot, lightweight is a more important design goal. Overweight limbs can cause the drive motor to be too large, and the increase in overall weight will shorten the robot standby time [1]. The main methods of lightweight in industrial products include the application of new lightweight materials, the use of advanced processing techniques and the use of optimized structures [2]. In recent years, topology optimization has played a large role in product lightweight [3]. The appearance of additive manufacturing technology further promotes the application of lightweight structures, which can make many new structures that can not be processed. The lattice structures proposed in recent years realize a variety of novel mechanical, heat transfer and electromagnetism characteristics on the macro level due to the geometry structure in the void and the different cell structures [4].

In medicine, artificial joints made of metal have been widely used. Since the stiffness of metal is greater than that of human skeleton, stress aggregation will occur in contact between metal and skeleton in human daily activities [5]. This accumulation of stress

© The Author(s), under exclusive license to Springer Nature Singapore Pte Ltd. 2023
H. Yang et al. (Eds.): ICIRA 2023, LNAI 14269, pp. 374–383, 2023.
https://doi.org/10.1007/978-981-99-6489-5_30

causes accelerated wear and tear in human bones, leaving sufferers suffering [6]. By controlling the relative density of lattice to improve the stiffness of metal materials, stiffness design of artificial joints and bones can be achieved to alleviate stress accumulation.

Bionic robot needs to consider standby time, power, explosive force, balance and other factors, which determines that its structure needs to have a high degree of integration, and its product quality is extremely high [7]. Therefore, on the basis of structural optimization, engineers and scientists learned from the hollow structure inside the skeleton and used lattice filling inside the structure to achieve a lighter material structure.

At present, there have been many researches on the design method of lattice structure and its macroscopic elastic parameters [8–11], but the influence of the relative density of lattice material on steel has not been quantified. Bionic bone structure design robot limbs, can play a better weight reduction effect. The performance of lattice filled tube is unknown, and the degree of influence of lattice on stiffness is still unknown. In the lattice design process, the shell with a single surface thickness is usually designed and stiffness is checked, and then lattice filling is added to achieve appearance and local filling. In addition, the internal parts of the robot structure are more complex, and the structure of the limbs usually needs more avoidance. In general, there will be a local lattice filled plate, which lacks theoretical guidance. Sheet material and pipe materials are often used in the design and manufacturing of industrial products. The leg/arm structure, shell and other parts of the robot are mostly designed by tubes or plates. Therefore, this paper will study the stiffness of plate, rod, tube and other structures commonly used in robot design, and explore the influence of lattice filling on it.

2   Stiffness of Lattice Filling Structure Filled Plate

2.1   A Subsection Sample

The stiffness of the plate is relatively easy to calculate, the knowledge of material mechanics can deduce its stiffness calculation formula. Take the lattice filled plate in Fig. 1(a) for example, the length, width and thickness of plate is l_c, b and h_1, respectively. The left side of the plate is fixed and the right side applied vertical load with bN, the influence of the internal lattice entity rate and the number of lattice layers on the stiffness of the plate is studied. The lattice is in form of rhomboid structure as shown in Fig. 1(b). The working condition of the plate is simplified as a plane strain problem, as shown in the longitudinal section of Fig. 1(c). The left side, upper and right side faces of the plate have solid areas with thickness of h_0. Besides the solid areas, filled with lattice structure, as shown in Fig. 1(d). The lattice length l_c is 2 mm. The layer number of lattice structure is m, therefore, the thickness $h_1 = l_c m + h_0$.

Orthogonal simulations were carried out on the three parameters of lattice layer number, rod diameter and plate length. The diameters of lattice rod is ϕ, in the simulation are 0.1 mm, 0.2 mm, 0.3 mm, 0.4 mm, 0.6 mm, 0.8 mm and 1.0 mm, respectively; the layer number of lattice is 2, 3, 4 and 5, respectively; the length of the plate is 30 mm, 50 mm, 70 mm and 90 mm, respectively. When the thickness of the plates filled with 2–5 layers of lattice is 5 mm, 7 mm, 9 mm, 11 mm respectively, the simulations is written by the way of length × thickness, such as a series of simulations with a length of 30 mm and a thickness of 5 mm, can be written as group 30 × 5.

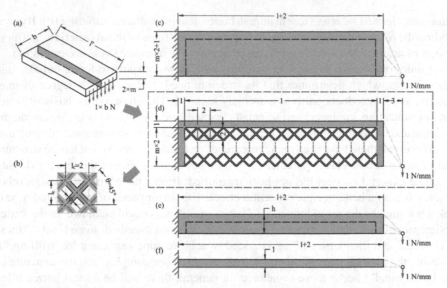

Fig. 1. Diagram of a lattice filler plate (a) plate and its longitudinal section are shown as equiaxial attempt; (b) lattice size diagram; (c) solid plate with same outer parameters of plate with lattice; (d) plate with lattice; (e) plate equal area of plate with lattice; (f) plate without lattice

The relative density of lattice structure is D_p,

$$D_p = 1 - \frac{\left(L_c - \sqrt{2}\phi\right)^2}{L_c^2} \tag{1}$$

In the simulation of length of 30 mm, 50 mm and 70 mm, the stiffness of plate with lattice is between solid plate of thickness h_1 with same outer parameters and solid plate of thickness h_0 without lattice, that is the stiffness of Fig. 1(d) is worse than Fig. 1(c) and better than Fig. 1(e) and (f). According to mechanics of materials, the stiffness formula of a 2D cantilever beam is as formula (2),

$$k = 4\frac{l^3}{Eh^3} \tag{2}$$

k is the stiffness of beam, mm/N, can be used for plate; l is the length of beam, mm; E is the Young's modulus, 4000 MPa.

The stiffness of lattice filled plate of 30/70/90 mm is shown in Fig. 2(a), (b), (c) and (d), respectively. The blue curves are FEM results of relative density from 0 to 1. The red dotted lines are stiffness of solid plate calculated according to formula (2), the upper is the stiffness of solid plate of h_1, and the bottom is that of h_0. As the relative density of lattice decreases, the lattice filled plate would loses stiffness. It is clear that the stiffness of lattice filled plate is better than the solid plate without lattice, which is the bottom limit in Fig. 2. The stiffness of lattice filled plate will decrease as the relative density increase, till it equals to the upper limit, which is the stiffness of solid plate with same outer parameters. When the relative density is above 0.4, decreased stiffness is small, and the stiffness begins to decrease dramatically when the relative density gradually less than 0.4, and this phenomenon is also observed in different lengths and layers of filling. Applying this principle reasonably designer can achieve considerable weight loss can be achieved through a small degree of stiffness reduction.

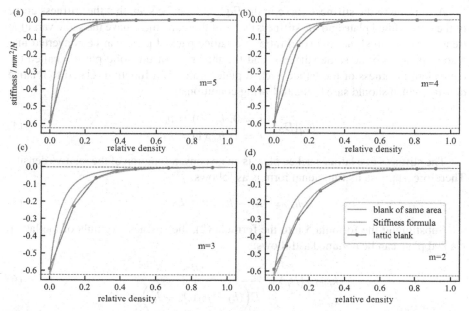

Fig. 2. Stiffness - relative density curve of lattice filled plate (a) thickness of 11 mm; (b) thickness of 9 mm; (c) thickness of 7 mm; (d) thickness of 5 mm

2.2 Stiffness Formula of Lattice Filled Plate

The upper and lower limits are not sufficient to quantitatively calculate the stiffness of lattice filled plates. The green curves in Fig. 2 are the stiffness of solid plate as same mass as lattice filled plate. The stiffness of lattice structure is less than that of solid plate with the same mass. The advantage of lattice structure is not the weight loss under equal strength, but the weight loss under equal part space, that is, lattice structure can fill the space more evenly. As can be seen in Fig. 2, there is little stiffness difference between lattice filled plate and equal area solid plate when the relative density is high, that is, the existence of lattice above a certain entity rate has little sacrifice to the stiffness.

Compared with the stiffness formula of solid plates, it is difficult to derive the stiffness of lattice filled plates directly. It can be concluded that the stiffness curves of solid plates with the same mass are geometrically related to the lattice filled plate. Since the upper and lower limits of stiffness can be calculated, the stiffness of lattice plate could be similar like formula 2, make it as $k_{lattice}$, it is a function related to l, h_0, h_1 and D_p, and should satisfy the following conditions,

$$k_{lattice}(D_p) \begin{cases} r = 0, k_{lattice} = 4\frac{l^3}{Eh_0^3} \\ r = 1, k_{lattice} = 4\frac{l^3}{Eh_1^3} \end{cases} \tag{3}$$

According to the stiffness curve in the Fig. 2, it can be seen that the stiffness curve of the lattice filled plate and the stiffness curve of the same mass have the same variation trend. It is assumed that the solid ratio of a lattice packed plate can be converted into a solid plate with the same stiffness, and the thickness of the solid plate is called the equivalent thickness of the lattice packed plate, which is a function related to relative density, which should satisfy the following conditions:

$$h_{eq}(D_p) \begin{cases} r = 0, h_{eq}(0) = h_0 \\ r = 1, h_{eq}(1) = h_1 \end{cases} \tag{4}$$

The stiffness of a lattice packed plate is an up convex function of the relative density. Therefore, suppose its functional form is as follows:

$$h_{eq} = (h_1 - h_0)D_p^a + h_0 \tag{5}$$

Substituting the formula 5 into the formula (2), the stiffness formula of the lattice packed plate can be obtained as follows:

$$k_{lattice}(D_p) = \frac{4l^3}{E\left((h_1 - h_0)D_p^a + h_0\right)^3} \tag{6}$$

By fitting the simulation results, the optimal parameter a in formula 6 is 1.3. The stiffness curves according to formula are orange curves as shown Fig. 2. The stiffness formula of lattice filled plate can describe its bending stiffness well. In the simulation results of each group, the maximum error value between FEM result and formula (6) is 7.2%.

2.3 Design Strategy with Finite Stiffness Loss

In the design of robot structure, it is of little significance to consider only the stiffness of the structure, and the deformation of the joint is the focus of the design. In the design of legged robot, the thigh structure can simplify the plate with a length of 500 mm, width of 70 mm and thickness of 40 mm. Motor and reducer is necessary to be placed inside the leg, the simple thin-wall structure is unable to provide support for equipment, therefore lattice filled plate is need. The design requires that the deflection value should be less than U_{lim}, which is 1 mm, under the condition of lateral 100 kg dead weight. If solid plate design is used, the displacement value is $U_{solid} = 0.51$ according to the formula 2, If lattice filled plate is adopted, when the rod diameter of lattice ϕ_1, and the displacement equals to U_{lim}. ϕ_1 can be calculated as follow,

$$\phi_1 = 2^{1.3}h_1 \sqrt{\left(\sqrt[3]{\frac{U_f}{U_{lim}}} - 1\right)\frac{1}{h_1 - h_0} + 1} \tag{7}$$

The above relation has two variables, which can only represent the relation between ϕ_1 and h_0. Using additive manufacturing, h_0 takes 1 mm as phenolic epoxy resin minimum thickness through AM method, the ϕ_1 is calculated as 1.7 mm.

Given the value of ϕ_1 and h_0, the area of longitudinal section is,

$$S(h_0) = l\left((h_1 - h_0)^{1.3} h_1 \sqrt{\left(\sqrt[3]{\frac{U_f}{U_{\lim}}} - 1 \right) \frac{1}{h_1 - h_0} + 1} + h_0 \right) \tag{8}$$

If, $h_1\left(\sqrt[3]{U_f / U_{\lim}} - 1 \right) = con$ and as known that $U_f/U_{\lim} < 1$, the derivative of the area formula is,

$$S'(h_0) = l\left(1 - \sqrt[1.3]{con\frac{1}{h_1 - h_0} + 1} - (h_1 - h_0)^{-\frac{1.3}{0.3}} \sqrt[1.3]{con\frac{1}{h_1 - h_0} + 1} \cdot con\frac{1}{(h_1 - h_0)^2} \right) \tag{9}$$

The value of derivative of area S is positive, that is, the area increases monotonically with h_0. Therefore, under the condition of the same mass, the smaller h_0 of the lattice packed plate is, the lighter the mass of the whole structure would be. In the design of lattice structure, the thickness value of the surface layer is selected according to the minimum thickness allowed by the processing method.

3 Stiffness of Lattice Filling Pipe

3.1 Relative Density Formula of BCC Lattice Structure

The longitudinal section of a lattice filled plate, is as same as longitudinal section of pipe filled with lattice. It is found in the experiment that the lattice filled pipe would also have a certain stiffness loss, similar to lattice filled plate. Take the BCC lattice structure as example, shown in Fig. 3(a) and (b), its lattice structure is shown in Fig. 3(b). BCC lattice structure is made up of 8 identical columnar structures, as shown in Fig. 3(c). The normal direction of plane B is (0, 1, 0) and that of plane C is (1, 1, 1), the Angle between the top and bottom of the cylinder is α. Each column structure is divided into six equal parts as shown in Fig. 3(d), and the volume of whole lattice cell is 96 times that of a single column, coordinate transformation is carried out with the column axis as the Z-axis. The normal vector of plane B after transformation is $(\sqrt{3}, 1, 2/\tan\alpha)$; given that the intercept of plane B and z-axis is $\sqrt{3}l_c/4$, then the equation of plane B is:

$$\sqrt{3}x + y + \frac{2}{\tan\alpha}\left(z - \frac{\sqrt{3}}{4}l_c \right) = 0 \tag{10}$$

Switch x and y to coordinate systems,

$$\begin{cases} x = r\sin\theta \\ y = r\cos\theta \end{cases} \tag{11}$$

The volume of lattice cell is,

$$V = 96 \int_0^R \int_0^{\frac{1}{3}\pi} \left(\frac{\sqrt{3}}{4}l_c - r(\sqrt{3}\sin\theta + \cos\theta)\frac{\tan\alpha}{2} \right) \cdot rdrd\theta$$

$$= 4\sqrt{3}\pi l_c R^2 - 16\sqrt{3}\tan\alpha \cdot R^3 \tag{12}$$

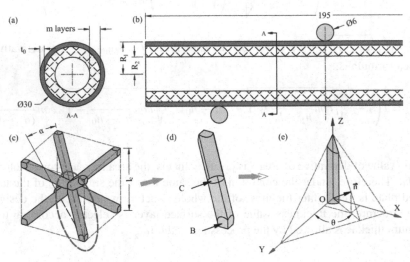

Fig. 3. Schematic diagram of a lattice filled pipe (a) cross section of pipe; (b) single lattice cell; (c) 1/8 column; (d) 1/96 volume of lattice cell

3.2 Deformation Characteristics of Lattice Filled Pipe During Bending

With the length of 200 mm and the diameter of $R_1 = 30$ mm, $R_0 = 0$ mm, the interior is lattice structure of $l_c = 3$ mm. The working condition of left end fixed and the right end applied 100 N vertical force, and orthogonal calculation of parameters t_0 and m is carried out. In Fig. 4(a), the dark and light blue curve are the vertical displacement of lattice pipe obtained by simulation and experiment, respectively. The green and orange curve is the pipe without lattice as same weight as lattice pipe, obtained by simulation and experiment, respectively. The relative density of 0.6 exceeded the accuracy of the processing equipment, so finite element simulation was used; for the sample with a relative density greater than 0.6, the length - diameter ratio of beam element is too small, which will distort the calculation, therefore, experiments are used. Obviously, solid bar has the worst stiffness, and lattice filled pipe have less stiffness than hollow pipe in the condition of same weight.

When the relative density is less than 0.06, the lattice filled pipe show better stiffness, which is different from the lattice filled plate. The lateral wall of the pipe enhances the stiffness, and the lattice filled pipe provides additional support around the wall. The equivalent stress distribution of lattice filled pipe is very even: with the support of lattice, the red area receives uniform tensile stress, while the hollow pipe receives more concentrated stress, as shown in Fig. 4(b) and (c).

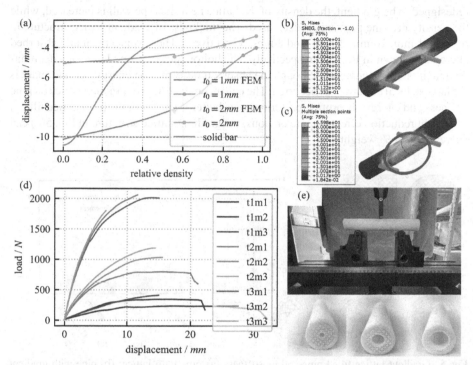

Fig. 4. Stiffness of lattice filled pipe and distribution of Mises stress (a) Stiffness of filled pipe, solid bar and hollow pipe; (b) Mises stress of hollow pipe; (c) Mises stress of lattice filled pipe; (d) displacement – load curve in 3 – points bending experiment; (e) experiment equipment of 3 – point bending

To prove the above inference, three-point bending tests with t_0 of 1 mm, 2 mm and 3 mm, layer number m from 1 to 3 were adopted, as shown in Fig. 4(e). The names of curves are in rule of thickness of wall and layer number. The stiffness of lattice with 2 layers is significantly enhanced than that of the 1 layer, while the additional 3rd layer has little influence on the stiffness, as shown in Fig. 4(d).

Reducing the weight of the structure by filling lattice can coast stiffness decreased. In the study of stiffness of lattice filled pipe above, it can be seen that with the increase of stiffness, the absorbed deformation energy will increase, which is a mechanical characteristic of lattice structure. The stress near the wall of the pipe is greater than that of near the axis of pipe, and the lattice near the axis has less support effect on energy absorption. This result shows that the main area of energy absorption is the near-wall lattice area. In the development of robot products, the energy absorption effect can be enhanced by adding lattice structures in the near-wall area to the parts that mainly play the role of buffer.

In view of this conclusion, it can be known that the lattice near the pipe axis has little effect on stiffness and energy absorption, so internal lattice form was redesigned as shown in Fig. 5. In order to further lightweight the product, the lattice type should be redesigned to be gradient, the density of the lattice near the pipe wall is increased, while the density near the pipe axis is decreased. The thickness of gradient lattice structure in pipe is 11 mm, 10 mm, 9 mm, and 8 mm, respectively. The displacement and absorbed energy are shown in Fig. 5(f) respectively. The hollow pipe with no lattice inside, it has the maximal displacement. Although the absorbed deformation energy per unit mass is the largest, local collapse has occurred. The enhancement effect of gradient lattice on pipe stiffness and energy absorption performance is better than that of uniform lattice filling, its weight reduction effect is quite obvious, the gradient lattice structure in Fig. 5(e) can decreased a 36% weight.

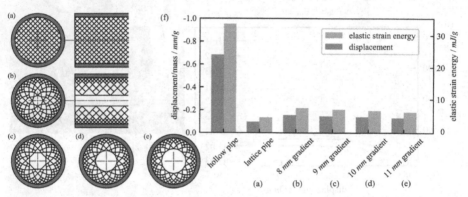

Fig. 5. Gradient lattice filled pipe and its stiffness (a) pipe with lattice; (b) pipe with gradient lattice of 11 mm; (c) pipe with gradient lattice of 9 mm; (d) pipe with gradient lattice of 7 mm; (e) pipe with gradient lattice of 5 mm

Not that the mass of each pipe in the Fig. 5 are not the same. Neither the displacement or deformation energy is meaningless. The simulation samples are in same outer size, but in different weight, the absorbed energy per unit mass and displacement are shown in Fig. 6. Therefore, the gradient lattice structure will have greater stiffness and absorb more energy at the same mass.

4 Conclusion

In this paper, lattice filling is carried out locally in common plate and pipe structures, and the stiffness of lattice structures under typical bending conditions is studied. The following conclusions are obtained. It is found that lattice filling can significantly reduce product weight and improve energy absorption effect at the cost of certain stiffness. Moreover, lattice can be used to disperse stress concentration, which is of great significance in product design.

(1) The lattice structure in the plate can reduce the weight at the cost of reducing the stiffness. The lattice filled plate is equivalent to a solid plate with the same stiffness. The formula for calculating the equivalent thickness and the stiffness of lattice filled plate is formula is proposed with maximum error is 7.2%

(2) Taking BCC lattice structure as target, the relative density calculation formula is derived. On this basis, the stiffness and energy absorption performance of the lattice packed pipe under load conditions are studied. It is pointed out that the lattice still reduces the weight at the cost of reducing the stiffness, but the stiffness reduction is not large because the pipe's side wall supports the stiffness more obviously.

(3) Through experiments and simulations, it is found that the near-wall lattice of the lattice filled tube has a greater contribution to the stiffness and energy absorption performance, while the biaxial lattice has a lesser influence. On this basis, the design idea of the gradient lattice packed tube is proposed. Through the research, it is found that the stiffness and energy absorption effect of the gradient lattice packed tube per unit mass is better than that of the uniform lattice packed tube.

References

1. Mohsen, A.: The rise of 3-D printing: the advantages of additive manufacturing over traditional manufacturing. Bus. Horiz. **60**, 677–688 (2017)
2. Sai, W., Xianlei, H., et al.: Design and experiment of V-shaped variable thickness rolling for rolled profiled strips. J. Mark. Res. **15**, 4381–4396 (2021)
3. Ole, S.: A 99 line topology optimization code written in Matlab. Struct. Multidisc. Optim. **21**, 120–127 (2001)
4. Janos, P., Ajit, P.: Review on design and structural optimisation in additive manufacturing: towards next-generation lightweight structures. Mater. Des. **183**, 108164 (2019)
5. Enrique, A., Daniel, B., et al.: Design of metallic bone by additive manufacturing. Scripta Mater. **164**, 110–114 (2019)
6. Jun, W., Niels, A.: Infill optimization for additive manufacturing - approaching bone-like porous structures. IEEE Trans. Visual Comput. Graph. **24**(2), 1127–1140 (2018)
7. Corrado, D.P., Giovanna, A.N.: 3D-printed biomimetic artificial muscles using soft actuators that contract and elongate. Sci. Robot. **7**(68), 1–8 (2022)
8. Boning, Y., Yuming, L.: Effective compressive elastic behavior of rhombic dodecahedron structure with and without border constraints. Compos. Struct. **259**, 113500 (2021)
9. Boning, Y., Yuming, L.: An analytical method to calculate effective elastic properties of mapped rhombic dodecahedron structures fabricated with electron beam melting. Mater. Today Commun. **32**, 103993 (2022)
10. Sabah, P., Afshin, Z.: Effect of geometrical parameters on the flexural properties of sandwich structures with 3D-printed honeycomb core and E-glass/ epoxy face-sheets. Structures **33**, 2724–2738 (2021)
11. Huang, Y., Xue, X., et al.: Effect of cross-sectional shape of struts on the mechanical properties of aluminium based pyramidal lattice structures. Mater. Lett. **202**, 53–56 (2017)

Analytical Backlash Model for 3K-type Planetary Gear Train with Flexure-Based Anti-backlash Carrier

Qinghao Du[1,2,3], Tuopu Zhang[1,2,3], Guilin Yang[1,2,3(✉)], Chin-Yin Chen[1,3], Weijun Wang[1,3], and Chi Zhang[1,3]

[1] Ningbo Institute of Materials Technology and Engineering, CAS, Ningbo, China
{duqinghao,zhangtuopu,glyang,chenchinyin,wangweijun,zhangchi}@nimte.ac.cn
[2] University of Chinese Academy of Sciences, Beijing, China
[3] Zhejiang Key Laboratory of Robotics and Intelligent Manufacturing Equipment Technology, Ningbo, China

Abstract. The 3K-type Planetary Gear Train (PGT) with a high reduction ratio and high backdrivability is suitable for enhancing the human-robot interaction performance of collaborative robots. However, the low accuracy of 3K-type PGT is an urgent problem. The backlash analysis of the 3K-type PGT is critical to evaluate its transmission accuracy. To calculate the backlash of 3K-type PGT directly based on the design parameters, an analytical backlash model is established based on an equivalent pinion-rack model. Moreover, the analytical backlash model is modified further for a novel 3K-type PGT with a flexure-based anti-backlash carrier to analyze the effects of the opening angle of the flexure-based carrier on the backlash. Through the simulations and experiments on the prototypes, the effectiveness and accuracy of the established analytical backlash model are verified.

Keywords: 3K-type planetary gear train · Flexure-based anti-backlash carrier · Analytical backlash model · Collaborative robots

1 Introduction

The 3K-type Planetary Gear Train (PGT) is a popular candidate reducer in robot joint actuators due to its high reduction ratio, low backdrive torque, and high bidirectional transmission efficiencies, especially in collaborative robots and rehabilitative robots with high requirements of Human-Robot Interaction (HRI) performance [1–3]. Many efforts were made on the optimization design method aiming to improve transmission efficiency of 3K-type PGT [4–6], but its low transmission accuracy still is a bottleneck for applications on robots, which is mainly caused by the significant backlash [7]. As such, the backlash analysis for 3K-type PGT is a critical issue. In the classical method, the backlash of the 3K-type PGT is usually implicit in the dynamic model, which is difficult to calculate

© The Author(s), under exclusive license to Springer Nature Singapore Pte Ltd. 2023
H. Yang et al. (Eds.): ICIRA 2023, LNAI 14269, pp. 384–397, 2023.
https://doi.org/10.1007/978-981-99-6489-5_31

through the design parameters directly. Therefore, an analytical backlash model for 3K-type PGT is desired to evaluate the design scheme simply.

The modeling for backlash of a compound PGT is complex due to the compound motion of multiple gear pairs. Many literature researched the effects of manufacturing errors on lost motion behavior of the simple 2K-H-type PGT [8–10], but few literature analyzed the backlash of the PGT with compound configurations [11,12]. However, these literature were focused on the compound PGT with conventional structures. While in our previous work, a backlash reduction approach based on a tweezer-like carrier is proposed for the 3K-type PGT, and a flexure-based anti-backlash carrier is designed according to the approach. The backlash of the novel 3K-type PGT cannot be obtained by the previous models conveniently.

In this paper, to analyze the backlash of the novel 3K-type PGT with the flexure-based carrier, an equivalent Pinion-Rack Model (PRM) model is introduced for 3K-type PGT. The analytical backlash models for 3K-type PGTs with conventional structures and with the flexure-based anti-backlash carrier are both established based on the equivalent pinion-rack model. The simulations and experiments are conducted to validate the accuracy of the proposed models. These analytical backlash models can be references to the parameter design of both gears and the flexure-based anti-backlash carrier.

This paper is organized as follows, in Sect. 2, the equivalent pinion-rack model is introduced and the analytical backlash model is derived for the conventional 3K-type PGT. In Sect. 3, the backlash reduction approach and a flexure-based carrier is introduced, and the analytical backlash model for the 3K-type PGT with the novel carrier is given. Verification of two analytical models are conducted through simulations and experiments respectively in Sects. 4 and 5. And the paper are concluded in Sect. 6.

2   Backlash Analysis for Conventional 3K-type PGT

2.1   Equivalent Pinion-Rack Model of 3K-type PGT

The structure of a 3K-type PGT is shown in Fig. 1(a). It consists of two-level planetary gear trains. The reduction ratio of a 3K-type PGT can be acquired by the Willis equations that:

$$i_s^g = \frac{1 + z_r/z_s}{1 - z_r z_q/z_g z_p},\qquad(1)$$

where z_i, $(i \in \{s, p, q, r, g\})$ is the tooth number of gears, when $z_r z_q$ is close to $z_r z_q$, a high reduction ratio can be achieved. The gears constitute three types of gear pairs, i.e., the sp-pair, the rp-pair, and the gq-pair. To analyze the motion of the 3K-type PGT in the backlash zone, an equivalent pinion-rack model is introduced. As shown in Fig. 1, the center components including the sun gear, the fixed gear ring, and the output gear ring are equivalent to racks, the rotations of them are transformed into the translations of racks. While the dual planet gears are equivalent to pinions, the rotations of which are equivalent to the rotations of pinions relative to the carrier.

According to the definition of the equivalent PRM, the position coordinates of the sun gear x_s, the carrier x_c and the dual planetary gear θ_p^c in PRM are given by:

$$\begin{cases} x_s = \theta_s r_s \cos\alpha \\ x_c = \theta_c r_c \cos\alpha \\ \theta_p^c = \theta_p - \theta_c \end{cases} \qquad (2)$$

where $\theta_s, \theta_c, \theta_p$ are the angular coordinates of the sun gear, the carrier, and the dual planet gear, respectively, in the original model of PGT. r_s and α are the pitch circle radius and the pressure angle of the sun gear, respectively, and r_c is the working radius of the carrier, which is equal to the reference center distance of the gear pairs in PGT. Moreover, considering the backlashes of gear pairs, the clearances are introduced into the PRM model and are arranged between pinions and racks, i.e. e_{sp}, e_{rp} and e_{gq}.

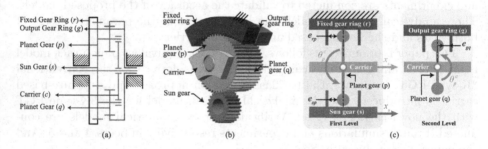

Fig. 1. Equivalent PRM of 3K-type PGT: (a) Diagram of 3K-type PGT structure; (b) Single-branch model of 3K-type PGT; (c) Scheme of equivalent PRM.

Based on the equivalent PRM, the motion of 3K-type PGT in the backlash zone is analyzed in the next subsection so as to establish the analytical backlash model.

2.2   Motion Analysis of 3K-type PGT in Backlash Zone

Considering the assumption that all clearances of three types of gear pairs are arranged symmetrically in the initial situation shown as Fig. 1(b), only one-direction motion is needed to be analyzed, and the translation direction of the equivalent sun rack is supposed to the right (sun gear rotates clockwise) in this subsection. According to the force analysis of 3K-type PGT in [4] that three gear pairs in a single branch can constitute one complete transmission chain, the motion to eliminate backlash is divided into three steps, which are shown in Fig. 2.

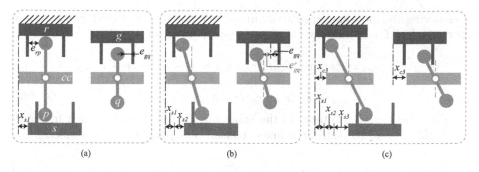

Fig. 2. Backlash elimination steps of 3K-type PGT: (a) Step 1; (b) Step 2; (c) Step 3.

Step 1. The sun rack generates a translational motion to eliminate the backlash of sp-pair e_{sp}, other components are static until the sun rack touches the planet gear p. Therefore, when the sun rack eliminates the backlash of sp-pair completely, the backlashes of other pairs are unchanged. The motion and residual backlash formulas for step 1 are as follows:

$$\begin{cases} x_{s1} = \theta_{s1} r_s \cos \alpha = e_{sp} \\ b_{sp1} = 0, \ b_{rp1} - e_{rp}, \ b_{gq1} = e_{gq} \end{cases} \tag{3}$$

where b_{spi}, b_{rpi} and b_{gqi} $(i = 1, 2, 3)$ are the residual backlashes of each gear pair respectively when the step i is finished. Note that all the subscript number of the variables in the following formulas denote the order of the step.

Step 2. The sun rack continues its translational motion to push the planet gear p, which produces a rotation to further eliminate the residual backlash of rp-pair b_{rp1}. Due to that the planet gears p and q are connected to each other, q rotates along with p and affects the backlash of gq-pair. According to the rotation direction of planet gear q, the residual backlash of gq-pair in step 2 increases. The carrier keeps static ($x_c = 0$) for that no load is applied to it in this step. The motion and residual backlash formulas for step 2 are given by:

$$\begin{cases} x_{s2} = \theta_{s2} r_s \cos \alpha - \theta_{p2}^c r_p \cos \alpha = b_{rp1} = e_{rp} \\ b_{sp2} = 0, \ b_{rp2} = 0 \\ b_{gq2} = e_{gq} + e_{gq}^r = e_{gq} + \theta_{p2}^c r_q \cos \alpha = e_{gq} + e_{rp} r_q / r_p \end{cases} \tag{4}$$

where r_p and r_q are the pitch circle radius of planet gear p and q, respectively.

Step 3. Due to that the gear ring of the first level r is fixed, more translational motion of the sun rack results in the linear motion of the carrier as well as the rotation of the planet gear q. Therefore, the compound motion of the carrier and the planet gear eliminates the residual backlash of gq-pair b_{gq2}. The linear motion of the carrier can be deduced by the reduction ratio relationship (5), and considering the motion of the carrier in the realistic model of PGT is a rotation, its equivalent linear motions on gq and sp-pair are given by (6).

$$x_{c3} = \theta_{c3} r_c \alpha = \theta_{s3}/i_s^c r_c \cos\alpha = \frac{z_s \theta_{s3}}{z_s + z_r} \cdot r_c \cos\alpha \tag{5}$$

$$x_{cgq} = x_{c3}(r_c + r_q)/r_c, \ x_{csp} = x_{c3} r_s/r_c \tag{6}$$

The planet gear q rotates in the same direction as step 2, which increases the backlash, and its equivalent linear motion on gq-pair can be obtained by:

$$x_{qgq} = -\frac{x_{s3} - x_{csp}}{r_p} \cdot r_q \cos\alpha \tag{7}$$

where $x_{csp} = x_{c3} r_s/r_c$ is the equivalent linear motion of carrier on sp-pair. When the planet gear q touches the output gear ring g, step 3 is finished. The motion and residual backlash formulas for step 3 are given by:

$$\begin{cases} x_{cgq} + x_{qgq} = b_{gq2} \\ b_{sp3} = 0, \ b_{rp3} = 0, \ b_{gq3} = 0 \end{cases} \tag{8}$$

Through these three steps, the backlashes of three gear pairs are eliminated completely, and the 3K-type PGT starts to transmit power. The total equivalent output backlash of 3K-type PGT can be given by:

$$\theta_{b,out} = 2(\theta_{s1} + \theta_{s2} + \theta_{s3})/i_s^g = \frac{2(x_{s1} + x_{s2} + x_{s3})}{i_s^g r_s \cos\alpha} \tag{9}$$

Substituting (3), (4), and (8) into (9), we obtain that:

$$\theta_{b,out} = \frac{2(e_{sp} + e_{rp})}{i_s^g r_s \cos\alpha} + \frac{2(e_{rp} r_q + e_{gq} r_p)(z_s + z_r)}{i_s^g [z_s(r_c + r_q)r_p - z_r r_s r_q] \cos\alpha} \tag{10}$$

For the standard gear, $r_i = m z_i/2$ $(i = s, p, q, r, g)$, where m is the modulus of gears. And according to the coaxial condition, $r_c = r_s + r_p = r_r - r_p = r_g - r_q$. Therefore, (10) for 3K-type PGT with standard gears is simplified as:

$$\theta_{b,out} = 2\frac{e_{sp}(r_r - r_g) + e_{rp}(r_g - r_s) + e_{gq}(r_r - r_s)}{r_g(r_r - r_s) \cos\alpha} \tag{11}$$

According to the dimension relationship of 3K-I-type PGT, $(r_r - r_s) > (r_g - r_s) \gg (r_r - r_g)$, which indicates that the backlashes of two inner gear pairs rp and gq have significant influences on the total backlash, while the backlash of sp-pair has a limited contribution.

3 Backlash Analysis for 3K-type PGT with Flexure-Based Carrier

3.1 Backlash Reduction Approach for 3K-type PGT

Considering the carrier of the 3K-type PGT is not loaded with torque, a backlash reduction approach based on a tweezer-like carrier is proposed in our previous work. The schematic diagram is shown in Fig. 3. The adjacent planet gears are repositioned back-to-back around central components so as to mesh with the sun gear and inner gear rings simultaneously along the opposite-side tooth surfaces under the pressure of spring. Whichever direction the sun gear rotates, at least one planet gear will mesh with the center gears without backlash. The adjacent planet gears are regarded as a pair of anti-backlash gears.

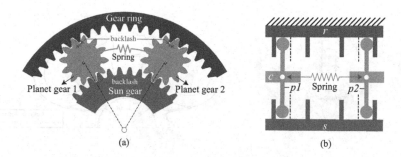

(a)   (b)

Fig. 3. Schematic diagram of the backlash reduction approach based on a tweezer-like carrier: (a) PGT model; (b) Equivalent PRM.

From the equivalent PRM shown in Fig. 3(b), the initial position of planet gears deviate from the central position of gear pairs (the black dot-dash line), which means the backlash of gear pair are rearranged asymmetrically in the initial situation.

3.2   Flexure-Based Anti-backlash Carrier for 3K-type PGT

To achieve the proposed approach, a flexure-based anti-backlash carrier is designed to ensure the compactness of the reducer. The arrangement of flexure-based carrier in the assembly of PGT and its structure are shown in Fig. 4.

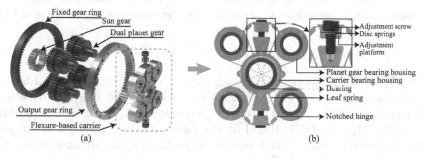

(a)   (b)

Fig. 4. Model of the proposed 3K-type PGT and flexure-based carrier: (a) Explosive view of the 3K-type PGT; (b) Sectional view of the flexure-based carrier.

The flexure-based carrier is installed at the output side of the reducer, which reduces the span of the two planet gears (p and q) and lowers the capsizing torque applying to the carrier. The flexure-based structure allows the carrier to deflect to push the adjacent planet gears back-to-back when the adjustment screws are tightened. Specifically, the deflection of the flexure-based carrier can be analyzed based on an equivalent five-bar mechanism, the notched hinges and the leaf springs are regarded as the revolute pairs, which are shown in Fig. 5.

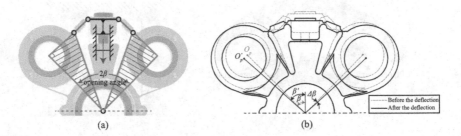

(a)   (b)

Fig. 5. Deflection analysis of flexure-based carrier: (a) Equivalent five-bar mechanism of carrier; (b) Deflection diagram of carrier.

In Fig. 5(b), $\Delta\beta = \beta' - \beta$ is the opening angle variation of the carrier, which is the critical parameter for establishing the backlash model. The relationship between the opening angle and the backlash is analyzed in the next subsection.

3.3   Analytical Backlash Model for 3K-type PGT with Flexure-Based Carrier

To simplify the model, the designed backlash of each gear pairs are supposed as an identical value e ($e_{sp} = e_{rp} = e_{gq} = e$), which is consistent with the practical design. As the equivalent PRM of the backlash reduction approach shown in Fig. 3(b), a stable structure is formed when both the external gear pairs and the inner gear pairs of adjacent planet gears mesh without backlash, which means the opening angle variation of carrier has the maximum value, which is obtained by:

$$\Delta\beta_{max} = \frac{e_{sp} + e_{gq}}{(r_s + r_r)} = \frac{e}{r_c} \tag{12}$$

According to the proposed backlash reduction approach, the initial backlash of each gear pairs is rearranged through repositioning the adjacent planet gears by the proposed flexure-based carrier. This repositioning changes the equilibrium state of the 3K-type PGT. Based on the force analysis, two equilibrium states of the dual planet gear 2 are observed depending on the opening angle of the carrier, which are shown in Fig. 6.

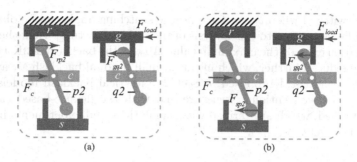

(a)   (b)

Fig. 6. Equilibrium states of the dual planet gear 2: (a) State 1; (b) State 2.

When the opening angle is small, the equilibrium state 1 is observed, the rp and gq-pairs of planet gear 2 are meshing, while the sp-pair is unengaged. In this situation, the backlash is derived based on the equivalent PRM proposed in Sect. 2, which is given by:

$$\theta_{b,out1} = \frac{2\theta_{b1}}{i_g^s \cos\alpha} \tag{13}$$

$$\theta_{b1} = \left[\frac{(r_s+r_r)(r_p+r_q)}{r_s(r_g r_p - r_r r_q)} + \frac{2}{r_s}\right]e - \frac{2(r_s+r_r)[r_g r_p(r_p-3r_q)+r_q(r_s r_p - r_s r_q + 2r_r r_q)]}{r_s(r_p-r_q)(r_g r_p - r_r r_q)}\Delta\beta \tag{14}$$

While when the opening angle is close to the maximum opening angle $\Delta\beta_{max}$, the equilibrium state 2 is observed, the sp and gq-pairs of planet gear 2 are meshing, the rp-pair is unengaged. Similarly, the backlash in this situation is derived as:

$$\theta_{b,out2} = \frac{2\theta_{b2}}{i_g^s \cos\alpha} \tag{15}$$

$$\theta_{b2} = \frac{2[r_g(r_p+3r_q)+r_p r_q - r_q^2]}{r_g r_s(r_p-r_q)}e - \frac{r_r(r_s+r_r)(r_p+3r_q)}{r_g r_s(r_p-r_q)}\Delta\beta \tag{16}$$

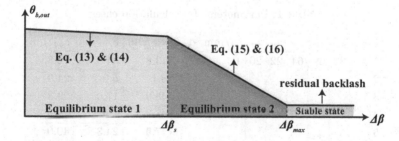

Fig. 7. Schematic diagram of the relationship between $\Delta\beta$ and the backlash of 3K-type PGT.

The relationship between $\Delta\beta$ and the backlash is depicted as Fig. 7. According to Fig. 7, Both (14) and (16) are linear equations, therefore, the two equilibrium states are switched when $\theta_{b1} = \theta_{b2}$, and the switching angle can be obtained as $\Delta\beta_s$. Besides, according to the analysis of the stable structure, when the opening angle variation exceeds the maximum value $\Delta\beta_{max}$, the backlash of 3K-type PGT can not be reduced further, which means a small residual backlash always exists.

Based on the PRM proposed in Sect. 2, analytical backlash models for 3K-type PGT with conventional structure and with the flexure-based carrier are both established, which are verified with simulations and experiments in Sects. 4 and 5, respectively.

4   Simulations

In the classical method, the dead zone models are introduced into the torsional dynamic model of each gear pair to obtain the total backlash. It is acquired from the stable transmission error when small loads T_{in} and $T_{out} = -i_s^g T_{in}$ are respectively applied on the input end and the output end of 3K-type PGT. Obviously, the backlash is implicit in the dynamic model and cannot be calculated directly. Employing the classical method as the reference, the proposed analytical backlash models of 3K-type PGT are verified in this section.

4.1   Verification of Analytical Backlash Model for Conventional 3K-type PGT

According to the analytical backlash model (11) proposed in Sect. 2.2, both dimension parameters of gears and the designed backlashes of each gear pairs affect the total backlash. Therefore, the total backlashes of nine cases are respectively calculated by the analytical backlash model and simulated by the classical method. These cases are divided into three sets, each of them having the same gear parameters and three sets of random designed backlashes. These parameters are listed in Table 1. The comparison results and the absolute errors are shown in Fig. 8.

Table 1. Parameters of 9 calculation cases.

Case	z_s	z_r	z_g	z_p	z_q	m/mm	$\alpha/°$	$e_{sp}/\mu m$	$e_{rp}/\mu m$	$e_{gq}/\mu m$
1	22	66	64	22	20	1	20	13.8	34.0	32.8
2								8.1	5.9	24.9
3								48.0	17.0	29.3
4	21	63	60	21	18			48.2	7.9	48.5
5								47.9	24.3	40.0
6								7.1	21.1	45.8
7	18	70	68	26	24			40.7	45.3	6.3
8								45.7	31.6	4.9
9								13.9	27.3	47.9

From the results, the calculated backlashes through the analytical model are very close to the simulated results from the classical method, the average relative error of these nine cases is only 0.14%, which means the analytical backlash model is accurate. The absolute errors of cases with the same gear parameters are constant from the Fig. 8(b), which are mainly because the elastic deformation of the gear teeth under the load of T_{in} are also considered in the transmission error from the classical method.

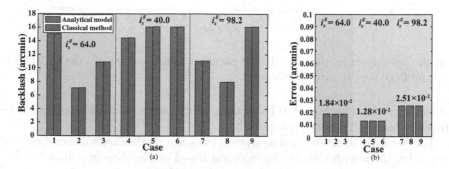

Fig. 8. Validation of analytical backlash model: (a) Results of the total backlashes from analytical model and classical method; (b) Absolute errors of two methods.

4.2 Verification of Backlash Model for 3K-type PGT with Flexure-Based Carrier

As mentioned in Sect. 3.3, in practice, the designed backlash of each gear pairs are usually set as an identical value e, and the proposed analytical backlash model for 3K-type PGT with flexure-based carrier mainly focuses on the relationship between the opening angle variation of carrier $\Delta\beta$ and the backlash $\theta_{b,out}$. A case is designed to validate the analytical backlash model, the gear parameters and designed backlash of this case are listed in Table 2. And the comparison results of the analytical backlash model and the classical method are shown in Fig. 9.

Table 2. Parameters of the designed case for 3K-type PGT with flexure-based carrier.

z_s	z_r	z_g	z_p	z_q	i_s^g	m/mm	α/°	e/μm
24	120	116	48	44	116	0.7	20	30

According to the results, the proposed analytical backlash model predicts the relationship between $\Delta\beta$ and $\theta_{b,out}$ accurately, the average relative error is 3.86%. The switching angle $\Delta\beta_s$ and the maximum opening angle variation $\Delta\beta_{max}$ are both observed by the two methods. From the results, the backlash of 3K-type PGT is reduced significantly with the increase of $\Delta\beta$, and the residual

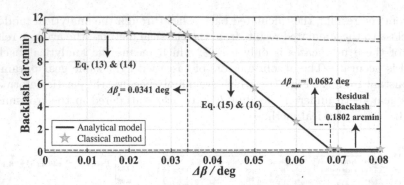

Fig. 9. Comparison results of analytical backlash model and the classical method for 3K-type PGT with flexure-based carrier.

backlash for this case is only 0.18 arcmin, which verifies the effectiveness of the proposed backlash reduction approach.

The accuracy of established analytical backlash models are validated through comparing them with the classical method based on the dynamic model considering the dead zone of gear pairs. Prototypes are fabricated and experiments are conducted in the next section to validate the analytical backlash models further.

5   Experiments

As shown in Fig. 10, three prototypes with various gear parameters are fabricated to validate the analytical backlash models for 3K-type PGT. Among them, prototype 2 is assembled with the flexure-based carrier to validate the effectiveness of the backlash reduction approach. The parameters and calculated backlashes $\theta_{b,out}$ through the analytical backlash model of these prototypes are listed in Table 3.

Table 3. Parameters and calculated backlash of the fabricated prototypes.

Prototype	z_s	z_r	z_g	z_p	z_q	i_s^g	m/mm	α/°	e/μm	$\theta_{b,out}$/arcmin
1	25	79	76	27	24	54.72	1	20	30	11.55
2	24	120	116	48	44	116	0.7	20	30	10.81
3	12	48	45	18	15	45	0.7	20	30	27.87

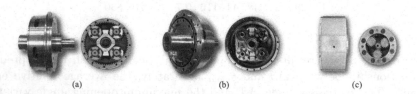

(a)   (b)   (c)

Fig. 10. Prototypes of 3K-type PGT for validation: (a) Prototype 1 with i_s^g of 54.72; (b) Prototype 2 with i_s^g of 116; (c) Prototype 3 with i_s^g of 45.

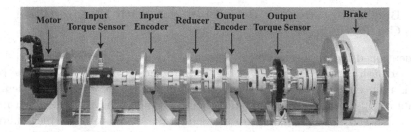

Fig. 11. Experimental bench for hysteresis curve measurement of PGT.

To obtain the backlashes of prototypes, the hysteresis curves are measured, and the experimental bench is shown in Fig. 11. The hysteresis curve is obtained by depicting the relationship between the input load and the quasi-static transmission error, which are respectively acquired by a torque sensor and dual encoders. The motor works in torque mode. To reduce the effects of elastic deformation and dynamic behavior, a torque with an small amplitude of 0.1Nm and with a slow period of 50 s is input to the PGT.

5.1 Backlash of Conventional 3K-type PGT Prototype

Hysteresis curves of three prototypes are measured, which are shown in Fig. 12. Note that the carrier of prototype 2 is not adjusted here, its opening angle variation $\Delta\beta$ is 0. The backlash of the three prototypes are 12.32 arcmin, 11.18 arcmin, and 29.94 arcmin, respectively. Compared with the calculated results listed in Table. 3, the relative errors are 6.25%, 3.31%, and 6.91%, respectively, which illustrates the proposed analytical backlash model is accurate. The errors are mainly caused by the manufacturing.

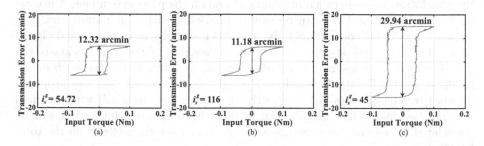

Fig. 12. Hysteresis curves of prototypes: (a) Prototype 1; (b) Prototype 2; (c) Prototype 3.

396   Q. Du et al.

5.2   Backlash of 3K-type PGT Prototype with Flexure-Based Carrier

As mentioned before, prototype 2 is assembled with the proposed flexure-based anti-backlash carrier. As shown in Fig. 13, after adjusting the carrier, the backlash is reduced significantly from 11.18 arcmin to 0.166 arcmin. The calculated results of this prototype by analytical backlash model have been shown in the Sect. 4.2 already. The relative error of residual backlash is 8.5%, which validates the effectiveness of the analytical backlash model for 3K-type PGT with the flexure-based carrier.

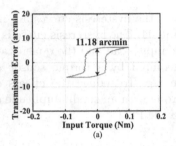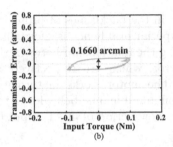

Fig. 13. Hysteresis curves of prototype 2: (a) Without adjustment; (b) With adjustment.

6   Conclusions

The analytical backlash models for the 3K-type PGT with conventional structure and with the flexure-based anti-backlash carrier are established in this paper based on an equivalent pinon-rack model. The two models are both validated by the simulation and experimental results. Based on the proposed models, the total backlash of 3K-type PGT can be simply predicted with gear parameters. The backlash model for conventional 3K-type PGT demonstrates that the designed backlashes of rp and gq-pairs are the main resources of the total backlash, the contribution of the designed backlash of sp-pair is limited. The backlash model for 3K-type PGT with flexure-based carrier demonstrates that the proposed backlash reduction approach is effective to reduce the backlash while a small residual backlash still exists. In the future, the manufacturing errors will be considered in the analytical backlash model to analyze their effects on the total backlash in detail.

Acknowledgment. This work was supported by the National Natural Science Foundation of China (Grant No. 92048201, No. U21A20121 and No. U20A20282) and the Zhejiang Province Key R&D Program (No. 2021C01067).

References

1. Brassitos, E., Jalili, N.: Design and development of a compact high-torque robotic actuator for space mechanisms. J. Mech. Robot. **9**(6), 061002 (2017)
2. Kanai, Y., Fujimoto, Y.: Torque-sensorless control for a powered exoskeleton using highly back-drivable actuators. In: IECON 2018–44th Annual Conference of the IEEE Industrial Electronics Society, pp. 5116–5121. IEEE (2018)
3. Liu, C., Liang, H., Ueda, N., Li, P., Fujimoto, Y., Zhu, C.: Functional evaluation of a force sensor-controlled upper-limb power-assisted exoskeleton with high backdrivability. Sensors **20**(21), 6379 (2020)
4. Matsuki, H., Nagano, K., Fujimoto, Y.: Bilateral drive gear-a highly backdrivable reduction gearbox for robotic actuators. IEEE/ASME Trans. Mechatron. **24**(6), 2661–2673 (2019)
5. Crispel, S., et al.: A novel wolfrom-based gearbox for robotic actuators. IEEE/ASME Trans. Mechatron. **26**(4), 1980–1988 (2021)
6. Xiao, R., Du, Q., Yang, G., Xiang, S., Zhang, C., Chen, C.Y.: MINLP-based design optimization of backdrivable 3k planetary gear drive for robot actuator. In: 2022 IEEE 17th Conference on Industrial Electronics and Applications (ICIEA), pp. 1316–1321. IEEE (2022)
7. Oba, S., Fujimoto, Y.: Hybrid 3k compound planetary reduction gearbox with a roller transmission mechanism. IEEE/ASME Trans. Mechatron. **27**(4), 2356–2366 (2021)
8. Butunoi, P.A., Stan, G., Ciofu, C., Ungureanu, A.L.: Research regarding backlash improvement for planetary speed reducers used in the actuation of industrial robots. Appl. Mech. Mater. **834**, 114–119 (2016)
9. Zhang, C., Dong, H., Dong, B., Wang, D.: A bi-directional drive model for lost motion behavior of planetary gear train. Mech. Mach. Theory **174**, 104885 (2022)
10. Guo, J., Bao, Z., Liu, C., Zhang, B.: Backlash analysis of gear transmission of parallel uniform planetary gear. J. Mech. Transm. **42**(7), 124–127 (2018)
11. Zhu, C., Xiao, N.: Backlash analysis of a new planetary gearing with internal gear ring. J. Chongqing Univ. **9**(3), 151–158 (2010)
12. Wang, Y., Yang, F.: Backlash analysis of compound planetary gear set in rotary actuators. In: IOP Conference Series: Materials Science and Engineering, vol. 470, p. 012022 (2019)

Design and Analysis of a Novel Membrane Deployable Solar Array Based on STACER Deployable Mechanism for CubeSats

Li Tingrui[1], Dong Kaijie[1](✉) (iD), Zhou Tianyu[1], and Li Duanling[2,3](✉) (iD)

[1] University of Science and Technology Beijing, Beijing 100083, China
dongkaijiedj@163.com
[2] Beijing University of Posts and Telecommunications, Beijing 100876, China
[3] Shaanxi University of Science and Technology, Xi'an 712000, China

Abstract. The CubeSat has witnessed rapid development and its application fields have continued to expand. To meet the demanding structural design and reliability requirements of satellite systems, as well as the growing power demands, this paper introduces a membrane deployable solar array for CubeSats based on STACER (MDSSC). Our study encompasses the design of a membrane folding method and an associated unfolding device. Additionally, an arc edge optimization method is employed to enhance the stress distribution along the membrane edge. Furthermore, a ground unfolding test was conducted to validate the suitability of the selected membrane folding method and the overall structural integrity.

Keywords: Deployable mechanism · solar array · Cube satellite · membrane structure

1 Introduction

CubeSat, characterized by its standardized size and specifications, represents a new generation of spacecraft. In comparison to traditional satellites, CubeSats possess compact dimensions, reduced weight, and operate at higher emission frequencies. They are frequently utilized in satellite launch experiments, with notable examples including the CUTE-1 test satellite from Japan, CanX-1 from Canada, and QuakeSat from the United States [1]. As the technology for CubeSats continues to advance, numerous universities and research institutions have embraced their potential for conducting scientific experiments, leading to a significant increase in satellite launches. Currently, CubeSats predominantly employ body-mounted solar arrays [2, 3], which are directly affixed to the satellite's surface. However, this method of integration suffers from inefficiency, resulting in limited energy generation. Consequently, it significantly constrains the orbital duration of CubeSats. Recognizing the advantages of lightweight construction and the potential for achieving large folding ratios, membranes have found wide application in various space structures, such as antennas, solar sails, solar arrays, and protective hoods. Furthermore, membranes exhibit the potential for widespread utilization in future spacecraft systems.

© The Author(s), under exclusive license to Springer Nature Singapore Pte Ltd. 2023
H. Yang et al. (Eds.): ICIRA 2023, LNAI 14269, pp. 398–410, 2023.
https://doi.org/10.1007/978-981-99-6489-5_32

In 2010, JAXA achieved a significant milestone by successfully launching the IKAROS solar sail and accomplishing on-orbit deployment. The membrane surface of the solar sail takes the form of a square with a side length of 14 m, which is composed of four triangular membranes, as depicted in Fig. 1(a) [4]. The deployment mechanism relies on the spin and centrifugal force generated by the four corner mass blocks to facilitate membrane deployment. The Planetary Society's LightSail-2 satellite, launched on June 25, 2019, made another notable advancement. As illustrated in Fig. 1(b), it achieved a deployment area of 32 square meters. This mission marked the first successful utilization of CubeSats for solar sail propulsion control [5].

Deployable Space Systems (DSS) has made significant progress in the development of a C-shaped composite rod-driven solar array known as ROSA, capable of generating 10 kW of power. Figure 1(c) illustrates the ROSA system [6].In the United States, ATK company has pioneered the development of regular polygon membrane solar arrays. These arrays are primarily driven by radial ribs, enabling flexible folding along the circumferential direction. The deployment surface is composed of triangular membrane units. Notably, in the 2008 Phoenix Mars exploration mission, the successful deployment of the UltraFlex solar arrays, with a diameter of 2.1 m, exemplified this technology, as depicted in Fig. 1(d) [7].

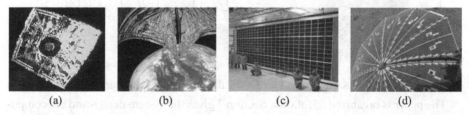

(a)   (b)   (c)   (d)

Fig. 1. Membrane structures: (a) JAXA's solar sail of IKAROS; (b) LightSail 2 solar sail; (c) ROSA solar arrays; (d) UltraFlex solar arrays.

As shown in Table 1, the current membrane deployable structure has a large volume and cannot satisfy the requirement of small-sized CubeSat. In 2019, Tokyo.

Table 1. Typical applications of space membrane structures

Type	Project Name	Research Unit	Time	Size (m)
Antenna	R3D2	DARPA	2019	Ø2.25
Solar sail	IKAROS	JAXA	2010	14 × 14
	LightSail-2	The Planetary Society	2019	5.66 × 5.66
Solar arrays	OrigamiSat-1	Tokyo Institute of Technology	2019	1 × 1
	ROSA	DSS	2010	\
Glare shield	JWST	NASA	2021	21.1 × 14.6

Institute of Technology designed a CubeSat OrigamiSat-1 (Fig. 2) based on CFRP [8], which successfully launched and verified the feasibility of the deployable membrane solar arrays. However, due to the insufficient stiffness of its boom, the membrane is prone to wrinkle, resulting in a decrease in the power generation efficiency of the solar arrays. Compared with CFPR, STACER, a one-dimensional linear deployment mechanism [9] as shown in Fig. 3, has the advantages of compact dimensions, large deployment length, self-driving and high stiffness. It has been applied to antennas, antenna support structures, linear actuators and sensor probes for many times. However, its application in deployable membrane solar arrays remains unexplored. Therefore, this paper presents a MDSSC, which can effectively improve the problem of low folding ratio and insufficient stiffness of deployable membrane solar arrays.

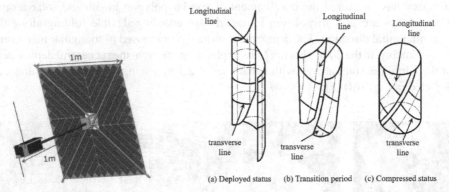

(a) Deployed status   (b) Transition period   (c) Compressed status

Fig. 2. OrigamiSat-1   **Fig. 3.** The deformation of lines marked on the steel strip

The paper is organized as follows. Section 2 gives the system design and the composition of important parts. The folding scheme design of the deployable thin deployable membrane solar arrays and the relationship between the crease length and the folding radius are introduced in Section 3. Subsequently, Section 4 outlines the force analysis after the membrane is unfolded. Section 5 presents the optimization scheme of the film arc edge. Section 6 introduces the prototype experiment. Finally, conclusions are drawn in Section 7.

2   Design of MDSSC

The Fig. 4 shows the components of MDSSC. Its stowed size is 100 mm × 100 mm × 130 mm, and the deployable membrane solar arrays is 900 mm × 900 mm.

As shown in Fig. 5, the platform load unit consists of a platform and a cover plate, with a space in between for accommodating electronic devices such as circuit boards and cameras. The baffle is connected to the side of the platform through a spring hinge, creating a wiring port outside the platform and a designated space suitable for other CubeSat interfaces. The control unit receives external instructions, and can control the working state of the release unit and the hold unit through motor rotation to realize the deployment of the deployable membrane solar arrays. In the release unit, the rolled column is connected to the STACER fixed in the retainer through the fiber rope. When the

STACER is compressed and folded in the retainer, it has a large strain energy, which is constrained by the hold unit. Following the release of the constraint as per instructions, the STACER extends to its designated length, thereby driving the expansion of the deployable membrane solar arrays. Hold unit includes hold block, base, hold plate. In the folding state, the hold block and the hold plate form an interlocking structure, restricting the movement of the baffle and the STACER. In the unfolded state, the magnetic force causes the hold block to move outward, releasing the constraints on the baffle and the STACER. This allows the baffle to move outward and the STACER to extend outward. The membrane employed is a 0.05mm-thick polyimide film, capable of being affixed to a flexible solar panel.

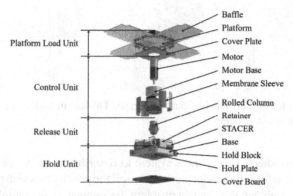

Fig. 4. Components of MDSSC

Figure 5 shows the working order of the deployment of the deployable membrane solar arrays.

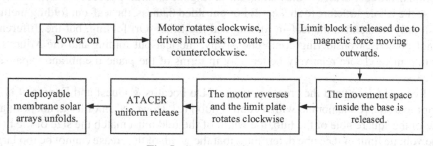

Fig. 5. System work process

3 Membrane Design

De Focatiis et al. have drawn inspiration from the unfolding of leaves and have proposed novel folding methods for membrane unfolded structures. These methods include the leaf-out folding, leaf-in folding, skew leaf-in folding, and Miura-Ori folding [10], as shown in Fig. 6. The leaf-out folding pattern is characterized by intersecting the midribs of multiple leaf units at one point, and the leaves point from the center to the outside. In contrast, the leaf-in folding method is to intersect the tips of multiple leaf units at one point, and the leaves face the center from the outside. In the leaf-in folding method, the angle of the broken line is changed to maintain the number of leaf units, and the skew leaf-in folding method can be obtained. As a special case of the skew leaf-in folding form, when the number of leaves n tends to infinity, a finite surface is generated, and the leaves are placed side by side along a straight line, which is the Miura-Ori folding model.

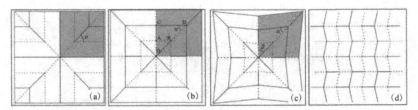

Fig. 6. Membrane folding: (a) The leaf-out folding; (b) The leaf-in folding; (c) The skew leaf-in folding; (d) The Miura-Ori folding

Xu et al. established a spring-mass system to describe the membrane material [11], proposed a criterion for self-contact pairs, and used the penalty function method to effectively solve the membrane self-contact problem. By comparing the membrane unfolding process of three folding methods: the leaf-out folding, the leaf-in folding and the Miura-Ori folding, the numerical simulation results show: (1) In terms of the unfolding stability, the unfolding process of the leaf-out folding method is relatively gentle, followed by the Miura-Ori folding method, while the leaf-in folding method has a large rigid body motion in the central area of the membrane during the unfolding process, which is easy to cause the whole structure to shake; (2) For unfolded flatness, the leaf-out folding method is slightly worse than the leaf-in folding and the Miura-Ori folding, but the difference is not obvious. Considering comprehensively, the leaf-out folding and the Miura-Ori folding methods are relatively better only in terms of the plane membrane expansion process.

Lee and Close used the crease pattern of De Focatiis & Guest and Furuya et al. to adapt to a square membrane with a central hub [12]. However, in order to adapt to any size of the square hole of the hub, the width of the fold must match the size of the hole. The volume limit of the cube determines that the width of the crease cannot be too large. Based on Lee's crease pattern, this paper improves the square vacancy and crease angle in the center of the pattern, and designs a membrane folding method that can be applied to any diameter hub, as shown in Fig. 7.

When the diameter of the hub wrapped by the membrane changes, the required two-dimensional plane diagram of the membrane structure can be designed according to the Eq. (1).

$$\frac{\pi D}{4} = 2S_1 \tan\theta - \left(L_2 - \frac{2S_1}{\cos\theta}\right)(\cos\theta - \sin\theta) \tag{1}$$

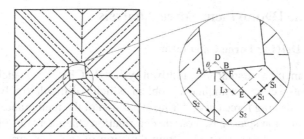

Fig. 7. Square membrane folding: (a) fold design; (b) details in inner ring of the membrane

where, D is the diameter of the hub, S_1 represents the width of the smaller folding area, S_2 represents the width of the larger folding area, L_1 represents the side length of the outer ring of the film, L_2 represents the side length of the inner ring of the membrane.

When the designer has determined the diameter of the hub D, the side length of the inner ring of the film L_2, and the width of the smaller folding area S_1, the angle θ can be solved by the Eq. (1). The values of S_2 and L_1 are determined by the diameter and height of the designed membrane after folding respectively, and have no significant effect on the membrane folding structure.

In order to make the membrane fit the hub better, this paper improved the equation proposed by Lee and Close, which describes the relationship between the crease length and wrapping radius of a single square membrane wound on the hub. The modified equation is specifically designed for the membrane configuration proposed in this paper, which exhibits k-fold rotational symmetry. In the case of a square design, the value of k is 4. For the first $1/k$ revolutions, the equation is rewritten as follows:

$$r\left(\frac{2\pi}{k}\right) = r(0) + h_+(0) + h_-\left(\xi\left(\frac{2\pi}{k}\right)\right) \tag{2}$$

and for the remainder of the pleat, equation is rewritten as

$$r(\theta) = r(\theta - \frac{2\pi}{k}) + h_+\left(\xi\left(\theta - \frac{2\pi}{k}\right)\right) + h_-(\xi(\theta)) \tag{3}$$

Figure 8 shows pleat width functions showing the thickness of the folded pleat on either side of the reference line and in total.

A numerical solver was implemented in MATLAB, utilizing a first-order Euler method with a fixed step size of 3.6°. Figure 9 illustrates the relationship between the package radius and the length along the crease. Crease patterns were computed for 0.2 mm thick parcel paper. The central pleats are 32.4 mm wide to form a central square hole with a width of 120 mm, and the remaining pleats are 65 mm wide. These dimensions were selected to provide a proof of concept for a deployable sheet that adheres to the 100 mm × 100 mm × 100 mm size constraint specified in the CubeSat standard, which is commonly employed for small spacecraft.

4 Membrane Deployment Force Analysis

4.1 STACER Driving Force Calculation

The deployable membrane solar array is driven by the STACER. The stretching process of STACER presents a complex nonlinear problem, which is difficult to solve statically. To ensure a suitable driving force curve during expansion of the membrane, Li constructed a deformation function space based on the deformation characteristics of the steel strip spiral tube. By identifying the main strain direction of the steel strip, the minimum deformation energy of the strip was calculated. Subsequently, the stretching force was determined using the principle of virtual work [13]. Figure 10 shows the mechanical parameters of STACER.

Fig. 8. Pleat width functions showing the thickness of the folded pleat on either side of the reference line and in total

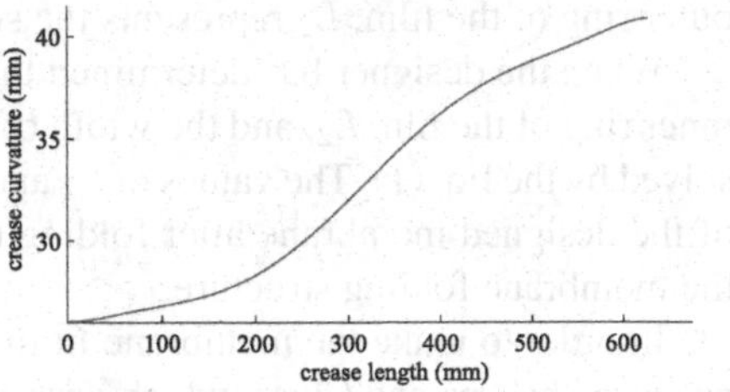

Fig. 9. The package radius to the length along the crease

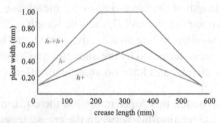

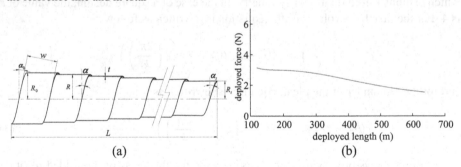

(a)   (b)

Fig. 10. STACER: (a) Mechanical Parameters [13]; (b) deployed force to length

Assuming that the STACER has zero initial stress when fully extended, and considering that it takes on a cylindrical shape when fully retracted, the parameters can be defined as follows: $\beta_0 = \pi/2 - \alpha$, $R_0 = R_1/\cos\beta_0$. The relationship between the driving force F of the STACER during the expansion process and the configuration parameters can be approximated using the following equation

$$F = \frac{Ewt^3}{24(1+\mu)r^3 \sin\beta_0} \cdot \left\{ \frac{\mu(1-\cos\beta_0)}{1-2\mu} + \left[\cos^2\psi_1 - \cos^2(\psi_1 + \beta_0)\cos\beta_0\right]^2 \right.$$
$$\left. + \left[\sin^2\psi_1 - \sin^2(\psi_1 + \beta_0)\cos\beta_0\right]^2 \right\} \tag{4}$$

where, w and t are the width and thickness of the STACER respectively. r is the radius corresponding to the end of the transition section, which is approximately equal to R_t. μ is the Poisson's ratio, and β is the spiral angle at the expansion. Figure 10 shows the relationship between the deployed force to deployed length of STACER.

According to Fig. 10(b), it can be seen that the STACER is fully extended in the transition section, and its stretching force tends to be stable.

4.2 Stress Calculation

The deployable membrane solar arrays differ from the ordinary planar membranes due to the presence of a square vacancy in the center. This vacancy serves not only as a positioning element for the membrane but also as a necessary design feature for folding. The presence of this vacancy can influence the propagation of stress within the membrane. Due to the unique structure of the regular quadrilateral in the deployable membrane solar arrays, the midpoint of each edge of the membrane and the midpoint of the regular quadrilateral lie on the same stress circle. This area represents the region with the lowest stress within the membrane. To study this stress distribution, the midpoint m of a straight edge of the quadrilateral membrane is selected as the focal point of the research, and the stress distribution is divided as illustrated in Fig. 11.

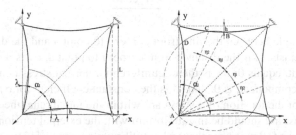

Fig. 11. Stress distribution of single-corner tensioned membrane: (a) stress arc in region I; (b) stress arc in region II.

The presence of a square vacancy in the center of the thin film solar wing provides an intermediate fixed boundary for the membrane. However, it is important to note that the tension at each point can still be transmitted to the midpoint m. The square vacancy primarily affects the stress distribution in its vicinity, while the overall stress transmission follows a similar pattern as that of a complete plane membrane. To evaluate the impact of the square vacancy, a finite element static analysis is conducted on two membrane structures with the same area. The tension applied is 20 N, and the stress distribution is shown in Fig. 12. It can be observed that the stress patterns in the two membranes are largely consistent. The stresses at the midpoints of the straight edges in both membranes are extracted for comparison. The equivalent stress of the complete planar film is 0.982 MPa, while the equivalent stress of the film with a square vacancy in the middle is 1.024 MPa. The resulting error is approximately 4.11%.

Indeed, the presence of a square vacancy in the middle of the thin film solar wing leads to a slight increase in stress along the straight edge of the membrane. However, the

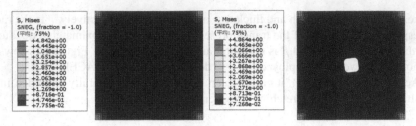

Fig. 12. Comparison of stress distribution between intact flat membrane and intermediate empty membrane

resulting error is quite small. Consequently, when analyzing the stress at the midpoint of the straight edge of the membrane arrays, it is acceptable to consider it as a complete plane membrane for practical purposes.

According to the superposition approach, the stress distribution in a corner tensioned rectangular membrane can be calculated by considering it as the superposition of its four single-corner tensioned states. Based on the solution provided by Timoshenko and Goodier [13] for a point force on a wedge tip with unit thickness, the stress at a random point a associated with corner i (i = 1,2,3,4) in polar coordinates can be described as

$$\sigma_r = \frac{k^* P \cos\theta}{2r_i} \tag{5}$$

where θ is the angle between the line from corner i to point a and the diagonal line on which corner i exists, r_i is the distance from corner i to point a, σ_r is the radial normal stress component, equals 0; σ_θ is the circumferential normal stress component, $\tau_{r\theta}$ is the shear stress component, is 0; and k^* is the constant coefficient for σ_r.

Regardless of the location of a stress arc within the membrane, the stress resultant on the same stress arc should be in equilibrium with the external tension load at corner 1. This leads to the following mechanical equilibrium equations [13]:

$$\begin{cases} 2\int_0^{\alpha_1} \dfrac{k^* P \cos^2\theta}{2r_1} r_1 d\theta = \dfrac{P}{2}, a \in \Omega_I \\ 2\int_0^{\eta_1} \dfrac{k^* P \cos^2\theta}{2r_1} r_1 d\theta + 2\int_{\eta_1+\eta_2}^{\alpha_1} \dfrac{k^* P \cos^2\theta}{2r_1} r_1 d\theta = \dfrac{P}{2}, a \in \Omega_{III} \end{cases} \tag{6}$$

where Ω_I, Ω_{II} represent region I, II, respectively. Solving equation gives the following expression of k^* in each region.

$$\begin{cases} k_1 = \dfrac{2}{\sin 2\alpha_1 + 2\alpha_1}, a \in \Omega_I \\ k_2 = \dfrac{2}{\sin 2\alpha_2 + \sin 2\eta_1 - \sin 2(\eta_1 + \eta_2) + 2\alpha_2 - 2\eta_2}, a \in \Omega_I \end{cases} \tag{7}$$

where

$$\eta_1 = \arctan\left(\frac{2(L-h)}{L}\right) - \frac{\pi}{4}, \alpha_2 = \frac{\pi}{4} - \arctan\left(\frac{2h}{L}\right) \tag{8}$$

η_2, α_1 can be obtained by solving the intersection point (x, y) of two circles O_2 and O_3

$$\eta_2 = \arctan\left(\frac{y_1}{x_1}\right) - \eta_1 - \frac{\pi}{4}, \alpha_1 = \arctan\left(\frac{y_2}{x_2}\right) - \frac{\pi}{4} \qquad (9)$$

The stress is converted from the polar coordinate system to the Cartesian coordinate system, where η represents the angle between the radial force and the x axis.

$$\begin{cases} \sigma_x = \sigma_r \cos^2 \lambda \\ \sigma_y = \sigma_r \sin^2 \lambda \\ \tau_{xy} = \sigma_r \sin \lambda \cos \lambda \end{cases} \qquad (10)$$

The stress is superposed in Cartesian coordinate system. According to the equation, the first principal stress and the second principal stress of the plane membrane can be determined. These values are then substituted into the equation to calculate the equivalent stress σ at each point of the film.

$$\begin{cases} \sigma_1 = \frac{\sigma_x + \sigma_y}{2} + \sqrt{\frac{(\sigma_x - \sigma_y)^2}{4} + \sigma_{xy}^2} \\ \sigma_2 = \frac{\sigma_x + \sigma_y}{2} - \sqrt{\frac{(\sigma_x - \sigma_y)^2}{4} + \sigma_{xy}^2} \end{cases} \qquad (11)$$

$$\overline{\sigma} = \sqrt{\frac{\sigma_1^2 + \sigma_2^2 + (\sigma_1 - \sigma_2)^2}{2}}$$

By substituting the values of $L = 900$ mm and $h = 0$ mm into the equations, we can calculate $k_1 = 0.7780$ and $k_2 = 0.9583$. Substituting these values back into the formula, we obtain $\sigma_1 = \sigma_4 = 0.0346$ MPa and $\sigma_2 = \sigma_3 = 0.0256$ MPa. Then, by transforming these stresses into the Cartesian coordinate system and performing stress superposition, we can obtain the stress at point m as $\sigma = 0.0687$ MPa. Comparing this theoretical value with the previous finite element simulation result, we find that the error is 5.79%. The finite element simulation takes into account the strain of the film, which may lead to slight inaccuracies in the simulation value. However, the error falls within an acceptable range and satisfies the calculation requirements.

5   Optimization Design of Membrane Arc Edge

The two adjacent triangular areas at the membrane point m are too small to paste the flexible solar panel, so the structure can be simplified here. The edge of the membrane is changed from a straight line to an arc edge [14], and the membrane folding is not affected. For the quarter of the membrane, we define the effective area as the area where the flexible solar panel is attached, as shown in the colored part of the Fig. 13. The section line part represents the reduced effective area due to the presence of the small triangular areas.

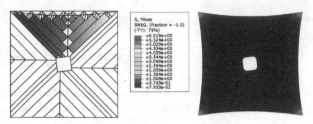

Fig. 13. Optimization design: (a) Effective area of membrane; (b) Membrane stress after arc edge optimization

After substituting the values of $L = 900$ mm and $h = 38$ mm into the Eqs. (6), (7), (8), (9), (10) and (11), the theoretical value of stress is 0.0793 Mpa, which is little different from the simulation results and within the acceptable range. After the arc edge optimization, the stress of the membrane is increased by 15.3%. Although the effective area is reduced by 11.6%, the membrane flatness is increased due to the stress increase, and the solar arrays power generation efficiency will also increase accordingly.

6 Prototype Experiment

Based on the preceding analysis, we have successfully designed the configuration and conducted arc edge optimization for the deployable membrane solar arrays. These design parameters were then implemented to construct a 1:1 test prototype. The unfoldment of MDSSC is shown in the Fig. 14. Under the stable connection of each system, the deployable membrane solar array is tested according to the flow chart, enabling systematic evaluation and verification of the system's performance.

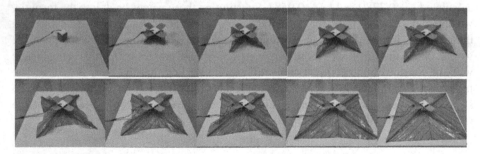

Fig. 14. Deployment test of deployable membrane on ground

Based on the test results, it is evident that the structure of the deployable membrane solar arrays is well-designed, exhibiting high membrane tension and successfully achieving the desired expansion. Notably, after the expansion, there were no signs of edge relaxation as confirmed by gently manipulating the membrane edge with a finger. This outcome highlights the significance of the arc edge design in facilitating stress propagation within the membrane and effectively mitigating edge stress. Consequently, these findings serve as compelling evidence for the reliability of the system.

7 Conclusion

In this paper, a design of deployable membrane solar arrays based on STACER for CubeSat is proposed. A deployable membrane solar arrays that can be wound on the hub is designed. The relationship between film thickness and crease curvature is analyzed, which provides a theoretical basis for membrane folding. The influence of the driving force of the STACER on the stress after the membrane is unfolded is analyzed, and the membrane structure is optimized. The ground experiment is successfully carried out to verify the feasibility of the scheme, which provides valuable experience and lessons for other research institutions or universities.

Acknowledgment. This study was co-supported by the National Natural Science Foundation of China (Grant No. 52175019), Beijing Natural Science Foundation (Grant No. 3212009, Grant No. L222038), Student Research Training Program of University of Science and Technology Beijing and Central Education and Teaching Reform Project.

References

1. Li, B.: Mechanical Characteristics Analysis of Tensioned Membrane Structure and Design of Triangular Prism Membrane Support Mast. Harbin Institute of Technology, Harbin China (2021). (in Chinese)
2. Ren, S., et al.: Overview of solar wing for CubeSat. Spacecraft Eng. **24**(2), 109–118 (2015). (in Chinese)
3. Hou, Y.: The Design and Application of Deployable Solar Array. Beijing University of Posts and Telecommunications, Beijing, China (2020). (in Chinese)
4. Sawada, H., et al.: Mission report on the solar power sail deployment demonstration of IKAROS. In: 52nd AIAA/ASME/ASCE/AHS/ASC Structures, Structural Dynamics and Materials Conference 19th AIAA/ASME/AHS Adaptive Structures Conference 13t. (2011)
5. Mansell, J., et al.: Orbit and attitude performance of the LightSail 2 solar sail spacecraft. In: AIAA Scitech 2020 Forum (2020)
6. Hoang, B., et al.: Commercialization of Deployable Space Systems' roll-out solar array (ROSA) technology for Space Systems Loral (SSL) solar arrays. In: IEEE Aerospace Conference 2016 (2016)
7. Murphy, D.: MegaFlex-the scaling potential of UltraFlex technology. In: 53rd AIAA/ASME/ASCE/AHS/ASC Structures, Structural Dynamics and Materials Conference 20th AIAA/ASME/AHS Adaptive Structures Conference 14th AIAA (2012)
8. Ikeya, K., et al.: Significance of 3U CubeSat OrigamiSat-1 for space demonstration of multifunctional deployable membrane. Acta Astronaut. **173**, 363–377 (2020)
9. Yu, C., et al.: A method for simulating STACER's deployment deformation. Chinese J. Theor. Appl. Mech. **48**(6), 1398–1405 (2016). (in Chinese)
10. De Focatiis, D.S.A., Guest, S.D.: Deployable membranes designed from folding tree leaves. Philos. Trans. Royal Soc. London Series A: Math. Phys. Eng. Sci. **360**(1791), 227–238 (2002)
11. Xu, Y., Guan, F.: Fold methods and deployment analysis of deployable membrane structure. Eng. Mech. **25**(5), 176–181 (2008)
12. Lee, N., Sigrid, C.: Curved pleat folding for smooth wrapping. Proc. Royal Soc. A: Math. Phys. Eng. Sci. **469**(2155), 20130152 (2013)
13. Li, B., et al.: Design and experiment of deployment mechanism for Mars subsurface radar. Chinese Space Sci. Technol. (2023)

14. Timoshenko, S.P., Goodier, J.N.: Theory of Elasticity, 3rd edn. McGraw-Hill, New York (1970)
15. Li, B., et al.: Stress Superposition Method and free vibration of corner tensioned rectangular thin membranes. Thin-Walled Struct. **159**, 107201 (2021)
16. Peng, T., et al.: Configuration design and optimization of deployable membrane sunshield for spacecraft. Chin. Space Sci. Technol. **43**(1), 129–138 (2023)

Graded Error Compensation Method for Heavy-Load Manipulators Based on Laser Tracking Measurement

Zhangwei Chen[1(✉)], Hongfei Zu[2], Xiang Zhang[3], Xuwen Chen[3], and Zhirong Wang[4]

[1] State Key Laboratory of Fluid Power and Mechatronic Systems, Zhejiang University, Hangzhou 310058, China
chenzw@zju.edu.cn
[2] School of Mechanical Engineering, Zhejiang Sci-Tech University, Hangzhou 310018, China
[3] Zhejiang Premax Co. Ltd, Ningbo 315048, China
[4] Testing, Standardization and Certification,
Changzhou Institute of Inspection, Changzhou 21 3000, China

Abstract. In order to meet the high positioning accuracy requirements of industrial application scenarios for manipulators, the motion accuracy of industrial manipulators is generally improved through error compensation. However, due to the presence of non-geometric errors such as friction and joint backlash, error compensation is usually a complex nonlinear problem. Therefore, the existing methods of improving the absolute positioning accuracy of manipulators through model parameter calibration are difficult to obtain good performance, especially for heavy-load manipulators. To solve the above problems, this manuscript proposes a graded error compensation method for heavy-load manipulators based on laser tracking measurement, which realizes the compensation of kinematics error and joint stiffness, and improves the positioning accuracy of the manipulator in the entire workspace. Firstly, the geometric parameters were modeled and compensated by combining the distance model and the Denavit-Hartenberg (DH) model. Then, joint stiffness errors were studied and compensated. Finally, experiments were conducted on a heavy-load manipulator to verify the feasibility and effectiveness of this method.

Keywords: Heavy-load Manipulators · DH Model · Error Compensation

1 Introduction

With the development of manipulator technology, industrial manipulators have been widely used in automotive assembly, 3C electronics, consumer entertainment, and other fields. However, due to its limited absolute positioning accuracy, most of the work is completed through Teach Pendant rather than offline programming [1, 2]. The deviation between the nominal kinematics model and the actual manipulator caused by machining errors, mechanical wear and other reasons greatly reduces the positioning accuracy of the manipulator. However, calibration can improve this issue by identifying a more accurate set of model parameters, thereby establishing a more accurate motion model for the manipulator.

© The Author(s), under exclusive license to Springer Nature Singapore Pte Ltd. 2023
H. Yang et al. (Eds.): ICIRA 2023, LNAI 14269, pp. 411–419, 2023.
https://doi.org/10.1007/978-981-99-6489-5_33

The calibration of industrial manipulators has always been a key research topic in both academia and industry, with the focus on modeling the error sources of manipulators [3, 4]. Errors can be mainly divided into geometric errors such as connecting rod length and non-geometric errors such as gear backlash. Previous studies have mostly focused on compensating for geometric errors, while neglecting non-geometric errors. However, non-geometric errors also play a crucial role in the positioning accuracy of the manipulator, accounting for approximately 8% to 10% of the total error. Judd et al. conducted experimental research on various error sources, such as geometric error, gear error, servo error, thermal variation error, etc., and proposed a method of adding a uniform matrix at the end of the manipulator to improve the accuracy of the manipulator [5]. Tan et al. proposed a method to describe the relationship between joint readings and position errors of manipulators in order to compensate for both geometric and non-geometric errors. The manipulator was calibrated using optimization methods such as genetic programming and artificial neural networks [6]. However, there are two issues with directly compensating for position using neural networks: (1) the model needs accurate training samples, but the training data obtained from the ideal inverse kinematics of the manipulator is inaccurate; (2) for heavy-load manipulators, the same set of spatial coordinates has different configurations, and the joint errors of different configurations vary greatly.

In response to the problem that the positioning accuracy of heavy-load is greatly affected by self-weight and load, this manuscript proposes a graded error compensation method based on laser tracking measurement. Firstly, the DH model is used to identify and compensate for the geometric errors of the entire workspace. After geometric error correction, the kinematics model will be more accurate. Then, the joint stiffness of the manipulator is modeled to compensate for errors caused by deformation of the special positioning joint. Finally, in order to verify the effectiveness and correctness of this method, comparative experiments were conducted based on a 6-axis industrial manipulator. Compared with traditional calibration methods, the calibration results of this method have better positioning accuracy.

2   Performance Measurement System of Industrial Manipulators

The experimental platform of this work is an industrial manipulator performance measurement system based on a laser tracker developed by Zhejiang University. The system mainly includes signal acquisition analyzer (MI-7208, ECON), laser tracker (VantageE, FARO), sensors, customized analysis software, etc., as shown in Fig. 1. The basic working principle of laser tracker is to determine the coordinates of the target by measuring two angles and a distance. These angles are measured by encoders installed on the vertex angle axis and azimuth axis, and the radial distance is measured by a fringe technology interferometer or absolute distance measuring instrument. Compared to the traditional measurement systems, this system possesses the following advantages:

(1) High measurement accuracy: the system measurement accuracy can reach 20 um.
(2) Large measurement range: the effective distance between measurement equipment and industrial manipulators can be as high as 80 m.

(3) Six-dimensional measurement. The system can simultaneously obtain the position and pose information of the manipulator, achieving six-dimensional measurement.

Fig. 1. Industrial Robot Performance Measurement System

3 Graded Error Compensation Method for Heavy-Load Manipulators Based on Laser Tracking Measurement

3.1 Kinematics Error Compensation Based on Distance Model and DH Model

The motion model of the manipulator in this manuscript is established based on the DH model [7], as shown in Fig. 2.

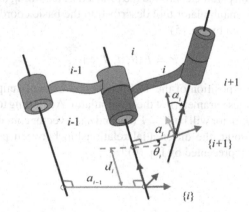

Fig. 2. DH Model Joint Coordinate System Conversion

The coordinate system is fixed on the joint axis of the manipulator. Two adjacent joint coordinate systems are connected by the homogeneous transformation matrix given by formula (1),

$$\begin{aligned}^{i-1}_iT &= trotz(\theta_i) * transal(a_i, 0.0)\\ &*transl(0, 0, d_i) * trotx(\alpha_i)\end{aligned} \qquad (1)$$

where $q = [\theta_i, a_i, d_i, \alpha_i]$ is the parameter vector, which represents the joint variable, connecting rod length, connecting rod offset, and connecting rod torsion angle, respectively. $Trot(*)$ is a (4x4) matrix of pure rotation transformation around the axis, and $Transl(*)$ is a (4x4) matrix of translation along the axis.

The position of the end effector of the manipulator can be obtained by multiplying the corresponding transformation matrix,

$$^0_{tool}T = ^{mea}_{base}T* \prod_{i=2}^{i=n} {}^{i-1}_iT *^n_{tool}T \qquad (2)$$

where represents the transformation matrix from the measurement coordinate system to the manipulator base coordinate system, including three translation transformations and three rotation transformations, as shown below,

$$\begin{aligned}^{mea}_{base}T &= transl(a_0, b_0, c_0) * trotx(\alpha_0)\\ &*troty(\beta_0) * trotz(\gamma_0)\end{aligned} \qquad (3)$$

where $^n_{tool}T$ represents the tool position transformation matrix related to the end effector of the manipulator,

$$^8_{tool}T = transl(a_{tool}, b_{tool}, c_{tool}) \qquad (4)$$

where $a_0, b_0, c_0, a_{tool}, b_{tool}, c_{tool}$ is the translation parameter along the joint axis and $\alpha_0, \beta_0, \gamma_0$ is the rotation parameter around the joint axis. According to the above formula, the center point of the manipulator tool described in the basic coordinate system of the manipulator can be given by Eq. (5),

$$P = F(\theta, a, d, \alpha) \qquad (5)$$

where P represents the position of the TCP at the end of the manipulator. (θ, a, d, α) represents the kinematics parameters of the manipulator. According to (5), the position of the manipulator end actuator will be $P = F(q)$, and q is a vector containing all kinematics parameters. For any joint, the differential relationship between position change and motion parameters is represented by Eq. (6) [8],

$$\delta_i T =_i T^a -_i T =_i T \Delta_i \tag{6}$$

The differential equation of kinematics parameters can be obtained through the derivative of transformation matrix, as shown in Eq. (7),

$$\delta_i T = \frac{\partial_i T}{\partial \theta_i} \delta\theta_i + \frac{\partial_i T}{\partial d_i} \delta d_i + \frac{\partial_i T}{\partial a_i} \delta a_i + \frac{\partial_i T}{\partial \alpha_i} \delta\alpha_i \tag{7}$$

TCP can also cause positional errors during the calibration process, and the differential equation for its transformation can be obtained from the following equation,

$$\delta_{tool} T = \frac{\partial_{tool} T}{\partial x_{tool}} \delta x_{tool} + \frac{\partial_{tool} T}{\partial y_{tool}} \delta y_{tool} + \frac{\partial_{tool} T}{\partial z_{tool}} \delta z_{tool} \tag{8}$$

According to the above formulas, the differential matrix from the base coordinate system to the tool coordinate system is as follows [9],

$$dp = B * dq \tag{9}$$

where $dp = d_{base}^{tool} T[1:3,4]$ is the position deviation vector, B is the Jacobian matrix represented by $dq = [\Delta\theta_1, \Delta a_1, \Delta d_1, \Delta\alpha_1, \Delta\theta_2, \Delta a_2, \Delta d_2, \Delta\alpha_2, \ldots, \Delta\theta_n, \Delta a_n, \Delta d_n, \Delta\alpha_n, \Delta x_{tool}, \Delta y_{tool}, \Delta z_{tool}]$. Formula (9) is a linearized equation including 35 unknown components. To solve this problem, it is only need to collect error information from 36 independent points.

3.2 Analysis and Modeling of Joint Deformation in Industrial Manipulators

The electromagnetic characteristic formula of a DC servo motor is [10]:

$$\tau_{output} = C_e \varphi\, i \tag{10}$$

where τ_{output} is the output torque value of the motor, C_e is the electromotive force constant, φ is the magnetic flux, and i is the joint current, which can be directly read from the controller of the manipulator. Taking the reducer as the research object, the torque relationship formula acting on each joint is shown in Eq. (11),

$$\tau_{input} = \tau_{gravity} + \tau_{friction} + \tau_{force} + \tau_{coriolis} + \tau_{centrifugal} \tag{11}$$

From the above equations, it can be seen that the input torque of each joint not only needs to offset the heavy torque caused by its own weight, but also needs to offset the friction torque between the joint transmission components and the external torque applied to the end of the manipulator. Due to the lack of movement of the industrial manipulator, the Coriolis centrifugal torque is negligible. The input torque of the reducer has the following relationship with the deformation,

$$\tau_{input} = k_i * \delta\theta_{ki} \tag{12}$$

where k_i is the stiffness coefficient of the first joint, $\delta\theta_{ki}$ is the joint angle error caused by the balance of different torques in the second joint. The stiffness matrix of the manipulator joint can be obtained as follows by ignoring the mutual influence between the stiffness of each joint,

$$K = \begin{bmatrix} k_1 & \cdots & 0 \\ \vdots & \ddots & \vdots \\ 0 & \cdots & k_n \end{bmatrix} \tag{13}$$

By substituting Eq. (12) into Eq. (10), the relationship between joint angle error and the current of each joint in the driver can be obtained

$$\delta\theta_{ki} = (C_e\varphi/k_i) * i \tag{14}$$

At this point, the flexibility matrix of the manipulator joint can be simplified as,

$$C = \begin{bmatrix} C_{e1}\varphi_1/k_1 & \cdots & 0 \\ \vdots & \ddots & \vdots \\ 0 & \cdots & C_{en}\varphi_n/k_n \end{bmatrix} \tag{15}$$

Finally, the joint angle deformation error can be obtained through the real-time read joint current value and joint angle value of the manipulator,

$$\theta_r = \theta_n + IC \tag{16}$$

where θ_n, θ_r are the joint angle vectors of the manipulator before and after joint deformation compensation (Fig. 3).

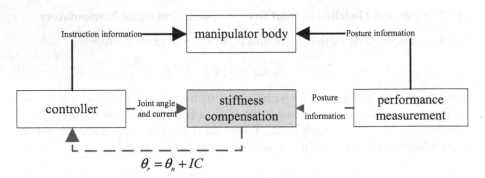

Fig. 3. Identification and compensation model of joint deformation of robots

4   Experimental Verification and Analysis

4.1   Acquisition of Error Data

The nominal parameters of kinematics parameters can be queried directly through the manual. This experiment mainly requires 50 points data for modeling DH model errors, which are measured once before and after DH parameter compensation.

Due to the vibration of the end effector of the industrial manipulator, the laser tracker will collect points and record coordinate values after the waiting period stabilizes. The three-dimensional position values required for modeling are tracked and measured by the laser tracker, and the corresponding joint values of each spatial point in the industrial manipulator can be read from the Teach Pendant. When obtaining data after DH parameter compensation, the driver current i of the manipulator at different positions is also required.

4.2 Experimental Results and Analysis

In order to prove the correctness and effectiveness of the method proposed in this manuscript, the graded error compensation method proposed in this manuscript and the traditional method were both used for the error compensation.

First, during the calibration process of the 6-axis heavy-load construction manipulator, the DH error model is used to calibrate the parameters of its motion model in the entire workspace, and the calibrated DH parameters are written back into the motion controller of the manipulator.

Then, the error grading compensation method is used to compensate for the same manipulator. In the first step, the distance-based DH model is used to compensate its kinematics parameters. The second step is to compensate for the angle error caused by joint deformation, as shown in Table 1 and Fig. 4.

Table 1. The error compensation results using the method proposed in this manuscript

	Average error (mm)	Minimum error (mm)	Maximum error (mm)
Before error compensation	6.48	2.49	12.33
After geometric error compensation	2.43	0.72	6.23
After joint deformation compensation	1.52	0.35	4.77

It can be seen that after geometric error and joint deformation error compensation, the average position error has been reduced from 6.48 mm to 1.52 mm, which is 14.04% higher than the traditional motion calibration method.

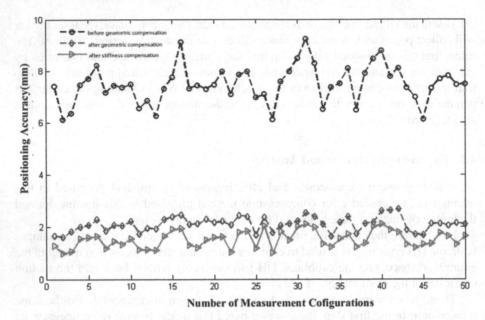

Fig. 4. Comparison of accuracy before and after error compensation by this method

5 Conclusion

In response to the problem that the positioning accuracy of heavy-load manipulators is greatly affected by self-weight and load, this manuscript proposed a graded compensation method for industrial manipulator error based on laser tracking measurement. Firstly, in the process of compensating for DH model errors, this manuscript introduced a distance model to reduce the errors introduced by coordinate system conversion during the modeling process. Then, a joint deformation error identification and compensation model was established. Finally, in order to verify the feasibility and effectiveness of the proposed method, calibration experiments were conducted on an industrial manipulator. The experimental results showed that the proposed method could improve the compensated accuracy by 14.04% compared with the traditional motion calibration method.

Acknowledgment. This work was supported by the "National Key R&D Program of China" (No.: 2022YFF0606003) and "Ningbo High tech Zone 2021 Major Science and Technology Special Project (Major Technological Innovation Project)" (No.: 2021DCX050012).

References

1. Zhao, S., Jia, X.: Research progress and trends in intelligent manufacturing and its core information equipment. Mechanical Science and Technology **36**(1), 16 (2017)
2. Wu, Y., Chen, J.: Research on the Development Strategies of China's Industrial Robot Industry 43–46 (2021)

3. Callegari, M., et al.: Industrial Robotics: Programming, Simulation and Applications 493–514 (2007)
4. Veitschegger, W.K., Wu, C.H.: Robot calibration and compensation. In: Robotics & Automation IEEE Journal of, pp. 643–656 (2016)
5. Judd, R.P., Knasinski, A.B.: A technique to calibrate industrial robots with experimental verification. IEEE Trans Robotics & Automation 6(1), 20–30 (1987)
6. Tan, Y., Sun, H., Jia, Q., et al.: New manipulator calibration method based on screw theory and distance error. J. Beijing Univ. Aeronau. Astronau. 32(9), 1104–1108 (2006)
7. Elatta, A.Y., Gen, L.P., Zhi, F.L., et al.: An overview of robot calibration. Info. Technol. J. 3(1), 74–78 (2004). https://doi.org/10.3923/itj.2004.74.78
8. Liu, Z., Chen, Y.: Robotics 24(5), 447–450 (2002)
9. Guiming, F., Wenjing, G., Tao, G., et al.: Calibration method of industrial robot kinematics parameters based on binocular vision and distance error model. Machine Tools and Hydraulics 49(15), 8 (2021)
10. Mao, C.: Research on motion calibration method of industrial serial manipulator. Zhejiang University (2020)

A Flexible Parallel Robotic Wrist Towards Transluminal Endoscopic Surgery

Jinpeng Diao[1], Chao Qian[1], Xiao Xiao[2], Xingguang Duan[1,3],
and Changsheng Li[1(✉)]

[1] School of Mechatronical Engineering, Beijing Institute of Technology,
Beijing 100081, China
lics@bit.edu.cn
[2] Yuanhua Robotics, Perception and AI Technologies Ltd., Shenzhen 518055, China
[3] Institute of Engineering Medicine, Beijing Institute of Technology,
Beijing 100081, China

Abstract. Transluminal endoscopic surgery has been widely used clinically for minimally invasive surgery (MIS). However, the size and dexterity of manipulators limit the development of this kind of surgical robot. To address this issue, we proposed a compact robotic wrist based on flexible parallel mechanisms with 4 degrees of freedom (DOFs), which is capable of dexterous manipulation in narrow cavity. The robotic wrist has an outer diameter of 4.5 mm with a 2.1 mm central tool channel. The kinematic model of the flexible parallel mechanism is established. The dexterity and coordination of the robotic wrist are demonstrated in terms of motion control in narrow and complex cavity, and pepper seed grasping.

Keywords: Surgical robot · Transluminal endoscopic surgery · Flexible parallel mechanism

1 Introduction

Minimally invasive surgery (MIS) is widely used clinically due to its advantages of smaller incisions, less bleeding, and faster recovery compared with open surgery [1–3]. As a MIS procedure, transluminal endoscopic surgeries such as endoscopy spinal and colonoscopy procedures have been a preferred option for surgeons and patients [4,5].

Transluminal endoscopic surgery relies on the integration of camera, light source, and tool channels within an endoscope, enabling surgeons to insert and maneuver surgical instruments through the tool channel for MIS operation [6].

This work was supported by the National Key Research and Development Program of China 2022YFB4703000, and the National Natural Science Foundation of China 62003045, and the Beijing Institute of Technology Research Fund Program for Young Scholars.

ⓒ The Author(s), under exclusive license to Springer Nature Singapore Pte Ltd. 2023
H. Yang et al. (Eds.): ICIRA 2023, LNAI 14269, pp. 420–430, 2023.
https://doi.org/10.1007/978-981-99-6489-5_34

However, most of the conventional surgical instruments suffer from the limitations of DOFs and flexibility, and the operating area is restricted [7,8]. With the development of surgical robots, robotic-assisted MIS has been widely studied [9–11]. The robotic wrist with smaller size and more DOF have become critical concerns in the field of transluminal endoscopic surgery.

Robotic wrists for transluminal endoscopic surgery can be divided into three types: tendon-driven mechanisms, continuum mechanisms, and parallel mechanisms. Depending on the particular application, these wrists should satisfy specific demands, including DOF, flexibility, and motion accuracy. Tendon-driven mechanisms [12–16] are popular choices in surgical robotics due to their ability to simplify manipulator design by enabling the actuation system to be placed at the remote end of the surgical workspace. However, the use of tendons also poses a significant challenge in terms of force transmission performance due to the friction force generated during actuation. Wang et al. presented a tendon-driven surgical drill [16] with an outer diameter of 4.5 mm and 3 DOFs to achieve dexterous operation in narrow cavity. Continuum mechanisms [17–22] consist of multiple DOFs that are distributed continuously, yet suffer from drawbacks such as low motion accuracy and small load capacity. Xu et al. presented a snake-like continuum mechanism [22] with an outer diameter of 4.2 mm and 3 DOFs, combined with error compensation to achieve precise movement. Parallel mechanisms [4,23–25] have features such as high accuracy and large load capacity, but it is challenging to achieve numerous DOFs with miniature size. Li et al. presented a flexible parallel mechanism [4] using NiTi rods instead of conventional rigid links to form an surgical arm with an outer diameter of 11mm and 5 DOFs. Incorporating flexible materials into the design of parallel mechanisms is an effective solution for simplifying configuration and achieving miniaturization.

In this paper, we proposed a compact and dexterous robotic wrist composed of a flexible parallel mechanism for transluminal endoscopic surgical robot. The contributions can be summarized as follows:

1) The robotic wrist is composed of 6 hyperelastic NiTi branch chains, which have 4 DOFs of motion under the size limit of 4.5mm outer diameter. Additionally, there is a 2.1mm tool channel in the middle of the robotic wrist. The hinge of the rigid mechanism is not required at the joint, which will greatly reduce the processing difficulty, and the flexibility of the mechanism itself provides a safety guarantee for the operation.

2) The kinematic model of the flexible mechanism is established. The motion function test of the prototype, the flexibility test of the narrow and complex cavity, and the pepper seed picking test under the simulated endoscope have been completed. Through the above tests, the flexibility and feasibility of the robotic wrist are verified.

This paper is organized as follows: Sect. 2 introduces the design of the robotic wrist, including spatial configuration and driving mode. Then the kinematic model is established as well as the workspace is analyzed. Section 3 demonstrates the flexibility and feasibility tests of the robotic wrist. The conclusions are summarized in Sect. 4.

2 Mechanical Design

2.1 Structure Design of the Robotic Wrist

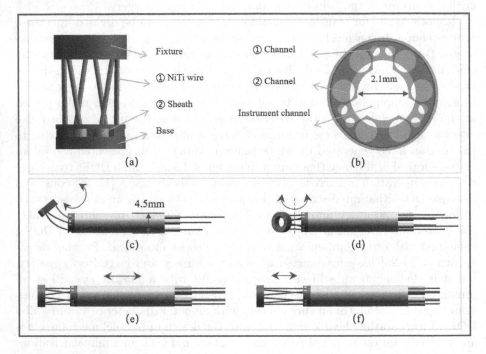

Fig. 1. Motion demonstration and configuration of a robotic wrist. (a) Spatial configuration; (b) The area of Channel distribution; (c)Yaw; (d) Pitch; (e) Overall axial displacement; (f) Local axial displacement.

This paper presents a novel robotic wrist with 4 DOFs, which enables it to perform surgical procedures within the human body via an instrument channel of an endoscopic platform. As shown in Fig. 1(a-b), the robotic wrist is a parallel mechanism composed of 6 hyperelastic branch chains. It has an outer diameter of 4.5 mm and an inner tool channel of 2.1 mm.

The adjacent NiTi rods are driven as a group, enabling 2 DOFs bending and 1 DOF axial movement. The length of the outer wrist sheath is adjustable to meet the requirements of different surgical channels. Its yaw and pitch angles, axial movement DOFs, and wrist length change DOF are depicted in Fig. 1(c-f).

This design overcomes the limitations of conventional rigid surgical instrument by removing redundant joints and replacing rigid links with NiTi rods. The mechanism provides sufficient strength and flexibility to resist deformation and damage caused by external forces. This mechanism demonstrates higher precision and load capacity compared to conventional flexible parallel mechanisms composed of 3 NiTi rods.

2.2   Kinematics Analysis

In the case of small deformations, the elastic rod deforms with constant curvature [26]. Moreover, due to the material properties of the elastic rod, the longitudinal length change is negligible. Table 1 is an overview of the symbols used in this section, and Fig. 2 is a schematic diagram of the kinematic model of the mechanism.

Table 1. The notation used in this section.

Order	Parameters	Description
1	$x_a O_a y_a$	Reference coordinate system
2	$x_b O_b y_b$	Moving coordinate system
3	α	Bending angles
4	β	Rotation angles
5	L_{ab}	Lengths of the imaginary center axes
6	R	Attitude matrix
7	P	Location matrix
8	T	Kinematic equations

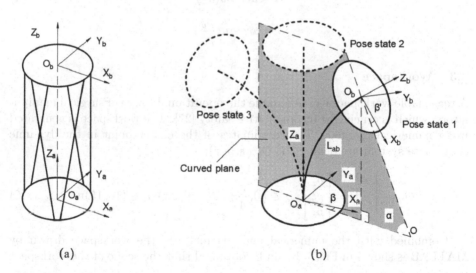

(a)   (b)

Fig. 2. Kinematic analysis of the robotic wrist. (a) Coordinate System; (b) Kinematic model parameters.

The coordinates of the end of the robotic wrist can be deduced from the geometric relationship by

$$O_b = \begin{bmatrix} x \\ y \\ z \end{bmatrix} = \begin{bmatrix} \cos\beta \cdot L/\alpha \cdot (1 - \cos\alpha) \\ \sin\beta \cdot L/\alpha \cdot (1 - \cos\alpha) \\ \sin\alpha \cdot L/\alpha \end{bmatrix} \tag{1}$$

The basic coordinate system $x_a O_a y_a$ undergoes 1 translation and 3 rotation transformations to obtain the moving coordinate system $x_b O_b y_b$, the homogeneous transformation matrix is T, and the rotation matrix is R.

$$R = \begin{bmatrix} c\alpha c^2\beta + s^2\beta & c\alpha c\beta s\beta - c\beta s\beta & s\alpha c\beta \\ c\alpha c\beta s\beta - c\beta s\beta & c\alpha s^2\beta + c^2\beta & s\alpha s\beta \\ -s\alpha c\beta & -s\alpha s\beta & c\alpha \end{bmatrix} \tag{2}$$

$$T = T_1 R_1 R_2 R_3 = \begin{bmatrix} R & P \\ 0 & 1 \end{bmatrix} = \begin{bmatrix} n_x & o_x & a_x & p_x \\ n_y & o_y & a_y & p_y \\ n_z & o_z & a_z & p_z \\ 0 & 0 & 0 & 1 \end{bmatrix} \tag{3}$$

The relationship between the joint angle α, β and the end pose is

$$\alpha = arccos(a_z) \tag{4}$$

$$\beta = arctan(\frac{p_y}{p_x}) \tag{5}$$

2.3   Workspace

A reasonable workspace can determine the operational range of surgical manipulators, which is crucial for intraoperative safety [27]. The workspace is generated using numerical methods. The coordinates of the center point in the dynamic coordinate system are denoted as O_b (x, y, z):

$$O_b = \begin{bmatrix} x \\ y \\ z \end{bmatrix} = \begin{bmatrix} p_x \\ p_y \\ p_z \end{bmatrix}, \alpha \in \left(0, \frac{\pi}{4}\right); \beta \in (0, 2\pi); L \in (10, 15)\text{mm} \tag{6}$$

Combined with the numerical analysis method, the workspace drawn by MATLAB is shown in Fig. 3. It can be obtained that the scope of the workspace is:

$$x \in (-5.59, 5.59); y \in (-5.59, 5.59); z \in (9, 15) \tag{7}$$

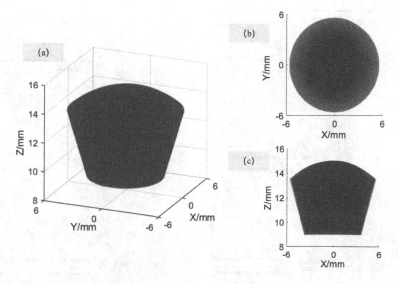

Fig. 3. Simulated workspace based on the kinematics of the robotic wrist. (a) Side view; (b) X-Y plane view; (c) X-Z plane view.

3   Experimental Evaluation

3.1   Mechanism Prototype

This test is set to demonstrate the configuration and kinematic performance of the robotic wrist. As shown in Fig. 4(a), the prototype is composed of NiTi rods, stainless steel outer casing, machined parts, and surgical forceps. Figure 4(b) shows the opening angle of the end surgical forceps. Figure 4(c-f) shows the 4 DOFs of the robotic wrist, with a maximum bending angle of 35°. The length of local and overall axial movement can be adjusted according to actual surgical needs. In this test, the length of local axial movement is longer than 15mm. The main parameters of the robot are shown in Table 2.

Table 2. The main parameters of the prototype.

Order	Parameters	Value
1	DOF	4
2	Maximum Diameter	4.5 mm
3	Diameter of the Surgical Tool Channel	2.1 mm
4	Maximal Bending Angle	35°
5	Minimum Length of the Wrist	1.5 mm
6	Maximum Length of the Wrist	>15 mm
7	NiTi Rod Diameter	0.3 mm

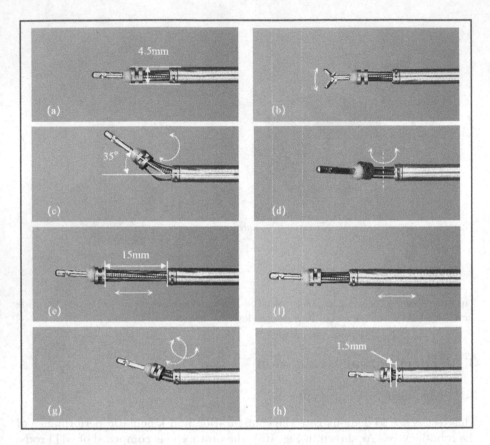

Fig. 4. The prototype of the robotic wrist and the effects of the primitive experiment.
(a) Prototype of the robotic wrist; (b) Surgical forceps opening and closing movement;
(c) Yaw motion of the wrist; (d) Pitch motion of the wrist; (e) Local axial movement of
the wrist; (f) Overall axial movement of the wrist; (g) Combined motion demonstration
in a small size scenario; (h) Minimum axial size of the wrist.

3.2   Performance Test

The proposed robotic wrist has the ability to move dexterously within narrow
and complex cavities. Flexibility and feasibility experiments are conducted to
verify the performances.

Flexibility Test. To verify the flexibility of the robotic wrist, the test shown
in Fig. 5 is proposed. Figure 5(a) shows the 3D-printed parts that simulate the
narrow and complex cavities of the human body. A large length is reserved
at the end of the robotic wrist to provide suitable length and flexibility for
entering the cavity. Figure 5(b-e) shows the process of robotic wrist entry. Since
the mechanism is sufficiently flexible, the end of the wrist is passively bent under
the constraints of the cavity during the entry process. Figure 5(f-h) demonstrates

the movement of the robotic wrist within the target area. The test results validate the flexibility of the robotic wrist.

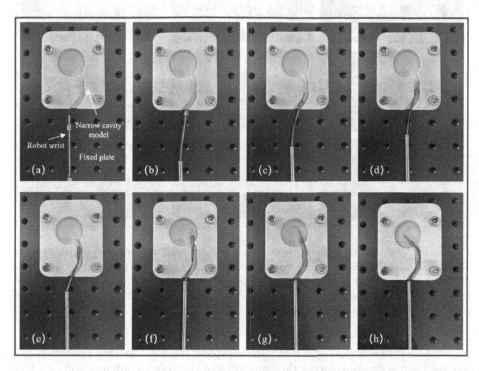

Fig. 5. Flexibility test in narrow and complex lumens. (a) The initial state before entering the complex narrow lumen. (b-e) The process of entering the cavity. (f-h) Movement of the robotic wrist in the target area.

Feasibility Test. The purpose of this experiment is to pick green pepper seeds under a simulated endoscope, and the operation process is shown in Fig. 6. The experimental setup, including a 3D-printed simulated endoscope platform with adjustable clamps and a miniature camera with a light source. A miniature camera with a light source was fixed at one end of the platform. The robotic wrist could enter the pepper through the tool channel, and complete the seed extraction operation under the view of the miniature camera. Figure 6(a-c) demonstrate the process of the robotic wrist picking pepper seeds from the outside.

The inside of the green pepper is a narrow cavity, which is similar to the environment of the cavity of the human body. The green pepper seeds are distributed on the inner wall of the cavity of the green pepper (Fig. 6(d)). Under the guidance of the endoscopic image, the operator manipulated the robotic wrist to the target area (Fig. 6(e-f)). The surgical forceps is controlled to collect the seeds (Fig. 6(g)). Subsequently, the harvested seeds were brought out to complete the operation (Fig. 6(h-i)). The results indicate that the robotic wrist can reach the

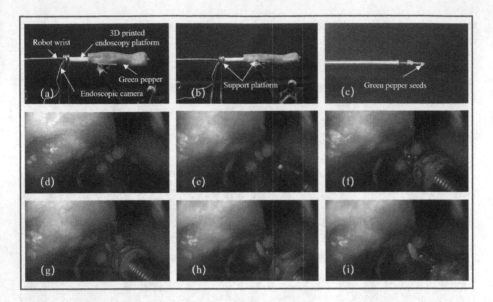

Fig. 6. Performance of picking green pepper seeds under a simulated endoscope. (a) The initial state of the robotic wrist before entering the green pepper; (b) The state after the robotic wrist picks out the green pepper seeds and exits; (c) The picked green pepper seeds; (d) The image captured inside the green pepper; (e-i) The process of picking seeds. (Color figure online)

target area under endoscopic view and complete the seed picking operation in a narrow cavity, demonstrating the feasibility of the robot configuration.

4   Conclusion

This paper presents a flexible robotic wrist specially designed for endoscopic surgery, which has a compact structure. The distal end of the wrist has 3 DOFs, in addition, the overall system has a translational DOF, enabling dexterous manipulation in confined space. Through numerical calculation and simulation using MATLAB software, the kinematic model is verified, and the workspace is obtained. Furthermore, the robotic wrist is validated in prototype experiments. The flexibility and feasibility of the robotic wrist structure are verified through the narrow and complex cavity movement and the pepper seed extraction test under the endoscope. However, in surgical robots, a more comprehensive driven system and kinematics model to achieve precise distal motion through master-slave control are required.

Future research will focus on exploring the characteristics of the flexible parallel mechanisms, designing efficient and reliable driven system, and establishing a complete kinematics model from the end pose to the drive system. This will enable the development of a more complete robotic surgery system, improving surgical precision and patient outcomes.

References

1. Alimoglu, O., et al.: Robot-assisted laparoscopic (RAL) procedures in general surgery. Int. J. Med. Robot. Comput. Assist. Surg. **12**(3), 427–430 (2016)
2. Chen, Y., et al.: The SHURUI system: a modular continuum surgical robotic platform for multiport, hybrid-port, and single-port procedures. IEEE/ASME Trans. Mechatron. **27**(5), 3186–3197 (2021)
3. Schoeggl, A., Maier, H., Saringer, W., Reddy, M., Matula, C.: Outcome after chronic sciatica as the only reason for lumbar microdiscectomy. Clin. Spine Surg. **15**(5), 415–419 (2002)
4. Li, C., Gu, X., Xiao, X., Lim, C.M., Ren, H.: A robotic system with multichannel flexible parallel manipulators for single port access surgery. IEEE Trans. Industr. Inf. **15**(3), 1678–1687 (2018)
5. Chen, Y., Zhang, S., Wu, Z., Yang, B., Luo, Q., Xu, K.: Review of surgical robotic systems for keyhole and endoscopic procedures: state of the art and perspectives. Front. Med. **14**, 382–403 (2020)
6. Khandge, A.V., Sharma, S.B., Kim, J.S.: The evolution of transforaminal endoscopic spine surgery. World Neurosurg. **145**, 643–656 (2021)
7. Li, C., et al.: A miniature manipulator with variable stiffness towards minimally invasive transluminal endoscopic surgery. IEEE Robot. Autom. Lett. **6**(3), 5541–5548 (2021)
8. Li, C., Gu, X., Xiao, X., Lim, C.M., Ren, H.: Flexible robot with variable stiffness in transoral surgery. IEEE/ASME Trans. Mechatron. **25**(1), 1–10 (2019)
9. Dupont, P.E., et al.: A decade retrospective of medical robotics research from 2010 to 2020. Sci. Robot. **6**(60), eabi8017 (2021)
10. Li, C., Gu, X., Xiao, X., Lim, C.M., Duan, X., Ren, H.: A flexible transoral robot towards Covid-19 swab sampling. Front. Robot. AI **8**, 612167 (2021)
11. Omisore, O.M., Han, S., Xiong, J., Li, H., Li, Z., Wang, L.: A review on flexible robotic systems for minimally invasive surgery. IEEE Trans. Syst. Man Cybern. Syst. **52**(1), 631–644 (2020)
12. Li, Z., Wu, L., Ren, H., Yu, H.: Kinematic comparison of surgical tendon-driven manipulators and concentric tube manipulators. Mech. Mach. Theory **107**, 148–165 (2017)
13. Hong, W., Schmitz, A., Bai, W., Berthet-Rayne, P., Xie, L., Yang, G.Z.: Design and compensation control of a flexible instrument for endoscopic surgery. In: 2020 IEEE International Conference on Robotics and Automation (ICRA), pp. 1860–1866. IEEE (2020)
14. Li, W., Shen, M., Gao, A., Yang, G.Z., Lo, B.: Towards a snake-like flexible robot for endoscopic submucosal dissection. IEEE Trans. Med. Robot. Bionics **3**(1), 257–260 (2020)
15. Thai, M.T., Phan, P.T., Hoang, T.T., Low, H., Lovell, N.H., Do, T.N.: Design, fabrication, and hysteresis modeling of soft microtubule artificial muscle (SMAM) for medical applications. IEEE Robot. Autom. Lett. **6**(3), 5089–5096 (2021)
16. Wang, Y., Zheng, H., Taylor, R.H., Au, K.W.S.: A handheld steerable surgical drill with a novel miniaturized articulated joint module for dexterous confined-space bone work. IEEE Trans. Biomed. Eng. **69**(9), 2926–2934 (2022)
17. Bergeles, C., Gosline, A.H., Vasilyev, N.V., Codd, P.J., Del Nido, P.J., Dupont, P.E.: Concentric tube robot design and optimization based on task and anatomical constraints. IEEE Trans. Robot. **31**(1), 67–84 (2015)

18. da Veiga, T.: Challenges of continuum robots in clinical context: a review. Progr. Biomed. Eng. **2**(3), 032003 (2020)
19. Hwang, M., Kwon, D.S.: Strong continuum manipulator for flexible endoscopic surgery. IEEE/ASME Trans. Mechatron. **24**(5), 2193–2203 (2019)
20. Gao, C., et al.: Fluoroscopic navigation for a surgical robotic system including a continuum manipulator. IEEE Trans. Biomed. Eng. **69**(1), 453–464 (2021)
21. Shang, J., et al.: An articulated universal joint based flexible access robot for minimally invasive surgery. In: 2011 IEEE International Conference on Robotics and Automation, pp. 1147–1152. IEEE (2011)
22. Xu, K., Simaan, N.: Actuation compensation for flexible surgical snake-like robots with redundant remote actuation. In: Proceedings 2006 IEEE International Conference on Robotics and Automation, 2006. ICRA 2006, pp. 4148–4154. IEEE (2006)
23. Li, C., King, N.K.K., Ren, H.: Preliminary development of a skull-mounted lightweight parallel robot toward minimally invasive neurosurgery. In: 2018 International Symposium on Medical Robotics (ISMR), pp. 1–6. IEEE (2018)
24. Gao, H., et al.: A miniature 3-DOF flexible parallel robotic wrist using niti wires for gastrointestinal endoscopic surgery. arXiv preprint arXiv:2207.04735 (2022)
25. Li, C., Gu, X., Xiao, X., Lim, C.M., Ren, H.: Cadaveric feasibility study of a teleoperated parallel continuum robot with variable stiffness for transoral surgery. Med. Biol. Eng. Comput. **58**, 2063–2069 (2020)
26. Xu, K., Simaan, N.: Analytic formulation for kinematics, statics, and shape restoration of multibackbone continuum robots via elliptic integrals. Mech. Robot. **107**, 58 (2010)
27. Du, H., et al.: Advancing computer-assisted orthopaedic surgery using a hexapod device for closed diaphyseal fracture reduction. Int. J. Med. Robot. Comput. Assist. Surg. **11**(3), 348–359 (2015)

Parameterizing the Dexterous Workspace of 6R Industrial Robots

Wenfei Wei[1], Guanghua Hu[1], Fengmin Chen[2], and Haifei Zhu[2(✉)]

[1] School of Mechanical and Automotive Engineering, South China University
of Technology, Guangzhou 510640, China
[2] School of Electromechanical Engineering, Guangdong University of Technology,
Guangzhou 510006, China
hfzhu@gdut.edu.cn

Abstract. To find the dexterous workspace of robot with regular shape, allowing for quicker and more accurate robot design and application, we proposed a method to parameterize the dexterous workspace of 6R industrial robots by the cross-sectional maximum ellipse. The cross-sectional boundary of the dexterous workspace was analyzed, the equations relating the maximum ellipse to the structural parameters were derived, and the parametrization of the dexterous workspace was realized via parameterizing the maximum ellipse. The effectiveness of the proposed method was verified through simulations and comparisons with the Iterative Regional Inflation by Semidefinite programming (IRIS) algorithm. The results exhibited that the proposed method achieved the same accuracy as the baseline IRIS algorithm with a relative error of less than 0.5%, but the consumption time was reduced by 91.3%. In addition, the significance of the proposed method was demonstrated by the application examples of the layout optimization and structural parameters determination of an industrial robot.

Keywords: Dexterous workspace · Darametrization · Maximum ellipse · Structural parameters

1 Introduction

Workspace analysis is necessary for tasks like trajectory planning and layout optimization for robots. The dexterous workspace is a crucial reference for guiding the design and execution of those tasks. The definition of the dexterous workspace varies depending on the type of robot and the tasks to be performed, and it essentially represents the area of the robot workspace that meets certain performance requirements [1].

Various scholars have suggested constructive approaches to determine a target workspace, including geometric method and discretization method. The representative of geometric method is [2], which determines the singularity-free workspace by geometric analysis. Monte Carlo methods and their improvements in discretization method are important for determining the boundaries of the target space. For example, Peidro et al. proposed a advanced Monte Carlo method

© The Author(s), under exclusive license to Springer Nature Singapore Pte Ltd. 2023
H. Yang et al. (Eds.): ICIRA 2023, LNAI 14269, pp. 431–442, 2023.
https://doi.org/10.1007/978-981-99-6489-5_35

based on Gaussian growth to find the workspace of the manipulator and obtain the boundary with high accuracy [3]. Zhi et al. processed the robot dexterous workspace by Monte Carlo method and polynomial fitting [4]. Others, such as branching and pruning method [5], can also determine the workspace very well. But the shape of the workspace determined by the above method is complex and irregular, making it difficult to easily apply the results to practical tasks.

Finding the target area with regular shape in the workspace is also the focus of scholars' research. Chablat et al. determined a largest cubic dextrous workspace [6]. Mousavi et al. obtained the maximum singularity-free ellipse of the 3-RPR planar parallel mechanism by convex optimization method [7]. Sirichotiyakul et al. used the sum-of-squares optimization technique to find the ellipse approximating the interior and exterior of the singularity-free space [8]. However, the workspace with regular shape determined by the optimization methods lacks the explicit mapping relationships with the influencing parameters, which is not conducive to further investigate the problem of optimizing structural parameters based on the demanded workspace.

This paper developed a new method to parameterize the dexterous workspace of 6R industrial robots based on cross-sectional maximum ellipse. Firstly, the problem of obtaining the dexterous workspace with regular shape determined by manipulability [9] was defined, and a method to parameterize this workspace by maximum ellipse was proposed. Then, the equations of the relationships between maximum ellipse and the structural parameters were derived to parameterize the dexterous workspace. To validate the proposed method, a series of simulations and comparisons were designed. Finally, the practical significance of the proposed method was demonstrated through application examples.

2   Problem Statement and Our Proposed Method

2.1   Problem Statement

This paper aims to determine the manipulability-based dexterous workspace D with regular shape of 6R industrial robots, and to establish clear correlations between the workspace characteristics and the structural parameters l. Meanwhile, the characteristics, including the center, shape and volume, are related only to the structural parameter l. The point x on the boundary B of the target workspace D satisfies the following equation:

$$B = f(l, x) \tag{1}$$

The specific expression of Eq.(1), which describes the relationships between the structural parameters l and the boundary B, is our main goal and the main problem. And what follows will be centered on this problem.

The position x of the end-effector of a common 6R industrial robot is determined by the first three joints [10]. Because of the symmetry of the workspace, we can study the only for the section with $\theta_1 = 0$. Thus the cross-sectional curve Q of boundary B is:

$$Q = g(l, x(\theta_2, \theta_3)) \tag{2}$$

The manipulability of a 6R industrial robot is given by [9]:

$$w = \sqrt{det(\boldsymbol{J}(\boldsymbol{\theta})\boldsymbol{J}^T(\boldsymbol{\theta}))} = |\boldsymbol{J}(\boldsymbol{\theta})| \tag{3}$$

where $\boldsymbol{J}(\boldsymbol{\theta})$ is the kinematic Jacobian matrix. The manipulability is independent of the first DoF [11] and can be expressed as:

$$w = w(\theta_2, \theta_3) \tag{4}$$

Combine Eqs.(2) and (4), and eliminate the variables θ_2 and θ_3 to obtain the equation:

$$\boldsymbol{Q} = g(\boldsymbol{l}, \boldsymbol{x}, w) \tag{5}$$

Generally speaking, the cross-sectional curve $\boldsymbol{Q}$ represented by Eq.(5) is complex and irregular, and needs to be replaced by a graph with regular shape to achieve our goal.

2.2 Our Proposed Method

To obtain the dexterous workspace with regular shape, ellipse is used to replace the cross-sectional curve $\boldsymbol{Q}$ of the boundary $\boldsymbol{B}$. We derive the mapping relationships between the characteristic parameters of the maximum inscribed ellipse of the curve $\boldsymbol{Q}$ and the structural parameters $\boldsymbol{l}$, using the theory of the inscribed ellipse. This enables us to solve the main problem described in Eq.(1). The method can be described specifically as follows:

Step1: Analyze the characteristics of the maximum inscribed ellipse $\boldsymbol{E}$ according to the properties of the curve $\boldsymbol{Q}$ like symmetry, where the equation of the ellipse is:

$$E = \{\boldsymbol{c} + \boldsymbol{A}\boldsymbol{u} : \boldsymbol{u} \in R^2, \|\boldsymbol{u}\| \le 1\} \tag{6}$$

where $\boldsymbol{A}$ and $\boldsymbol{c}$ are the parameter matrix and the center of the ellipse $\boldsymbol{E}$, respectively.

Step2: Determine the contact points $\boldsymbol{u}_i$ between the ellipse $\boldsymbol{E}$ and the curve $\boldsymbol{Q}$, combine Theorem 1 in [12] to build the association of the ellipse $\boldsymbol{E}$ with the structural parameters $\boldsymbol{l}$.

Theorem 1. *If an ellipsoid $\boldsymbol{E}$ contained in convex body $\boldsymbol{K}$ is the maximal inscribed ellipsoid of $\boldsymbol{K}$ if and only if there exists a multiplier vector $\boldsymbol{\lambda} = (\lambda_1, ..., \lambda_k) > 0, 0 \le k \le n(n+3)/2$, and contact points $\{\boldsymbol{u}_i\}_1^k$ such that:*

$$A^2 = \sum_{i=1}^{k} \lambda_i(\boldsymbol{u}_i - \boldsymbol{c})(\boldsymbol{u}_i - \boldsymbol{c})^T$$

$$0 = \sum_{i=1}^{k} \lambda_i(\boldsymbol{u}_i - \boldsymbol{c}) \tag{7}$$

$$n = \sum_{i=1}^{k} \lambda_i$$

$$\boldsymbol{u}_i \in \partial \boldsymbol{K} \cap \partial \boldsymbol{E}, i = 1, ..., k$$

Step3: Derive the expressions for the association of the parameter matrix A and the center c with the structural parameters l by the boundary conditions. The expressions are:

$$A = m(l, w)$$
$$c = n(l, w) \quad (8)$$

However, the Eq.(8) is often systems of equations with complex solution processes.

Equation(8) represents the explicit relationships between the cross-sectional maximum inscribed ellipse E of the boundary B and the structural parameters l, and is the key to realize parameterizing dexterous workspace D. By using Eq.(8) and rotation, we can accurately obtain the ring-shaped dexterous workspace and determine the structural parameters based on the workspace requirements.

3   Derivation

3.1   Find the Cross-Sectional Boundary

Without loss of generality, taking the 6-DoF ABB IRB120 manipulator as an example, and the structural parameters are d_1, a_2, a_3, d_4, as show in Fig. 1. The manipulability of the manipulator is:

$$w = |(a_2c_2 + a_3c_{23} + d_4s_{23})a_2(d_4c_3 - a_3s_3)| \quad (9)$$

On the xoz plane, the end-effector position (x, y, z) can be expressed as:

$$x = a_2c_2 + a_3c_{23} + d_4s_{23}$$
$$y = 0 \quad (10)$$
$$z = a_2s_2 + a_3s_{23} - d_4c_{23}$$

To simplify Eq.(9), let $sin\varphi_1 = d_4/\sqrt{d_4^2 + a_3^2}$, $cos\varphi_1 = a_3/\sqrt{d_4^2 + a_3^2}$, and combine Eqs.(9) and (10) to obtain the simplified equation as:

$$w = | - xa_2\sqrt{d_4^2 + a_3^2}sin(\theta_3 + \varphi_1)| \quad (11)$$

Considering the inverse kinematic equation $\binom{0}{1}\mathbf{T})^{-1}\binom{0}{6}\mathbf{T}) = \frac{1}{6}\mathbf{T}$, substitute the parameter φ_2 satisfying $sin\varphi_2 = a_3/\sqrt{d_4^2 + a_3^2}$, $cos\varphi_2 = d_4/\sqrt{d_4^2 + a_3^2}$ and Eq.(9) into inverse kinematic equation to obtain the equation for θ_3 as follows:

$$\sqrt{d_4^2 + a_3^2}sin(\theta_3 + \varphi_2) = \frac{(x^2 + (z - d_1)^2 - (a_2^2 + a_3^2 + d_4^2))}{2a_2} \quad (12)$$

Let $a = a_2^2$, $c = d_4^2 + a_3^2$, then combine Eqs.(11) and (12) to obtain the equation of the cross-sectional curve Q of the boundary. The equation is:

$$w^2 = \frac{1}{4}x^2(4ac - (x^2 + (z - d_1)^2 - (a + c))^2) \quad (13)$$

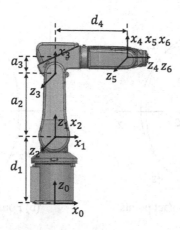

Fig. 1. ABB IRB120 manipulator

3.2 Calculate the Maximum Inscribed Ellipse

The curve $\boldsymbol{Q}$ represented by Eq.(13) is symmetric about $z = d_1$, so to simplify Eq.(13), let $d_1 = 0$ and $z = h(x)$, there is:

$$h(x) = \sqrt{a + c - x^2 + \frac{2}{x}\sqrt{acx^2 - w^2}} \qquad (14)$$

According to $0 \le k \le n(n+3)/2$ in Theorem 1, the number k of contact points between the curve $\boldsymbol{Q}$ and its inscribed ellipse is no more than 5. Since the curve $\boldsymbol{Q}$ is symmetric about $z = 0$ and continuous, the number k of the contact points is three or four, as shown in Fig. 2. We assume that Fig. 2(a) is correct, then the contact point $u_1(x_1, 0)$ satisfies:

$$\frac{1}{4}x_1^2(4ac - (x_1^2 - (a+c))^2) - w^2 = 0 \qquad (15)$$

And there exists a point $u_m(x_1, z_m)$ which is on the curve. Substitute $u_m(x_1, z_m)$ into Eq.(13) to get:

$$\frac{1}{4}x_1^2(4ac - (x_1^2 + z_m^2 - (a+c))^2) - w^2 = 0 \qquad (16)$$

Combine Eqs.(15) and (16) to obtain equation as:

$$z_m^2 = a + c - x_1^2 \qquad (17)$$

Obviously $a + c > x_1^2$, so the assumption holds that the curve $\boldsymbol{Q}$ has only three contact points with its maximum inscribed ellipse.

According to Fig. 2(a), it is known that the short axis of the ellipse is on the line $z = 0$ and the long axis is parallel to the z axis. Therefore, let the center $\boldsymbol{c}$ of the ellipse be $(x_c, 0)$ and the lengths of the semi-short and semi-long

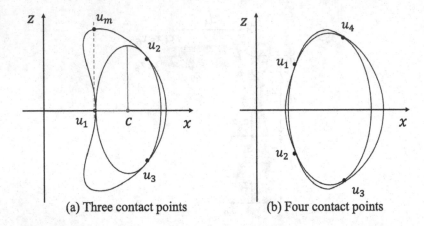

(a) Three contact points   (b) Four contact points

Fig. 2. Geometric relationship between the curve and the inscribed ellipse

axes be l_a, l_b, respectively. Substitute these parameters into Eq.(6) to obtain the expressions of the parameter matrix A and the center c:

$$A = \begin{bmatrix} l_a & 0 \\ 0 & l_b \end{bmatrix} \qquad c = \begin{bmatrix} x_c \\ 0 \end{bmatrix} \tag{18}$$

Substitute $u_1(x_1, 0)$, $u_2(x_2, h(x_2))$, $u_3(x_2, -h(x_2))$ into Eq.(7), and combine Eqs.(7) and (18) to obtain the following equation:

$$\begin{aligned}
x_c &= \frac{1}{3}(2x_2 + x_1) \\
l_a &= \frac{2}{3}(x_2 - x_1) \\
l_b &= \frac{2}{\sqrt{3}} h(x_2)
\end{aligned} \tag{19}$$

According to (19), the area of the inscribed ellipse is:

$$S = \frac{4\pi}{3\sqrt{3}}(x_2 - x_1)h(x_2) \tag{20}$$

The area of the ellipse is maximum when Eq.(20) obtains extreme value, that is, $\partial S/\partial x_2 = 0$. Expand the equation $\partial S/\partial x_2 = 0$ and simplify it to get:

$$a + c - x_2^2 + \frac{2}{x_2}\sqrt{acx_2^2 - w^2} + (x_2 - x_1)(-x_2 + \frac{w^2}{x_2^2\sqrt{acx_2^2 - w^2}}) = 0 \tag{21}$$

3.3   Parameterize the Dexterous Workspace

After the aforementioned derivation, it is evident that Eqs.(14), (15), (18), (19) and (21) are the explicit forms of Eq.(8), providing a satisfactory answer to the primary question posed in Eq.(1). Corresponding to the proposed method and Eq.(8), we apply Eqs.(14), (15) and (19) to obtain the contact points u_1, u_2 and u_3 of the ellipse E and curve Q, and then utilize Eqs.(18) and (19) to deduce the parameter matrix A and center c of the ellipse E based on structural parameters $a(a = a_2^2), c(c = a_3^2 + d_4^2)$, and the manipulability w. By rotating the ellipse E around the first joint axis, the ring-shaped dexterous workspace, which has the explicit relational equations with structural parameters, is obtained.

4   Simulations and Comparisons

4.1   Simulations

The structural parameters of ABB IRB120 are $d_1 = 0.30\,\mathrm{m}$, $a_2 = 0.27\,\mathrm{m}$, $a_3 = 0.07\,\mathrm{m}$, $d_4 = 0.34\,\mathrm{m}$, and the manipulability is $w = 0.0225$. Because the results are independent of d_1, so let $d_1 = 0.00\,\mathrm{m}$.

Firstly, to check the accuracy of the curve represented by Eq.(13), the manipulability on the xoz plane is introduced and compared with the curve determined by the manipulability w, as shown in Fig. 3(a). Then, the cross-sectional maximum inscribed ellipse is obtained shown in Fig. 3(b), where the ellipse parameters are $x_c = 0.4369\,\mathrm{m}$, $l_a = 0.1439\,\mathrm{m}$, $l_b = 0.3647\,\mathrm{m}$, and the parameter matrix A and the center c are:

$$A = \begin{bmatrix} 0.1439 & 0 \\ 0 & 0.3647 \end{bmatrix} \qquad c = \begin{bmatrix} 0.4369 \\ 0 \end{bmatrix} \qquad (22)$$

Finally, the ring-shaped dexterous workspace is obtained by rotating the ellipse around the first joint axis, as in Fig. 3(c), with the expression:

$$\frac{(\sqrt{x^2 + y^2} - 0.4369)^2}{0.1439^2} + \frac{z^2}{0.3647^2} = 1 \qquad (23)$$

4.2   Comparisons

In order to further verify the correctness of the proposed method, the IRIS algorithm [13], a method for computing large ellipsoidal regions of obstacle-free space, is used to obtain the target ellipse, and then the results are compared with those in Sect. 4.1. The steps for finding the target ellipse are as follows:

Step1: Rasterize the xoz plane in the x and z directions at 0.005 intervals and calculate the manipulability at the vertices.

Step2: Generate square virtual obstacles at the vertex where the manipulability is in the range of $[0.8w, 0.95w]$, where $w = 0.0225$, so as to construct an obstacle-free space surrounded by obstacles, as show in Fig. 4.

Step3: Apply the IRIS algorithm to find the local maximum ellipse after setting the initial point P_i, and take the center c_i of current maximum ellipse as next initial point P_{i+1}. The distance e between the two consecutive initial points is calculated as follows:

$$e = \|P_{i+1} - P_i\|_2 \qquad (24)$$

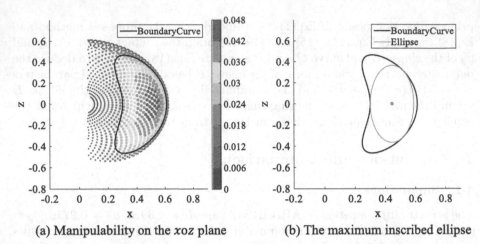

(a) Manipulability on the xoz plane   (b) The maximum inscribed ellipse

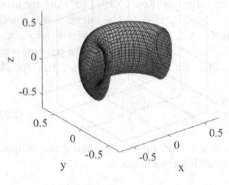

(c) The dexterous workspace

Fig. 3. The results of simulations

Step4: When the distance e satisfies $e \leq \varepsilon, \varepsilon \to 0^+$, the iteration of the algorithm terminates and the obtained ellipse is regarded as the global maximum ellipse.

The structural parameters are set to be consistent with the simulations in Sect. 4.1 and the results are shown in Fig. 4 and Table 1. From the initial point P_0 to P_2, the local maximum ellipses containing initial points are obtained, and the dashed line with arrows indicates the process of moving the center of the ellipse.

The work station is the computer equipped with a Core I5-12600KF, and the operating memory is 32 GB. Table 1 shows the comparisons of the results obtained by the two methods. Obviously, the errors of parameters are very small, so our method is correct. In terms of time consumed, our method is superior to the IRIS algorithm where the time spent is influenced by the number of obstacles.

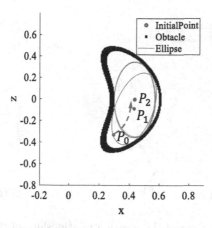

Fig. 4. The process of obtaining the maximum ellipse by IRIS

Table 1. The comparisons of the results obtained by two methods.

Items	S/m^2	$l_a/$ m	$l_b/$ m	$x_c/$ m	Time$/s$
Baseline(IRIS)	0.1641	0.1432	0.3648	0.4349	42.010
Our method	0.1649	0.1439	0.3647	0.4369	3.637
Errors	0.488%	0.489%	−0.027%	0.460%	−91.3%

5   Applications

The cross-sectional maximum inscribed ellipse plays a crucial role in parameterizing the dexterous workspace of 6R industrial robots. Therefore, taking the maximum ellipse as a bridge to illustrate the application of the proposed method in both optimizing the layout of the workpieces and determining the structural parameters.

5.1   Optimize the Layout of Workpieces

During the mission analysis, the proposed method is applied to precisely obtain the cross-sectional maximum ellipses of the dexterous workspace determined by different manipulability w, as shown in Fig. 5. The ellipse w_1, w_2, w_3 are determined by the manipulability $w = 0.008, 0.0225, 0.032$, respectively, and their inner regions represent the approximate non-singular space, the workspace satisfying general task requirements, and the workspace with excellent kinematic performance, respectively. Therefore, the layout of the task objects, which contain workpieces A, B and C, need to be optimized. According to Fig. 5, workpieces B and C need to be moved completely to the non-singular space.

Usually, it is necessary to consider the layout of the workpieces on the 3D space, and we need to analyze the position relationships by the equation similar to Eq.(23).

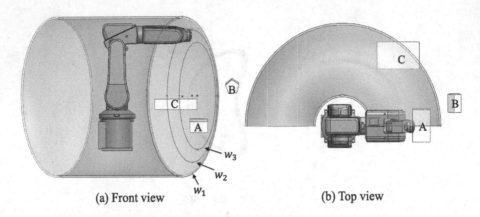

(a) Front view   (b) Top view

Fig. 5. The analysis of the position relationships of the workpieces

5.2   Determine Structural Parameters

The requirements for the dexterous workspace are transferred to the maximum ellipse, so the parameters x_c, l_a and l_b become the focus of attention. When only an ellipse parameter is required, there are two structure parameters $a(a = a_2^2)$ and $c(c = a_3^2 + d_4^2)$ $(a_3 = const)$ corresponding to it, so it is necessary to establish some rules to make the number of required parameters the same as the number of influencing parameters.

When only an ellipse parameter is required, the rule can be only $a(d_4 = const)$ or $c(a_2 = const)$ will change, or keeping $c = ka$. For example, we can substitute the requirement $l_a = 0.18$ and the constraint represented by the rule into the Eqs.(14), (15), (19) and (21) to determine the structural parameters. The results are shown in Fig. 6 and the rows $E_1 - E_3$ in Table 2. When two parameters are required, the structural parameters can be obtained by combining Eqs.(14), (15), (19) and (21). The curve E_4 in Fig. 6 is the result for the parameters $l_a = 0.21$, $l_b = 0.48$ and the data corresponds to the row E_4 in Table 2. However, when three parameters are required, only two of them can be satisfied exactly, while the other one is greater than the required value.

Table 2. The determination of structural parameters a_2, d_4 under different rules.

Rules	Ellipse	$l_a/$m	$l_b/$m	$a_2/$m	$d_4/$m
Initial	E_0	0.1439	0.3647	0.27	0.34
Only a	E_1	0.18	0.4291	0.3220	0.34
Only c	E_2	0.18	0.4378	0.27	0.4108
$c = ka$	E_3	0.18	0.4296	0.3120	0.3514
a and c	E_4	0.21	0.48	0.3547	0.3558

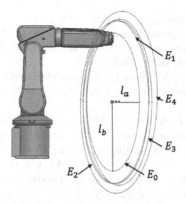

Fig. 6. The required cross-sectional ellipses

6 Conclusions

In this study, the manipulability was selected as dexterity index and a method to parameterize the dexterous workspace of 6R industrial robots by cross-sectional maximum ellipse was proposed. The related equations between the structural parameters and the parameters of the maximum ellipse were derived. The parametrization of the ring-shaped dexterous workspace was realized. Then, the simulations of ABB IRB120 manipulator and the comparisons based on IRIS algorithm showed that the method proposed is accurate and efficient. Finally, the practical significance of the proposed method was illustrated through application examples of the layout optimization and structural parameters determination of ABB IRB120 manipulator.

Acknowledgements. This work was supported in part by the Research and Development Programs in Key Areas of Guangzhou (Grant No. 202103020004), the Natural Science Foundation of Guangdong Province (Grant No. 2022A1515010806, 2020A1515010698), and the Guangzhou Science and Technology Plan Project (Grant No. 2023B01J0046).

References

1. Valsamos, C., Moulianitis, V., Synodinos, A., Aspragathos, N.: Introduction of the high performance area measure for the evaluation of metamorphic manipulator anatomies. Mech. Mach. Theory **86**, 88–107 (2015)
2. Kaloorazi, M.H.F., Masouleh, M.T., Caro, S.: Determination of the maximal singularity-free workspace of 3-DOF parallel mechanisms with a constructive geometric approach. Mech. Mach. Theory **84**, 25–36 (2015)
3. Peidró, A., Reinoso, Ó., Gil, A., Marín, J.M., Payá, L.: An improved Monte Carlo method based on gaussian growth to calculate the workspace of robots. Eng. Appl. Artif. Intell. **64**, 197–207 (2017)

4. Zhi, X., Bai, W., Yeatman, E.M.: Kinematic parameter optimization of a miniaturized surgical instrument based on dexterous workspace determination. In: 2021 6th IEEE International Conference on Advanced Robotics and Mechatronics (ICARM), pp. 112–118. IEEE (2021)
5. Bohigas, O., Manubens, M., Ros, L.: A complete method for workspace boundary determination on general structure manipulators. IEEE Trans. Robot. **28**(5), 993–1006 (2012)
6. Chablat, D., Wenger, P., Majou, F., Merlet, J.P.: An interval analysis based study for the design and the comparison of three-degrees-of-freedom parallel kinematic machines. Int. J. Robot. Res. **23**(6), 615–624 (2004)
7. Mousavi, M.A., Masouleh, M.T., Karimi, A.: On the maximal singularity-free ellipse of planar 3-RPR parallel mechanisms via convex optimization. Robot. Comput. Integr. Manuf. **30**(2), 218–227 (2014)
8. Sirichotiyakul, W., Patoglu, V., Satici, A.C.: Efficient singularity-free workspace approximations using sum-of-squares programming. J. Mech. Robot. **12**(6), 061004 (2020)
9. Yoshikawa, T.: Manipulability of robotic mechanisms. Int. J. Robot. Res. **4**(2), 3–9 (1985)
10. Gotlih, K., Kovac, D., Vuherer, T., Brezovnik, S., Brezocnik, M., Zver, A.: Velocity anisotropy of an industrial robot. Robot. Comput. Integr. Manuf. **27**(1), 205–211 (2011)
11. Gotlih, K., Troch, I.: Base invariance of the manipulability index. Robotica **22**(4), 455–462 (2004)
12. Güler, O., Gürtuna, F.: Symmetry of convex sets and its applications to the extremal ellipsoids of convex bodies. Optim. Methods Softw. **27**(4–5), 735–759 (2012)
13. Deits, R., Tedrake, R.: Computing large convex regions of obstacle-free space through semidefinite programming. In: Akin, H.L., Amato, N.M., Isler, V., van der Stappen, A.F. (eds.) Algorithmic Foundations of Robotics XI. STAR, vol. 107, pp. 109–124. Springer, Cham (2015). https://doi.org/10.1007/978-3-319-16595-0_7

Design and Kinematic Analysis of a Mobile Parallel Mechanism with Over Constrained Branch Chains

Yuang Xia[1](✉), Chunyan Zhang[1], and Xinyue Yu[2]

[1] School of Mechanical and Automotive Engineering, Shanghai University of Engineering Science, Shanghai 201620, China
1370529242@qq.com
[2] Weilai Automobile (Anhui) Co., Ltd., Hefei 230061, Anhui, China

Abstract. In this paper, a multi-mode mobile parallel mechanism with over-constrained branches is designed to explore the influence of over-constrained branches on the stability of the mechanism in motion, and the mechanism motion and the realization of each mode are verified by motion simulation and physical production. Firstly, the schematic diagram is designed, and the mechanism configuration is designed according to it. A multi-mode mobile parallel mechanism with constrained branches is obtained, and its over-constrained branches arc judged; The linkage group equivalent method is used to analyze the degrees of freedom of each mode of the mechanism; Kinematic analysis of the mechanism is carried out to solve the position coordinates of each point; Compare and analyze the branch chain of the mechanism with or without over-constraint, solve the centroid coordinates according to the ZMP theory, and use MATLAB to draw and compare the centroid of the mechanism at the time of movement.

Keywords: Over constrained branch chain · Mobile parallel mechanism · Multi-mode · Kinematic · Stability

1 Introduction

Overrestrained mechanism has the advantages of large stiffness, simple structure and high precision, and is widely used in engineering [1, 2]. The same component is subject to two or more constraints of the same nature, which means that the component is subject to excessive constraints, which is called "over-constraints" [3]. Institutions with public constraints or over-constraints are called over-constrained institutions [4]. The earliest over-constrained mechanism is the classic Sarrus linkage mechanism proposed by Sarrus [5]. Later, there are researches on space single closed-loop over-constrained mechanisms, such as Bennett 4R linkage mechanism and Bricard 6R linkage mechanism.

Many scholars have done a lot of research on the effect of constraint characteristics on mechanism performance. Liu Xiaofei et al. [6] conducted a dynamic comparative analysis of the 6PUS + UPU and 6PUS parallel mechanism, and proved that the dynamic performance of the parallel mechanism could be improved when the constrained branch

© The Author(s), under exclusive license to Springer Nature Singapore Pte Ltd. 2023
H. Yang et al. (Eds.): ICIRA 2023, LNAI 14269, pp. 443–455, 2023.
https://doi.org/10.1007/978-981-99-6489-5_36

was massless. By comparing 2RPU/UPR/RPR + R + P and 2RPU/UPR + R + P, Xu Zhenghe [7] found that the mechanism with overconstraint has better stiffness performance. Gosselin [8], Han Bo et al. [9], Liu Wenlan et al. [10] applied the constrained parallel mechanism in antenna device by taking advantage of its high stiffness. Hu Bo et al. [11] proposed a novel over-constrained 2RPU + UPU mechanism, in which two RPU branches provide over-constraints and improve the dynamic performance of the mechanism. It can be seen that the stiffness and other properties of the mechanism can be significantly improved by introducing excessive constraints into the mechanism, but whether to improve the kinematic stability of the mechanism needs to be further studied. Although some scholars increase its stability by designing multi-closed-loop mechanisms, such as Xun Zhiyuan 's three-orthogonal parallelotron rolling mechanism, Xiangzhi Wei et al.' s spherical rolling mechanism, Huifang Gao et al. 's novel coupling mechanism containing regular triangular bicones, However, the above mechanism is a single motion mode, which cannot be applied to multiple terrains and can not be switched between modes according to working conditions.

Generally, in the mobile parallel mechanism with overconstrained branch chains, the overconstrained branch chains are directly connected to the platform. In this paper, a schematic diagram of the mechanism with no connection between the constrained branch chains and the platform was designed. The design configuration was designed based on the four-bar mechanism and the constrained branch chain as the ontology, and the constrained branch chain of the design mechanism was over-constrained and the influence of the constrained branch chain on the stability of the multi-mode mobile parallel mechanism was explored. The kinematic and stability analysis of each motion mode of the mechanism proves that the multi-mode mobile parallel mechanism with overconstrained branch chain is more stable, and the motion of the mechanism and the realization of each mode are verified by simulation and prototype production.

2   Mechanism Analysis

2.1   Overconstraint Decision Theory of Mobile Parallel Mechanism

The parallel mechanism is essentially a family of spatial multi-ring mechanisms, consisting of moving platform, fixed platform and n linkage branches. As shown in Fig. 1, when the parallel mechanism moves, the linkage group in contact with the ground is defined as a static platform, and the moving linkage group is called a moving platform. Constraints of the parallel mechanism in the moving process are judged by the linkage parameter matrix. A coordinate system is established on the fixed platform in Fig. 4. The end of any branch of the link group can be represented by the link group parameter formula(1), where α, β, γ is the angular motion parameter, and represents the angular displacement of the link group along the X, Y and Z directions.x, y, z are linear motion parameters, representing the amount of movement of the rod group along the X, Y, and Z directions. A zero value in α, β, γ, x, y, z indicates that there is a binding or binding couple in this direction.

$$G=(\alpha\ \beta\ \gamma\ ;\ x\ y\ z)\tag{1}$$

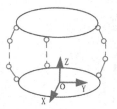

Fig. 1. General structure diagram of parallel mechanism

M is used to represent the bar group parameter matrix composed of all the branch chain bar group parameters, namely:

$$M = \begin{bmatrix} \alpha_1 & \beta_1 & \gamma_1 & x_1 & y_1 & z_1 \\ \alpha_2 & \beta_2 & \gamma_2 & x_2 & y_2 & z_2 \\ \vdots & \vdots & \vdots & \vdots & \vdots & \vdots \\ \alpha_n & \beta_n & \gamma_n & x_n & y_n & z_n \end{bmatrix} \tag{2}$$

In Formula (2) $R_x = \begin{bmatrix} \alpha_1 & \alpha_2 & \cdots & \alpha_n \end{bmatrix}$, $R_y = \begin{bmatrix} \beta_1 & \beta_2 & \cdots & \beta_n \end{bmatrix}$, $R_z = \begin{bmatrix} \gamma_1 & \gamma_2 & \cdots & \gamma_n \end{bmatrix}$, R_x ، R_y ، R_z represents the angular column vectors of all branch chains in the X, Y and Z directions; $T_x = \begin{bmatrix} x_1 & x_2 & \cdots & x_n \end{bmatrix}$, $T_y = \begin{bmatrix} y_1 & y_2 & \cdots & y_n \end{bmatrix}$, $T_z = \begin{bmatrix} z_1 & z_2 & \cdots & z_n \end{bmatrix}$, T_x ، T_y ، T_z represents line column vectors of all branch chains in the X, Y, and Z directions. Base point displacement parameter. $O_B = \cap_{k=1}^{L} G_k^{gz}$.

If there are two or more zero elements in the above angular column vector or line column vector, it is said to be multi-zero angular column vector or multi-zero line column vector. If there are multi-zero angular column vectors in matrix M, it means that there are overconstraint pairs in the direction corresponding to the zero element. If there are multiple zero line column vectors that satisfy the geometric conditions of coaxial, coplanar and spatial parallelism, it indicates that there are overconstraints. If the matrix does not contain multiple zero column vectors, then there is no overconstraint.

2.2 Description of Multi-Mode Mobile Parallel Mechanism with Constrained Branch Chains

A multi-mode mobile parallel mechanism with constrained branch chains is designed in this paper. Figure 2 shows the 3D model diagram of the mechanism and its schematic diagram. Figure (a) shows the 3D model diagram of the mechanism and Figure (b) shows the schematic diagram of the mechanism. The mechanism consists of 32 rods, 28 rotating pairs, 12 U pairs and 2 platforms. In Fig. 2 (a), two rods are connected through the central motion pair to form a component, as shown in Fig. 3.

2.3 The Mechanism Overconstrains the Judgment

First, the organization as a whole is judged to be over-constrained, and the loop is divided according to the basic conditions of over-constrained organizations, as shown in Table 1,

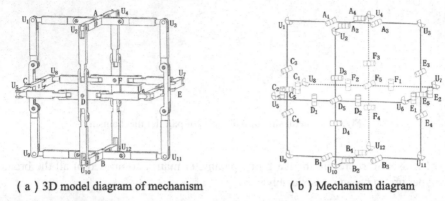

(a) 3D model diagram of mechanism   (b) Mechanism diagram

Fig. 2. Three-dimensional model diagram and schematic diagram of multi-mode mobile parallel mechanism with constrained branch chain

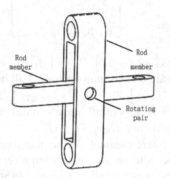

Fig. 3. Component model diagram

which can be loop $BU_{10}DU_6EU_{11}B$, loop DU_2AU_3E, loop BU_9CU_5D, loop CU_1A, loop $BU_{12}FU_8C$, loop FU_4A, loop EU_7F.

Loop $BU_{10}DU_6EU_{11}B$ can BE regarded as a loop formed by kinematic chain $BU_{10}D$ and chain $DU_6EU_{11}B$ connected through component D. Kinematic chain BED is connected by kinematic chain BE and ED through component E. Loop DU_2AU_3E: The loop is a closed loop formed by connecting component D and component E of the first loop with a series moving chain DU_2AU_3E; Loop BU_9CU_5D: The loop connects component D and component A of the first loop with a series moving chain BU_9CU_5D to form a closed loop; Loop CU_1A: The loop is composed of A member C of the third loop and A of the second loop connected with a series chain CU_1A to form a closed loop; Loop $BU_{12}FU_8C$: The loop is composed of a member C of the third loop and a member B of the first loop connected with a series moving chain $BU_{12}FU_8C$ to form a closed loop; Loop FU_4A: The loop consists of A component F of the fifth loop and A of the second loop connected with a series chain FU_4A to form a closed loop; Loop EU_7F: The loop consists of a closed loop consisting of a member F of the fifth loop and a member E of the first loop connected with a series moving chain EU_7F. Table 2 shows the division of each loop and the matrix of rod group parameters.

Table 1. Division of each loop

Loop	Loop one	Loop two	Loop three	Loop four
Mechanism representation				

Loop	Loop five	Loop six	Loop seven
Mechanism representation			

The bar group parameter matrix of the mechanism can be written as:

$$M = \begin{pmatrix} \alpha\ \beta\ 0;\ x\ 0\ z \\ \alpha\ \beta\ \gamma;\ x\ y\ z \\ \alpha\ \beta\ 0;\ x\ 0\ z \\ \alpha\ \beta\ 0;\ 0\ y\ z \\ \alpha\ \beta\ 0;\ x\ 0\ z \\ 0\ \beta\ \gamma;\ x\ y\ z \\ \alpha\ \beta\ 0;\ 0\ y\ z \\ \alpha\ 0\ 0;\ 0\ y\ z \\ \alpha\ 0\ \gamma;\ x\ y\ z \\ \alpha\ \beta\ 0;\ x\ 0\ z \\ \alpha\ \beta\ 0;\ x\ 0\ z \\ 0\ \beta\ 0;\ x\ 0\ z \\ \alpha\ 0\ \gamma;\ x\ y\ z \\ 0\ 0\ \gamma;\ x\ 0\ z \end{pmatrix} \tag{3}$$

Multiple zero angular column vectors exist in the parameter matrix of the linkage group, so there are overconstraints in the mechanism.

Next, it is determined whether the constraint branch chain has a constraint effect on the connected member, as shown in Fig. 4 (a), which is the three-dimensional top view of the constraint branch chain, and (b) its structural relationship diagram.In Figure (b), the "U" in the box represents the motion pair, and the rotation pair connected to the

Table 2. Division of each loop and pole group parameter matrix

Loop	Bar group parameter matrix
Loop $BU_{10}DU_6EU_{11}B$	$M_1=\begin{pmatrix} G_{BD} \cup G_D \\ G_{BED} \end{pmatrix}=\begin{pmatrix} \alpha\ \beta\ 0;\ x\ 0\ z \\ \alpha\ \beta\ \gamma;\ x\ y\ z \end{pmatrix}$
Loop DU_2AU_3E	$M_2=\begin{pmatrix} G_{DA} \cup G_A \\ G_{EA} \\ G_D \\ G_E \end{pmatrix}=\begin{pmatrix} \alpha\ \beta\ 0;\ x\ 0\ z \\ \alpha\ \beta\ 0;\ 0\ y\ z \end{pmatrix}$
Loop BU_9CU_5D	$M_3=\begin{pmatrix} G_{BCD} \\ G_D \\ G_A \end{pmatrix}=\begin{pmatrix} \alpha\ \beta\ 0;\ x\ 0\ z \\ 0\ \beta\ \gamma;\ x\ y\ z \end{pmatrix}$
Loop CU_1A	$M_4=\begin{pmatrix} G_{AC} \\ G_C \end{pmatrix}=\begin{pmatrix} \alpha\ \beta\ 0;\ 0\ y\ z \\ \alpha\ 0\ 0;\ 0\ y\ z \end{pmatrix}$
Loop $BU_{12}FU_8C$	$M_5=\begin{pmatrix} G_{BFC} \\ G_C \end{pmatrix}=\begin{pmatrix} \alpha\ 0\ \gamma;\ x\ y\ z \\ \alpha\ \beta\ 0;\ x\ 0\ z \end{pmatrix}$
Loop FU_4A	$M_6=\begin{pmatrix} G_{FA} \\ G_A \\ G_F \end{pmatrix}=\begin{pmatrix} \alpha\ \beta\ 0;\ x\ 0\ z \\ 0\ \beta\ 0;\ x\ 0\ z \end{pmatrix}$
Loop EU_7F	$M_7=\begin{pmatrix} G_{EF} \\ G_E \\ G_F \end{pmatrix}=\begin{pmatrix} \alpha\ 0\ \gamma;\ x\ y\ z \\ 0\ 0\ \gamma;\ x\ 0\ z \end{pmatrix}$

member is named:

$$I_m(I = C, D, E, F, = 1, 2) \tag{4}$$

"S" represents the member of the branch chain, and the member of the constraint branch chain has constraint effect on each other." → "represents the direction of the constraint, and the horizontal line represents the connection relation. The mechanism and constraint branch chain have symmetry. Taking component D as an example, the analysis is carried out. It is assumed that component C and component D are frames. Component D and branch chain $R_C U_5 R_D$, $R_{D2} U_6 R_{E1}$ form a closed loop. In kinematic chain CU_5DU_6E, rod S_{11}, S_{12}, S_{21}, S_{22} is connected through kinematic pair to form a closed loop, which is closed through a single kinematic pair. Therefore, the parameter

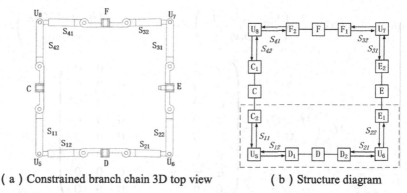

(a) Constrained branch chain 3D top view   (b) Structure diagram

Fig. 4. Constraint branch chain overlooking 3D diagram and structure diagram

matrices of rod group of kinematic chain $R_C U_5 R_D$, $R_{D2} U_6 R_{E1}$ are:

$$M_1 = \begin{pmatrix} G_{CU_5} \cup G_{U_5} \\ G_{U_5D} \end{pmatrix} = \begin{pmatrix} \alpha\ 0\ \gamma\ \ 0\ 0\ 0 \\ 0\ 0\ \gamma\ \ 0\ 0\ 0 \end{pmatrix}; M_2 = \begin{pmatrix} G_{D_2U_6} \cup G_{U_6} \\ G_{U_6R_{E_1}} \end{pmatrix} = \begin{pmatrix} \alpha\ 0\ \gamma\ \ 0\ 0\ 0 \\ 0\ 0\ \gamma\ \ 0\ 0\ 0 \end{pmatrix}$$

Vector of motion parameters of base point $O_1^D = \begin{pmatrix} 0\ 0\ \gamma\ 0\ 0\ 0 \end{pmatrix}$, $O_2^D = \begin{pmatrix} 0\ 0\ \gamma\ 0\ 0\ 0 \end{pmatrix}$, it is known that member D has the degree of freedom of rotation around the axis. Moving chain $R_{C2}U_5 R_{D1}$ and moving chain $R_{D2}U_6 R_{E1}$ form a closed loop through memberD, and the bar group parameter matrix of the whole loop is:

$$M_3 = \begin{pmatrix} M_1 \cup \begin{pmatrix} G_D \\ 0 \end{pmatrix} \\ M_2 \end{pmatrix} = \begin{pmatrix} \alpha\ \beta\ \gamma\ 0\ 0\ 0 \\ 0\ 0\ \gamma\ \ 0\ 0\ 0 \\ \alpha\ 0\ \gamma\ \ \ 0\ 0\ 0 \\ 0\ 0\ \gamma\ \ \ 0\ 0\ 0 \end{pmatrix} \tag{5}$$

$T_x = \begin{bmatrix} 0\ 0\ 0\ 0 \end{bmatrix}^T, T_y = \begin{bmatrix} 0\ 0\ 0\ 0 \end{bmatrix}^T, T_z = \begin{bmatrix} 0\ 0\ 0\ 0 \end{bmatrix}^T$, There are multiple zero line column vectors in the matrix, and it shows that there are four parallel binding forces in the x, y and z directions, and there are common constraints.

$$M_4 = \begin{pmatrix} G_{RC_1F} \cup G_F \\ G_{RF_1U_7R_{E_2}} \end{pmatrix} = \begin{pmatrix} \alpha\ \beta\ \gamma\ 0\ 0\ 0 \\ 0\ 0\ \gamma\ \ 0\ 0\ 0 \\ \alpha\ 0\ \gamma\ \ \ 0\ 0\ 0 \\ 0\ 0\ \gamma\ \ \ 0\ 0\ 0 \end{pmatrix} \tag{6}$$

Among them: $G_{RC_1F} = \begin{pmatrix} G_{RC_1U_8} \cup G_{U_8} \\ G_{U_8RF_2} \end{pmatrix}$, $G_{RF_1U_7RE_2} = \begin{pmatrix} G_{RF_1U_7} \cup G_{U_7} \\ G_{U_7RE_2} \end{pmatrix}$.

$$M = \begin{pmatrix} M_3 \cup G_E \\ M_3 \end{pmatrix} = \begin{pmatrix} \alpha & \beta & \gamma & & 0 & 0 & 0 \\ 0 & 0 & \gamma & & 0 & 0 & 0 \\ \alpha & 0 & \gamma & & 0 & 0 & 0 \\ 0 & 0 & \gamma & & 0 & 0 & 0 \\ \alpha & \beta & \gamma & & 0 & 0 & 0 \\ 0 & 0 & \gamma & & 0 & 0 & 0 \\ \alpha & \beta & \gamma & & 0 & 0 & 0 \\ 0 & 0 & \gamma & & 0 & 0 & 0 \end{pmatrix} \tag{7}$$

$$T_x = \begin{bmatrix} 0 & 0 & 0 & 0 & 0 & 0 & 0 & 0 \end{bmatrix}^T \tag{8}$$

$$T_y = \begin{bmatrix} 0 & 0 & 0 & 0 & 0 & 0 & 0 & 0 \end{bmatrix}^T \tag{9}$$

$$T_z = \begin{bmatrix} 0 & 0 & 0 & 0 & 0 & 0 & 0 & 0 \end{bmatrix}^T \tag{10}$$

There are multiple zero line column vectors in the matrix, and it shows that there are 8 parallel binding forces in the x, y and z directions, and there are over-binding forces, so the constraint branch chain is over-constrained branch chain.

3 Kinematic Analysis

3.1 Quadrilateral Pattern

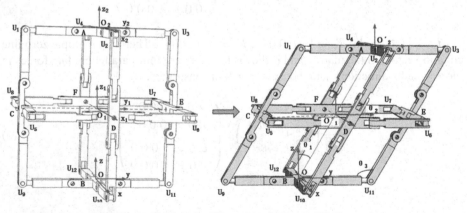

Fig. 5. Quadrilateral rolling mode motion model diagram

Figure 5 shows the kinematic model diagram of the mechanism in quadrilateral rolling mode. With center O_2 of platform A as the origin, the coordinate system is established with axis $O_2-x_2y_2z_2$, x_2 along the direction of O_2U_2, axis y_2 along the direction of O_2U_3, and axis z_2 can be obtained according to the right hand rule. With the center of the plane where the overconstrained branch chain is located as the origin of O_1, the coordinate system $O_1-x_1y_1z_1$, x_1 axis and x_2 axis are in the same direction, y_1 axis and y_2 axis are in the same direction, z_1 axis can be obtained according to the right hand rule, and the space coordinate of the mechanism is $O-xyz$. Assume that the mechanism moves along the positive direction of axis y, and after the motion Angle θ_1 is set, the Angle between axis $\theta_1 \subset \left(0, \frac{\pi}{2}\right)$, origin O_2 becomes O_2', O_1 becomes O_1', $O_2'O$ and axis z is θ_1, and the plane where the overconstrained branch chain is located has two rotations, one is rotated around the axis of rotation pairs D_5 and F_5, and the rotation Angle is set to θ_2. In this process, only the motion coordinate on this plane will change. The other is the rotation that occurs with respect to the spatial coordinate system, where the input Angle of the mechanism is $\angle BU_{11}E = \theta_3$, where the relation between θ_1 and θ_3 is $\theta_3 = \frac{\pi}{2} + \theta_1$, where $\theta_3 \subset \left(\frac{\pi}{2}, \pi\right)$.

The mechanism moves θ_1 Angle, and the rotation transformation matrix of this process is:

$$R_1 = \begin{bmatrix} 1 & 0 & 0 \\ 0 & C\theta_1 & -S\theta_1 \\ 0 & S\theta_1 & C\theta_1 \end{bmatrix} \qquad (11)$$

Among them: $C\theta_1 = \cos\theta_1$, $S\theta_1 = \sin\theta_1$.

After moving from Angle θ_1, each motion pair on the plane where platform A is located can be expressed in the space coordinate system $O - xyz$ as follows:

$$\begin{bmatrix} A_{mx}^O \\ A_{my}^O \\ A_{mz}^O \end{bmatrix}^T = [R_1]\begin{bmatrix} A_{mx}^{O_2} \\ A_{my}^{O_2} \\ A_{mz}^{O_2} \end{bmatrix}^T + \begin{bmatrix} x_2' \\ y_2' \\ z_2' \end{bmatrix}^T , \quad \begin{bmatrix} U_{ix}^O \\ U_{iy}^O \\ U_{iz}^O \end{bmatrix}^T = [R_1]\begin{bmatrix} U_{ix}^{O_2} \\ U_{iy}^{O_2} \\ U_{iz}^{O_2} \end{bmatrix}^T + \begin{bmatrix} x_2' \\ y_2' \\ z_2' \end{bmatrix}^T .$$

Assuming that the motion of the plane where the constraint branch chain is located is completed step by step, first rotates θ_2 angles around axis x_1, then rotates θ_1 angles around axis x, then the rotation transformation matrix of the plane motion pair where it is located is:

$$R = R_1R_2 = \begin{bmatrix} 1 & 0 & 0 \\ 0 & C\theta_1C\theta_2 - S\theta_1S\theta_2 & -(S\theta_1C\theta_2+S\theta_2C\theta_1) \\ 0 & S\theta_2C\theta_1+S\theta_1C\theta_2 & C\theta_1C\theta_2 - S\theta_1S\theta_2 \end{bmatrix} \qquad (12)$$

Therefore, the rotation pair at U pair $U_i(i = 5\ 8)$ and component C, D, E and F can be expressed in the space coordinate system $O - xyz$ as:

$$I_m^O = [R]I_m^{O_1} + O_1'(I = C, E, m = 1, 2, 5)I_m^O = [R_1]I_m^{O_1} + O_1'(I = C, E, m = 3, 4)$$
$$I_m^O = [R]I_m^{O_1} + O_1'(I = D, F, m = 1, 2)I_m^O = [R_1]I_m^{O_1} + O_1'(I = D, F, m = 3, 4, 5)$$
$$U_i^O = [R]U_i^{O_1} + O_1(i = 5\ 8)$$

3.2 Spherical Mode

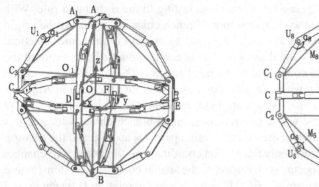 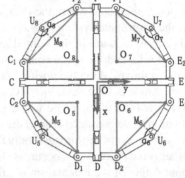

(a) Spherical kinematic mode l   (b) Top view of spherical mode overconstrained branch chain

Fig. 6. Kinematic model diagram of spherical rolling mode

Figure 6 shows the kinematic model of spherical rolling mode. Coordinate system $O - xyz, O - xyz$ is established with center O of the plane where the overconstrained branch chain is located as the origin. According to the geometric characteristics of the mechanism, the lines $A_m B_m$, $C_m D_m$ and $E_m F_m (m = 1\ 4)$ are perpendicular to each other, their intersection point is set as $O_i (i = 1\ 12)$, and then connected successively to $I_m J_n (I, J = A\ F, m, n = 1\ 4)$, so that triangle $O_i I_m J_n$ constitutes a right triangle, taking right triangle $O_1 A_1 C_3$ as an example,O_1 is a right Angle,$O_1 A_1 \perp O_1 C_3$.The length of $O_i I_m$ is set to $d_p (p = 1\ 6)$, the $O_i I_m$ in the positive and negative directions along the z axis is d_1 and d_2 respectively, the $O_i I_m$ in the positive and negative directions along the x axis is d_3 and d_4 respectively, and the $O_i I_m$ in the positive and negative directions along the y axis is d_5 and d_6 respectively, and the relationship can be obtained:

$$O_i I_m^2 + O_i J_n^2 = |I_m J_n|^2 \tag{13}$$

Suppose the Angle between the member at $U_i (i = 1\ 12)$ is $\alpha_i (i = 1\ 12)$, then:

$$|I_m J_n|^2 = 2l^2 (1 - \cos \alpha_i) \tag{14}$$

According to Eqs. (4) and (5), it can be obtained:

$$O_i I_m^2 + O_i J_n^2 = 2l^2 (1 - \cos \alpha_i) \tag{15}$$

$$d_p^2 + d_q^2 = 2l^2 (1 - \cos \alpha_i)(p, q = 1\ 6) \tag{16}$$

U_i can be obtained:

$$U_i = \begin{bmatrix} \frac{l}{2} + M_{ix} \pm \sqrt{\dfrac{\left(l^2 - M_{ix}^2 - M_{iy}^2\right)M_{iy}^2}{M_{i,x}^2 + M_{i,y}^2}} \\ \frac{l}{2} + M_{iy} \mp \dfrac{M_{ix}}{M_{iy}}\sqrt{\dfrac{\left(l^2 - M_{ix}^2 - M_{iy}^2\right)M_{iy}^2}{M_{ix}^2 + M_{iy}^2}} \\ 0 \end{bmatrix} \quad (i = 5\ 8) \tag{17}$$

Among them: $\begin{bmatrix} M_5 \\ M_6 \\ M_7 \\ M_8 \end{bmatrix} = \frac{1}{2}\begin{bmatrix} d_3 & -d_6 & 0 \\ d_3 & d_5 & 0 \\ -d_5 & d_4 & 0 \\ -d_4 & -d_6 & 0 \end{bmatrix}\begin{bmatrix} M_5 \\ M_6 \\ M_7 \\ M_8 \end{bmatrix} = \frac{1}{2}\begin{bmatrix} d_3 & -d_6 & 0 \\ d_3 & d_5 & 0 \\ -d_5 & d_4 & 0 \\ -d_4 & -d_6 & 0 \end{bmatrix}$

Plane coordinate of closed-loop $ACBE$ is $O - yz$, then:

$$U_i = \begin{bmatrix} \frac{l}{2} + M_{ix} \pm \sqrt{\dfrac{\left(l^2 - M_{ix}^2 - M_{iy}^2\right)M_{iy}^2}{M_{i,x}^2 + M_{i,y}^2}} \\ 0 \\ \frac{l}{2} + M_{iz} \mp \dfrac{M_{ix}}{M_{iz}}\sqrt{\dfrac{\left(l^2 - M_{ix}^2 - M_{iz}^2\right)M_{iz}^2}{M_{ix}^2 + M_{iz}^2}} \end{bmatrix} \quad (i = 1, 3, 9, 11) \tag{18}$$

Among them: $\begin{bmatrix} M_1 \\ M_3 \\ M_9 \\ M_{11} \end{bmatrix} = \frac{1}{2}\begin{bmatrix} 0 & -d_6 & d_1 \\ 0 & -d_6 & -d_2 \\ 0 & d_5 & -d_2 \\ 0 & d_5 & d_1 \end{bmatrix}.$

Plane coordinate of closed-loop $ADBF$ is $O - xz$, then:

$$U_i = \begin{bmatrix} 0 \\ \frac{l}{2} + M_{iy} \pm \sqrt{\dfrac{\left(l^2 - M_{iy}^2 - M_{iz}^2\right)M_{iz}^2}{M_{iy}^2 + M_{iz}^2}} \\ \frac{l}{2} + M_{iz} \mp \dfrac{M_{ix}}{M_{iz}}\sqrt{\dfrac{\left(l^2 - M_{ix}^2 - M_{iz}^2\right)M_{iz}^2}{M_{ix}^2 + M_{iz}^2}} \end{bmatrix} \quad (i = 2, 4, 10, 12) \tag{19}$$

Among them: $\begin{bmatrix} M_2 \\ M_4 \\ M_{10} \\ M_{12} \end{bmatrix} = \frac{1}{2}\begin{bmatrix} d_3 & 0 & d_1 \\ d_3 & 0 & -d_2 \\ -d_4 & 0 & -d_2 \\ -d_4 & 0 & d_1 \end{bmatrix}\begin{bmatrix} M_2 \\ M_4 \\ M_{10} \\ M_{12} \end{bmatrix} = \frac{1}{2}\begin{bmatrix} d_3 & 0 & d_1 \\ d_3 & 0 & -d_2 \\ -d_4 & 0 & -d_2 \\ -d_4 & 0 & d_1 \end{bmatrix}$

4 Influence of Overconstrained Branch Chain on Mechanism Stability

ZMP in the y direction is:

$$y_{ZMP} = \frac{\sum_{i=1}^{n} m_i(\ddot{z}_i + g)y_i - \sum_{i=1}^{n} m_i\ddot{y}_i z_i - \sum_{i=1}^{n} I_{ix}\ddot{\Omega}_{ix}}{\sum_{i=1}^{n} m_i(\ddot{z}_i + g)} \tag{20}$$

where: m_i is the mass of each component,$\ddot{z}_i$、$\ddot{y}_i$ is the acceleration of the center of mass of each component in the coordinate system,y_i、z_i is the center of mass coordinate of each component in the coordinate system,I_{ix} is the moment of inertia of each bar member around the X-axis,$\dot{\Omega}_{ix}$ is the angular acceleration of each component around the X-axis, and g is the acceleration of gravity. Since the mechanism is in uniform motion and the angular velocity is constant, the angular acceleration is 0 (Table 3).

Table 3. Relationship between modes y_{ZMP} and θ_3

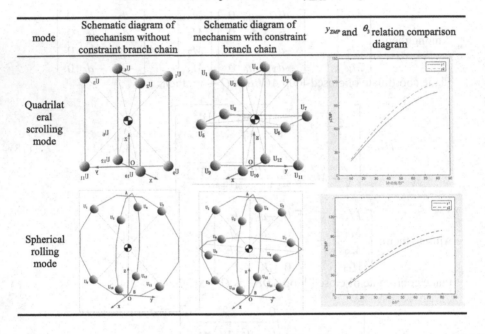

5 Summary

(1) Based on the four-bar mechanism and the constrained branch chain as the body, a multi-mode mobile parallel mechanism with constrained branch chain was constructed. The situation that the over-constrained branch chain was not connected to the platform was analyzed. After the judgment of over-constrained branch chain, a multi-mode mobile parallel mechanism with over-constrained branch chain was obtained.

(2) Because the mechanism is a spatial multi-loop mechanism, the coupling between the branch chains will occur when it moves. And the kinematic analysis of two modes of the mechanism: quadrilateral rolling mode and spherical rolling mode is carried out.

(3) The influence of over-constrained branch chains on the stability of the mechanism was analyzed. The relationship between the motion of the mechanism with or without over-constrained branch chains and Angle y_{ZMP} was compared and analyzed. The comparative analysis diagram was drawn by Matlab, and the stability performance of the mechanism with over-constrained branch chains was better.

References

1. Kong, X.W., Gosselin, C.M.: A class of 3-DOF translational parallel manipulators with linear input-output equations (2002)
2. Gosselin, C.M.: Development and experimentation of a fast 3-DOF camera-orienting device. International Journal of Robotics Research (1997)
3. Sarrus, P.T.: Note sur la transformation des mouvements rectilignes alternatifs, en mouvements circulaires; et reciproquement
4. Gosselin, C.M., Éric, St.-P.: Development and Experimentation of a Fast 3-DOF Camera-Orienting Device. The International Journal of Robotics Research 16(5), 619–630 (1997)
5. Wei, X., Tian, Y., Wen, S.: Design and locomotion analysis of a novel modular rolling robot. Mech. Mach. Theory 133(4), 23–43 (2019)
6. Gao, H., Liu, J., Yu, Y.: Design and motion analysis of a novel coupled mechanism based on a regular triangular bipyramid. Int. J. Adv. Rob. Syst. 13(6), 172988141667813 (2016)
7. Zhang, C.Y., Xie, M.J., Zhang, D.: Kinematic analysis and optimization of a multi-mode mobile parallel Mechanism. Machine Design & Research (2018)
8. Zhang, C.Y., Wan, Y., Zhang, D., et al.: A new mathematical method to study the singularity of 3-RSR multimode mobile parallel mechanism. Mathematical Problems in Engineering (2019)
9. Liu, X.Y., Zhang, C.Y., Ni, C., et al.: A reconfigurable multi-mode walking-rolling robot based on motor time-sharing control. Industrial Robot (2019). ahead-of-print(ahead-of-print)
10. Zhang, C., Wan, Y., Zhang, D., et al.: A New Mathematical Method to Study the Singularity of 3-RSR Multimode Mobile Parallel Mechanism. Mathematical Problems in Engineering (2019)
11. Xun, Z.Y., Yao, Y.A., Li, Y., et al.: A novel rhombohedron rolling mechanism. Mechanism and Machine Theory (2016)

Design and Analysis of Space Extra Long Deployable Telescopic Boom Based on Cable Drive

Zhou Su[1], Lin Li[1], Qiuhong Lin[1], Jingya Ma[1], Duanling Li[2,3](✉) (iD), and Qiang Cong[1]

[1] Beijing Institute of Spacecraft System Engineering, Beijing 100094, China
[2] Beijing University of Posts and Telecommunications, Beijing 100876, China
liduanling_bupt@163.com
[3] Shaanxi University of Science and Technology, Xi'an 712000, China

Abstract. Due to its excellent structural rigidity and large storage ratio, the scope of application expands continuously for the rope-driven deployable telescopic boom. Considering the future requirements on application of the extra-long deployable telepic boom in space, a method of design and analysis for the extra-long deployable telepic boom is proposed in this paper on the basis of rope transmission. Through experimentation, the contact stiffness of the cone of the deployable telescopic boom is determined. When the fit force of the cone reaches a certain level, the contact stiffness of the cone of the deployable telescopic boom tends to stabilize. Given the large flexibility of the extra-long deployable telescopic boom, a numerical calculation method of multiple differential equations is produced in this study for the large displacement flexible rods that can be applied to the extra-long deployable telescopic boom. By comparing the results of numerical calculation with those of final element simulation analysis, it is verified that when the stiffness of cone fit is consistent, the deployed extra-long deployable telescopic boom is equivalent to a large deformation and large displacement flexible beam for analysis. The results of numerical calculation are consistent with the results of final element analysis.

Keywords: Deployable mechanism · Telescopic boom · Differential equations · Numerical calculation · Cable drive

1 Introduction

As a typical one-dimensional linear deployable structure, the deployable telescopic boom consists of multiple closely-spaced coaxial circular tubes of different diameters, and the deployment device is generally the tube positioned on the symmetric axis. In order to ensure sufficient stiffness of post-deployment extension boom for the deployable telescopic boom tube, there must be a sufficient overlay length allowed between the adjacent tube units, which however makes it difficult to achieve the maximum deployment length in theory. After completion of the mechanical fit, the adjacent telepic boom elements are fitted through mechanical surfaces to build a relatively stable rod structure.

© The Author(s), under exclusive license to Springer Nature Singapore Pte Ltd. 2023
H. Yang et al. (Eds.): ICIRA 2023, LNAI 14269, pp. 456–467, 2023.
https://doi.org/10.1007/978-981-99-6489-5_37

Typically applied to form an extra long baseline, deployable telescopic boom functions as the main support and deployable structure for large deployable solar wings and large aperture antennas. Besides, it is capable to withstand heavy loads in the orbit. In the future, deployable telescopic boom can also be applied as the main support structure for planetary surface buildings [1, 2].

Figure 1 illustrates the typical application of the deployable telescopic boom. To be specific, Fig. 1(a) shows the deployable telescopic boom of North Grumman (prototype and product), prototype: a STEM drive, an extended length of 34.3 m, a storage ratio of 1:12, a driving force of 445N, a diameter of 314 mm; product: JWST-Mid BOOM deployable telescopic boom, a deployment length of about 6 m [3]. Figure 1(b) shows the OXFORD-SPACE SYETEM deployable telescopic boom, prototype: a STEM driven, a deployment length of 15 m, a storage ratio of 1:7, a weight of 35 kg, and a diameter of 290 mm.

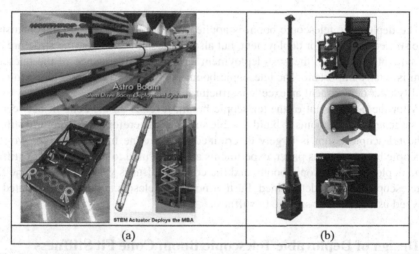

Fig. 1. Telescopic Boom: (a) North Grumman's deployable telescopic boom; (b) OXFORD-SPACE SYETEM's deployable telescopic boom.

In general, the driving mechanism of the deployable telescopic boom consists of screw drive deployable telescopic boom, cable drive deployable telescopic boom and STEM drive deployable telescopic boom, etc (Fig. 2).

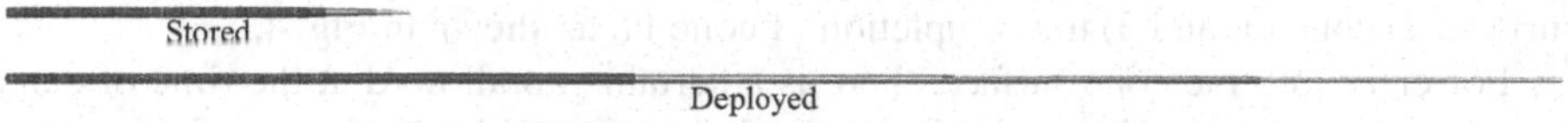

Stored

Deployed

Fig. 2. Telescopic Boom stored and deployed

In this paper, a deployable telescopic boom type deployable mechanism is designed on the basis of cable drive linkage driven deployment mechanism, which consists mainly of multiple sets of cable driven deployable telescopic boom type mechanisms.

When the cable is used for driving, the cable-driving device is installed at the end where the mechanism is connected to the base, with the cable arranged back and forth in the cylinder through pulleys. The winding drum in the rotating device that drives the cable winds the cable around itself. By generating a driving force to pull the cable, the mechanism can be deployed and stored [4] (Fig. 3).

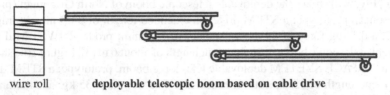

wire roll   **deployable telescopic boom based on cable drive**

Fig. 3. Cable drive principle -telescopic boom

The deployable telescopic boom is applied not only as the driving mechanism of some spacecraft loads for deployment, but also as the main load-bearing structure after deployment. Therefore, the post-deployment structural performance of the telescopic boom is vitally important. The telescopic boom is required to ensure a high structural stability after deployment an excellent structural stiffness.

After the deployment of the telescopic boom, it relies on the cone fit between the two-stage telescopic booms to build a stable structure. Therefore, the structural stiffness of the telescopic boom is largely determined by the cone fit between the two-stage telescopic booms. In this paper, experiments are performed to test the cone fit stiffness of the deployable telescopic boom, and the contact stiffness value after the cone fit of the telescopic boom is determined. Furthermore, the telescopic boom is simulated and analyzed using the cone surface fit stiffness.

2 Design of Deployable Telescopic Boom Cone Fit Stiffness

Usually, the taper fit of ground mechanical equipment is purposed to make the taper fit by applying a fast impulse. In this case, the cone fit is reliant mainly on the deformation induced by surface extrusion, and there exists a certain friction force, which makes the cone fit very tight. Therefore, it is equivalent to a rigid part in practice.

However, the speed of deployment is very low for the deployable telescopic boom through the cable transmission. During the deployment of the deployable telescopic boom, there are three processes involved in the cone fit: 1) the entry into the cone surface, 2) cone fit, and 3) the completion of cone fit, as shown in Fig. 4.

For entry into the cone surface, there is a certain gap allowed at the time of entry into the cone surface. The main function of the cone fit is the friction force. After the cone fit force reaches a certain level and the cone surface is matched, the surface extrusion deformation force remains dominant. Also, frictional resistance occurs to a certain extent. In the figure, F_1 is the cone fit force, F_2 is the friction force, and F_3 is the extrusion deformation force.

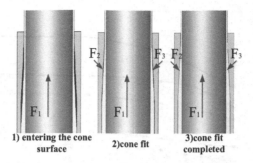

1) entering the cone surface   2)cone fit   3)cone fit completed

Fig. 4. Cone fitting process of telescopic Boom

Considering the characteristics of the cable transmission deployable telescopic boom, the fit stiffness test of the cone fit is designed. Firstly, the cone fit force of the telescopic boom is increased progressively. Then, the stiffness obtained after the fit of the cone is tested after each load of the cone fit force is applied. The contact stiffness test of the cone fit of each two-stage telescopic boom is illustrated in the figure below (Fig. 5).

Fig. 5. Telescopic boom test piece- telescopic boom contact stiffness of cone fit test

The curve of relationship between the loading force and stiffness of the cone surface is reflective of the relationship between the stiffness and the cone fit force. It can be seen from the figure that the contact stiffness shows an increasing trend with the rise of the cone fit force. When the cone fit force reaches a certain level, however, the value of stiffness remains unchanged. At this time, the cone fit can be treated as completed. In the course of cone fit, the resulting cone fit force is applied to obtain the contact stiffness of the cone-surface fit. After matching of the taper surface, the telescopic boom can be viewed as the rod with a complete structure in theory (Fig. 6).

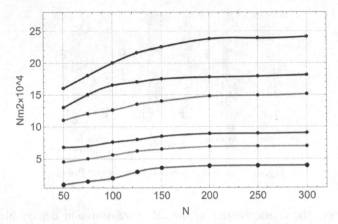

Fig. 6. Curve of the relationship between loading force and stiffness of the conical surface

The above experiments are performed to determine not only the cone fit force of the telescopic boom but also the contact stiffness of cone fit of the telescopic boom, which is crucial for the subsequent analysis.

3 Large Displacement Differential Equations for Flexible Rods

After deployment of the telescopic boom, the cone fits tightly, achieving a consistent contact stiffness, while the telescopic boom is treated as a rod structure in theory. When conventional problems are dealt with, the deflection of a rod can be calculated using the traditional deflection formula in the mechanics of materials. However, due to the large flexibility of the extra-long telescopic boom, large deformation and displacement will occur under the condition of large load at the end of the telescopic boom. The conventional deflection formula is not suitable for calculating large deformation and large displacement scenarios. In this chapter, the differential equations intended for the flexible rods with large deformation and large displacement are introduced and deduced to support the numerical calculation and analysis of post-deployment large deformation and large displacement occurring to extra-long telescopic boom.

To establish the equation, it is usually assumed that the length of the rod axis remains unchanged during deformation. Although the displacement and deformation in the other two directions are large, the axial deformation is still small. The figure below shows the infinitesimal balance rod element suitable for the flexible rods with large deformation and large displacement, in the form of tensor (Fig. 7).

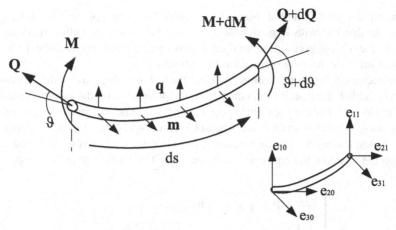

Fig. 7. Infinitesimal balance rod element

By projecting an infinitely flexible rod element with internal and external loads onto a plane, a 6th degree differential equation for large deformation and large displacement can be derived [5], which is suitable for the fast numerical calculation of large displacement in the plane. The large displacement differential equation used to describe the stress deformation state of a flexible rod is expressed as follows:

$$
\begin{cases}
\dfrac{dx}{ds} = \cos \vartheta \\[2mm]
\dfrac{dy}{ds} = \sin \vartheta \\[2mm]
\dfrac{d\vartheta}{ds} = \dfrac{M}{EI} + \dfrac{d\vartheta_0}{ds} \\[2mm]
\dfrac{dQ_x}{ds} + q_x = 0 \\[2mm]
\dfrac{dQ_y}{ds} + q_y = 0 \\[2mm]
\dfrac{dM}{ds} = Q_x \sin \vartheta - Q_y \cos \vartheta
\end{cases}
\tag{1}
$$

The first three equations are used to calculate the ratio of motion and elasticity, while the remaining ones are used to describe the balance of the rod. The forces Q_x and Q_y are assigned to a fixed cartesian coordinate system, M is moment, s indicates the curvature of the non-deformed rod axis, $d\vartheta_0/ds$ is the initial curvature of the rod, and EI is the bending stiffness of the cross-section.

The 6th degree differential equation is established using a plane coordinate system. For the flexible rod with large displacement and subjected to multi-directional loads in space, the 12th degree differential equations can be used [6], and the 12th degree equations are written in the space coordinate system.

The vector equilibrium equation describes the rod in a coupled coordinate system. In order to establish the equilibrium equation in the projection on the coordinate axis, it is necessary to represent the vector in the corresponding basis, such as the basis $\{e_i\}$ related to the cross-section axis. In this case, it must be remembered that not only the projections of the corresponding vectors depend on ε, but also the unit vectors of the basis $e_i(\varepsilon)$. Through the formula, the equation can be entered. The local derivative is expressed as follows:

$$\begin{cases} \dfrac{d\mathbf{Q}}{d\varepsilon} + \mathbf{P} + \chi \times \mathbf{Q} = \mathbf{0}, \\ \dfrac{d\mathbf{M}}{d\varepsilon} + \mathbf{e}_1 \times \mathbf{Q} + \chi \times \mathbf{M} + \mathbf{T} = \mathbf{0}, \\ \mathbf{M} = A(\chi - \chi_0^{(1)}), \\ L_1 \dfrac{d\vartheta}{d\varepsilon} + L_2 \chi_0^{(1)} - A^{-1}\mathbf{M} = \mathbf{0}, \\ \dfrac{d\mathbf{u}}{d\varepsilon} + \chi \times \mathbf{u} + (l_{11} - 1)\mathbf{e}_1 + l_{21}\mathbf{e}_2 + l_{31}\mathbf{e}_3 = \mathbf{0} \end{cases} \tag{2}$$

where:

$$\mathbf{P} = \mathbf{q} + \sum_{i=1}^{n} \mathbf{P}^{(i)}\delta(\varepsilon - \varepsilon_i); \quad \mathbf{T} = \mu + \sum_{v=1}^{\rho} \mathbf{P}^{(v)}\delta(\varepsilon - \varepsilon_v) \tag{3}$$

$$L_1 = \begin{bmatrix} \cos\theta_2\cos\theta_3 & 0 & -\sin\theta_2 \\ -\sin\theta_2 & 1 & 0 \\ \sin\theta_2\cos\theta_3 & 1 & \cos\theta_2 \end{bmatrix};$$

$$L_2 = \tag{4}$$

$$\begin{bmatrix} \cos\theta_2\cos\theta_3-1 & \cos\theta_2\sin\theta_3\cos\theta_1 + \sin\theta_2\sin\theta_1 & \cos\theta_2\sin\theta_3\sin\theta_1 - \sin\theta_2\cos\theta_1 \\ -\sin\theta_2 & \cos\theta_1\cos\theta_3 - 1 & \cos\theta_3\sin\theta_1 \\ \sin\theta_2\cos\theta_3 & \sin\theta_2\sin\theta_3\cos\theta_1 - \cos\theta_2\sin\theta_1 & \sin\theta_2\sin\theta_3\sin\theta_1 + \cos\theta_2\cos\theta_1 - 1 \end{bmatrix};$$

where, L_1 and L_2 are rotation matrices, used to participate in the calculation of the rotation angle in the case of large displacement; $\mathbf{Q}$ and $\mathbf{M}$ are vectors of internal forces and moments; $\mathbf{P}$ and $\mathbf{T}$ are vectors of external forces and moments; $\mathbf{q}$ is external distributed load vector; $\mathbf{u}$ is the displacement vector; χ is curvature vector; $\mathbf{e}_i$ basis vectors; A is section stiffness matrix.

The forces and moments $\mathbf{q}$, $\mathbf{P}^{(i)}$, μ and $\mathbf{T}^{(v)}$ entering into Eqs. (1) in the most general case can depend on the displacements of the points of the axial line of the rod u_j and the rotation angles of the associated axes ϑ_j. The analytical dependence of the load vectors on u_j and ϑ_j in each particular problem is considered to be known.

If the load is follower, then the components of the vectors $\mathbf{q}$, $\mathbf{P}^{(i)}$, μ and $\mathbf{T}^{(v)}$, in the coupled axes remain unchanged at any finite angles of rotation ϑ_j of the coupled axes.

If the forces are dead and equilibrium equations in coupled axes (1.1) are used, then rotation matrices should be used.

The equilibrium equations of a rod in the projections on related axes. To solve most problems, it is simpler to study the equilibrium of rods using the equations in projection onto coupled axes. In addition, the components Q_i and M_i of the vectors $\mathbf{Q}$ and $\mathbf{M}$ have a clear physical meaning in the coupled axes (Q_1 is an axial force, Q_2 and Q_3 are shear forces, M_1 is a torque moment, and M_2 and M_3 are bending moments).

4 Numerical Calculation and Simulation Analysis of Extra Long Deployable Telescopic Boom

Considering the practical working conditions at the end of the loaded deployable telescopic boom, the 12th-order differential equation is used and the finite element analysis is conducted in this paper to analyze and calculate the large deformation and large displacement occurring to the deployable telescopic boom. Then, the analytical results are compared.

The deployable telescopic boom has a total of 6 stages. The post-deployment length is 22.5 m, the cylinder diameters are 160 mm, 140 mm, 120 mm, 100 mm, 80 mm, and 60 mm, the equivalent elastic modulus of the material is 120 Gpa, and the Poisson's ratio is 0.3.

The coordinate system of the deployable telescopic boom is shown in the figure below, in which point o indicates the coordinate origin (Fig. 8).

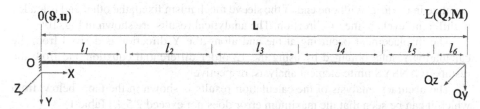

Fig. 8. Schematic diagram of deployable telescopic boom under load

The initial conditions are as follows. The end of the telescopic boom is fixed, and the loads Q_z and Q_y are applied at the initial end.

In this context, $Q_z = 0$, Q_y applies different loads:

$$Q_y = \{50N, 75N, 100N, 150N, 200N, 300N\}.$$

The deployed telescopic boom is equivalent to an extra-long flexible rod with a variable cross-section, and the 12th differential equations are used to perform numerical calculation. The boundary conditions are as follows:

$$\{\vartheta_1(0),\ \vartheta_2(0),\ \vartheta_3(0),\ u_1(0), u_2(0), u_3(0)\} = \{0, 0, 0, 0, 0, 0\};$$
$$\{Q_1(L), Q_2(L), Q_3(L), M_1(L),\ M_2(L), M_3(L)\} = \{0, Q_y, Q_z, 0, 0, 0\}.$$

The calculation results are summarized as shown in the figure below (Fig. 9):

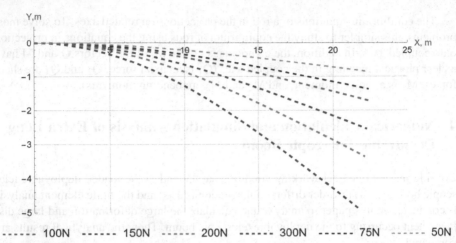

Fig. 9. Change in displacement of member under different loads in the Q_y direction (the 12th degree differential equation)

The finite element analysis is carried out in ANSYS by setting not only the contact and friction boundary conditions between each two-level telescopic boom but also the contact stiffness at the contact position of each two-level telescopic boom [7]. Also, the value of the contact stiffness is defined as the value of the contact stiffness that tends to stabilize in the test. With one end of the sleeve mechanism fixed, the other end is loaded to different levels in the Q_y direction. The analytical results are shown in Fig. 10:

The displacement occurring at the end along the Y direction is derived from the calculation results obtained by using the 12-order differential equation and from the results of ANSYS finite element analysis, respectively.

The accuracy analysis of the calculation results is shown in the table below, from which it can be seen that the maximum error does not exceed 2.5% (Table 1).

It can be concluded from above that the deployable telescopic boom under different loads can be treated as equivalent to a complete flexible rod for calculation and analysis after the expansion of the deployable telescopic boom if the contact stiffness of the cone fit stabilizes. Also, it is verified that the 12th degree differential equation of the large flexible rod is applicable to calculate the deployable telescopic boom numerically.

Considering the deployable telescopic boom which is subjected to space load, the 12th degree differential equation is used to analyze the situation of the telescopic boom being subjected to multi-directional load in space.

The boundary conditions are set as follows. The end of the sleeve is fixed, and the loads Q_z and Q_y are applied at the initial end.

In this condition, $Q_z = \{50\ N, 75, 100\ N, 150\ N, 200\ N, 300\ N\}$, $Q_y = \{50\ N, 75, 100\ N, 150\ N, 200\ N, 300\ N\}$. The analysis results are shown in the figure below (Fig. 11).

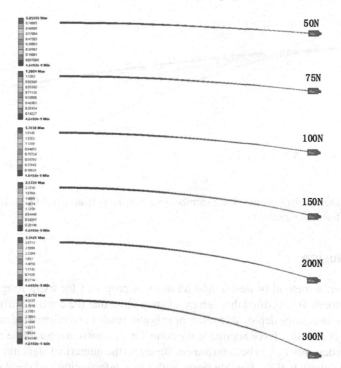

Fig. 10. Change in displacement of member under different loads in the Q_y direction (ANSYS)

Table 1. Comparison of displacement results in the y direction of the end

Load value	50 N	175 N	100 N	150 N	200 N	300 N
ANSYS	0.855	1.280	1.704	2.533	3.343	4.875
12th D.E	0.834	1.312	1.721	2.543	3.387	4.844
Accuracy	1.4%	2.5%	1%	0.4%	1.5%	0.6%

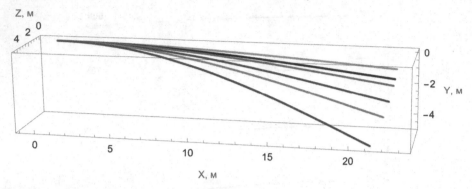

Fig. 11. Change in displacement of the member under different loads in the Q_z and Q_y directions (the 12th differential equation)

5 Conclusion

In this paper, a method of design and analysis is proposed for extra-long deployable telescopic boom. It is verified through experimentation that the contact stiffness of cone fitting in the two-stage deployable telescopic boom tends to stabilize gradually with the increase of cone fitting force applied to the cone. On this basis, a reasonable contact stiffness of the cone surface can be determined. Based on the numerical algorithm of the 12th differential equation of the flexible beam with large deformation and displacement, the change in displacement of the loaded deployable telescopic boom is analyzed. Through a comparison with the results of the finite element software analysis, it is discovered that the extra-long deployable telescopic boom is equivalent to a flexible rod with variable cross-section after the telescopic boom is deployed. Therefore, the numerical algorithm of the differential equation of the flexible rod is applicable to the analysis and calculation of the deployable telescopic boom. This numerical algorithm contributes more solutions to calculating and analyzing the large deformation and displacement occurring to the extra-long deployable telescopic boom on orbit in space.

Acknowledgment. This study was co-supported by the National Natural Science Foundation of China (Grant No. 52175019), Beijing Natural Science Foundation (Grant No. 3212009, Grant No. L222038).

This study was co-supported by the Foundation of China(No. 51675017) and Civil Astronautics Pre-Research Project during the "13th Five-Year Plan" (No D020205).

References

1. Puig, L., Barton, A., Rando, N.: A review on large deployable structures for astrophysics missions. Acta Astronautica. **67**(12), 1226 (2010)
2. Belvin, W.K., Straubel, M., Wilkie, W.K., et al.: Advanced deployable structural systems for small satellites. In: Proceedings of AVT-257/RSM-041 (2016)
3. Mehran, M., Chris, S.: Design and performance of the telescopic tubular mast. The 41st Aerospace Mechanisms Symposium, Jet Propulsion Laboratory, pp. 127140 (2012)

4. Xu, K., Li, L., Bai, S., et al.: Design and analysis of a metamorphic mechanism cell for multistage orderly deployable/retractable mechanism. Mech. Mach. Theory **111**, 85–98 (2017)
5. Гаврюшин, С.С., Барышникова, О.О., Борискин, О.Ф.: Численные методы проектирования гибких упругих элементов. Калуга.: ГУП «Облиздат» (2001)
6. Светлицкий В.А. Механика стержней: Ч. 1. М.: Высшая школа (1987)
7. Thomas, J.R.H.: The Finite element method linear statics and dynamic element analysis. Courier Corporation (2012)

Extenics Networking Method of Generalized Deployable Units

Hangjia Dong and Tuanjie Li[(✉)]

School of Mechano-Electronic Engineering, Xidian University, Xi'an 710071, China
`tjli888@126.com`

Abstract. A new kind of mechanisms named the generalized deployable mechanism is proposed and defined in this paper, which is made up of not only the traditional rigid members, but also the flexible components, springs, cables, pretensioned prismatic joints, pre-tensioned revolute joints, compliant hinges and so on. The extension basic-elements including the matter-element, relationship-element and affair-element are introduced to correspond to the generalized deployable unit, common elements and their combination, respectively. The common elements are the common generalized links or generalized kinematic pairs to connect two generalized deployable units. Based on the summarized assembly types of generalized deployable units, the networking rules of generalized deployable units are proposed to form the generalized deployable kinematic chains. Combining the extension basic-elements with the networking rules, we establish the generating procedure of generalized deployable kinematic chains. The networking processes of four-bar and six-bar generalized deployable units are taken as examples to illustrate and validate the networking method.

Keywords: generalized deployable mechanism · generalized deployable unit · extension basic-elements · networking rules · assembly types

1 Introduction

The deployable mechanism is proposed by Pinero in the 1960s [1]. Deployable mechanisms, also named as deployable structures [2], can vary their shape automatically from a compact, packaged configuration to an expanded, operational configuration. The first engineered deployable structures were used as stabilization booms on early spacecraft. Later on, more complex structures were devised for solar arrays, communication reflectors and telescopes [3–5]. The deployable mechanisms are composed of the same deployable units due to modular design. The deployment and retraction of deployable units depend on the elastic deformation of springs, flexible components or cable driven. Thus, deployable units include not only the traditional rigid links and kinematic pairs, but also the flexible components, springs, cables, preloaded kinematic pairs and flexible hinges. We define them as the generalized deployable units which are composed of the generalized links and generalized kinematic pairs [6]. Generalized links include the flexible members, springs, and cables etc. Generalized kinematic pairs include the preloaded kinematic pairs and flexible hinges etc. The generalized deployable mechanisms are generated by assembling generalized deployable units.

© The Author(s), under exclusive license to Springer Nature Singapore Pte Ltd. 2023
H. Yang et al. (Eds.): ICIRA 2023, LNAI 14269, pp. 468–483, 2023.
https://doi.org/10.1007/978-981-99-6489-5_38

With the development of deployable mechanisms, it is possible to evolve new configurations meeting the requirements of engineering applications. The configuration synthesis is the effective method to address the key problem. The configuration synthesis of traditional mechanisms is one of the hotspot issues. Early configuration synthesis mainly depended on the experience and inspiration. Until the 1960s, the topological graph theory was introduced to describe the mechanisms and lots of configuration synthesis methods were advanced. Gantes [7] investigated the geometric modeling and design methodology of the deployable structures featuring stable and stress-free states in both the deployed and collapsed configurations. Warnaar and Chew [8, 9] studied the generation of deployable truss modules with graph theory. Chen and You [10] conducted lots of researches in the field of monocyclic constraint mechanisms on the basis of Bennett and Myard mechanisms, and some new space deployable mechanisms generated. The generalized deployable mechanism, which is composed of the generalized unit, is a system that can vary their shape automatically from a compact, packaged configuration to an expanded, operational configuration. The combination of generalized units may generate all sorts of deployable mechanisms with different performances. In recent years, the networking technologies of deployable units have been developed. Liu and Chen [11] have created a number of deployable blocks based on the Myard linkage and built large deployable assemblies with these blocks. Chen and You [12] dealt with deployable structures formed by interconnected Bennett linkages to form arch, cylindrical and helical shapes with a single degree of mobility. Huang et al. [13] studied a method for the mobile connection between single loop deployable mechanisms. With this method, lots of deployable units can be used to build a large deployable mechanical network. In recent years, we analyzed the structural characteristics and mobility of planar generalized mechanisms [14], and developed the configuration synthesis of generalized deployable units and mechanisms [6, 15]. In this paper, we proceed from the generalized deployable units, and develop the configuration synthesis of generalized deployable mechanisms with extenics theory. Extenics theory was created by Yang and Cai in 1983 [16]. It is a newly emerging discipline with contradictory problems as its research objects, intelligent management of contradictory problems as its main research content and extension methods as its main research methods. There are three characteristics of extenics: formalized, logical and mathematics characteristics. The extension basic-elements including matter-element, relationship-element and affair-element are correspond to the generalized deployable unit, common elements and their combination respectively. Based on the summarized assembly types of generalized deployable units, the networking rules of generalized deployable units are proposed to form the generalized deployable kinematic chains. Combined extension basic-elements with the networking rules, we establish the generating procedure of generalized deployable kinematic chains,

2 Extenics and Extension Knowledge Space

2.1 Extenics

Extenics is a subject that uses a formalized and logical method to discover the extensibility of matters [16]. Extenics defines the concept of basic-element, which is used to describe the information of the objects, characteristics, and numerical values. The matter-element, affair-element and relationship-element are the three basic elements which are the logical cells of extenics. It is expressed as:

$$B = (O, C, V) = \begin{bmatrix} Object & c_1 & v_1 \\ & c_2 & v_2 \\ & \vdots & \vdots \\ & c_n & v_n \end{bmatrix} \tag{1}$$

where, $O(Object)$ indicates the object, operation or relationship, $C = [c_1\ c_2 \cdots c_n]^T$ indicates the characteristics of the object, $V = [v_1\ v_2\ \cdots v_n]^T$ are the values of characteristics.

The physical entities of generalized deployable mechanisms can correspond to the three basic-elements: matter-element, affair-element, and relationship-element in extenics. The generalized deployable unit is treated as the matter-element. The common elements, the common generalized links and kinematic pairs connecting two generalized deployable units, are treated as the relationship-element. The generalized deployable mechanism formed by generalized deployable units is treated as the affair-element. The affair-element is the combination of matter-elements and relationship-elements. For the purpose of simplicity, the matter-element, affair-element and relationship-element can be expressed by graph, as shown in Table 1.

Table 1. The graph expression of basic-elements

Basic-elements	Physical entity	Diagram
Matter-element	Generalized deployable unit	◯
Relationship-element	Common elements	
Affair-element	Generalized deployable mechanism	☐

2.2 Extension Knowledge Space

The logic base of extenics is extension theory containing three pillars: basic-element theory, extension set theory and extension logic. The extension set theory is an important conception used to categorize things dynamically and describe the quantitative and qualitative changes [17]. The core conception of extension set is extension field including positive and negative extension fields which are called as extension knowledge space. In order to transform the basic-element of extension field into the element of extension knowledge space, some concepts and algorithms of extenics are introduced as follows.

Definition 1: The extension knowledge space of an extension basic-element is a $n+1$ dimensional space, where n is the dimension of the basic-element. Every element in the space shows the unique state of extension basic-element.

Definition 2: $B_0 = (O_0, c_0, v_0)$, $B = (O, c, v)$ are called as the basic-element and the additive basic-element respectively. If a transformation T makes $TB_0 = B_0 \oplus B$, the T is referred to as the additive transformation of B_0.

Definition 3: The operation of transforming an extension basic-element in extension field into an element in extension knowledge space is called as the mapping. The operation of transforming an element of extension knowledge space into an extension basic-element is called as the inverse mapping, as shown in Fig. 1. Thus, each extension basic-element corresponds to an element of extension knowledge space.

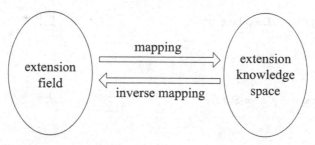

Fig. 1. Extension field and extension knowledge space

3 Assembly Types of Generalized Deployable Units

The generalized deployable mechanism is composed of generalized units. The combination of generalized units may generate all sorts of configurations with different performances. The classical assembly types of generalized deployable units are summarized as shown in Table 2.

Table 2. Assembly types of generalized deployable units

Basic types	Type1	Line type (Solar panel)	
	Type2	Loop type (AstroMesh deployable antenna [18])	
	Type3	Star type (Umbrella antenna [19])	
Hbrid types	Type4	Star-Loop type	
	Type5	Loop-Loop type	
	Type6	Line-Star type	
	Type7	Loop-Line type	
	Type8	Star-line type	

4   Networking Method of Generalized Deployable Units

The extenics provide the formulated expression of generalized deployable units. So the corresponding generalized deployable mechanisms can be obtained by the transformation of extenics. Based on these considerations, we propose the networking method of generalized deployable units as follows.

4.1 Extension Knowledge Space

The generalized deployable units include the cables, flexible components, and preloaded kinematic pairs etc. The weighted values in the configuration matrix and the graphical representations are defined to express the types of the generalized links and generalized kinematic pairs, as shown in Tables 3 and 4.

Table 3. Types of generalized links

Generalized links	Weighted values	Graphical representation
Rigid link	1	
Flexible link	2	
Spring	3	
Cable	4	

Table 4. Types of generalized kinematic pairs

Generalized kinematic pairs	Weighted values	Graphical representation
Revolute pair	5	
Preloaded hinge	7	
Flexible hinge	8	
Fixed joint	9	

The common elements are the common generalized links and generalized kinematic pairs connecting two generalized deployable units. Not all of the generalized links or generalized kinematic pairs can be regarded as the common elements. Some rules are needed to select the common elements. Such as the springs, cables, preloaded hinges and fixed joints can not be regarded as the common elements.

4.2 Networking Expression

(1) Matter-elements networking expression

The affair-element matrix represents the assembly of some matter-elements and expressed by a $N \times 5$ matrix as follows.

$$\begin{bmatrix} n & gn & ga & \boldsymbol{gb} & gc \\ 0 & gn_1 & ga_1 & \boldsymbol{gb_1} & gc_1 \\ \vdots & \vdots & \vdots & \vdots & \vdots \\ 0 & gn_n & ga_n & \boldsymbol{gb_n} & gc_n \end{bmatrix} \tag{2}$$

where, the number of rows N, is equal to the number of generalized deployable units n is the identifier of affair-element matrix. The elements in the second column indicate the serial number of generalized deployable units. The elements in the third, fourth, fifth columns indicate the weighted values of generalized kinematic pairs, generalized links, and generalized kinematic pairs constituting a simple opened chain which will connect to another generalized deployable unit, of which the elements in bold font in the matrix stand for the common elements. The common elements can be changed by the weighted values which stand for the type of common elements. For example, Fig. 2 shows the topological graph, networking process and formed generalized deployable mechanism. The labels 1, 2, 3 and 4 are the identifier of affair-elements.

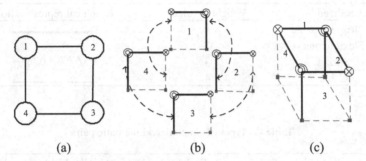

(a)   (b)   (c)

Fig. 2. Networking process of a generalized deployable kinematic chain. (a) Topological graph, (b) Networking process, (c) Generalized deployable kinematic chain.

The corresponding affair-element matrix is:

$$\begin{bmatrix} 1\ 1\ 7\ 1\ 9 \\ 0\ 2\ 7\ 1\ 9 \\ 0\ 2\ 8\ 2\ 9 \\ 0\ 3\ 8\ 2\ 9 \\ 0\ 3\ 7\ 1\ 9 \\ 0\ 4\ 7\ 1\ 9 \\ 0\ 4\ 8\ 2\ 9 \\ 0\ 1\ 8\ 2\ 9 \end{bmatrix} \tag{3}$$

(2) Affair-elements networking expression

The affair-element represents the networking result of some matter-elements. We can also define the affair-elements networking matrix as follows, which includes three parts: the assembly type T, the number of affair-elements A, and the property of common element Q.

$$\begin{bmatrix} N & 0 & 0 \\ 0 & T & v_1 \\ 0 & A & v_2 \\ 0 & Q & v_3 \end{bmatrix} \tag{4}$$

where, T stands for one of eight assembly types shown in Table 2. N is the identifier of the affair-elements networking matrix. v_1, v_2, v_3 are the values of T, A and Q respectively.

For example, if four affair elements are assembled by the type 8 in Table 2, the rigid link and flexible link are selected as common elements, the corresponding affair-elements networking matrix is:

(3) Mapping

For the specified generalized deployable unit, choose the generalized links and generalized kinematic pairs as the common elements. The combination of common elements can be ensured. For example, if a revolute pair and a rigid link act as the common elements, the combination of them includes three elements: revolute pair with revolute pair, rigid with link rigid link, revolute pair with rigid link.

The mapping is an additive transformation: $TB_i = B_0 \oplus B_i$, i is the mapping number, B_0 is the simple opened chains matrix, B_i is the common elements matrix which can be determined by one element in the combination. They are expressed as follows.

$$B_0 = \begin{bmatrix} n & gn & ga & \mathbf{0} & gc \\ 0 & gn_1 & ga_1 & \mathbf{0} & gc_1 \\ \vdots & \vdots & \vdots & \vdots & \vdots \\ 0 & gn_n & ga_n & \mathbf{0} & gc_n \end{bmatrix} \tag{6}$$

$$B_i = \begin{bmatrix} n & 0 & 0 & \mathbf{gb} & 0 \\ 0 & 0 & 0 & \mathbf{gb_1} & 0 \\ \vdots & \vdots & \vdots & \vdots & \vdots \\ 0 & 0 & 0 & \mathbf{gb_n} & 0 \end{bmatrix} \tag{7}$$

The affair-element matrix can be generated by the mapping $TB_i = B_0 \oplus B_i$, that is

$$\begin{bmatrix} n & gn & ga & \mathbf{gb} & gc \\ 0 & gn_1 & ga_1 & \mathbf{gb_1} & gc_1 \\ \vdots & \vdots & \vdots & \vdots & \vdots \\ 0 & gn_n & ga_n & \mathbf{gb_n} & gc_n \end{bmatrix} = \begin{bmatrix} n & gn & ga & \mathbf{0} & gc \\ 0 & gn_1 & ga_1 & \mathbf{0} & gc_1 \\ \vdots & \vdots & \vdots & \vdots & \vdots \\ 0 & gn_n & ga_n & \mathbf{0} & gc_n \end{bmatrix} \oplus \begin{bmatrix} n & 0 & 0 & \mathbf{gb} & 0 \\ 0 & 0 & 0 & \mathbf{gb_1} & 0 \\ \vdots & \vdots & \vdots & \vdots & \vdots \\ 0 & 0 & 0 & \mathbf{gb_n} & 0 \end{bmatrix} \tag{8}$$

The generated affair-element matrix corresponds to a generalized deployable kinematic chain. All the affair-element matrixes constitute the extension knowledge space.

4.3 Networking Steps

The networking steps can be concluded as follows.

1) Choose a generalized deployable unit as the matter-element.
2) Determine an assembly type from the three basic assembly types shown in Table 2.
3) Choose the generalized links and/or generalized kinematic pairs as the common elements between the two matter-elements.
4) Define mapping and generate the extension knowledge space. And each element in the space is an affair-element.

5) Choose an assembly type for the affair-elements from the five hybrid types shown in Table 2.
6) Choose the common element and define the mapping. Then obtain the extension knowledge space of all the affair-elements and generate the generalized deployable kinematic chains.

The basic idea of the networking method is to generate the extension knowledge space from the extension field by the mapping. First, choose the generalized deployable unit and common elements. Then, define mapping. Finally, generate the extension knowledge space. If necessary, the extension knowledge space can be regarded as a new extension field to generate a larger extension knowledge space using the same way for the complex generalized deployable kinematic chains.

5 Examples

5.1 Networking of Four-Bar Generalized Deployable Unit

A four-bar generalized deployable unit as shown in Fig. 3 is chosen as an example to illustrate the networking method. If the assembly type is the line type (Type1) shown in Table 2, the simple opened chains matrix is

$$B_0 = \begin{bmatrix} 1 & 1 & 5 & 0 & 9 \\ 0 & 2 & 5 & 0 & 9 \\ 0 & 2 & 8 & 0 & 9 \\ 0 & 3 & 8 & 0 & 9 \\ 0 & 3 & 5 & 0 & 9 \\ 0 & 4 & 5 & 0 & 9 \end{bmatrix} \tag{9}$$

Fig. 3. A generalized deployable unit

The common elements matrix B_1 is

$$B_1 = \begin{bmatrix} 1 & 0 & 0 & 1 & 0 \\ 0 & 0 & 0 & 1 & 0 \\ 0 & 0 & 0 & 2 & 0 \\ 0 & 0 & 0 & 2 & 0 \\ 0 & 0 & 0 & 1 & 0 \\ 0 & 0 & 0 & 1 & 0 \end{bmatrix} \tag{10}$$

Then the mapping T is applied to B_1, $TB_1 = B_0 \oplus B_1$, and

$$
\begin{bmatrix}
1 & 0 & 0 & 1 & 0 \\
0 & 0 & 0 & 1 & 0 \\
0 & 0 & 0 & 2 & 0 \\
0 & 0 & 0 & 2 & 0 \\
0 & 0 & 0 & 1 & 0 \\
0 & 0 & 0 & 1 & 0
\end{bmatrix}
\oplus
\begin{bmatrix}
1 & 1 & 5 & 0 & 9 \\
0 & 2 & 5 & 0 & 9 \\
0 & 2 & 8 & 0 & 9 \\
0 & 3 & 8 & 0 & 9 \\
0 & 3 & 5 & 0 & 9 \\
0 & 4 & 5 & 0 & 9
\end{bmatrix}
=
\begin{bmatrix}
1 & 1 & 5 & 1 & 9 \\
0 & 2 & 5 & 1 & 9 \\
0 & 2 & 8 & 2 & 9 \\
0 & 3 & 8 & 2 & 9 \\
0 & 3 & 5 & 1 & 9 \\
0 & 4 & 5 & 1 & 9
\end{bmatrix}
\tag{11}
$$

The corresponding networking result is shown in Fig. 4.

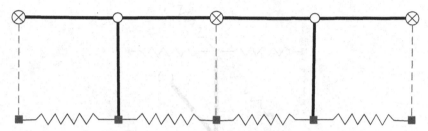

Fig. 4. The networking result according to line assembly type

With the same method, if the assembly type is the loop type (Type 2) shown in Table 2, the corresponding affair-element matrix is

$$
\begin{bmatrix}
2 & 1 & 9 & 0 & 5 \\
0 & 2 & 9 & 0 & 5 \\
0 & 2 & 9 & 0 & 8 \\
0 & 3 & 9 & 0 & 8 \\
0 & 3 & 9 & 0 & 5 \\
0 & 4 & 9 & 0 & 5 \\
0 & 4 & 9 & 0 & 8 \\
0 & 1 & 9 & 0 & 8
\end{bmatrix}
\oplus
\begin{bmatrix}
2 & 0 & 0 & 1 & 0 \\
0 & 0 & 0 & 1 & 0 \\
0 & 0 & 0 & 2 & 0 \\
0 & 0 & 0 & 2 & 0 \\
0 & 0 & 0 & 1 & 0 \\
0 & 0 & 0 & 1 & 0 \\
0 & 0 & 0 & 2 & 0 \\
0 & 0 & 0 & 2 & 0
\end{bmatrix}
=
\begin{bmatrix}
2 & 1 & 9 & 1 & 5 \\
0 & 2 & 9 & 1 & 5 \\
0 & 2 & 9 & 2 & 8 \\
0 & 3 & 9 & 2 & 8 \\
0 & 3 & 9 & 1 & 5 \\
0 & 4 & 9 & 1 & 5 \\
0 & 4 & 9 & 2 & 8 \\
0 & 1 & 9 & 2 & 8
\end{bmatrix}
\tag{12}
$$

The networking result is shown in Fig. 5.

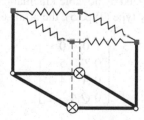

Fig. 5. The networking result according to loop assembly type

If the assembly type is the star type (Type 3) shown in Table 2, the corresponding affair-element matrix is

$$
\begin{bmatrix} 3 1 5 0 9 \\ 0 2 5 0 9 \\ 0 3 5 0 9 \\ 0 4 5 0 9 \end{bmatrix} \oplus \begin{bmatrix} 3 0 0 1 0 \\ 0 0 0 1 0 \\ 0 0 0 1 0 \\ 0 0 0 1 0 \end{bmatrix} = \begin{bmatrix} 3 1 5 1 9 \\ 0 2 5 1 9 \\ 0 3 5 1 9 \\ 0 4 5 1 9 \end{bmatrix} \tag{13}
$$

The networking result is shown in Fig. 6.

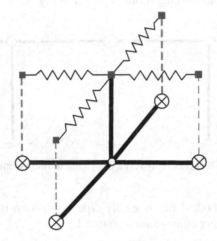

Fig. 6. The networking result according to star assembly type

From the above networking results, we have obtained an extension knowledge space including three affair-elements. For the star-loop assembly type (Type 4), the affair-elements networking matrix is

$$
\begin{bmatrix} 1 & 0 & 0 \\ 0 & T & 4 \\ 0 & A & 4 \\ 0 & Q & 4 \end{bmatrix} \tag{14}
$$

The corresponding generalized deployable kinematic chain is shown in Fig. 7.
For the loop-loop assembly type (Type 5), the affair-elements networking matrix is

$$
\begin{bmatrix} 1 & 0 & 0 \\ 0 & T & 5 \\ 0 & A & 4 \\ 0 & Q & 4-1 \end{bmatrix} \tag{15}
$$

The corresponding generalized deployable kinematic chain is shown in Fig. 8.

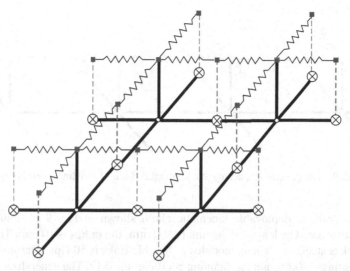

Fig. 7. The generalized deployable kinematic chain of star-loop assembly type

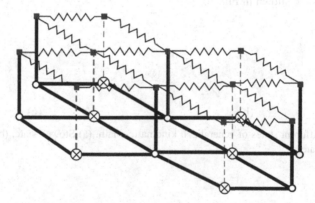

Fig. 8. The generalized deployable kinematic chain of loop-loop assembly type

For the star-line (Type 6) assembly type, the affair-elements networking matrix is

$$\begin{bmatrix} 1 & 0 & 0 \\ 0 & T & 6 \\ 0 & A & 2 \\ 0 & Q & 4 \end{bmatrix} \tag{16}$$

The corresponding generalized deployable kinematic chain is shown in Fig. 9.

It can be seen from above that the networking of basic assembly types of generalized deployable units can be described with the affair-element matrix, and the networking of hybrid assembly types can be described with the affair-elements networking matrix. The two matrixes are obtained by different mappings and include all topological information of generalized deployable kinematic chains.

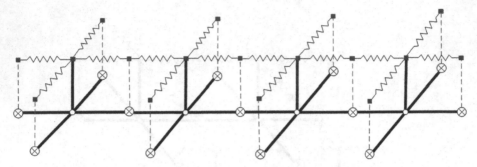

Fig. 9. The generalized deployable kinematic chain of star-line assembly type

The generalized deployable kinematic chain shown in Fig. 9 is simulated with ADAMS software. The length of the link is 500 mm, the radius is 10 mm. The material of rigid link is steel. The Young modulus of flexible links is 50 Gpa. The stiffness coefficient of springs is 0.66, and the damping coefficient is 0.17. The generalized kinematic chain is actuated by the stored spring strain energy. The folded state, deployment and deployed state are shown in Fig. 10.

(a)   (b)   (c)

Fig. 10. The different states of generalized kinematic chain. (a) Stowed state, (b) Deployment, (c) Deployed state.

5.2 Networking of Six-Bar Generalized Deployable Unit

A six-bar generalized deployable unit as shown in Fig. 11 is chosen as another example to illustrate the networking method.

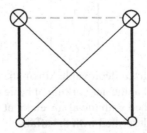

Fig. 11. A six-bar generalized deployable unit

If the assembly type is the loop type (Type 2), the corresponding affair-element matrix is

$$
\begin{bmatrix}
1\ 1\ 8\ 0\ 5 \\
0\ 2\ 8\ 0\ 5 \\
0\ 2\ 8\ 0\ 5 \\
0\ 3\ 8\ 0\ 5 \\
0\ 3\ 8\ 0\ 5 \\
0\ 4\ 8\ 0\ 5 \\
0\ 4\ 8\ 0\ 5 \\
0\ 1\ 8\ 0\ 5
\end{bmatrix}
\oplus
\begin{bmatrix}
0\ 0\ 0\ 1\ 0 \\
0\ 0\ 0\ 1\ 0 \\
0\ 0\ 0\ 1\ 0 \\
0\ 0\ 0\ 1\ 0 \\
0\ 0\ 0\ 1\ 0 \\
0\ 0\ 0\ 1\ 0 \\
0\ 0\ 0\ 1\ 0 \\
0\ 0\ 0\ 1\ 0
\end{bmatrix}
=
\begin{bmatrix}
1\ 1\ 8\ 1\ 5 \\
0\ 2\ 8\ 1\ 5 \\
0\ 2\ 8\ 1\ 5 \\
0\ 3\ 8\ 1\ 5 \\
0\ 3\ 8\ 1\ 5 \\
0\ 4\ 8\ 1\ 5 \\
0\ 4\ 8\ 1\ 5 \\
0\ 1\ 8\ 1\ 5
\end{bmatrix}
\tag{17}
$$

The networking result is shown in Fig. 12.

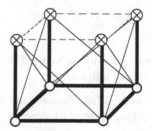

Fig. 12. The networking result according to Eq. (17)

If the above affair-element is assembled by the loop-line type (Type 7), the affair-elements networking matrix is

$$
\begin{bmatrix}
1 & 0 & 0 \\
0 & T & 7 \\
0 & A & 2 \\
0 & Q & 2-8
\end{bmatrix}
\tag{18}
$$

The corresponding generalized deployable kinematic chain and its prototype are shown in Fig. 13, which is the folding articulated square truss mast developed by AEC-Able Engineering Company [20]. This example illustrates the extenics networking method is effective.

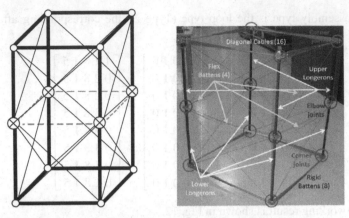

Fig. 13. The generalized deployable kinematic chain and its prototype

6 Conclusions

This paper proposes the extenics networking method of generalized deployable units. The specific work can summarize as follows.

(1) The concepts of matter-element, affair-element, and relationship-element are introduced. The extenics networking method of generalized deployable units has been proposed.
(2) The assembly types of generalized deployable units are summarized.
(3) The extensics networking expression method and the networking steps are presented.
(4) A planar four-bar and six-bar generalized deployable units are as examples to illustrate the extenics networking method.

Acknowledgment. This project is supported by National Natural Science Foundation of China (Grant No. 51775403).

References

1. Pinero, E.P.: Expandable space framing. Prog. Arch. **43**(6), 154–155 (1962)
2. Pellegrino, S.: Deployable Structures. Springer Vienna (2001)
3. Li, T.J.: Deployable analysis and control of deployable space antenna. Aerosp. Sci. Technol. **18**(1), 42–47 (2014)
4. Tibert, G.: Deployable tensegrity structures for space applications. Ph.D. Thesis, Royal Institute of Technology (2002)
5. Mruthyunjaya, T.S.: Kinematic structure of mechanisms revisited. Mech. Mach. Theory **38**(4), 279–320 (2003)
6. Li, T.J., Jiang, J., Dong, H.J., Zhang, L.: Configuration synthesis of generalized deployable units via group theory. Mechanical Sci. **7**(2), 201–208 (2016)
7. Gantes, C.: A design methodology for deployable structures. Ph.D. Thesis, Massachusetts Institute of Technology (1991)

8. Warnaar, D.B., Chew, M.: Kinematic synthesis of deployable-foldable truss structure using graph theory, part 1: graph generation. Transaction of the ASME. J. Mech. Des. 117(1), 112–116 (1995)

9. Warnaar, D.B., Chew, M.: Kinematic synthesis of deployable-foldable truss structure using graph theory, part 2: generation of Deployable Truss module design concepts. transaction of the ASME. J. Mech. Des. 117(1), 117–122 (1995)

10. Chen, Y., You, Z.: Two-fold symmetrical 6R foldable frame and its bifurcations. Int. J. Solids Struct. 46(25), 4504–4514 (2009)

11. Liu, S.Y., Chen, Y.: Myard linkage and its mobile assemblies. Mech. Mach. Theory 44(10), 1950–1963 (2009)

12. Chen, Y., You, Z.: On mobile assemblies of bennett linkages. Proceedings of the Royal Society A 464(2093), 1275–1293 (2008)

13. Huang, H.L., Deng, Z.Q., Li, B., et al.: Mobile assemblies of large deployable mechanisms. JSME J. Space Eng. 5(1), 1–14 (2012)

14. Li, T.J., Jiang, J., Deng, H.Q.: Analysis of structural characteristics and mobility of planar generalized mechanisms. Iranian J. Science and Technology-Transactions of Mechanical Eng. 41(1), 25–34 (2017)

15. Chen, C.C., Li, T.J., Tang, Y.Q.: Configuration synthesis of generalized mechanism based on screw theory. Iranian J. Science and Technology-Transactions of Mechanical Eng. 43(S1), 1013–1021 (2019)

16. Yang, C., Cai, W.: Extenics: Theory, Method and Application. Science Press, Beijing (2013)

17. Cai, W., Yang, C.Y., Zhao, Y., et al.: New development of the basic theory of extenics. Engineering Sci. 12(1), 40–45 (2004)

18. Thomson, M.K.: The Astromesh deployable reflector. IEEE Antennas and Propagation Society International Symposium (1999)

19. Amend, C., Nurnberger, M., Oppenheimer, P., et al.: A novel approach for a low-cost deployable antenna. Proceedings of the 40th Aerospace Mechanisms Symposium, NASA Kennedy Space Center (2010)

20. Gross, D., Messner, D.: The able deployable articulated mast-enabling technology for the shuttle radar topography mission. Proceedings of the 33rd Aerospace Mechanisms Symposium (1999)

Research on Foot Slippage Suppression of Mammal Type Legged Robot based on Optimal Force Allocation

Yufei Liu[1,2(✉)], Yongyao Li[1,2], Zeyuan Sun[1,2], Dongdong Zheng[1,2], Ruiwei Liu[3], Chao Chen[4], Boyang Xing[1,2], and Zhirui Wang[1,2]

[1] Unmanned Center, China North Vehicle Research Institute, Beijing 100072, China
liuyufei_hit@163.com
[2] Collective Intelligence and Collaboration Laboratory, Beijing 100072, China
[3] College of Naval Architecture and Ocean Engineering, Guangzhou Maritime University, Guangzhou 510725, China
[4] Shandong Artificial Intelligence Institute, Qilu University of Technology (Shandong Academy of Sciences), Jinan 250014, China

Abstract. Heavy-duty robots such as hexapod and quadruped robots exhibit tremendous potential with their high payload ability and terrain adaptability. This paper introduces a slippage estimation and suppression approach for mammal type legged robot that traverses uneven and transition stage from a flat surface to sloped terrain. An optimal force allocation method under contact constraints is developed to minimize the linear and quadratic costs in the commands and constrained contact forces. Extensive experiments have been conducted, and the results have demonstrated the effectiveness of the proposed control approach.

Keywords: Heavy-duty robots · Slippage estimation and suppression · Optimal force allocation

1 Introduction

Multi-legged robots exhibit tremendous potential in the case of rough or steep sloped terrains. Heavy-duty legged robots can play an important role in transporting supplies over rough terrain, and they can help disaster rescue and perform outdoor exploration [1].

Heavy-duty legged robots can be classified as hydraulically and electrically driven robots. TITAN XI is another hydraulically driven quadruped robot with a mass of 6800 kg and can work on steep slopes [2]. Addie and Kenzo [3] presents an optimal impedance controller based on body inertia to adapt the uneven and soft terrain; this method is used on COMET-IV hexapod robot, which is approximately 2120 kg with a payload of 400 kg, aims to perform disaster rescues. Athlete is the most representative of large-scale electrically driven robots; the trunk of its body has a hexagonal frame with a total weight of approximately 1440 kg, and its improved motion planning enables traverse various terrains [4].

© The Author(s), under exclusive license to Springer Nature Singapore Pte Ltd. 2023
H. Yang et al. (Eds.): ICIRA 2023, LNAI 14269, pp. 484–494, 2023.
https://doi.org/10.1007/978-981-99-6489-5_39

Due to the feet of legged robots were not in contact with the ground at all times. The estimation algorithm can be applied in different terrains and is immune to feet slippage. A robust estimation method of walking legged robots was presented based on the proprioceptive sensors data fusion [5]. Okita presented slippage estimation algorithm based on the Unscented Kalman Filter, and the data are from the IMU and accelerometer data [6]. The impact of walking gait and energy efficiency on the performance of the robot under different friction environments are analyzed [7]; and also proposed two adaptive slippage strategies to achieve the walking of quadruped robot.

The optimization of contact interactions is crucial for maintaining stability and high tracking performance. Mistry et al. [8] presents an analytically solution by using orthogonal decomposition to eliminate constraint forces, and it avoids drawback of relying on the complex dynamics projections. The pseudo-inverse formulations are presented by Jiang [9] to optimize the force distribution; the sum of the squares of contact forces is minimized and the optimal force distribution can be obtained. Righetti et al. [10] develops an inverse-dynamics controller to minimize the quadratic cost and reduce slipping on varying terrains; the ability of the controller is demonstrated using the humanoid and quadruped robots. The optimal force distribution and control of quadruped robots under external disturbances are presented in Li et al. [11]; in this method, an adaptive neural network is adopted to handle perturbations based on the hybrid motion/force control. The humanoid robot Atlas can walk on stones with sharp surfaces without any prior knowledge of the terrain; a quadratic program is used to optimize the cost function based on the whole-body momentum control framework [12, 13]. However, slippage suppression based on optimal interactions on various terrains have rarely been experimentally studied with mammal type legged robots.

The main contribution of this paper is to propose slippage suppression method for mammal type legged robot based on optimal force allocation. The foot-terrain slippage estimation method based on state estimation is applied. The optimal force allocation method can detect the slippage rate and suppress the slippage. This paper is organized as follows: Sect. 2 introduces the data fusion method. Slippage estimation are presented in Sect. 3. Section 4 introduces optimal force allocation. Finally, comprehensive experiments are presented in Sect. 5. The conclusions are given in Sect. 6.

2 Data Fusion Method

In order to obtain the velocity information of the robot body, it is necessary to integrate the acceleration signal of sensor, and the velocity error gradually increases with time. Therefore, it is necessary to calibrate the acceleration data to suppress the error of velocity calculation. The acceleration error of the IMU can be calculated by the scaling factor and the deviation value of each axis. The three-axis static model can be expressed as:

$$\begin{cases} f_x = G_{ax}\hat{f}_x + B_{ax} \\ f_y = G_{ay}\hat{f}_y + B_{ay} \\ f_z = G_{az}\hat{f}_z + B_{az} \end{cases} \tag{1}$$

where G_{ax}, G_{ay} and G_{az} are the scaling factors of each axis, B_{ax}, B_{ay} and B_{az} are the deviation values of acceleration for each axis.

The estimated values of each axis acceleration are:

$$\hat{f}_{x,k-1} = (f_x - \hat{B}_{x,k-1}) \cdot \hat{G}_{x,k-1} \tag{2}$$

When the estimated value does not reach the true value, there exists acceleration error. In order to compensate the error in real time, an error model needs to be established, and the error value between the calculated value and the true value can also be calculated. The static model of acceleration can be transformed as:

$$\beta_1 \hat{f}_x^2 + \beta_2 \hat{f}_x + \beta_3 \hat{f}_y^2 + \beta_4 \hat{f}_y + \beta_5 \hat{f}_z^2 + \beta_6 \hat{f}_z + 1 = 0 \tag{3}$$

Inertial navigation acceleration measurement value after calibration can be calculated as:

$$\beta = (\mathbf{S}^T \mathbf{S})^{-1} \mathbf{S}^T \upsilon \tag{4}$$

The state variable differential equation of the prediction model is derived, and the equations of the velocity, acceleration and angular acceleration of the trunk body are obtained as:

$$\begin{cases} \dot{p} = v \\ \dot{v} = \mathbf{T}_B^N (\hat{f} - b_f - w_f) \\ \dot{e} = \mathbf{T}_B^N (\hat{w} - b_w - w_w) \end{cases} \tag{5}$$

In accordance with the feedback correction principle, the estimated deviation values can be feedback to the calculation process. The correction vectors of the position, velocity and attitude are obtained as:

$$\begin{bmatrix} p_c(k-1) \\ v_c(k-1) \\ \varepsilon_c(k-1) \end{bmatrix} = \begin{bmatrix} p_{IMU}(k-1) \\ v_{IMU}(k-1) \\ \varepsilon_{IMU}(k-1) \end{bmatrix} - \begin{bmatrix} \delta\hat{p}_{k-1} \\ \delta\hat{v}_{k-1} \\ \delta\hat{\varepsilon}_{k-1} \end{bmatrix} \tag{6}$$

Thereafter, the estimations of the state are formulated as:

$$\begin{bmatrix} \hat{p}(k) \\ \hat{v}(k) \\ \hat{e}(k) \end{bmatrix} = \begin{bmatrix} p_c(k-1) \\ v_c(k-1) \\ \varepsilon_c(k-1) \end{bmatrix} + \begin{bmatrix} v_c(k-1)\Delta t + C_B^W(\tilde{f} - b_f - w_f)\Delta t^2/2 \\ C_B^W(\tilde{f} - b_f - w_f)\Delta t \\ C_B^W(\tilde{w} - b_w - w_w)\Delta t \end{bmatrix} \tag{7}$$

The state estimators provided position, velocity and attitude vectors which were further compared to the values obtained by Mocap system.

3   Slippage Estimation

In order to prevent and compensate for the invalid slippage of the foot terrain contact process, the slippage estimation method for the mammal type hexapod and quadruped robots based on the dynamic model. The body velocity estimation value and the foot tip velocity estimation value are fused based on the EKF, and the foot slippage of the robot can be estimated [14].

When the legged robot walking by the mammal type, the robot can walk in forward direction. Slippage estimation method is proposed based on the single leg dynamics model. Suppose that the robot walks in the forward direction and do not consider the turn, and it relies on the movement of the hip joint and knee joint simplified, as shown in Fig. 1.

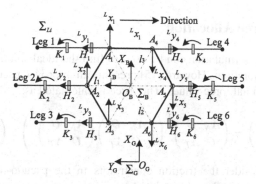

Fig. 1. Slip model of trunk body for mammal type

The angle between the hip joint and the normal direction is q_H, and the angle between the knee joint and the normal direction is q_K. The position of the foot tip for the supporting phase represents the slippage displacement. The input slippage variables for dynamic system are defined. According to the single-leg slippage model for mammal-type legged robot walking, the position vector of the two-link can be obtained as:

$$\mathbf{p}_K = \begin{bmatrix} {}^L P_{sy} + L_K \sin q_K \\ {}^L P_{sz} + L_K \cos q_K \end{bmatrix}$$
$$\mathbf{p}_H = \begin{bmatrix} {}^L P_{sy} + L_K \sin q_K + L_H \sin q_H \\ {}^L P_{sz} + L_K \cos q_K + L_H \cos q_H \end{bmatrix} \tag{8}$$

The kinetic energy of the robot's single-leg movement for mammal-type legged robot walking is:

$$T = \frac{1}{2} M_K \dot{\mathbf{p}}_k^T \dot{\mathbf{p}}_k + \frac{1}{2} M_H \dot{\mathbf{p}}_H^T \dot{\mathbf{p}}_{II} + \frac{1}{2}(J_K \dot{q}_K^2 + J_H \dot{q}_H^2) \tag{9}$$

The potential energy of the hexapod robot for the mammal type legged robot walking can be expressed as:

$$V = M_K g({}^L P_{sz} + I_K \cos q_K) \mid M_H g({}^L P_{sz} + L_K \cos q_K + L_H \cos q_H) \tag{10}$$

The general form of the equation for single leg movement according to Lagrange equation:

$$\mathbf{D_d}(\mathbf{q})\ddot{\mathbf{q}} + \mathbf{B_d}(\mathbf{q}, \dot{\mathbf{q}})\dot{q} + \mathbf{G_d}(\mathbf{q}) - \mathbf{C_d}\mathbf{u} - \mathbf{E_d}\mathbf{F} = 0 \tag{11}$$

where the $\mathbf{D_d}(\mathbf{q})$ is Inertia matrix, and the $\mathbf{B_d}(\mathbf{q})$ is Coriolis matrix, and the $\mathbf{G_d}(\mathbf{q})$ is Gravity matrix and $\mathbf{u}$ is joint torque.

According to the single leg Lagrange equation, the forward slippage acceleration model is obtained as:

$$^L\ddot{P}_{sy} = ((M_K L_K + L_K M_H)(\dot{q}_K^2 \sin q_K - \ddot{q}_K \cos q_K) + M_H L_H (\dot{q}_H^2 \sin q_H \\ -\ddot{q}_H \cos q_H) + F_T)/(M_K + M_H) \tag{12}$$

4 Optimal Force Allocation

The pseudo-inverse formulation can be used to find the ideal solution which is closest to the origin of all solutions. Howard [15] presents an improved pseudo-inverse method to calculate the optimal force values. The force is calculated as:

$$\begin{pmatrix} F_N \\ F_T \end{pmatrix} = \begin{pmatrix} A_N & O \\ O & A_T \end{pmatrix}^T \left(\begin{pmatrix} A_N & O \\ O & A_T \end{pmatrix} \begin{pmatrix} A_N & O \\ O & A_T \end{pmatrix}^T \right)^{-1} \begin{pmatrix} B_N \\ B_T \end{pmatrix} \tag{13}$$

In order to consider the friction constraints in the pseudo-inverse method, the equilibrium equations can be reformulated as:

$$\begin{cases} f_{Txi} = K_{xi}\mu_i f_{zi} \\ f_{Tyi} = K_{yi}\mu_i f_{zi} \end{cases} \tag{14}$$

Defining the supporting phase has three legs, and the tangential equilibrium equation can be formulated as:

$$A_K K_T = B_T \tag{15}$$

The solution for the friction duty factors is given by:

$$K_T = A_K^T (A_K A_K^T)^{-1} B_T \tag{16}$$

The pseudo-inverse solutions for the foot forces are given by Eq. (14).

However, this method only solves the equilibrium equation without considering the constraints of the hexapod robot. Such as the slippage on the different terrains or the joint torques provided by the actuators.

For a hexapod robot, the force and moment vectors that act at the center of the body are denoted by $W_B = \begin{bmatrix} ^B F_x & ^B F_y & ^B F_z & ^B M_x & ^B M_y & ^B M_z \end{bmatrix}$, and the forces at the supporting legs are represented by $^L f = \begin{bmatrix} ^L f_{xi} & ^L f_{yi} & ^L f_{zi} \end{bmatrix}$. The statics of a multi-contact hexapod robotic system is shown in Fig. 2.

In order to balance the forces and moments between the trunk body and each leg, the equilibrium equations are formulated as:

$$AF = -W \tag{17}$$

where $F = \begin{bmatrix} ^L f_{x1} & ^L f_{y1} & ^L f_{z1} & \cdots & ^L f_{x6} & ^L f_{y6} & ^L f_{z6} \end{bmatrix}^T$. $A \in \mathbf{R}^{6 \times 18}$ is calculated as:

$$A = \begin{bmatrix} I_3 & \cdots & I_3 \\ R_1 & \cdots & R_n \end{bmatrix} \tag{18}$$

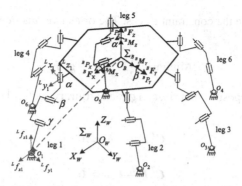

Fig. 2. The statics of a multi-contact hexapod robotic system

R_i is formulated as a skew symmetric matrix:

$$R_i = \begin{bmatrix} 0 & -{}^L P_{zi} & {}^L P_{yi} \\ {}^L P_{zi} & 0 & -{}^L P_{xi} \\ -{}^L P_{yi} & {}^L P_{xi} & 0 \end{bmatrix} \tag{19}$$

In the normal direction, the equilibrium equations of the moment for the robot body are formulated as:

$$\begin{cases} \sum_i {}^L f_{zi} + \sum_j m_j g = 0 \\ \sum_i {}^L f_{zi}({}^L P_{xi} - {}^B P_x) + \sum_j m_j g({}^L P_{xj} - {}^B P_x) = 0 \\ \sum_i {}^L f_{zi}({}^L P_{yi} - {}^B P_y) + \sum_j m_j g({}^L P_{yj} - {}^B P_y) = 0 \end{cases} \tag{20}$$

where m_j is the weight of each leg; ${}^L P_{xi}$ and ${}^L P_{yi}$ are the positions of feet; ${}^L P_{xj}$ and ${}^L P_{yj}$ are the positions of legs; ${}^B P_x$ and ${}^B P_y$ are the positions of trunk body.

In the tangential direction, the forces of trunk body satisfy the equilibrium equation:

$$\begin{cases} \sum_i {}^L f_{xi} = m_B \ddot{a}_{Bx} \\ \sum_i {}^L f_{yi} = m_B \ddot{a}_{By} \\ \sum_i {}^L f_{yi}({}^L P_{xi} - {}^B P_x) - \sum_i {}^L f_{xi}({}^L P_{yi} - {}^B P_y) = I_B \ddot{\gamma}_B \end{cases} \tag{21}$$

where m_B is the weight of robot; a_{Bx} and a_{By} are the acceleration of robot; I_B is the inertial tensor of the robot; $\ddot{\gamma}_B$ is the yaw acceleration of the body.

The solutions to the contact forces are not unique, thus, an optimal method is chosen to minimize the command and constraint forces. The quadratic programming (QP) method is chosen to minimize the constraint forces. The objective functions for the QP method is as follows:

$$\text{Minimize } \frac{1}{2}F^T G F + g^T F \qquad (22)$$

G is a symmetric positive matrix, and g is an arbitrary vector. The desired constraints are calculated as:

$$C_A^T F + C_W = 0 \qquad (23)$$

$$C_Z^T F + C_{z0} \geq 0 \qquad (24)$$

$$\sqrt{\left(C_X^T F\right)^2 + \left(C_Y^T F\right)^2} \leq \mu \cdot C_Z^T F \qquad (25)$$

where $C_A = A^T, C_W = W$, and C_X, C_Y and C_Z are the vectors in the forward, tangential and normal directions, respectively. C_{z0} is threshold value for the normal force in the stance phase.

According to Eq. (17), there are six linear equations with eighteen unknown variables. Equation (17) is simplified as follows:

$$\begin{bmatrix} A_p & A_r \end{bmatrix} \begin{bmatrix} F_p \\ F_r \end{bmatrix} = \hat{W} \qquad (26)$$

where A_p is the matrix for the particular solution, A_r is the matrix for the unknown variables, F_p represents the particular forces of F, F_r represents the unknown solutions of F. The free variable F_r may then be rewritten using the following form:

$$F_r = A_r^{-1}\left(\hat{W} - A_p F_p\right) \qquad (27)$$

The solution of the forces is obtained as:

$$F = F_0 + N F_r \qquad (28)$$

where $F_0 = \begin{bmatrix} A_p^{-1}\hat{W} & 0 \end{bmatrix}^T$ is the particular solution for F, and $N = \begin{bmatrix} -A_p^{-1}A_r & 1 \end{bmatrix}^T$ is the matrix that maps F_r onto W.

The force allocation problem formulated from the QP method is calculated using Eqs. (22) – (25). On substituting Eq. (28) into Eq. (22), the solution in the QP form is obtained as follows:

$$\text{Minimize } g^T F_0 + g^T N F_r + \frac{1}{2}F_0^T G F_0 + \frac{1}{2}F_0^T G N F_r$$
$$+ \frac{1}{2}F_r^T N^T G F_0 + \frac{1}{2}F_r^T N G N F_r \qquad (29)$$

Solving the unknown force by Lagrange method, and the target equation for solving the force is transformed into the Lagrange function:

$$L(\mathbf{F}, \lambda) = \frac{1}{2}F_r^T G_r F_r + g_r^T F_r - \lambda^T(A_r F_r - \mathbf{b}_w) \qquad (30)$$

The stagnation conditions for the target equation are as follows:

$$\nabla_F L = G_r F_r + g_r - A_r \lambda = 0$$
$$\nabla_\lambda L = A_r F_r - b_w = 0 \tag{31}$$

The equation can be transformed into a linear system:

$$\begin{bmatrix} G_r & -A_r \\ -A_r^T & 0 \end{bmatrix} \begin{pmatrix} F_r \\ \lambda \end{pmatrix} = - \begin{pmatrix} g_r \\ b_w \end{pmatrix} \tag{32}$$

The Lagrange matrix is symmetric but not positive, and its inverse matrix can be expressed as:

$$\begin{bmatrix} G_r & -A_r \\ -A_r^T & 0 \end{bmatrix}^{-1} = \begin{bmatrix} H & -T \\ -T^T & U \end{bmatrix} \tag{33}$$

The vectors in the Lagrange inverse matrix are:

$$H = G_r^{-1} - G_r^{-1} A_r (A_r^T G_r^{-1} A_r)^{-1} A_r^T G_r^{-1}$$
$$T = G_r^{-1} A_r (A_r^T G_r^{-1} A_r)^{-1} \tag{34}$$
$$U = -(A_r^T G_r^{-1} A_r)^{-1}$$

The optimal force solutions of the unknown values are:

$$F_r^* = -g_r H + T b_w$$
$$\lambda^* = b_w T^T - b_w U \tag{35}$$

5 Experimental Verification

The experimental systems of hexapod robot named ElSpider and quadruped robot named Panda5 include proprioceptive and external measurement equipments. The IMU has an advantage of dependence on real-time gravity. The accelerations and angular velocities can be integrated over time to derive the position, velocity of the trunk body. The acceleration in the IMU frame have been periodically measured in the experiments; and forward kinematic is adopted to calculate the velocity to further determine the measurement model in the data fusion method.

Mocap system consists of four cameras and six position markers; furthermore, a rigid body model in Mocap frame is incorporated. The cameras are placed in the four corners of the experimental field and they are immobile during the whole experiment. The experimental measurement systems for hexapod and quadruped robots are shown in Fig. 3.

The hexapod robot adopts the tripod gait walking, and slippage estimation data of hexapod trunk body and stance feet for hexapod robot are analyzed on the tile terrain. The slippage estimation of stance feet for hexapod and quadruped body are analyzed on soft terrain as shown in Fig. 4.

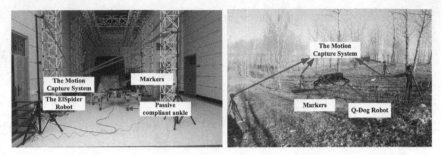

Fig. 3. The internal and external measurement system for hexapod and quadruped robots

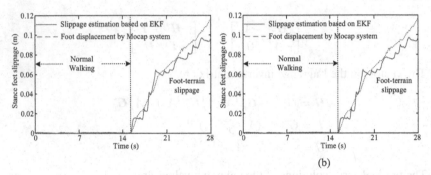

Fig. 4. Comparison results of the slipping displacement for the stance feet of the hexapod (a) and quadruped robot (b)

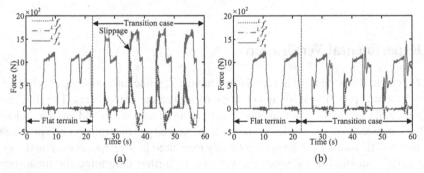

Fig. 5. Experiments of force allocation in the transition terrain: (a) forces of front leg 1 without the slippage suppression method; (b) forces of front leg 1 with the slippage suppression method.

According to the calculated foot slip acceleration, the foot-terrain slippage displacement of hexapod and quadruped robots can be estimated and the comparison data by the Mocap system verifies the effectiveness of the slippage estimation algorithm. We can see that the different legs in the stance phase can support the trunk body simultaneously, and the legs on the sloped surface or horizontal plane can exert approximately the same normal forces in the transition stage. Thus, the optimal force allocation method can suppress the slippage effectively (Fig. 5).

6 Conclusion

In this study, we investigate a data fusion method based on EKF. The data of accurate velocity and slippage estimation of hexapod and quadruped robots are from the kinematics, IMU and foot force information. Optimal force allocation under contact constraints is presented to minimize the tangential forces during locomotion on flat, uneven, sloped and harsh terrains. Given a desired body trajectory, the forces are optimized at each instant. The verification experiments of the slippage suppression method have been performed. Future work will aim to fuse the state estimator with the visual information to detect the foot slippage more accurate for the legged robots.

References

1. Zhuang, H., Gao, H., Deng, Z., Ding, L., Liu, Z.: A review of heavy-duty legged robots. Science China 57(2), 432–437 (2014)
2. Hodoshima, R., Doi, T., Fukuda, Y., Hirose, S., Okamoto, T., Mori, J.: Development of a quadruped walking robot to work on slopes. IEEE/RSJ International Conference on Intelligent Robots and Systems (IROS) (2004)
3. Irawan, A., Nonami, K.: Optimal impedance control based on body inertia for a hydraulically driven hexapod robot walking on uneven and extremely soft terrain. J. Field Robotics 28(5), 690–713 (2011)
4. Hauser, K., Bretl, T., Latombe, J., Harada, K., Wilcox, B.: Motion planning for legged robots on varied terrain. Int. J. Robot. Res. 27(11), 1325–1349 (2008)
5. Wawrzyński, P., Możaryn, J., Klimaszewski, J.: Robust estimation of walking robots velocity and tilt using proprioceptive sensors data fusion. Robot. Auton. Syst. 66, 44–54 (2015)
6. Okita, N., Sommer, H.J.: A novel foot slip detection algorithm using unscented Kalman Filter innovation. American Control Conference, pp. 5163–5168 (2012)
7. Takemura, H., Deguchi, M., Ueda, J.: Slip-adaptive walk of quadruped robot. Robot. Auton. Syst. 53(2), 124–141 (2005)
8. Mistry, M., Buchli, J., Schaal, S.: Inverse dynamics control of floating base systems using orthogonal decomposition. IEEE International Conference on Robotics and Automation, pp. 3406–3412 (2010)
9. Jiang, W.Y., Liu, A.M., Howard, D.: Optimization of legged robot locomotion by control of foot-force distribution. Trans. Inst. Meas. Control. 26(4), 311–323 (2004)
10. Righetti, L., Buchli, J., Mistry, M., Kalakrishnan, M., Schaal, S.: Optimal distribution of contact forces with inverse-dynamics control. Int. J. Robot. Res. 32(3), 280–298 (2013)
11. Li, Z., Ge, S., Liu, S.: Contact-Force Distribution Optimization and Control for Quadruped Robots Using Both Gradient and Adaptive Neural Networks. IEEE Transactions on Neural Networks and learning Systems 25(25), 1460–1473 (2014)
12. Wiedebach, G., et al.: Walking on partial footholds including line contacts with the humanoid robot atlas. humanoid robots (Humanoids), 2016 IEEE-RAS 16th International Conference on (2016)
13. Koolen, T., et al.: Design of a momentum-based control framework and application to the humanoid robot atlas. Int. J. Humanoid Robotics 13(1), 1650007 (2016)

494   Y. Liu et al.

14. Yufei, L., Boyang, X., Wang, Z., Lei, J.: Research on foot slippage estimation of mammal type legged robot. International Conference on Intelligent Robotics and Applications (ICIRA) (2021)
15. Howard, D., Jiang, W.Y., Liu, A.M.: Optimization of legged robot locomotion by control of foot-force distribution. Trans. Inst. Meas. Control. 26(4), 311–323 (2004)

Evaluation of Wearable Robots
for Assistance and Rehabilitation

Improved Notch Filter Method for Vibration Suppression of Flexible Joint Robots with Harmonic Reducers

Zhihong Zhu[1], Kejian Wang[1], Xing Zhou[1,2], Qian Sun[1], Ran Ju[1], Meng Gao[2], and Shifeng Huang[1,2(✉)]

[1] the National CNC Engineering Technology Research Center,
Huazhong University of Science and Technology, Wuhan 430074, China
d201677154@hust.edu.cn
[2] Foshan Institute of Intelligent Equipment Technology, Foshan 528000, China

Abstract. Mechanical resonance affects the performance of robot trajectory tracking. Notch filter (NF) is an effective method to solve resonance problems. However, because the NF introduces phase lag and the resonance frequency of robot is low, the NF will cause system instability. Therefore we propose an improved notch filter (INF) to improve the phase delay near the notch frequency. On the other hand, because the resonance frequency varies with robot's posture, it's difficult to determine the notch frequency. This paper studies the robot with harmonic reducers (HRs) as transmission components. Based on the electro-mechanical coupling system, we analyze the transfer functions of multiple excitation sources to motor velocity and link velocity. Then we confirm that the main resonant excitation source is harmonic component of transmission error (HCTE) in HRs. Therefore the notch frequency can be set priorly by commend velocity. Finally, the validity of the INF method was verified on a flexible joint robot.

Keywords: Notch filter · Robot resonance · Harmonic reducer

1 Introduction

With the rapid development of industrial automation and intelligence, robots are widely used in welding, spraying, assembly, handling and mechanical processing. Harmonic reducers (HRs) are widely used in robots because of their capacity to achieve high precision, minimize clearance, large reduction ratios, and maintain a compact size. These features make them particularly well-suited for small and medium-sized robots.

However, the use of HRs also increases the joint flexibility of the robot, leading to unwanted vibrations. When an excitation source produces a frequency that matches the resonance frequency of the robot, it can trigger destructive resonance behavior. To suppress vibration, scholars have conducted extensive research on robot vibration suppression. Various vibration suppression strategies have been

© The Author(s), under exclusive license to Springer Nature Singapore Pte Ltd. 2023
H. Yang et al. (Eds.): ICIRA 2023, LNAI 14269, pp. 497–508, 2023.
https://doi.org/10.1007/978-981-99-6489-5_40

proposed, including singular perturbation control [5], backstepping control [8], robust control based on disturbance observer [9], and state observer [11]. Based on the estimated position of the link-side, vibration suppression of the robot can be achieved using the pole placement method [10].

Among the methods, the NF [1,2,4,6,7] is widely used to effectively suppress the resonance problem in mechanical systems. Notably, the NF is easy to implement and is commonly utilized in mechanical systems with elastic transmission to address high-frequency mechanical resonance issues. Reference [7] analyzed the dual-mass system and realized the adaptive tuning process of NF parameters through fast FFT analysis. Iwasaki M [4] focuses on suppressing the resonance phenomenon of robots with HRs. Based on this, this paper conducts a further analysis of robot resonance and compares the vibration suppression effects between NF and INF. However, accurately calculating the mechanical frequency of each axis is challenging due to the time-varying inertia of the link, which is also studied.

The novel contributions of this article are the following. 1) Determining that the HCTE is the main source of resonant excitation in robots with HRs. 2) Proposing INF to solve the system instability caused by the phase lag of NF. 3) Setting notch frequency by command velocity avoiding calculation of robot resonance frequency.

This paper is organized as follows. In Sect. 2, we analyze the influence of multiple excitation sources based on the electro-mechanical coupling system on robot vibration. In Sect. 3, INF is proposed to address the resonance phenomenon. And a scheme for setting the notch frequency is introduced. Experimental evaluations are conducted in Sect. 4. Finally, Sect. 5 concludes this paper.

2 Robot Resonance Analysis

Robot is highly nonlinear and strongly coupled dynamic systems, which is difficult to analyze directly by classical control theory. In addition, the link inertia is time-varying, and the stiffness of the robot also follows a nonlinear model, which makes the vibration form of the robot more complex. In order to analyze the resonance phenomenon of robots, a dual-mass system model is used to describe robots with flexible joints, as shown in Fig. 1.

In Fig. 1, the reducer can be considered as an equivalent torsion spring and then the dynamic model is established as:

$$
\begin{aligned}
T_m &= J_m \ddot{q}_m + T_s \\
T_s &= K(q_m - q_l) + C_s(\omega_m - \omega_l) \\
T_s + T_l &= J_l \ddot{q}_l
\end{aligned}
\tag{1}
$$

where T_m is the electromagnetic torque, T_s is the torsion spring torque, T_l is the link-side torque (including gravity and the coupling force between the links); J_m is the motor inertia, J_l is the link inertia; K is the torsion spring stiffness, C_s is the torsion spring damping coefficient; q_l and q_m are the link position and the motor position, ω_l and ω_m are the link velocity and the motor velocity, respectively. In the later analysis, the damping coefficient C_s is small and neglected.

The transfer function from T_m to ω_m can be obtained by Eq. (1):

$$G_1(s) = \frac{\omega_m}{T_m} = \frac{J_l s^2 + K}{J_m J_l s^3 + K(J_m + J_l)s} = \frac{s^2 + \omega_{ARF}^2}{J_m(s^2 + \omega_{NTF}^2)s} \tag{2}$$

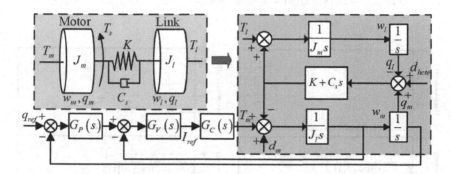

Fig. 1. Two mass system and robot servo control system

Equation (2) indicates that the flexible joint will introduce a pair of conjugate zeros ω_{ARF} and poles ω_{NTF}, which respectively represent the anti-resonance frequency and resonance frequency of the robot.

$$\omega_{ARF} = \sqrt{\frac{K}{J_l}}, \omega_{NTF} = \sqrt{\frac{K(J_m + J_l)}{J_m J_l}} \tag{3}$$

The introduction of harmonic components with frequency ω_{NTF} in the electromagnetic torque T_m will cause the mechanical system to resonate.

The preceding analysis focuses on the robot resonance phenomenon caused by the input electromagnetic torque without considering the servo system control. However, the vibration phenomenon caused by HCTE in HRs is more common in robots. In Fig. 1, the HCTE d_{hcte} and the motor-side disturbance torque d_m are added to the servo system control, and the command position q_{ref} is the system input. The servo system control is a typical cascade control system consisting of position loop $G_P(s)$, velocity loop $G_V(s)$, and current loop $G_C(s)$. Normally, the transfer function of the current loop can be viewed as 1.

$$G_P(s) = k_{pp}, G_V(s) = k_{vp} \tag{4}$$

As the command position q_{ref} contains no high-frequency components, this paper aims to analyze the effects of d_{hcte}, d_m, T_l on the system, specifically on the link velocity ω_l and motor velocity ω_m. The transfer functions can be derived as follows:

$$G_{den} = (J_m J_l s^4 + K(J_m + J_l)s^2 + (J_l s^2 + K)(k_{pp}k_{vp} + k_{vp}s))$$

$$G_{d_{hcte}To\omega_m} = \omega_m(s)/d_{hcte}(s) = -KJ_l s^3/G_{den}$$

$$G_{d_m To\omega_m} = \omega_m(s)/d_m(s) = (J_l s^3 + Ks)/G_{den}$$

$$G_{T_l To\omega_m} = \omega_m(s)/T_l(s) = Ks/G_{den} \qquad (5)$$

$$G_{d_{hcte}To\omega_l} = \omega_l(s)/d_{hcte}(s) = K(J_m s^3 + k_{vp}s^2 + k_{pp}k_{vp}s)/G_{den}$$

$$G_{d_m To\omega_l} = \omega_l(s)/d_m(s) = Ks/G_{den}$$

$$G_{T_l To\omega_l} = \omega_l(s)/T_l(s) = (J_m s^3 + k_{vp}s^2 + Ks + k_{pp}k_{vp}s)/G_{den}$$

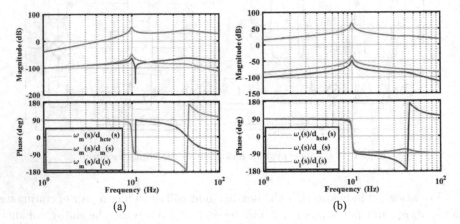

Fig. 2. Electro-mechanical coupling system Bode diagram. (a).Bode diagram of the excitation source to motor velocity. (b).Bode diagram of the excitation source to link velocity

Figure 2 shows the bode diagram of Eq. (5). It can be seen that each excitation source can cause resonance in electro-mechanical coupling system. Equation (5) reveals that all transfer functions share the same denominator. Moreover, the servo parameters k_{pp}, k_{vp} also affect the distribution of the transfer function poles and alter the resonance frequency. Unlike Eq. (3), the resonance frequency of the mechanical system is determined by the mechanical structure alone but the servo parameters change the resonance frequency considering the servo control.

It is essential to note that these transfer functions exhibit distinct frequency response behaviors. For instance, the bode diagrams of the transfer functions from d_{hcte} and d_m to ω_m feature a second resonance peak. And the bode diagrams of the transfer function from d_{hcte} to ω_m has an anti-resonance peak. We will rely on these differences to demonstrate that HCTE d_{hcte} is the excitation source that causes resonance behavior in Sect. 4. Furthermore, the primary frequency component of the HCTE is the harmonic signal with twice the frequency of the wave generator input [3], which increases the likelihood of inducing resonance in the system.

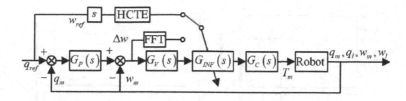

Fig. 3. Servo control system with INF

3 Improved Notch Filter Method

In order to solve the resonance, the INF is added after the output of the velocity loop to suppress vibration, as shown in Fig. 3. The NF is written as:

$$G_{NF}(s) = (s^2 + kp\omega_n s + \omega_n^2)/(s^2 + k\omega_n s + \omega_n^2) \qquad (6)$$

where ω_n is the notch frequency, p is the notch depth coefficient, and k is the notch width coefficient. INF transfer function is written as:

$$G_{INF}(s) = \frac{s^2 + kp\omega_n s + \omega_n^2}{s^2 + k(\omega_n + \omega_d)s + (\omega_n + \omega_d)^2} \frac{(\omega_n + \omega_d)^2}{\omega_n^2} \qquad (7)$$

where ω_d is the frequency offset.

The Bode diagrams of the NF and INF are shown in Fig. 4(a), both of which can attenuate the signal at the notch frequency to achieve the effect of vibration suppression. However, the NF will bring a 90° phase lag. In a system where the robot resonance frequency is only between $10 \sim 30\text{Hz}$, it can lead to system instability. INF can improve the phase lag characteristics brought about by the NF. After adding NF and INF, the Bode diagrams of the transfer function from d_{hcte} to ω_m and ω_l are shown in Fig. 4(b) and Fig. 4(c). From the amplitude response diagram, both NF and INF can reduce the response amplitude at the resonance frequency. But from the phase diagram, it can be found that the phase mutation of the NF is severe, resulting in system instability. From the pole-zero distribution diagram of Figure Fig. 4(d), it can be found that the poles of the NF are distributed in the right half plane, while the INF is in the left half plane. Therefore, the INF can keep the system stable while suppression vibration.

Figure 5(a) is the Bode plot of the INF for different width coefficients. As the width factor increases, the phase improvement function of INF decreases. Figure 5(b) shows the Bode diagram of INF under different frequency offsets. When $\omega_d = 0$, the INF degenerates into a NF without phase improvement function. As ω_d increases, the phase improvement becomes more and more pronounced, but the new formant peak is introduced with increasing magnitude.

Both the NF and the INF have difficulty in parameter setting, especially the setting of the notch frequency. We know that the inertia of the robot link varies with its pose, so the resonance frequency of the system also changes with the pose, which brings great difficulties to the parameter setting of the notch frequency.

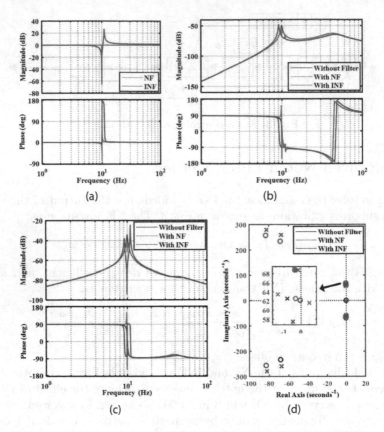

Fig. 4. Comparison of NF and INF. (a) NF and INF. (b) Bode diagram of d_{hcte} to ω_m transfer function. (c) Bode diagram of d_{hcte} to ω_l transfer function. (d) System zero-pole distribution

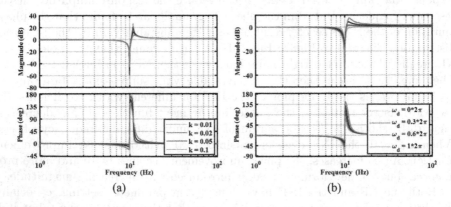

Fig. 5. Effect of different parameters on improved notch filter.(a) Comparison of Bode diagrams with different width coefficients of INF.(b) Comparison of Bode diagrams with different Frequency Offset of INF

However, it is also extremely difficult to analyze the resonance frequency of the robot through online FFT. Accurate identification of the resonance frequency in the robot requires sufficient sampling points to obtain FFT results with a small enough resolution. It has been explained above that the main resonance excitation source of the robot using the HRs is the HCTE d_{hcte}. Therefore, according to the characteristics of the main frequency components of d_{hcte}, this paper calculates the theoretical frequency value of HCTE through command velocity calculation to set the notch frequency of the INF, as shown in Fig. 3. That is to say, the INF no longer traps the resonance frequency of the robot, but weakens the main frequency component of the HCTE d_{hcte}. When the frequency of HCTE reaches the resonance frequency of the robot, the INF can suppress resonance behavior. The frequency-variable notch filter is shown in Fig. 6, and its notch frequency changes with the command velocity.

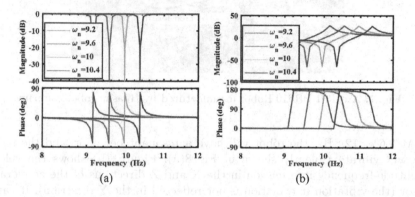

Fig. 6. Variable notch frequency Bode plot. (a) NF. (b) INF

4 Experiment

This paper conducts experiments on the robot shown in Fig. 7, which is provided by Foshan Institute of Intelligent Equipment Technology. An acceleration sensor is installed at the load center to measure the vibration data of the link-side.

4.1 Verification of Resonant Excitation Source

First, the motor feedback velocity and link velocity (acceleration sensor acquisition) at different operating velocitys are collected and analyzed. The 100% running velocity of the second joint motor is $960r/min$.

Analyze the feedback velocity of motor and link, then draw the amplitude-frequency diagram as shown in Fig. 8. It can be seen from the motor velocity amplitude-frequency diagram that there are two resonance peaks, and there is no anti-resonance peak. Compared with Fig. 2, it can be considered that the resonance behavior of a robot with HRs is determined by the HCTE. When the

504   Z. Zhu et al.

motor command velocity is in the 30% ∼ 40% velocity range, the vibration is relatively severe. And the frequency of HCTE d_{hcte} at this time is:

$$f_{ate} = 960 \times (30\% \sim 40\%)/60 \times 2r/min = 9.6 \sim 12.8\,Hz \tag{8}$$

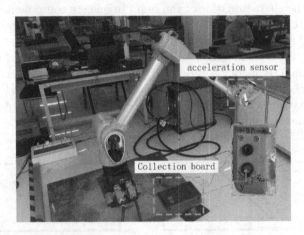

Fig. 7. An HSR-BR610 Robot manufactured by Huashu robot company

At $9.6 \sim 12.8\,Hz$, the robot will have a resonant behavior, and the motor-side will vibrate violently shown in Fig. 8(a). Figure 8(b) shows the velocity amplitude-frequency information in the X and Z directions of the acceleration sensor (the vibration information is not reflected in the Y direction). It can be seen that the link-side also produces severe vibration at this frequency.

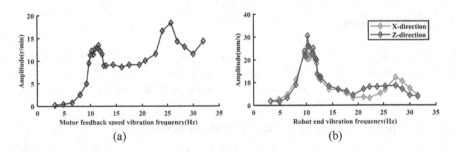

Fig. 8. Robot vibration analysis.(a) Motor feedback velocity frequency spectrum.(b) Acceleration sensor collecting velocity frequency spectrum

In order to verify the feasibility of setting ω_n by calculating the frequency of HCTE through command velocity, the theoretical frequency of HCTE and the vibration frequency of the robot's actual feedback motor velocity were compared.

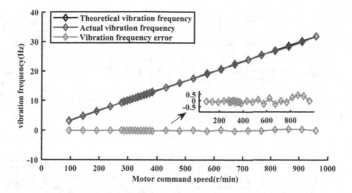

Fig. 9. Comparison of theoretical vibration frequency and actual vibration frequency

The calculation formula of theoretical angular transmission error frequency is shown in Eq. (8), and the comparison results are shown in Fig. 9. It is worth noting that the primary vibration frequency of the motor feedback velocity deviates from the theoretical angular drive error frequency by less than 0.5Hz. It is further proved that the resonance excitation source of the robot equipped with the HRs is HCTE. The accuracy of the theoretical HCTE frequency also proves the reliability of calculating ω_n from the command velocity.

4.2 Vibration Suppression Effects of NF and INF

In the above-mentioned full-velocity measurement experiment, it was found that the robot would vibrate in the 30% ∼ 40% velocity range, and reach the vibration peak value at 34% velocity. Therefore, the vibration suppression strategies are mainly aimed at this velocity range to verify. The collected data includes motor-side feedback velocity, electromagnetic torque, acceleration sensor X-direction velocity and Z-direction velocity. An FFT analysis is performed on these data, and the frequency and amplitude with the largest vibration are taken. Then the amplitude-frequency diagram is drawn as shown in Fig. 10. The trend of four graphs is same, which can well reflect the vibration suppression effect. In practical applications, we pay more attention on the link-side. So this paper takes Fig. 10(c) as an example to compare the experimental results of NF and INF. It can be found that in the 9.5 ∼ 11Hz velocity range, the NF fails, and even causes system instability and aggravates the robot vibration. The INF has a good inhibitory effect on robot resonance, and the vibration amplitude is suppressed from $25mm/s$ to about $5mm/s$.

As shown in Fig. 11, we verify the impact of different width coefficients on vibration suppression performance. In order to ensure that the NF is effective, a comparison is made at a velocity of 39%. Collecting the acceleration and velocity information of the acceleration sensor, analyze the vibration amplitude. In the velocity and acceleration information on the link-side, it can be observed that the vibration amplitude decreases. At this velocity, both the NF and the INF can

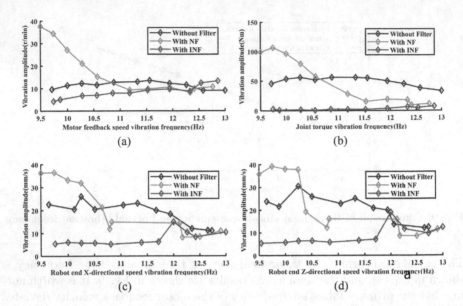

Fig. 10. Vibration suppression effect of NF and INF. (a) Motor feedback velocity. (b) Electromagnetic torque. (c) Acceleration sensor X-direction velocity. (d) Acceleration sensor Y-direction velocity

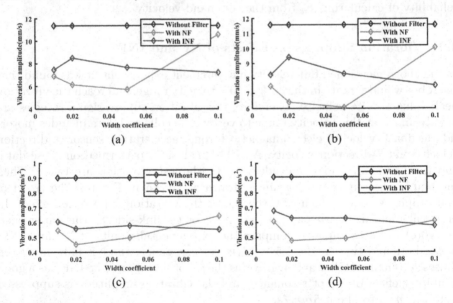

Fig. 11. Vibration suppression effect of different notch width coefficients. (a) Acceleration sensor X-direction velocity. (b) Acceleration sensor Z-direction velocity. (c) Acceleration sensor X-direction acceleration.(d) Acceleration sensor Y-direction acceleration

suppression vibration. The NF works best when ω_d is small. As the ω_d increases, the phase lag of the NF increases, and the notch effect becomes invalid. More seriously, NF will cause system instability at lower speeds, but the INF can still work effectively.

5 Conclusion

This paper focuses on analyzing the resonance of robots using HRs. First, it investigates the difference of resonance behavior between mechanical system and electro-mechanical coupling system. Next, the excitation sources in the electro-mechanical coupling system are analyzed, and their transfer function bode diagrams are presented. Experimental results demonstrate that the resonance excitation source in robots with HRs is HCTE. Furthermore, it discusses the instability caused by the phase lag of the NF and an INF is proposed. To solve the problem of determining the notch frequency, the theoretical HCTE frequency is calculated by command velocity. Finally, the validity of INF is verified by experiments.

Acknowledgements. We greatly acknowledge the funding of this work by National Natural Science Foundation of China, U19A2072. And we would like to thank for the help and support of Foshan institute of intelligent Equipment Technology.

References

1. Bahn, W., Kim, T.I., Lee, S.H., et al.: Resonant frequency estimation for adaptive notch filters in industrial servo systems. Mechatronics **41**, 45–57 (2017)
2. Chen, Y., Yang, M., Long, J., Hu, K., Xu, D., Blaabjerg, F.: Analysis of oscillation frequency deviation in elastic coupling digital drive system and robust notch filter strategy. IEEE Trans. Industr. Electron. **66**(1), 90–101 (2018)
3. Ghorbel, F.H., Gandhi, P.S., Alpeter, F.: On the kinematic error in harmonic drive gears. J. Mech. Des. **123**(1), 90–97 (2001)
4. Iwasaki, M., Nakamura, H.: Vibration suppression for angular transmission errors in harmonic drive gearings and application to industrial robots. IFAC Proc. Vol. **47**(3), 6831–6836 (2014)
5. Kim, J., Croft, E.A.: Full-state tracking control for flexible joint robots with singular perturbation techniques. IEEE Trans. Control Syst. Technol. **27**(1), 63–73 (2017)
6. Kumagai, S., Ohishi, K., Shimada, N., Miyazaki, T.: High-performance robot motion control based on zero-phase notch filter for industrial robot. In: 2010 11th IEEE International Workshop on Advanced Motion Control (AMC), pp. 626–630. IEEE (2010)
7. Lee, D.H., Lee, J., Ahn, J.W.: Mechanical vibration reduction control of two-mass permanent magnet synchronous motor using adaptive notch filter with fast Fourier transform analysis. IET Electr. Power Appl. **6**(7), 455–461 (2012)
8. Pham, M.N., Hamelin, P., Hazel, B., Liu, Z.: A two-stage state feedback controller supported by disturbance-state observer for vibration control of a flexible-joint robot. Robotica **38**(6), 1082–1104 (2020)

9. Sariyildiz, E., Oboe, R., Ohnishi, K.: Disturbance observer-based robust control and its applications: 35th anniversary overview. IEEE Trans. Industr. Electron. **67**(3), 2042–2053 (2019)
10. Szabat, K., Orlowska-Kowalska, T.: Vibration suppression in a two-mass drive system using pi speed controller and additional feedbacks-comparative study. IEEE Trans. Industr. Electron. **54**(2), 1193–1206 (2007)
11. Szabat, K., Tran-Van, T., Kamiński, M.: A modified fuzzy Luenberger observer for a two-mass drive system. IEEE Trans. Industr. Inf. **11**(2), 531–539 (2014)

Design of a Locust-Like Robot Based on Metamorphic Mechanism

Lu Liu[1], Xiaoli Jia[1(✉)], Aqing Xin[1], Jinglong Zhang[1], and Liaoliang Ke[2]

[1] College of Machinery and Storage and Transportation Engineering, China University of Petroleum (Beijing), Beijing 102249, People's Republic of China
xljia@cup.edu.cn
[2] School of Mechanical Engineering, Tianjin University, Tianjin 300072, China

Abstract. In this paper, a locust is used as the bionic object to design a locust robot based on a variable cell mechanism that couples two modes of movement, jumping and fluttering, with a focus on the design and simulation of the jumping mechanism and fluttering mechanism of the locust robot. The jump mechanism is composed of incomplete gears, springs and connecting rods, while the flutter mechanism is composed of worm gears and double cranks and double rockers. A push-pull solenoid is used to achieve instantaneous merging and separation of the mechanism based on the construction of a class of variable cells. The constraint equations and neighbouring chain matrix are also used to describe the constitutive characteristics of the variable cell mechanism and the variable cell process. The simulation results show that the movement process of the model is basically the same as that of the locust, which verifies the feasibility of the bionic structure.

Keywords: Locust-like Robot · Metamorphic Mechanism · Constraint Equation

1 Introduction

Bionics is a technical science that studies the structure, properties, principles, and behaviors of biological systems, and provides new design ideas, working principles, and system composition for engineering technology [1]. The research field of mobile bionic robots has shifted from fixed-point operations in a structured environment to autonomous operations in an unstructured environment, such as interstellar exploration, military reconnaissance, field rescue, and archaeological reconnaissance activities. Many insects have very strong hind leg jumping muscles, which has always attracted the interest of researchers, and thus made significant progress in biological research and insect-inspired jumping robots [2].

Locust has a strong jumping ability and can pause and jump over a long distance. Hence, locusts are often used as imitation objects of bionic jumping robots. Stability analysis method has been used by many scholars to achieve jumping stability through real-time control of the robot's jumping legs.

Sarfogliero and others designed a four-legged jumping robot "Grillo" based on the observation and analysis of the biological characteristics of leafhoppers. The jumping

© The Author(s), under exclusive license to Springer Nature Singapore Pte Ltd. 2023
H. Yang et al. (Eds.): ICIRA 2023, LNAI 14269, pp. 509–521, 2023.
https://doi.org/10.1007/978-981-99-6489-5_41

height of the jumping robot is 100 mm and the horizontal distance is 200 mm, which is about twice and four times its body length, respectively [3]. Inspired by the legs of desert locusts, V.Zaitsev et al. built a locust-like robot prototype with a jumping mechanism that mimics the structural characteristics of the locust femur and tibia with equal-length legs [4]. The prototype can jump up to 3.1 m in height and 3 m in jump distance.

In terms of the bionic flapping-wing mechanism, Gerdes et al. [5] has created three generations of miniature coaxial dual flapping-wing aircraft, the miniature version of Delft DelFly I aircraft, the most noteworthy feature of this aircraft is its visual stability; DelFly II Reduce the wingspan to 28 cm, can fly forward at a speed of 7 m/s, and even fly backward at a speed of -1 m/s. DelFly Micro is the smallest among them (The wingspan is only 10 cm) and the world's lightest (3.07 g) flapping-wing micro-aircraft. Germany's Festo (FESTO) company successfully imitated the principle of bird flight and studied a "SmartBird" bionic bird resembling a seagull.

Although the jumping robot can overcome large obstacles and move in a more complicated terrain environment due to its instantaneous explosiveness and discreteness of footing, its trajectory is difficult to control and it is easy to overturn during jumping. Flapping-wing robot not only integrates the lifting, hovering and propulsion functions into a flapping-wing system, but also has the characteristics of light weight and high flexibility. However, the current flapping-wing robot lacks a leg mechanism and requires additional power during take-off. There will be a big impact when landing, and the internal structure will be easily damaged.

The above-mentioned single movement mode has certain defects, such as insufficient environmental interaction ability and large landing impact. In the process of evolution, locusts have evolved a more competitive movement mode, not only for jumping performance, but also for jumping heights that can reach several times their body length. They can also rely on their wings to glide in the air to maintain their posture stability. Therefore, the introduction of metamorphic mechanism makes the jumping motion and flapping motion of the locust-like robot independent of each other and has a certain degree of coupling, which helps to make up for the shortcomings of a single motion mode, and further improves the function of the organism itself. It conforms to the movement mechanism of natural organisms.

In this study, a design method of locust-like robot mechanism based on metamorphic mechanism is proposed. The jump mechanism and the flapping wing mechanism are coupled to design the robot body structure. The simulation results show that the mechanism design method of the locust-like robot is feasible.

2   Design of Locust-Like Robot Based on Metamorphic Mechanism

2.1   Design and Analysis of Robot Energy Storage System and Flapping Wing Mechanism

Energy Storage System Design. Springs are used to simulate the tendons of the hind feet of locusts as the energy storage components of the locust-like robot. The structure diagram of the locust-like robot energy storage system is shown in Fig. 1, and its parameters are shown in Table 1.

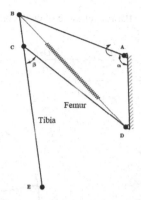

Fig. 1. Structure diagram of energy storage system

Table 1. Parameter table of each component of energy storage

parameter	l_{AB}	l_{BC}	l_{CD}	l_{DA}	l_{CE}
length (mm)	150	58	175	100	175

Design and Analysis of Flapping Wing Mechanism. The flapping wing system uses a symmetrical double-crank and double-rocker mechanism as shown in Fig. 2. This section selects the right side for analysis, as shown in Fig. 3.

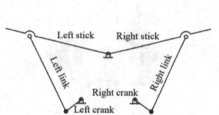
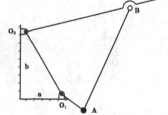

Fig. 2. Structure diagram of flapping wing system

Fig. 3. Schematic diagram of right flapping wing system

The flapping-wing creature has a longer flapping time and a shorter flapping time during flight. Therefore, the quick-return characteristics of the flapping-wing mechanism should be considered in the design of this section. The extreme angle $\theta - 36°$, and the calculation results of the dimensions of each component are shown in Table 2.

The structure of the locust wings was considered to design a flexible wing with a rigid front edge and a flexible tail. The structure of the wing veins intersects each other, and the wing surface is wrapped with a thin film to form a 1/4 ellipse, as shown in Fig. 4. The three-dimensional model of the flapping-wing mechanism of the locust-like robot is shown in Fig. 5. It can be seen from Fig. 5 that the maximum swing angle of a single wing is 40°, and the limit angle of a single-sided shot is 20°.

Table 2. Parameter table of each component

parameter	l_{O_1A}	l_{AB}	l_{O_2B}	a	b
size (mm)	10	40	50	15	25.98

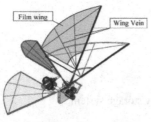

Fig. 4. Wing shape diagram of Flapping wing mechanism

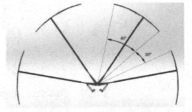

Fig. 5. Schematic diagram of right flapping wing system

2.2 Metamorphic Mechanism Design

Structural Design of Metamorphic Mechanism. Based on the design of the jumping mechanism and the flapping-wing mechanism, the motion characteristics of the push-pull electromagnet are used to design the transmission system of the locust-like robot into a metamorphic mechanism with metamorphic function.

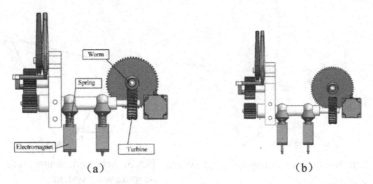

Fig. 6. Two forms of metamorphosis mechanism (a) merged state; (b) separated state

Push-pull electromagnets are used to realize the instantaneous merging or separation between the worm wheel and the worm. The worm wheel and the worm have a certain load force during the transmission process. If only the push-pull electromagnet is used to realize the separation and meshing of the worm wheel and the worm, problems of instability and toothing will occur. Therefore, the worm gear shaft can be supported by the compression spring, and a certain deformation space is provided, so that the worm gear and the worm can be meshed and transmitted smoothly.

The combined state is the normal meshing of the worm wheel and the worm, as shown in Fig. 6(a). The separated state is the disengagement of the worm wheel and the worm, as shown in Fig. 6(b).

Metamorphic Matrix Analysis. The establishment of the constraint function **C** is based on the analysis of the constraint characteristics of the movement pair of the metamorphic mechanism, and the restraint ability and degree of the movement pair are taken into consideration. The matrix method is used to construct a kinematic chain adjacency matrix **A** with constraint functions as elements to describe and analyze the configuration and changes of metamorphic mechanisms. The metamorphic mechanism has 3 stable states A, B, C and 6 metamorphic states A → B, B → C, C → B, B → A, A → C, C → A, as shown in Fig. 7.

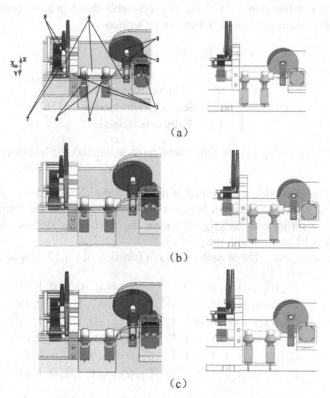

(a)

(b)

(c)

Fig. 7. Three steady states of metamorphic mechanism (a) Steady state A; (b) Steady state B; (c) Steady state C

where 1-worm body, drive motor, electromagnet and sliding groove, 2-motor gear, 3-gear 11 and worm, 4-gear 12, worm gear, shaft 7, 5-shaft sleeve, 6-double compression spring, 7- Right crank gear 13, 8-left crank gear 14.

The metamorphic source kinematic chain of the metamorphic mechanism has 8 components and 8 kinematic pairs, and the chain adjacency matrix can be expressed as

$$A_i^{(8)} = \begin{pmatrix} 0 & C_{12} & C_{13} & C_{14} & C_{15} & C_{16} & C_{17} & C_{18} \\ C_{12} & 0 & C_{23} & 0 & 0 & 0 & 0 & 0 \\ C_{13} & C_{23} & 0 & C_{34} & 0 & 0 & 0 & 0 \\ C_{14} & 0 & C_{34} & 0 & C_{45} & 0 & 0 & 0 \\ C_{15} & 0 & 0 & C_{45} & 0 & C_{56} & 0 & 0 \\ C_{16} & 0 & 0 & 0 & C_{56} & 0 & 0 & 0 \\ C_{17} & 0 & 0 & 0 & 0 & 0 & 0 & C_{78} \\ C_{18} & 0 & 0 & 0 & 0 & 0 & C_{78} & 0 \end{pmatrix} \tag{1}$$

The constraint function $C(t)$ in Eq. (1) represents the degree of constraint of the motion pair in various directions, which can be written as

$$C(t) = (C_1, C_2, C_3, C_4, C_5, C_6)^T \tag{2}$$

$$C(i) = \begin{cases} 0 & \text{Unconstrained} \\ [0, 1] & \text{Semi - constrained } i \in [1, 6] \\ 1 & \text{Fully constrained} \end{cases} \tag{3}$$

The first three in Eq. (3) are movement constraints, and the last three are rotation constraints.

a) State A: The shaft sleeve is located at the top of the sliding groove, which can be regarded as a fixed connection between the shaft sleeve and the frame. 6- double compression spring is in the original length, the worm gear meshes with the worm, and the gear 12 meshes with the gear 13.

In this state, the value of each constraint function in Eq. (2) can be expressed as

$$\begin{aligned} C_{12}(t) &= (1, 1, 1, 1, 0, 1)^T & C_{23}(t) &= (0, 0, 0, 0, 1, 0)^T \\ C_{13}(t) &= (1, 1, 1, 1, 0, 1)^T & C_{34}(t) &= (1, 1, 1, 0, 0, 1)^T \\ C_{14}(t) &= (1, 1, 0, 0, 1, 1)^T & C_{45}(t) &= (0, 1, 1, 0, 1, 1)^T \\ C_{15}(t) &= (1, 1, 1, 1, 1, 1)^T & C_{56}(t) &= (0, 0, 0, 0, 0, 0)^T \\ C_{16}(t) &= (1, 1, 1, 1, 1, 1)^T & C_{78}(t) &= (0, 0, 0, 1, 0, 0)^T \\ C_{17}(t) &= (1, 1, 1, 0, 1, 1)^T & C_{18}(t) &= (1, 1, 1, 0, 1, 1)^T \end{aligned} \tag{4}$$

Then Eq. (1) can be expressed as

$$A_A^{(8)} = \begin{pmatrix} 0 & C_{12} & C_{13} & C_{14} & 1 & 1 & C_{17} & C_{18} \\ C_{12} & 0 & C_{23} & 0 & 0 & 0 & 0 & 0 \\ C_{13} & C_{23} & 0 & C_{34} & 0 & 0 & 0 & 0 \\ C_{14} & 0 & C_{34} & 0 & C_{45} & 0 & 0 & 0 \\ 1 & 0 & 0 & C_{45} & 0 & 0 & 0 & 0 \\ 1 & 0 & 0 & 0 & 0 & 0 & 0 & 0 \\ C_{17} & 0 & 0 & 0 & 0 & 0 & 0 & C_{78} \\ C_{18} & 0 & 0 & 0 & 0 & 0 & C_{78} & 0 \end{pmatrix} \tag{5}$$

In this state, the 6-double compression spring is in its original state, and the members 5 and 6 can be regarded as being fixedly connected to the frame. Therefore, Eq. (5) can be simplified, which can be written as

$$
A_A^{(6)} =
\begin{pmatrix}
0 & C_{12} & C_{13} & C_{14} & C_{17} & C_{18} \\
C_{12} & 0 & C_{23} & 0 & 0 & 0 \\
C_{13} & C_{23} & 0 & C_{34} & 0 & 0 \\
C_{14} & 0 & C_{34} & 0 & 0 & 0 \\
C_{17} & 0 & 0 & 0 & 0 & C_{78} \\
C_{18} & 0 & 0 & 0 & C_{78} & 0
\end{pmatrix}
\tag{6}
$$

b) b) State B: The sleeve moves along the sliding groove, the worm gear meshes with the worm, and the gear 12 meshes with the gear 13. The metamorphic matrix in this state can be expressed as

$$
A_A^{(8)} =
\begin{pmatrix}
0 & C_{12} & C_{13} & C_{14} & C_{15} & 1 & C_{17} & C_{18} \\
C_{12} & 0 & C_{23} & 0 & 0 & 0 & 0 & 0 \\
C_{13} & C_{23} & 0 & C_{34} & 0 & 0 & 0 & 0 \\
C_{14} & 0 & C_{34} & 0 & C_{45} & 0 & 0 & 0 \\
C_{15} & 0 & 0 & C_{45} & 0 & C_{56} & 0 & 0 \\
1 & 0 & 0 & 0 & C_{56} & 0 & 0 & 0 \\
C_{17} & 0 & 0 & 0 & 0 & 0 & 0 & C_{78} \\
C_{18} & 0 & 0 & 0 & 0 & 0 & C_{78} & 0
\end{pmatrix}
\tag{7}
$$

C_{56} in Eq. (7) is semi-constrained, $C_{56} \in [0, 1]$.

$$
\begin{aligned}
&C_{12}(t) = (1, 1, 1, 1, 0, 1)^T & &C_{23}(t) = (0, 0, 0, 0, 1, 0)^T \\
&C_{13}(t) = (1, 1, 1, 1, 0, 1)^T & &C_{34}(t) = (1, 1, 1, 0, 0, 1)^T \\
&C_{14}(t) = (1, 1, 0, 0, 1, 1)^T & &C_{45}(t) = (0, 1, 1, 0, 1, 1)^T \\
&C_{15}(t) = (1, 1, 0, 1, 1, 1)^T & &C_{56}(t) = (0, 0, C_{56}, 0, 0, 0)^T \\
&C_{16}(t) = (1, 1, 1, 1, 1, 1)^T & &C_{78}(t) = (0, 0, 0, 1, 0, 0)^T \\
&C_{17}(t) = (1, 1, 1, 0, 1, 1)^T & &C_{18}(t) = (1, 1, 1, 0, 1, 1)^T
\end{aligned}
\tag{8}
$$

3) State C: The shaft sleeve is located at the bottom of the sliding groove, the 6-dual compression spring is in a compressed state and locked, and the components 4, 5, 6, 7, and 8 can be regarded as being fixedly connected to the frame. The metamorphic matrix at this time can be expressed as

$$
A_C^{(8)} =
\begin{pmatrix}
0 & C_{12} & C_{13} & 1 & 1 & 1 & 1 & 1 \\
C_{12} & 0 & C_{23} & 0 & 0 & 0 & 0 & 0 \\
C_{13} & C_{23} & 0 & 0 & 0 & 0 & 0 & 0 \\
1 & 0 & 0 & 0 & 1 & 0 & 0 & 0 \\
1 & 0 & 0 & 1 & 0 & 1 & 0 & 0 \\
1 & 0 & 0 & 0 & 1 & 0 & 0 & 0 \\
1 & 0 & 0 & 0 & 0 & 0 & 0 & 1 \\
1 & 0 & 0 & 0 & 0 & 0 & 1 & 0
\end{pmatrix}
\tag{9}
$$

It can be seen from Eq. (9) that the state C can be simplified to three components, and the simplified metamorphic matrix can be written as

$$A_C^{(3)} = \begin{pmatrix} 0 & C_{12} & C_{13} \\ C_{12} & 0 & C_{23} \\ C_{13} & C_{23} & 0 \end{pmatrix} \tag{10}$$

2.3 The Overall Structure of the Locust-Like Robot

The position of the center of mass is the main parameter that affects the dynamic performance of the robot. The distribution of the center of mass can be achieved by adjusting the position of the flapping-wing mechanism in the locust-like robot, which as showen as Fig. 8 and Table 3.

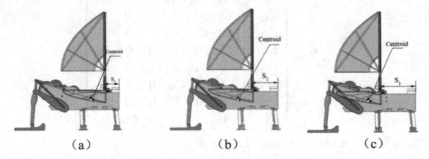

(a)   (b)   (c)

Fig. 8. Overall structure of the locust-like robot (a) Position 1; (b) Position 2; (c) Position 3

Table 3. Performance comparison of various plastic materials

serial number	s_1	s_2	s_3
length(mm)	10	140	200

3 Simulation and Result Analysis

3.1 Control Process of Locust-Like Robot

The control process of a motion cycle of the locust-like robot includes: jumping mechanism control, flapping-wing mechanism control and metamorphic mechanism control, as shown in Fig. 9. The entire control process is realized by a single drive motor, and the key is to activate timing control for the main components.

In the take-off stage, the restraint on the spring can be released only after the incomplete gear is completely disengaged, so as to avoid the energy loss and the motor reversal caused by loosening the spring in advance.

In the airborne phase, the motor can be decelerated appropriately to avoid greater impact during the process of metamorphosis. At the same time, the metamorphosis mechanism must be triggered before reaching the highest point to obtain a good flapping effect, and the flapping movement can be realized after the metamorphosis is completed.

In the landing stage, the spring that is restored to its original length has a stretching margin and the forefoot and midfoot together absorb the impact when landing.

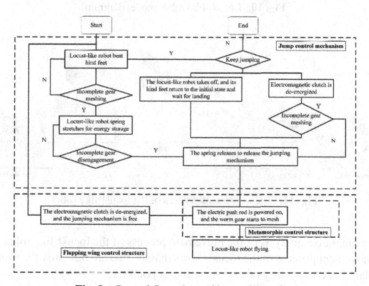

Fig. 9. Control flow chart of locust-like robot

3.2   Kinematics Simulation and Result Analysis

ADAMS is used to simulate and analyze the kinematics and dynamics of the established locust-like robot model. The locust robot model is imported into ADAMS and related parameters are set, as shown in Fig. 10. The movement process of the locust-like robot is shown in Fig. 11.

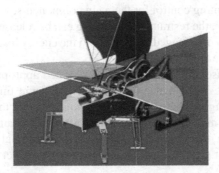

Fig. 10.   Locust-like robot model diagram

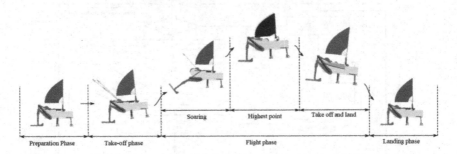

Fig. 11.   The movement process of the locust-like robot

The comparative analysis of the movement process of the locust-like robot (Fig. 11) and the movement process of the locust shows that the two are basically the same, which verifies the bionic feasibility of the locust-like robot model.

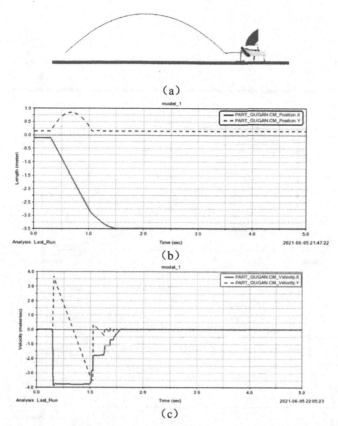

Fig. 12. Movement curve of the center of mass of the locust-like robot (without flapping wings) (a) The trajectory of the center of mass; (b) The horizontal and vertical displacements of the center of mass change; (c) The horizontal and vertical velocity variation of centroid

Figure 13(a) shows the centroid motion curve of the locust-like robot, which shows that the locust-like robot is in the preparation stage at 0−0.25 s; the locust-like robot is in the take-off phase at 0.25−0.50 s; the locust-like robot is at 0.50−1.30 s. It is in the airborne stage; at 1.30−2.00 s, the locust-like robot is in the landing stage. Through the comparison of Fig. 12 (a) and Fig. 13(a), it can be obtained that the locust-like robot in which the metamorphic mechanism couples the jumping motion and the flapping wing motion has a stronger motion ability than in the single motion mode.

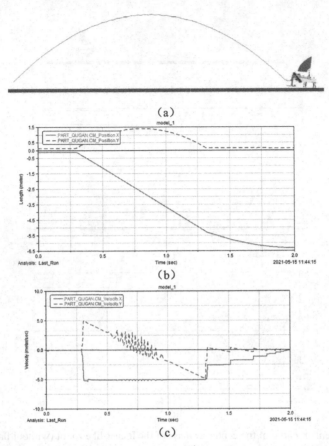

Fig. 13. Movement curve of the center of mass of the locust-like robot (a) The trajectory of the center of mass; (b) The horizontal and vertical displacements of the center of mass change; (c) The horizontal and vertical velocity variation of centroid

4   Conclusion

A locust-like robot based on metamorphic mechanism that couples jumping motion and flapping wing motion was designed in this study.

a) Design of locust-like robot. The jumping mechanism and the flapping-wing mechanism with quick-return characteristics were designed based on the structural characteristics and measurement parameters of the locust, and the corresponding kinematic analysis and selection design were carried out. Then the component metamorphosis principle in the metamorphosis mechanism is used as the bionic basis, using push-pull electromagnets to couple the jumping mechanism and the flapping wing mechanism. And constraint equations are used to construct metamorphic matrix to describe the structural characteristics and changes of metamorphic mechanism.

b) Simulation analysis. The kinematics simulation analysis of the locust-like robot model is carried out. The biomimetic feasibility of the locust-like robot is verified by analyzing that the movement process of the model is consistent with that of the locust.

Future studies could try to use spherical hinges to realize twisting, swinging, and folding motion processes to enhance its bionicity and athletic ability. A locust-like robot based on metamorphosis mechanism was developed in this work, and further experiments can be conducted in the future to verify the feasibility of the proposed method.

References

1. Ren, K., Yu, J.: Research status of bionic amphibious robots: a review. Ocean Eng. **227**(8), 108862 (2021)
2. Han, C., Yu, M., Pan, H., et al.: About the design of a new bionic robot with four legs for competition. In: MATEC Web of Conferences, vol. 336, p. 03003 (2021)
3. Scarfogliero, U., Fei, L., Chen, D., et al.: Jumping mini-robot as a model of scale effects on legged locomotion. In: IEEE International Conference on Robotics & Biomimetics, pp. 853–858. IEEE (2007)
4. Zaitsev, V., Gvirsman, O., Hanan, U.B., et al.: Locust-inspired miniature jumping robot. In: 2015 IEEE/RSJ International Conference on Intelligent Robots and Systems (IROS). IEEE (2015)
5. Gerdes, J.W., Gupta, S.K., Wilkerson, S.A.: A review of bird-inspired flapping wing miniature air vehicle designs. In: ASME 2010 International Design Engineering Technical Conferences and Computers and Information in Engineering Conference, pp. 57–67 (2010)

A Reconfigurable Cable-Driven Hybrid Robot Synchronous Calibration Method Considering Multiple Mapping Relationships

Yonghua Guo[1], Wangru Zhu[1], Wanquan Liu[1], and Jianqing Peng[1,2]($\boxtimes$)

[1] School of Intelligent Systems Engineering, Shenzhen Campus of Sun Yat-sen University, Shenzhen 518107, China
pengjq7@mail.sysu.edu.cn
[2] Guangdong Provincial Key Laboratory of Fire Science and Technology, Guangzhou 510006, China

Abstract. Reconfigurable cable-driven hybrid robot (RCDHR) has strong interaction ability with the environment, and can perform tasks in a wide workspace, especially suitable for high altitude, complex and other operating environments. The rapid deployment of RCDHRs in emergency situations requires rapid determination of kinematics parameters, manipulator-platform and hand-eye relationships. The traditional methods need to firstly identify the kinematics parameters by self-calibration methods, and then solve the hand-eye relationship through the closed-chain relationship of the homogeneous matrix. The process is complex and lengthy. Based on this, this paper proposes a fast synchronous calibration method for RCDHRs. Based on the inverse kinematics model of the cable-driven parallel robot (CDPR), an optimization model including unknown quantities of the fixed anchors, manipulator-platform and hand-eye relationships is established. Then, the Levenberg-Marquardt optimization method is used to solve the synchronous calibration equation. Furthermore, an RCDHR model consisting of 8 parallel cables and 6 serial joints was built in *CopperliaSim* software to collect and produce calibrated data by comparing it with real values in typical application scenarios. The simulation results show that the position method achieves position accuracy and attitude accuracy of the order of 10^{-1} (mm) and 10^{-2} (°), respectively, further demonstrating the effectiveness and applicability of the method.

Keywords: Synchronous calibration · cable-driven hybrid robot · reconfigurable · kinematics

This work was supported in part by the National Key R&D Program of China under Grant 2022YFB4703103, the National Natural Science Foundation of China under Grant 62103454, the Guangdong Basic and Applied Basic Research Foundation under Grant 2019A1515110680, the Shenzhen Municipal Basic Research Project for Natural Science Foundation under Grant JCYJ20190806143408992, and the Shenzhen Science and Technology Program under Grant JCYJ20220530150006014.

© The Author(s), under exclusive license to Springer Nature Singapore Pte Ltd. 2023
H. Yang et al. (Eds.): ICIRA 2023, LNAI 14269, pp. 522–533, 2023.
https://doi.org/10.1007/978-981-99-6489-5_42

1 Introduction

RCDHR consists of a cable-driven platform and a rigid serial robot (RSR). It combines the advantages of cable-driven parallel robot (CDPR) and RSR, including: (1) rapid deployment, which means that it has the ability to quickly build and produces a marked effect in complex environments [1]; (2) high load ratio, which can provide sufficient supporting force for the serial robot [2]; (3) the mobile platform and the joint of the serial robot can be synchronously changed to quickly reaching the desired pose [3]; (4) Wide workspace with high operational flexibility [4, 5]. Compared with traditional RSRs, RCDHR has a cable-driven mobile platform as the base of the manipulator that can move in vast spaces, and its end-effector can flexibly perform complex operations [5]. Due to the outstanding performance, RCDHRs will have rich applications in scenarios such as disaster rescue, aerial construction, and large-scale equipment inspection [1–3, 6–11].

When deploying cable-driven robots, it is necessary to recognize the kinematics parameters of the robot. The existing methods are mainly divided into high-precision instrument calibration and self-calibration [13]. The first method is to obtain parameter information directly through tiltmeter, laser tracker and other instruments. The second method bases the relationship between the physical structure and kinematics of the robot to calculate parameters indirectly without external instruments. Borgstrom *et al.* [3] used a laser tracker to measure the relative distance of fixed anchor points of NIMS3D (Networked Info Mechanical System 3D), and then calculated the coordinates of each fixed anchor point based on geometric relationships. The least squares method was used to establish a cable length error optimization model. Another method established an error model between the iterative pose of the mobile platform and the pose measured by laser trackers [12]. Yuan *et al.* [13] made full differentiation on the kinematics model of CDPR, after which they deduced the transfer model of the pulley angle errors to the kinematics parameters. Borgstrom *et al.* [1] constructed an optimization model for kinematics parameters based on the slight change of cable length and cable force after the incremental displacement of the mobile platform. Wang *et al.* [14] established a general calibration model, proposed a configuration search method based on the matrix perturbation theory, and verified it on the kinematics parameter calibration of a CDPR.

Unlike simple CDPRs, RCDHRs require additional determination of manipulator-platform and hand-eye relative relationships. The existing multi robot hand-eye calibration methods are usually divided into the $AXB = YCZ$ problem, where A, B, and C are known quantities derived from the serial joint sensor or visual sensor in the closed-chain homogeneous transformation relationship, and X, Y, Z are unknown homogeneous matrices to be solved. Ma *et al.* [15] proposed a probabilistic solution method for the $AXB = YCZ$ problem, using the variational form of the problem to gradually solve various unknown quantities. Peng *et al.* [16] deduced a hybrid calibration model based on the kinematics model of multilink cable-driven hyper redundant manipulators (MCDHMs). The particle swarm optimization algorithm was used to solve the hybrid calibration problem. Wang *et al.* [17] proposed a method to calculate the initial estimated solution of the $AXB = YCZ$ problem using the closed form of Kronecker-product, which improves the speed of iterative convergence. However, for RCDHRs, the homogeneous transformation relationship between the mobile platform coordinate system and the world coordinate system needs to be obtained through the forward kinematics, which requires the identification of kinematics parameters first. Therefore, it is difficult to establish the closed-chain form of homogeneous matrix representation. The existing methods cannot effectively solve the calibration problem of the RCDHRs.

This paper proposes a synchronous calibration method for RCDHR. This method establishes the closed-chain relationship of the calibration problem through the forward kinematics model of the RCDHR and the cooperative calibration object. The length of cables is directly observed and obtained through the winch control motor encoder. Levenberg-Marquardt optimization algorithm is utilized to synchronously solve fixed anchor points, manipulator-platform, and hand-eye relationships. When arranges RCDHR in application scenarios, this method can quickly determine unknown quantities.

The following structure is arranged as follows: Sect. 2 defines the established coordinate system and states the synchronization calibration problem of the RCDHR. Section 3 elaborates on the method proposed in this paper. Section 4 builds a 14° of freedom (DOF) RCDHR simulation model and verifies the proposed method on this example. Finally, Sect. 5 is the summary of the paper.

2 Synchronous Calibration Problem Statement

A RCDHR with $m + n$ degree of freedom is shown in Fig. 1, where m is the number of cables and n is the number of joints of the manipulator. For the convenience of the expression, we agreed that the world frame $\{W\}$ is established on the cooperative marker and aligned with the cooperative marker frame, $\{P\}$ is the mobile frame with the origin located at the center of mass of the mobile platform, $\{M\}$ is the base frame of the manipulator, $\{V\}$ is the frame of camera that is suspended at the end link of the manipulator, $\{E\}$ is the end-effector frame of the serial robot, $\{T\}$ is the cooperative marker frame, $^{W}A_i$ is the coordinate of the i-th fixed anchor with respect to the world frame, $^{P}r_i$, $^{W}r_i$ are the coordinates of the i-th mobile platform anchor with respect to the mobile frame and the world frame, respectively, $^{W}L_i$ is the vector of the i-th cable relative to the world frame, l_i is the length of the i-th cable, $i = 1, 2, \cdots, m$.

When deploys RCDHRs in different application scenarios, the positions of fixed anchors, manipulator installation position, and camera installation position will all change. Thus, these parts of parameters need to be re identified. The mobile platform does not change after production, which can be considered that the coordinates of the mobile anchors in the mobile frame, $^{P}r_i$, have been determined in advance.

Assuming that the pose of the moving platform relative to the world frame is $^{W}X_p$, and the joint angle group of the RSR is Θ, the generalized pose of the RCDHR can be expressed as $Q = \left[^{W}X_p^{T}, \Theta^{T} \right]^{T}$. The lengths of the cables are controlled by the winch motors, which drive the platform to change its pose. The joint angle group, Θ, is changed by the serial robot joint controllers.

From the above analysis, the synchronization calibration problem of RCDHRs can be expressed as: under constant known parameters, given N sets of measurement data of cable length and joint angle, the positions of fixed anchors, the homogeneous matrix between the mobile frame and the base frame, and the homogeneous matrix of hand-eye can be synchronously calibrated. Due to the mutual conversion between homogeneous

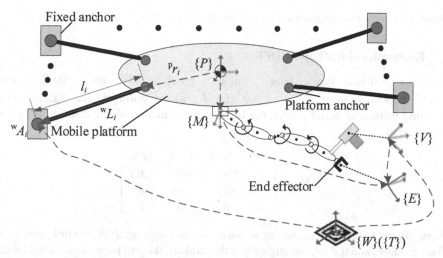

Fig. 1. Schematic diagram of synchronous calibration problem for RCDHRs (the purple lines in the figure represent the unknown quantities to be solved, while the blue lines represent the known quantities or observable sensor measurements). (Color figure online)

matrix and cartesian pose, the latter representation is used as the variable to be solved in this paper.

3 Synchronous Calibration Method

According to the transformation relationship between homogeneous matrix, rotation matrix and position vector, the homogeneous matrix of the frame f_2 with respect to the frame f_1 can be expressed as follows:

$$^{f_1}\boldsymbol{H}_{f_2} = \begin{bmatrix} ^{f_1}\boldsymbol{R}_{f_2} & ^{f_1}\boldsymbol{T}_{f_2} \\ \boldsymbol{O}_{1\times3} & 1 \end{bmatrix} \tag{1}$$

where, $^{f_1}\boldsymbol{R}_{f_2}$, $^{f_1}\boldsymbol{T}_{f_2}$ are the rotation matrix and the position vector of the frame f_2 with respect to the frame f_1, respectively, $\boldsymbol{O}_{1\times3}$ is a 1×3 zero matrix.

According to (1), $^{f_1}\boldsymbol{R}_{f_2}$ and $^{f_1}\boldsymbol{T}_{f_2}$ can be calculated by $^{f_1}\boldsymbol{H}_{f_2}$ as follows:

$$\begin{aligned} ^{f_1}\boldsymbol{R}_{f_2} &= {}^{f_1}\boldsymbol{H}_{f_2}(1:3, 1:3) \\ ^{f_1}\boldsymbol{T}_{f_2} &= {}^{f_1}\boldsymbol{H}_{f_2}(1:3, 4) \end{aligned} \tag{2}$$

Assuming that the pose of the frame f_2 with respect to the frame f_1 is $^{f_1}\boldsymbol{X}_{f_2} = [x, y, z, \gamma, \beta, \alpha]^{\mathrm{T}}$, according to the relationship between homogeneous matrix and cartesian pose, the rotation matrix and the position vector of the frame f_2 with respect to the frame f_1 can be calculated as:

$$^{f_1}\boldsymbol{R}_{f_2} = \begin{bmatrix} c\alpha c\beta & c\alpha s\beta s\gamma - s\alpha c\gamma & c\alpha s\beta c\gamma + s\alpha s\gamma \\ s\alpha c\beta & s\alpha s\beta s\gamma + c\alpha c\gamma & s\alpha s\beta c\gamma - c\alpha s\gamma \\ -s\beta & c\beta s\gamma & c\beta c\gamma \end{bmatrix} \tag{3}$$

$$^{f_1}\boldsymbol{T}_{f_2} = [x, y, z]^{\mathrm{T}}$$

where, $s\,(\cdot)$ and $c\,(\cdot)$ represent $\sin\,(\cdot)$ and $\cos\,(\cdot)$, respectively.

3.1 Kinematics of RSR and CDPR

Assuming that the joint angle group of the RSR with n-DOF is $\boldsymbol{\Theta} = [\theta_1, \theta_2, \cdots, \theta_j, \cdots, \theta_n]^{\mathrm{T}} (1 \leq j \leq n)$, according to the standard D-H modeling method of serial robots, the homogeneous matrix of adjacent joints can be calculated as:

$$
^{j-1}\boldsymbol{H}_j = \begin{bmatrix} c\theta_j & -s\theta_j c\alpha_j & s\theta_j s\alpha_j & a_j c\theta_j \\ s\theta_j & c\theta_j c\alpha_j & -c\theta_j s\alpha_j & a_j s\theta_j \\ 0 & s\alpha_j & c\alpha_j & d_j \\ 0 & 0 & 0 & 1 \end{bmatrix}
\tag{4}
$$

where, $c\theta_j = \cos\theta_j$, $s\theta_j = \sin\theta_j$, $c\alpha_j = \cos\alpha_j$, $s\alpha_j = \sin\alpha_j$, a_j, d_j, α_j are link length, the offset distance, and the torsion angle, θ_j is the angle of the j-th joint of the serial robot.

The homogeneous matrix of the end-effector frame with respect to the base frame can be further expressed as:

$$
^{b}\boldsymbol{H}_e = {}^{0}\boldsymbol{H}_n = \prod_{j=1}^{n} {}^{j-1}\boldsymbol{H}_j
\tag{5}
$$

where, $^{0}\boldsymbol{H}_n$ is the homogeneous matrix of the last joint frame with respect to the base frame.

According to Eqs. (2) and (5), the rotation matrix and position vector, $^{e}\boldsymbol{R}_b$ and $^{e}\boldsymbol{T}_b$, can be calculated respectively, namely:

$$
^{e}\boldsymbol{R}_b = {}^{e}\boldsymbol{H}_b(1:3, 1:3) = \left(^{b}\boldsymbol{H}_e\right)^{-1}(1:3, 1:3)
$$
$$
^{e}\boldsymbol{T}_b = {}^{e}\boldsymbol{H}_b(1:3, 4) = \left(^{b}\boldsymbol{H}_e\right)^{-1}(1:3, 4)
\tag{6}
$$

As shown in Fig. 1, the i-th cable vector and cable length can be calculated based on the inverse kinematics of CDPR, thus,

$$
^{w}\boldsymbol{L}_i = {}^{w}\boldsymbol{A}_i - {}^{w}\boldsymbol{r}_i
\tag{7}
$$

$$
l_i = \left\| {}^{w}\boldsymbol{L}_i \right\|_2
\tag{8}
$$

3.2 Synchronous Calibration Model

Assuming that the homogeneous matrix of the cooperative marker relative to the camera is $^{v}\boldsymbol{H}_w$, according to (2), the rotation matrix and position vector of the camera relative to the world frame, $^{w}\boldsymbol{R}_v$ and $^{w}\boldsymbol{T}_v$, can be expressed as follows:

$$
^{w}\boldsymbol{R}_v = {}^{w}\boldsymbol{H}_v(1:3, 1:3) = \left(^{v}\boldsymbol{H}_w\right)^{-1}(1:3, 1:3)
$$
$$
^{w}\boldsymbol{T}_v = {}^{w}\boldsymbol{H}_v(1:3, 4) = \left(^{v}\boldsymbol{H}_w\right)^{-1}(1:3, 4)
\tag{9}
$$

Agreed that ^bX_p is the cartesian pose of the mobile frame with respect to the base frame, and ^vX_e is the cartesian pose of the end-effector frame with respect to the camera frame. The rotation matrices, ^bR_p and ^vR_e, together with the position vector, ^bT_p and ^vT_e, can be further calculated by (3), where, ^bR_p and ^bT_p are respectively the rotation matrix and position vector of the mobile frame with respect to the base frame, ^vR_e and ^vT_e are respectively the rotation matrix and position vector of the end-effector frame with respect to the camera frame.

Expanding (7), the relationship between the coordinates of the mobile anchors and the known and unknown quantities in the world frame can be expressed as follows:

$$
\begin{aligned}
^wr_i &= {}^wT_v + {}^wR_v \cdot {}^vT_e + {}^wR_e \cdot {}^eT_b + {}^wR_b \cdot {}^bT_p + {}^wR_p \cdot {}^pr_i \\
&= {}^wT_v + {}^wR_v \cdot {}^vT_e + {}^wR_v \cdot {}^vR_e \cdot {}^eT_b \\
&\quad + {}^wR_v \cdot {}^vR_e \cdot {}^eR_b \cdot {}^bT_p + {}^wR_v \cdot {}^vR_e \cdot {}^eR_b \cdot {}^bR_p \cdot {}^pr_i
\end{aligned}
\tag{10}
$$

where, ^wR_e, ^wR_b and ^wR_p are rotation matrices of the end-effector frame, the base frame and the mobile frame relative to the world frame, respectively.

According to Eqs. (7)–(8), the equation between the cable length and the known and unknown quantities is established as follows:

$$
\begin{aligned}
l_i = \Big\| {}^wA_i - \big({}^wT_v + {}^wR_v \cdot {}^vT_e + {}^wR_v \cdot {}^vR_e \cdot {}^eT_b + \\
{}^wR_v \cdot {}^vR_e \cdot {}^eR_b \cdot {}^bT_p + {}^wR_v \cdot {}^vR_e \cdot {}^eR_b \cdot {}^bR_p \cdot {}^pr_i \big) \Big\|_2
\end{aligned}
\tag{11}
$$

Thus, the synchronous calibration model of the RCDHR can be represented as:

$$
l_i = f\left({}^wA_i, {}^pr_i, {}^bX_p, {}^vX_e, {}^vH_w, {}^bH_e \right)
\tag{12}
$$

The equation shown in Eq. (12) can be solved through iterative optimization methods. Assuming that the iterative solution values of ^bX_p, ^vX_e and ^wA_i are $^b\widetilde{X}_p$, $^v\widetilde{X}_e$ and $^w\widetilde{A}_i$, respectively, the error models for the true value and the solution value of the length of the i-th cable can be established by:

$$
\begin{aligned}
^bX_p, {}^vX_e, {}^wA_i &= \arg\min \sum_i^m \left\| l_i - \widetilde{l}_i \right\|_2 \\
\widetilde{l}_i &= f\left({}^w\widetilde{A}_i, {}^pr_i, {}^b\widetilde{X}_p, {}^v\widetilde{X}_e, {}^vH_w, {}^bH_e \right) \\
i &= 1, 2, \cdots, m
\end{aligned}
\tag{13}
$$

where, $\widetilde{l}_i$ is the solution value of the length of the i-th cable, $\|\cdot\|_2$ represents the binomial function, the true cable length value can be obtained from the measurement of the winch connected to the cable, and we believe that this measurement value is absolutely accurate.

For m-DOF RCDHRs, m sets of Eq. (11) can be established for each generalized pose. The quantities to be identified include a total of $18 + 3m$ unknown parameters. Therefore, to fully solve the calibration problem, at least $floor\left(\frac{18+3m}{m}\right)$ sets of data from different poses are required, where floor $(\cdot)$ represents the upward rounding function. However, when using the least squares method, the more sets of calibration data, the more accurate the calibration results. Thus, N is usually more than $floor\left(\frac{18+3m}{m}\right)$.

Assuming that the upper right superscript k represents the k-th calibration data group, the objective optimization function for synchronous calibration using N sets of data can be further expressed as:

$$^b X_p, {}^v X_e, {}^w A_i = \arg\min \sum_k^N \sum_i^m \left\| l_i^{(k)} - \widetilde{l_i^{(k)}} \right\|_2$$

$$\widetilde{l_i^{(k)}} = f\left({}^w\widetilde{A}_i, {}^p r_i, {}^b\widetilde{X}_p, {}^v\widetilde{X}_e, {}^v H_w^{(k)}, {}^b H_e^{(k)} \right) \tag{14}$$

$$k = 1, 2, \cdots, N,$$

$$i = 1, 2, \cdots, m$$

where, $l_i^{(k)}$ and $\widetilde{l_i^{(k)}}$ are the measurement value and solution value of the length of the i-th cable in the k-th dataset.

The optimization problem shown by Eq. (14) can be solved using the L-M optimization algorithm [18]. The selection of initial iteration values can help for faster convergence. We agreed that $^b\widetilde{X}_p^{(0)}$ represents the initial iteration value of the pose for $^b X_p$, $^v\widetilde{X}_e^{(0)}$ represents the initial iteration value of the pose for $^v X_e$, and $^w\widetilde{A}_i^{(0)}$ represents the initial iteration value of the fixed anchor position in the world frame. The initial iteration values will be discussed in the following subsection.

3.3 Selection of Initial Iteration Values

By using prior knowledge, the iterative initial values of the quantities to be calibrated can be given, which enables faster convergence. When deploying RCDHRs, the initial coordinates of the fixed anchors $^w\widetilde{A}_i^{(0)}$ can be estimated as approximate values by the relative position between the anchor points and the cooperative marker. For RCDHRs, the serial robot is usually installed on the upper or lower surface of the mobile platform, so $^b\widetilde{X}_p^{(0)}$ can be selected as $\left[0, 0, {}^h/_2, 0, 0, 0\right]^T$ or $\left[0, 0, -{}^h/_2, 0, 0, 0\right]^T$, where h represents height of the mobile platform. For hand-eye cameras installed for reconstruction, the conversion relationship between the camera physical frame and the end-effector is similar to the previous one. Therefore, $^v\widetilde{X}_e^{(0)}$ can be selected as the cartesian pose value of the end-effector frame with respect to the camera frame when the camera has not been replaced. When installing the camera for the first time, it can be selected as $[0, 0, 0, 0, 0, 0]^T$.

4 Simulation

As shown in Fig. 2, a RCDHR model based on *CopperliaSim* software is constructed, which consists of 8 cables and 6 serial joints. Through it, the proposed calibration method can be verified. In the simulation, an UR5 manipulator is used as the serial robot. The apriltag QR code serves as a collaborative marker [19]. The serial robot is installed on the upper surface of the mobile platform. The visual sensor is suspended at the end link of the robotic arm to obtain images of cooperative marker. The size of the mobile platform is 0.5 m × 0.8 m × 0.1 m, and the mobile anchors is considered to be located on the diagonal of the rectangular body of the platform. The standard D-H parameters of the UR5 are shown in Table 1.

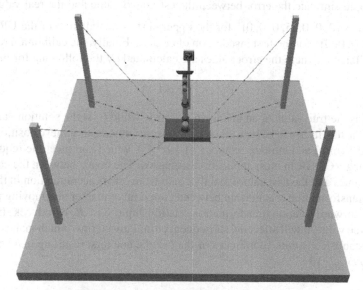

Fig. 2. Simulation scenario of the RCDHR

Table 1. Kinematics of UR5 serial robots

Name	θ_j	d_j/m	a_j	α_j
Joint 1	0	0.0746	0	$\pi/2$
Joint 2	0	0	−0.4251	0
Joint 3	0	0	−0.3921	0
Joint 4	0	0.1092	0	$\pi/2$
Joint 5	0	0.0947	0	$-\pi/2$
Joint 6	0	0.0750	0	0

The generalized pose of the RCDHR is changed through length changes of cables and joints motion of the UR5. As shown in Fig. 3, every time the generalized pose is changed, ensure that the complete shape of the cooperative marker can be observed by the Kinect v1 camera. Afterwards, the length of cables, angles of the UR5, and homogeneous matrix $^{V}H_{w}$ are recorded as one set of data. When the number of data groups obtained is greater than or equal to N ($N = 40$ in this simulation), stop the data acquisition process. Then the method proposed in this paper is used for synchronous calibration. In addition, during the simulation process, the true values of the unknown quantities are obtained through the application programming interface (API) in *CopperliaSim*, i.e., $^{b}X_{p}$, $^{v}X_{e}$ and $^{w}A_{i}$.

Before using L-M algorithm to solve the problem, $^{w}\widetilde{A}_{i}^{(0)}$ is assumed that the true value plus normal distribution disturbance with standard deviation of 0.3 and mean value of 0, to simulate the error between the estimated value and the real value. $^{b}\widetilde{X}_{p}^{(0)}$ is selected as $[0, 0, 0.05, 0, 0, 0]^{T}$ for the upper surface installation of the UR5. $^{v}\widetilde{X}_{e}^{(0)}$ is $[0, 0, 0, 0, 0, 0]^{T}$ for the first installation of camera. Finally, the calibration results are shown in Table 2, where the error values are calculated by the following formula:

$$err = \left\| (\cdot) - \widetilde{(\cdot)} \right\|_{2} \tag{15}$$

where, $(\cdot)$ is the true value of an unknown quantity, while $\widetilde{(\cdot)}$ is the solution value.

From the results, it can be seen that our proposed method can achieve positional accuracy of 10^{-1} (mm) and attitude accuracy of 10^{-2} (°), which can meet the requirements of deploying RCDHR in most application scenarios. The errors between the calibration solution values and the true values mainly come from errors accumulation in the homogeneous transformation relationship between cooperative marker and moving platform. When the forward rotation transformation relationship (i.e., $^{w}R_{v}$) produces slight error with the true value, it will affect the subsequent cumulative terms, which makes it impossible to establish accurate coordinates of the mobile anchors, resulting in a small error between $l_{i}^{(k)}$ and $\widetilde{l_{i}^{(k)}}$.

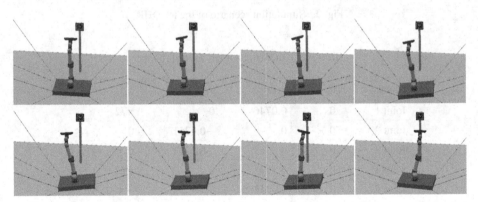

Fig. 3. Acquisition process of simulation datasets

Table 2. True values and solution values of the unknown quantities

Name	True value				Solved value		err	
	Position (m)		Attitude (°)		Position (m)	Attitude (°)	Position (10^{-4}m)	Attitude (10^{-2}°)
${}^{w}A_1$	x	-0.7000	$-$		-0.7002	$-$	7.3043	$-$
	y	-2.0000			-2.0004			
	z	2.9749			-2.9744			
${}^{w}A_2$	x	-0.7000	$-$		-0.6999	$-$	3.7814	$-$
	y	-2.0000			-2.0000			
	z	0.0251			0.0255			
${}^{w}A_3$	x	-0.7000	$-$		-0.7002	$-$	8.5794	$-$
	y	2.0000			2.0004			
	z	0.0251			0.0244			
${}^{w}A_4$	x	-0.7000	$-$		-0.7002	$-$	2.8634	$-$
	y	2.0000			1.9999			
	z	-2.9749			-2.9751			
${}^{w}A_5$	x	1.1000	$-$		1.0997	$-$	4.2270	$-$
	y	-2.0000			-2.0002			
	z	-2.9749			-2.9747			
${}^{w}A_6$	x	1.1000	$-$		1.1000	$-$	2.1557	$-$
	y	-2.0000			-1.9998			
	z	0.0251			0.0252			
${}^{w}A_7$	x	1.1000	$-$		1.1000	$-$	8.0180	$-$
	y	2.0000			2.0004			
	z	0.0251			0.0244			
${}^{w}A_8$	x	1.1000	$-$		1.0997	$-$	4.6618	$-$
	y	2.0000			1.9998			
	z	-2.9749			-2.9752			
${}^{b}X_p$	x	-0.0478	γ	0.0082	-0.0478	-0.0011	1.3636	0.4375
	y	0.0370	β	0.0001	0.0369	-0.0002		
	z	-0.0640	α	-0.0013	-0.0639	0.0110		
${}^{v}X_e$	x	0.0141	γ	0	0.0141	-0.0018	0.3858	1.5471
	y	0.0824	β	0	0.0824	-0.0002		
	z	-0.0293	α	0	-0.0292	-0.0040		

5 Conclusion

This paper proposed a synchronous calibration method for RCDHRs. Based on the inverse kinematics of CDPR, the closed-loop relationship between the length of cables, the calibration unknown quantities, the observable known quantities are derived. A *CopperliaSim* simulation model consisting of 8 parallel drive cables and 6 serial joints was built. The calibration results indicate that the position accuracy and attitude accuracy of the proposed method reach the order of 10^{-1} (mm) and 10^{-2} (°) respectively, which can meet the goal of quickly and accurately deploying RCDHRs.

References

1. Borgstrom, P.H., et al.: NIMS-PL: a cable-driven robot with self-calibration capabilities. IEEE Trans. Rob. **25**(5), 1005–1015 (2009)
2. Albus, J., Bostelman, R., Dagalakis, N.: The NIST ROBOCRANE. J. Robot. Syst. **97**(3) (1992)
3. Borgstrom, P.H., et al.: Design and implementation of NIMS3D, a 3-D cabled robot for actuated sensing applications. IEEE Trans. Rob. **25**(2), 325–339 (2009)
4. Yang, G., Pham, C.B, Yeo, S.H.: Workspace performance optimization of fully restrained cable-driven parallel manipulators. In: 2006 IEEE/RSJ International Conference on Intelligent Robots and Systems, pp. 85–90 (2006)
5. Gouttefarde, M.: Static analysis of planar 3-dof cable-suspended parallel robots carrying a serial manipulator. In: New Trends in Mechanism and Machine Science: Theory and Industrial Applications, pp. 363–371 (2017)
6. El-Ghazaly, G., Gouttefarde, M., Creuze, V.: Hybrid cable-thruster actuated underwater vehicle-manipulator systems: a study on force capabilities. In: 2015 IEEE/RSJ International Conference on Intelligent Robots and Systems, pp. 1672–1678 (2015)
7. Osumi, H., Utsugi, Y., Koshikawa, M.: Development of a manipulator suspended by parallel wire structure. In: 2000 IEEE/RSJ International Conference on Intelligent Robots and Systems, pp. 498–503 (2000)
8. Qi, R., Rushton, M., Khajepour, A., et al.: Decoupled modeling and model predictive control of a hybrid cable-driven robot (HCDR). Robot. Auton. Syst. **118**, 1–12 (2019)
9. Sacchi, N., Simetti, E., Antonelli, G., et al.: Analysis of hybrid cable-thruster actuated ROV in heavy lifting interventions. In: 2022 IEEE/RSJ International Conference on Intelligent Robots and Systems, pp. 8430–8435 (2022)
10. Takemura, F., Enomoto, M, Tanaka, T., Denou, K., Kobayashi, Y., Tadokoro, S.: Development of the balloon-cable driven robot for information collection from sky and proposal of the search strategy at a major disaster. In: 2005 IEEE/ASME International Conference on Advanced Intelligent Mechatronics, pp. 658–663 (2005)
11. Qian, S., Zi, B., Shang, W.W., et al.: A review on cable-driven parallel robots. Chin. J. Mech. Eng. **31**(1), 1–11 (2018)
12. Zhang, Z., Xie, G., Shao, Z., et al.: Kinematic calibration of cable-driven parallel robots considering the pulley kinematics. Mech. Mach. Theory **169**, 104648 (2022)
13. Yuan, H., You, X., Zhang, Y., et al.: A novel calibration algorithm for cable-driven parallel robots with application to rehabilitation. Appl. Sci. **9**(11), 2182 (2019)
14. Wang, H., Gao, T., Kinugawa, J., et al.: Finding measurement configurations for accurate robot calibration: Validation with a cable-driven robot. IEEE Trans. Rob. **33**(5), 1156–1169 (2017)

15. Ma, Q., et al.: Probabilistic approaches to the AXB=YCZ calibration problem in multi-robot systems. Auton. Robot. **42**, 1497–1520 (2018)
16. Peng, J., Xu, W., Wang, F., et al.: A hybrid hand–eye calibration method for multilink cable-driven hyper-redundant manipulators. IEEE Trans. Instrum. Meas. **70**, 1–13 (2021)
17. Wang, G., Li, W., Jiang, C., et al.: Simultaneous calibration of multicoordinates for a dual-robot system by solving the AXB=YCZ problem. IEEE Trans. Rob. **37**(4), 1172–1185 (2021)
18. Levenberg, K.: A method for the solution of certain non-linear problems in least squares. Q. Appl. Math. **2**(2), 164–168 (1944)
19. Olson, E.: AprilTag: A robust and flexible visual fiducial system. In: 2011 IEEE International Conference on Robotics and Automation, pp. 3400–3407 (2011)

Wearable Robots Improve Upper Limb Function In Stroke Patients

Yunfeng Zhang, Yihao Chen, Min Zhuang, Zuojun Cao, Jue Liu, and Jing Tian[✉]

Department of Rehabilitation Medicine, Huashan Hospital, Fudan University, Shanghai, China
karentianjing@126.com

Abstract. Wearable upper limb robots can improve motor performance of stroke patients. The Armeo Spring, a wearable upper limb robot designed by Swiss company Hocoma, has been developed specifically to strengthen the upper limbs of stroke patients and improve treatment outcomes. The purpose of this article is to introduce this novel upper limb rehabilitation robot into the training of clinical daily activities. Armeo Spring is an upper limb mechanical structure with multiple joints and degrees of freedom, equipped with force and position sensors. Based on force control algorithms and real-time data monitoring, and targeting the patient's active control strategy, the machine structure, motor actuators, sensors, and safety protection aspects have been optimized, and a game-based human-machine interaction method is used to train patients. This article introduces the design and development of the robot, as well as clinical experimental evaluations and verifications in stroke patients. Clinical research results confirm that the wearable upper limb robot can improve upper limb function in stroke patients.

Keywords: Wearable robots · Stroke · Upper limb function

1 Introduction

Stroke refers to acute cerebrovascular disease, a focal vascular neurological dysfunction syndrome characterized by acute onset, symptoms lasting more than 24 h, or death [1]. A study that searched relevant data and literature between 1990 and 2010 found that more than 60% of stroke deaths worldwide occurred in developing countries, and the incidence is still increasing in low- and middle-income countries [2]. In China, the age-standardized prevalence, morbidity, and mortality rates for stroke in the last three decades were 1114.8/100,000, 246.8, and 114.8/100,000 person-years, respectively [3]. Stroke is the second leading cause of death and the third leading cause of disability worldwide [4]. Although the mortality rate of stroke patients has decreased significantly with advances in medical technology, unfortunately, the rate of disability after stroke remains high [5]. According to relevant data, 55%–75% of patients still have limited motor function 3–6 months after stroke onset, which greatly affects their quality of life and ability to perform activities of daily living [6]. Studies have noted that somatosensory impairment is common after stroke; 7–53% have impaired tactile sensation, 31–89% have impaired stereo vision, and 34–64% have impaired proprioception, with about two-thirds of people

© The Author(s), under exclusive license to Springer Nature Singapore Pte Ltd. 2023
H. Yang et al. (Eds.): ICIRA 2023, LNAI 14269, pp. 534–542, 2023.
https://doi.org/10.1007/978-981-99-6489-5_43

experiencing upper extremity dysfunction after a stroke, affecting the quality of daily life [7, 8]. Upper limb dysfunction directly and severely affects patients' quality of life, and therefore improving upper limb motor function is also a core element of rehabilitation [9].

Currently, traditional rehabilitation of stroke limb dysfunction relies on one-on-one unassisted, high-intensity training by rehabilitation therapists. Routine rehabilitation can help stroke patients improve upper limb motor function to a certain extent, but the effectiveness of rehabilitation is affected by various factors such as the level of competence of the therapist and the patient's compliance. In addition, conventional rehabilitation training often has disadvantages such as difficulty in maintaining training intensity, cumbersome training process, lack of timely feedback on training effects, and lack of objective evaluation data [10]. Upper limb robotics is an emerging therapeutic technology for upper limb dysfunction in stroke patients that provides high precision and repetitive training [11]. It was found that upper limb robots can avoid these disadvantages of traditional upper limb rehabilitation described above. First, the rehabilitation robot can maintain the training intensity without fatigue and can quantify and record the training content to provide personalized rehabilitation training to patients. It can also reduce clinical labor costs and improve treatment efficiency; the fun nature of the treatment process can also improve patient compliance [12].

The currently clinically applied upper limb rehabilitation robots can be divided into exoskeleton robots, end-effector robots, functional electrical stimulation-assisted upper limb rehabilitation robots, upper limb rehabilitation robots based on surface electromyographic signals, upper limb rehabilitation robots based on virtual reality technology, and upper limb rehabilitation robots based on brain-computer interfaces. In this study, we will focus on exploring the effectiveness of a wearable 3D upper limb multi-joint rehabilitation robot in upper limb motor function training. The wearable upper limb rehabilitation robot is a human-computer wearable device that integrates intelligence and mechanical power. It is small in size and light in weight, and it can meet various rehabilitation training needs of patients by supporting and pulling the joints of the wrist, forearm, upper arm, and other parts of the upper limb to guide them through rehabilitation training [13]. The most typical is the MIT-ManuS, a robotic system for upper limb rehabilitation developed at MIT in 1991. It uses a tandem five-link structure of selective compliance assembly robotic arm (SCARA) with two degrees of freedom at the end of the arm to assist patients in horizontal rehabilitation training of the shoulder and elbow joints. Patients with upper extremity movement disorders are tracked by the robot to complete passive range of motion training according to a preset trajectory, and appropriate damping can also be added to assist patients in muscle strength training [14]. A wearable upper limb exoskeleton based on mirror therapy was developed by Kyeong SK et al. at the Korea Institute of Science and Technology [15]. Other typical wearable multidimensional upper limb rehabilitation robots include the U-Rob upper limb rehabilitation exoskeleton designed and developed by ISLAM at the University of Wisconsin, USA [16], the passive upper limb rehabilitation robotic system-REHAROB developed by Toth, Hungary [17], and the CADEN-7 developed by the University of Washington [18].

Although upper limb rehabilitation robots are widely used in rehabilitation clinical work and have achieved good therapeutic effects, the evaluation of their clinical effects is still lacking due to the low quality of clinical trial evidence and small sample size. Therefore, the use of quantitative and clinical evaluation will be beneficial for the design of the structure, function, and auxiliary methods of rehabilitation robots.

2   System Overview

2.1   Function Description

The system can provide sufficient support for the upper extremity to assist patients with upper extremity dysfunction for functional training and can also give visual biofeedback of the patient's upper extremity function. It is suitable for early neurological and post-operative orthopedic rehabilitation to train patients' proprioceptive and neuromuscular control.

The Armeo Spring system (shown in Fig. 1) consists of an arm weight reduction support system, an enhanced performance feedback system, and an evaluation reporting tool. The Arm Weight Reduction Support System helps patients regain and improve motor control by providing weight reduction support to the damaged arm and hand, while helping patients to train voluntary, repetitive movements in the three-dimensional workspace, serving to preserve residual motor function, promote voluntary, high-intensity repetitive movements and increase the amount of movement in the three-dimensional spatial range; The autonomic software shared in this enhanced performance feedback system provides patients with a variety of motivational exercises and games to enhance the user's neuroplasticity and motor relearning ability. Using games to simulate routine activities in daily life and giving motivating and rewarding repetitive tasks can engage patients to train more effectively for longer periods of time. In addition, the system provides timely performance feedback and adjusts the training intensity according to the user's needs and actual performance.

The Armeo Spring system also has a database that can be used to manage individual treatment plans. The database provides a standardized assessment reporting tool that provides accurate feedback on the user's upper extremity mobility. Its record of each training session and the content of the assessment provide important reference value for clinical decision making.

2.2   Mechanical Configurations and Sensory System

This section will focus on the hardware description of the Armeo Spring System Arm Weight Reduction Support System. The system consists of a multi-joint robotic arm that provides support for the upper extremity and assists the patient in upper extremity motor function training as well as visual biofeedback training.

The multi-joint robotic arm is equipped with springs to support the entire arm from shoulder to hand, which can be adjusted to compensate for the partial weight of the patient's arm, enhance residual function and neuromuscular control, thus performing assisted active movement in three-dimensional space and assisting patients with upper limb motor dysfunction in functional upper limb functional rehabilitation training. The arm support force can be steplessly adjusted, with a forearm support force of 0.7–2.4 kg and an upper arm support force of 0.5–3.8 kg.

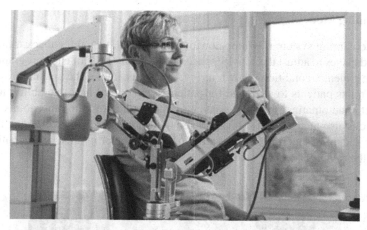

Fig. 1. System Overview of Armeo Spring system

The multi-joint robot arm can perform wrist flexion/extension, forearm rotation forward/backward, elbow flexion/extension, shoulder flexion/extension, horizontal inversion/abduction, internal rotation/external rotation, and other dimensions. In addition, the shoulder, forearm, and wrist joints of the robotic arm can be single-joint locked or multi-joint locked to avoid joint movements of the patient and facilitate the emergence of separate movements of the patient. To adapt to patients with different motor dysfunctions, the length of each part of the multi-joint robotic arm can be steplessly adjusted and can be quickly converted from left to right. The length of the forearm can be adjusted from 290–390 mm, the length of the upper arm from 220–310 mm, and the height of the robotic arm can also be adjusted within the range of 85–125 cm to suit patients of different heights, and the mainframe also has a special base design to suit patients with limited mobility in wheelchairs.

The multi-joint robot arm is equipped with seven high-precision angle sensors and one high-precision grip force sensor. These sensors are connected to a computer and can display the angle of each joint activity, muscle strength, and grip force of the upper limb in real time to realize real-time situational simulation visual biofeedback training of the entire upper limb or individual joints. The robotic arm can also be paired with a manipulator that can be infinitely adjusted to the size of the patient's hand. The strength of the spring can be adjusted according to the patient's hand muscle tension to optimize the assistive force throughout the range of motion of the fingers. This function is particularly suitable for patients with high flexor muscle tone and weak extensor muscles and can assist patients in completing palmar and finger extension movements. This robotic manipulator contains 1 angle sensor, and 2 pairs of anatomical angle couplers for finger movement, making the robotic arm, pressure sensing handle, and robotic hand together to form an overall upper limb motion chain, allowing simultaneous visual biofeedback rehabilitation training from shoulder off to fingers using the same software.

2.3 Training Mode

The Armeo Spring system is equipped with more than 20 visual feedback training programs and games to adjust the activity space and difficulty level of each program according to the patient's condition (shown in Fig. 2). For example, the special grip training program trains patients to grip, and for patients who do not have the ability to grip, it can be set to automatic grip, so that patients can continue to train other joints. In addition, there is also a close-to-life scenario simulation visual feedback training program, including shopping supermarkets and other ADL training programs, so that patients can improve their ADL ability.

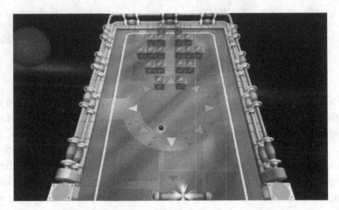

Fig. 2. Visual feedback training programs

The Armeo Spring system also has a variety of tests, including a single-joint range of motion in the single plane of motion, multi-joint 3D spatial motion, and upper extremity motion accuracy, which can be readily evaluated and reported on for a single-joint range of motion in the single plane of motion, multi-joint 3D spatial and coordination, and upper extremity motion accuracy.

3 Experiments and Results

The evaluation experiments of the Armeo Spring robot have been conducted in the Earth Huashan Hospital in Shanghai China. The operation and related parameters of the robot are set by experienced therapists.

3.1 Subjects Recruitment

Total 44 stroke patients were admitted in this research program. They were inpatients in Earth Huashan Hospital from January 2018 to October 2019. The inclusion and exclusion of participants were listed as follows:

Inclusion Criteria: Aged 20 to 80 years old; Hemiparetic stroke patients, Brunnstrom stage between II to IV; According to the "National Cerebrovascular Disease Conference" (2010 edition), diagnosed as stroke; Stroke duration>3 months; voluntary signing of informed consent and willingness to participate in this body.

Exclusion Criteria: Skeletal instability (unfixed fractures, severe osteoporosis), open skin injuries to the upper extremities, wearing of upper extremity orthoses; Instability of vital functions: contraindications to pulmonary or cardiac circulation (instability or these functions require mechanical support); inability to maintain sitting balance, severe postural reflex impairment, severe motor coordination impairment, ataxia; Paresthesia; shoulder subluxation or shoulder pain; severe spasticity or contractures; severe visual impairment (the patient cannot see the points displayed on the computer screen); Severe cognitive impairment and inability to cooperate; Seizure phase.

Characteristics for the group are summarized with means (and standard deviations) in Table 1.

Table 1. Characters of Participants ($x \pm s$)

	n	Age	Disease duration (month)
Experiment	23	43.22 ± 16.13	3.83 ± 3.79
Control	21	47.33 ± 13.12	6.62 ± 8.58

3.2 Experiment Procedure

A random number table was used to assign the participants randomly to either the experimental group or the control group. All participants received regular individualized rehabilitation training, including physical therapy, occupational therapy, task-oriented training of the upper extremities.

The control group added a manual repetitive movement training, 20 min each time and five times per week to the usual treatment. Training movements are set according to the patient's different functional status, including flexion and extension of the elbow, dorsal extension or palmar wrist flexion by some simple equipment; repeatedly wipe the table or wall; Pronation or A random number table was used to assign the participants randomly to either the experimental group or the control group. All participants received regular individualized rehabilitation training, including physical therapy, occupational therapy, task-oriented training of the upper extremities. Supronation of forearms with the help of gymnastic sticks. The experimental group added an Armeo Spring upper limb robot-assisted treatment to the usual treatment, each for 20 min, 5 times a week. The upper limb robot-assisted treatment plan is set by an experienced therapist and includes: (1) adjusting the length of the upper limb robotic arm according to the length of the patient's upper arm and forearm. (2) Adjust and reduce weight according to the patient's motor function state and arm weight, so that the patient is in the best assisted active movement state. (3) Select games according to the patient's motor function status, each game corresponds to different repetitive movements of the upper limbs, 3–4 games are selected each time, and the time of each game is generally 3–5 min. Such as ballooning (shoulder abduction/adduction); rubbing shredded carrots (elbow flexion and extension); football goalkeeper (forearm internal rotation/external rotation); Rescue of small animals (integrated exercise, including wrist flexion/extension, hand grasping); Driving games (mixed sports, improve ADL). (4) After each training, it can be compared with the previous training performance, and the therapist can evaluate the patient's motor function status according to the actual data, and give the patient guidance and encouragement in time; During training, the therapist adjusts the difficulty of the game or changes the game according to the improvement of the patient's motor function. If there is any discomfort or endangering the patient's life and health during training, the training should be terminated immediately, and the reason should be ascertained before deciding whether to continue robot-assisted training.

Evaluation Method: The evaluations were made by one physiatrist who was blind to the group of the participants. The evaluations were measured at before and after. During the study, we also monitored if the adverse events or safety problems to avoid secondary damage to subjects during training. The functional evaluations include functional comprehensive assessment, (FCA) and Fugl-Meyer assessment-upper extremity (FMA-UE).

:

Statistical Analysis: SPSS 23.0 software was used for statistical analysis, while $P < 0.05$ is statistically significant.

Table 2. FCA in different time points (x ± s)

Group	n	FCA1	FCA2	t	P
Experiment	23	68.33 ± 13.53	82.87 ± 9.96	9.35	0.00*
Control	21	72.46 ± 14.63	74.08 ± 14.45	3.92	0.001*
t	–	–0.972	2.366		
P	–	0.336	0.023*		

* means $P < 0.05$

3.3 Clinic Data Analysis

Functional comprehensive assessment: As shown in Table 2, at baseline, there were no significant difference between experiment group and control group ($P > 0.05$). There were significant differences between the two groups before and after training ($P < 0.05$), and the experimental group had significant differences after training compared with the control group ($P < 0.05$).

Fugl-Meyer assessment-upper extremity: As shown in Table 3, at baseline, there were no significant difference between experiment group and control group ($P > 0.05$).

Table 3. FMA-UE in different time points (x ± s)

Group	n	FMA-UE1	FMA-UE2	t	P
Experiment	23	26.43 ± 19.64	32.04 ± 21.30	4.156	0.000*
Control	21	21.90 ± 15.57	26.57 ± 15.86	3.459	0.002*
t	–	0.842	0.959		
P	–	0.404	0.343		

* means P<0.05

There were significant differences between the two groups before and after training ($P < 0.05$), but there was no significant difference between the experimental group and the control group after training ($P > 0.05$).

4 Conclusion

The anti-gravity support system of wearable upper limb robots can help patients perform three-dimensional directional exercises more easily while reducing the weight of the upper limb. This promotes early active movement and enhances motor function. The FCA scale is a comprehensive assessment tool of the patient's ability to self-care and survive in their community. It objectively reflects the patient's ADL ability. The results of this study showed that the FCA score of patients who underwent upper limb wearable robot training was significantly higher than the control group. This indicates that the application of upper limb wearable robots to stroke patients can effectively improve upper limb motor function recovery and improve daily living abilities.

Compared to conventional rehabilitation therapy, the upper limb robot-assisted system has a situation simulation biofeedback system and a large game library. The therapist can select suitable games for the patient based on their functional status and interests. This allows the patient to engage in targeted, progressive and high-repetition active movement training [19]. If a patient does a 20-min traditional repetitive movement training, they can become easily fatigued and lose focus. This system helps patients improve their attention, maintain physical energy, increase interest and motivation in training. The driving game in particular can simulate driving and different paths and scenarios, making the exercise more interesting. This helps improve the patient's motor function while gradually experiencing the process of recovery in daily life, thereby building their confidence in rehabilitation and willingness to take an active role in their recovery.

References

1. Sacco, R.L., Kasner, S.E., Broderick, J.P., et al.: An updated definition of stroke for the 21st century: a statement for healthcare professionals from the American heart association/American stroke association. Stroke 44(7), 2064–2089 (2013)
2. Feigin, V.L., et al.: Global and regional burden of stroke during 1990–2010: fndings from the global burden of disease study 2010. Lancet 383, 245–254 (2014)

3. Wang, W., et al.: Prevalence, Incidence, and mortality of stroke in China: results from a nationwide population-based survey of 480687 adults. Circulation **135**, 759–771 (2017)
4. Kim, A.S., Cahill, E., Cheng, N.T.: Global stroke belt: geographic variation in stroke burden worldwide. Stroke **46**, 3564–3570 (2015)
5. Sarti, C., Rastenyte, D., et al.: International trends in mortality from stroke, 1968 to 1994. Stroke **31**(7),1588–1601 (2000)
6. Abo, M., Kakuda, W., Momosaki, R., et al.: Randomized, multicenter, comparative study of NEURO versus CIMT in poststroke patients with upper limb hemiparesis: the neuro-verify study. Int. J. Stroke **9**(5), 607–612 (2014)
7. Connell, L., Lincoln, N., Radford, K.: Somatosensory impairment after stroke: frequency of different deficits and their recovery. Clin. Rehabil. **22**, 758–767 (2008)
8. Nakayama, H., Jorgensen, H.S., Raaschou, H.O., Olsen, T.S.: Compensation in recovery of upper extremity function after stroke: the copenhagen stroke study. Arch. Phys. Med. Rehabil. **75**, 852–857 (1994)
9. Pollock, A., Farmer, S.E., Brady M.C., et al.: Interventions for improving upper limb function after stroke. Cochrane Datab. Syst. Rev. (Online), 11 (2013)
10. Babaiasl, M., Mahdioun, S.H., Jaryani, P., Yazdani, M.: A review of technological and clinical aspects of robot-aided rehabilitation of upper-extremity after stroke. disability and rehabilitation. Assistive Technol. **11**(4), 263–280 (2016)
11. Chang, W.H., Kim, Y.: Robot-assisted therapy in stroke rehabilitation. Stroke **15**(3), 174–181 (2013)
12. Riener, R.: Robot-aided rehabilitation of neural function in the upper extremities. Acta Neurochir. Suppl. **97**(Pt 1), 465–471 (2007)
13. Riener, R., Nef, T., Colombo, G.: Robot-aided neurorehabilitation of the upper extremities. Med. Bio. Eng. Comput. **43**(1), 2–10 (2005)
14. Hogan, N., Krebs, H.I., Charnnarong, J., et al.: MIT-MANUS: a workstation for manual therapy and training. In: SPIE Proceedings: Telemanipulator Technology, vol. 1833, pp. 161–165 (1993)
15. Kyeong, S., Na, Y., Kim, J.: A mechatronic mirror-image motion device for symmetric upper-limb rehabilitation. Int. J. Precision Eng. Manufact. **21**(1), 947–956 (2020)
16. Islam, M.R., Assad-Uz-Zaman, M., Brahmi, B., Bouteraa, Y., Wang, I., Rahman, M.H.: Design and development of an upper limb rehabilitative robot with dual functionality. Micromachines **12**(8), 870 (2021)
17. Toth, A., Fazekas, G., Arz, G., Jurak, M., Horvath, M.: Passive robotic movement therapy of the spastic hemiparetic arm with REHAROB: report of the first clinical test and the follow-up system improvement. In: 9th International Conference on Rehabilitation Robotics, pp. 127–130. ICORR 2005, Chicago, IL, USA (2005)
18. Perry, J.C., Rosen, J.: Design of a 7 degree-of-freedom upper-limb powered exoskeleton. In: The First IEEE/RAS-EMBS International Conference on Biomedical Robotics and Biomechatronics, pp. 805–810. BioRob 2006, Pisa, Italy (2006)
19. McDowd, J.M., Filion, D.L., Pohl, P.S., et al.: Attentional abilities and functional outcomes following stroke. J. Gerontol. B Psychol. Sci. **58**(1), 45–53 (2003)

Design and Evaluation of a Pelvic-Assisted Gait Training Robot for Mobility Improvement in Stroke Patients

Rong-Rong Lu, Er-Kang Xie, Tian-Hao Gao, Yan-Hua, and Yu-Long Bai$^{(\boxtimes)}$

Department of Rehabilitation Medicine, Huashan Hospital, Fudan University, No. 12 Middle Wulumuqi Road, Shanghai 200040, China
dr_baiyl@fudan.edu.cn

Abstract. Periodic task-specific repetitive movements have been shown to improve motor performance in stroke patients. As a typical periodic task-specific repetitive movement, gait training with wearable devices might be effective in improving mobility in stroke patient. In this study, we designed a pelvic-assisted gait training robot and evaluated its effectiveness in clinical practice. Equipped with force and position sensors, this robot features a pelvic structure with multiple degrees of freedom. Its mechanical structure, motor actuators, sensors, and safety protection features have been optimized for patient-active control strategies based on force control algorithms and real-time monitoring. In this study, we assessed whether stroke patients could benefit from this training and improve their mobility. We randomly assigned 33 stroke patients to either the experimental group, which underwent pelvic-assisted gait training, or the control group, which received gait training supervised by a physical therapist. We assessed lower extremity mobility, motor function, and activities of daily living before and after the intervention After intervention, participants in the experimental group walked more independently than those in the control group. Also, ability of maintaining balance in participants in the experimental group also improved significantly. The results of this preliminary study indicated that pelvic-assisted gait training not only reduced the burden on therapists and provided high-intensity training but also produced quantitative evaluation results that might help us design better training protocols for stroke patients.

Keywords: Pelvic-supported gait training · Stroke · Mobility · Balance

1 Introduction

Stroke is the second most common cause of death worldwide and its prevalence is projected to increase in the coming years in parallel with the increase of life expectancy [1]. Despite the great improvements in the management of the acute phase of stroke, some residual disability persists in most patients thus requiring rehabilitation [2], causing heavy economic burden to families and society [3]. The most common impairment after

---

R.-R. Lu and E.-K. Xie—Contributed equally to this work.

© The Author(s), under exclusive license to Springer Nature Singapore Pte Ltd. 2023
H. Yang et al. (Eds.): ICIRA 2023, LNAI 14269, pp. 543–553, 2023.
https://doi.org/10.1007/978-981-99-6489-5_44

stroke is hemiplegia [4, 5]. So gait impairments is common in stroke patients regardless of their disease duration. Decreased mobility after stroke is associated with an increased risk of fall and a decreased quality of life [6]. Thus, restoring mobility is one of the major rehabilitative goals. The recommended rehabilitative approaches include task-oriented physical training of walking, high intensity and repetitive gait training which focuses on taking full advantage of residue motor function. Physical therapists usually conduct gait training by manual assistance of the trunk, pelvis and legs which places heavy burden on them and might impede the effectiveness of training. The use of robots in rehabilitation can not only alleviate physicians from the substantial load of training tasks but also assess patients' recovery status by analyzing the data recorded during robotic training. Given its advantages in terms of accuracy and reliability, rehabilitation robotics could offer an effective approach to enhance the recovery outcomes following stroke. Thus, there is an urgent demand for rehabilitation robots [7].

Several types of rehabilitation robots for lower limb have been developed. These can be classified into four types: robots with a single degree of freedom, wearable robots, suspended gait robots, and sitting or lying gait robots. Robots with a single degree of freedom are limited in their training capabilities, and wearable robots require the patient to have independent walking ability. This study would focus on suspended gait robots for rehabilitation training.

The Lokomat [8, 9], developed by Hocoma AG, was the first driven gait orthosis to improve the walking movements of gait-impaired patients. LOPES [10, 11], designed by Veneman et al., is a gait rehabilitation robot that automatically adapts to each patient's gait to assist them in standing up and walking. Other common suspended gait trainers include the Haptic Walker [12], LokoHelp [13, 14], and Gangtrainer GT 1 [15, 16] made in Germany.

The lower limb robot used in our study provides pelvic unloading support and allows control of three degrees of freedom of pelvic motion (rotation, tilt, and translation). Sensors are used to obtain the pelvic position and interaction force data during the walking process, providing real-time information on pelvic motion. Additionally, the training difficulty can be adjusted by restricting the pelvic degrees of freedom based on the patient's mobility, partially opening or fully opening all degrees of freedom. This unloading support is different from previous lower limb robots as it does not restrict the natural movement of the legs. In a fully open state, it provides a realistic and natural gait training environment, maintaining the natural movement trajectory of the pelvis and aiming to restore the natural gait as much as possible.

In the present study, a pelvic assisted lower limb robot was designed and assessed in stroke patients to see how it can assist with gait training. The new robot can alleviate the burden on therapists during training, analyze data collected during the training process, and evaluate the patient's rehabilitation progress. This study provides an overview of the pelvic-assisted rehabilitation robot and compares it with traditional gait training supervised by the physiotherapists. Based on the preliminary results, we also evaluate the application of pelvic-assisted gait training robots in clinical scenario

2 Methods

2.1 System Overview

In order to assist stroke patients in training with the treadmill, the system should be able to support them in standing and walking scenario. The pelvic-assisted gait training robot (Fig. 1) consists of five components: the column system, pelvis system, operation system, treadmill, and virtual reality (VR) system. The column system comprises a lead screw, linear rail, and servo motor. By driving the motor, the lead screw moves up and down to adjust the position of the system for the patients during gait training. The pelvis system is a multi-DOF mechanical system with a dynamic weight reduction function. The operation system provides a simplified user interface for the therapists to operate. Multiple training modes are designed for patients in different disease duration using the treadmill system. During the training, patients could interact with the VR system. Finally, safety protection mechanisms are integrated into the whole system to prevent secondary damage to the patients during training.

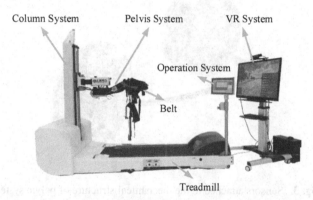

Fig. 1. System overview of pelvic-assisted lower limb robot

The main part of this pelvis assisted gait training robot is the pelvis system which could simulate pelvic motion and provides body weight support during training. As shown in Fig. 2, the pelvis system is connected to the column system to adjust the patient's posture during training. It is designed as a parallelogram mechanism, which allows for pelvic left and right movement. The lateral movement is achieved around the horizontal axis, while torsion movement can be accomplished around the rotating axis. The sensor attached to the pelvic system could obtain the position and interaction force data during training, providing real time information on pelvic motion (Fig. 3).

The hardware system is composed of a controller, a force sensor, a motor, and a motor driver. To adjust the height of the system, two servo motors were employed for the column system, while the treadmill system was controlled by another motor. The column motor is equipped with an absolute encoder to measure position and velocity, whereas the treadmill motor is equipped with an incremental encoder.

Four training modes have been designed for different patients, and would be discussed in detail below.

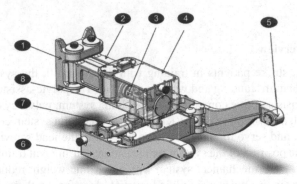

Fig. 2. Mechanical Structure of pelvic system. 1-Foundation support, 2-Back Four-link mechanism, 3-the horizontal axis, 4-the connection box, 5-Force sensor, 6-bracket, 7-Forward Four-link mechanism, 8-shaft.

Fig. 3. Sensors attached to the mechanical structure of pelvic system

The Constant Velocity Mode allows therapists to set individualized speeds for different patients. The setting speed would not be changed during the training. To alter the setting speed, the training must be stopped and the new speed should be set. This mode provides a safe training environment for patients since the speed is chosen based on the mobility of the patients.

In the Following Mode, therapists can set a maximum speed to ensure patient safety. Here a controller was designed to adjust the force error (difference between target force and actual force value from the force sensor) and to control the treadmill speed. In this mode, patients to walk in appropriate speed.

In the Resistance Mode, patients must overcome the resistance force. Using the preset resistance force threshold, the velocity is calculated with the actual force sensor value, and patients can then begin training at the expected speed. Furthermore, the Following Mode is a special case of the Resistance Mode, where the resistance value is set to zero.

The Disturbance Mode is quite different from the three previously mentioned training modes, and is used to improve patients' balance and anti-falling abilities. Therapists can set the acceleration, disturbance number, disturbance direction, and period time values to generate a small displacement, which allows us to observe patients' reactions to sudden movements and train their balance abilities.

2.2 Study Overview

This study was a single-center, single-blind, randomized controlled trial. The SE-NaturaGait1® robot (Shanghai Electric Group, Shanghai, China) system is indicated for using by hemiparetic stroke patients during their gait training under the supervision of a physical therapist. This study was approved by the Institutional Review Boards of Huashan Hospital. The research was performed in accordance with the Declaration of Helsinki. Written informed consent was obtained from all participants.

2.2.1 Participants

Stroke patients (both inpatients and outpatients from Rehabilitation Department, Huashan Hospital) were admitted in this study. The inclusion and exclusion criteria were listed as follows:

Inclusion criteria: age between 20 and 80 years old; diagnosed with hemiparetic stroke and Brunnstrom stage of the lower limb between II to IV; diagnosed as stroke according to the 2010 edition of the "National Cerebrovascular Disease Conference"; disease duration between 14 days to 12 months; and voluntary signing of informed consent indicating a willingness to participate.

Exclusion criteria: In combination with severe cardiopulmonary liver and kidney dysfunction, not suitable for rehabilitation, eg in the past 6 months, due to any cause of congestive heart failure (CHF) attack or aggravation need to change the dosage, diet or any heart attacks that needs to be admitted to hospital were seen as CHF; Known CHF with valvular disease; open thoracic cardiac surgery (coronary artery bypass or valve replacement); acute myocardial infarction within 3 months; acute MI on admission with signs or symptoms, including electrocardiogram findings; suspected aortic dissection on admission; acute arrhythmia with hemodynamic instability (including any tachycardia or bradycardia); liver dysfunction (more than 1.2 times the normal range); serum creatinine, urea nitrogen exceeds 1.2 times the normal range; existing acute or chronic lung disease); poor blood pressure and blood glucose control, blood pressure test for systolic blood pressure $> = 140$ mmHg, diastolic blood pressure $> = 90$ mmHg; Acute disease such as acute infection, fracture or dislocation (fracture or dislocation in healing period which is not properly fixed); Participating in other relevant clinical researchers at the same time; Pregnant or plan for pregnancy; History of malignant tumor; Contraindications for using lower limb rehabilitation robots.

2.2.2 Study Protocol

A random number table was utilized to randomly assign participants to either the experimental group or the control group. All participants underwent their assigned treatment for three weeks, five times per week, consisting of 45 min of individualized rehabilitation training based on their motor impairment. The experimental group received 20 min of training with the pelvic-assisted gait training robot (Fig. 4), while the control group received 20 min gait training supervised by an experienced physical therapist. The parameters of the gait training were limited to a controllable range, such as the weight unloading ratio being restricted to [5%, 30%] and the walking speed being limited to [0.6, 1.6] m/s.

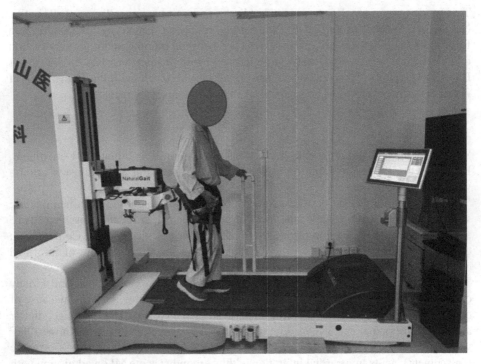

Fig. 4. Patients training with pelvic-assisted lower limb robot

2.2.3 Primary and Secondary Outcome

The primary outcome was the score of Functional Ambulation Category (FAC), reflecting the participants' gait independence. Secondary outcome measures included motor function (Fugl-Meyer Assessment of Motor Recovery of the lower extremities), static and dynamic balance ability (Berg Balance Scale scores) and ability to perform activities of daily living (Modified Barthel Index). Outcome measures were evaluated for each participant at baseline, after the 7th intervention, and immediately after the completion of the entire training program by a blinded physiatrist.

2.2.4 Statistical Analysis

SPSS 19.0 was used for statistical analysis. The measurement data was expressed in terms of two independent sample t test or Wilcoxon rank sum test to compare the results of the experimental group and the control group at different evaluation time points. The paired t test was used to compare the results of the participants at different time points within the group. Two-sided statistical tests were performed and the level of significance was set at $\alpha = 0.05$.

3 Results

3.1 Participants

Thirty-three stroke patients were admitted in this study. All of them have completed all the interventions and assessments. Eighteen were in the experimental group and fifteen were in the control group. There were no significant differences in age and disease duration between the two groups (P > 0.05) (Table 1).

Table 1. Demographic Characters

Group	N	Age	Disease duration (month)
Experimental Group	18	56.17 ± 15.10	4.89 ± 3.14
Control Group	15	52.33 ± 16.94	4.23 ± 3.35

3.2 Functional Ambulation Category (FAC)

As shown in Table 2, at baseline, there were no significant difference between experimental group and control group (P > 0.05). After intervention, the experimental group improved significantly (P < 0.05) while there was no significant improvement in the control group (P > 0.05). But there's no significant difference between the experimental group and control group after the intervention (P > 0.05). This indicated that the walking independence in experimental group improved significantly.

Table 2. FAC

Group	n	Baseline	After 7th intervention	After 15th intervention	P
Experimental	18	2.83 ± 1.34	3.33 ± 1.41	3.72 ± 1.32*	0.003
Control	15	2.60 ± 2.10	2.80 ± 1.93	2.80 ± 1.93	0.189
P	–	0.701	0.368	0.115	

3.3 Fugl-Meyer Assessment (FMA)

As shown in Table 3, at baseline, there were no significant difference between experimental group and control group (P > 0.05). Significant improvement occurred in both group after training (P < 0.05). This indicated both training could improve the motor impairment significantly.

Table 3. FMA

Group	n	Baseline	After 7th intervention	After 15th intervention	P
Experimental	18	21.33 ± 6.82	25.44 ± 3.57	27.28 ± 4.14*	0.002
Control	15	23.67 ± 5.07	24.67 ± 4.03	25.93 ± 3.90*	0.018
P	–	0.281	0.561	0.348	

3.4 Berg Balance Scale (BBS)

The results are presented in Table 4, at baseline, there were no significant difference between experimental group and control group (P > 0.05). Significant improvement occurred in both group after intervention (P < 0.05). This indicated that the posture control ability improved significantly in both groups.

Table 4. BBS

Group	n	Baseline	After 7th intervention	After 15th intervention	P
Experimental	18	23.89 ± 8.51	28.50 ± 4.67	29.94 ± 4.68*	0.004
Control	15	21.33 ± 11.36	24.20 ± 9.89	24.67 ± 9.82*	0.041
P	–	0.466	0.111	0.052	

3.5 Barthel Index (BI)

The results are presented in Table 5, at baseline, there were no significant difference between experimental group and control group (P > 0.05). Significant improvement occurred in both group after training (P < 0.05). This indicated that the independence of activity of daily life improved significantly in both groups.

Table 5. BI

Group	n	Baseline	After 7th intervention	After 15th intervention	P
Experimental	18	64.72 ± 18.03	73.89 ± 19.06	77.50 ± 17.17*	0.000
Control	15	66.67 ± 23.20	71.33 ± 22.87	73.00 ± 23.74*	0.000
P	–	0.788	0.729	0.533	

4 Discussion

Motor impairment is the most common impairment in stroke patients. When concerning rehabilitation of lower extremity, mobility is among the first priority. There are many factors might affect the mobility and gait pattern in stroke patients. Thus, gait training should incorporate various sensory inputs, experiences, learning, and motor training to trigger neural pathways for compensation [17].

Gait training could be provided via therapist and robots. Compared with gait training supervised by therapist, robot-assisted gait training has certain advantages, including early initiation in severely dependent patients, less effort for physiotherapists, longer duration and higher intensity of gait, more physiological and reproducible gait patterns, and the possibility to measure a patient's performance [18]. Currently, there exist four major categories of lower limb robotics, mainly the tethered exoskeletons, end-effector devices, untethered exoskeletons and patient-guide suspension systems [19]. Although many clinical trials have been designed, the results of these studies did not support the efficacy of robot assisted gait training. In this study, we found similar results. Although our results indicated that after intervention, the FAC score in the experimental group has improved significantly. Considering the small sample size and the preliminary nature of our study, it should be cautious to made concrete conclusion. But we do think from certain point of view, robot assisted gait training could provide some advantages. For example, it could increase the time of training, saving labor resources, and to modify the working environment of the therapists.

Different lower limb robots focus on different aspect of gait training. Applying gait training robots at different disease duration might better enhance mobility. For example, exoskeleton robots covering the lower extremity combined with treadmill could provide the chance of gait training in early subacute stage. End-effector-based systems simulate trajectories in the stance and swing phases during gait training [20]. Patient-guided suspension systems are non-anchored robotic walking frames that allow overground, supported walking and provide a harness and/or trunk or pelvic support during walking. And this is the robot system used in this study.

From patients' perspective of view, they wanted start gait training as early as possible in a saft manner. They also need certain amount of gait training. Gait training once a day might not meet their needs. While walking training supervised by the therapist in the early disease stage consumes manpower and might have safety issues. Providing robot assisted gait training could meet patients' needs and compensate the aforementioned disadvantages.

In this study, we found the mobility in the experimental group improved significantly. But other behavioral assessments didn't show significant improvement. There may be several reasons might account for the results. First, mobility is a practical skill, and gait training might directly improve walking ability. However, in terms of improving motor function, simple gait training may not lead to significant improvements in motor function. Furthermore, although weight support technique might achieve early access to walking ability, it also decreased the proprioceptive input during walking, which might affect balance to some extent. Thirdly, the limited sample size in this study may also have an impact on the research results.

In the future, we would further modify the equipment based on the results of this study, for example, how to balance weight bearing and timing of walking training. And modify training protocols to better enhance the mobility of stroke patients.

Acknowledgements. This work was supported by National Key Research and Development Program of China (No 2022YFC3601200). The SE-NaturaGait1® robots used in this study was provided by Shanghai Electric GeniKIT Medical Science and Technology Co., LTD.

References

1. Global, regional, and national burden of stroke and its risk factors, 1990–2019: a systematic analysis for the Global Burden of Disease Study 2019. Lancet Neurol. **20**, 795–820 (2021)
2. Virani, S.S., et al.: Heart disease and stroke statistics-2020 update: a report from the American heart association. Circulation **141**, e139–e596 (2020)
3. Chen, W.W., et al.: Summary of china cardiovascular disease report 2016. Chin. Circ. J. **32**, 521–530 (2017)
4. Pollock, A., et al.: Interventions for improving upper limb function after stroke. Cochrane Db. Syst. Rev. (11), CD010820 (2014)
5. Stinear, C.M., Lang, C.E., Zeiler, S., Byblow, W.D.: Advances and challenges in stroke rehabilitation. Lancet Neurol. **19**, 348–360 (2020)
6. Hu, X.L., et al.: Effectiveness of functional electrical stimulation (FES)-robot assisted wrist training on persons after stroke. In: 2010 Annual International Conference of the IEEE Engineering in Medicine and Biology, pp. 5819–5822 (2010)
7. Zhu, Y., Zhen, R., Liu, H., Meng, S.: The research of rehabilitation robots BCI technology based on EEG. In: International Conference on Computer Science and Software Engineering, pp. 1107–1110, 12–14 December 2008. IEEE, Wuhan (2008)
8. Hidler, J., Wisman, W., Neckel, N.: Kinematic trajectories while walking within the Lokomat robotic gaitorthosis. Clin. Biomech. **23**(10), 1251–1259 (2008)
9. Wirz, M., Zemon, D.H., Rupp, R., Scheel, A., Colombo, G.: Effectiveness of automated locomotor training in patients with chronic incomplete spinal cord injury: a multicenter trial. Arch. Phys. Med. Rehabil. **86**, 672–689 (2005)
10. Fleerkotte, B.M., Koopman, B., Buurke, J.H., van Asseldonk, E.H., van der Kooij, H., Rietman, J.S.: The effect of impedance-controlled robotic gait training on walking ability and quality in individuals with chronic incomplete spinal cord injury: an explorative study. J. Neuroeng. Rehabil. **11**, 26 (2014)
11. Veneman, J.F., Kruidhof, R., Hekman, E.E.G., Ekkelenkamp, R., van Asseldonk, E.H.F., van der Kooij, H.: Design and evaluation of the LOPES exoskeleton robot for interactive gait rehabilitation. IEEE Trans. Neural Syst. Rehabil. Eng. **15**(3), 379–386 (2007)

12. Schmidt, H., Hesse, S., Bernhardt, R., Kruger, J.: Haptic-Walker-a novel haptic foot device. ACM Trans. Appl. Percept. **2**(2), 166–180 (2005)
13. Freivogel, S., Mehrholz, J., Husak-Sotomayor, T., Schmalohr, D.: Gait training with the newly developed 'LokoHelp'-system is feasible for non-ambulatory patients after stroke, spinal cord and brain injury. a feasibility study. Brain Injury. **22**, 7 (2008)
14. Freivogel, S., Schmalohr, D., Mehrholz, J.: Improved walking ability and reduced therapeutic stress with an electromechanical gait device. J. Rehabil. Med. **9**, 734–739 (2009)
15. Werner, C., Frankenberg, S.V., Treig, T., Konrad, M., Hesse, S.: Treadmill training with partial body weight support and an electromechanical gait trainer for restoration of gait in subacute stroke patients: a randomized crossover study. Stroke. **33**(12), 2895–2901 (2002)
16. Pohl, M., Werner, C., Holzgraefe, M., Kroczek, G., Mehrholz, J., Wingendorf, I., et al.: Repetitive locomotor training and physiotherapy improve walking and basic activities of daily living after stroke: a single-blind, randomized multicentre trial (Deutsche GAngtrainerStudie, DEGAS). Clin. Rehabil. **21**(1), 17–27 (2007)
17. Poli, P., Morone, G., Rosati, G., Masiero, S.: Robotic technologies and rehabilitation: new tools for stroke patients' therapy. Biomed. Res. Int. 153872 (2013)
18. Schwartz, I., Meiner, Z.: Robotic-assisted gait training in neurological patients:who may benefit? Ann. Biomed. Eng. **43**, 1260–1269 (2015)
19. Esquenazi, A., Talaty, M.: Robotics for lower limb rehabilitation. Phys. Med. Rehabil. Clin. N. Am. **30**(2), 385–397 (2019)
20. Hesse, S., Waldner, A., Tomelleri, C.: Innovative gait robot for the repetitive practice of floor walking and stair climbing up and down in stroke patients. J. Neuroeng. Rehabil. **28**(7), 30 (2010)

Effect of Lower Limb Exoskeleton Robot on Walking Function of Stroke Patients

Yuean Yang and Jiamin Lu[✉]

Department of Rehabilitation Medicine, Huashan Hospital, Fudan University, Fudan, China
84720042@qq.com

Abstract. Objective: To study the clinical effect of lower limb exoskeleton robot on walking function of stroke patients with hemiplegia.

Methods: 46 stroke patients with hemiplegia were divided into control group (conventional rehabilitation therapy + conventional gait training) and experimental group (conventional rehabilitation therapy + robot-assisted gait training), 23 cases, 5 times/week, a total of 4 weeks. Before treatment and 4 weeks after treatment, balance function was assessed using a three-stage balance scale in sitting and standing positions, Brunnstrom lower limb staging, lower limb score on the Fugl-Meyer Motor Function Rating Scale (FMA), Functional ambulation category scale to assess lower limb motor function and walking ability.

Results: After 4 weeks of treatment, the experimental group showed improvement in sitting balance and orthostatic balance after treatment, while the control group showed improvement only in sitting balance. The motor function and walking function of the experimental group and the control group were improved after treatment, and the motor function of the experimental group was better than the control group.

Conclusion: The use of lower limb exoskeleton robot can effectively improve the balance function, motor function and walking function of patients in the convalescent stage of stroke, and promote the rehabilitation of patients.

Keywords: Stroke · Exoskeleton Robot · Walking

1 Introduction

Stroke is one of the major chronic noninfectious diseases threatening the health of Chinese people, as well as the primary cause of premature death and disability due to disease, with five characteristics: high incidence, high disability rate, high mortality rate, high recurrence rate and high economic burden. According to the China Stroke Prevention and Treatment Report, the incidence rate of stroke in China was 201/100,000 in 2019. In 2018, about 1.94 million people died of stroke, accounting for 22.3% of the total mortality rate of Chinese residents [1]. With the gradual deepening of aging in China, the number of stroke patients is bound to increase, which will become a major burden for families and society.

Dyskinesia of stroke patients will greatly affect patients' ability of daily living activities and quality of life, and is the second leading cause of disability worldwide [2].

© The Author(s), under exclusive license to Springer Nature Singapore Pte Ltd. 2023
H. Yang et al. (Eds.): ICIRA 2023, LNAI 14269, pp. 554–563, 2023.
https://doi.org/10.1007/978-981-99-6489-5_45

Impaired walking function is one of the most common dysfunction in stroke patients. Walking control is very complex, lower limb muscle strength decreased, hypoesthesia, trunk control and deterioration of balance coordination function have serious impact on walking function in stroke patients. In order to improve patients' daily activity ability and quality of life, walking training should be an important part of rehabilitation therapy.

With the development of walking rehabilitation training technology, transcranial Direct Current Stimulation, tDCS [3], electronic biofeedback technology, balance instrument [4] and robot-assisted walking training can effectively improve the therapeutic effect. Among them, Robot Assisted Gait Training is one of the popular rehabilitation treatment directions in recent years. Several studies and reviews have confirmed that robot-assisted gait can provide good therapeutic effects [5].

Traditional walking training relies heavily on the therapist's personal experience and technology. Robot-assisted walking training can realize automatic intelligent training, and save the therapist's physical strength and resources. Robot-assisted gait training provides sensory motor training to the patient, giving the patient the same plantar pressure and proprioceptive stimulation in both lower limbs at each stage of the walking cycle. The treatment time of robot gait training is longer and the process is more stable. Repeated sensory stimulation input induces neural recombination in the cerebral cortex and subcortical regions. [6].

Aiwalker exoskeleton robot has the advantages of small size, easy to move and wide clinical application. It can also carry out walking training for patients with weak motor function. The Aiwalker exoskeleton robot has been recognized for its safety and feasibility, but its effect on walking function in stroke patients still needs to be further explored to clarify its clinical performance and application prospects.

2 Data and Methods

2.1 General Information

Forty-six convalescent stroke patients admitted to the Rehabilitation Medicine Department of Huashan Hospital Affiliated to Fudan University from January 2021 to December 2021 were selected as the research objects. There were 23 patients in control group, including 16 males and 7 females, 12 patients with cerebral infarction and 11 patients with cerebral hemorrhage, aged 18–75 years old, with an average age of (54.3 ± 12.4) years old. There were 23 patients in experimental group, there were 17 males and 6 females, 8 patients with cerebral infarction and 15 patients with cerebral hemorrhage, aged 18–76 years old, with an average age of (48.7 ± 16.2) years old. There was no significant difference in the general data between the two groups (P > 0.05). (Table 1).

2.2 Inclusion Criteria

(1) Inclusion criteria: the subjects had unilateral limb paralysis caused by stroke for the first time in clinical practice, the course of disease was less than 12 months, and the subjects were between 18 and 80 years old; Weight <85 kg, height 150 cm−185 cm. (2) Exclusion criteria: basic vital signs are unstable and rehabilitation training is not suitable; Severe joint disease or osteoporosis of the lower extremities: severe spasms of the lower extremities with limited range of motion.

2.3 Device

Aiwalker Exoskeleton robot (produced by Beijing Ai-Robotics Technology Co., LTD.) consists of a mechanical body (including leg lever, sole, driving device), mobile support platform, equipment controller, and binding. The machine is made of titanium alloy and stainless steel and weighs about 80 kg. The exoskeleton robot is mounted on a four-wheeled mobile support platform to support the patient's lower back and provide balance control. At the same time, it can provide patients with real ground rehabilitation walking training. [7] The rotation centers of the hip and knee motors shall be on the same axis as the rotation centers of the user's hip and knee joints, respectively. The exoskeleton is attached to the user's waist, thighs, calves and feet with straps (see Fig. 1).

The Aiwalker Exoskeleton robot's drive control system controls both hip and knee joints to achieve a bionic gait. The drive control system includes controller (coordinate synchronization between multiple drivers), driver (drive circuit system), brushless DC motor, harmonic reducer, information acquisition unit (relative code disk, absolute code disk), output shaft, etc. The controller is responsible for outputting the moving gait and coordinating the synchronized coordinated motion between the four drivers. At the same time, according to the angular speed of the motor shaft and the angular position of the output shaft, the motion parameters of the driver are adjusted in real time to control the motion state of the leg shaft (see Fig. 2).

The Aiwalker Exoskeleton robot provides enough strength to assist the robot in walking without the need for active strength in the lower extremities. The thigh and calf rods are designed to be retractable, and the waist width can be adjusted to accommodate users of different heights and body types.

Hip and knee angles can be adjusted according to the patient's needs. The maximum range of motion of the hip joint is $33°$ flexion and $23°$ extension. The maximum range of motion of the knee joint is $53°$ flexion and $23°$ extension. The device provides four different angles of gait to suit different patients. The gait cycle can be adjusted between 2.45 and 5.25 s depending on the patient's needs. With the given human-like gait as the training control system, the standard gait was input, the dynamics and kinematics models of human lower limbs were established, the motion output of lower limb structure was calculated and controlled, and the patients were driven to carry out passive movements of lower limbs (see Fig. 3).

2.4 Methods

The control group received routine rehabilitation therapy + routine gait training, including good limb placement; Draft training; Turn over transfer training; Trunk and lower limb joint motion control training; Muscle strength training; Separate motor training. Routine gait training includes balance training and flat walking training. Conventional rehabilitation treatment 40 min/time, conventional gait training 20 min/time, once/day, 5 times/week, a total of 4 weeks.

Routine rehabilitation treatment + robot-assisted gait training in the experimental group was the same as that in the control group. Robot-assisted gait training was carried out by therapists assisting patients, including: (1) Human body size was measured before use, including pelvis width and great calf length. (2) Trained therapists adjust the equipment to the appropriate size according to the size of each patient and assist the patient to use the machine. (3) Fasten the straps to fix the patient's waist, legs and feet on the corresponding positions of the device to complete the device wearing. (4) The step length and gait cycle suitable for patients were selected for training. Routine rehabilitation treatment 40 min/time, robot-assisted gait training 20 min/time, once/day, 5 times/week, a total of 4 weeks.

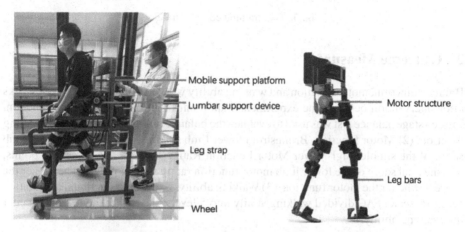

Fig. 1. Structures of Aiwalker Exoskeleton robot

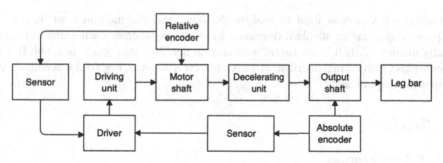

Fig. 2. Drive control system of Aiwalker Exoskeleton robot

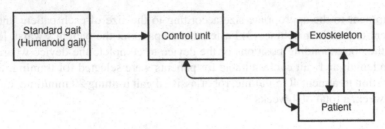

Fig. 3. Gait training control strategy

3   Outcome Measures

Balance function, motor function and walking ability were compared before and 4 weeks after intervention between the experimental and control groups. (1) Balance function. Three - stage balance test was used to evaluate the balance function of sitting and standing position. (2) Motor function. Brunnstrom lower limb staging was used; The lower limb score of the simple Fugl-Meyer Motor Function Rating Scale (FMA) was 0–2 points, and the total score of the lower limb motor function rating was 34 points. The higher the score, the better the motor function. (3) Walking ability. Using the Functional ambulation category scale, FAC divided walking ability into 5 levels, the higher the level, the better the walking ability.

3.1   Statistical Analysis

Spss20.0 software was used to analyze the data, and the measurement data were expressed as mean $\pm$ standard deviation. First, check whether each variable is normally distributed. If it is consistent with normal distribution, t test is adopted; if it is inconsistent with normal distribution, rank sum test is adopted. $P < 0.05$ was considered statistically significant.

4   Results

4.1   Balance Function

There was no difference between the experimental group and the control group in sitting and standing balance before and after treatment. The experimental group showed significant improvement in sitting balance and orthostatic balance after treatment, while the control group only showed significant improvement in sitting balance after treatment (Table 2).

4.2 Motor Function

The motor function of experimental group and control group improved significantly after treatment. After treatment, Brunnstrom lower limb staging in experimental group was significantly better than that in control group (Table 3).

4.3 Walking Function

The walking function of the experimental group and the control group improved significantly after treatment. There was no significant difference in walking function between the two groups after treatment (Table 4).

The difference in balance function, motor function and walking ability between the two groups before and after treatment was statistically significant. In sitting balance, standing balance, brunnstrom lower leg stage and FAC, the difference before and after treatment was greater in the experimental group than in the control group (Table 5).

Table 1. Comparison of baseline data between the two groups

Group	Age (years)	Gender		Stroke type	
		Male	Female	Cerebral infarction	Cerebral hemorrhage
Control group	54.3 ± 12.4	16	7	12	11
Experimental group	48.7 ± 16.2	17	6	8	15
Z/X^2	−1.375	0.107		1.415	
P	0.169	0.743		0.234	

Table 2. Comparison of balance functions between the two groups

Group	Sitting balance		P	Standing balance		P
	Baseline	Post treatment		Baseline	Post treatment	
Control group	1.74 ± 1.14	1.91 ± 1.04	0.049	0.78 ± 0.95	0.95 ± 0.90	0.08
Experimental group	1.83 ± 1.11	2.35 ± 0.94	0.001	0.83 ± 0.71	1.35 ± 0.94	0.001
Z	−0.251	−1.592	—	−0.495	−1.441	—
P	0.802	0.111	——	0.621	0.150	——

Table 3. Comparison of motor function between the two groups

Group	Brunnstrom stage of lower extremity		P	FMA score of lower extremity		P
	Baseline	Post treatment		Baseline	Post treatment	
Control group	2.74 ± 1.14	2.91 ± 1.16	0.046	11.65 ± 7.99	13.83 ± 7.44	0.017
Experimental group	3.09 ± 1.07	3.68 ± 1.04	0.005	14.27 ± 8.26	17.91 ± 8.26	0.000
Z	−1.095	−2.372	—	−1.331	−1.616	—
P	0.274	0.018	—	0.183	0.106	—

Table 4. Comparison of walking function between the two groups

Group	Functional ambulation category scale, FAC		Z	P
	Baseline	Post treatment		
Control group	0.57 ± 0.73	0.83 ± 0.89	−2.449	0.014
Experimental group	0.57 ± 0.79	1.35 ± 1.11	−4.025	0.000
Z	−0.087	−1.583	—	—
P	0.931	0.113	—	—

Table 5. Comparison of the effects of balance function, motor function and walking ability between the two groups before and after treatment

Group	Sitting balance, Post treatment-Baseline	Standing balance, Post treatment-Baseline	FMA score of lower extremity, Post treatment-Baseline	Brunnstrom stage of lower extremity, Post treatment-Baseline	FAC, Post treatment-Baseline
Control group	0.17 ± 0.39	0.14 ± 0.35	2.17 ± 4.53	0.17 ± 0.39	0.26 ± 0.45
Experimental group	0.52 ± 0.59	0.52 ± 0.51	3.64 ± 4.08	0.59 ± 0.85	0.78 ± 0.52
Z	−2.221	−2.711	−1.328	−2.077	−3.251
P	0.026	0.007	0.184	0.038	0.001

5   Discussion

Stroke patients with hemiplegia sequelae, motor dysfunction seriously affect their ability to daily life. The exoskeleton robot combines medical theory with robot technologies such as sensing, control, information acquisition and mobile computing to realize the

Effect of Lower Limb Exoskeleton Robot

support function similar to human lower limb skeleton, joint controllable flexion and extension activities and real ground gait walking. The patient is provided with strength support during training by walking through high-intensity repetitive exercise.

In this study, Aiwalker exoskeleton robot was used to assist gait training instead of conventional gait training, which has a good effect. Balance function, motor function and walking function were improved in the experimental group, and the degree of improvement was greater than that in the control group. Lin [8] et al. applied the exoskeleton robot for walking training and found that the patients' trunk control and balance functions were significantly improved. Literature reports that the use of rehabilitation robots for trunk stability rehabilitation training of stroke patients can effectively improve patients' balance ability, lower limb function and walking independence [9]. Repeated gait training can promote the reconstruction of symmetrical walking pattern [10].

One of the most widely used robot-assisted gait training devices is Lokomat, from Hocoma, a Swiss company. Lokomat is equipped with a weight loss support system and dynamic gait orthotics on the surface of the hip and knee joints for use on running platforms. The therapist can conduct walking rehabilitation training according to the individual gait pattern of the patient. The exoskeleton drives the leg to achieve a walking motion in the sagittal plane, and four rotatory joint flexion drives the hip and knee flexion and extension. Studies have found that lokomat and other robot-assisted therapy combined with traditional physical therapy can more effectively improve the gait function of patients with post-stroke movement disorders, and at the same time, the walking support is reduced, the stride frequency is increased, and the stride speed is increased [11–13]. Lokomat belongs to the body weight support treadmill training with exoskeleton rehabilitation robot, which is composed of lower limb gait correction driving device, weight bearing system, treadmill and control system, etc., [14] covering a large area. And this kind of treadmill equipment is only suitable for a specific gait trajectory, and the environmental stimulation is relatively simple.

ReWalk is an exoskeleton robot developed by Israeli company Rewalk Robotics [15]. he robot is composed of exoskeleton mechanical legs, waist support, flat crutches and backpack. Mechanical legs can control flexion and extension of hip and knee joints; The waist bracket is used to link the mechanical legs and the backpack on both sides; Batteries and control systems are integrated in the backpack [16]. Rewalk lower limb rehabilitation robot can assist patients with lower limb paralysis to stand, walk, turn and go up and down stairs, with strong flexibility [17]. But this kind of robot is mainly suitable for the bilateral upper limb function intact lower limb motor dysfunction patients, more suitable for paraplegia patients rather than hemiplegia patients.

Post-stroke rehabilitation training emphasizes early intervention, early intervention, higher brain plasticity, greater recovery potential. Aiwalker exoskeleton robot can provide stable trunk support and lower limb power, so that patients who are unable to stand and walk can also have early walking training. The external frame can ensure that the center of gravity of patients during walking training does not exceed the external boundary, and there is no risk of falling, so as to ensure the safety of patients in walking training. Repeated stimulation of sensation in the muscles and skin of the lower extremities helps patients recover proprioception and plantar pressure perception, thereby improving walking function.

Aiwalker exoskeleton robot allows patients to carry out walking training on the real ground in a richer training environment, which can more effectively promote cerebral cortex remodeling and further improve motor function. At the same time, it also increases the interest of training, and improves patients' treatment compliance and tolerance. However, the Aiwalker exoskeleton robot can only perform passive walking training at present, without the active participation of the patient. Studies have shown that the outcome of motor learning after stroke is influenced by patients' active involvement [18], motivation and feedback [19]. Therefore, robot-assisted passive walking training has limited training effect on patients.

The exoskeleton robot can improve balance function, motor function and walking ability in stroke patients, and its efficacy is comparable to, and in some aspects even better than, traditional walking training. Robot-assisted walking training can reduce the physical burden of therapists and improve the efficiency of rehabilitation.

6 Conclusion

The Aiwalker exoskeleton robot can effectively improve the balance function, motor function and walking function of patients in the convalescent stage of stroke, and promote the rehabilitation of patients.

Funding. This study was supported by Beijing Ai-Robotics Technology Co., Ltd, Beijing, China.

References

1. Liyuan, P., et al., Projected global trends in ischemic stroke incidence, deaths and disability-adjusted life years from 2020 to 2030. Stroke **54**(5), 1330−1339 (2023)
2. Feigin, V.L., et al.: Global, regional, and national burden of neurological disorders, 1990–2016: a systematic analysis for the global burden of disease study 2016. Lancet Neurol. **18**(5) (2019)
3. Etienne, O., et al.: The effects of anodal transcranial direct current stimulation on the walking performance of chronic hemiplegic patients. Neuromodulation J. Int. Neuromodul. Soc. **23**(3) (2020)
4. Min, Z., et al.: Effects of visual feedback balance training with the Pro-kin system on walking and self-care abilities in stroke patients. Medicine **99**(39) (2020)
5. Antonio, R.F., L.P. Joan, and F.L.J. M., Systematic review on wearable lower-limb exoskeletons for gait training in neuromuscular impairments. J. Neuro Eng.Rehabil. 18(1), 1−21 (2021)
6. Wallard, L., et al., Effects of robotic gait rehabilitation on biomechanical parameters in the chronic hemiplegic patients. Neurophysiol. Clin./Clin. Neurophysiol. **45**(3), 215−219 (2015)
7. Sijing, C., et al.: Safety and feasibility of a novel exoskeleton for locomotor rehabilitation of subjects with spinal cord injury: a prospective, multi-center, and cross-over clinical trial&#13. Front. Neurorobotics, **16**, 848443 (2022)
8. Lin, L.-F., et al.: A novel robotic gait training system (RGTS) may facilitate functional recovery after stroke: a feasibility and safety study. NeuroRehabilitation **41**(2), 453−461 (2017)

9. Hong, M.J., et al.: Effects of trunk stabilization training robot on postural control and gait in patients with chronic stroke: a randomized controlled trial. International journal of rehabilitation research. Internationale Zeitschrift fur Rehabilitationsforschung. Revue internationale de recherches de readaptation, **43**(2) (2020)
10. Banala, S.K., et al.: Robot assisted gait training with active leg exoskeleton (ALEX). IEEE Trans. Neural Syst. Rehabil. Eng. Publ. IEEE Eng. Med. Bio. Soc. **17**(1), 2–8 (2009)
11. Schwartz, I., et al.: the effectiveness of locomotor therapy using robotic-assisted gait training in subacute stroke patients: a randomized controlled trial. PM&R **1**(6), 516–523 (2009)
12. Calabrò, R.S., et al.: Robotic neurorehabilitation in patients with chronic stroke: psychological well-being beyond motor improvement. International journal of rehabilitation research. Internationale Zeitschrift fur Rehabilitationsforschung. Revue internationale de recherches de readaptation. **38**(3), 219–225 (2015)
13. Giovanni, T., et al.: Conflicting results of robot-assisted versus usual gait training during postacute rehabilitation of stroke patients: a randomized clinical trial. International journal of rehabilitation research. Internationale Zeitschrift fur Rehabilitationsforschung. Revue internationale de recherches de readaptation **39**(1), 29 (2016)
14. Hidler, J., Wisman, W., Neckel, N.: Kinematic trajectories while walking within the Lokomat robotic gait-orthosis. Clin. Biomech. **23**(10), 1251–1259 (2008)
15. Alberto, E., et al.: The ReWalk powered exoskeleton to restore ambulatory function to individuals with thoracic-level motor-complete spinal cord injury. Am. J. Phys. Med. Rehabil. **91**(11), 911–921 (2012)
16. Zeilig, et al., Safety and tolerance of the ReWalk? exoskeleton suit for ambulation by people with complete spinal cord injury: a pilot study. J. Spinal Cord Med. **35**(2), 96–101 (2012)
17. Yang, A., et al.: Assessment of in-hospital walking velocity and level of assistance in a powered exoskeleton in persons with spinal cord injury. Top Spinal Cord Inj. Rehabil. **21**(2), 100–109 (2015)
18. Alain, K.-L., Lumy, S., Cohen, L.G.: Role of voluntary drive in encoding an elementary motor memory. J. Neurophysiol. **93**(2), 1099–1103 (2005)
19. Holden, M.K.: Virtual environments for motor rehabilitation. Cyberpsychol. Behavior. **8**(3), 187–211 (2005)

Design and Control of a Novel Underactuated Soft Exosuit

Wei Yang[1] , Lianghong Gui[1] , Luying Feng[1], Canjun Yang[2],
and Qiaohuan Cao[1(✉)]

[1] Ningbo Innovation Center, Zhejiang University, Ningbo 315100, China
qh_cao2023@163.com
[2] College of Mechanical Engineering, Zhejiang University, Hangzhou 310027, China

Abstract. Soft exosuit is widely researched to assist walking. Lacking of physical compliance in hip exosuits restricts wearing comfort of the system. This paper presents design and control of an underactuated hip exosuit with soft series elastic actuator (SSEA) that exhibits customized physical compliance. The actuation module is mounted on the backpack, and each motor is responsible for hip flexion and extension of one side. In high level control, a phase oscillator model was used for assistive force generation. In low level control, PID controllers were applied for flexion and extension forces tracking, respectively. Experimental results indicate the proposed hip exosuit can assist walking with physical compaliance and provide suitable force at the accurate timing. This work enables studies of exosuits with underactuated mechanism and actuator with physical compliance to pave the way for application of wearable robots in real-world.

Keywords: Soft exosuit · Soft series elastic actuator · Under-actuated mechanism · Physical compliance · Walking assistance

1 Introduction

Wearable exoskeletons have great potential in enhancing human locomotion and walking efficiency by providing additional assistive forces required by the human body [1]. For a healthy user, portable and lightweight hip joint assistive devices are desirable and effective in reducing energy expenditure during human walking [2]. Current hip exoskeletons can be categorized into two main groups based on their structural design: anthropomorphic rigid structures and soft structures [3], among them, rigid structures are often bulky and face challenges such as mechanical joint limitations and misalignment with biological joints [4]. On the other hand, soft exosuits provide a reliable and comfortable means to enhance user mobility without restricting movement or introducing incompatible degrees

Research supported by Ningbo Science and Technology Innovation 2025 Project (No. 2020Z022 and 2020Z082), Ningbo Public Welfare Project (No. 2021S082), and Key Research and Development Project of Zhejiang Province (No. 2022C03029).

© The Author(s), under exclusive license to Springer Nature Singapore Pte Ltd. 2023
H. Yang et al. (Eds.): ICIRA 2023, LNAI 14269, pp. 564–575, 2023.
https://doi.org/10.1007/978-981-99-6489-5_46

of freedom between the user and the exoskeleton. Therefore, soft exosuits have become a current research focus [5,6].

Many existing soft exosuits are driven by motors combined with Bowden cables [7,8]. While the force application direction is unrestricted, the assistance provided by these systems lacks a certain degree of passive compliance, resulting in a relatively high level of rigidity during fast movements. Improvements have been made by researchers such as S. M. Cox et al. [9], who introduced a modification by incorporating springs in series with the Bowden cables. This modification enables passive compliance in ankle joint assistance, enhancing the overall flexibility of the exoskeleton system. However, transferring this approach to hip joint exosuits presents difficulties due to the proximity of the cables to the thigh muscles. During walking, the thigh exhibits considerable swing amplitude, and the presence of springs in such a configuration may lead to potential muscle compression.

In order to address these challenges, A. T. Asbeck et al. [10] opted to utilize elastic bands as the means of force transmission for hip joint assistance, aiming to avoid the aforementioned issues. However, this approach comes at the cost of relinquishing the benefits of Bowden cables, which allow for force guidance in any desired direction. Consequently, the flexion actuator and extension actuator are mounted on the anterior and posterior sides of the user's waist, respectively.

This paper introduces a novel concept called the soft series elastic actuator (SSEA), which combines the merits of both approaches above. The proposed SSEA comprises a motor-driven Bowden cable or a tension cable that is serially connected with a soft elastic element, as illustrated in Fig. 1. The proposed SSEA not only allows for effective force transmission to the desired region but also exhibits excellent passive compliance and human-body compatibility. Furthermore, by employing a high torque-to-weight ratio quasi-direct drive motor as the core component of the SSEA, it achieves reduced weight and superior

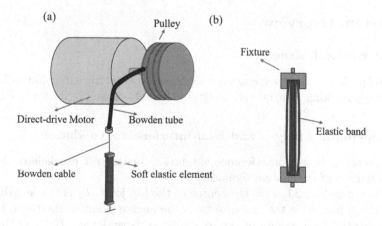

Fig. 1. Soft series elastic actuator (SSEA) structure. (a) Elements of SSEA. (b) Customized flexible element with modularized elastic bands.

back-drivability. Besides being lightweight, the ease of donning and adaptability to different body types are important concerns for researchers. Similar to the modular design proposed by C. Nesler et al. [11], This work offers customizable compliant elastic elements based on users' specific needs for passive compliance, different numbers of elastic bands can be connected in parallel. Additionally, the thigh attachment, tension cables, and soft elastic element can be easily separated, allowing for convenient wearing and removal.

Most of the research on flexible hip exoskeletons has focused on unidirectional assistance (either hip flexion or hip extension) [12,13]. Only a few studies have explored bidirectional assistance [14], Q. Chen et al. typically employ two motors for actuation of a hip joint, one for flexion and another for extension, which increases the overall weight of the exoskeleton. In contrast, E. Tricomi et al. [15] adopted an underactuated approach, using a single motor on the anterior side to assist both legs in flexion without extension. In this work, an underactuated approach is adopted, utilizing a single motor for bidirectional assistance of a hip joint at different times, significantly reducing the weight of the system.

The contributions of this paper can be summarized as follows:

(1) Innovatively, the concept of SSEA is proposed, combining the advantages of Bowden cable and elastic band drivetrain. The SSEA provides controllable force transmission direction, exhibits passive compliance, and ensures good conformity with the human thigh. A quasi-direct drive motor is selected to achieve excellent back-drivability performance.
(2) Modular design of an exosuit is proposed, which allows for convenient donning and doffing, as well as the selection of corresponding serial elastic modules based on individual needs.
(3) Underactuated design, for the first time, utilizes a single motor for bidirectional assistance in both flexion and extension for one hip joint, effectively reducing the weight of the exosuit.

2   System Overview

2.1   Mechanical Structure

The novel underactuated soft exosuit is designed to assist hip extension and flexion during daily walking. The overall design of this soft exosuit is shown in Fig. 2.

2.2   Kinematic Analysis and Non-interference Validation

In this section, the non-interference validation on the soft exoskeleton is given by the analysis of the motion dynamics.

As shown in Fig. 2.b, O is the center of the hip joint, L_1 is the length of the human thigh bar, L_2 is the distance from the anchor point to the thigh bar, B_1 and B_2 are the force points of the exoskeleton drive device, B_1C_1 is the front Bowden cable, B_2C_2 is the rear soft rope, θ is the hip joint angle, reflecting the walking gait.

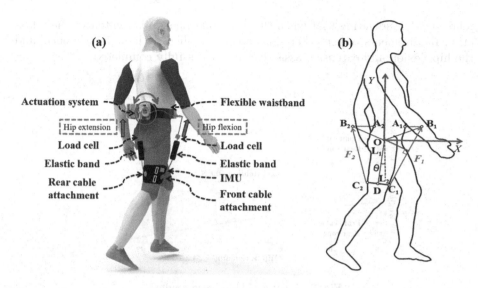

Fig. 2. System overview. (a) Overall design of the exosuit. (b) Kinematic analysis diagram.

According to the dynamic model, the moving path of the front cable and the rear soft rope can be calculated. Assume that the coordinate of C_1 is (x_1, x_2) and that of C_2 is (x_2, y_2). By measuring the physiological parameters of the wearer, $L_1 = 0.36$ m, $L_2 = 0.08$ m.

When the hip joint is in the stage of flexion movement, the calculation process is as follows:

$$x_1 = L_1 \cdot sin\theta + L_2 \cdot cos\theta, \tag{1}$$

$$y_1 = L_2 \cdot sin\theta - L_1 \cdot cos\theta, \tag{2}$$

$$x_2 = L_1 \cdot sin\theta - L_2 \cdot cos\theta, \tag{3}$$

$$y_2 = -L_2 \cdot sin\theta - L_1 \cdot cos\theta. \tag{4}$$

Assuming that the coordinates of B_1 and B_2 are (x_3, y_3) and (x_4, y_4) respectively, the two parts of the path are calculated as follows:

$$L_3 = \sqrt{(x_1 - x_3)^2 + (y_1 - y_3)^2}, \tag{5}$$

$$L_4 = \sqrt{(x_2 - x_3)^2 + (y_2 - y_3)^2}. \tag{6}$$

The two paths are similarly calculated when the hip joint is in the extension phase.

The final calculation results are shown in Fig. 3. It can be seen from the calculation results that during the two movements of hip flexion and extension, the cable on the working side always changes more rapidly than that on the relaxed side, indicating that when the cable on one side is tightened, the relaxation requirements of the other side can be satisfied without interference, and the hip flexion and extension assist can be successfully completed.

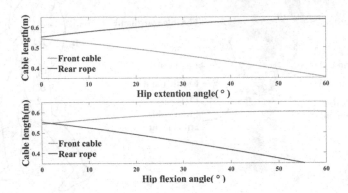

Fig. 3. Results of kinematic analysis.

3   Controler Design

The human-machine interaction performance of a soft exosuit is highly contingent upon its control strategies. The control architecture of the novel underactuated soft exosuit basically consists of two components: (1) high-level control, which is responsible for the overall planning of assistance, including the workflow of underactuated motors, gait phase estimation, and generation of desired reference forces at the low-level control; (2) low-level control, which is responsible for controller design to track the reference force provided by the high-level control, aiming to accomplish the assistive task.

3.1   High-Level Control Strategy

Working Principle. The underactuated soft exosuit was designed to utilize a single motor to assist both hip flexion and extension during the whole walking process. In the natural walking process of the human body,, the gait cycle can be divided into two phases: the swing phase, which extends from toe-off to heel strike, and the stance phase, which spans from heel strike to toe-off. The swing phase involves the leg extending from maximum hip extension (MHE) to maximum hip flexion (MHF). Therefore, the motor needs to rotate to drive the Bowden cable on the anterior side of the thigh to apply flexion assistance. Conversely, in the stance phase, the motor needs to rotate in the opposite direction to drive the cable on the posterior side of the thigh for extension assistance. The specific workflow is illustrated in Fig. 4.

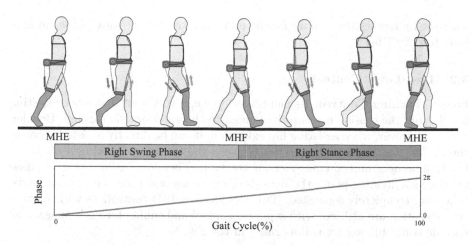

Fig. 4. Walking assistance principle of the underactuated soft exosuit.

Gait Phase Estimation. In the process of human-machine interaction, exoskeletons need to understand the user's locomotion intentions. Common methods include discrete gait event detection based on plantar pressure sensors and continuous gait phase estimation based on IMUs. Continuous gait phase estimation can generate continuous control references for the low level control. Therefore, phase oscillator (PO), as a robust continuous gait phase estimation algorithm, is adopted. Its principle is to calculate the phase angle based on the thigh segment's angle and angular velocity collected by an IMU and convert the phase angle from 0–2π to 0–100%, which can be obtained by

$$\varphi = \arctan 2\left(\dot{\theta}, \theta\right), \tag{7}$$

where θ and $\dot{\theta}$ represent the hip joint flexion/extension angle and angular velocity, respectively, obtained from the IMU fixed on the human thigh. To enhance the control performance of the algorithm, adaptive phase shifting and scaling are applied to the acquired angle and angular velocity:

$$\hat{\theta}(t) = s(t) \times (\theta(t) + \alpha(t)),$$
$$\hat{\dot{\theta}}(t) = \dot{\theta}(t) + \beta(t), \tag{8}$$

where $\alpha(t)$ and $\beta(t)$ represent the translation parameters calculated from the hip joint and angular velocity, respectively, and $s(t)$ denotes the scaling parameter.

Assist Force Profile Planning. Once the gait phase of human motion is obtained, it is necessary to generate the corresponding reference force for the low-level controller to track. Since the torque exerted by the biological hip joint resembles a sinusoidal signal, the force profile can be described as

$$\tau_m = \kappa \sin \varphi, \tag{9}$$

where κ represents the scaling factor, and ϕ represents the gait phase ranging from 0 to 2π [16].

3.2 Low-Level Control

Force Tracking Control. As mentioned above, it is evident that when assisting hip flexion, the tension needs to be guided to the anterior side through Bowden cables. However, when assisting hip extension, it can be directly assisted through the cables. The friction terms differ between the two cases, making it challenging to employ a unified controller for tracking. Therefore, using the gait phase of 50% as a dividing point, the periods of extension assistance and flexion assistance are completely separated. Two feedforward PID controllers with friction compensation are utilized, with separate control and tuning for each phase. The specific control flowchart is illustrated in the Fig. 5.

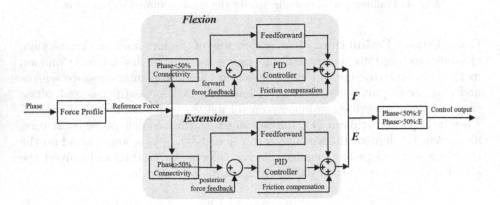

Fig. 5. Block diagram of underactuated force tracking control.

4   Experiment and Result

The proposed underactuated soft exosuit, along with the electronic devices and controllers, was built in this study. Excluding the battery, the total weight of the soft exosuit is 2.85 kg. Fig. 6 illustrates the human-machine system control architecture. Each leg is equipped with a PMSM motor (RMD-L-7025 28T, MYACTUATOR Ltd, Suzhou, China), an IMU (WT901CTTL, Wit-motion Ltd, Shenzhen, China), and a tension sensor (JLBS-MD-50kg, JN-sensor Ltd, Anhui, China). The motor has a rated torque of 1.6 Nm, which, after conversion through pulleys and cables to the hip joint end, can provide an assist torque of 8–10 Nm. The IMU is used to collect thigh segment angles and angular velocities for gait phase estimation, while the tension sensor acquires tension data for feedback control.

A Raspberry Pi 4B (The Raspberry Pi Foundation, Cambridge, UK) served as the data intermediary device, collecting motor current feedback, tension sensor data, and IMU data. The collected data was transmitted via UDP to the host PC running MATLAB R2022a's Simulink Real-Time environment. The control algorithm was implemented in Simulink, and the control commands were sent back to the Raspberry Pi 4B. The Raspberry Pi 4B promptly relayed the commands to the motor, enabling closed-loop force feedback control. Simulink operated at a frequency of 1 kHz, while the IMU sampling rate was 150 Hz, the tension sensor operated at 100 Hz, and the motor control frequency was 100 Hz.

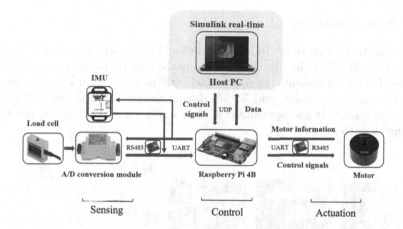

Fig. 6. Hardware architecture of the exosuit.

4.1 Experimental Protocol

Except for the human wearing component in Experiment I, all experiments in this study were conducted on an imitation human experimental platform, where the exoskeleton was fixed to the platform and the end anchor point was fixed. An IMU was used to simulate the swinging motion of the thigh during human walking by regular shaking, generating continuous gait phases. Experiment I verified the rationality of the exoskeleton's structural design, Experiment II validated the effectiveness of the high-level gait phase estimation algorithm and torque generation, and Experiment III assessed the performance of the low-level force tracking. All research-related ethics for this experiment have been approved by the Ethics Committee of the College of Biomedical Engineering and Instrument Science, Zhejiang University (Ethics Approval Number: 202255).

During Experiment I. A participant (weight: 67 kg, height: 170 cm, age: 22) was involved in the wearing experiment. The participant wore the exosuit and perform actions such as leg lifting, leg swinging, and leg pressing to test the degrees of freedom provided by the exosuit. Subsequently, the back-driving forces of the exosuit were measured on the platform, along with the tension on the opposite side during extension and flexion assistance, to validate the underactuated performance and back-driving performance of the exosuit.

During Experiment II. Real-time data from the IMU was collected to support the operation of the high-level planning algorithm. The algorithm computed the gait phase and the corresponding reference forces. This experiment aimed to validate the effectiveness of the high-level control strategy.

During Experiment III. The underactuated force tracking control algorithm was executed to assess the performance of the low-level force tracking.

4.2 Experimental Results

Experiment I. Figure 7.a illustrates the achievable motion patterns by the wearer, revealing that the subject's motion in the sagittal plane is generally unrestricted. Figure 7.b presents the motor back-driving force, with a maximum force of 3.98 N during extension and 5.26 N during flexion. This figure also demonstrates the tension in the opposite side, during flexion and extension assistance, remains close to zero.

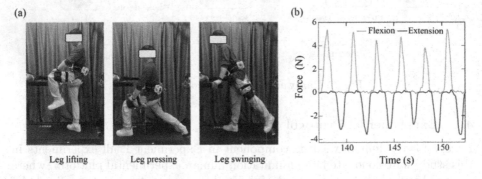

Fig. 7. Physical compliance test. (a) Demonstration of the range of motion allowed by the exosuit. (b) Back-driving force during flexion-extension movement.

Experiment II. The results of the high-level control strategy is shown in Fig. 8, including the collected angles and angular velocities, as well as the computed continuous gait phase and reference force signals. The results demonstrate good linearity of the gait phase and smoothness of the generated reference force profile, which can meet the requirements of the low-level control.

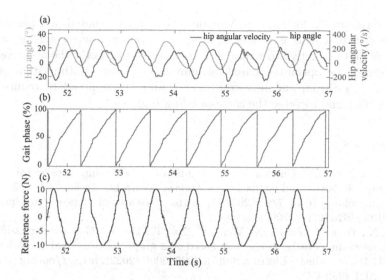

Fig. 8. Experimental results of high-level control strategy. (a) Hip angle and angular velocity. (b) Continuous gait phase. (c) Generated assistive force profile.

Experiment III. Figure 9 presents the performance of the low-level force tracking control, illustrating the effectiveness of the force control in tracking desired force profile.

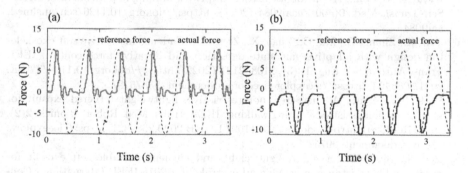

Fig. 9. Low-level force tracking results. (a) Force tracking during flexion. (b) Force tracking during extension.

5   Discussion and Conclusion

The overall aim of this study is to design a soft exosuit with SSEAs that ensure physical compliance. Experimental results indicate that the designed exosuit can assist hip flexion and extension adaptively according to the wearer's locomotion state and the proposed underactuated force tracking control is applicable to track desired force profile for the SSEA model. The underactuated and quasi-direct drivable design scheme is beneficial to system compact and weight reduction, which are quite sensitive to wearable robots. In future work, the assistive force profile should be optimized based on human-in-the-loop optimization or user preference algorithm, and new controller would be proposed to reduce force tracking error and increase the corresponding bandwidth.

References

1. Yang, C., et al.: Current developments of robotic hip exoskeleton toward sensing, decision, and actuation: a review. Wearabl. Technol. 3, e15 (2022). https://doi.org/10.1017/wtc.2022.11, https://www.cambridge.org/core/product/identifier/S2631717622000111/type
2. Wu, X., Yuan, Y., Zhang, X., Wang, C., Xu, T., Tao, D.: Gait phase classification for a lower limb exoskeleton system based on a graph convolutional network model. IEEE Trans. Industr. Electron. 69(5), 4999–5008 (2022). https://doi.org/10.1109/TIE.2021.3082067
3. Wang, X., Guo, S., Qu, B., Bai, S.: Design and experimental verification of a hip exoskeleton based on human-machine dynamics for walking assistance. IEEE Trans. Human Mach. Syst. 53(1), 85–97 (2023). https://doi.org/10.1109/THMS.2022.3217971
4. Sposito, M., Di Natali, C., Toxiri, S., Caldwell, D.G., De Momi, E., Ortiz, J.: Exoskeleton kinematic design robustness: an assessment method to account for human variability. Wearable Technol. 1, e7 (2020). https://doi.org/10.1017/wtc.2020.7
5. Awad, L.N., et al.: A soft robotic exosuit improves walking in patients after stroke. Sci. Transl. Med. 9(400), eaai9084 (2017). https://doi.org/10.1126/scitranslmed.aai9084
6. Tan, X., Zhang, B., Liu, G., Zhao, X., Zhao, Y.: Cadence-insensitive soft exoskeleton design with adaptive gait state detection and iterative force control. IEEE Trans. Autom. Sci. Eng. 19(3), 2108–2121 (2022). https://doi.org/10.1109/TASE.2021.3066403, https://ieeexplore.ieee.org/document/9387549/
7. Park, E.J., et al.: A hinge-free, non-restrictive, lightweight tethered exosuit for knee extension assistance during walking. IEEE Trans. Med. Robot. Bionics. 2(2), 165–175 (2020). https://doi.org/10.1109/TMRB.2020.2989321, https://ieeexplore.ieee.org/document/9075258/
8. Bae, J., Siviy, C., et al.: A lightweight and efficient portable soft exosuit for paretic ankle assistance in walking after stroke. In: 2018 IEEE International Conference on Robotics and Automation (ICRA), pp. 2820–2827. IEEE, Brisbane, QLD (2018). https://doi.org/10.1109/ICRA.2018.8461046, https://ieeexplore.ieee.org/document/8461046/
9. Cox, S.M., Rubenson, J., Sawicki, G.S.: A soft-exosuit enables multi-scale analysis of wearable robotics in a bipedal animal model. In: 2018 IEEE/RSJ International Conference on Intelligent Robots and Systems (IROS), pp. 4685–4691. IEEE, Madrid, October 2018. https://doi.org/10.1109/IROS.2018.8593911, https://ieeexplore.ieee.org/document/8593911/
10. Asbeck, A.T., Schmidt, K., Walsh, C.J.: Soft exosuit for hip assistance. Robot. Autonom. Syst. 73, 102–110 (2015). https://doi.org/10.1016/j.robot.2014.09.025, https://linkinghub.elsevier.com/retrieve/pii/S0921889014002103

11. Nesler, C., Thomas, G., Divekar, N., Rouse, E.J., Gregg, R.D.: Enhancing voluntary motion with modular, backdrivable, powered hip and knee orthoses. IEEE Robot. Autom. Lett. **7**(3), 6155–6162 (2022). https://doi.org/10.1109/LRA.2022.3145580, https://ieeexplore.ieee.org/document/9691920/

12. Chen, L., et al.: A portable waist-loaded soft exosuit for hip flexion assistance with running. Micromachines. **13**(2), 157 (2022). https://doi.org/10.3390/mi13020157, https://www.mdpi.com/2072-666X/13/2/157

13. Cao, W., et al.: A lower limb exoskeleton with rigid and soft structure for loaded walking assistance. IEEE Robot. Autom. Lett. **7**(1), 454–461 (2022). https://doi.org/10.1109/LRA.2021.3125723, https://ieeexplore.ieee.org/document/9606603/

14. Chen, Q., Guo, S., Wang, J., Wang, J., Zhang, D., Jin, S.: Biomechanical and physiological evaluation of biologically-inspired hip assistance with belt-type soft exosuits. IEEE Trans. Neural Syst. Rehabil. Eng. **30**, 2802–2814 (2022). https://doi.org/10.1109/TNSRE.2022.3209337, https://ieeexplore.ieee.org/document/9903060/

15. Tricomi, E., et al.: Underactuated soft hip exosuit based on adaptive oscillators to assist human locomotion. IEEE Robot. Autom. Lett. **7**(2), 936–943 (2022). https://doi.org/10.1109/LRA.2021.3136240, https://ieeexplore.ieee.org/document/9655470/

16. Yang, W., Xu, L., Yu, L., Chen, Y., Yan, Z., Yang, C.: Hybrid oscillator-based no-delay hip exoskeleton control for free walking assistance. Industr. Robot. Int. J. Robot. Res. Appl. **48**(6), 906–914 (2021). https://doi.org/10.1108/IR-02-2021-0038, https://www.emerald.com/insight/content/doi/10.1108/IR-02-2021-0038/full/html

Morphology Design of Soft Strain Sensors with Superior Stability for Wearable Rehabilitation Robots

Qian Wang[1], Seyram Ofori[2], Qiulei Liu[3], Haoyong Yu[2], Shuo Ding[2(✉)], and Haitao Yang[3(✉)]

[1] Department of Material Science Engineering, National University of Singapore, 9 Engineering Drive 1, Singapore 117575, Singapore
[2] Department of Biomedical Engineering, National University of Singapore, 4 Engineering Drive 3, Singapore 117583, Singapore
bieding@nus.edu.sg
[3] Frontiers Science Center for Flexible Electronics, Northwestern Polytechnical University, 127 West Youyi Road, Xi'an 710072, China
iamhtyang@nwpu.edu.cn

Abstract. Accurate human motion tracking by wearable sensors is critical for wearable robots in rehabilitation, but existing sensing technologies have several limitations, such as unaffordability, poor stability, and reliability concerns. Through the sensor morphology design, this research focuses on the development of robust soft strain sensors using crumpled single-walled carbon nanotubes (SWCNTs). Compared to planar sensors, crumpled SWCNTs sensors exhibit wide working strain ranges, robust cycling performance, and superior mechanical stability. These sensors were integrated into a rehabilitation exoskeleton and successfully monitored elbow deformation and muscle activity by sensitive, stable, and reliable signals, indicating great potential in replacing EMG and inertial sensors to provide accurate and immediate feedback for optimized operations in rehabilitation tasks. This technology provides a cost-effective, wearable, and privacy-friendly solution for motion monitoring in rehabilitation robots, improving the effectiveness and convenience of rehabilitation treatment for people with physical disabilities.

Keywords: Strain sensor · Crumpled microstructures · Sensor stability · Rehabilitation robots

1 Introduction

Real-time monitoring of human motion to track joint kinematics and dynamics for closed-loop control in motion is a crucial technology for wearable robots in rehabilitation [1, 2]. To achieve accurate motion tracking, optical capture systems that consist of a set of camera arrays have been widely adopted, but it suffers from several limitations. First, such an optical system is generally too heavy and fixed, which is not compatible with

© The Author(s), under exclusive license to Springer Nature Singapore Pte Ltd. 2023
H. Yang et al. (Eds.): ICIRA 2023, LNAI 14269, pp. 576–583, 2023.
https://doi.org/10.1007/978-981-99-6489-5_47

wearable robots that move freely in unlimited space [1]. Second, it generally requires a strong Graphics Processing Unit (GPU) to analyze the recorded images or videos, proposing the concerns of energy consummation for long-term usage [3]. Third, optical capture systems suffer from privacy issues [1, 4]. It records detailed visual information about user's body proportions and physical appearance, putting identity information at risk of compromise or misappropriation in certain situations.

In addition to optical capture systems, wearable sensors, such as inertial sensors, electromyography (EMG) sensors, and soft strain sensors, have emerged as an alternative approach to monitoring human motions [1, 2, 5–7]. These sensors can be easily attached to body joints/bodies and track human kinematics by collecting joint accelerations and angular velocities, monitoring muscular activities, or measuring skin/textile deformations. However, each kind of wearable sensor faces challenges during body motion monitoring. Firstly, inertial sensors suffer from inherent integration drift, particularly in the plane perpendicular to gravity, and the obtained inertial information is often affected by noise and requires frequent signal recalibration [8]. Moreover, EMG sensors suffer from noisy signals which show low sensitivity and require specialized software to analyze the data [3, 6]. Besides, as for soft strain sensors, most of them show inferior mechanical stability, affecting the overall performance and accuracy during long-term motion tracking [8–10].

In this study, instead of EMG and inertial sensors where the application challenges are attributed to their inalterable structures and working mechanisms, we focused on soft strain sensors for wearable rehabilitation robots by overcoming the long-term stability issue through sensor morphology design. Basically, we prepared crumpled SWCNTs which serve as a promising soft strain sensor. Compared to a planar sensor device that can only withstand only 10% strain with bad cycling performance, the crumpled SWCNTs sensor showed > 100% working strain and robust cycling performance up to 5,000 cycles. Afterward, we applied the crumpled SWCNTs sensor in a rehabilitation exoskeleton with the aim of helping physically disabled people. As a result, the developed SWCNTs sensors not only can accurately detect joint deformations but also are capable of monitoring muscular activities with high sensitivity in real-time. With this technology, patients can receive immediate feedback on their movements, enabling the exoskeleton to effectively assist in adjusting and optimizing their movements, showing high potential to replace EMG and inertial sensors during rehabilitation tasks.

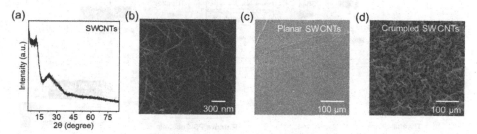

Fig. 1. (a) XRD pattern of SWCNTs. (b) SEM image of SWCNTs network. (c,d) Top-down SEM image of planar SWCNTs and crumpled SWCNTs sensors.

2 Results and Discussion

In this work, SWCNTs were selected for the fabrication of strain-sensing layers. The X-ray diffractometer (XRD) pattern of SWCNTs displays a representative peak at 22.81°, indicating the presence of a crystalline structure (Fig. 1a). The top-down SEM image of the SWCNTs shows a network of thin, cylindrical tubes that are randomly arranged and interconnected, forming a complex and intricate network (Fig. 1b). Scanning electron microscope (SEM) images of a planar SWCNTS film prepared by vacuum filtration exhibit a flat and uniform surface (0.5 mg mass loading on a circular area with 3.8 cm diameter, see the image in Fig. 1c). Figure 1d shows the SEM image of a crumpled SWCNTs film which displays a highly textured and interconnected web-like structure with numerous folds and creases, resulting in a distinctive and intricate surface texture.

The schematic illustration of the SWCNTs sensor fabrication process is shown in Fig. 2. Firstly, planar SWCNTs strain sensors (planar indicates there are no pre-deformations on the SWCNTs layer) were prepared by transferring the freestanding SWCNTs film onto an elastomeric ecoflex substrate. To prepare the crumpled SWCNTs strain sensor, a polystyrene shrink film with biaxial pre-strain was first cut into rectangles, washed with ethanol, dried under nitrogen gas flow, and treated with oxygen plasma. The planar SWCNTs film was carefully transferred onto the plasma-treated shrink film followed by overnight drying. Afterward, the planar SWCNTs coated polystyrene film was heated in an oven at 140 °C for 5 min without constraints for biaxial shrinkage. The shrunk sample was then coated with 2 mm ecolfex and immersed in ethyl acetate to dissolve the polystyrene substrate to obtain the ecoflex-coated SWCNTs device, which was sequentially rinsed with ethyl acetate and then served as a strain sensor. It is valuable to mention that such preparation method can be easily scaled up to produce a large number of sensors simultaneously. Firstly, the utilized materials, including SWCNTs, elastic substrates, polystyrene shrink film, are relatively cheap and readily accessible. Secondly, the preparation process entails precisely defined steps and parameters that can be accurately replicated, ensuring consistent results across multiple production cycles during batch processing.

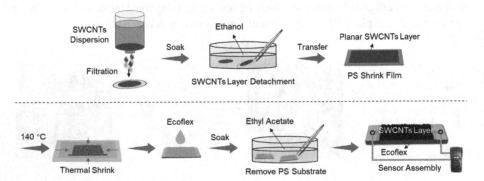

Fig. 2. Schematic illustration of crumpled SWCNTs strain sensor fabrication.

Figure 3a and 3b present the strain sensing curves of planar and crumpled SWC-NTs sensors, respectively. Basically, the planar sensor showed a narrow working window <10% strain. In contrast, the crumpled sensor demonstrates a much wider strain response till 100%. This phenomenon is attributed to the different crack propagation behaviors between planar and crumpled SWCNTs sensors. Herein, we performed in situ electron microscopy studies and finite element analyses (FEAs) to investigate how the morphology of the sensing layer affects the crack propagation behavior and consequently the resistance change. As depicted in Fig. 3 c-ii, at a strain of 10%, the planar SWCNTs sensor exhibits prominent perpendicular cracks throughout the entire section. This observation aligns with the FEA results, which indicate that the central region of the planar SWCNTs layer experienced significant localized strains when subjected to uniaxial strain. These localized strains ultimately resulted in the formation of large cracks perpendicular to the axis of applied stress, which cut off the conductive pathways quickly. On the other hand, Fig. 3 c-iii, iv displays the structural evolutions of a crumpled SWCNTs sensor under uniaxial strains. Different from planar sensors where cracks grew quickly, there were tiny cracks even under 60% strain, because the localized strains were concentrated along

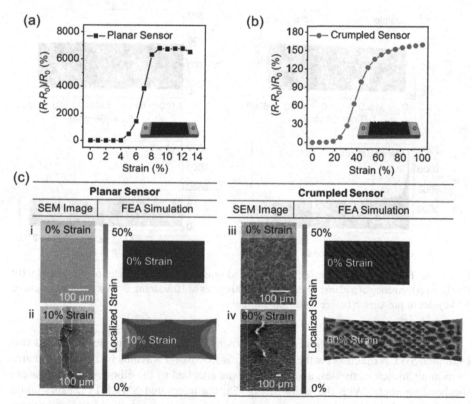

Fig. 3. (a,b) Resistance-strain profiles of planar and crumpled sensors. (c) FEA simulation of strain distribution and in situ SEM images of planar and crumpled SWCNTs sensors under various uniaxial strains.

the valley of crumple textures (see FEA results in Fig. 3c), resulting in the formation of short and widely distributed cracks. This kind of crumples-confined crack growth enabled the resulting sensor to show a much wider working window until 100%.

Furthermore, stability tests were performed on both the crumpled and planar SWC-NTs strain sensors. Considering their crack propagation mechanism, to enhance the mechanical stability, both planar and crumpled sensors experienced a pre-stretching treatment to induce mature crack patterns before usage (500 times of cyclic loading, 10% strain for the planar sensor and 100% for the crumpled sensor). After the pre-stretching experiments, the crumpled sensor was tested with an additional 5000 cycles under 100% strain, and the results exhibited exceptional stability (Fig. 4a). In contrast, the planar sensor showed worse stability during the additional 5000 cycles test where the sensor signals decreased and fluctuated a lot, as shown in Fig. 4b. Considering the large working strain as well as the good sensing stability, we adopted crumpled SWC-NTs sensors to integrate with a wearable exoskeleton to validate their performance in practicality.

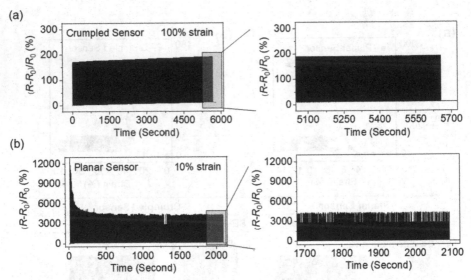

Fig. 4. (a) The cycling performance of a crumpled sensor under 5000 cycles of 100% strain. (b) Cycling performance of a planar sensor under 5000 cycles of 10% strain. Both sensors experienced 500 cycles of pre-stretch before collecting the data,

With the exoskeleton application, as shown in Fig. 5, we strategically placed two crumpled SWCNTs sensors at the elbow (Fig. 5a). Sensor-1 was attached to the upper arm to monitor muscle activities, and sensor-2 was attached to the elbow joint to measure the bending angle. With the setup in Fig. 5a, the integrated SWCNTs sensors could record the real-time resistance changes during movements, including bending without and with load (2.5 kg, see Fig. 5b). As shown in Fig. 5c, both sensors 1 and 2 are able to recognize the bending motion of the arm. Notably, in Fig. 5d, sensor 1 showed an obvious resistance increase (from 21.4 Ω to 22.3 Ω) when subjected to a load of 2.5 kg, due to an increase in muscle tension. This demonstrates the sensor's ability to monitor muscle activity. Afterward, we evaluate the sensing performance regarding the elbow joint bending. According to Fig. 5e, during the elbow movements, sensor-2 showed sensitive and consistent signals with the professional 3D motion capture Vicon system outcomes, showing high potential for joint monitoring tasks. Herein, a slight signal lag can be observed due to the hysteresis effects from flexible substrate, this limitation can be effectively mitigated by replacing the current flexible substrate with a low hysteresis alternative. It is worth mentioning that our crumpled SWCNTs sensors also address the privacy issues associated with optical capture systems. As it is designed to provide a more abstract representation of human motion by measuring joint deformation and muscle activity, offering localized and personalized monitoring, minimizing the risk of identity exposure and location tracking, and reducing the risk of unauthorized surveillance.

In the end, we performed the sensing experiments with a wearable robot for arm rehabilitation (see the setup in Fig. 5a), where both the SWCNTs sensor and EMG sensor signals were recorded simultaneously for comparisons. According to the results in Fig. 5f, when the volunteer moved the right arm with a 2.5 kg dumbbell without the exoskeleton assistance, both SWCNTs and EMG sensors showed remarkable signal responses regarding the arm motions. Meanwhile, when powering on the exoskeleton to help the movements, the arm muscle activity was much reduced. Accordingly, the attached SWCNTs sensor-1 showed obviously reduced signals but could still track the muscle movements with periodic peaks. As a comparison, the EMG sensor showed nearly no signal peaks during this stage to track the muscle activity, due to its low sensing sensitivity. The higher sensitivity of the SWCNTs sensor is due to the ability to conform to the body and muscle shape, which allows tight contact with the muscle thus provides more sensitive measurements to subtle changes in muscle activity compared to rigid EMG sensors. In addition, SWCNTs have excellent electrical conductivity, enabling the sensor to detect even weak electrical signals generated by muscle contractions with high sensitivity. These results indicated unique advantages of our developed SWCNTs sensor with accurate, sensitive, stable sensing performance regarding the rehabilitation robotic applications. In addition to sensing characteristics, our SWCNTs sensors also offer distinct merits, including cost-effectiveness, excellent wear resistance, and tight integration with textiles, which were significant as well for the broad and large-scale applications for rehabilitation. However, for the practical application in real working scenarios, the long-term stability of the developed sensors in different extreme environments and the integration with different types of wearable devices need to be further explored.

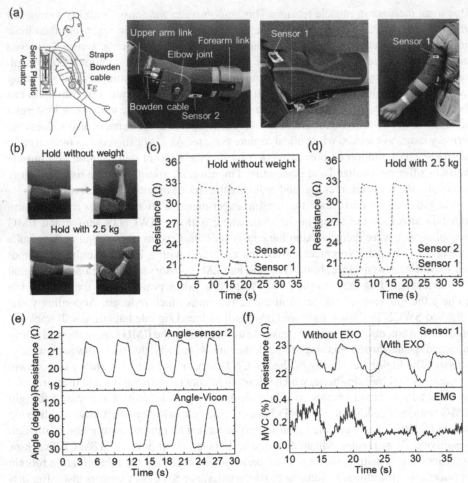

Fig. 5. (a) Exoskeleton setup diagram and sensor positions. (b) Diagram of the elbow and muscle deformation of the arm from expansion to bending under non-weight-bearing and weight-bearing 2.5 kg. (c,d) Resistance change of crumpled SWCNTs sensor 1 and sensor 2 attached to the arm during the flexion movement under non-weight-bearing and weight-bearing 2.5 kg respectively. (e) Correspondence between the elbow angle calibrated by the Vicon system and the resistance change of crumpled SWCNTs sensor 2 during the elbow joint action. (f) The variation of the resistance of crumpled SWCNTs sensor 2 and the EMG sensor signal with and without the assistance of the exoskeleton (EXO) at the elbow joint.

3   Conclusion

In conclusion, through decorating crumpled microstructure into the SWCNTs layer, this study presents a robust soft strain sensor for monitoring arm motion and giving real-time and reliable feedback in a wearable rehabilitation robot. With the unique crumpling morphology design, the developed SWCNTs sensor showed robust cyclic performance and a wide working range > 100% strain. These flexible sensors were able to detect joint deformation and monitor muscle activity in real-time with high sensitivity. We further integrated the crumpled SWCNTs sensors with a rehabilitation exoskeleton, which provided instant and reliable feedback corresponding to the movement of disabled people. Compared with conventional inertial and EMG sensors, this study demonstrates the high potential of crumpled SWCNTs strain sensors to be an economical, durable, and highly integrated alternative to motion monitoring for wearable rehabilitation robots, making rehabilitation more effective and accessible to physically disabled people.

References

1. Zhou, H., Hu, H.: Human motion tracking for rehabilitation—a survey. Biomed. Signal Process. Control **3**, 1–18 (2008)
2. Homayounfar, S.Z., Andrew, T.L.: Wearable sensors for monitoring human motion: a review on mechanisms, materials, and challenges. SLAS Technol. **25**, 9–24 (2020)
3. Jeong, H., et al.: Miniaturized wireless, skin-integrated sensor networks for quantifying full-body movement behaviors and vital signs in infants. Proc. Natl. Acad. Sci. **118**, e2104925118 (2021)
4. Yahya, M., et al.: Motion capture sensing techniques used in human upper limb motion: a review. Sens. Rev. **39**, 504–511 (2019)
5. González-Villanueva, L., Cagnoni, S., Ascari, L.: Design of a wearable sensing system for human motion monitoring in physical rehabilitation. Sensors **13**, 7735–7755 (2013)
6. Zhang, W., Tomizuka, M., Byl, N.: A wireless human motion monitoring system for smart rehabilitation. J. Dyn. Syst. Meas. Control **138**, 111004 (2016)
7. Pang, M., Guo, S., Huang, Q., Ishihara, H., Hirata, H.: Electromyography-based quantitative representation method for upper-limb elbow joint angle in sagittal plane. J. Med. Biol. Eng. **35**, 165–177 (2015)
8. Roetenberg, D., Luinge, H., Slycke, P.: Xsens MVN: Full 6DOF Human Motion Tracking Using Miniature Inertial Sensors (2013)
9. Chen, J., et al.: An overview of stretchable strain sensors from conductive polymer nanocomposites. J. Mater. Chem. C **7**, 11710–11730 (2019)
10. Wang, Y., et al.: Wearable and highly sensitive graphene strain sensors for human motion monitoring. Adv. Funct. Mater. **24**, 4666–4670 (2014)

The Feasibility, Safety and Efficacy of Robot-Assisted Gait Training Based on a Wearable Ankle Robot in Stroke Rehabilitation

Rui Huang[1], Shuaishuai Han[1], Ling Jin[2], Jianhua Zhou[2], Xiaoxiao Chen[2], Shichen Ruan[2], and Haoyong Yu[1(✉)]

[1] National University of Singapore, Singapore, Singapore
`bieyhy@nus.edu.sg`
[2] Nanjing Ruihai Bo Rehabilitation Hospital, Nanjing, China

Abstract. Background and Purpose. The purpose of this study was to investigate the feasibility, safety and efficacy of robot-assisted gait training with a newly developed wearable ankle robot in patients with subacute or chronic stroke.

Methods. Three patients with subacute or chronic ischemic stroke were enrolled and completed the three-day robot-assisted gait training based on a wearable ankle robot. The primary outcome is the safety of the newly developed ankle robot. The secondary outcomes include the improvement of gait function (assessed by 10 MWT, 6 MWT, TUG), improvement of FD (assessed by IMU), improvement of lower limb impairment (assessed by FMA-LE scale), and improvement of balance function (assessed by BBS).

Results. The improvement of 10MWT, 6MWT and TUG were observed in all three patients. It's worth mentioning that the maximal changes of 10MWT, 6MWT and TUG of the three patients exceeded the MCID of each index. However, the change of FMA-LE and BBS were minimal and were lower than the MCID. Additionally, no adverse event is observed during the training period.

Conclusion. The ankle robot has good safety and robustness in clinical practice, and could induce considerable improvement in locomotor function in patients with subacute or chronic stroke of Brunnstrom V ~ VI stage. Robot-assisted gait training with this ankle robot can be adopted for rehabilitation of patients with subacute or chronic stroke in further longer term and larger scale clinical trial.

Keywords: Robot-assisted Gait Training · Wearable Ankle Robot · Stroke Rehabilitation

1 Introduction

Stroke is a leading cause of movement disability globally, affecting up to 80.1 million people by 2030 [1]. The improvement in gait function is the goal most often requested by stroke patients [2]. Foot drop (FD) is a typical symptom of stroke gait dysfunction, which occurs in about 20% ~ 30% of stroke survivors [3, 4]. FD decreases speed and

© The Author(s), under exclusive license to Springer Nature Singapore Pte Ltd. 2023
H. Yang et al. (Eds.): ICIRA 2023, LNAI 14269, pp. 584–594, 2023.
https://doi.org/10.1007/978-981-99-6489-5_48

increases the risk of fall due to asymmetry, instability and disruption in weight acceptance and transfer, which reduces the quality of life and needs long-term rehabilitation [5, 6]. Conventional treatments include physiotherapy, functional electrical stimulation (FES) and traditional ankle-foot orthosis (AFO) [7–9], while none of them is ideal currently [6, 10]. According to the characteristics of neuroplasticity and clinical experience, an early rehabilitation program with high intensity and frequency is advocated in the clinical practice of stroke rehabilitation [11, 12], which leads to overwhelming pressure on the physical therapists of a limited amount [13]. Besides, these therapies highly depend on the therapist individuals and inevitably face the problems of non-standardization, labor-intensiveness and subjectiveness in evaluation [14].

To overcome these shortcomings, recent decades have witnessed the rapid development of robot-assisted gait training (RAGT), which has shown remarkable potential in gait rehabilitation [15–20]. However, until now, researchers have not reached a consensus on the efficacy of RAGT [21–23], including RAGT with ankle robot [24–27]. Even in two of the controlled RCTs of ankle rehabilitation robots with relatively large sample sizes, the results were contradictory [19, 20]. Hence, most of the robotic use is confined to research instead of clinical practice. The uncertainty of RAGT efficacy mostly attributed to three reasons. First, most of the investigated robots are outdated and unable to give scope to the real benefit of RAGT. The bulky design and stiff actuation provide an incompliant experience for patients, studies only focus on the kinematic performance instead of clinical effectiveness, with a rather small sample size and lack of controlled groups [28]. Last and most importantly, most of the measurements were relatively simple and rough, which were hard to capture minor changes of patient performance [19, 20].

In this context, we have developed a novel ankle rehabilitation robot with the most advanced technologies including compliant actuation, compliant force control, cable transmission, force-based assistance strategy, which can help patients learn correct gait patterns and regain gait symmetry. As a novel self-developed rehabilitation robot, the clinical feasibility of the device needs to be validated. Therefore, to explore the possibility of further meaningful RCT and sensitive indicators, we applied it in three post-stroke patients to evaluate the primary feasibility, safety and efficacy in gait rehabilitation.

2 Methods

2.1 Participants

Individuals with first-ever stroke who fulfill the following criteria were eligible for inclusion: (1) 35 ~ 70 years old; (2) clinical diagnosis of stroke (cerebral infarction, primary intracerebral haemorrhage, subarachnoid haemorrhage); (3) 3 months after primary stroke; (4) brunnstrom V ~ VI stage; (5) able to walk at least 10 m independently (without auxillary devices); (6) walking speed: 0.4 ~ 0.8 m/s; (7) height < 180 cm; (8) weight < 80 kg; (9) able to provide consent to take part in the study and to comply with the requirements of the protocol. Exclusion criteria were more than one stroke (patients with a previous transient ischemic attack (TIA) may be invited to participate) or serious cardiovascular events in the past three months or have a history of other neurological and musculoskeletal diseases or previous use of other lower limb rehabilitation robots.

Patients were recruited by announcement in hospital for patients with rehabilitation needs. The subjects and data-gathering phases were blinded to the data analyst. All participants gave their written informed consent to individual patient data reporting before participating in the study (Table 1).

Table 1. The baseline data of patients

	Patient 1	Patient 2	Patient 3
Sex	Male	Male	Male
Age	35	66	53
Body height (cm)	177	174	172
Body mass (Kg)	77	72	76
Stroke onset (months)	7	4	6
Stroke type	ischemic stroke	ischemic stroke	ischemic stroke
Brunnstrom stage	VI	V	V
Comorbidity	None	Hypertension	None
Affect site	Right	Right	Right
Case description	has already well recovered from the stroke and has mild drop-foot	serve drop foot and shank muscle weakness	serve drop foot, strephenopodia and knee hyperextension
Habitual mobility aids	None	Unilateral walking cane	None
Baseline 10MWT speed (m/s)	0.85	0.65	1.57
Baseline 6MWT (m)	161	112	265
Baseline TUG (s)	21.7	29.9	16.5
Baseline Berg Balance scale	44	45	38
Baseline FMA-LE scale	18	25	22
Baseline peak of foot lift angle($°$)	18.0	2.2	4.3

2.2 Wearable Ankle Robot

The ankle robot used in this study is developed independently by NUS Biomedical Engineering laboratory. Following Fig. 1 shows a brief description of the ankle robot prototype. More details can also be found in our previous publication [29].

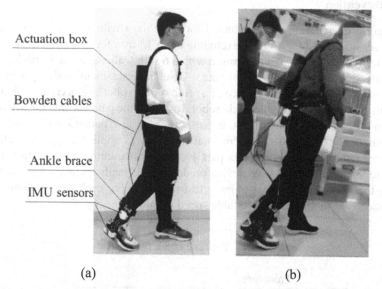

(a)   (b)

Fig. 1. Wearable rehabilitation ankle robot. (a) The robot is composed of an actuation box which contains a compliant actuator, a microcontroller, a battery and other electronics. (b) A patient is doing rehabilitation training with assistance from the ankle robot.

The wearable rehabilitation robot is composed of three parts: actuation box, Bowden cable transmission and wearable ankle frame. The actuation box is attached to an upper body brace so that a user can wear it. In this robot, a special compliant actuator called series elastic actuator (SEA) is adopted for achieving the controllability of assistive force and comfortable human-robot interaction.

Compared to the position control based robotic assistance, force-based assistance can meet the practical operating principles of physical rehabilitation and will be safer during applications. The adopted SEA can generate up to 16 Nm assistive torque at the ankle joint, which is high enough to provide dorsi-flexion or plantar flexion assistance for stroke patients. Bowden cable will transfer the force from actuation box to the ankle frame joint. Benefit from the cable transmission, the actuation and ankle frame are separated. In this case, the ankle frame on lower limb weighs only 500g. A lightweight distal structure will improve the wearing comfort and make the device more acceptable for patients. The ankle frame is equipped with two IMU sensors for detecting the real-time moving information of the patient. Based on the sensory information of IMU sensors, the ankle robot can detect the patient's gait phases and apply assistive forces accordingly. The data collection and implementation of control algorithm are performed by a micro-controller in the actuation box.

The entire robot weighs approximately 3 kg and the user can wear it for long-time training during rehabilitation or even daily living.

2.3 Intervention

The training intervention was conducted for three days with 1 session per day. Each training session lasted for 45 min (excluding extra 15 min for preparation), which was divided into 5 parts, each part comprised with a 6-min walking and a 3-min break.

In part 1, patients were asked to take a baseline assessment: walking without the ankle robot. Then, under the guidance of a professional robot engineer, the affected side was equipped with the wearable ankle robot. In part 2, the patients walked with passive device mode as a wearing test. Next, in part 3 training test, patients walked with active device mode. 70 N force (~2.3 N*m joint torque) was applied for ground clearance assistance. After training, there was part 4 set to post-training wearing test. Patients needed to walk with the passive device mode again. Finally, patients walked without wearing the ankle robot as post-training test in part 5. For each part, patients walked independently at their most comfortable speed (Table 2).

Table 2. Timeline of Study design

Timeline	Procedure
Day 1	Patient recruitment, consent obtaining
Day 2	Training of therapist, patient discussion
Day 3	Baseline assessment, Gait training & data collection
Day 4	Gait training & data collection
Day 5	Gait training & data collection, outcome assessment
Day 13	Retainability assessment

2.4 Outcome Measures

Outcome measures were evaluated for each participant at baseline, after three-day training and 1 week after the end of the training to evaluate the retainability of the improvement. Meanwhile, the walking distance, speed, and peak of foot lift angle (q) were recorded at each session.

Primary outcome of this study was safety measured by adverse events. Secondary outcomes include motor and balance function assessed by 10-m walking test (10MWT), 6-min walking test (6MinWT), timed up and go test (TUG), Fugl-Meyer Assessment Lower Extremity Motor Sub-Score (FMA-LE) and Berg Balance Scale (BBS). In addition, we measured the peak of foot lift angle.

2.5 Statistical Analysis

This is a preliminary study comparing the data from different timepoints of the single-armed patients. The Shapiro-Wilks and Levene tests, respectively, are used to determine whether data have a normal distribution and whether their variance is homogeneous. Baseline differences are evaluated using t-tests. Also, the t-test is used to investigate changes in any outcome measure caused by gait training. P-values under 0.05 are regarded as significant.

3 Results

Generally, no adverse event is observed during the training period of the patients, which showed considerable clinical safety and feasibility of the ankle rehabilitation robot.

3.1 The Peak Foot Lift Angle

The peak foot lift angle was recorded during every training session. Therefore, it reflected the dynamic change of the patients' gait function.

Subject 1 has already well recovered from the stroke and has mild drop-foot. His testing result largely varies because of his personal active reactions. During some training sessions, subject 1 showed fatigue and some negative feedback. This may be the main reason for the unreasonable experimental results. Subject 2 has severe drop foot and shank muscle weakness. The gait rehabilitation robot can effectively assist his ground clearance. Even though the assistance was not provided in part 2 and part 4, positive effects could still be observed. This might be benefited by the surprising fact that the rigid mechanical design of our ankle robot helps to correct the strephenopodia, which is usually accompanied by drop-foot. Subject 3 has severe drop foot, strephenopodia and knee hyperextension. Because of individual reasons of the patients, the last two tests on Day 1 were not conducted. The gait rehabilitation robot can effectively assist his ground clearance. Even though the assistance was not provided in part 2 and part 4, positive effects could still be observed. By assisting the ground clearance, the knee hyperextension was also surprisingly corrected during training (Fig. 2).

3.2 The Gait Function and Lower Limb Impairment

The 10MWT, 6MWT, and TUGT, FMA-LE, BBS were assessed at the baseline, after the three-day training and 1-week post-training.

For patient 1, the 10MWT raised from 0.85m/s to 0.93m/s, which was stable 1-week post-training. His TUGT gradually decreased from 21.7, 20.9 to 19.3 s, and his 6MWT increased from 161, 163 to 172 m at the three time points. His FMA-LE increased from 18 to 19 after training and was stable 1-week post-training. His BBS did not change during the training period.For patient 2, the 10MWT raised from 0.65 m/s to 0.73 m/s, which decreased to 0.67 m/s 1-week post-training. His TUGT decreased from 29.9 s to 24.5 s and was stable at 24.5 s 1-week post-training. His 6MWT increased from 112, 120 to 130 m at the three time points. His FMA-LE increased from 25 to 26 after training, and

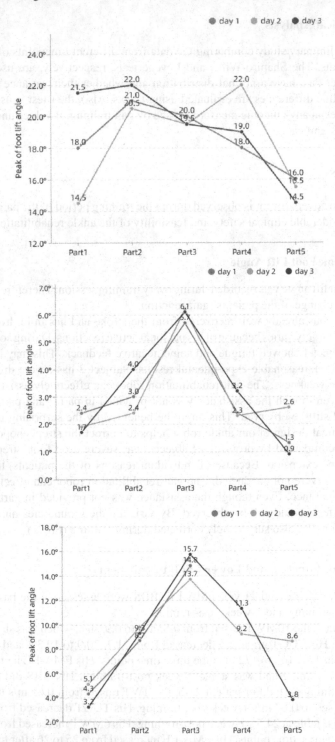

Fig. 2. The peak foot lift angle of three patients

was stable 1-week post-training. His BBS did not change after training, but increased from 45 to 47 at one week post training. For patient 3, the 10MWT raised from 1.57 m/s, 1.61 m/s to 1.72 m/s. His TUGT decreased from 16.5 s,17.0 s to 13.3 s. His 6MWT increased from 265, 291 to 387 m at the three time points. His FMA-LE did not change after training, but increased from 22 to 23 at one-week post-training. His FMA-LE did not change after training, but increased from 38 to 41 at one-week post-training (Fig. 3).

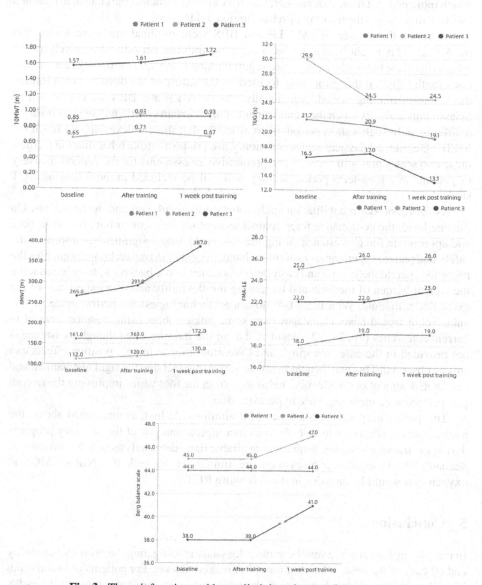

Fig. 3. The gait function and lower limb impairment of three patients

4   Discussion

The results showed that the three-day training of the novel rehabilitation ankle robot could considerably improve the patients' gait function in general. Improvement of 10MWT, 6MWT and TUGT were observed in all three patients. Additionally, the maximal changes of 10MWT, 6MWT and TUG of the three patients exceeded the MCID of each index, which indicated that these indexes were sensitive enough to detect the change in patient's gait function during the training of rehabilitation ankle robot.

However, the change of FMA-LE and BBS were minimal and were lower than the MCID. This might be due to the rather short training period and relatively rough sensitivity of the two scales. The common gait training often lasts for 6 weeks and at least one month [30], but this pilot study focused on the safety of the device, which limited the length of training period. Additionally, the FMA-LE and BBS are not quantified assessments and only when the improvement attains certain criteria will the result shows a difference. In such a short period, it's reasonable that these indexes did not reach the MCID. Despite, as classical scales commonly used in post-stroke rehabilitation studies, these two scales may still serve as comprehensive assessments for the general recovery of patients in a long-term period, so they will still be included in the following RCT study.

As for robot, our rehabilitation ankle robot equips with two core technologies. On the one hand, the compliance force control technology helps the robot provide in-time and appropriate force assistance during the gait cycle, which significantly improves the safety and patient experience. On the other hand, the cable-driven technology enables the robot to separate the engine and calculation modules into a backpack, largely reducing the weight burden of the limb and increasing the flexibility and user experience of the exoskeleton module. With these two advanced technologies, the performance of this ankle robot would have advantages over some ankle robots using position control in current researches [26, 31, 32]. Besides, during the training, even though assistance is not provided in the case "Wearing" and "Wearing after training", positive effects can still be observed. This may benefit from the surprising fact that the rigid mechanical and one DOF design of our ankle robot helps to correct the foot varus, improving the overall gait performance including knee hyperextension.

This preliminary work has a series of limitations. At first, as mentioned above, the training period is short, which leads to an incomplete analysis of the recovery progress during the training sessions. With more available data, data analysis will be carried out. Secondly, the dimensions of assessment are limited, for this seek, the fNIRS, EMG and oxygen cost would be included in the following RCT.

5   Conclusion

In this preliminary study, a small sample pilot study investigating the primary feasibility and efficacy of the ankle rehabilitation robot was conducted. For patients of brunnstrom V ~ VI stage, the ankle rehabilitation showed good safety and robustness in three-day clinical practice, and induced considerable improvement in scales and tests reflecting the gait function. A longer training period, larger sample size and more assessment dimensions should be applied to further evaluate the characteristic of the ankle rehabilitation robot.

References

1. Collaborators G B D S.: Global, regional, and national burden of stroke, 1990-2016: a systematic analysis for the global burden of disease study 2016. Lancet Neurol **18**(5), 439-458 (2019)
2. Grefkes, C., Fink, G.R.: Recovery from stroke: current concepts and future perspectives. Neurol. Res. Pract. **2**, 17 (2020)
3. Cho, K.H., Lee, J.Y., Lee, K.J., et al.: Factors related to gait function in post-stroke patients. J. Phys. Ther. Sci. **26**(12), 1941–1944 (2014)
4. Prenton, S., Hollands, K.L., Kenney, L.P.J., et al.: Functional electrical stimulation and ankle foot orthoses provide equivalent therapeutic effects on foot drop: A meta-analysis providing direction for future research. J Rehabil Med **50**(2), 129–139 (2018)
5. Peishun, C., Haiwang, Z., Taotao, L., et al.: Changes in gait characteristics of stroke patients with foot drop after the combination treatment of foot drop stimulator and moving treadmill training. Neural Plast. **2021**, 9480957 (2021)
6. Kwon, J., Park, J.H., Ku, S., et al.: A soft wearable robotic ankle-foot-orthosis for post-stroke patients. IEEE Robotics and Automation Letters **4**(3), 2547–2552 (2019)
7. Santos, G.F., Jakubowitz, E., Pronost, N., et al.: Predictive simulation of post-stroke gait with functional electrical stimulation. Sci. Rep. **11**(1), 21351 (2021)
8. Yan, T., Hui-Chan, C.W., Li, L.S.: Functional electrical stimulation improves motor recovery of the lower extremity and walking ability of subjects with first acute stroke: a randomized placebo-controlled trial. Stroke **36**(1), 80–85 (2005)
9. Karniel, N., Raveh, E., Schwartz, I., et al.: Functional electrical stimulation compared with ankle-foot orthosis in subacute post stroke patients with foot drop: a pilot study. Assist. Technol. **33**(1), 9–16 (2021)
10. Alnajjar, F., Zaier, R., Khalid, S., et al.: Trends and technologies in rehabilitation of foot drop: a systematic review. Expert Rev. Med. Devices **18**(1), 31–46 (2021)
11. Coleman, E.R., Moudgal, R., Lang, K., et al.: Early rehabilitation after stroke: a narrative review. Curr. Atheroscler. Rep. **19**(12), 59 (2017)
12. Hu, J.: Research on robot fuzzy neural network motion system based on artificial intelligence. Comput. Intell. Neurosci. **2022**, 4347772 (2022)
13. Ploughman, M., Kelly, L.P.: Four birds with one stone? Reparative, neuroplastic, cardiorespiratory, and metabolic benefits of aerobic exercise poststroke. Curr. Opin. Neurol. **29**(6), 684–692 (2016)
14. Fan, W., Zhang, Y., Wang, Q.M., et al.: An interactive motion-tracking system for home-based assessing and training reach-to-target tasks in stroke survivors-a preliminary study. Med. Biol. Eng. Comput. **58**(7), 1529–1547 (2020)
15. Rodgers, H., Bosomworth, H., Krebs, H.I., et al.: Robot assisted training for the upper limb after stroke (RATULS): a multicentre randomised controlled trial. Lancet **394**(10192), 51–62 (2019)
16. Dijk, W.V., Meijneke, C., Kooij, H.V.D.: Evaluation of the achilles ankle exoskeleton. IEEE Trans. Neural Syst. Rehabil. Eng. **25**(2), 151–160 (2017)
17. Thalman, C.M., Hsu, J., Snyder, L., et al.: Design of a soft ankle-foot orthosis exosuit for foot drop assistance. In: Proceedings of the 2019 International Conference on Robotics and Automation (ICRA), F 20–24 May 2019 (2019)

18. Fong, J., Rouhani, H., Tavakoli, M.: A therapist-taught robotic system for assistance during gait therapy targeting foot drop. IEEE Robotics and Automation Letters 4(2), 407–413 (2019)

19. Lee, M., Kim, J., Hyung, S., et al.: A compact ankle exoskeleton with a multiaxis parallel linkage mechanism. IEEE/ASME Trans. Mechatron. 26(1), 191–202 (2021)

20. Conroy, S., Roy, A., Magder, L., et al.: Treadmill Integrated Robot-Assisted Ankle Dorsiflexion Training for Stroke Rehabilitation: A Randomized Controlled Trial (2020)

21. Mirelman, A., Bonato, P., Deutsch, J.E.: Effects of training with a robot-virtual reality system compared with a robot alone on the gait of individuals after stroke. Stroke 40(1), 169–174 (2009)

22. Wu, Y.N., Hwang, M., Ren, Y., et al.: Combined passive stretching and active movement rehabilitation of lower-limb impairments in children with cerebral palsy using a portable robot. Neurorehabil. Neural Repair 25(4), 378–385 (2011)

23. Moucheboeuf, G., Griffier, R., Gasq, D., et al.: Effects of robotic gait training after stroke: a meta-analysis. Ann. Phys. Rehabil. Med. 63(6), 518–534 (2020)

24. Wiart, L., Rosychuk, R.J., Wright, F.V.: Evaluation of the effectiveness of robotic gait training and gait-focused physical therapy programs for children and youth with cerebral palsy: a mixed methods RCT. BMC Neurol. 16, 86 (2016)

25. Bergmann, J., Krewer, C., Bauer, P., et al.: Virtual reality to augment robot-assisted gait training in non-ambulatory patients with a subacute stroke: a pilot randomized controlled trial. Eur. J. Phys. Rehabil. Med. 54(3), 397–407 (2018)

26. Yeung, L.F., Ockenfeld, C., Pang, M.K., et al.: Randomized controlled trial of robot-assisted gait training with dorsiflexion assistance on chronic stroke patients wearing ankle-foot-orthosis. J. Neuroeng. Rehabil. 15(1), 51 (2018)

27. Rampeltshammer, W.F., Keemink, A.Q.L., Kooij, H.V.D.: An improved force controller with low and passive apparent impedance for series elastic actuators. IEEE/ASME Trans. Mechatron. 25(3), 1220–1230 (2020)

28. Khalid, Y.M., Gouwanda, D., Parasuraman, S.: A review on the mechanical design elements of ankle rehabilitation robot. Proc. Inst. Mech. Eng. H 229(6), 452–463 (2015)

29. Zhong, B., Guo, K., Yu, H., Zhang, M.: Toward gait symmetry enhancement via a cable-driven exoskeleton powered by series elastic actuators. IEEE Robot. Automat. Lett. 7(2), 786–793 (2022)

30. Schroder, J., Truijen, S., Van Criekinge, T., et al.: Feasibility and effectiveness of repetitive gait training early after stroke: a systematic review and meta-analysis. J Rehabil Med 51(2), 78–88 (2019)

31. Beom-Chan, L., Dae-Hee, K., Younsun, S., et al.: Development and assessment of a novel ankle rehabilitation system for stroke survivors. Annu Int. Conf. IEEE Eng. Med. Biol. Soc. 2017, 3773–3776 (2017)

32. Yeung, L.F., Lau, C.C.Y., Lai, C.W.K., et al.: Effects of wearable ankle robotics for stair and over-ground training on sub-acute stroke: a randomized controlled trial. J. Neuroeng. Rehabil.Rehabil. 18(1), 19 (2021)

3D Printing Soft Robots

Design and Control of a Miniature Soft Robotic Fish Actuated by Artificial Muscles

Moise Tsimbo, Yida Zhu, Yihan Yang, and Erbao Dong(✉)

CAS Key Laboratory of Mechanical Behavior and Design of Materials,
Department of Precision Machinery and Precision Instrumentation,
University of Science and Technology of China, Hefei 230026, China
tsimbomax@mail.ustc.edu.cn, ebdong@ustc.edu.cn

Abstract. In this article, we present the design, fabrication and control of a miniature soft robotic fish (SoRoFAAM-2) that mimics subcarangiform swwimmers. The soft body is designed by a suitable integration of several soft and smart materials by layer bonding technology. The versatility of the designed soft body endows SoRoFAAM-2 with multiple BCF-based locomotion modes among which subcarangiform is the most prevalent. The actuator skeleton is made up of an artificial muscle module that acts as the muscle and skeleton of SoRoFAAM-2. From a phenomenological model of SMA-wire we present a dynamics model of the artificial muscle module. This model is then used in simulation to identify a suitable heating strategy. Subsequently, the large number of integrated soft and smart materials with their known nonlinear, hysteresis and viscoelastic behaviour led us to use nonparametric models to develop the control system of SoRoFAAM-2. In fact, through experimentation, we develop two non-parametric models, viz. the relationship between the flapping frequency and the duty time on the one hand, and the relationship between the duty time and the actuation current on the other hand. The control system is implemented in a microcontroller that drives a programmable DC power supply to control SoRoFAAM-2. SoRoFAAM-2 is 200 mm long and weighs 25.5 g. Swimming experiments show that SoRoFAAM-2 has good bionic fidelity and swims like living fish. In particular,it has a Strouhal number of 0.43 which is quite close to that of living fish.

Keywords: Soft robotic fish · Biomimetic robot · Swimming modes · Artificial muscle · Shape memory alloy · Nonparametric model

1 Introduction

Recently, soft robotic fish have received substantial attention from the scientific community. This has been reflected in the design of soft robotic fishes for various purposes. Ranging from soft robotic fish as an experimental platform to soft robotic fish for underwater life exploration and monitoring. Moreover, the majority of these works have focused on the use of soft robotic fish as experimental platforms to better understand fish swimming mechanisms. This is primarily

© The Author(s), under exclusive license to Springer Nature Singapore Pte Ltd. 2023
H. Yang et al. (Eds.): ICIRA 2023, LNAI 14269, pp. 597–609, 2023.
https://doi.org/10.1007/978-981-99-6489-5_49

due to two facts, viz. experiments on living fish are difficult, and servomotor-based robotic fish have shown their limitations.

In fact, experimentation on living fish is not only difficult but also requires a long experimental protocol for the results to be meaningful [1]. This approach has enabled scientists in the 20th century to understand the basic swimming mechanism and develop dynamics model of swimming bodies, referred to as the large amplitude elongated body theory, and to understand fish physiology in general [2]. However, this approach is somewhat limited as the range of controllability that the experimenter exerts on living fish in the course of experiments is quite limited. This limitation led scientists to use servomotor technology to design robotic fish. Experiments performed with these servomotor-driven robotic fish allowed the understanding and systematic definition of underwater propulsion efficiency [3]. However, servomotor based robotic fishes turned out to have a low bionic fidelity as they were heavy, large, difficult to scale down, noisy, less compliant and lacked continuous deformability.

Soft and smart materials, with their unique ability of sensing and actuation embodied within the same material, have allowed researchers to design more bionic robotic fish, which are noiseless, highly scalable, and deforming as living fish. This includes, for instance the soft robotic designed by Shintake et al., which has a Strouhal number of 0.47, quite close to that of living fish [4]. In addition, Marchese et al. have designed a soft robotic fished actuated by a fluidic elastormer and capable of escape maneuvers. This relatively good resemblance has motivated researchers to use soft robotic fish as an experimental platform to better understand fish swimming mechanism. In fact, Zhang et al. designed hybrid robotic fish to investigate the swarming behaviour of animals [5]. Berlinger et al. investigated the relationship between speed, frequency and the shape of the caudal fin [6]. Wolf et al. have used a pneumatically actuated soft robotic fish to investigate the effect of the backbone stiffness of fish and undulation frequency on swimming performance [7]. The role of retractable morphic fins on stability and maneuverability has also been investigated [8,9] Katzschmann et al. designed a soft robotic fish for underwater life exploration [10].

However, the design of soft robotic fishes presents new challenges. In fact, soft and smart material-based actuators are mainly handmade. In addition, most soft and smart materials do not yet have constitutive models and present nonlinear and hysteresis behaviour in the working range of interest. Thus, modelling and control of soft and smart material-based actuators and hence soft robotic fish present a nontrivial challenge. This is the reason why most soft robotic fish designed in the literature are open-loop controlled. In addition, there is a lack of integrated simulation environments where researchers can numerically analyse soft robotic fish. We hope that the increasing interest in soft robotic fish will infer that of these related areas which limit the present potential of soft robotic fish compared to their living contre-parts.

Several soft and smart materials have been used to design soft robotic fish. Among them, elastomers (fluidic and dielectric) [4,5,11–13] and SMA wires [14–16] are the most commonly used in soft robotic fish design. Elastomers have a very large residual strain of approximately 215% but with a very low achievable stress of approximately 0.6 MPa [17]. When ed with electricity, dielectric elastomers require a high voltage of the order of a few kilo-volts. In addition, elastomers have an efficiency of 60 to 80%. SMA wires have very high actuation stress up to 200 MPa (Flexinol^{TM} wires, made by Dynalloy^{TM}). In addition, they have self-sensing capability by means of their electrical resistance. However, the maximum residual strain of SMA-wire is 5 to 10%. The most significant advantage of SMA-wires with respect to other smart materials is their extremely high power density. The high power-density and actuation stress have been the primary guidelines in our choice of SMA-wire to design a miniature soft robotic fish mimicking subcarangiform swimmers.

SoRoFAAM-2 is designed to mimic subcarangiform swimmers. In fact, fish swimming modes are classified into Body/Caudal Fin (BCF) and Median/Paired Fin (MPF) based locommotions. Approximately 85% of living fish use BCF as the primary propulsion means [18]. In addition, BCF based locomotion is in turn subdivided into angiliform, subcarangiform, carangiform, thunniform and ostraciiform locomotions. These locomotion modes differ from each other by the wavelength of the wave travelling the fish body during, or the portion fish's body use in, the undulatory motion. In fact, anguiliform and ostraciiform swimmers use almost the entire body and only the caudal-fin, respectively. Subcarangiform, carangiform and thunniform swimmers use the posterior half, one-third and 10%, respectively, of the body [19]. As little has been done on bionic subcarangiform swimmers compared to the others, we have chosen in this work to mimic subcarangiform swimmers. Table 1 summarizes the design specifications of SoRoFAAM-2.

Table 1. Design specifications of SoRoFAAM-2.

Symbol	Description	Specification
m	Mass (in g)	25
v	Volume (in cm^3)	30
U	Cruise Velocity (in BL/s)	$U \geq 1$
S_t	Strouhal number	$0.15 \leq S_t \leq 0.4$
S_h	Head swing factor	$0.15 \leq S_h \leq 0.4$
M_r	Maneuverability from rest	$M_r < 0.4$

2   Materials and Methods

2.1   Design and Fabrication of the Artificial Muscle Module

It is well known that BCF swimmers produce undulatory motion by alternating contraction of the muscles, referred to as myomeres, on both sides of their body. In our biomimetic design, we mimic this feature by designing an artificial muscle module (AMM) composed of two one-sided artificial muscles (AMs) and a flexible/restoring element. Each one-sided AM is responsible for bending the artificial module in one direction when activated while the flexible element improves the elasticity property of the AMM and hence provides a restoring moment.

Each one-sided AM is composed of 2 printed circuit boards (PCBs) and a set of SMA wires (see Fig. 1.a). The SMA wires are organised in two channels (C1 and C2) and each channel consists of two SMA wires arranged in parallel both electrically and mechanically. In Fig. 1.a, COM refers to the common high electrical potential of SMA wires, which in this work is V_{DD}. In Fig. 1.b the SMA-wire based skeleton is placed in a mould to prestrain the SMA wires by the desired percentage and provide a permanent load that will be used for cyclic prestraining. Then, PDMS (polydimethilsiloxane, Silgard 184) was mixed at a ratio of 10:1 (PDMS:curing agent) and degassed in a vacuum chamber, poured into the mould and placed in an oven at 45 °C for 3 h. Figure 1.c shows the cured structure, single-sided AM, after demoulding. To fabricate the AMM two single-sided AMs are used with a spring steel sheet and adhesive glue (super glue 502). Both single-sided AMs are bonded on both sides of the spring steel sheet. Figure 1.e shows the cross sectional view of the bonded structure and Fig. 1.f shows a photo of the fabricated prototype.

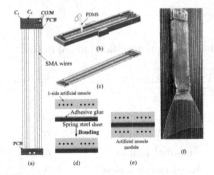

Fig. 1. Fabrication steps of the artificial muscle module. (a) Muscle skeleton; (b)moulding of the PDMS around the muscle skeleton; (c)single-sided artificial muscle; (d)adhesive process of the artificial muscle module; (e) cross sectional view of the artificial muscle module; (f)fabricated prototype.

2.2   Design and Fabrication of SoRoFAAM-2

SoRoFAAM-2 is designed to primarily mimic subcarangiform swimmers, although as we will see in Sect. 4 the versatility of the AMM and soft materials used endow SoRoFAAM-2 of several BCF-based locomotion modes. Thus, from a swim point of view, its tail and caudal fin are the most important elements. In fact, as subcarangiform swimmers use only their half posterior part to generate undulations, the head of SoRoFAAM-2 is 3D printed with a resin-based 3D printer. The posterior half part is soft and compliant and made up of soft and smart materials. To begin with the fabrication process, a caudal fin is cut from a flexible plastic sheet of 0.5 mm and bonded at one end of the AMM (Fig. 2.a. Then the other end of the AMM is fixed on the 3D printed head (Fig. 2.b). To make the tail, the AM is placed inside a mould and a Flexible Polyurethane Foam (FPF) is poured onto (Fig. 2.c). The FPF used is FlexFoam-iT!^{TM} 6 manufactured by Smooth-On in the USA. Parts A and B are first stirred separately, mixed at a 105:100 (A:B) weight ratio, stirred well for 25 s and poured rapidly within 15 s. This FPF expands in approximately 5 min and cures in 2 h. Figure 2.d shows the fabricated prototype which has a total length of 200 mm and weighs 25.5 g.

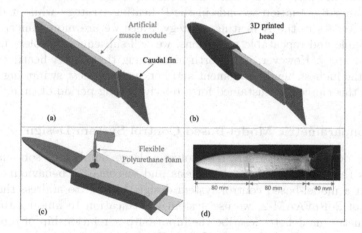

Fig. 2. Fabrication steps of SoRoFAAM-2. (a) AMM with caudal fin; (b)AMM and head bonding; (c) Tail fabrication; (d)Fabricated prototype.

3   Modelling and Control

3.1   Dynamic Model of the Artificial Muscle Module

The values of the parameters of the AM module used in this paper, obtained by DMA and DSC, can be found in Table 2 of ref. [20]. From reference [20], the thermomechanical model of the AMM can be expressed under reasonable assumptions as

$$
\begin{bmatrix} \dot{\epsilon} \\ \dot{T} \\ \dot{\varepsilon} \end{bmatrix} = \begin{bmatrix} \dfrac{\mu_T \frac{i^2 R - hS(T-T_{na})}{\rho V c}}{1+\mu_\sigma k \varepsilon_L \frac{E(\epsilon)}{E(\epsilon)+k} - \mu_T \frac{H}{c}} \\ \dfrac{i^2 R - hS(T-T_{na})}{\rho V c} + \dfrac{H\dot{\epsilon}}{c} \\ \dfrac{E(\epsilon)\varepsilon_L}{E(\epsilon)+k}\dot{\epsilon} \end{bmatrix} \tag{1}
$$

when $A_s + \frac{\sigma}{C_A} \leq T \leq A_f + \frac{\sigma}{C_A}$. Where ϵ, T, and ε are martensite volume fraction, temperature and strain of SMA-wire, respectively. E and σ are the Young's modulus of elasticity and stress in the SMA-wire, respectively. Figures 3.b and 3.d depict the simulation results of the thermomechanical response of the AMM over 10 s with two heating strategies. Figures 3.a and 3.c show the actuation signals in the P and A heating strategies respectively. In these later figures CHX-Y signifies channel X of the Y AM and R and L stand for right and left sides, respectively. T and T_{ON} represent the heating (or actuation) period and the duration of the Joule heating of SMA-wire, respectively. Subsequently, we will refer to T_{ON} as duty time. Figure 3.b shows that, having in mind that the martensite phase transformation temperatures are approximately 50°C, alternatively heating channels on one side of the AMM over the actuation periods drastically improve the cooling of the SMA-wire. As a result, the bending range in Fig. 3.d decreases by only 5% after 6 actuation seconds in the P heating strategy while it decreases by 55% after 6 s in the A heating strategy. Since we are more concerned with having stable and repeatable actuations, we will subsequently solely use the P heating strategy. However, it is worth mentioning that the A heating strategy leads to the highest bending moment and hence the highest swimming velocity, although this cannot be sustained for a relatively long period of time [20].

3.2   Nonparametric Model-Based Control System Design

Since the design of SoRoFAAM-2 evolves a large number of soft and smart materials that have nonlinear, hysteresis and viscoelastic behaviours, we will not adopt a model-based control system design. Indeed, to address the control problem of SoRoFAAM-2, we use system identification techniques to develop nonparametric models to describe the input-output relationship of processes of interest viewed as black boxes in Fig. 4. Black box 1 in this figure nonparametrically models the heat transfer problem from SMA-wire → PDMS → FPF → water by answering the following question: at a given flapping frequency what is the maximum duty time, T_{ON}, that will not lead to heat accumulation within a characteristic duration of interest? Black box 2 nonparametrically models the phase transformation of the SMA-wire coupled to the entire structure of SoRoFAAM-2 and answers the following question: at a given constant heating current, I, what is the required duty time, T_{ON}, to produce a desired actuation? Figs. 5.a and 5.b show the input-output descriptions of black boxes 1 and 2, respectively, obtained experimentally. These nonparametric models are obtained at 0.2 Hz and 1.75 A, respectively. We have numerically implemented

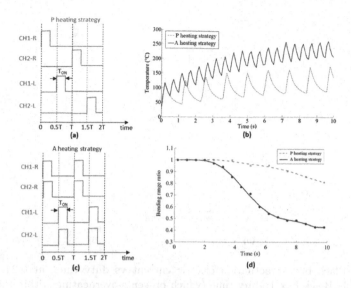

Fig. 3. a. actuation signals in the P heating strategy; b. heat transfer simulation of the artificial muscle module; c. actuation signals in the A heating strategy; d. simulation of the mechanical response of the artificial muscle module.

them in a microcontroller (STM32F103C8). As shown in Figs. 4 and 6, the outputs of these black boxes are used by the microcontroller to drive, through serial communication, a DC power supply that powers SoRoFAAM-2. The microcontroller board is equipped with a wireless communication module (nRF24L01) which serves as an interface to remotely control the operations from a laptop (see Fig. 6). Figure 7.a shows the schematic of the control circuit of any channel of SMA-wire of SoRoFAAM-2 and Fig. 7.b shows a photo of the PCB used to control SoRoFAAM-2.

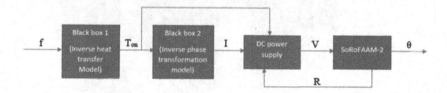

Fig. 4. Block diagram of the control system of SoRoFAAM-2.

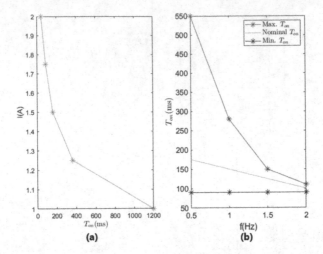

Fig. 5. a. Black box 2: actuation electric current vs duty time, at 0.2 Hz flapping frequency; b. Black box 1: duty time (which prevents overheating within the duration of interest) vs actuation frequency when $I = 1.75$ A.

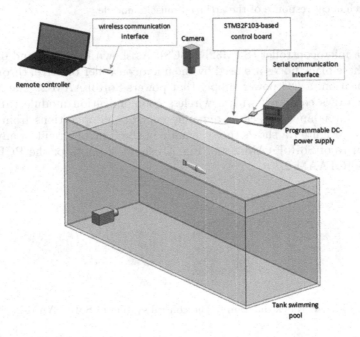

Fig. 6. Photo of the overall control unit of SoRoFAAM-2.

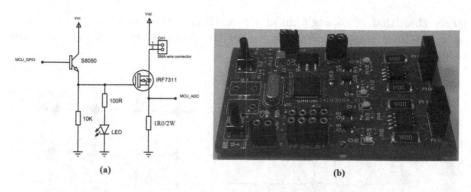

Fig. 7. a. Schematic of the control circuit of the SMA-wire channels; b. Photo of the control PCB.

4   Results and Discussion

Figure 8 shows photos of SoRoFAAM-2 during cruising and turning at 1 Hz. Table 2 shows the swimming performance of SoRoFAAM-2 at 1 Hz. More specifically, the maximum velocity in cruising when swimming at 1 Hz is 140 mm/s which corresponds to 0.67 BL/s. The head swing factor [20] of SoRoFAAM-2 is 0.61 and is slightly larger than that of living fish. The tail beat peak-to-peak amplitude was measured as 60 mm leading to a Strouhal number $S_t = 1 \cdot 60/140 \equiv 0.43$. Although this Strouhal number does not lie within the range of that of living fish it is quite close to that range (see Fig. 9.b). This means that the propulstion efficiency of SoRoFAAM-2 is better than previously reported ones. The maximum angular velocity of SoRoFAAM-2 when turning at 1 Hz is 60°/s and the minimum turning radius is 80 mm. Thus, the maneuverability [20] of SoRoFAAM-2 is $M_r = 0.4$. Figure 9.a shows the maneuverability of soft robotic fish from the literature. Although, the maneuverability from rest of SoRoFAAM-1 is slightly better than that of SoROFAAM-2 (0.15 vs 0.4), SoRoFAAM-2 can be considered more maneuverable in general than SoRoFAAM-1 since its maximum angular velocity is approxima eight times that of SoRoFAAM-1. By clamping the head of SoRoFAAM-2, its natural frequency of vibration was measured as 6.6 Hz. This frequency is similar to the flapping frequency of several living fish (such as mackerel) when cruising at high speed (typically, $U > 4$ BL/s). This signifies that the proposed AMM has a high potential in mimicking living fish.

By varying the actuation current, duty time and flapping frequency, the versatility of the AMM and soft body endow SoRoFAAM-2 with multiple BCF-based locomotion modes. Figure 10 depicts several BCF-based locomotion modes of SoRoFAAM-2. At low actuation current and duty time, SoRoFAAM-2 exhibits thunniform locomotion while at intermediate values it exhibits carangiform locomotion. Above 1.5 Amps or 275 milliseconds duty time it exhibits subcarangiform locomotion. We see that the subcarangiform locomotion domain is much larger than that of carangiform and thunniform. More specifically, our design decisions have led to the satisfaction of the requirement of designing a sub-carangiform swimmer.

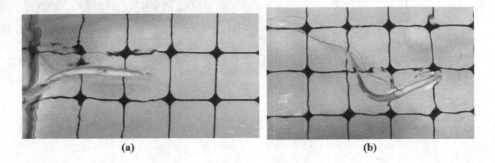

(a)   (b)

Fig. 8. Photo of SoRoFAAM-2 during a. cruising; b. turning, at 1 Hz.

Table 2. Swimming performance of SoRoFAAM-2 at 1 Hz.

Symbol	Description	Value
U	Cruise velocity (in BL/s)	0.67
$\dot{\theta}$	Angular velocity (in °/s)	60
S_t	Strouhal number	0.43
S_h	Head swing factor	0.61
M_r	Maneuverability from rest	0.4

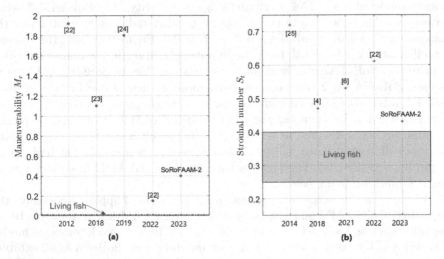

(a)   (b)

Fig. 9. Evolution of a. Maneuverability in BCF-based locomotion; b. Strouhal number, of soft robotic fish with smart-material-made actuators from the literature.

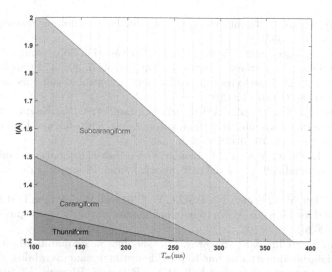

Fig. 10. Swimming modes of SoRoFAAM-2 as a function of the actuation current and duty time at 1 Hz flapping frequency.

5   Conclusion and Perspectives

In this paper, we have presented the design, fabrication, modelling, control and locomotion analysis of a miniature soft robotic fish actuated by artificial muscles (SoRoFAAM-2). SoRoFAAM-2 has multiple locomotion modes and a natural frequency of vibration matching that of living fish. This clearly shows the high potential of the integration of soft and smart materials in mimicking living creatures. In addition, SoRoFAAM-2 has good maneuverability and a Strouhal number, which is close to that of living fish. This also shows the high potential of this design in mimicking living fish. As the natural frequency of vibration of SoRoFAAM-2 matches the flapping frequency of some living fish when cruising at high speed, SoRoFAAM-2 may reach living fish's swimming speed if is was actuated at its natural frequency of vibration. However, the bandwidth of our control system does not include this frequency. This is the primary limitation of the current work and we will address it in our subsequent work. In addition, the fact that SoRoFAAM-2 is tethered largely increases the power consumption and deteriorates the reliability of SMA-wire resistance feedback for bending angle control. In our subsequent work we will embed both the control board and battery in the head of SoRoFAAM-3.

References

1. Webb, P.W.: Kinematics of pectoral fin propulsion in cymatogaster aggregata. J. Exp. Biol. **59**, 697–710 (1973)
2. Webb, P.W.: Form and function in fish swimming. Sci. Am. **251**, 72–82 (1984)

3. Triantafyllou, M.S., Triantafyllou, G.: An efficient swimming machine. Sci. Am. **272**(3), 64–70 (1995)
4. Shintake, J., Cacucciolo, V., Shea, H.R., Floreano, D.: Soft biomimetic fish robot made of dielectric elastomer actuators. Soft Robot. **5**, 466–474 (2018)
5. Zhang, Z., et al.: Global vision-based formation control of soft robotic fish swarm. Soft Robot. **8**, 310–318 (2020)
6. Berlinger, F., Saadat, M., Haj-Hariri, H., Lauder, G.V., Nagpal, R.: Fish-like three-dimensional swimming with an autonomous, multi-fin, and biomimetic robot. Bioinspir. Biomim. **16**, 026018 (2021)
7. Wolf, Z., Jusufi, A., Vogt, D.M., Lauder, G.V.: Fish-like aquatic propulsion studied using a pneumatically-actuated soft-robotic model. Bioinspir. Biomim. **15**, 046008 (2020)
8. Triantafyllou, M.S., Winey, N., Trakht, Y., Elhassid, R., Yoerger, D.R.: Biomimetic design of dorsal fins for AUVs to enhance maneuverability. Bioinspir. Biomim. **15**, 035003 (2020)
9. Randeni, S., Mellin, E.M., Sacarny, M., Cheung, S., Benjamin, M., Triantafyllou, M.S.: Bioinspired morphing fins to provide optimal maneuverability, stability, and response to turbulence in rigid hull AUVs. Bioinspir. Biomim. **17**, 036012 (2022)
10. Katzschmann, R.K., DelPreto, J., MacCurdy, R., Rus, D.: Exploration of underwater life with an acoustically controlled soft robotic fish. Sci. Robot. **3**, 3449 (2018)
11. Marchese, A.D., Onal, C.D., Rus, D.: Autonomous soft robotic fish capable of escape maneuvers using fluidic elastomer actuators. Soft Robot. **1**(1), 75–87 (2014)
12. Li, T., et al.: Fast-moving soft electronic fish. Sci. Adv. **3**, e1602045 (2017)
13. Feng, H., Sun, Y., Todd, P.A., Lee, H.P.: Body wave generation for anguilliform locomotion using a fiber-reinforced soft fluidic elastomer actuator array toward the development of the eel-inspired underwater soft robot. Soft Robot. **7**, 233–250 (2019)
14. Li, J., He, J., Wang, Y., Kai, Yu., Woźniak, M., Wei, W.: A biomimetic flexible fishtail embedded with shape memory alloy wires. IEEE Access **7**, 166906–166916 (2019)
15. Coral, W., Rossi, C., Curet, O.M., Castro, D.: Design and assessment of a flexible fish robot actuated by shape memory alloys. Bioinspir. Biomim. **13**, 056009 (2018)
16. Kim, H., Heo, J.-K., Choi, I., Ahn, S., Chu, W.-S.: Shape memory alloy-driven undulatory locomotion of a soft biomimetic ray robot. Bioinspir. Biomim. **16**, 066006 (2021)
17. Kin, J., Kim, J.W., Kim, H.C., Zhai, L., Ko, H., Muthoka, R.M.: Review of soft actuator materials. Int. J. Precis. Eng. Manuf. **20**, 2221–2241 (2019)
18. Sfakiotakis, M., Lane, D., Davies, J.: Review of fish swimming modes for aquatic locomotion. IEEE J. Ocean. Eng. **24**, 237–252 (1999)
19. Raj, A., Thakur, A.: Fish-inspired robots: design, sensing, actuation, and autonomy-a review of research. Bioinspir. Biomim. **11**, 031001 (2016)
20. Tsimbo Fokou, M.R., Xia, Q., Jin, H., Xu, M., Dong, E.: A soft robotic fish actuated by artificial muscles (Sorofaam-1). J. Bionic Eng. **20**, 1–14 (2023)
21. Brinson, L.: One-dimensional constitutive behavior of shape memory alloys: thermomechanical derivation with non-constant material functions and redefined martensite internal variable. J. Intell. Mater. Syst. Struct. **4**, 229–242 (1993)
22. Kim, S.H., Shin, K., Hashi, S., Ishiyama, K.: Magnetic fish-robot based on multi-motion control of a flexible magnetic actuator. Bioinspir. Biomim. **7**, 036007 (2012)

23. Berlinger, F., et al.: A modular dielectric elastomer actuator to drive miniature autonomous underwater vehicles. In: 2018 IEEE International Conference on Robotics and Automation (ICRA), pp. 3429–3435 (2018)
24. Shaw, H., Thakur, A.: Shape memory alloy based caudal fin for a robotic fish: design, fabrication, control and characterization. In: Proceedings of the Advances in Robotics 2019 (2019)
25. Hubbard, J., et al.: Monolithic IPMC fins for propulsion and maneuvering in bioinspired underwater robotics. IEEE J. Oceanic Eng. **39**, 540–551 (2014)

A Single-DOF Quadrilateral Pyramid Deployable Unit and Its Networking Mechanism

Jinwei Guo, Jianliang He, and Guoxing Zhang$^{(\boxtimes)}$

School of Mechanical Engineering, Jiangsu University of Science and Technology,
Zhenjiang 212100, China
1473733099@qq.com

Abstract. A space deployable mechanism with high unfolding ratio, strong scalability, and stable structure has potential applications in the aerospace field. A pyramid basic deployable unit with good composability and expandability is studied, which can be used to construct large-scale spatial deployable mechanisms. Firstly, the principle of basic unit folding is analyzed, and the configuration design of the basic unit is carried out using the spatial multi closed-loop mechanism configuration synthesis method with added constraint branches. Then, the screw theory and the link dismantling method are used to analyze the DOF of the pyramid unit, and geometric derivatives are applied to solve the motion characteristics of the unit nodes. Furthermore, three network expansion methods for pyramid unit mechanisms are proposed, resulting in three large-scale expandable spatial mechanisms. Finally, three-dimensional models of three types of extension mechanisms are established and the motion simulation analysis are conducted to verify the effectiveness of the configuration design and extension methods. The research results can provide theoretical reference for the design and application of spatial deployable mechanisms with large aperture and high unfolding ratio.

Keywords: Quadrilateral pyramid · deployable mechanism · unfolding characteristics · network expansion · single-DOF

1 Introduction

The significant feature of deployable structures is the ability to convert the maximum space envelope volume to the minimum space envelope volume, which has advantages such as high aspect ratio, stable structure, and flexible working methods. As one of the cutting-edge technologies in the international aerospace field, space deployable structures have become a cutting-edge research topic in space science and technology. Over the years, key technologies of space deployable structures have made breakthroughs in deployable mechanisms, cable membrane shape finding, dynamic analysis, reliable environmental adaptability analysis and verification [1–5].

Deployable mechanisms are different from general series/parallel mechanisms. They are spatial multi closed-loop mechanisms composed of multiple basic units. Therefore, the basic unit configuration and expansion methods of deployable mechanisms that meet

© The Author(s), under exclusive license to Springer Nature Singapore Pte Ltd. 2023
H. Yang et al. (Eds.): ICIRA 2023, LNAI 14269, pp. 610–621, 2023.
https://doi.org/10.1007/978-981-99-6489-5_50

the above characteristics still need to be continuously explored. Phocas et al. [6] studied a reconfigurable deployable linkage mechanism applied in the field of architecture. Sun et al. [7] studied a circular mesh deployable antenna mechanism based on H-type deployable units. Chen et al. [8] demonstrated the design and networking method of deployable mechanisms based on the classic linkage mechanism Bennett. Meng et al. [9] proposed a novel basic unit with good composability and expandability. Yang et al. [10] studied a novel deployable mechanism with composite springs for loading, promoting its application in aerospace. Lyu et al. [11] designed an isosceles trapezoidal prism deployable unit, and proposed a geometric construction method using this unit to approximate smooth plane curve. Takamatsu et al. [12] proposed a deployable truss concept configuration and construction mode for large antennas. Tian et al. [13] innovatively designed a networking method for rib modules and their large-sized modular deployable antenna mechanisms. Guo et al. [14, 15] proposed a modular tetrahedral deployable mechanism and conducted research on its mechanical properties, structural design, and comprehensive performance. Wang et al. [16] proposed a joint transformation configuration synthesis method for spatial deployable units and innovatively designed a petal shaped spatial deployable mechanism. Huang et al. [17, 18] designed an improved petal shaped deployable mechanism, which has a simple structure and good mechanical properties.

The above literates propose various high-performance deployable unit mechanisms, some of which can form large-scale spatial deployable mechanisms through networking, but there are problems such as low unfolding ratio and weak scalability. Most deployable mechanisms are complex multi loop mechanisms, which pose great challenges in configuration synthesis, motion analysis, and expansion methods. Exploring spatial deployable mechanisms with high unfolding ratio, strong scalability, and stable structure is of great research significance.

2 Quadrilateral Pyramid Basic Deployable Unit Mechanism

Quadrilateral geometric units can be used as the basic components of large planes, with good symmetry and high scalability. If the four vertices of a quadrilateral are to be folding, the four nodes need to move towards the center of the quadrilateral. A translational joint (P) can be used between each node and the center of the quadrilateral to describe the motion characteristics of the nodes, as shown in Fig. 1. In addition, considering the arbitrariness of the center point of each node in the height direction during the folding process, a slider is connected to the central axis, and four nodes are connected to the slider, so that the folding center can move freely in the height direction. In order to ensure the synchronization of the folding of the three nodes, select the center O point as the center of the circumscribed circle of the quadrilateral $ABCD$. As long as the four nodes have the same movement input as the central slider, the four nodes can reach the central axis at the same time. According to the principle of quadrilateral four node folding mentioned above, only distance changes occur between the four nodes A, B, C, and D, and the direction of movement and expansion between adjacent nodes remains unchanged, always following the direction of the connecting line between the two nodes at the initial position. Therefore, a constraint branch chain that can move in this direction can be added between adjacent nodes, enabling them to follow the original motion and structurally limiting the relative motion of the two nodes.

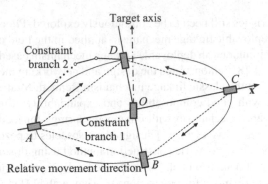

Fig. 1. Folding schematic diagram

Based on the motion of the nodes during the folding, it is assumed that all four nodes are folded towards the target axis through the P joint. After adding constraint branches between adjacent nodes, the constraint branch and the two P joints form a closed loop, which can be regarded as a parallel mechanism composed of two branches. The P joint connected to one node is regarded as branch 1, and the P joint and constraint branch connected to another node are regarded as branch 2. For example, adding a constraint branch chain between nodes A and B as shown in Fig. 1, the closed-loop mechanism should only have one DOF according to the node motion requirements. Among the constraint branches that meet the above constraint conditions, the structure of P branch and RRR branch is the simplest. The triangle folding mechanism formed by adding three P joint constraint branches and RRR constraint branches is shown in Fig. 2, respectively. The constraint branch structurally restricts two adjacent nodes from synchronously moving towards the central slider.

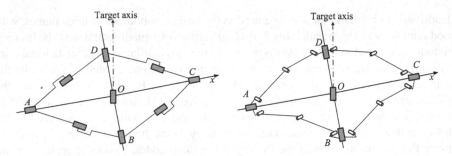

Fig. 2. 4P-4P mechanism and 4RRR-4P mechanism

The quadrilateral folding mechanism obtained by adding constraint branches mentioned above is a planar mechanism in the fully unfolded state, with low stiffness. Therefore, virtual constraint branches can be added in the plane determined by each node and the folding target axis to improve the overall stiffness of the mechanism. Taking node A as an example, the virtual constraint branch chain added should be able to follow the movement of node A in the direction of the AO line. Among all virtual constraint branches that meet the motion requirements, the branch chain structure with RR virtual constraint is the simplest. The mechanisms formed by adding virtual constraint branch chain RR to the quadrilateral folding mechanism shown in Fig. 2 are shown in Fig. 3, respectively. When using this virtual constraint branch chain, the position of the central slider changes regularly along the target axis with the folding motion of the nodes.

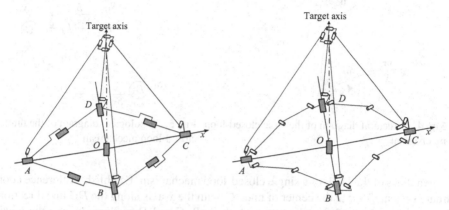

Fig. 3. 4P-4RR mechanism and 4RRR-4P mechanism with virtual constraint branch RR added

The virtual constraint branch chain, as well as the branch chain composed of the moving joint and center slider of node A along the AO line direction, are used to ensure that node A is close to the target axis along the AO line direction. Therefore, the branch chain composed of the moving joint and center slider of node A along the AO line direction can be removed, and only the virtual constraint branch chain is retained, and other nodes are also the same. In addition, considering that the folding volume of mechanisms with P joints is much smaller than that of mechanisms with only R joints, the 4RR-4RRR pyramid unit mechanism composed of RR virtual constraint branches and RRR constraint branches is preferred.

3 DOF and Kinematics Analysis of the 4RR-4RRR Pyramid Unit Mechanism

3.1 DOF Analysis

The 4RR-4RRR pyramid unit can be decomposed into one triple closed loop mechanism and one RRR (S_{18}, S_{19}, and S_{20}) kinematic chain. Among them, the triple closed loop mechanism is composed of three 7R single closed loop mechanisms sharing two web members. Due to the symmetry of the structure, the RRR motion chain mentioned above is a redundant constraint branch chain, which does not affect the DOF of the entire tetrahedral unit. Therefore, the DOF of the 4RR-4RRR pyramid unit are the same as those of the three closed-loop mechanism. Next, the DOF of the three closed-loop mechanism will be analyzed. The structural diagram and topology diagram of the three closed-loop mechanism are shown in Figs. 4 and 5, respectively.

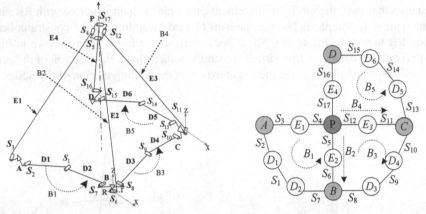

Fig. 4. Structural diagram of the three closed-loop mechanism

Fig. 5. Topological diagram of the three closed-loop mechanism

Analysis of the DOF of a single closed-loop mechanism. Establish a reference coordinate system C-xyz at the center of node C, with the x-axis along the DC line direction, the z-axis perpendicular to the plane where A, B, C and D are located, and the y-axis determined by the right-hand rule. The representation of the unit motion screw of branch chain RR and RRRRR in the reference coordinate system is

$$\begin{cases} \$_{m13}^{C} = \left(0\ b_{13}\ c_{13}\ 0\ -x_{13}c_{13}\ x_{13}b_{13} \right)^{T} \\ \$_{m14}^{C} = \left(0\ b_{13}\ c_{13}\ -b_{13}z_{14}\ -x_{14}c_{13}\ x_{14}b_{13} \right)^{T} \\ \$_{m15}^{C} = \left(0\ b_{13}\ c_{13}\ 0\ -x_{15}c_{13}\ x_{15}b_{13} \right)^{T} \\ \$_{m16}^{C} = \left(a_{16}\ b_{16}\ 0\ 0\ 0\ x_{16}b_{16} \right)^{T} \\ \$_{m17}^{P} = \left(a_{16}\ b_{16}\ 0\ -b_{16}z_{17}\ a_{16}z_{17}\ x_{17}b_{16} - a_{16}y_{17} \right)^{T} \end{cases} \quad (1)$$

$$\begin{cases} \$_{m11}^{C} = \left(a_{11}\ b_{11}\ 0\ 0\ 0\ 0 \right)^{T} \\ \$_{m12}^{C} = \left(a_{11}\ b_{11}\ 0\ -b_{11}z_{12}\ a_{11}z_{12}\ x_{12}b_{11} - a_{11}y_{12} \right)^{T} \end{cases} \quad (2)$$

where $\left(a_{i}\ b_{i}\ c_{i} \right)$ refers to the direction vector of S_{i}, and $\left(x_{i}\ y_{i}\ z_{i} \right)$ refers to the position vector of the center of S_{i} in the reference coordinate system.

Calculate the reciprocal screw of Eqs. (1) and (2), respectively, and the constraint screw applied to P can be expressed as:

$$\$_{r1}^{P} = \left(0\ 0\ 0\ -b_{16}c_{13}\ a_{16}c_{13}\ -a_{16}b_{13} \right)^{T} \quad (3)$$

$$\begin{cases} \$_{r2}^{P} = \left(0\ 0\ 0\ 0\ 0\ 1 \right)^{T} \\ \$_{r3}^{P} = \left(0\ 0\ 0\ b_{11}\ -a_{11}\ 0 \right)^{T} \\ \$_{r4}^{P} = \left(a_{11}\ b_{11}\ 0\ 0\ 0\ 0 \right)^{T} \\ \$_{r5}^{P} = \left(x_{12}\ y_{12}\ z_{12}\ 0\ 0\ 0 \right)^{T} \end{cases} \quad (4)$$

where $\$_{r1}^{P}$ represents the constraint couple perpendicular to the revolute joint in the constraint chain ($S_{13}, S_{14}, S_{15}, S_{16}, S_{17}$), $\$_{r2}^{P}$ represents the constraint couple along the z-axis, $\$_{r3}^{P}$ represents the constraint couple parallel to the xy plane, $\$_{r4}^{P}$ represents the constraint force parallel to the axis of the revolute joint at both ends of the link E_3 through the origin of the coordinate system, and $\$_{r5}^{P}$ represents the constraint force along the axis of the link E_3 through the origin of the coordinate system.

Taking the union of Eqs. (3) and (4) and solving its reciprocal screw, the kinematic screw of P relative to C can be expressed as:

$$\$_{mP}^{C} = \left(0\ 0\ 0\ -b_{11}\ a_{11}\ \frac{x_{12}b_{11} - y_{12}a_{11}}{z_{12}} \right)^{T} \tag{5}$$

Similarly, the kinematic screw of P relative to B can be expressed as:

$$\$_{mP}^{B} = \left(0\ 0\ 0\ -b_{5}\ a_{5}\ \frac{x_{5}b_{5} - a_{5}y_{5}}{z_{5}} \right)^{T} \tag{6}$$

Finally, the kinematic screw of A relative to B can be solved as:

$$\$_{mA}^{B} = \left(0\ 0\ 0\ 1\ 0\ 0 \right)^{T} \tag{7}$$

This screw represents movement along the x-axis. Similarly, it can be concluded that D also has a DOF of movement along the AB line direction relative to C. In the single closed-loop mechanism ($S_5, S_6, S_8, S_9, S_{10}, \$_{mP}^{C}$), the application of screw theory can obtain that C only has one DOF of movement along the BC line direction relative to B. Therefore, considering the dismantled RRR (S_{18}, S_{19}, and S_{20}) kinematic chains, the 4RR-4RRR pyramid unit mechanism is a single DOF mechanism, which can achieve synchronous unfolding motion with unchanged orientation of the four nodes on the bottom surface with only one actuation.

3.2 Kinematics Analysis

It can be known from the DOF analysis that the node orientation of the unit mechanism is always unchanged in the process of movement. Therefore, during the kinematics analysis, the node can be simplified as a rigid body node with orientation, and the axis of the motion joint connected between the node and each member intersects at this point. Taking the 4RR-4RRR mechanism shown in Fig. 6 as an example, the displacement and velocity of each node during the unit motion process are analyzed.

The reference coordinate system O-XYZ is established at point P. The origin O coincides with point P, with the X-axis parallel to the bottom edge AB, the Y-axis parallel to the bottom edge BC, and the Z-axis along the centerline of the pyramid unit. According to the geometric constraints, it can be concluded that

$$AE = EH = m \sin \varphi \tag{8}$$

$$AH = \sqrt{2}m \sin \varphi = l \sin \theta \tag{9}$$

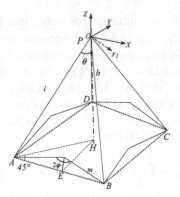

Fig. 6. Kinematics analysis diagram of 4RR-4RRR mechanism

Thus, it can be concluded that

$$\sin \theta = \frac{\sqrt{2}m \sin \varphi}{l} \tag{10}$$

There also exists

$$OH = l \cos \theta \tag{11}$$

Thus, the position vectors of A, B, C, and D can be obtained as

$$\begin{cases} \vec{A} = (-m \sin \varphi \ -m \sin \varphi \ -l \cos \theta) \\ \vec{B} = (m \sin \varphi \ -m \sin \varphi \ -l \cos \theta) \\ \vec{C} = (m \sin \varphi \ m \sin \varphi \ -l \cos \theta) \\ \vec{D} = (-m \sin \varphi \ m \sin \varphi \ -l \cos \theta) \end{cases} \tag{12}$$

The velocity at point A can be expressed as the cross product of the angular velocity of the web PA and the position vector of the web, i.e.

$$V_A = \vec{\omega}_{VA} \times \vec{A} \tag{13}$$

and

$$\vec{\omega}_{VA} = r_1 \dot{\theta} = \left(\sqrt{2}/2 \ -\sqrt{2}/2 \ 0 \right)^T \dot{\theta} \tag{14}$$

where r_1 refers to the unit vector perpendicular to the plane APH.

Taking the derivative of Eq. (10) yields

$$\dot{\theta} = \frac{\sqrt{2}m \cos \varphi \dot{\varphi}}{l \cos \theta} \tag{15}$$

It can be concluded that

$$V_A = \vec{\omega}_{VA} \times \vec{A} = \left(\tfrac{\sqrt{2}}{2}l \cos \theta \ \tfrac{\sqrt{2}}{2}l \cos \theta \ -\sqrt{2}m \sin \varphi \right)^T \cdot \frac{\sqrt{2}m \cos \varphi \dot{\varphi}}{l \cos \theta} \tag{16}$$

$$V_B = \vec{\omega}_{VB} \times \vec{B} = \left(-\frac{\sqrt{2}}{2}l\cos\theta \quad \frac{\sqrt{2}}{2}l\cos\theta \quad -\sqrt{2}\,m\sin\varphi \right)^T \cdot \frac{\sqrt{2}\,m\cos\varphi\,\dot{\varphi}}{l\cos\theta} \quad (17)$$

$$V_C = \vec{\omega}_{VC} \times \vec{C} = \left(-\frac{\sqrt{2}}{2}l\cos\theta \quad -\frac{\sqrt{2}}{2}l\cos\theta \quad -\sqrt{2}\,m\sin\varphi \right)^T \cdot \frac{\sqrt{2}\,m\cos\varphi\,\dot{\varphi}}{l\cos\theta} \quad (18)$$

$$V_D = \vec{\omega}_{VD} \times \vec{D} = \left(\frac{\sqrt{2}}{2}l\cos\theta \quad -\frac{\sqrt{2}}{2}l\cos\theta \quad 0 \right)^T \cdot \frac{\sqrt{2}\,m\cos\varphi\,\dot{\varphi}}{l\cos\theta} \quad (19)$$

4 Expanding the Networking of Pyramid unit Mechanisms

Three expansion methods based on the quadrilateral characteristics of the bottom surface of the pyramid unit mechanism are proposed. ① The bottom quadrilateral is a square, and at this point, the pyramid unit mechanism is linearly arranged along the two-dimensional direction of the XY plane, and infinite expansion can be achieved, as shown in Fig. 7(a); ② The bottom quadrilateral is a square. At this point, three pyramid unit mechanisms are arranged in a circular array, and the peripheral nodes of the units are sequentially connected to form an irregular hexagonal closed-loop composite mechanism. Using this composite mechanism as an extension unit, six unit circular arrays are arranged again to obtain a circular extension mechanism, which can also achieve infinite expansion, as shown in Fig. 7(b); ③ Considering the infinite expansion of a regular hexagon, the bottom quadrilateral is designed as a rectangle, and the expansion method is the same as ②, as shown in Fig. 7(c).

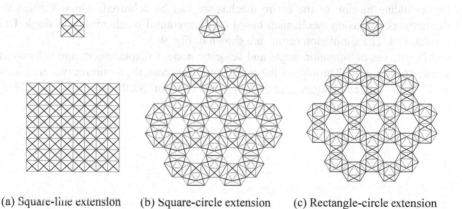

(a) Square-line extension   (b) Square-circle extension   (c) Rectangle-circle extension

Fig. 7. Basic combination units and networking expansion methods

The above three expansion methods can all achieve the networking of deployable spatial mechanisms of any size. Taking the extension of the 4RR-4RRR quadricone unit line-type as an example, starting from node A, the four quadricone units connected to it and their closed-loop mechanism are shown in Fig. 8. Four pyramid units form a closed loop by sharing four synchronous folding links, and the mechanism is analyzed as a single DOF closed loop mechanism.

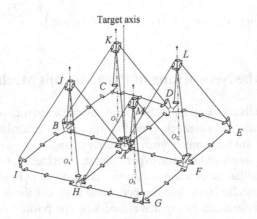

Fig. 8. 16RR-12RRR Mechanism

The ADAMS dynamic simulation software was applied to simulate and analyze the folding and unfolding motion of the extension mechanisms. Adding a rotation actuation at the middle rotation joint of any synchronous link supporting chain, the folding/unfolding motion of the entire mechanism can be achieved, which verified that the network extension mechanism based on the pyramid mechanism is a single DOF mechanism. The simulation results are shown in Fig. 9.

The curves of actuation angle and velocity, node A displacement and velocity are shown in the Fig. 10. Throughout the entire motion process, the motion curves are smooth without any sudden changes, and the mechanism motion is effective and reasonable.

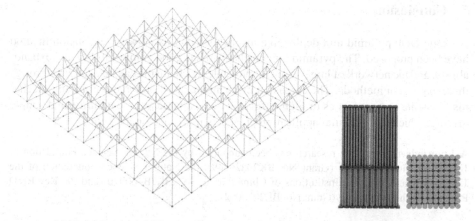

(a) Unfolding and folding configurations of square-line extension mechanisms

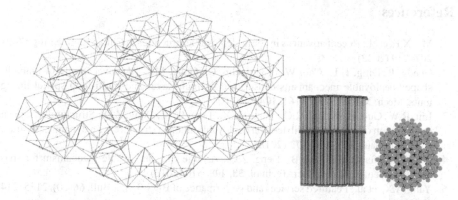

(b) Unfolding and folding configurations of square-circle extension mechanisms

Fig. 9. Motion simulation of extended mechanisms

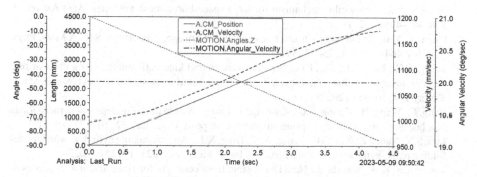

Fig. 10. Curves of actuation and node *A*

5 Conclusion

A single DOF pyramid unit deployable mechanism and its network expansion method have been proposed. The pyramid unit mechanism has good composability and expandability, and the network of large spatial deployable mechanisms can be achieved through three expansion methods. The extension mechanism based on the pyramid unit mechanism has the characteristics of high unfolding ratio, appreciable scalability, and simple driving, which has potential application prospects in the aerospace field.

Acknowledgements. This research has been supported by the Natural Science Foundation of Jiangsu Province of China (Grant No. BK20220649), the Natural Science Foundation of the Jiangsu Higher Education Institutions of China (Grant No. 23KJB460010) and the Key R&D Project of Jiangsu Province (Grant No. BE2022062).

References

1. Ma, X.F., et al.: Recent advances in space-deployable structures in China. Engineering **17**(10), 207–219 (2022)
2. Cheng, P., Ding, H.F., Cao, W.A., Gosselin, C., Geng, M.C.: A novel family of umbrella-shaped deployable mechanisms constructed by multi-layer and multi-loop spatial linkage units. Mech. Mach. Theory **161**, 104169 (2021)
3. Liu, R.W., Guo, H.W., Liu, R.Q., Wang, H.X., Tang, D.W., Deng, Z.Q.: Structural design and optimization of large cable–rib tension deployable antenna structure with dynamic constraint. Acta Astronaut. **151**, 160–172 (2018)
4. Qi, X.Z., Huang, H.L., Li, B., Deng, Z.Q.: A large ring deployable mechanism for space satellite antenna. Aerosp. Sci. Technol. **58**, 498–510 (2016)
5. Yang, Y.X., et al.: Featured services and performance of BDS-3. Sci. Bull. **66**(20), 2135–2143 (2021)
6. Phocas, M.C., Christoforou, E.G., Dimitriou, P.: Kinematics and control approach for deployable and reconfigurable rigid bar linkage structures. Eng. Struct. **208**, 110310 (2020)
7. Sun, Z.H., Zhang, Y.Q., Yang, D.W.: Structural design, analysis, and experimental verification of an H-style deployable mechanism for large space-borne mesh antennas. Acta Astronaut. **178**, 481–498 (2021)
8. Chen, Y., You, Z.: On mobile assemblies of Bennett linkage. Proc. Royal Soc. A Math. Phys. Eng. Sci. **464**(2093), 1275–1293 (2008)
9. Meng, Q.Z., Liu, X.J., Xie, F.G.: Structure design and kinematic analysis of a class of ring truss deployable mechanisms for satellite antennas based on novel basic units. Mech. Mach. Theory **174**, 104881 (2022)
10. Yang, C., Wang, B., Zhong, S.C., Zhao, C.M., Liang, W.: On tailoring deployable mechanism of a bistable composite tape-spring structure. Composit. Commun. **32**, 101171 (2022)
11. Lyu, S.N., Yao, P.F., Xiao, H., Zhang, W.X., Ding, X.L.: Approximating cylinders with bundle-folding plane-symmetric Bricard linkages. Int. J. Mech. Sci. **221**, 107231 (2022)
12. Takamatsu, K.A., Onoda, J.: New Deployable truss concepts for large antenna structures or solar concentrators. J. Spacecr. Rocket. **28**(3), 330–338 (1991)
13. Tian, D.K., et al.: Design and kinematic analysis of a multifold rib modular deployable antenna mechanism. Mech. Sci. **13**(1), 519–533 (2022)

14. Guo, J.W., Zhao, Y.S., Xu, Y.D., Zhang, G.X.: Mechanics analysis and structural design of a truss deployable antenna mechanism based on 3RR-3URU tetrahedral unit. Mech. Mach. Theory **171**, 104749 (2022)
15. Guo, J.W., Zhao, Y.S., Xu, Y.D., Zhang, G.X., Yao, J.T.: A novel modular deployable mechanism for the truss antenna: assembly principle and performance analysis. Aerosp. Sci. Technol. **105**, 105976 (2020)
16. Wang, R.G., Sun, J.X., Dai, J.S.: Design analysis and type synthesis of a petal-inspired space deployable-foldable mechanism. Mech. Mach. Theory **141**, 151–170 (2019)
17. Huang, H., Guan, F.L., Pan, L.L., Xu, Y.: Design and deploying study of a new petal-type deployable solid surface antenna. Acta Astronautica **148**(JUL.), 99–110 (2018)
18. Huang, H., Cheng, Q., Zheng, L., Yang, Y.: Development for petal-type deployable solid-surface reflector by uniaxial rotation mechanism. Acta Astronaut. **178**(2), 511–521 (2021)

A Rigid-Soft Pneumatic Wrist with Fixed Rotation Axes and Active Jamming Variable Stiffness Mechanisms

Kehan Ding, Li Jiang[(✉)], and Ruichen Zhen

State Key Laboratory of Robotics and System, Harbin Institute of Technology, Harbin, China
jiangli01@hit.edu.cn

Abstract. The wrist can greatly enhance the manipulative performance of dexterous hands. In addition, due to the flexibility of soft materials, the soft wrist has obvious advantages in environmental adaptability and safety. However, existing soft wrists often have small motion curvatures and cannot modulate stiffness. Inspired by the human wrist, we proposed a rigid-soft pneumatic wrist design with fixed axes, realizing variable stiffness through jamming mechanisms. The wrist is composed of two rotary joints in series to achieve pronation/supination and flexion/extension motions. Each joint is driven by two opposite-mounted actuators, resulting in active bidirectional movement. The pre-stretched mounting of pneumatic actuators eliminates the stiffness torque effects. Both joints have independent jamming stiffening mechanisms controlled by air pressure and require no additional power source, which makes the stiffness control more flexible. Experimental results demonstrated that the maximum output torques of the two joints reached 1.18 Nm and 1.40 Nm, and the jamming mechanism increased the stiffness of the joints by 55.3% and 67.2% in the practical test, respectively. The proposed rigid-soft wrist provides a feasible solution for enhancing the manipulative ability of soft dexterous hands.

Keywords: Robotic wrist · Variable stiffness · Soft pneumatic actuator · Rigid-soft structure

1 Introduction

With the progress of science and technology, robotic dexterous hands are being increasingly used in the industrial field [1]. As the end effector of the robot system, dexterous hands can achieve manipulations such as grasp, pinch, and other actions [2], and both rigid and flexible dexterous hands have been extensively investigated [3]. Many previous studies about robotic hands focused on fingers and palms, while the wrist has received less attention. But the wrist joint plays an important role in the performance of the robotic hand, improving the operation dexterity and accuracy significantly [4].

Rigid mechanisms can easily achieve 3 degrees of freedom (DOF) similar to the human wrist, but in unstructured application scenarios, rigid structures often lack adequate adaptability, and it is easy to harm the operating objects. Consequently, there are

© The Author(s), under exclusive license to Springer Nature Singapore Pte Ltd. 2023
H. Yang et al. (Eds.): ICIRA 2023, LNAI 14269, pp. 622–634, 2023.
https://doi.org/10.1007/978-981-99-6489-5_51

certain safety problems in the interaction with fragile products and organisms [5]. Soft robotics are rapidly progressing in recent years due to their exceptional capacity for environmental adaptation caused by inherent compliance [6], and the soft wrist has also attracted attention to solving adaptability and safety problems in unstructured environments [7]. A soft wrist with a modular design used for underwater environments has been proposed, which is capable of delicate manipulation at depths of more than 2300m under hydraulic actuation [8]. A soft wrist driven by independent cables has been developed, achieving variable stiffness based on a novel jamming mechanism [9]. Bending and twisting motion is achieved by a soft wrist driven by four parallel air chambers, whose helical structure provides more possibilities for driving modes [10]. A spring-actuated soft wrist has been investigated, using a new learning framework to meet the needs of human-robot interaction [11]. In the field of rehabilitation for patients with wrist injuries, a soft wearable wrist equipped with Origami actuators has been proposed, with eight drivers in a unitized design [12]. At the same time, one of the most significant challenges for soft robots is variable stiffness, because its inherent flexibility brings advantages in terms of environmental adaptation, but also means a smaller force output [13]. The jamming-based variable stiffness system has recently received a lot of attention from researchers [14] and is used in many kinds of soft robot designs [15]. For example, a soft gripper with passive variable stiffness based on jamming stiffening has been studied [16]. A particle jamming pneumatic finger for robust grasping is investigated [17]. A novel fabric-based versatile and stiffness-tunable soft gripper was proposed [18]. A flexible robot with a wide range of adjustable stiffness based on the jamming principle has been developed [19].

However, the current soft wrists generally face two significant obstacles. First, existing soft wrists have small curvature of motions and no fixed axis of rotation, which brings inconvenience to the subsequent motion planning. Second, there has been limited research on soft wrists with adjustable stiffness, which greatly limits their adaptability to multiple tasks.

In this paper, a rigid-soft pneumatic wrist with fixed rotating axes is presented, and each joint has an independent active adjustable stiffness mechanism based on jamming stiffening. The rigid-soft design allows bending motions of the wrist to be constrained by rigid components, allowing for large curvature deformations that improve the dexterity of the wrist and facilitate the control of wrist movements. Four actuators in the wrist provide a bidirectional drive for both joints, and the pre-stretched mounting method eliminates non-linear effects on torque and position, which are caused by actuator folding. When the wrist is required to carry external loads and prevent positional changes, the variable stiffness mechanisms provide additional antagonistic torques for wrist stability. The resistance torque of the jamming mechanism can be adjusted by air pressure, and each joint has an independent stiffness mechanism, which significantly improves wrist dexterity, further enhancing the ability to adjust the stiffness to different task requirements. A series of wrist experiments have also been performed. The two joints' maximum output torques were 1.18 Nm and 1.40 Nm, respectively, and the jamming mechanism increased the stiffness of the joints by 55.3% and 67.2% in the practical test.

2 Design of the Wrist

2.1 Motion and Structure Analysis of Human Wrist

As one of the most complex joints in the human body, the wrist can not only achieve dexterous movement but also achieve large force output, thus greatly improving the operation ability of human hands.

The wrist has three degrees of freedom, known as pronation/supination, flexion/extension, and radial/ulnar deviation [20], and each motion corresponds to a forward and reverses motion about the axis. For the wrist of most healthy individuals, the maximum range of motion of the pronation/supination, flexion/extension, and radial/ulnar deviation is 76°/85°, 75°/75°, and 20°/45°, respectively, as shown in Fig. 1. However, in daily life, the maximum range of motion of the wrist is often not fully utilized. The three ranges that can accommodate the majority of requirements are 65°/77°, 50°/70°, and 18°/40° [21–23].

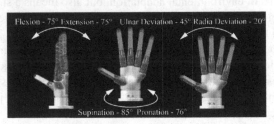

Fig. 1. The DOF and range of motion of the human wrist, and the soft hand in the illustration has been introduced in our previous research [24, 25].

2.2 Soft Wrist Design with Jamming Mechanism

Inspired by the human wrist, we propose a 2DOF variable stiffness wrist design. Although the three degrees of freedom structure of the human wrist allows for significantly increased flexibility in handling, the radial/ulnar deviation motion does not extend the range of motion of the palm relative to the forearm obviously because of the coupling between the motions. At the same time, more freedoms result in more complex structures, which makes design challenging. From the perspective of reducing the complexity of joints and achieving greater dexterity with as little freedom as possible, the proposed wrist keeps two DOFs of pronation/supination and flexion/extension. The main design parameters of the soft wrist are shown in Table 1.

The wrist is composed of rigid bones and flexible parts. It consists of two rotating joints in series to achieve pronation/supination and flexion/extension movements, which are referred to as the upper and lower joints respectively. Each joint has an independent variable stiffness mechanism and two symmetrically mounted pneumatic actuators. The structure of the soft wrist is illustrated in Fig. 2.

Table 1. Parameters of the pneumatic soft wrist

Feature	Parameter
Total length: L	172 mm
Maximum width: D	87 mm
Number of actuators	4
Upper and lower joint actuator natural length: l_{n1}, l_{n2}	33 mm, 40mm
Upper and lower joint actuator mounting length: l_{m1}, l_{m2}	41 mm, 52mm
Actuator thickness: h_a	3 mm
Number of variable stiffness mechanisms	2
Upper and lower joint locking rod blade length: l_{b1}, l_{b2}	10 mm, 14 mm
Upper and lower joint flexible film thickness: h_{f1}, h_{f2}	1.5 mm, 3 mm
Upper and lower joint flexible film diameter: d_{f1}, d_{f2}	32 mm, 52 mm
Particle diameter: d	3 mm
Total weight	346 g

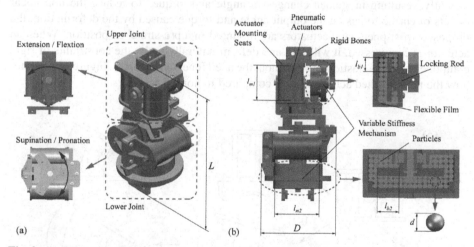

Fig. 2. Design of the pneumatic soft wrist. (a) The overall structure of the wrist and its mode of movement. (b) Front view of the wrist and cross-section view of the variable stiffness mechanism. Relevant parameters are explained in Table 1.

The pneumatic actuator is a three-layer, single-air-chamber construction formed of an inner silicone layer, a fiber strengthening layer, and an outer silicone layer from inside to outside, as illustrated in Fig. 3(a). The inner silicone layer, made of hard silicone material with strong tensile strength and the ability to withstand large air pressure, is the base of the air chamber. The fiber reinforcing layer is the fiber wound on the inner silicone layer, enhancing the pressure-bearing capacity and limiting the radial deformation of

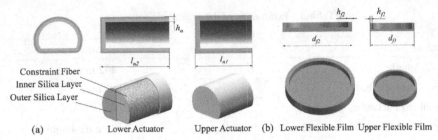

Fig. 3. The structure of flexible parts. (a) The pneumatic actuator structure of the upper and lower joints. (b) The structure of flexible films for variable stiffness mechanisms in upper and lower joints. Relevant parameters are interpreted in Table 1.

the air chamber. The outer silicone layer plays the role of protecting and fixing the fiber-strengthening layer, thus its material is much softer than the inner silicone layer.

Since the actuators are mounted symmetrically in each joint, if one of them extends under pressure, the other actuator must be compressed and folded. When the actuators are in a natural state, a large force is required to compress and fold them because of their stiffness. Once the deformation occurs, most of the reaction force will be released instantly, resulting in sudden changes in angle and torque. To reduce the non-linear effects of elastic forces on the output angle and torque caused by the deformation, the proposed wrist pneumatic actuators are mounted in a pre-stretched position. When an actuator is compressed, it will fold and deform naturally under the constraints of rigid components and its elastic forces, without the need for external forces. Figure 4 illustrates how the pre-stretched actuators work compared to normal actuators.

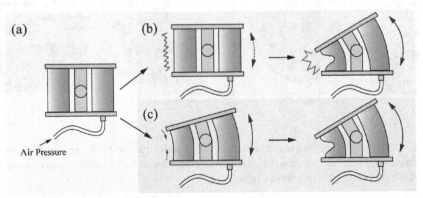

Fig. 4. The working principle of pre-stretch-mounted pneumatic actuators. (a) The initial state of the actuators and joint. (b) The working condition of an actuator installed in a natural state, with obvious antagonism on the compressed side and an abrupt change when rotation occurs. (c) The working condition of a pre-stretched actuator, with its bending naturally under its restoring force and producing a small impedance force.

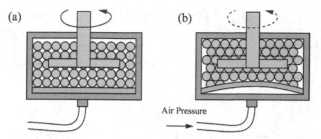

Fig. 5. The working principle of the variable stiffness mechanism. (a) The initial state of a variable stiffness mechanism, in which it can rotate freely with little resistance. (b) The working state of a variable stiffness mechanism, in which the particles are squeezed by the flexible film, and the locking rod is subjected to resistance when rotating.

The variable stiffness is realized by the jamming mechanism, which consists of a rigid shell, a locking rod, blocking particles, and a flexible film. When there is no increase in air pressure, the particles are loose and there is no squeezing pressure between them, therefore the locking rod can rotate freely relative to the rigid shell with little resistance. When the air pressure is increased, the flexible film deforms and compresses the particles. Because the particles squeeze each other, the resistance of the lock rod also increases, which is finally reflected in the rise of the rotational impedance force of the joint. In the case of sufficient air pressure, the force required for the wrist joint to rotate at the same angle by the external load will be significantly increased, thus achieving the effect of enhancing stiffness. Figure 5 illuminates how the jamming mechanism works, and the structure of flexible films is shown in Fig. 3(b).

2.3 Material and Fabrication

Materials of the inner silicone layer and the outer silicone layer in the pneumatic actuator are Dragon Skin 10 and Ecoflex 00-30, respectively. The material of the fiber strengthening layer is the glass-fiber string fixed by the outer silicone layer and grooves on the inner silicone layer. Dragon Skin 10 is also selected as the material for the flexible film of the variable stiffness mechanism. Rigid parts of the wrist are made of 3D-printed resin, which is both lightweight and strong. Sil-Poxy (Smooth-on, USA) is selected for adhesive fixation of silicone and resin. The manufacturing process of the actuator is illustrated in Fig. 6.

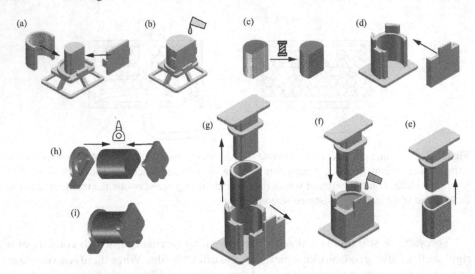

Fig. 6. Fabrication process of the pneumatic actuator. (a) Assemble the mold for the inner silicone layer. (b) Pour silicone (Dragon Skin 10) into the mold. (c) Wrap glass-fiber strings around the inner silicone layer. (d) Assemble the outer mold for the outer silicone layer. (e) Install the air chamber on the inner mold. (f) Pour silicone (Ecoflex 00-30) into the outer mold and then inserted the inner mold and gas chamber into the outer mold. (g) Disassemble the mold to get the air chamber. (h) Adheres the air chamber to the mounting seat with glue (Sil-Poxy). (i) The complete structure of the pneumatic actuator.

3 Experiments

3.1 Pneumatic Actuator Characteristics

The characteristics of pneumatic actuators determine the motion state of the joint and the static force output, and the state of the actuator is completely controlled by the air pressure. Therefore, it is necessary to test the relationships between the air pressure and the angular displacement of the joint, as well as the output torque. The test platform is shown in Fig. 7.

The platform consists of an air pump, a 12V DC power supply, a valve, a torque sensor, and a camera. IR2010-02-A from SMC is selected as the valve, and the torque sensor is the DYDJ-104 with a range of 5 Nm and an accuracy of 0.3%. The torque sensor is fixed to the joint to be measured and is mounted on a fixed base, and the torques can be read directly from its display when the air pressure changes. The joint angles are measured visually. The air pressure is added to actuators after zeroing the joint rotation, which causes the two 2D codes to rotate relative to each other. The program then calculates the angle relative to the initial position once the camera has captured the image information. Each test was repeated for eight sets under the same conditions, and the averages were taken as the final data.

Figure 8(a, b) exhibits the barometric output torque relationships at different positions of the upper and lower joints, which conform to the linear relationship and have almost the same slope. The output torque of the joint tends to decrease with the increase in

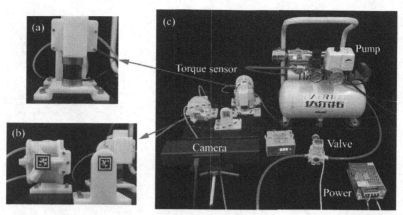

Fig. 7. The experimental test platform. (a) The torque test and torque sensor. (b) The angle test and QR code tag for visual angle measurement. (c) The overall structure of the platform.

angular position, and the spacing between their curves is uniform. The upper and lower joints reach their maximum output torques of 1.18 Nm and 1.40 Nm, respectively, in the initial position and at an air pressure of 110 kPa.

The barometric angular displacement curves of pronation/supination and flexion/extension joints are illustrated in Fig. 8(c), and the barometric pressure and angular displacement exhibit a non-linear relationship. To avoid interference between components, the maximum rotation angle of the joint is limited to about 45°. Since this is only the range of a single direction, the total range of rotation of the joint is ±45°. Figure 8(d) reveals the natural recovery torques of the upper and lower joints at different positions, which are entirely generated by the elastic deformation of the actuator itself.

3.2 Jamming Mechanism Characteristics

The effect of the variable stiffness mechanism is controlled by air pressure. In this paper, the variable stiffness characteristics of the wrist are discussed with the example of the lower joint, and the relationship between the resistance torque and the air pressure input of the jamming mechanism at the lower joint is shown in Fig. 8(e).

The torque increases linearly with increasing air pressure. The jamming mechanism starts to have a significant resistance torque of about 0.45 Nm at 30 kPa; when the air pressure rises to 110 kPa the resistance torque reaches 1.80 Nm. Compared to the output torque of the actuator illustrated in Fig. 8(a, b), the variable stiffness mechanism is able to produce a greater resistance torque when the joint is rotated to an arbitrary position. Therefore, the variable stiffness mechanism can provide the wrist with a large additional resistance torque when the wrist needs to be held in posture under external loads. Consequently, the stiffening function of the jamming mechanism can significantly improve the stability of the wrist.

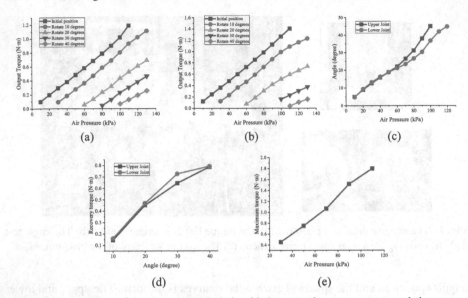

Fig. 8. The experimental data curves. (a) Relationship between the output torque and air pressure of the upper joint at different angular positions. (b) Relationship between the output torque and air pressure of the lower joint at different angular positions. (c) Relationship between rotation angle and air pressure of upper and lower joints. (d) Relationship between recovery torque and angular position of upper and lower joints. (e) Relationship between maximum impedance torque of variable stiffness mechanism and air pressure of the lower joint.

3.3 Soft Wrist Motion and Variable Stiffness Experiment

Physical tests are carried out on a single joint to visually assess the wrist's real functional capacity. In the experiment shown in Fig. 9, the weight of the object being lifted is 585 g, and the distance between the suspension point and the rotation axis of the joint is 200 mm.

Fig. 9(a) and Fig. 9(b) illustrate the torque changes in the upper and lower joints, respectively. With the increase in actuator air pressure, the object is significantly lifted.

Figure 9(c) and Fig. 9(d) demonstrate the flexural stiffness of the upper and lower joints. The air pressure of the upper and lower joint actuators is 80 kPa and 50 kPa, and the joints rotate at a certain angle after the load is installed. After the load is removed, the joints return to the initial position shown in the control group. If the pressure of the variable stiffness mechanisms is increased and the load is installed again, the rotation angle of the joint gradually decreases. Experimental results of joint variable stiffness are shown in Fig. 10, indicating that the upper joint stiffness rose by 55.3% at 120 kPa and the lower joint stiffness increased by 67.2% at 100 kPa.

Figure 11 illustrates the range of motion of the soft wrist, which is fitted with a rigid-soft, five-fingered dexterous hand [24, 25]. The initial position of the wrist and the ultimate position of each joint are shown, and it is illustrated how the soft wrist increases the dexterous hand's range of motion.

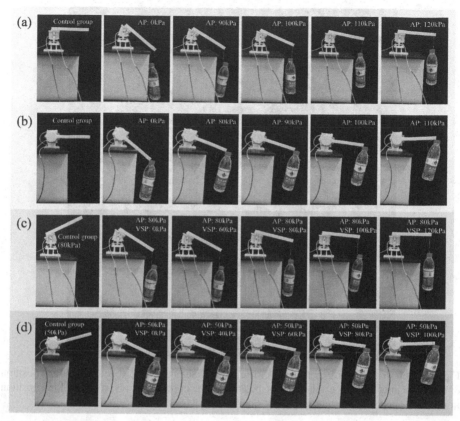

Fig. 9. The joint characteristic tests. (a) Torque output test of upper joint. (b) Torque output test of lower joint. (c) Variable stiffness characteristic test of upper joint. (d) Variable stiffness characteristic test of lower joint. AP stands for actuator pressure, and VSP stands for variable stiffness pressure.

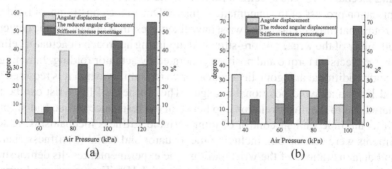

Fig. 10. Experimental results of joint variable stiffness. (a) Variable stiffness test of upper joint. (b) Variable stiffness test of lower joint.

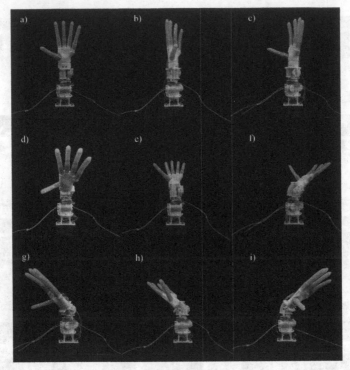

Fig. 11. Soft wrist motion experiment. (a) The initial state of the wrist. (b, c) The limiting position of the lower joint only. (d, e) The limiting position of the upper joint only. (f–i) The limit position in which the upper and lower joints work simultaneously.

4 Conclusions and Future Work

In this work, we suggested a rigid-soft wrist equipped with pre-stretched actuators and jamming mechanisms. The specific structure of the wrist is clarified in detail, including the fabrication process of the pneumatic actuator. Due to the constraints of rigid components, rotational movements of the wrist have fixed axes, thus enhancing the dexterity and controllability of the wrist. The pre-stretched mounting approach of actuators eliminates non-linear effects on torque and position generated by actuator folding. Jamming mechanisms add additional antagonistic torques for wrist stability when it is required to carry external loads and avoid positional changes. The stiffness of the wrist can be flexibly modulated due to the linear relationship between the resistance torque and air pressure, as well as the independent control of joint variable stiffness mechanisms. A series of experiments were carried out, including the actuator and variable stiffness characteristics, and demonstrations of the wrist motion. The experimental results demonstrate that both joints of the wrist have a range of motion of $\pm 45°$. The upper and lower joints' maximum driving torques are 1.18 Nm and 1.40 Nm, respectively, while the variable stiffness mechanisms' maximum torques are 0.80 Nm and 1.80 Nm. In the experiment of lifting a load, the stiffness of the upper and lower joints increased by 55.3% and 67.2%, respectively. In conclusion, the proposed soft wrist not only has fixed axes for each joint but also has bidirectional actuators with a large output torque, which greatly improves the flexibility of the wrist. The jamming mechanism is equipped to provide a large blocking torque to help the wrist carry external loads, and the blocking torque can be adjusted individually for each joint by pneumatic pressure, which significantly improves the stability of the wrist. This design greatly enhances the operational capabilities of the soft hand developed in our previous work [24, 25], enabling it to meet the demands of a wide range of operational tasks.

The future work will focus on four issues: increasing the DOF of the wrist, enhancing the actuator, improving the variable stiffness mechanism, and developing a wrist control system. For the DOF, we will attempt to add the radial/ulnar deviation motion and reduce the size of the wrist. For the pneumatic actuator, we will try to increase its output torque and range of motion. For the jamming mechanism, exploring principles of variable stiffness and improving the adjustable range of stiffness will be a major part of our work. For the control system, control schemes for the wrist and collaborative wrist-hand control algorithms will be investigated.

References

1. Kadalagere Sampath, S., Wang, N., Wu, H., et al.: Review on human-like robot manipulation using dexterous hands. Cogn. Comput. Syst. **5**(1), 14–29 (2023)
2. Yu, C., Wang, P.: Dexterous manipulation for multi-fingered robotic hands with reinforcement learning: a review. Front. Neurorobot. **16**, 861825 (2022)
3. Billard, A., Kragic, D.: Trends and challenges in robot manipulation. Science **364**(6446), eaat8414 (2019)
4. Fan, H., Wei, G., Ren, L.: Prosthetic and robotic wrists comparing with the intelligently evolved human wrist: a review. Robotica **40**(11), 4169–4191 (2022)
5. Rus, D., Tolley, M.T.: Design, fabrication and control of soft robots. Nature **521**(7553), 467–475 (2015)
6. Laschi, C., Mazzolai, B., Cianchetti, M.: Soft robotics: Technologies and systems pushing the boundaries of robot abilities. Sci. Robot. **1**(1), eaah3690 (2016)
7. Xu, Y.: Design and simulation of a soft robotic device for wrist rehabilitation. In: 2020 3rd International Conference on Advanced Electronic Materials, Computers and Software Engineering (AEMCSE), pp. 697–701. Shenzhen, China (2020)
8. Kurumaya, S., Phillips, B.T., Becker, K.P., et al.: A modular soft robotic wrist for underwater manipulation. Soft Rob. **5**(4), 399–409 (2018)
9. Zhou, J., Cao, H., Chen, W., et al.: Bioinspired soft wrist based on multicable jamming with hybrid motion and stiffness control for dexterous manipulation. IEEE/ASME Trans. Mech. (2022)
10. Chen, G., Lin, T., Ding, S., et al.: Design and test of an active Pneumatic Soft Wrist for Soft Grippers. Actuators. MDPI **11**(11), 311 (2022)
11. Hamaya, M., Tanaka, K., Shibata, Y., et al.: Robotic learning from advisory and adversarial interactions using a soft wrist. IEEE Robot. Autom. Let. **6**(2), 3878–3885 (2021)
12. Liu, S., Fang, Z., Liu, J., et al.: A compact soft robotic wrist brace with origami actuators. Front. Robot. AI **34** (2021)
13. Yang, Y., Li, Y., Chen, Y.: Principles and methods for stiffness modulation in soft robot design and development. Bio-Des. Manufac. **1**(1), 14–25 (2018)
14. Manti, M., Cacucciolo, V., Cianchetti, M.: Stiffening in soft robotics: a review of the state of the art. IEEE Robot. Autom. Mag. **23**(3), 93–106 (2016)

15. Fitzgerald, S., Delaney, G., Howard, D.: A review of jamming actuation in soft robotics. Actuators **9**(4), 104 (2020)
16. Li, Y., Chen, Y., Yang, Y., et al.: Passive particle jamming and its stiffening of soft robotic grippers. IEEE Trans. Rob. **33**(2), 446–455 (2017)
17. Zhou, J., Chen, Y., Hu, Y., et al.: Adaptive variable stiffness particle phalange for robust and durable robotic grasping. Soft Rob. **7**(6), 743–757 (2020)
18. Kim, Y.J., Cheng, S., Kim, S., et al.: A novel layer jamming mechanism with tunable stiffness capability for minimally invasive surgery. IEEE Trans. Rob. **29**(4), 1031–1042 (2013)
19. Zhao, Y., Shan, Y., Zhang, J., et al.: A soft continuum robot, with a large variable-stiffness range, based on jamming. Bioinspir. Biomim. **14**(6), 066007 (2019)
20. Bajaj, N.M., Spiers, A.J., Dollar, A.M.: State of the art in artificial wrists: A review of prosthetic and robotic wrist design. IEEE Trans. Rob. **35**(1), 261–277 (2019)
21. Marshall, M.M., Mozrall, J.R., Shealy, J.E.: The effects of complex wrist and forearm posture on wrist range of motion. Hum. Factors **41**(2), 205–213 (1999)
22. Ryu, J., Cooney, W.P., III., Askew, L.J., et al.: Functional ranges of motion of the wrist joint. J. Hand Surg. **16**(3), 409–419 (1991)
23. Nelson, D.L., Mitchell, M.A., Groszewski, P.G., et al.: Wrist range of motion in activities of daily living. Adv. Biomech. Hand Wrist 329–334 (1994)
24. Zhen, R., Jiang, L., Li, H., et al.: Modular bioinspired hand with multijoint rigid-soft finger possessing proprioception. Soft Rob. **10**(2), 380–394 (2023)
25. Zhen, R., Jiang, L.: Rigid skeleton enhanced dexterous soft finger possessing proprioception. In: 2022 IEEE/RSJ International Conference on Intelligent Robots and Systems (IROS), pp. 5402–5408. IEEE (2022)

Author Index

© The Editor(s) (if applicable) and The Author(s), under exclusive license
to Springer Nature Singapore Pte Ltd. 2023
H. Yang et al. (Eds.): ICIRA 2023, LNAI 14269, pp. 635–637, 2023.
https://doi.org/10.1007/978-981-99-6489-5

Printed in the United States
by Baker & Taylor Publisher Services

Printed in the United States
by Baker & Taylor Publisher Services